Criminal Justice in America

Criminal Justice in America

Advisory Editor
ROBERT M. FOGELSON

Editorial Board
RICHARD C. LARSON

JEROME H. SKOLNICK

LLOYD L. WEINREB

A History of the
Penal, Reformatory and Correctional Institutions of the State of New Jersey

Analytical and Documentary

HARRY ELMER BARNES

ARNO PRESS
A New York Times Company
New York • 1974

Reprint Edition 1974 by Arno Press Inc.

Reprinted from a copy in
  The University of Illinois Library

Criminal Justice in America
ISBN for complete set: 0-405-06135-8
See last pages of this volume for titles.

Manufactured in the United States of America

Library of Congress Cataloging in Publication Data

Barnes, Harry Elmer, 1889-1968.
  A history of the penal, reformatory, and correctional
institutions of the State of New Jersey.

  (Criminal justice in America)
  Reprint of the author's thesis, Columbia, 1918, which
was printed by MacCrellish & Quigley, Trenton, N. J.
  Bibliography: p.
  1. Correctional institutions--New Jersey--History.
I. Title. II. Series.
HV9475.N5B3 1974   365'.9749   74-3817
ISBN 0-405-06137-4

A History of the

Penal, Reformatory and Correctional Institutions of the State of New Jersey

Analytical and Documentary

HARRY ELMER BARNES, A.M.,

Lecturer in History, Columbia University. Sometime University Fellow in Historical Sociology, and Bayard Cutting Fellow in the History of Thought and Culture, Columbia University

---

SUBMITTED IN PARTIAL FULFILLMENT OF THE REQUIREMENTS FOR THE DEGREE OF DOCTOR OF PHILOSOPHY, IN THE FACULTY OF POLITICAL SCIENCE, COLUMBIA UNIVERSITY

TRENTON, N. J.
MacCRELLISH & QUIGLEY COMPANY
1918

CONTENTS

PART I. ANALYTICAL.

(3)

PAGE.

PART II. DOCUMENTARY.

Table of Contents. 9

LIST OF ILLUSTRATIONS

LIST OF DIAGRAMS OF GROUNDS AND BUILDINGS

Part I

ANALYTICAL

GENERAL INTRODUCTION

The history of the penal, reformatory, and correctional institutions of New Jersey is a subject of more than local interest, being in fact little less than a study in the social history of the United States. New Jersey's penal institutions and penological ideas and procedure did not develop in isolation, but as a part of the general current of penal development in this country. In view of the fact that New Jersey experimented with practically all of the chief types of penal institutions which have been tried in this country, including the Quaker workhouses, the congregate prisons, the Pennsylvania system of solitary confinement, and the Auburn system, which combined both the congregate and the solitary systems, there probably is no state which recapitulates better than New Jersey the essential features of the evolution of penal, reformatory, and correctional institutions in the United States.

During more than a century of its history the penal and correctional institutions of New Jersey were limited to the county jails and the few scattered workhouses, which were erected mainly in conjunction with the almshouses. In the jails there was no approach to anything like a differentiated treatment of delinquents. In them were herded promiscuously those convicted of crime and those awaiting trial; those of all ages and both sexes; those convicted of all varieties of crimes punishable by imprisonment; those of all mental states—normal, feeble-minded, neurotic, insane, epileptic. The workhouses were employed for the most part as an agency for suppressing vagrancy.

The first step towards a differentiated treatment of crime and criminals came with the erection of a state prison in 1797–8. This provided for a differentiation between those convicted of the more serious crimes and those convicted of petty offenses or awaiting trial. It did not, however, attempt any differentiation on the basis of age, sex, or mental state. Children and adults, male and female, sane and insane, were confined in contiguity.

(13)

The next attempt at differentiation came with the erection of the state hospital for the insane at Trenton in 1848. This provided for the treatment of the more important types of mental disorder, though no adequate provision was made for removing the insane from the prison.

During the next quarter of a century there was active agitation to provide a means of differentiating the treatment of criminals on the basis of sex, age, and degree of criminality. The first important accomplishment in this direction was the erection of reform schools for juvenile delinquents at Jamesburg and Trenton, in 1865 and 1871. Juvenile delinquents, if not guilty of major crimes, could then be removed from their degrading confinement in the state prison or the worse county jails and receive the properly specialized treatment which their circumstances demanded. No provision for the differentiated treatment of the less serious type of adult delinquents was made until the erection of the reformatories at Rahway and Clinton Farms in 1901 and 1913. The provision of the reformatory and correctional institutions at Jamesburg, Trenton, Rahway, and Clinton Farms marked a double process of differentiation, in that they not only called for a diversity of treatment according to age, sex, and degree of criminality, but also from the fact that they were clearly differentiated from the prison and jails in making reformation rather than punishment their chief aim.

Along with this development of a properly differentiated system for treating the delinquent population, has gone the growth of specialized institutions for dealing with the defective class, which was once treated indiscriminately along with the delinquent classes when its members were guilty of criminal action. The institution for the feeble-minded at Vineland, opened in 1898, the village for epileptics at Skillman, opened in the same year, and the state colonies for feeble-minded males, opened during 1916, provided scientific treatment for large numbers of those who would today be confined in the state prison or the county jails, if the ideas and institutions of 1840 now prevailed.

Finally, within the last quarter of a century, beginnings have been made in what is likely to be an important future development, namely, the non-institutional care of the less pronounced and confirmed types of delinquents, particularly delinquent minors. The developments along this line have, up to the present, consisted chiefly in the adoption of parole systems by all the state penal, reformatory, and correctional institutions; a more liberal use of the suspended sentence and probation; and the authorization, by the law of 1910, of the commitment of delinquent minors to the care of the State Board of Children's Guardians, a body created by an act of March 24, 1899.

If the following pages have succeeded in presenting a clear, even if an incomplete, picture of the different stages through which this general development has taken place in New Jersey, the aims of the writer will have been achieved.

THE COLONIAL PERIOD

CRIMINAL CODES AND
PENAL INSTITUTIONS

CHAPTER I

THE CRIMINAL CODES AND PENAL INSTITUTIONS OF COLONIAL NEW JERSEY.

I. THE SETTLEMENT OF THE COLONY OF NEW JERSEY.

1. THE ORIGIN OF NEW JERSEY.

In the early part of 1664, Charles II of England granted to his brother, the Duke of York, who afterwards became James II, the Dutch province of New Netherland.[1] The Duke proceeded

[1] *New Jersey Archives*, Vol. I, pp. 3–8.

to wrest the province from the Dutch by military force and rechristened it New York.

On June 23rd of the same year the Duke transferred that part of New York which now constitutes New Jersey to Lord John Berkeley and Sir George Carteret. The new grant was designated New Jersey, as a tribute to Carteret's vigorous defence of the Island of Jersey for the Stuarts during the Puritan wars.[1]

2. THE DIVISION OF THE PROVINCE OF NEW JERSEY.

The original joint proprietorship did not long endure. In 1673 Berkeley sold his share of the province to a group of prominent English Quakers. Out of this purchase was constructed the province of West Jersey. It constituted that portion of the province west of a line run from Little Egg Harbor to a point on the Delaware River, 41° N., a short distance north of the Delaware Water Gap.[2]

West Jersey was the largest portion in area, embracing 4,595 square miles, as compared with 2,981 square miles for East Jersey. East Jersey was, naturally, the most thickly populated, and by the beginning of the eighteenth century it had a population of about 10,000, or three times that of West Jersey.[3]

3. THE EARLY POPULATION OF EAST AND WEST JERSEY.

The original population of East Jersey was extremely heterogeneous. In what is now Bergen county, the Dutch were predominant. In Essex and Middlesex counties, Puritan New Englanders from New Haven colony, Connecticut, constituted a majority of the population. They brought with them the democratic political institution of the town-meeting. Quakers and Baptists from Long Island settled Monmouth county, while

[1] *New Jersey Archives*, Vol. I, pp. 8–14. E. P. Tanner, *The Province of New Jersey, 1664–1738*, p. 3.

[2] Tanner, op. cit., pp. 6, 10–11.

[3] Ibid., pp. 10–11, 29.

Scottish immigrants populated the region around Perth Amboy
in Middlesex county. Many Germans settled around New Brunswick in Middlesex county. This composite nature of the population of East Jersey doubtless goes a long way toward accounting for its "turbulent" political history and the harsh criminal
codes deemed necessary to preserve order.[1]

The population of West Jersey was more homogeneous. There
were a few Swedes, but the mass of the population were middle-
class Englishmen, at first mainly Quakers. As compared with
East Jersey, West Jersey enjoyed a peaceful and harmonious
existence, and its mild and advanced Quaker criminal and penal
codes contrasted most favorably with the crude and harsh enactments of East Jersey.[2]

II. The Administrative System of Colonial New Jersey.

1. East Jersey.

The general government of East Jersey was vested by the
proprietors in a governor, a council of from six to twelve members chosen by the governor, and an assembly of twelve chosen
by the freemen of the province. It was empowered to make all
laws for East Jersey which did not interfere with the laws of
England and the fundamental charter of the colony, and to erect
all public buildings and institutions.[3]

Counties were first created in New Jersey by the act of 1675,
in East Jersey, which marked out four divisions of the province
for the purpose of organizing local judicial systems and juris-
dictions. In 1683 these districts were definitely designated as the
counties of Bergen, Essex, Middlesex, and Monmouth. Somerset county was created out of Middlesex in 1688. There were,
thus, in East Jersey at the time of the union of 1702, five coun-

[1] Ibid., pp. 26–8.
[2] Ibid., pp. 28–9.
[3] Ibid., pp. 82–4.

ties.   In East Jersey the county during the seventeenth century was more of a territorial unit for judicial convenience than a local self-governing unit.   The inhabitants of East Jersey generally were strongly attached to the system of town government and the town and village rather than the county were the units of local self-government.[1]

There was no real demarcation of townships until 1692 in East Jersey.   Then an act of the legislature allowed the inhabitants of the counties, under the warrants of justices of the peace, to ascertain and set the limits of the towns.   Upon the basis of the results of this survey was passed the act of 1693 marking out the boundaries of the various towns.[2]

2. WEST JERSEY.

The organization of the government of West Jersey constituted the first application of Quaker principles to political administration.   The frame-work of the government was arranged by the famous *West Jersey Concessions* of 1677.   The general government was vested by the proprietors in a governor, a council and an elective assembly of one hundred.   The assembly possessed almost absolute political power and strictly limited the powers of the governor and council.[3]

The first counties in West Jersey were created by the survey of 1681, from the results of which Burlington, Gloucester, and Salem counties were marked out.   Cape May county was created in 1692.   Unlike the situation in East Jersey, the county in West Jersey was the vital local political unit and the center of the

[1] Osgood, *The American Colonies in the Seventeenth Century,* Vol. II, pp. 183, 285; Crecraft, *The Government of Hudson County, New Jersey,* p. 5; Howard, *Local Constitutional History of the United States,* pp. 365–6; Lee, *New Jersey as a Colony and a State,* Vol. I, pp. 263–4; Field, *The Provincial Courts of New Jersey,* pp. 5ff; Fairlie, *Local Government in Counties, Towns, and Villages,* pp. 29–30.

[2] Lee, op. cit., pp. 273–4; Osgood, op. cit., p. 174.

[3] Tanner, op. cit., pp. 113–14. *New Jersey Archives,* Vol I, pp. 241–270.

organization of local political life. In West Jersey the towns were created chiefly as constabularies.[1]

3. THE UNITED ROYAL PROVINCE OF NEW JERSEY, 1702–1776.

In the year 1702 the divided proprietary provinces of East and West Jersey were united in the royal province of New Jersey.

Up to 1738 New Jersey did not have a separate governor, the chief executive being the royal governor of New York, who spent little time in New Jersey, except when attending the legislative sessions. In 1738, after years of petitioning, New Jersey was granted the privilege of having a separate governor appointed by the Crown.[2]

The legislative powers were lodged in a council of twelve appointed by the Crown, and in an assembly of twenty-four members, two each being elected by the towns of Perth Amboy and Burlington, and ten each by the freeholders of what had been East and West Jersey.[3]

The council acted in an advisory capacity to the governor; constituted a court of highest appeal in the province; and had, in theory, equal legislative powers with the assembly, but in fact could not initiate money bills.[4]

While the assembly theoretically possessed only equal legislative powers with the council, it was in reality the most powerful and aggressive branch of the legislature.[5]

The legislature adopted the rather awkard and expensive practice of meeting alternately at Perth Amboy and Burlington, a custom which it adhered to with humorous tenacity against the wishes of the governors, probably because of the jealousy between the eastern and western portions of the state.[6]

---

[1] Lee, op. cit., pp. 264–6, 275.
[2] Tanner, op. cit., pp. 166f., E. J. Fisher, *New Jersey as a Royal Province, 1738–1776*, pp. 24, 73.
[3] Tanner, op. cit., pp. 259, 318.
[4] Fisher, op. cit., p. 48.
[5] Ibid., p. 73.
[6] Tanner, op. cit., pp. 166f. Fisher, op. cit., p. 73.

Under the united royal province four additional counties were created—Hunterdon out of Burlington in 1714; Morris out of Hunterdon in 1739; Cumberland out of Salem in 1748; and Sussex out of Morris in 1753.[1] The procedure in constructing a new county was essentially the following—the inhabitants of a portion of any given county would petition the legislature for a separate county government; the legislature upon granting the petition would determine the boundaries of the new county, authorize the new county officials to erect the necessary county buildings, and extend to the new county the general laws of the province.[2] Under the royal province there were four methods of creating towns—by direct action of the provincial legislature; by court orders; by the action of commissioners appointed by the provincial government; and by charter obtained from the governor. Of these methods the first was the most common.[3]

The system of local government in New Jersey has always been a very complicated matter. In the first place, the purely local government has been a mixture of town and county government and, in the second place, further to complicate matters, the provincial and state government has generally tended to infringe upon the proper jurisdiction of the counties. Again, in neither the colonial period, nor in the period since the formation of the state has the method or amount of local government been uniform throughout the state. During the united provincial period— from 1702 to 1776—the local government of New Jersey was a curious mixture of provincial and local powers. In the county, the chief executive officer, the sheriff, was an appointee of the governor, subject to the approval of the council. The county justices of the peace were also appointed by the governor, according to the Ordinance of 1704, thus making the strictly local judiciary appointees of the central provincial government. On the other hand, the county boards of chosen freeholders were

[1] Lee, op. cit., pp. 268–9. Warren county was created in 1824; Passaic and Atlantic in 1837; Mercer in 1838; Hudson in 1840; Camden in 1844; Ocean in 1850; and Union in 1857.
[2] Crecraft, op. cit., pp. 8–9.
[3] Lee, op. cit., pp. 275–6.

elected by the local authorities at an annual election held on the second Tuesday in March. The county financial administration was vested in a board consisting of two chosen freeholders and the county justices of the peace, thus combining in its composition both provincial and local and elective and appointive elements. This board retained these powers until 1798, when the justices were removed from the board and the financial administration given over to the freeholders alone. The town government was organized by the law of 1717, which directed the inhabitants of all towns to elect annually assessors and collectors of taxes. If they failed to do this the county justices of the peace were ordered to appoint such officers. Constables, one or more for each township, were to be appointed annually by the court of general sessions. Thus, by the appointment of the constables by a body which was itself appointed by the governor and represented the central provincial government, the local autonomy of even the township was infringed by the provincial government.[1] As far as the county jails were concerned, the control of the erection and repairs was put in the hands of the justices of the peace and the county board of chosen freeholders, a body which grew out of the act of 1693 in East Jersey allowing the inhabitants of each county to elect one or more men to meet with the justices of the peace to adjust the debts of the county and assess the taxes to meet the debts. As will be pointed out below, the acts of 1710 and 1714 vested the financial control of the jails in the board of chosen freeholders and the justices of the peace of each county, while from 1683 onward the sheriff was clothed with the executive power over the county jails.[2]

[1] L. Q. C. Elmer, *The Constitution and Government of the Province and State of New Jersey*, in *The Collections of the New Jersey Historical Society*, Vol. VII, pp. 7–8, 18–19. Fairlie, op. cit., pp. 27–9, 76–7.

[2] Crecraft, op. cit., p. 6. Howard, op. cit., pp. 365–7; Osgood, op. cit., p. 176; see below, pp. 42, 45.

III. The Judicial Organization, the Criminal Codes, and the Penal Institutions of Colonial New Jersey.

I. THE JUDICIAL ORGANIZATION.[1]

a. *East Jersey.*

The province of East Jersey established its court system in 1675. Monthly justices' courts for the trial of petty disputes not involving more than forty shillings were provided in each town. County courts were to meet twice each year in each county. An assize or provincial court was to meet annually at Woodbridge. The place of meeting of this last court was later changed to Elizabethtown and Perth Amboy. The governor and his council constituted the highest court of appeals.[2]

b. *West Jersey.*

In West Jersey, courts of justices of the peace having jurisdiction in cases of petty offences and disputes not involving more than forty shillings were provided for each town. County courts were to meet four times each year in Burlington and Salem. A court of appeals was established in 1693 A court of "capital jurisdiction" was provided. Finally, the assembly constituted the highest court of the province, and among other duties and powers had to pass upon all sentences to capital punishment before they could be carried into execution.[3]

c. *The United Royal Province.*

The judicial organization of the united province was provided for in the Ordinance of 1704. There were to be justices' courts for the towns, which met without any jury and tried cases of

---

[1] On this subject see Field, *The Provincial Courts of New Jersey.*

[2] Tanner, op. cit., pp. 458ff. Howard, *Local Constitutional History of the United States,* pp. 365–6.

[3] Tanner, op. cit., pp. 460ff.

debt and trespass involving sums less than forty shillings. In the counties there was to be a court of general sessions meeting four times each year and also a court of common pleas likewise meeting four times a year and trying all cases triable at common law. For the province a supreme court of appeals was provided to meet in May at Perth Amboy and in November at Burlington. In addition, the supreme court justices might also, in their discretion, hold courts in the separate counties. Finally, the governor and council constituted the highest court of appeal in special cases. This colonial judicial system, established in 1704, possesses more than antiquarian interest as it persisted through the colonial period and became the basis of the present judicial organization of the State of New Jersey.[1]

2. THE CRIMINAL CODES OF COLONIAL NEW JERSEY.

a. *East Jersey.*

In May, 1668, the first general assembly of New Jersey met at Elizabethtown and enacted a criminal code. This was reënacted with very little change on December 9, 1675, and constituted the basis of East Jersey criminal procedure.[2]

This code was a characteristic expression of the severe Puritan conceptions of criminal justice which had been brought into

[1] Tanner, op. cit., pp. 462-3; Fisher, op. cit., pp. 240-41. Howard, op. cit., p. 367.

[2] Aaron Leaming and Jacob Spicer, *The Grants, Concession and Original Constitutions of the Province of New Jersey,* pp. 78-84, 104-110. (References are to the reprint of 1881.) See Documents in Part II, pp. 343-7.

Edwin F. Hatfield, *A History of Elizabeth, New Jersey,* N. Y., 1868, p. 125. Hatfield states that the code of 1668 of East Jersey was taken almost verbatim from the famous Hempstead or Connecticut Code of 1650. This code is reproduced in *The Public Records of the Colony of Connecticut,* compiled by J. H. Trumbull, Hartford, 1850, Vol. I, pp. 509ff., and in *The Laws of New Haven Colony,* edited by S. Andrus, Hartford, 1822. Cf. C. H. Levermore, *The Republic of New Haven,* pp. 152-3.

As a matter of fact, however, the Jersey code of 1668 closely resembles the earlier, cruder, and more summary Connecticut code of "Capitall Lawes" enacted by the general court in December, 1642, from which the code of 1650 was largely copied; see Trumbull, op. cit., pp. 77-8. See Documents, Part II, pp. 341-3.

New Jersey by the settlers from New Haven colony. It is an exceedingly interesting document as it illustrates not only the severity of the criminal codes of the time, but also the comparatively small part that imprisonment played in theories of punishment at that time. The punishment prescribed for the various crimes was almost exclusively fine or corporal punishment, the latter taking the form of death, mutilation, branding, the stocks, or whipping. The idea of imprisonment as a generally accepted mode of punishment, which later developed, was derived partially from the European institution of the workhouse, which was in process of development from the middle of the sixteenth century, and in part from the Quaker experiments in penal institutions which were worked out in West Jersey and Pennsylvania. The Quakers were far less dominated by the sentiments of the Levitical Code than the Puritans, and their reluctance to employ the death penalty naturally led them to look with favor upon imprisonment at hard labor as a relatively humane and effective mode of punishment.

In the East Jersey Codes of 1668 and 1675 the death penalty was prescribed for murder, perjury, buggery, sodomy, abduction, rape, witchcraft, assault by children upon their parents, conspiracy, the third offence of burglary and robbery, and the fourth offence of thievery.[1]

Arson was to be punished by compelling the offender to make full satisfaction to the injured party, or suffer death or such other punishment as the court might prescribe. For burglary

As many of the Puritan settlers in East Jersey came from New Haven Colony, there is little doubt that a direct connection exists between the Connecticut codes of 1642 and 1650, and the East Jersey codes of 1668 and 1675. The Connecticut codes of 1642 and 1650 are a particularly fine expression of Puritan ideas of criminal justice. They were even more harsh than the East Jersey code; pertinent Scripture being quoted in support of the death penalty for each of the twelve capital crimes:—idolatry, witchcraft, blasphemy, murder, poisoning, buggery, sodomy, adultery, rape, abduction, perjury, insurrection. There may thus be some basis for Hatfield's claim that in the East Jersey code of 1668 "Puritan austerity was tempered with Dutch indifference." However, a perusal of the Jersey code is sufficient to convince one that the tempering process was not carried very far.

[1] Leaming and Spicer, pp. 78–84.

or robbery the offender was compelled to make full restitution for the first offence and to be branded with a T on the hand, doubtless signifying "Thief." A second offence required restitution and the brand of an R on the forehead, signifying "Robber." Death was prescribed for the third offence. For theft, treble restitution was prescribed for the first offence; treble restitution and such punishment as the court might dictate for the second and third offences; and death for the fourth. Adultery was to be punished by divorce, corporal punishment, banishment, any or all at the discretion of the court. Fornication required compulsory marriage, fine, or corporal punishment, as the court might decree, and security for the care of the potential offspring. "Concerning that beastly vice, drunkenness," it was enacted that the guilty party was to be fined one shilling for the first offence, two for the second, and three shillings six pence for all subsequent repetitions. On default of fine, corporal punishment was ordered and the stocks were decreed for unruly drunkards. Swearing was to be punished by a fine of one shilling, one-half of which went to the public treasury and one-half to the informant. Those who could not furnish a satisfactory explanation of their absence from home after nine o'clock in the evening were to be punished according to the discretion of the court. Resistance to the public authorities was to be punished by fine or corporal punishment as the court might decree. Finally, it was enacted that the death penalty was not to be inflicted except according to the laws of the province and only after conviction upon the testimony of two or more witnesses.[1]

As has been pointed out above, this code of 1668 was formally reënacted as the criminal code of East Jersey in 1675.[2]

The Puritan influence in East Jersey was further manifested in the Law of October, 1677, forbidding the profaning of the Sabbath. Householders or tavern-keepers who allowed drinking, tippling, or disorderly conduct on their premises on the Sabbath were to be punished by a fine of ten shillings for the first

[1] Leaming and Spicer, Ibid.
[2] Ibid., pp. 104-10. Hatfield, op., cit., p. 185.

offence and of twenty shillings for each succeeding offence. All
disorderly persons found on the premises were to receive two
hours in the stocks.[1]

In spite of the generally harsh and severe nature of these early
Puritan codes it is only fair to point out that in one important
respect these codes were greatly in advance of those in vogue
at the present time. They aimed as far as possible to compel the
offender to make *restitution* to society and to the victim of his
unlawful conduct, while the laws of the present day have so concentrated upon the ascertaining of guilt and the fixing of the
punishment of the offender that they have practically left out of
consideration the matter of exacting restitution to the injured
party or his relatives.

In 1681–1682 a group of Quakers, among them William Penn,
gained administrative control of East Jersey through its purchase from the heirs of Carteret for £3400. While they never
constituted any significant proportion of the population of East
Jersey, their controlling interest in the government was reflected
in the changes in the regulation and administration of criminal
procedure. This Quaker influence was immediately felt in the
new criminal and civil code drawn up for East Jersey in 1682.
The penalties exacted for criminal offences were less severe and
jails were provided for confinement, but this method of punishment was mainly employed in the case of debtors. The sections
of the code relating to civil cases testified to the development of
a more settled agricultural industry, as it prescribed the procedure
to be followed in regard to the legal complications which would
inevitably arise in an agricultural society. It is interesting to
note that in formulating the legal rules to be followed in adjudi-
cating civil cases the inhabitants of East Jersey drew as freely
upon the Mosaic code as they had in formulating the criminal
codes of 1668 and 1675.[2]

[1] Leaming and Spicer, p. 124.
[2] Leaming and Spicer, op. cit., pp. 233–9. Hatfield, op. cit., pp. 210–11, 217–
18. Osgood, *The American Colonies in the Seventeenth Century,* Vol. II,
p. 191.

As to the criminal offences it was provided that murder should be punished by the death penalty, though accident and self-defence should be accorded the same consideration as in the English common law. If a thief or burglar be caught alive he was to make double restitution or be sold for his offence. A citizen was to be relieved from all responsibility if he killed a thief or burglar in the act. Buggery was to be punished with death. Fornication required a compulsory marriage, and if the girl's parents refused this, the offender was to pay damages as the court decreed. If a man should run away with the wife of another and either or both return they were to receive ten lashes on the back. Six months' absence of a wife under such circumstances were to release the husband from all responsibility acquired by his marriage to the woman. If convicted of perjury, the offender was to receive the sentence that the accused might have received or did receive; to make full satisfaction to the wronged person; and to be put on record as a perjurer and excluded from all future entry into court as a witness. "Affliction" of widows or orphans was to be dealt with at the discretion of the court. Work was forbidden on the "Lord's Day."[1]

The following provisions were made for the more important civil cases which might arise or had arisen. It was decreed that if a man were gored and killed by an ox or beast, the beast should be forfeited to the nearest relative of the deceased, and if the owner had been warned of the unruly nature of his beast he was also to be fined as the court should decide. If a person should dig a pit and not fence it adequately and his neighbor's beast should fall in it, he must make restitution and might keep the beast. If a man's beast should kill that of a neighbor, the two animals were to be sold and the receipts divided. If a person should steal any domesticated animals he was compelled to make five-fold restitution. Full restitution was decreed for feeding one's stock on the land or products of another or for damages from a careless setting of fires. If borrowed property was stolen and the thief captured, double restitution was decreed,

[1] Leaming and Spicer, op. cit., pp. 233-9.

and, if the thief was not apprehended, the court was to decide the matter justly. If a borrowed beast should die the borrower was to pay in full unless the owner was present. In the case of death of a hired beast the full responsibility lay with the owner.[1]

As to criminal procedure it was provided that all trials were to be by a jury of twelve men and that in criminal and capital cases such a trial was to be preceded by a grand jury indictment. Jails were to be provided in all counties, but primarily as places of detention of accused rather than for the punishment of condemned. Bail was to be allowed on sufficient security.[2]

It was evidently considered that further legislation was needed in addition to this general code, for in the same session it was enacted that "prophane swearing" was to be punished by a fine of two shillings six pence, or by three hours in the stocks; that drunkenness was to have penalty of a fine of five shillings or six hours in the stocks; that incest was to be punished as a felony; that adultery was to be punished by a fine of from five to fifty pounds; that fornication was to be penalized by three months in jail or a fine of five pounds; and, finally, that "prophaning the Lord's Day" should require a punishment of a fine of five shillings for the first offence and of ten shillings for all succeeding offences, with two hours in the stocks in case of a default of fines.[3]

Such were the rather crude and primitive criminal codes of Puritan East Jersey, the harsh provisions of which, so characteristic of the period, created little need for penal institutions.

b. *West Jersey.*

The first provisions for the administration of justice in West Jersey were embodied in the famous constitution of the province drawn up by the Quaker proprietors in 1677 and entitled "The Concessions and Agreements of the Proprietors, Freeholders,

[1] Ibid.
[2] Ibid.
[3] Ibid., pp. 240–246.

and Inhabitants of the Province of West Jersey in America."
The "Concessions" have been called by a competent historian
"the broadest, sanest, and most equitable charter draughted for
and body of Colonists up to that time.[1]

As contrasted with the East Jersey codes of 1668 and 1675
the juridical provisions of this Quaker instrument of government
were remarkably mild and advanced. The penalties were mild
and elastic, the mode and degree of punishment usually being
left to the discretion of the court to fit the circumstances. Absolute freedom of "opinion and worship" was decreed, and equally
remarkable for that period, the imprisonment of honest debtors
was forbidden.[2]

The commissioners of the province were to see that justice was
executed according to the laws of the province, and they were
given power to suspend sentences they thought unjust and to
appeal them to the next session of the assembly. The accused
or condemned were to be kept in safe custody in the meantime,
a provision which necessitated the maintenance of jails. It was
further enacted that no fees should be paid by inmates to officers
of prisons.[3]

No person was to be convicted except by a jury of his neigh-
bors and the accused was to have the privilege of rejecting thirty-
five jurors without any cause being stated and an indefinite number upon good cause. Three justices were to sit with the jurors
in all counties, but they were merely to pronounce the sentence
imposed by the jury. Conviction had to be based upon the sworn
testimony of at least two reputable witnesses and perjury was to
be punished in civil cases by requiring the perjurer to receive
the sentence of the accused or convicted person, and in criminal

[1] Andrews, *Colonial Self-Government*, pp. 121–122.
[2] Leaming and Spicer, op. cit., pp. 382–411. The "Concessions and Agreements" are also to be found in the *New Jersey Archives*, Vol. I, pp. 250–66.
See Documents, Part II, pp. 347–351.
See *The Colonial Records of Pennsylvania*, Phil., 1852, Vol. I, pp. 37–42,
for the Quaker Criminal Code of Pennsylvania. Cf. A. C. Applegarth, *The
Quakers in Pennsylvania*, pp. 30–49.
[3] Leaming and Spicer, op. cit., pp. 382–411.

3 P

cases by a severe fine and for a second offence, exclusion from all public offices and from employment in the province. All trials were to be in public "that justice may not be done in a corner nor in any covert manner" and that all "may be free from slavery and oppression." [1]

Any one attempting to subvert the fundamental laws of the province was liable to trial for treason. Robbery and theft were to be punished by compelling two-fold restitution or such punishment as a jury of twelve should deem fit, though it was not to extend to death or mutilation. Assault and battery were to be punished according to the decision of a jury to fit the circumstances. While treason and murder were formally capital offences, the death penalty was not to be inflicted until the case was reviewed by the following session of the assembly. In all cases except treason, murder, and felony the person preferring the charges was given the privilege of withdrawing the charges at any time, and thus stopping the proceedings, and of remitting the penalty after conviction. [2]

The criminal and juridical provisions of the "Concessions and Agreements" of 1677 were reënacted by the general assembly meeting at Burlington in November, 1681. The only changes of any importance were that restitution for robbery was thereafter to be four-fold rather than two-fold, and it was expressly provided that imprisonment should be accompanied by hard labor. [3]

Shortly after 1680 there came a Puritan immigration into West Jersey from East Jersey, from New England, and from England itself. Puritan influence was reflected in the increasing severity of the criminal legislation of West Jersey after 1681.

The addition to the criminal code enacted by the assembly of March, 1683, provided that swearing should be punished by a fine of two shillings or three hours in the stocks; drunkenness by a fine of three shillings four pence or five hours in the stocks; and whoredom as the court should decree. [4]

[1] Ibid.
[2] Ibid.
[3] Ibid., pp. 426–34.
[4] Ibid., p. 460.

The act of October, 1693, decreed that a fine of six shillings should be imposed for profaning the Lord's Day.[1]

In May, 1694, an act was passed for the punishment of whoredom and adultery. A fine of five pounds was imposed if both were unmarried and of ten pounds if either was married. If the fine was not paid the guilty parties were to submit to a severe whipping.[2]

Finally, in May, 1700, it was provided that for the proper punishment of burglary, in addition to the making of four-fold restitution, for the first offence the guilty person was to receive thirty-nine lashes on the back; for the second offence thirty-nine lashes and be branded with a letter T on the forehead; and for the third offence to be branded with a T on the cheek, be imprisoned for twelve months at hard labor, and be whipped with thirty-nine lashes each month during his confinement. The particular virtue attached to thirty-nine lashes was probably drawn by association from the thirty-nine books of the Old Testament.[3]

Thus the criminal code of West Jersey, which began as a mild expression of Quaker ideas of justice, had by the close of the century, through Puritan immigration, begun to take on many of the characteristics of the severe criminal procedure of the code of Puritan East Jersey.

c. *The Criminal Codes of the United Royal Province, 1702–76.*

There were no marked changes in the criminal code after the union of East and West Jersey. As has been already pointed out, the criminal codes of the Eastern and Western provinces had tended towards a general similarity. The harsh code of East Jersey had been moderated by the influence of the Quaker proprietors after 1682, while the mild Quaker code of West Jersey became more and more severe and intolerant with the increased Puritan immigration into this portion of the colony. These early

[1] Ibid., p. 519.
[2] Ibid., pp. 527–8.
[3] Ibid., pp. 573–4.

criminal codes with their modified sumptuary legislation were carried over into the united province and still later had an important influence on the formation of the criminal code of the state in 1796.[1]

The Puritan restrictions on "immorality" were reënacted in May, 1704, with hardly any change from the form they had taken late in the previous century in the codes of both East and West Jersey.[2]

New Jersey evidently began to suffer in the first half of the eighteenth century from the English practice of deporting criminals, for on July 8, 1730, a law was passed "imposing a duty on persons convicted of heinous crimes, and to prevent poor and impotent persons from being imported into the province of New Jersey." A duty of five pounds was levied on all convicts imported into the province and the importer was obliged to give a bond of fifty pounds guaranteeing their good behavior for one year.[3]

By the middle of the century the colony of New Jersey had so far developed that it became troubled with some of the vices common to established societies, and, in December, 1748, an act was passed "for the more effective preventing of lotteries, playing of cards and dice, and other gaming for lucre of gain; and to restrain the abuse of horse racing within this colony for the future." [4] That these "evil tendencies" were not easily curbed may be gathered from the passage of a more stringent law in December, 1761, "effectually to prevent horse racing and gaming in the Province of New Jersey." [5]

[1] William and Andrew Bradford, *The Acts of the General Assembly of New Jersey,* 1703–1730, Philadelphia, 1732, pp. 3–5. *New Jersey Archives,* Vol. II, p. 511.

[2] Bradford, op. cit., pp. 3–5.

[3] Ibid., pp. 276–7. *New Jersey Archives,* Vol. XIV, p. 438. Cf. O. M. Dickerson, *American Colonial Government,* pp. 245–6.

[4] Samuel Allinson, *The Acts of the General Assembly of New Jersey,* 1702–1776, pp. 187ff.

[5] Ibid., pp. 241–4. That horse stealing was also becoming a menace to the peace and security of the colony may be inferred from the succession of severe laws passed to root out the practice. *New Jersey Archives,* Vol. XVIII, pp. 103, 474.

By the beginning of the second half of the eighteenth century the practice of imprisonment for debt was evidently proving a burdensome failure, for in December, 1761, a law was passed providing that a man who owed debts of less than fifty pounds could indenture himself as a servant to anyone who was willing to assume the payment of the debt and would thereby be free from arrest.[1] That this did not solve the problem is evident from the act of December, 1771, decreeing that, whereas imprisonment for debt had proved unsatisfactory, a debtor might assign his whole estate to his creditors, reserving only his tools or implements of trade and one bed and bedding, not to exceed ten pounds value in all, and thereafter be forever discharged from such debts as were outstanding at the time. This law of 1771 was an early expression of the modern bankruptcy laws. This privilege was not to be open to unmarried debtors under forty years of age. This latter type of debtor was compelled to render satisfaction by indentured servitude to his creditors.[2]

An act somewhat related to these, which were designed to relieve the colony from the expense of maintaining debtors in prison, was passed in December, 1775, and provided that those condemned for criminal offences and who did not have sufficient funds to pay their fines or fees might be sold for a term not to exceed five years to any person or persons who were willing to pay the said fines or fees.[3]

Such were the chief characteristics of the New Jersey criminal codes in the colonial period. A harsh and severe Levitical code in Puritan East Jersey was modified by Quaker influences in the government. The mild Quaker code of West Jersey was rendered more vigorous by Puritan immigration. These two codes were thus gradually assimilated through mutual interaction and interpenetration of the social forces which

[1] Allinson, op. cit., p. 244.

[2] Ibid., pp. 356–63. Imprisonment for debt was finally abolished in 1846, only after prolonged agitation.

[3] Ibid., p. 491. The growing expense of maintaining penal institutions is also reflected in laws relieving sheriffs and preventing the immigration of criminals. *New Jersey Archives,* Vol. XVIII, pp. 105, 256, 326.

brought them into being and were carried over into the united province and perpetuated throughout the colonial period. Toward the end of this period the criminal codes were forced to readjust themselves to curb vices inherent in a more developed society and to escape the expense connected with an unwise detention of debtors and petty offenders, for whom imprisonment was not intended or adapted as a punishment. Attention may now be turned to the consideration of the origin and development of penal institutions during the colonial epoch.

3. THE PENAL INSTITUTIONS OF COLONIAL NEW JERSEY.

a. *General Observations on the Origins of the Penal Institutions of New Jersey.*

New Jersey is noteworthy in the history of penal institutions, in that it shared with Pennsylvania the distinction of being the first definitely and consistently to employ the Quaker practice of utilizing the workhouse as the basis of the penal system.

The workhouse was not a Quaker invention. It had a considerable vogue in Europe as early as the seventeenth century. However, it was employed in Europe more for the repression of vagabonds and beggars than for the punishment of condemned criminals. The criminal codes of that day, as has already been pointed out, made little use of imprisonment as a method of punishing crime. Criminals were punished rather by fines, corporal punishment, and later by banishment and deportation. The European prisons of that time were designed mainly to confine debtors and political offenders and to detain accused persons pending their trial and disposition.[1]

However, though the Quakers did not originate the idea of the workhouse or imprisonment at hard labor, it was their theory of punishment which made possible the extensive employment of imprisonment at hard labor as a system of punishment and the

[1] J. F. Stephen, *A History of the Criminal Law of England*, Vol. I, p. 57; F. H. Wines, *Punishment and Reformation*, pp. 115–116.

basis of a penal system. Being extremely averse to the whole-sale employment of capital punishment and the cruel methods of physical torture then practiced, the Quakers naturally fell back upon the alternative of imprisonment at hard labor as the chief agency in protecting society from the criminal and in effecting the punishment and reformation of the latter.[1]

The Quaker criminal code of 1681 in West Jersey distinctly provided for the workhouse as the basis of the penal system. While East Jersey never went far beyond the conventional use of the jail system as a place of detention for the accused and of imprisonment for debtors and those unable to pay their fines, Quaker influence permeated East Jersey to some extent and was evident in the laws of 1682 providing for a system of jails, and in the later provision that was made for workhouses in some counties of East Jersey.

When the Quaker population in New Jersey became outnumbered and submerged by the immigration of other elements, particularly from the beginning of the eighteenth century, the Quaker theory and practice in penology gradually died out and New Jersey reverted in general to the older and less rational county jail system, in which detention rather than punishment, determent, or reformation was the main object sought and achieved. In this system any approach to a proper differentiation, classification, and effective punishment, reformation, or employment of those confined was practically impossible. The few workhouses which were erected before the Revolutionary War were practically the only visible remains of Quaker influences in the penology of New Jersey, and the workhouses soon lost most of their characteristics as penal institutions.

In Pennsylvania, the Quaker theory and practice of basing the penal system upon the workhouse received a longer and more thorough and general application. The laws framed by Penn and his associates for the government of Pennsylvania in 1682

[1] See Penn's *Frame of the Government of the Province of Pennsylvania, together with Certain Laws Agreed Upon in England*, 1682, in *The Colonial Records of Pennsylvania*, Phil., 1852, Vol. I, p. 38. Cf. W. R. Shepherd, *A History of Proprietary Government in Pennsylvania*, pp. 225-316.

provided that "all prisons shall be workhouses for felons, vagrants, and loose idle persons; whereof one shall be in every county."[1] It was from Quaker Pennsylvania, in the main, that the modern prison system, based upon the employment of prisoners at hard labor, spread through the colonies and was later adopted by many of the states in the early national period. The extraordinary diffusion of these Quaker ideas and practices in penal administration was in all probability due to the fact that the Quakers were first in the field with penological ideas which in any sense harmonized with the general growth and development of humanitarian tendencies in the eighteenth and early nineteenth centuries, and also to the central and dominating situation and position of Philadelphia in this country between 1750 and 1825. From the United States it was introduced into the practice of Europe through the recommendation of such investigators of penal systems as the Englishman, Wm. Crawford, and the Frenchmen, Beaumont and De Tocqueville. After the Quaker influence in New Jersey died out, neither the colony nor the state attained to any special prominence in the history of American penology until about 1830. At that time New Jersey exerted an influence upon the other states by its speedy imitation of the famous Pennsylvania system of solitary confinement in 1833, and its tenacious adherence to this system until after all other states except Pennsylvania had abandoned it.[2]

b. *East Jersey.*

A jail system was provided for East Jersey by the act of March, 1682, but, as has been suggested above, it was designed for the detention rather than the punishment and reformation of offenders. It enacted that,

"In each county there shall be a common gaol, which shall be for fellons, vagrants, and idle persons, and safely to keep all persons committed to goal for debt before or after judgment."[3]

[1] *The Colonial Records of Pennsylvania*, Philadelphia, 1852, Vol. I, p. 38.
[2] See below, pp. 96–7, 102–3.
[3] Leaming and Spicer, op. cit., p. 235.

Provision for carrying this law into execution was made by the act of the following year, decreeing,

"Whereas, by several Acts of Assembly, it has been heretofore provided that in every county shall be built and provided a common gaol, and in every town a convenient pound. Be it enacted by the Governor, Council, and Deputies in General Assembly met and assembled, and by the authority of the same, that in every county the justices of the peace at their next Quarter Sessions, next after the publishing hereof, or so many thereof as shall meet at said sessions, shall order, assess, and make a rate or tax upon the inhabitants of each county, for the building and maintaining in each county a common gaol and in each town a pound, and shall also order and constitute collectors for the same, and shall also order, contract, and agree with workmen for making and erecting the said gaols and pounds, which said rate and tax so assessed, imposed or taxed, the said collectors shall levy by distress upon non-payment thereof, and pay into the hands of such person or persons, as the said justices shall order, to the end aforesaid."[1]

The penal system of East Jersey, then, provided for nothing beyond the antique county jail system with the emphasis placed on detention rather than punishment or reformation. Though it was much less important in the history of penology than the workhouse system of West Jersey, it was much more closely connected with the subsequent penal system of colonial New Jersey, which in the main adopted the county jail system.

c. *West Jersey.*

The provision of the acts of the assembly of West Jersey in 1681 that condemned persons, especially those condemned to death, should be kept in safe custody until their cases were reviewed by the governor and general assembly at the next session of the legislature, necessitated the provision of jails for the confinement of such persons.[2]

In the same session the workhouse system was made an integral part of the jail or prison system by the law which decreed that "all persons to be committed to prison for criminal causes shall be compelled to work for their daily bread during the time

[1] Leaming and Spicer, op. cit. p. 268.
[2] Leaming and Spicer, op. cit., p. 427.

of their commitment in such work as they shall be able to perform." [1]

The significant aspect of this adoption of the workhouse plan by the West Jersey Quakers is that they employed it not merely as an adjunct to the almshouse to suppress vagrancy and pauperism, but as a penal institution for the punishment and reformation of convicted criminals. This action, which was essentially an innovation as compared with European procedure, was further developed by the Pennsylvania Quakers, was imitated in time by most of the other states and constitutes one of the most significant contributions made by the United States to the development of penal institutions.

d. *The United Royal Province of New Jersey, 1702–76.*

When the united royal province of New Jersey was constituted in 1702, it was natural that the county jail system of East Jersey, which was much the most populous division of the province, should dominate the penal procedure of the united province rather than the Quaker workhouse system of West Jersey.

The first important law passed in the united province which made provision for a jail system in the colony was that of January, 1709–1710, which provided for the building and repairing of jails and courthouses in the several counties of the province. As far as chronological priority is concerned, this act may be regarded as the historical origin of the New Jersey practice of delegating the power to build and repair the county jails and courthouses to a board of chosen freeholders.[2]

This act apparently was not carried into effect, for it was followed by the important act of February 28, 1714, giving two chosen freeholders and the justices of the peace in each county the authority to raise money to build and repair jails and courthouses. It provided that "whereas gaols and courthouses are

[1] Ibid., p. 434.
[2] *New Jersey Archives,* Vol. XIII, p. 398.

absolutely necessary for the administration of Justice and putting the Laws into Execution," the inhabitants of each county should meet annually on the second Tuesday in March and elect two freeholders who should meet with the justices of the peace of each county "and agree upon such sum and sums of money as shall be needful for repairing such gaols and courthouses as are already built and for building such as are waiting." The freeholders and justices were empowered to appoint assessors and collectors to raise the necessary funds to build or repair the said courthouses and jails and to designate managers to carry the work into execution.[1]

That the provisions of this act were to some extent carried out is to be gathered from a number of later acts granting permission to rebuild jails and courthouses which had burned down. The following acts throw some light on the situation:

On July 8, 1730, an act was passed authorizing the building of a new courthouse and jail in Monmouth county to replace the original structure which had burned down.[2]

A similar act was passed on March 15, 1739, providing for the rebuilding of the recently burned jail and courthouse of Somerset county.[3]

An act of July 31, 1740, allowed the inhabitants of Essex county to repair the courthouse and jail at Newark.[4]

Cumberland county was created in 1748, when an act was passed authorizing the construction of a jail and courthouse, according to the provisions of the act of 1714.[5]

Likewise, Morris county was empowered to erect its first courthouse and jail by an act of June 8, 1753, and the new county of Sussex, which had just been constructed out of a part of Morris county, was given a similar authorization by another act of the same date. Apparently Sussex county did not avail itself of the

[1] Bradford, op. cit., pp. 42-4. This is also given in Allinson, op. cit., pp. 14-16. See Documents, Part II, pp. 351-354.
[2] Allinson, op. cit., pp. 92-3.
[3] Ibid., pp. 107-8.
[4] Ibid., pp. 116-118.
[5] Ibid., pp. 154-5.

opportunity, for, in 1761, the citizens of that county petitioned the legislature for permission to build a courthouse and jail, and their request was granted by an act of December 12, 1761.[1]

By an act of December 7, 1763, the citizens of New Brunswick, Middlesex county, were authorized to repair their courthouse and their jail, the latter being in "such decay" that it was unfit for the confinement of prisoners and unequal to the task of safely detaining them in custody.[2]

An act of June 28, 1766, providing for the rebuilding of the courthouse and jail in Perth Amboy in Middlesex county which had burned down, and an act of March 11, 1774, granted similar authority to the citizens of Cape May county who had likewise lost their courthouse and jail by fire.[3]

In view of the general empowering act of February 28, 1714, it is difficult to understand why these separate acts, just enumerated, were necessary, but whatever may have been their legal value they serve the historian in reconstructing the picture of the penal institutions of the later colonial period.[4]

As far as one can judge by the few drawings and rough cuts of the jails of the colonial period, even those constructed after the middle of the eighteenth century were rather crude frame structures, highly combustible and ill-adapted for the safe confinement of offenders.[5]

The acts enumerated above providing for the erection of new jails reveal the large percentage of jails which were destroyed by fire. Instances of jail-breaking were even more numerous. From the newspaper notices preserved in the volumes of the *New Jersey Archives,* one learns that in the period from 1720 to 1765 one or more escapes were advertised as having taken place

[1] Ibid., pp. 195–6, 240–41.

[2] Ibid., pp. 259–60.

[3] Ibid., pp. 283–4; 458–60.

[4] There is little doubt that these separate acts were passed as a result of the peculiar relation which has always existed in New Jersey between the counties and the commonwealth, resulting in a general tendency on the part of the central government to infringe on the jurisdiction of the counties, and a jealous resistance of this policy by the counties.

[5] See Plate XV, opposite page 332.

in Bergen, Burlington, Cumberland, Gloucester, Hunterdon, Middlesex, Monmouth, Morris, Salem, and Somerset counties.[1]

These instances of jail-breaking were by no means limited to the occasional escape of a single minor offender, but were in many cases little if anything short of a virtual emptying out of the jail. Many desperate criminals, some awaiting an execution of the death penalty, effected their escape and were never recaptured. Thus the jails of colonial New Jersey, which openly abandoned any attempt at the reformation of offenders, also failed, to a considerable extent, in fulfilling their elementary function of protecting society through the detention of criminals. In this respect, however, they were not essentially different from those in the remainder of the colonies.

e. *The Administration of the County Jails.*

The administration of the county jail system in New Jersey has been vested from the beginning in the sheriff and his subordinates. As early as March, 1683, an act was passed in East Jersey authorizing the governor to appoint a high sheriff for the province and a sheriff for each of the four counties.[2]

When the jail system and the office of sheriff were first constituted in East Jersey no provision was made for raising funds to maintain the jails and support the sheriffs. Samuel Moore, the newly appointed sheriff and "keeper of the common gaol" of Middlesex county, soon sent a petition to the legislature "setting forth his former great cost and charge in keeping and maintaining the prisoners without any allowance for the same, which charge is yet continued upon him, there being no provision to this day made for him." [3]

[1] *New Jersey Archives,* Vol. XI, pp. 52, 58, 65, 154, 187, 193, 200, 213, 223, 293, 317, 332, 358, 480, 483, 493, 507; Vol. XX, pp. 81, 128, 170-1, 409, 604; Vol. XXIV, pp. 58, 59, 61, 80, 90, 110, 111, 116, 206, 207, 221, 226, 227, 246, 357, 374, 377, 406, 443, 447, 448, 470, 471, 479, 518, 560, 587, 676. See Documents, Part II, pp. 354-356.
[2] *New Jersey Archives,* Vol. XIII, pp. 10-12, 24. Howard, op. cit., p. 366. Tanner, *The Province of New Jersey,* pp. 257-8.
[3] *New Jersey Archives,* Vol. XIII, p. 84.

The council resolved that such allowance be made to Moore that his office would no longer be a drain on his resources, but would encourage him to undertake its duties.[1] That the resolution was never extended to all of the other counties of the province is evident from the introduction of a bill in May, 1683, to provide for the punishment of sheriffs who refused to accept their office and execute its duties. The council declared, however, that it was unreasonable to punish a sheriff severely for refusing to accept his office when no salary or reward had been provided for the office.[2] That the difficulty was not satisfactorily adjusted at the time is apparent from the act of October, 1686, directing that the sheriffs hold office for one year and that they be fined twenty pounds if they refused to accept the office.[3]

After the union of East and West Jersey in 1702 there was little change in the administrative system of the county jails. As before, the sheriffs were appointed by the governor with the consent of the council. The reluctance to hold the office of sheriff varied with the locality and the individual. There were several acts passed compelling those appointed to accept the office under penalty of a heavy fine, but, at the same time, there was a number of acts aimed at prohibiting a sheriff from holding office more than one year and from using unfair means to achieve his appointment.[4] The lack of any uniform system of providing funds to maintain the jails, and the curious variation in the apparent desirability of the office of sheriff, would seem to warrant the conclusion that the value of the office varied with the industry and ingenuity of the individual sheriffs.

In the period between 1708 and 1748 a series of acts was passed providing that the sheriffs give security for the faithful execution of their office. The act of March, 1708, provided that the sheriff of Burlington county should give a bond of five hun-

[1] Ibid.
[2] Ibid., pp. 87–88.
[3] Ibid., p. 164.
[4] Ibid., pp. 89, 163–4; Vol. XIV, pp. 218–19; Vol. XVI, pp. 358–60; Elmer, *The Constitution and Government of the Province and State of New Jersey, in Collections of the New Jersey Historical Society*, Vol. VII, pp. 7ff., 18.

dred pounds; the sheriff of the other counties except Bergen and
Cape May three hundred; and in Bergen and Cape May one
hundred pounds.[1]   In May, 1720, this was reënacted with the
change that the bond required in Burlington county was reduced
to three hundred pounds.[2]   In March, 1736, it was provided that
the bond for all counties except Bergen, Cape May, and Somerset, should be four hundred pounds, and, for these counties, it
should be two hundred.[3]

It was not until 1748 that a series of acts provided for a
uniform administration of the county jails and the office of
sheriff in New Jersey.   On January 19, 1748, "in order to
oblige the Sheriffs of the several Counties, Cities, Boroughs,
and Towns—corporate, within this colony, to a more strict and
impartial Execution of their several Offices, and for the better
securing the Rights of the Crown, and the properties of the
People," an act was passed regulating the bonds of sheriff, the
method of taking oath, and the term of office and residence qualifications of the sheriffs.[4]

As a guarantee of faithful performance of the duties of
the office of sheriff, it was enacted that the bond should be eight
hundred pounds for all counties except Cape May, for which a
bond of two hundred pounds was deemed sufficient.[5]

The sheriffs were compelled to take the long oath of office provided for in the act of 1722, which included a declaration of
loyalty to the House of Hanover and of disbelief in transubstan-
tiation and in the efficacy of the adoration of the Virgin.[6]

As to the term of office of the sheriff, it was decreed that no
sheriff or undersheriff should hold office more than three years,
nor serve a second term until after an interval of three years.   In
addition, the law prescribed that no one could hold the office of

[1] *New Jersey Archives,* Vol. XIII, p. 314.
[2] Ibid., Vol. XIV, p. 141.
[3] Ibid., p. 522.
[4] Allinson, op. cit., pp. 156.
[5] Ibid.
[6] Ibid., pp. 156-7.   These humorous phases of the oath were prescribed for
all officers by a decree of the Crown.

sheriff who had not been a freeholder in the given county for at least three years before his appointment.[1]

The sheriff's fees, and his expenses in maintaining prisoners in the county jail, were provided for in the general "Fees Act" of February 18, 1748. This law, which was passed "for the better enabling the Judges and Justices of this colony to ascertain and tax Bills of Cost, and for making provision by law for the payment of the services of the several officers of the Colony, and for preventing the said officers from taking exhorbitant fees," fixed in detail the fees which the sheriff was to receive for his services in civil and criminal cases and provided an allowance of six pence per day for "victualling every prisoner" in the county jail.[2] This provision of six pence per day for the prisoners in the county jails was later deemed insufficient, and the act of December 21, 1771, raised the allowance to nine pence per day.[3]

In the early colonial period, when the population was scattered and the duties of the sheriff were not particularly exacting, the sheriff also directly supervised the administration of the county jail.[4] However, all the contemporary evidence goes to show that before the middle of the eighteenth century the present practice had arisen of detailing an undersheriff to assume the immediate supervision of the jail, thus leaving the sheriff free to discharge his duties as the chief executive officer of the county.[5]

f. *The Colonial Workhouses.*

In addition to the county jails, the laws of the royal province of New Jersey provided for the erection and maintenance of *workhouses,* but these were as much a part of the almshouse system as of the penal institutions. Instead of being based on the Quaker practice of combining the workhouse and the jail or

[1] Ibid., pp. 158–9.
[2] Ibid., p. 164.
[3] Ibid., p. 354.
[4] *New Jersey Archives,* Vol. XIII, p. 84.
[5] Cf. Allinson, op. cit., p. 104.

prison, the workhouse system, which was developed in New Jersey in the eighteenth century, was modeled primarily after the European practice of employing the workhouse for the suppression of pauperism and disorderly conduct, rather than as a basis of the penal system. However, there can be no doubt that the workhouse system which was adopted in New Jersey, together with the influence of the Quaker procedure in Pennsylvania, were the determining factors in the adoption of the principle of imprisonment at hard labor in the New Jersey state prison in 1798.

The legal foundations of the New Jersey workhouse system were laid by the directions given by Queen Anne, in 1702, to Lord Cornbury, the newly-appointed governor of the province. These instructed Lord Cornbury "to endeavor with the assistance of the Council to provide for the raising of stocks, and the building of public workhouses, in convenient places for the employing of poor and indigent people." [1]

It was nearly half a century, however, before these instructions bore any practical fruits. The first workhouse was provided for in the act of December 16, 1748, which gave the county of Middlesex the authority to erect a poorhouse, a workhouse, and a house of correction in Perth Amboy.[2]

The enacting clause of this law throws considerable light upon the contemporary opinion as to the nature and purpose of the workhouse system. It stated,

"Whereas divers of the Inhabitants of the County of Middlesex have humbly certified to the General Assembly by their petition that the numbers of poor people have of late years very much increased within the said county, and that, for the better regulation and government of the said county, it is highly necessary that a poorhouse shall be erected within the same for the maintenance and employment of such poor persons as may become chargeable to the several cities and townships within the said county, and for the educating and bringing up of poor children in some honest and industrious way; as also a workhouse and House of Correction for setting to work and punishing all vagrants, vagabonds, and pilferers, and all idle and disorderly

[1] *New Jersey Archives*, Vol. II, p. 532.
[2] See Documents, Part II, pp. 356–364.

4 P

persons, servants, and slaves within the limits of the said county, and the
depressing of vice and immorality.
  "Be it enacted   .   .   ." [1]

It was provided that the following classes should be sent to
the poorhouse and workhouse—the destitute of all classes; poor
children under fourteen; and disorderly or insubordinate slaves
or servants upon application of their masters.[2]

It was further decreed that "all Rogues, Vagrants, Vagabonds,
and Sturdy Beggars, and other idle and disorderly persons, which
shall be found wandering or misbehaving themselves" should be
sent to the "House of Correction." [3]

It was also provided by this act of 1748, that the managing
committee of the workhouse and house of correction might receive as inmates persons sent from other counties and boroughs
upon the payment of appropriate fees to be agreed upon by the
contracting parties.[4]

One more combination of poorhouse, workhouse, and house of
correction was created by the act of June 21, 1754, "to enable
the Mayor, Recorder, Aldermen, and Common Councilmen of
the free Borough and Town of Elizabeth, to build a Poorhouse,
Workhouse, and House of Correction, within the said Borough;
and to make Rules, Orders, and Ordinances for the governing
of the same." [5] The enacting clause of this bill proclaimed the
same general purposes that were enumerated in the act for Middlesex county in 1748. It declared that the act was passed,

"To the intent that the poor of the said borough may be better employed
and maintained; poor children educated and brought up in an honest and
industrious way; as also for setting to work and punishing all vagrants,
vagabonds, pilferers, and all idle and disorderly persons, servants and slaves
within the said borough; for the encouragement of honesty and industry,
and suppressing of vice and immorality, and better government of the said
boroughs." [6]

[1] Allinson, op. cit., pp. 179–80.
[2] Ibid., pp. 182–185.
[3] Ibid., p. 184.
[4] Ibid., p. 186.
[5] Ibid., p. 198.
[6] Ibid.

The various specific provisions of the bill were so similar to those of the Perth Amboy act of six years earlier, that there can be no doubt that the plans for the Elizabeth institution were modeled after those of the one at Perth Amboy. The bill provided for the commitment of the same general classes and for the admission of inmates from other counties upon a payment of six pence per day for each person so admitted.[1]

While there is little evidence as to the type of work provided in the two workhouses of colonial New Jersey, there is little reason to suppose that the inmates were employed at particularly productive labor. Work was provided in the early workhouses for its supposed deterrent effect in suppressing crime, rather than with a view to its economic possibilities. It is probable that, like the European workhouses of the time, the labor varied from the more crude and elementary manual labor, such as grinding corn and coarse weaving and spinning, to such devices as the treadmill, which had no productive possibilities whatever.[2]

IV. SUMMARY.

The situation, then, in regard to the penal institutions of colonial New Jersey before the formation of the state, may be briefly characterized as follows:

(1) There was no central provincial or state penal institution provided for during the colonial period. Corporal punishment in its various phases, including death, whipping, branding, and the stocks, was almost exclusively employed as a punishment for crimes, and thus created little necessity for penal institutions.

(2) The county jails were the basis of the penal system, and were, in fact, the only real penal institutions in the conventional sense of the term.

There were at the close of the colonial period thirteen counties in the state of New Jersey, each of which had at least one jail. Though it is impossible to know just how many towns had local jails, there is little doubt that in counties containing several pop-

---

[1] Ibid., pp. 198–202.
[2] Wines, *Punishment and Reformation*, pp. 115.ff.

ulous towns, each town had its local jail. This is known to have been the case in Middlesex county, where both Perth Amboy and New Brunswick had separate jails. The single county jail seems to have been the rule.

(3) The jail system was then, as now, to a very great degree, a failure as a penal and reformatory agency.

There was no clear differentiation between the treatment of those condemned for crime and those accused and awaiting trial.

There was no provision for differentiation in the treatment of criminals according to age, sex, or criminal record.

There was no strict or scientific differentiation in the reception, detention, and treatment of the criminal, the feeble-minded, and the insane.

No provision being made for the useful employment of those confined in the county jails, the jail system was not only a failure from the standpoint of penology, but also from the standpoint of economics. From the middle of the eighteenth century the jail system had become a serious financial burden to the province, and thus initiated the condition of economic failure which has characterized the penal institutions of New Jersey from that time to the present.

The jail system afforded a certain degree of protection to society from the criminal element, but even this rudimentary function of a penal system was but partially fulfilled, as there were a large number of escapes.

(4) As imprisonment for debt was the rule, the jail was related to the almshouses as a place for the detention of the poor, with which it was also connected by the link of the workhouse and house of correction, which received both criminals and paupers.

With the exception of the few houses of correction and workhouses, there was no provision whatever for the reformatory function of penal servitude. These were, moreover, provided for by but two counties, and normally received only petty offenders, mostly of a type not detained in a penal institution.

(5) The workhouse and house of correction were more a part of the crude system of social relief than of the penal system, and the beneficial results which might have been obtained from an extension of these institutions into the penal system were almost entirely lost.

CHAPTER II

THE ORIGIN AND FAILURE OF THE FIRST STATE PRISON OF NEW JERSEY

*(NEW JERSEY'S EXPERIENCE WITH
THE CONGREGATE SYSTEM, 1797-1836)*

CHAPTER II

THE ORIGIN AND FAILURE OF THE FIRST STATE PRISON OF NEW JERSEY, 1797–1836.

I. THE FIRST CRIMINAL CODE OF THE STATE OF NEW JERSEY.

The criminal codes and traditions of colonial New Jersey were worked over and systematized as the first criminal code of the state of New Jersey, and this code was put upon the statute books by the act of March 18, 1796. While it was an improvement over the East Jersey code of 1668, many of the vestiges of barbarism were allowed to remain, and in moderation it fell short of the Quaker West Jersey criminal codes of more than a century earlier.

The death penalty was provided for treason, murder, and petit treason and for the second offence of manslaughter, sodomy, rape, arson, burglary, robbery and forgery.[1]

The following were the maximum penalties provided for the lesser crimes, the minimum sentences not being specified: *arson,* fifteen years imprisonment; *abduction,* twelve years imprisonment; *blasphemy,* twelve months imprisonment, a fine of two hundred dollars, or both; *bribery,* five years imprisonment, a fine of eight hundred dollars, or both; *burglary,* ten years imprisonment; *conspiracy,* two years imprisonment, a fine of five hundred dollars, or both; *corruption of jury,* one year imprisonment, a

---

[1] *The Laws of the State of New Jersey,* revised and published under the authority of the Legislature, by William Paterson, Newark, 1800, pp. 208–221.

fine of three hundred dollars, or both; *extortion,* two years imprisonment, a fine of four hundred dollars, or both; *fraud,* three years imprisonment, a fine of one thousand dollars, or both; *fornication,* a fine of fourteen dollars; *adultery,* a fine of one hundred dollars or six months imprisonment; *impersonating Jesus Christ,* six months imprisonment, a fine of one hundred dollars, or both; *incest,* eighteen months imprisonment, a fine of five hundred dollars, or both; *larceny* under six dollars, one year imprisonment, a fine of thirty dollars, or both; *larceny* above six dollars, ten years imprisonment, a fine of five hundred dollars, or both; *maiming or disfiguring,* seven years imprisonment, a fine of one thousand dollars, or both; *manslaughter,* three years imprisonment, a fine of one thousand dollars, or both; *open lewdness,* twelve months imprisonment, a fine of one hundred dollars, or both; *perjury* or subornation of perjury, seven years imprisonment, a fine of eight hundred dollars, or both; *forgery,* ten years imprisonment; *rape,* fifteen years imprisonment; *robbery,* fifteen years imprisonment; *sodomy,* twenty-one years imprisonment.[1]

Debtors were to be kept in close confinement, though separate from criminals, and the sheriff was held liable for their debts if they were allowed to escape.[2]

If a sheriff voluntarily allowed a prisoner to escape who was sentenced to death, the death penalty was to be exacted of the sheriff.[3]

All offences not provided for in the penal code were to be tried by the courts according to the common law, and no appeal was allowed in any trial of a criminal offence.[4]

It was also enacted that those sentenced to imprisonment at hard labor should be confined in the county jails until other institutions were provided.[5]

---

[1] Ibid., pp. 208–18.
[2] Ibid., p. 206.
[3] Ibid., p. 216.
[4] Ibid., p. 220.
[5] Ibid., p. 221. This penal code of 1796 was reënacted with practically no changes on February 17, 1829. See J. Harrison, *A Compilation of the Public Laws of New Jersey,* 1833, pp. 221–45.

While this code was in many ways harsh and primitive, it contrasted most favorably with the criminal law of England at this time, which provided capital punishment for about two hundred crimes, and hence left little need for any penal institutions. The one conspicuous and significant feature of this first penal code of the state of New Jersey was that it provided for a liberal use of *imprisonment at hard labor* as a mode of punishment, a procedure contrasting strongly with the early colonial codes of East Jersey which disposed of most crimes by fines or corporal punishment. The first criminal code of the state of New Jersey, then, created a definite need of a more advanced system of penal institutions than had heretofore existed. Attention may now be turned to the first step in providing for this necessity, namely, the erection of a state prison.

II. THE ORIGIN OF THE FIRST STATE PRISON OF NEW JERSEY.

The first move towards the erection of a state prison for New Jersey came on March 1, 1797, when Jonathan Doan was commissioned by the Legislature to purchase from Peter Hunt a tract of six and one-half acres of land in the town of Lamberton, now in the city of Trenton, as a site for the new state prison.[1]

Work, apparently, was immediately begun, as the report of the legislative committee, which was directed to investigate the progress of the state prison, stated that, on October 24, 1797, the work on the prison had been in progress for one hundred and eighty days, and that £5,710 had already been expended on the construction. It was estimated that £4,511 would be required to complete the additional work which was needed to carry out the original plan for the prison.[2]

By the latter part of the year 1799, the new prison was ready for occupation, having been built at a cost of £9,842, and it gave rise to a considerable amount of just pride on the part of the

[1] *Acts of the Twenty-first General Assembly*, March 1, 1797, pp. 189–90. See Documents, Part II, pp. 367–8.

[2] *Journal of the Proceedings of the Legislative Council of the State of New Jersey*, Nov., 1797, pp. 16–17. See Documents, Part II, pp. 369–70.

state government.[1] Some of the penological ideas which dominated the minds of the builders of the original state prison are
reflected in the inscription which they placed over the door and
which ran as follows:

LABOR, SILENCE, PENITENCE.
THE PENITENTIARY HOUSE,
ERECTED BY LEGISLATIVE
AUTHORITY.
RICHARD HOWELL, GOVERNOR.
IN THE XXII YEAR OF
AMERICAN INDEPENDENCE,
MDCCXCVII
THAT THOSE WHO ARE FEARED
FOR THEIR CRIMES
MAY LEARN TO FEAR THE LAWS
AND BE USEFUL.
HIC LABOR, HOC OPUS.

The influence of the ideas of the Quakers of Philadelphia is
readily apparent in this inscription. In addition to the emphasis
upon hard labor as a punishment, this inscription gives evidence
of some rudimentary grasp of the deterrent and reformatory
aspects of punishment by imprisonment. This original state
prison, with some minor alterations, is still standing in the city
of Trenton and has been used as the State Arsenal since 1837.

III. The System of Administration in the First State Prison.

The legal and administrative basis of the newly created state
prison system was provided for in the act of February 15, 1798,
"making provision for carrying into effect the 'Act for the Punishment of Crimes'." [2]

The administrative system in its general outline and nomen-
clature, which was created by this act, has persisted with minor
changes down to the present day.

[1] Ibid., Nov. 6, 1798; Feb. 11, 1799; June 1, 1799; Nov. 6, 1799.
[2] See Documents, Part II, pp. 371-77.

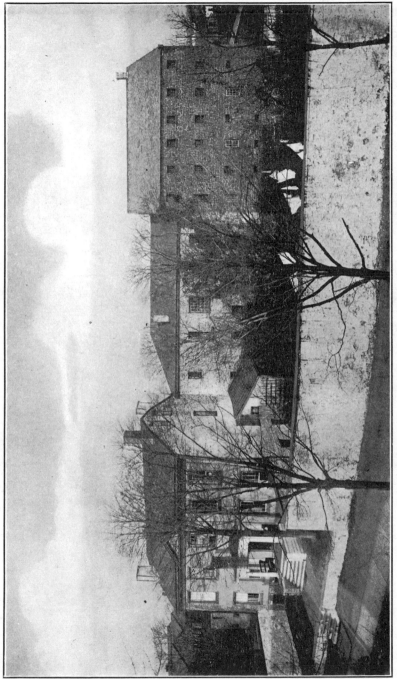

PLATE I. The First State Prison of New Jersey, 1797–1836.

The most important officials connected with the administration of the state prison were the board of inspectors. In fact, not again until the law of 1914, were the inspectors granted such extensive powers as by the law of 1798. There were to be eight inspectors, appointed annually by a joint meeting of the legislature.[1] Within the general limitations prescribed by the laws of the state, the inspectors were given the authority to make all rules and regulations for the actual administration of the prison, and the keeper was compelled to respect and obey these regulations under penalty of fine and removal.[2] The inspectors were also to appoint the keeper and fix his salary, and to exercise supervision over the keeper's appointment of his subordinates.[3] Again the inspectors were to have general supervisory authority over the industrial operations within the prison and were to check up the accounts of the keeper.[4] Finally, it was provided that they should meet once in three months at the state prison and elect two of their number to be acting inspectors. These acting inspectors were required to visit the prison weekly and make appropriate observations and reports to the board.[5]

The chief administrative officer of the state prison was the keeper, appointed by the inspectors. Subject to the supervisory powers of the inspectors, the keeper was to appoint the subordinate officials; was to have immediate charge of the industry of the prison; and was to maintain the discipline of the prison.[6] The maximum punishment which the keeper might inflict was confinement in a dungeon for two days on a diet of bread and water. If this did not prove sufficient the inspectors were given the authority to extend this type of punishment over a period of six days.[7] Considering the penological ideas of the

[1] *Acts of the Twenty-second General Assembly of the State of New Jersey,* February 15, 1798, p. 285.

[2] Ibid., pp. 285-6.

[3] Ibid., pp. 284-5.

[4] Ibid., pp. 282-3.

[5] Ibid., p. 285. By an act of November 19, 1799, it was decreed that the inspectors should receive one dollar per day for their services. By the act of May 30, 1820, this was increased to one dollar and fifty cents.

[6] Ibid., p. 282.

[7] Ibid., p. 284.

period with which we are concerned, this decreed punishment was certainly relatively mild and humane. In fact, the laws of New Jersey in this respect have been fairly enlightened, and the distressing inhumanities, which investigations have from time to time revealed, have never had any legal sanction.

It was further provided in this act that the condemned prisoners should be removed from the county jails to the state prison as soon as it was completed and ready for occupancy.[1] Thereafter, all prisoners sentenced to a term of imprisonment longer than six months were to be transferred from the jails to the state prison within twenty days of their conviction, while those sentenced to a term of less than six months were to be confined in the county jails.[2]

The prisoners confined in the state prison were to be "employed at labor of the hardest and most servile kind," and were to labor as many hours as the season permitted, namely, eight hours in November and December, nine hours in February and October, and ten hours for the rest of the year.[3] If any of the prisoners should prove especially industrious and the products of their labor should exceed the costs of prosecution and maintenance, then the prisoners were to be given one-half of the excess profit thus created.[4] The keeper was also stimulated to additional vigilance and energy by being allowed a percentage of five per cent. on all sales of prison-made products.[5]

[1] Ibid., p. 285.

[2] Ibid., pp. 280–81. The act of February 20, 1799, conferred upon the Board of Chosen Freeholders in each county the authority to erect workhouses in connection with the county jails, to which were to be committed all persons sentenced to six months or less of hard labor. Paterson, op. cit., pp. 378–80. This salutary provision was scarcely made use of; as late as 1850, only one county out of thirteen investigated had erected and maintained a workhouse. See the *Memorial of the New Jersey Prison Reform Association*, January 25, 1850, p. 4.

[3] Ibid., p. 282.

[4] Ibid., p. 283. This item of excess earnings of the prisoners was never systematically entered in the accounts of the prison. The committee of 1830 found that in 1829 the prisoners had thus entitled themselves to $133.

[5] Ibid., p. 284. The percentage allowance to the keeper was abolished by law of May 30, 1820.

IV. PRISON MAINTENANCE AND PRISON LABOR IN THE FIRST STATE PRISON.

The system of providing for prison maintenance, which was introduced into the new state prison by the law of February 15, 1798, was awkward, was a failure from the first, and, ultimately, was given up in disgust. Instead of providing for the maintenance of the prison out of the state treasury and then applying the proceeds from the labor of the prisoners on this account, the crude procedure was adopted of charging all inmates with the cost of their prosecution and their maintenance, thus opening a personal account with each prisoner. The prisoners were charged twenty cents per day for their board, with an extra charge for clothes, light and heat.[1] The product of each prisoner's labor was to be balanced against the charges for his prosecution and maintenance. As was pointed out above, industrious prisoners were to be rewarded by having one-half of the excess of their productive labor over their expenses, while, on the other hand, the act of December 1, 1802, provided that the inspectors of the state prison should not allow any prisoner to be discharged until he had paid, by his labor, the whole cost of prosecution and maintenance.[2] However, the lack of proper facilities for productive labor in the new prison made it practically impossible for many of the prisoners to equal or exceed the cost of their maintenance. Consequently, to remedy the situation, the law of 1802 was repealed by that of March 1, 1804, which stipulated that the inspectors might liberate prisoners, even if they owed a debt to the prison at the time of their discharge, if it could be proved that they had labored industriously and had no property with which to pay such debt.[3] A law of December 4, 1807, provided that discharged prisoners

[1] *Report of the Committee of the Legislature on the Regulation of the State Prison,* February 22, 1804. *Votes of the Assembly,* Twenty-eighth Assembly, 1804, pp. 147–155. *Report of the Joint Committee of the Legislature,* Novem-12, 1822, in *Votes of the Assembly,* Forty-seventh Assembly, pp. 77–9.

[2] J. Bloomfield, *The Laws of New Jersey,* 1811, p. 25.

[3] Ibid., p. 121.

who owed debts were liable, with their property, for these debts.[1] Finally, it was recommended in 1822 that the whole system of personal charges against the prisoners be abolished, as few ever paid the charges, and the only result of this regulation was a distortion and confusion of the prison accounts.[2]

It would be a grievous error, however, to state, as some writers have done, that there was no attempt or intention upon the part of the legislature of New Jersey to make the original state prison system, as far as possible, self-supporting. All the evidence available goes to show that the officials viewed with grave concern the economic failure of the prison, and made serious, though unscientific, attempts to remedy the situation. It was the generally conceded and practically irremediable defects in the industrial arrangements of the old prison which, to a large degree, led to its abandonment and the erection of a new one in 1833–36.[3]

The report of the committee of the legislature rendered on February 22, 1804, relative to the conditions existing at the state prison, gives an illuminating picture of the industrial situation at the prison during the early years of its existence. Nail-making was the chief productive industry, employing forty out of the sixty-one employed inmates. This remained the most important industry of the prison until it was destroyed by English competition after the War of 1812. The remaining twenty-one were engaged chiefly in the domestic activities of the prison and in repair work. Eight prisoners from age and illness were not employed. The prisoners were paid according to the number of nails which they made and received on an average about three shillings per day if they performed what was scheduled as a day's labor. Out of this income they were required to pay twenty cents per day for board, in addition to paying for heat, light, and general service. Therefore, only the most industrious

[1] Ibid., pp. 122–4.
[2] *Votes of the Assembly*, Forty-seventh Assembly, 1822, pp. 77–9. See Documents, Part II, pp. 390–91.
[3] Ibid., 1817, pp. 33–36; Ibid., Forty-ninth Assembly, 1824, pp. 104–6; Ibid., Fifty-first Assembly, 1826, p. 134.

convicts were able to accumulate a surplus, and the majority ended their term with a balance against them. The products of the prison were sold by the keeper, who was the selling agent as well as the industrial manager of the prison. Apparently some of the nails were sold on a permanent contract, while the rest were sold in the open market. There was, then, at the beginning, an application of both the contract (piece-price) and the public account methods of disposing of prison-made products.[1]

Such, in brief outline, was the original state prison system of the state of New Jersey. The forces and influences leading to its origin are not difficult to discover. In the first place, there were the Quaker influences in the adjoining state of Pennsylvania, as well as those which lingered in western New Jersey. These made towards a more liberal use of imprisonment as a mode of punishment, and towards the procedure of keeping all prisoners employed, both for the moral and physical welfare of the prisoners and for the economical conduct of the institution. These influences are readily apparent in the New Jersey penal code of 1796, and in the act of 1798, which directed that all inmates of the state prison be employed at hard labor.[2] In the second place, by the third quarter of the eighteenth century the county jails were becoming overcrowded and were beginning to be a serious economic burden. In the third place, the recent formation of a self-governing commonwealth had stimulated the growth of state self-consciousness and promoted the development of activities of state-wide significance. Finally, the erection of state prisons in neighboring states, particularly Pennsylvania, brought into play the powerful factor of imitation.

In spite of the crudities of this early state prison from the standpoint of both architecture and scientific penology, the fact

[1] *Votes of the Assembly,* Twenty-eighth Assembly, 1804, pp. 147–155. See Documents, Part II, pp. 377–391.

[2] The influence of the Quaker theory of a prison as a workhouse or house of correction upon the origin of the first state prison of New Jersey is readily apparent in the discussions preceding the enactment of the law of 1797, in which the proposed prison was usually referred to as a "house of correction." See *Journal of the Legislative Council,* 1796, p. 62.

must not be overlooked that it marked a very great advance over
the previous system of confining the condemned in the county
jails. In the first place, it provided for that very necessary differentiation between the treatment of those accused of crime and
of those convicted. In the second place, it made provision for the
employment of the inmates, thus eliminating in part, at least,
that demoralizing idleness which has from the first characterized
the county jail system. Finally, while the industrial equipment
and the economic notions in the prison were extremely crude
and elementary, it must be admitted that even this feeble attempt
to introduce a rational system of prison labor was a great advance in an economic sense over the county jail system, in which
no real attempt was made to make the institution self-supporting.

Unfortunately, the defects of the system were quite as obvious.
Aside from failing to provide a place of commitment for those
receiving a sentence of less than six months, the state prison did
not provide for any differentiation in treatment according to the
classes of offenders, or the mental states of the prisoners, nor did
it take into account the age or sex of those committed. Hardened recidivists, first termers, the insane, men and women, boys
and girls, were all imprisoned within the same walls and confined in contiguity. The prisoners of each sex were allowed
to associate freely. The prison was constructed on the congregate plan, after the model of the Walnut Street Prison, of Philadelphia, and until 1820 there was little attempt at solitary confinement during day or night, and it was not until the opening
of the second state prison in 1836 that solitary confinement became the rule.[1] As the report of the investigating committee in
1830 pointed out, the facilities for communication were better
between prisoners than between the keeper and his subordinates
or between the prison officials and the prisoners. The very vital
reformatory function of a penal institution was, thus, almost
entirely ignored at the origin of the New Jersey state prison
system.

[1] *Journal of the Legislative Council,* November 5, 1798, pp. 16–17. See
Documents, Part II, pp. 369–70; 402ff.; 428ff.; 436ff.

V. The Decline and Failure of the Congregate System in New Jersey.

I. THE TREND TOWARDS SOLITARY CONFINEMENT.

The two most outstanding defects in the original state prison system in New Jersey were the evils inherent in the promiscuous association of the congregate system, and the expense due to the partial failure of the industrial system. As a consequence, the relatively short history of the first state prison in New Jersey was, to a very great degree, the record of successive attempts to remedy these defects, which culminated in a frank recognition of the failure of the system and of the necessity of reconstructing the whole prison scheme. The attempt to remedy the evils of the old congregate system of confinement will first be considered.

As early as 1802, the joint committee of the legislature on the state prison recommended the erection of permanent cells in the north wing of the prison for the solitary confinement of a number of the prisoners.[1] There is no record, however, that anything came of the suggestion, but about fifteen years later the agitation was revived with sufficient strength to cause action to be taken. In 1816 a committee of the legislature was appointed to examine into the desirability of constructing a tier of from fifty to seventy-five cells in the prison. This committee reported in January, 1817, that such a plan was not feasible, but recommended the erection of a new building to hold sixty cells. Their recommendation was not acted upon.[2] In February of the same year the joint committee of the legislature reported in favor of the segregation of the more vicious criminals and urged the construction of cells for this purpose. This committee also criticized the practice of sending to the state prison those who had received a prison sentence of less than one year. Their request, however, was likewise ignored.[3] Finally, the inspectors of the

---

[1] *Journal of the Legislative Council,* 27th session, 1802, pp. 176–7.
[2] *Votes of the Assembly,* 41st General Assembly, January 8, 1817, p. 80.
[3] Ibid., pp. 176–7.

state prison presented a memorial to the legislature in February, 1818, in which, ten years before the opening of the famous Eastern Penitentiary of Pennsylvania, there were set forth the essential arguments in favor of the Pennsylvania system of solitary confinement. The inspectors recommended the segregation of the worst offenders in a block of cells so that these criminals might be better punished, the remainder saved from moral contamination, and the deterrent effect of imprisonment be strengthened.[1] They expressed their opinion of the proposed method of segregation or solitary confinement in the following words:

"This, with due deference to your honors, would, we conceive, be the most effectual means of lessening the number of convicts sent for high crimes, as the circumstances of separate confinement would soon get abroad among that class of society, which would, no doubt, prevent a number from violating our most excellent laws, and would ultimately, we have no doubt, be the means of bringing about a reformation in those who should unhappily become the subjects of such a mode of punishment."[2]

This pressure led to the provision for an extensive addition to the prison building, which was completed in 1820, and, by 1821, twenty-one out of ninety-nine prisoners were kept in solitary confinement, the law of May 31, 1820, having authorized the solitary confinement of prisoners convicted of arson, manslaughter, rape, blasphemy, perjury, burglary, robbery, forgery, assault, theft of more than fifty dollars, and house-breaking.[3] The success from this partial adoption of the system of solitary confinement was not as great as had been anticipated, for the joint committee, in its report on the state prison submitted on December 5, 1826, declared the system of solitary confinement to have been a failure in practically every respect. The committee declared that the morals of those in solitary confinement showed no improvement, as contrasted with the moral tone of those sentenced to hard labor. Again, the practice of solitary confinement left no possibility for acquiring valuable habits of

[1] Ibid, 42d General Assembly, February 3, 1818, pp. 130–6. See Documents, Part II, pp. 387–90.

[2] Ibid., p. 136.

[3] Ibid., 47th Assembly, 1822, pp. 77–9. *The Laws of New Jersey,* revised and published by Joseph Justice, Trenton, 1821, p. 739. See the diagram opposite page 68.

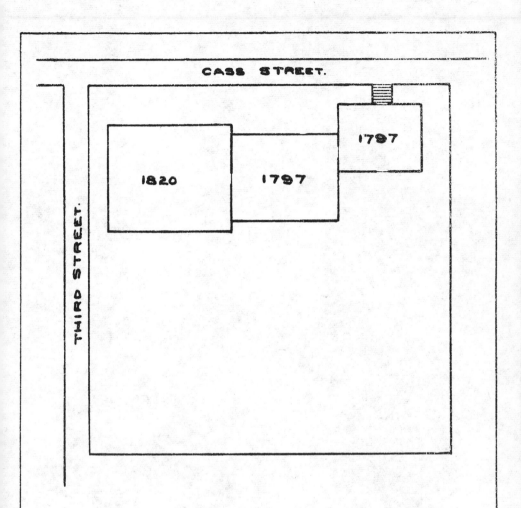

CASS STREET.

THIRD STREET.

1820

1797

1797

THE ORIGINAL STATE PRISON
OF NEW JERSEY.

ERECTED IN 1797 AND EXTENDED
IN 1820.

industry or skill in manual labor, thus leaving the discharged convict with little opportunity to do anything except reënter his profession of crime. The ideal prison system was said to consist in employment at hard labor in the congregate system by day and solitary confinement by night.[1] There was thus presented at this early period a criticism of what was to be known as the Pennsylvania system of prison regulation and administration, and a recommendation of the adoption of what later came to be known as the Auburn system.

This recommendation of solitary confinement by night, and of the prevention of conversation during the congregate work by day, was enacted as law by the act of March 7, 1828, which provided that the prisoners were to be isolated in separate cells by night, so far as was possible, and that all conversation between prisoners was to be prohibited.[2] How far from possible either of these provisions was of enforcement will be revealed later, in the analysis of the report of the committee on prison discipline of 1830. Suffice it to say that any attempt to work out a rational system of penal administration was quite impossible within the limitations imposed by the architecture of the first prison building. The recognition of the futility of hoping to remedy the situation without a new prison was one of the chief influences which forced a decision to that effect a few years later.

2. THE INDUSTRIAL ADMINISTRATION OF THE ORIGINAL STATE PRISON.

The attempts, which were made between 1798 and 1833, to put the state prison on a sounder industrial basis, were equally futile. There was no definite supervisor of industry provided for the prison by the law of 1798, which determined the administrative procedure of the state prison. The keeper, in addition to his other duties, was delegated to act as the purchasing agent

---

[1] Ibid., 51st General Assembly, 1826, p. 134. See Documents, Part II, pp. 393-6.

[2] *Acts of the 52d General Assembly,* 1827-8, pp. 212-13. It is worthy of note that New Jersey thus tried out on a limited scale both the Auburn and the Pennsylvania systems of confinement before finally adopting the Pennsylvania system for the new state prison in 1833-6.

for the prison, as supervisor of the prison industry, and as agent for the prison products. Naturally, these extra duties were rather indifferently performed in the face of many difficulties, though up to 1820 the keeper was stimulated to greater energy by the provision that he was to receive a commission of five per cent. on the sale of all prison-made products.[1] The difficulties experienced in having the keeper act as the sales agent of the prison were to a certain degree eliminated by the law of May 30, 1820, which repealed the commission of five per cent. to the keeper and authorized the inspectors to appoint a sales agent for the prison at such a place as they deemed most desirable.[2]

In addition to this initial defect of the lack of a trained supervisor of industry, the construction and distribution of the crude and primitive "shops" were such that the limited number of underkeepers and guards could maintain little discipline, and much time and material were wasted and many of the products carelessly made.[3] There is little evidence that the reward offered to industrious convicts had any marked effect in stimulating their efforts; the more fundamental defects of the industrial system served to offset all the good which could have come from this provision.

In addition to these general administrative defects in the industrial system, there was a large amount of contemporary protest against sending to the prison those sentenced for less than one year. It was held that it was impossible to teach them any type of useful industry in so short a period, and the cost of transporting them to the prison was as great as for long-term prisoners. In spite of the numerous protests against this practice, no legal action seems to have been taken.[4]

A most determined effort to remedy the industrial situation was made by the joint committee of the legislature in its report

---

[1] *Acts of the 22d General Assembly,* 1798, pp. 282–3.
[2] *Laws of New Jersey,* revised and published by Joseph Justice, Trenton, 1821, p. 732.
[3] *Votes of the Assembly,* 54th General Assembly, 1829–1830, pp. 171, 172–5.
[4] Ibid., 41st General Assembly, 1817, p. 81. Ibid., 42nd General Assembly, 1818, p. 134.

of 1824. The committee expressed its regret over the uniform loss to the state which was occasioned by the industrial failure of the prison system, a loss, which in the previous year had amounted to over six thousand dollars. The committee reported that it was hard to get suitable productive employment for the prisoners and agreed that the situation was altogether discouraging. They recommended that the criminal law be altered so that the short-term criminals, who could not be taught any trade, might be segregated in cells so that they would not be contaminated by contact with the confirmed criminals. They further urged that the inspectors be chosen from among expert mechanics and manufactureres and be given power to make the needed alterations in the prison shops so that the prison industry might be put on a business-like and efficient basis.[1]

However, these recommendations came to naught, and the notable report of 1830 revealed the fact that the industrial basis of the prison was as inefficient in 1830 as it had been at any previous time in the history of the institution.

The very elementary and limited industrial operations in the first state prison, as late as 1825, are revealed by the report of the joint committee of the legislature of that year, which catalogues the occupations of the prisoners who were employed at productive labor. Out of the forty prisoners so employed, eight were engaged at weaving, three at spooling, seven at shoe-making, five at sawing stone, two at plaster pounding, two at spinning, one as a tailor, one as a cooper, one as a basket-maker, two as blacksmiths, one as a carpenter, two as cooks, two at cutting wood, one at washing, and two as waiters. The total loss sustained by the institution in the year 1825 was $4,794.43, including the salaries of the officials and the cost of the transportation of prisoners.[2]

The report submitted by the renowned investigating committee of 1830 presents a vivid picture of the industrial operations of the prison during the preceding year. In 1829, out of a total

[1] Ibid., 49th General Assembly, 1824, pp. 104–6.
[2] Ibid., 50th General Assembly, 1825, p. 93.

of ninety convicts, eighty-four were employed. Sixteen were employed at shoe-making (known also as cordwaining); thirty-nine at weaving; two as coopers; four at sawing stone; three as tailors; five at spinning; and fifteen in various phases of the domestic service of the prison. The average daily earnings of the shoe-makers were 18 cents 9 mills; of the weavers, 12 cents and of the remaining twenty-nine employed, 5 cents. The average daily earnings were thus 10 cents 4 mills, while the total daily cost of maintaining the convicts, including the salaries of the officers, was 18 cents 6 mills. The cost of maintenance alone during 1829 was $3,081.50, and the salaries paid were $3,117.50. The total receipts or earnings were $3,427.98, thus making the prison a loss for the year of $2,771.02. The committee assigned this unprofitable condition of the prison industries to the lack of proper supervision of the labor of the convicts, and to the failure of the contractors to furnish the prisoners with enough labor to keep them working continuously. The industrial administration of the prison was at that time carried on almost entirely under that type of the contract system known as the "piece-price" system, in which the contractors paid a certain price per piece for the product of the labor of the prisoners. That the prices allowed were not high may be seen from the fact that the total amount of excess earnings accumulated by all the prisoners during 1829 was only $133, while most of them earned much less than the cost of maintenance.[1]

3. LEGAL DEVELOPMENTS IN PENAL ADMINISTRATION, 1797–1836.

There were no important legal innovations in the development of the state prison between 1798 and 1830. The penal code of 1796 was reënacted with very slight changes on February 17, 1829;[2] and likewise the act of 1798, regulating the administration of the state prison, was reproduced with no important altera-

[1] Ibid., 54th General Assembly, 1830, pp. 180–183, 186.
[2] J. Harrison, *A Compilation of the Laws of New Jersey,* 1833, pp. 221–45.

tions on February 23, 1829. The only changes of any significance in the provisions for prison administration in this act of
1829, were that there were but five inspectors provided for, and
the appointment of the principal keeper was taken from the inspectors and put in the control of the same joint-meeting of the
legislature that elected the inspectors.[1]

4. THE PRISON INVESTIGATION OF 1829–30.

Having now briefly surveyed the chief characteristics of the
first prison system of New Jersey, pointed out its contributions
and defects, and summarized the unsuccessful attempts to eliminate these deficiencies, one is now in a position to examine the
famous report of the Legislative Committee on Prison Discipline of 1830—the most important document in the history of
New Jersey penal institutions up to that time, and both an epi-
taph of the old system and a prophecy of a new order.[2]

This report, which was a crushing indictment of the original
prison system of New Jersey, was inspired and guided, to a considerable degree, by Louis Dwight, the distinguished Secretary of
the Boston Prison Discipline Society from 1826 to 1853, the most
commanding figure in prison reform in the United States during
that period. It thus represents the comment of the best penological knowledge of the day upon what was admittedly an unsatisfactory prison system.

The purpose of the report, as expressed in the introduction,
was to show that any adequate system of discipline was impossible in the old state prison, and that the old prison system was
quite as much a failure from the economic standpoint as from
the disciplinary.[3]

The first criticisms were passed on the *construction* of the
prison. In the first place, it was found that the office of the
principal keeper was so remote from the rest of the prison that

[1] Ibid., pp. 250–260.
[2] See Documents, Part II, pp. 396–423.
[3] *Votes of the Assembly,* 54th General Assembly, February 11, 1830, p. 170.

he could neither see nor hear what was going on in the cells or the shops.[1]　Next, it was shown that there were not nearly enough cells to allow solitary confinement at night.　In some cases three or four prisoners were put in one large cell.　The cells were so arranged that unrestricted conversation was possible among the prisoners, and between them and persons outside the prison, while, strangely enough, the guards were completely shut off from the prisoners, when in their cells, by solid doors.　This made free and easy inspection by the guards quite impossible, and invited the planning and execution of plots for escape from the prison.[2]　Again, the prison shops were not compactly and uniformly located, but were so scattered about that the given force of guards were unable to enforce any kind of discipline, a condition which resulted in the partial demoralization of the industry of the prison and the waste of much time and material.[3] The prison cookhouse was poorly inspected, and was so constructed and located that food might be easily passed to and from the street outside.[4]　The hospital was located in a miserably ventilated room and was very indifferently inspected.[5]　The chapel was cramped and difficult of access.[6]　Finally, the sentry's box was not so located as to secure a commanding view of the prison yard.　It was possible for persons to approach or leave the prison from three sides without being seen by the sentry.[7]

The *system of discipline* was not less severely criticized than the prison construction, though it was made clear that the unscientific construction of the prison was largely responsible for the most serious faults in the discipline of the prison.　The head keeper was unable to inspect the prison with any facility, and the guards, discouraged by their excessive duties and the hopelessness of any effort at their effective execution,

[1] Ibid., pp. 170–71.
[2] Ibid., p.　171.
[3] Ibid.
[4] Ibid.
[5] Ibid.
[6] Ibid., pp. 171–2.
[7] Ibid., p.　172.

tended towards an attitude of general laxity and of familiarity with the prisoners. Unrestricted intercourse was allowed between the prisoners of each sex, and the guards freely exchanged commodities with the prisoners and even took articles made by the prisoners out of the prison and sold them.[1] There were so many scattered departments in the prison shops that more than double the available number of guards would have been required to maintain any degree of effective discipline. As it was, the prisoners had to be left alone, and idleness, waste and disorder were the natural and inevitable results.[2] The prisoners were allowed to do practically as they pleased in their cells at night. They spent much of their time nights and on Sunday in making various articles, including very useful rope ladders, and in imparting instruction in the latest and most approved criminal methods. Fights were frequent in the cells, these often resulting in very serious wounds. The prisoners were well informed through their windows of all that was going on outside of the prison, and carried on a profitable trade with the outside world through these windows. So many articles were hidden by the prisoners that it was not only impossible to take an accurate inventory of the prison equipment, but it was also uncertain when extensive plans were maturing for a serious riot or escape. Riots in the prison were frequent, some attaining alarming proportions. Finally, there existed a large "Staunch-Gang," a secretly organized band of the most desperate prisoners, whose avowed purpose was to break up the discipline of the prison and to devise and execute plans for escape.[3]

In view of the foregoing conditions, it was not at all surprising that since the prison had been built there had been one hundred and eight escapes, a number equaling one-twelfth of all the prisoners committed.[4]

The committee discovered that the *punishments* practiced in the prison were extremely barbarous and quite beyond anything

[1] Ibid., pp. 172–173.
[2] Ibid., p. 173.
[3] Ibid., pp. 172–8.
[4] Ibid., pp. 178–9.

that the law permitted. However, the committee was of the opinion that the penal system and the prison architecture, rather than the personal depravity of the prison officials or the unruly nature of the prisoners, were primarily responsible for the existence of such modes of punishment. The committee discovered that in some extreme cases men were strapped on their backs in unheated cells in the winter and not released from this position for twenty days at a time. Many cases of physical disability resulted from this severe punishment, and in twenty years ten prisoners were known to have died from its effects. What was, perhaps, the most striking example of barbarism discovered was the treatment of a fourteen-year-old boy who was confined in the prison in free association with the most hardened criminals. The boy, being undersized, was small enough to crawl through the prison grating, and the prison officials hit upon the astounding device of putting on him an iron yoke which fitted around his neck and kept his arms extended some twenty inches apart on a level with his shoulders. This yoke device was a common method of restraining unruly cattle, but cattle were usually favored with a wooden instead of an iron yoke.[1] In concluding their indictment of the barbarous methods of punishment, the committee thus expressed their view of the responsibility:

"If the prison were so constructed as to separate the men at night and keep them perfectly still, and thus break up such combinations as that of the staunch gang; and if the shops were so constructed as to admit of a constant inspection, so as to keep the prisoners in their places, at their work in silence, there would be comparatively little need of severe punishments, because rebellion and villainy would be prevented in the very beginning."[2]

It is evident that the *reformatory* and *deterrent* functions of imprisonment were scarcely realized in such a system. The committee pointed out the very large number of recommitments and the absence of any record of a case of complete reformation, though in Auburn the reported cases of reformation totaled over fifty per cent. of the discharged prisoners.[3]

[1] Ibid., pp. 179–80.
[2] Ibid., p. 180.
[3] Ibid., p. 181.

The committee found that the number of guards provided was less than half what was needed for maintaining adequate *discipline* in such a poorly constructed prison. There were but three guards provided to watch and direct ninety prisoners.[1]

As an *industrial* institution, the old prison was pointed out to be a hopeless failure. The average yearly loss since 1800 had been $5,304. This loss was caused by the fact that not enough contractors could be found who would supply work to the prisoners; that the awkward construction of the prison and the insufficient number of guards prevented a careful supervision of the work that was done; and finally, that the state lost much of the income from the finished work through bad debts which might have been collected if the prison had been provided with an efficient financial agent. That the economic failure of the prison was due to the system in vogue was the committee's opinion, as based upon the experience of the Wethersfield prison in Connecticut, where the old prison, similar to that of New Jersey, brought an average deficit to the state of over $8,000, while the new prison produced a surplus above all expenses of over $3,000.[2]

The committee concluded its report by the following vigorous summary:

"Thus, the committee on the state prison has endeavored to submit the facts in the case now before them in a full and impartial manner. These have produced in the minds of the committee an unanimous opinion that the *construction* of the prison is altogether wrong, and does not admit of being essentially corrected in the old establishment. The *discipline,* in consequence, in great part, of the construction, may be called disorder rather than discipline. The *escapes* have been, so far as our knowledge extends, without a parallel, principally in consequence of the imperfection of the buildings. The *punishments,* from the same disadvantages in construction, have been very severe, to prevent riots, insurrections, and escapes. The committee greatly lament the facts in evidence on this part of the subject. The *deaths* are more numerous than they would be in a prison well constructed and well ventilated. The *recommitments* are numerous in proportion to the number of convicts, and the cases of reformation, few or none; because the men are associated together day and night for the purposes of mutual corruption, and this cannot be prevented in the buildings.

[1] Ibid., pp. 169, 185-6.
[2] Ibid., pp. 180-83, 186.

"The *expense* of supporting the establishment is very heavy, and this too, in great part, because the men cannot be kept at their business. . . .

"The committee, therefore, recommend with entire unanimity the building of a new prison, on the general plan of those at Auburn, in New York, and at Wethersfield, in Connecticut."[1]

This report is important in many ways. In the first place, it constitutes an excellent analysis of the generally deplorable condition of the first state prison in New Jersey. It further demonstrates that the whole system was radically wrong, and that the construction of the prison was the chief cause for the worst defects in the prison administration. Again, it throws light upon the character of the most advanced penological ideas of the first third of the last century. It shows that the reformatory and deterrent functions of imprisonment were clearly perceived, but that the chief requisites of a prison were held to be humane confinement and sound economic administration. Finally, this report illustrates how at this relatively early period there was a powerful interaction between the Eastern states in regard to penal procedure and prison reform. The dominating ideas of the report were inspired by the Boston Prison Discipline Society which had many members in New Jersey, and the main recommendations that were made were based on the most advanced examples of prison architecture and penal administration which then existed.

While there is little danger that one will draw too dark a picture of the conditions in the New Jersey state prison in 1830, it must be remembered that the situation was not relatively bad. While the penal code and the prison architecture and administration of New Jersey were scarcely abreast of those in some of the neighboring states, notably, Massachusetts, Connecticut, and New York, they compared favorably with those in the majority of the states of the country. It must further be remembered that the prison system of the United States, in general, was so greatly in advance of the European procedure that the leading European countries sent representatives to visit our advanced institutions

[1] Ibid., pp. 186–7. The committee of 1830 was made up of A. Howell, Amzi Dodd, Chas. Hillard, Littleton Kirkpatrick, Ferdinand Schenck, and Isaac Hinchman.

and report upon the possibility of adapting them to European conditions. The old prison found few defenders in the face of the crushing indictment presented by the report of the committee of 1830, and its subsequent history belongs most properly with the origin of the new prison, a subject to which attention may now be directed.

CHAPTER III

THE SECOND STATE PRISON SYSTEM OF NEW JERSEY

*(THE PENNSYLVANIA
SYSTEM, 1836-1860)*

CHAPTER III

THE SECOND STATE PRISON SYSTEM OF NEW JERSEY, 1836–1860.

I. THE REORGANIZATION OF THE NEW JERSEY STATE PRISON SYSTEM—THE ADOPTION OF THE PENNSYLVANIA SYSTEM.

After the report of the committee of 1830 had been submitted the problem of the prison system in the state of New Jersey was no longer whether or not the old prison could be retained and improved, but rather, what type of prison system would be adopted to replace the old one. This report gave impetus to the already powerful attacks upon the discredited congregate system of confinement and it found few defenders.

Even a month before the report of 1830 was submitted, Governor Peter D. Vroom, Jr., who had an advance copy of the report in his hands, attacked the old prison system very vigorously in his annual message of January 7, 1830. His remarks were essentially in accord with the opinions expressed by the committee. He stated that the best prison system consisted in congregate work by day, and isolation by night. He expressed himself as of the opinion that reformation was the primary object to be sought in any successful prison system.

(83)

He thus summarized his views as to the utter failure of the prison system then in vogue:

"Penitentiaries upon the old plan, in which every prisoner can communicate in the course of the day with his fellow-prisoners, and where from necessity, a number are enclosed together in the same apartment during the night, have no terrors for those who are already hardened in profligacy and crime. The temporary loss of liberty ceases to be a privation to them, when, mingling with kindred spirits, they rehearse the daring or craftiness of former achievements, or devise plans for the accomplishment of future mischief. The young soon lose all sense of shame, and are gradually initiated in all the mysteries of villainy, while the old add crime to crime, until reformation becomes hopeless. Such institutions are schools of vice, and offences of the most aggravated character are often committed within their very walls. They are also expensive. Not being able to support themselves they are a continual tax upon the people." [1]

In concluding his remarks on the state prison, the Governor contrasted with the administrative and economic failure of the New Jersey prison, the conspicuous success in both of these respects of the new state prison at Wethersfield, Connecticut. [2]

On October 28 of the same year, the Governor stated that while some improvement had been made in the state prison in the last year there was little ground for any hope that anything short of a new prison would remedy the situation. [3]

A committee from the assembly was appointed to report on this part of the Governor's message. The committee reported that the old prison was an utter failure as a deterrent institution. There had been a great increase of crime in the state, due, they thought, to the failure of the deterrent influence of the old state prison, which had become so crowded that from two to four convicts had to be put in cells designed for solitary confinement, and old abandoned and unsafe calls had to be occupied. They also pointed out the serious economic failure of the old prison by showing that it had cost the state $165,000 in thirty years, a sum

[1] *Votes of the Assembly*, 54th General Assembly, 1829–30, p. 79.
[2] Ibid., p. 80.
[3] Ibid., 55th General Assembly, 1830–31, p. 13.

equal to one-third of all the taxes raised in the state for all purposes during that period. They insisted that it would be entirely useless further to repair the old prison, as its faulty and inadequate construction destroyed all possibilities of satisfactory discipline. The committee reported several cases of barbarous punishment, among them the following: "Your committee saw a convict in a damp, cold, unheated cell, with his hands and feet chained to the floor. He was sitting on a wooden stool, with a blanket around his shoulders, and your committee were told by the keeper that he had been in that situation three or four days and nights, on an allowance of nothing but cold water." The committee held that a satisfactory prison system would eliminate all necessity of such severe punishment, and expressed themselves as of the unanimous opinion that New Jersey should have a new prison modelled on that at Wethersfield, Connecticut.[1]

In their annual report of November 15, 1831, the joint committee of the legislature on the state prison continued the onslaughts on the old prison system. They summed up thus their opinion of its defects:

"Your committee are satisfied that from the malconstruction of the prison buildings, its inadaptedness to the purposes of a rigid and wholesome police, and the constant recurring necessity for additions and repairs, the state must look in vain for any permanent improvement in its annual exhibits.

"Independent of the necessary deficiency in its moral government, and the fearful, but too probable apprehension, that it contributes more to the increase than to the diminution of crime, to the obduracy than to the reformation of the offender, thereby perverting all the legitimate objects of punishment, it must from all these sources forever prove a waste gate for the revenues of the State."[2]

The committee unanimously advised the erection of a new state prison situated on a good water power. They estimated

---

[1] *Votes of the Assembly,* 55th General Assembly, 1830–1831, pp. 93–4. In this and previous recommendations of the Auburn-Wethersfield system is to be seen the influence of Louis Dwight, the most ardent and effective advocate which this system had. Dwight did more than any other person in fastening the Auburn system on the United States.

[2] Ibid., 56th General Assembly, 1831, p. 99.

the cost of the new prison at $30,000, which they considered very low indeed, in view of the fact that many of the counties in New Jersey had without any difficulty erected court houses and jails costing $25,000. The committee called attention to an additional defect of the old state prison, namely, that it made no provision for the care of insane prisoners, and they reported that there were in the prison at that time nine insane inmates, who were further breaking up the discipline of the institution and needed some other disposition.[1]

In his message of January 11, 1833, Governor Samuel L. Southard carried on the campaign of his predecessors against the old state prison. He insisted upon the imperative necessity of building a new prison. He recommended that the old prison be converted into a state arsenal, the arms and ammunition of the state having hitherto been deposited in the State House, which was, in the opinion of the Governor, a dangerous practice.[2]

The same general view was expressed four days later by the joint committee of the legislature on the erection of a new state prison.[3] The report of this committee on January 15, 1833, is one of the most important documents in the history of New Jersey penology. Its significance lies in the fact that it represents the transition of opinion in New Jersey from favoring the Wethersfield and Auburn type of prison to favoring the new Pennsylvania system of solitary confinement, which had just been put into operation in the famous "Eastern Penitentiary of Pennsylvania," opened in 1829 after forty years of vigorous activity by the Quaker Prisoners' Aid and Prison Reform Society of Philadelphia. In the earlier discussions as to what type of prison should be adopted in place of the old one, the committees had unanimously favored the Auburn-Wethersfield system, but

[1] Ibid., p. 100. It was most unfortunate that the advice of this committee to build the new prison in the open country on a good water power was not followed. The lack of water power and the inability to expand without crowding the prison yard have been serious handicaps to the industry and discipline of the state prison at Trenton.

[2] Ibid., 57th General Assembly, 1832-3, p. 105.

[3] See Documents, Part II, pp. 436-44.

the recent success of the new Pennsylvania type of prison administration had evidently won over New Jersey opinion, in spite of the fact that continual solitary confinement had been vigorously condemned after its first trial in New Jersey between 1820 and 1826.

In their report the committee held that there was no possibility of satisfactorily remodeling the old prison. They further insisted upon the urgent necessity of providing a new and better system, as the amount of crime in New Jersey had increased by fifty per cent in three years on acount of the flocking of criminals to New Jersey who were alleged to have been attracted there by the notorious defects of the system of prison discipline. The committee thus expressed its opinion regarding the total failure of the congregate prison system in New Jersey, as a deterrent agency:

"There is one fact we cannot fail to repeat, that our prison, instead of deterring from the commission of crime, has actually invited its perpetrators from other States; and that the number of our convicts is steadily increasing from this cause. . . . It offers to them all the allurements of that kind of society which they have long been accustomed to submit in other places of confinement; and at the same time holds out a prospect of a speedy escape. To this may be attributed the great number of our convicts, and as long as it continues, we may expect our prison to be filled. Within the last three years the number has increased from eighty-seven to one hundred and thirty, being an increase of fifty per cent."

The committee expressed itself as of the opinion that the prevention of crime was the real object of punishment and they held that this was to be achieved by deterrence and reformation. They contended that social defence rather than cruel punishment should be made the purpose of confinement. The committee asserted that the two most advanced prison systems in the world were those of the state prison at Auburn, New York, and the Eastern Penitentiary of Pennsylvania.

The committee expressed itself as in favor of adopting the Pennsylvania system. The reversal of opinion in favor of the Pennsylvania system was due in part to the prominence of the venerable penological traditions of Philadelphia; in part to the

proximity of Philadelphia to Trenton; and, finally, to the real
or supposed virtues of the Pennsylvania system which were as
ably expressed to the committee by John Haviland, the architect
of the Eastern Penitentiary, and by the Quaker exponents
of that system, as those of the Auburn-Wethersfield system
had been to earlier committees by Louis Dwight and his
associates. The committee gave the following reasons for
their decision, which admirably sum up the alleged advantages
of the Pennsylvania system: Solitude is the most powerful
agent in effectual individual reformation, as it gives an unex-
celled opportunity for self examination, self reproach, and the
desire to reform. Again, the possibility of individual moral
instruction is bound to make one feel more deeply the condemnation, "Thou art the man!" Solitary confinement makes
preaching in the corridors of the prison more effective, as one
is left to his own meditation. None of the inmates in a prison
conducted on the principle of solitary confinement can know
the others personally, and hence they cannot reproach one
another with criminality, when released. In addition to these
moral and social advantages of the solitary confinement system,
it is also an economic success, in that it allows effective individual labor in each cell. This individual labor is also a
stronger deterrent of crime, since it is more of a punishment
than work in association with others. The success of the Pennsylvania system from the standpoint of deterrence was seen by
the fact that there had been no recommitments as yet to the
Eastern Penitentiary. In view of all these considerations the
committee unanimously recommended the building of a new
state prison on the lines of the Eastern Penitentiary of Pennsylvania. It was estimated that the new prison would cost $150,-
000 and plans for its construction were submitted, which had
been drawn by John Haviland.[1]

The following quotation from the report of this committee
constitutes what is probably the most striking statement to be

[1] *Votes of the Assembly,* 57th General Assembly, 1832–33, pp. 142–153. See
also *Journal of the Legislative Council,* 1833, pp. 64–74.

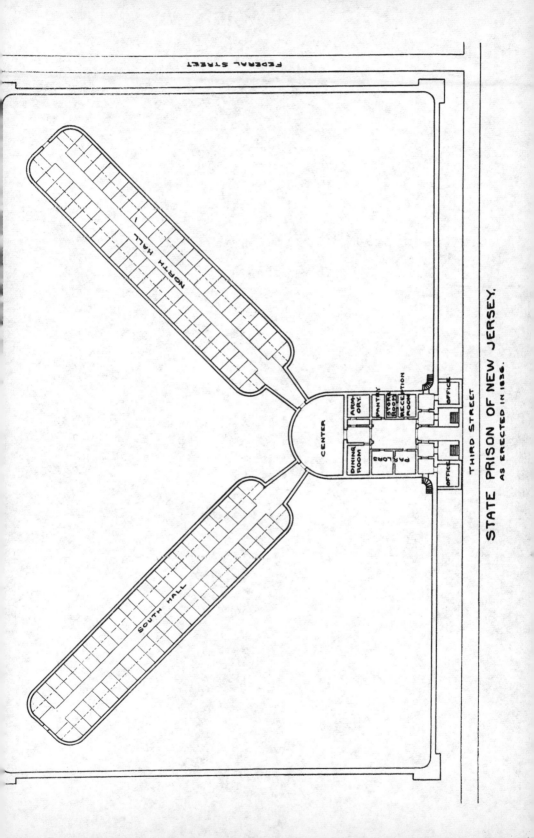

STATE PRISON OF NEW JERSEY.

AS ERECTED IN 1836.

found in the public documents of New Jersey relative to the alleged reformatory influence of the system of solitary confinement:

"It is found by experiment, indeed it is a part of the philosophy of our nature, that the most powerful agent in the work of individual reformation is *solitude.*

"In this position the mind of man is necessarily cast upon itself; its powers, passions, habits and propensities are all before it.—The mass of his life is surveyed with a scrutiny that it never encountered before; and conscious as in his prison house he must be, that escape is hopeless, he continues the unwelcome task of self examination, till his obduracy is subdued, his disposition humble and teachable, and he, prepared to receive with gladness such moral and religious instruction as may be best adapted to his circumstances. In the eloquent and emphatic language of another, 'If any circumstances can be imagined, calculated to impress the warning, the encouragements, the threats or the hopes of religion upon the mind, it must surely be those of the convict in his cell, where he is unseen and unheard, and where nothing can reach him but the voice which must come to him as it were from the other world, telling him of things, which perhaps never before entered into his mind; telling him of God, of eternity, of future reward and future punishment, of suffering far greater than the mere physical endurances of the present life, and of joy infinitely beyond the pleasures he may have experienced. These instructions frequently discover to the guilty tenant of the cell, what seems often not to have occurred to him, the simple fact, that he has a spiritual nature, and that he is not the mere animal which his habits and hitherto uncontrolled propensities would indicate. And this is a discovery which alone may and does effect a great change in a man's whole character. He feels that he is a being superior to what he had thought himself, and that he is regarded as one having higher powers than he had supposed. This first step in the path of improvement is a prodigious one; a new ambition is awakened, and the encouragement of it is the principal thing now needed. This encouragement it is a part of the system to give.'"

These vigorous recommendations were too strong and frequent for even legislative inertia to resist, and on February 13, 1833, a law was passed which decreed that a new state prison should be erected following the plan of construction adopted in the Eastern Penitentiary of Pennsylvania.[1] The prison was to be designed to contain one hundred and fifty

---

[1] Josiah Harrison, *A Compilation of the Laws of New Jersey,* 1833, pp. 443-4. The design of the Eastern Penitentiary was probably suggested by the prison of Ghent, Belgium, built about 1773. See Wines, *Punishment and Reformation,* p. 133.

prisoners, according to the principle of separate confinement at hard labor.[1] It was to be erected on lands adjacent to the old state prison and so arranged that one hundred and fifty more cells might be added when needed. Joseph Kaighn, Charles Parker, and William R. Allen were appointed commissioners to have charge of erecting the new prison, and $130,000 were appropriated toward its erection. It was recommended that convicts be employed as far as possible in building the prison.[2] It was ordered that the old prison be converted into the state arsenal, as had previously been suggested.[3]

The advocates of prison reform in New Jersey were as optimistic in their anticipation of the success which the new system would achieve, as they had been hopeless of reforming the old system of congregate confinement. Governor Vroom, who was serving his second term in 1834, was especially hopeful over the prospects of the new system. In his message of October 29th, 1834, he expressed himself as of the opinion that the new prison promised to be the best in the United States. Though he had in 1830 warmly advocated the adoption of the Auburn-Wethersfield type of prison, he was now as thoroughly in favor of the new Pennsylvania system. So effective did he believe the new prison system to be, that he reported that though the new prison was only partially constructed, the very fear of being confined therein had caused a marked falling off in the crimes committed in New Jersey. The Governor expressed his opinion in the following manner regarding this truly remarkable deterrent virtue which was supposed to reside in the Pennsylvania system:

"But a few years ago there were upwards of one hundred and fifty convicts within the walls at one time. The sensible diminution experienced within the last two years, is attributed by the warden to the fear of confinement in the new prison, entertained by those whose business it is to vio-

[1] The prison was actually built so that it could contain 192 cells. See the diagram opposite page 88.
[2] J. Harrison, *Compilation of the Laws of New Jersey,* 1833, pp. 443–444.
[3] *Acts of the 61st Legislature,* 1837, pp. 159–60. *Votes of the Assembly,* 62d General Assembly, 1837, pp. 13–14.

PLATE II. The Second State Prison of New Jersey, 1836 to 1884.

late the law. That this is true to a certain extent I have no doubt; and it encourages us to hope that the number of prisoners will in the future be permanently lessened."

The Governor summarized his reflections as to the anticipated reformatory influences of the Pennsylvania system in the following paragraph:

"The plan of solitary confinement, with labor, adopted by the State, is gaining friends among those who have devoted much attention to the subject. It is peculiarly fitted for that profitable meditation which tends to reform the unfortunate convict, reclaim him from vice, and finally restore him to the bosom of society. This is the blessed end we have principally in view; and if it shall be attained in any good degree, our best hopes will be realized." [1]

The new state prison was opened in 1836, having been built at an initial cost of $179,429. [2]

The joint committee on the state prison, in its first annual report after the new prison had been put into operation, presented a most favorable view of the effect produced by the new prison system. In the first place, it had been a conspicuous economic success, having produced a net balance in favor of the state, including the salaries of officers, of $1,741.41 during the first year of its operation, as compared with a deficit of $1,352.31 for the last year of the old prison. But the committee was even more pleased over what was believed to be its unquestionable reformatory influence. The committee's views on this subject were expressed in the following paragraph:

"It is, however, the moral condition of the convicts, and the efficiency of the punishment, which afford to the friends of humanity, and the lovers of the social order, the principal recommendation of the system; and this cannot but be peculiarly gratifying to those liberal philanthropists who, through evil as well as good report, firmly sustained their onward and unwavering course in promoting their benevolent object." [3]

[1] *Votes of the Assembly*, 59th General Assembly, 1834, pp. 14–15.
[2] *Journal of the Legislative Council*, 61st Session, 1837, pp. 238–41. A description of the new prison by a contemporary, accompanied by elaborate drawings, is to be found in Demetz and Blouet, *Rapports sur les pénétenciers des États-unis*, Paris, 1837, Appendix, pp. 65ff.
[3] *Votes of the Assembly*, 62d General Assembly, 1837, pp. 155ff.

The report of the board of inspectors of the state prison for the same year (1837) was equally optimistic.[1] This document is probably the best expression of the extreme satisfaction which was felt in New Jersey over the newly adopted prison system. The superiority of the new Pennsylvania system of solitary confinement in every sense, moral, disciplinary, hygienic, and economic was duly emphasized, and it was confidently supposed that the problems of prison administration in New Jersey had been satisfactorily solved, as far as they involved the choice of a system of prison administration. The following excerpt from the report of the inspectors is one of the most confident statements of the disciplinary and reformatory value of solitary confinement:

"Amongst the numerous advantages of this system, the following might be mentioned. The isolated situation of the convict, affords the keeper the very best opportunity to study and know his disposition, his character and his propensities, and to regulate his treatment of him accordingly; besides, there is no means by which any of the convicts, in the adjoining cells, can interfere with, or operate against, this judicious course of treatment; add to this, the strict privation of intercourse, from every human being, except the officers in the daily discharge of their duties or the casual appearance of an 'official visitor'; the unhappy man, cut off thus from the world, is thrown back upon himself, and sooner or later the 'monitor' placed within will speak. In proof of this, we have witnessed, (in a visit to one of the cells but a few days since) the powerful athletic frame tremble in agony, and the big pearly drops steal down the manly cheek, whilst the conscience-stricken convict, in deep distress of mind, related to us his first departure from the path of duty, in 'despising a mother's advice,' and 'disregarding a father's authority'; and this, the small commencement of a career of crime, which has terminated in the lonely cell of a prison.

"In solitary confinement here, every prisoner who can read, has placed within his reach 'the Word of Life, which is able to make wise unto salvation;' and we have good reason to believe, that not a few of these unfortunate men, peruse it daily to advantage, as their orderly conduct abundantly testifies."

So optimistic were the inspectors regarding the potentialities of the newly adopted system of prison administration and discipline that they asserted their belief that it would soon be the "only one known to civilized society." The inspectors thus summarized their opinion as to the prospects of the new Pennsylvania system:

[1] Ibid., pp. 64–74. See Documents, Part II, pp. 445–53.

"We are sincerely desirous to see every obstacle to the prosperity of this infant institution, removed out of the way; considering, as we do, that the Pennsylvania system of separate confinement, with labor and instruction, adopted here, is likely, ere long, to be the only one known to civilized society. At this period of its existence here, it requires cautious, mild treatment. Our hope for its welfare is in the combined wisdom of an intelligent Legislature, every member of which is its particular guardian; who we doubt not will extend to it that fostering care, which, under a benign and gracious Providence, may render its salutary discipline signally instrumental in restoring to society many of those wanderers from the path of virtue and of peace, reformed and amended, living monuments of the wisdom, benevolence, and humanity of its founders." [1]

Unfortunately, they were mistaken, and the new Pennsylvania system had an even shorter existence in New Jersey than did the older congregate system, notwithstanding the fact that New Jersey clung to the Pennsylvania system longer than any other state except Pennsylvania itself.

II. The Trial and Failure of the Pennsylvania System of Prison Administration in New Jersey, 1836–1860.

I. General Tendencies in the Trial of the Pennsylvania System in New Jersey.

The history of the Pennsylvania system in New Jersey in its broadest aspects is essentially the record of the gradual and reluctant recognition of its failure. By 1838 the reports of the prison officials showed unmistakable signs of a decline in that exuberant optimism that had characterized the period of the construction and opening of the new prison. In his annual report of 1838, the keeper admitted that the newly adopted system of solitary confinement apparently had little influence in decreasing the amount of crime committed within the state.[2]

In their report of November 5, 1839, the board of inspectors stated that while the experiences of the past year had not shaken their confidence in the system of solitary confinement, yet candor

[1] Ibid., p. 74.
[2] *Votes of the Assembly*, 63d General Assembly, 1838, pp. 45–7.

demanded that they admit that the mental and physical health of the prisoners had been impaired to a certain degree as a result of this type of imprisonment. They held, however, that the lack of opportunity for vicious association was important enough to offset the unhygienic aspects of solitary confinement.[1]

But the most vigorous and intelligent assaults upon the new system came from the prison physician, James B. Coleman, whose persistent and unanswerable criticism of the detrimental physical and mental effects of solitary confinement did more than anything else, except the economic failure of the new prison, to cause the ultimate relinquishment of the Pennsylvania system in New Jersey.[2] His annual report for 1839 is an admirable analysis of the fundamental defects in the system of solitary confinement. He pointed out the deteriorating effect of solitary confinement on the physical health of the prisoners through the impossibility of taking normal methods of exercise. But even worse was its effect upon the mental health of the prisoners, it leading to solitary vices and mental degeneration. The choice between the congregate and the solitary type of confinement, he held, was fundamentally the problem as to whether vicious association is more to be deplored than mental and physical deterioration. He said:

"It is for others to determine whether the old discipline, hardening the vicious in their crimes while it preserves the body in its full vigor, so that at the expiration of the sentence the convict may go forth a more accomplished rogue than he entered the prison, is to be preferred to another, which, while it subdues the evil passions, almost paralyzing them for want of exercise, leaves the individual, if still a rogue, one who may be easily detected."[3]

In this report for 1841, Dr. Coleman reported that experiments in putting prisoners together in cells had had a beneficial physical and mental effect. He also pointed out the dangerous possibilities which lurked in the practice of pardoning the insane to get them out of the prison, and correctly insisted upon the correla-

[1] *Journal of the Legislative Council,* 64th Session, 1839, pp. 76-9.
[2] See Documents, Part II, pp. 457-62.
[3] *Journal of the Legislative Council,* 64th Session, 1839, pp. 80-83.

tion between mental defects and crime. He quoted at length from Dr. Combe, a leading psychologist of that period, as substantiating his claim that solitary confinement operated against the instinctive human tendency to associate, and resulted in mental deterioration.[1]

His report for 1843 made it clear that everything which was possible "within the law," and much that was not legally permissible, was being done to avoid carrying out a strict application of the system of solitary confinement. In other words, at this early period, it was apparent that the Pennsylvania system had been abandoned in the strict sense of the word, though it was long after adhered to in theory. He also pointed out the difficulties which came from the presence of insane prisoners whose outcries disturbed the minds and discipline of the other prisoners.[2]

Dr. Coleman remained an implacable enemy of the system of solitary confinement during his whole term of office, reiterating year after year the facts and arguments which have been presented above.

Dr. Coleman was not alone in his condemnation of the system. Even the board of inspectors, as early as 1840, betrayed a lack of confidence in the views expressed by the board in 1837, and admitted that there was little evidence that the system of solitary confinement was producing any moral reformation of the prisoners. While they were convinced that it was better adapted for this purpose than other systems, they agreed that the exponents of the system had claimed quite impossible results from it as to its disciplinary, reformatory, and economic virtues. They protested against giving long term sentences under this system of confinement, holding that ten years of solitary confinement was enough to destroy the strongest constitution.[3]

From this time to the close of the "fifties," the reports of the inspectors and of the joint committees of the legislature, in so far

[1] *Votes of the Assembly,* 66th General Assembly, 1841, pp. 189–92.
[2] Ibid., 68th General Assembly, 1843, pp. 170–71. For typical reports of Dr. Coleman, see Documents, Part II, pp. 457–62.
[3] *Votes of the Assembly,* 65th General Assembly, 1840–41, pp. 212–16. See Documents, Part II, pp. 453–7.

as they related to the effects of the system of solitary confinement, monotonously repeated the same criticisms, namely, that
while the system was actually accomplishing practically nothing
that had been claimed for it in the beginning, nevertheless, it was
the most perfect in existence. Its failure to accomplish the
desired results was not usually correctly ascribed to the inherent
defects of the system, so clearly exposed by Dr. Coleman, nor
to the fact that overcrowding and inefficient administration prevented the system from having a fair opportunity to exhibit its
virtues in New Jersey, but was attributed to that ever-present
refuge for personal incompetence—"an overruling Providence."

Not only was the system of solitary confinement an administrative and disciplinary failure in New Jersey, but it also soon
became an economic failure. Though it had started by creating
a surplus over expenses, by the "fifties" a deficit was the rule,
and this increased steadily until by the middle of that decade the
enemies of the "solitary" system were able to enlist the economic
argument on their side.[1]

Notice that the Pennsylvania system was doomed in New Jersey, came in the annual message of Governor Rodman M. Price
in January, 1857, in which the administrative and economic failure of that system was frankly admitted. He summed up his
views as follows:

"No revenue has been derived from the State Prison; indeed, it is becoming a heavy charge upon the state. My observation is that the present system of prison discipline is inhuman, and has practically failed to answer the
purposes of its establishment—the better to reform convicts—beside being
more expensive than the old system of the workhouse. My clear judgment is
that the system should be changed. Solitary confinement has a prejudicial
influence, mentally and physically."[2]

A special legislative committee was appointed to report on this
part of the governor's message. Its report is important as marking the last official defence of the system of solitary confinement
in New Jersey. The burden of the arguments of the committee

[1] *Appendix to the House Journal*, 1856, Document E, pp. 5–6. The balance
against the prison in this year was $8,322.
[2] *Annual Message of the Governor*, 1857, p. 9.

was the valid contention that the Pennsylvania system had not received a fair trial in New Jersey owing to the imperfect physical equipment of the prison and the interference of political considerations with efficient administration. If the Pennsylvania system in New Jersey had been a failure, it was maintained by the committee that such fact had little or no bearing on the value of the system itself when scientifically and methodically conducted.[1]

However, the views of the governor prevailed and the act of March 18, 1858, allowed the re-establishment of workshops and the congregate system of employment,[2] though little was accomplished by the state to bring about the restoration of the shop system until the passage of the acts of March 22, 1860, and February 16, 1861, which made appropriations for carrying this work into execution. The practical activities taken in this direction were inspired, to a large degree, by the attacks upon the old system by Governors William A. Newell, and Charles S. Olden, the successors of Governor Price.

2. THE LEGAL AND ADMINISTRATIVE CHANGES DURING THE PERIOD OF THE PENNSYLVANIA SYSTEM.

The legal phases of the history of the prison system during the domination of the Pennsylvania system in New Jersey were not particularly important.

The penal code, first framed in 1796, and re-enacted with no vital changes in 1829, was embodied with no very significant alteration in the "revision of 1846." The only important variations were a slight decrease in the employment of the death penalty and a corresponding extension of the use of imprisonment as a substitute.[3] The penal code embodied in the act of April 16, 1846, commuted the death penalty for a second con-

[1] *Votes of the Assembly,* 81st General Assembly, 1857, pp. 655ff. See Documents, Part II, pp. 474-7.
[2] *Acts of the 82nd Legislature,* 1858, p. 453. See Documents, Part II, pp. 479-80.
[3] *Revised Statutes of New Jersey,* 1847, pp. 256-284.

7 P

viction of manslaughter, sodomy, rape, arson, burglary, robbery, and forgery, which had been prescribed in the codes of 1796 and 1829, into imprisonment for not more than double the duration of the first sentence.

The evils of the antiquated system of imprisonment for debt which had in part called into existence the New Jersey Howard Society of 1833, and for years incurred the wrath of Louis Dwight and his associates of the Boston Prison Discipline Society, were done away with by the law of April 15, 1846, which forbade imprisonment for debt save in cases of palpable fraud.[1]

When the new constitution for the state was adopted in 1844, the offices of principal keeper and inspector of the state prison were provided for in the constitution, thus preventing any change in their term of office or method of selection through statutory law. It was provided that:

"The state treasurer and the keeper and inspectors of the state prison shall be appointed by the senate and general assembly in joint meeting.

"They shall hold their offices for one year, and until their successors shall be qualified into office."[2]

The legal basis of the administration of the state prison was organized by the law of February 27, 1838, and was re-established in the "Act for the Government and Regulation of the State Prison," of April 16, 1846.[3] This act of 1846 had no great significance, however, as it did little more than to re-enact, in a general way, the provisions of the laws of 1829 and 1838 regarding the choice, election, and duties of the officers of the state prison, though, of course, it could not provide for the choice of the keeper and the inspectors, whose selection had been regulated by the newly adopted constitution.[4] The only changes introduced by the laws of 1838 and 1846 related to the details of the routine of. prison administration, which had to be altered to some extent in being adapted to the Pennsylvania system.

[1] *Revised Statutes of New Jersey*, 1847, pp. 323–325.
[2] *Constitution of New Jersey*, 1844, Art. VII, Sec. ii, par. 3.
[3] Elmer, *Digest of the Laws of New Jersey*, 1838, pp. 392ff. *Revised Statutes of New Jersey*, 1847, pp. 302–313.
[4] *Revised Statutes of New Jersey*, 1847, pp. 302–313.

The act of February 9, 1848, provided for the appointment of a moral instructor and a teacher at a salary of $400 per year.[1] Previous to this time, the religious services at the prison had been conducted by clergymen who had either volunteered their services or had been scantily paid by the paltry appropriations provided for this purpose by the legislature, and by contributions from philanthropic citizens of New Jersey and from the Prison Discipline Society of Boston.

The remaining act of importance relating to the state prison in this period was that of March 18, 1858, which provided for the legal termination of the system of solitary confinement in New Jersey by allowing the revival of the system of congregate workshops.[2]

3. THE INDUSTRIAL HISTORY OF THE PENNSYLVANIA SYSTEM IN NEW JERSEY.

The legal foundations of the organization of the industrial operations of the prison were laid by the act of February 27, 1838, and repeated without any significant changes in the act of April 16, 1846. It was enacted that each prisoner on every day except Sunday should be kept "strictly at hard work, of some sort in which the work is least liable to be spoiled by ignorance, neglect or obstinancy, and in which the materials cannot be easily embezzled or destroyed." The principal keeper was vested with the powers and duties of industrial manager of the state prison, being required to provide the stock and implements necessary for the industrial operations of the prison, and being authorized to receive all payments for prison-made products and for the contracted labor of the prisoners. In addition to acting himself as a selling agent for the prison, the principal keeper was authorized to appoint such additional selling agents as he deemed necessary who should receive a commission on all sales. The principal keeper was further authorized to contract with any person for the labor of all or a part of the convicts in the

[1] *Acts of the 72nd Legislature,* 1848, p. 255.
[2] *Acts of the 82nd Legislature,* 1858, p. 453.

prison. Definite legal provision was thus made for both the public account and the contract systems in the acts of 1838 and 1846. Some legal provision was also made for the state use system by the clause which decreed that as far as possible the prison should be supplied with prison-made products. It was provided that the labor of the prisoners should be determined by the age and capacity of the men. A separate account was to be opened for each prisoner and he was to receive the benefit from all surplus labor or overwork when the total product of his labor exceeded the cost of maintenance. The immediate supervision of the industrial activities of the prison was governed by the provision that the principal keeper might appoint industrial instructors when the labor was conducted on the public account system, and that the contractors might bring in instructors for the industries which were conducted by them.[1]

Under the Pennsylvania system of solitary confinement in cells and the carrying on of all industries within individual cells, the industrial operations of the prison were necessarily those simple and elementary activities which could be conducted in the isolation of separate cells. Chair-making, weaving, and shoe-making (cordwaining) were the chief, and almost the only, productive industries during the twenty years of the operation of the Pennsylvania system in New Jersey, chair-making being the most profitable of the three. The nature and condition of the industries may be gathered from the financial statements of 1845 and 1853, two normal years. In 1845 the net income from the chair-making industry was $7,153; from weaving, $2,301; and from shoe-making, $1,713.[2] In 1853 the net return from the chair-making industry was $11,622; from shoe-making, $6,200; and from weaving, $853.[3] As will be pointed out below,

---

[1] Elmer, *Digest of the Laws of New Jersey,* 1838, pp. 392ff. *Revised Statutes of New Jersey,* 1847, pp. 302ff.

[2] *Annual Report of the State Prison,* 1845, in *Senate Journal,* 1846, pp. 28, 188, 191. The salaries in 1845 aggregated $5,576, and the total loss sustained, including salaries, was $294.

[3] *Annual Report of the State Prison,* 1853, pp. 7–15, in *Appendix to the Senate Journal,* 1854, Document B. The prison was a total loss in 1853, including salaries, of $4,962. For the details of prison industry during this period see Documents, Part II, pp. 467–74.

the products from these industries were chiefly contracted for in advance.

From this brief summary of the nature of the industries of the prison during this period attention may be turned to the method by which they were organized and administered.

At the outset, the abolition of the workshops carried with it a partial decline in the application of the old contract or "piece-price" system and an increased reliance upon the public account system, namely, the direction of the work of the convicts by the prison officials, and the sale of the finished products to outsiders to defray, as far as possible, the expenses of the maintenance of the prison.[1] As has already been shown, this plan was at first financially successful, paying a surplus into the state treasury of over $1,700 in the first year of the operation of the new prison.[2] However, the difficulties of overseeing the work when performed by many isolated individuals, the lack of any distinct financial agent or industrial manager, and the accumulation of bad debts, caused the ultimate downfall of the industrial system. By 1840 the annual loss of the state prison had reached $15,883, including salaries.[3] The inspectors were alarmed at the condition and earnestly advised the appointment of a financial agent, as authorized by the law of February 27, 1838, to aid the keeper in selling the prison-made goods and in collecting the debts owing the prison.[4] However, it was deemed wise to make a more sweeping change, and from 1841 to 1858 the contract system, which had existed along with the public account system, was much more extensively employed, the contractors furnishing the raw material and then taking the finished product, thus relieving the prison officials of the trouble of finding a market for the prison-made goods.[5] There is little evidence that any

---

[1] *Report of the Board of Inspectors,* November 6, 1837, in *Journal of the Legislative Council,* 1838, pp. 71–80. *Votes of the Assembly,* 65th General Assembly, 1840, p. 248.

[2] *Journal of the Legislative Council,* 1838, p. 73.

[3] See Documents, Part II, pp. 465–6.

[4] *Votes of the Assembly,* 65th General Assembly, 1840, pp. 212–16, 246–49.

[5] Ibid., 66th General Assembly, 1841, p. 42.

extensive application was made of the crude contract system of leasing outright the labor of a large number of the prisoners, whose industrial activities were to be entirely conducted and supervised by agents of the contractors, as became the rule after 1860. In his report of 1844 the keeper stated that an attempt had been made by his predecessor to lease out the labor of fifty men to Howe and Co. of New York for the making of shoes, but that the experiment had proved subversive of the discipline of the prison and had been terminated early in his incumbency of the office.[1] The "piece-price" form of the contract system, supplemented by the public account system, appears to have been the typical mode of industrial administration of the state prison during most of the period of the trial of the Pennsylvania system in New Jersey.

For the most of the decade after 1841, except for temporary fluctuations due to the general industrial conditions in the country, the finances of the prison were maintained on a fairly satis-factory basis. By 1847 the total loss including salaries was only $1,000, and in 1848 it was proudly reported that the prison was earning more than ever before in its history.[2] But this period of prosperity was short-lived. The overcrowding of the cells, and the interference of politics with efficient administration, together with fundamental difficulties in the administration of the industrial system, soon cut down the earning capacity of the prison and by 1856 the institution was again becoming a serious loss to the state. In that year the balance against the prison was $8,322, in addition to salaries aggregating over $10,000.[3] The panic of 1857 "came upon the heels" of this industrial decline in the prison, and the period of the passing of the Pennsylvania system was one of serious economic loss to the state.

The failure of both the public account and the contract systems of employment, when carried on in connection with the individual labor of convicts isolated in their cells, led to a

[1] *Annual Report of the Keeper of the State Prison, 1844, in Senate Journal,* 1845, pp. 264–266.
[2] *Votes of the Assembly, 72nd General Assembly, 1848, p. 36.*
[3] *Appendix to the Journal of the House, 1856, Doc. E., pp. 5–6.*

movement to restore the system of congregate employment in workshops, which had existed on a small scale during the period of this first state prison. Legal provision for the establishment of congregate workshops was made by the law of March 18, 1858, which appropriated $500 for the construction of prison workshops, and decreed that "the keeper of the state prison is hereby authorized from time to time to employ in the said workshops as many of the convicts in the said prison as may be deemed expedient for the interests of the institution." [1] Action according to the provisions of this act was urged by Governor William A. Newell in his message of 1859. He advised the building of workshops and a more extensive employment of the practice of disposing of convict labor to contractors. He further advised that workhouses be constructed in connection with the county jails and that the "short termers" be transferred there from the state prison.[2] The joint committee of the legislature on this part of the governor's message entirely concurred in these opinions of the governor and unanimously recommended the re-establishment of the congregate workshop system which had been legally authorized by the act of the previous year.[3]

In his message of the following year, Governor Newell stated that contractors themselves had erected some workshops within the prison yard and that even this partial re-establishment of the workshop system had proved a success. He vigorously recommended a state appropriation to carry on the necessary work of building more workshops, so that all available convicts might be employed.[4] The inspectors reiterated the Governor's opinions and recommendations, and the keeper reported that, even with this incomplete establishment of the workshop system, the prison had earned $1,089 over the expenses of maintenance, exclusive of the salaries of the prison officials which

[1] *Acts of the 82d Legislature*, 1858, p. 453.
[2] *Appendix to the Journal of the Senate*, 1859, pp. 8–10.
[3] Ibid., pp. 352–3. See Documents, Part II, pp. 477–9.
[4] Ibid., 1860, pp. 9–12.

aggregated over $13,000.[1] These vigorous recommendations met with some degree of response from the legislature and the act of March 22, 1860, appropriated $17,000 for the erection of a new wing and new workshops, and further appropriation of $2,243 for the same purpose was made by the act of February 16, 1861.[2] As the system of solitary confinement at night was continued, in so far as it was possible in view of the limited capacity of the prison, it is not inaccurate to say that these acts, in fact, established the Auburn system of congregate work by day and isolation by night, which had been rejected in favor of the Pennsylvania system in 1833. Along with this adoption of the congregate workshops there went an almost complete adoption and acceptance of the system of leasing outright the labor of the convicts to contractors.[3]

4. PRISON DISCIPLINE AND ADMINISTRATION UNDER THE PENNSYLVANIA SYSTEM.

The legal organization of prison administration and discipline was furnished by the general organizing law of February 27, 1838, which provided for the regulation of the newly constructed prison. However, the provisions of this law were by no means new or original, being little more than a slight revision of the law of 1829, so changed as to be adapted to the system of solitary confinement. The general provisions as to the nature, choice and tenure of the official force were practically unchanged. The general supervision of the prison was vested, as before, in a board of inspectors elected yearly by the joint-session of the legislature. The chief executive officer was the principal keeper, chosen annually, as under the regulation of the law of 1829, by the same joint-session that elected the inspectors. It was enacted that the principal keeper should visit each occupied cell twice

---

[1] Ibid., pp. 454–5, 458, 473–484.
[2] *Acts of the 84th Legislature*, 1860, pp. 600–601; *Acts of the 85th Legislature*, 1861, p. 29.
[3] *Annual Report of the State Prison*, 1861, pp. 9, 17–18; 1862, p. 10.

weekly and that he should assign a certain number of prisoners to each deputy who should visit each prisoner assigned to him in his cell three times daily. The salient "solitary" and "silent" characteristics of the Pennsylvania system were thoroughly safeguarded from a legal standpoint, though the law was little respected after a few years of the trial of the system. It was decreed that no prisoner should be taken from his cell except to save his life, and then only upon the certificate of the physician that such action was necessary. Even in such a case it was ordered that the greatest precautions should be taken to prevent any association with another prisoner. It was also explicitly enacted that no keeper or deputy should enter into any conversation whatever with any prisoner beyond what was absolutely indispensible to the execution of the duties of prison administration. The only opportunity for conversation which was legally permissible was with properly certified clergymen, who might be admitted "to guide and intensify the communion of each prisoner with his soul and Saviour." [1]

It has been pointed out above in connection with Dr. Coleman's cricitisms of the Pennsylvania system that the legal provisions for solitary confinement were little respected. By 1841 the increase of insanity and nervous and physical "breakdowns" among the prisoners led to the practice of putting two prisoners in a cell, and it was not long before it became a general custom to allow a limited degree of exercise in the open air, though these departures from the prescribed legal course of administration occurred only in the case of those in a serious condition of health, and so were not adequate to solving the problem of association or exercise for the general prison population. [2] The failure to provide for a proper exercising space in the second state prison at Trenton was undoubtedly a primary cause of the speedy

[1] Elmer, *Digest of the Laws of New Jersey*, 1838, pp. 392ff. Cf. *Votes of Assembly*, 57th General Assembly, 1832-3, pp. 142-153; Ibid., 62d General Assembly, 1837, pp. 64-74; *Report of the Moral Instructor*, 1852, in *Appendix to the Journal of the Senate*, 1852, pp. 175-181. See Documents, Part II, pp. 462-5.

[2] *Votes of the Assembly*, 1841, pp. 189-192.

decline and failure of the Pennsylvania system in New Jersey, as compared with its long existence in the Eastern Penitentiary of Pennsylvania which has been in operation since 1829.

But considerations of mental and physical hygiene were not the only cause of the rapid abandonment of the strict and literal appli_ cation of the principle of solitary confinement in the prison at Trenton. The prison population had increased by 1845 to such a degree that all the available cells were occupied, and from that time on, the multiple occupation of the cells became the rule until the abandonment of the system.[1] By 1860 there were three hundred and forty-six prisoners in the prison to be confined in one hundred and eighty available cells.[2] Thus the very pressure of physical circumstances prevented any long and thorough application of the Pennsylvania system in New Jersey, though it was tried long enough to prove that it was bound to be a failure when conducted without adequate exercising facilities.

There is little extant evidence available regarding the infliction of punishment in the prison under the Pennsylvania system. The legal maximum of six days in a dark cell on bread and water, which had been enacted in the law of 1798, was retained in that of 1838 and that of 1846. It seems safe to generalize to the effect that excessive punishments were not practiced during any considerable portion of this period. There is little mention of any such occurrences in the contemporary literature, and it is probable that the activity of prison reform associations at this time would have brought such abuses to the public notice if they had existed. The cases of inhuman punishment reported by the Commission on Prison Discipline in 1869 probably indicate a reversion to the policy of inflicting harsh punishments during the last decade of the existence of the Pennsylvania system in New Jersey. In 1846 shower-baths were adopted in the prison as a method of punishment which was designed as a more humane

[1] *Appendix to the Journal of the Senate*, 1852, p. 170; *Appendix to the Journal of the Senate*, 1856, Document E, p. 17.
[2] *Appendix to the Journal of the Senate*, 1860, p. 467.

substitute for the dungeon. They were given up two years later, however, as too dangerous to be extensively employed.[1]

5. TENDENCIES IN PRISON REFORM 1836–1860.

a. *General Reform Movements.*

The most interesting aspect of the history of the penal institutions of New Jersey during the era of the Pennsylvania system was the prominence of movements for prison reform. It was at this time that prison reform was first assuming serious proportions in Europe, and the advanced American experiments in penal institutions were the object of admiring investigation by the foremost figures in European penal reform. This interaction between the more enlightened individuals and associations of both continents was reflected in America by the activities of the influential Boston Prison Discipline Society, which was country-wide in its activities from 1826–1853, and in the various state organizations for prison reform whose aims were modelled on those of this quasi-national organization.

The first prison reform organization in New Jersey was the *Prison Instruction Society,* organized in 1833, which was composed of such eminent men as Governor Southard, L. Q. C. Elmer, Professor John Maclean, of Princeton, and Keeper

---

[1] Bathing facilities for hygienic purposes were not introduced until many years later. Dr. Taylor, the prison physician, in his report for 1854, gave out the startling information that although the prison had been in operation nearly twenty years there had never been any bathing facilities provided beyond the wash-basins in each cell. The disgraceful nature of this condition is readily apparent when one reflects that many of the prisoners were committed after having spent months in the dirty country jails and were then forced to spend years in the state prison without this simplest and most elementary of hygienic conveniences. Dr. Taylor pointed out that in the Eastern Penitentiary facilities were provided for bathing every two weeks, and advocated the provision of similar opportunities at Trenton.

Joseph Yard, of the state prison.[1] The purpose of this society
was expressed as follows :

"The chief object of this society shall be, to extend to the convicts in the
Prisons of this state the benefits of the Sabbath school system of instruction,
and also to furnish them with preaching.
"In connection with the foregoing objects, provision shall also be made for
inquiring into the relative efficiency of different modes of prison discipline,
and of different modes of instruction."[2]

This society with its primary theological aim, was characteristic of the period. The spiritual welfare of the prisoners was
made the chief motive in agitating for the reform of the criminal code and the penal institutions.

In the same year that the Prison Instruction Society was
organized, the *New Jersey Howard Society,* named in honor of
the English prison reformer, John Howard, was established, its
chief purposes being to attack the barbarous practice of imprisoning debtors, which still persisted in New Jersey, and to urge better
provision for the care of the insane and the reformation of delinquent minors.[3]

The next movement toward prison reform in New Jersey
centered around the efforts of Miss Dorothea L. Dix, to secure
adequate provision for the insane and idiotic inmates of the
county jails, almshouses, and the state prison. For years prison
officials had pointed out the serious difficulties imposed upon
them by the presence of the insane in the institution.[4] In her
notable Memorial of January, 1845, Miss Dix, who, in addition
to being one of the foremost reformers and philanthropists of
her day, was for that time an unusually enlightened and well-

[1] The first annual report of this society, which is reproduced in the *Eighth
Annual Report of the Prison Discipline Society of Boston,* 1833, pp. 95-102,
is one of the best summaries in existence of the main developments in
penology and penal institutions in America during the first third of the last
century. See Documents, Part II, pp. 427-35.

[2] *Eighth Annual Report of the Prison Discipline Society of Boston,* 1833,
pp. 16-17. See Documents, Part II, pp. 480-2.

[3] Ibid., *Ninth Annual Report,* 1834, pp. 85, 93.

[4] Ibid., *Twelfth Annual Report,* 1837, p. 26; *Fourteenth Annual Report,*
1839, pp. 11-14.

informed student of recent developments in psychiatry, demonstrated that as early as 1839 there were 252 insane males and 163 insane females and 93 male idiots and 103 female idiots in the state of New Jersey.[1] This insane and idiotic population, which received no adequate treatment, was thus much larger than the total population of the state prison at that time. Miss Dix's convincing statistics and her eloquent appeal for a rational treatment of the mentally abnormal classes bore fruit in the establishment of the state hospital for the insane and idiotic at Trenton in 1848. However, though the state hospital took care of the insane in the state prison at that time, adequate provision was not made for the transferring to the state hospital of convicts who might afterward become insane, and the state prison therefore continued to be hampered by the presence of insane inmates for the rest of the century.[2]

The most pretentious organization for penal reform which was developed during this period, was the *New Jersey Prison Reform Association* organized in Trenton in 1849. This association included among its members many of the most prominent citizens of the state. Daniel Haines was president of the society, Ex-Governor Vroom was vice-president, and Samuel Starr, Moral Instructor of the state prison, was secretary. The designs of the association were thus expressed in its constitution:

"*First.*—The improvement of the prisons and jails of the State.

"*Secondly.*—The physical, moral and religious betterment of prisoners therein, especially the improvement of juvenile offenders and the provision of more appropriate means than now exist in the state for their proper punishment and reformation.

"*Thirdly.*—The due encouragement of all such convicts on their discharge, as shall have conducted themselves well during their imprisonment and who on professed resolutions of amendment, desire aid in procuring by their labor

[1] *Memorial of Dorothea L. Dix to the New Jersey Legislature on the Insane in the New Jersey County Jails, Almshouses and the State Penitentiary,* Trenton, January, 1845, pp. 5–23. *Twentieth Annual Report of the Prison Discipline Society of Boston,* 1845, p. 20.

[2] Cf. *Annual Report of the State Prison,* 1916, pp. 41–2.

the means of an honest livelihood, and in regaining the blessings of a reputable character."[1]

This association was thoroughly organized throughout the state in county committees co-ordinated through a central state committee. Its chief activities were centered about the improvement of the condition of the jails and the state prison, and the attempt to secure for the state of New Jersey a "House of Refuge" or a reformatory for minors, who were then confined in the state prison or the county jails along with the most hardened criminals. The first annual report of the society, which was published in 1850, presented a caustic indictment of the barbarous county jail system of New Jersey, which was based on a detailed investigation by members of the society of the county jails of thirteen counties of the state. In summing up their Memorial to the Legislature on the subject of the county jails, they made the following recommendations:

"Let then wise, well considered, and judicious enactments be passed, that shall provide for the strict enforcement of *hard labor,* for the proper separation of the hardened criminal from those younger in vice, and from those merely committed for trial, as also of the sexes; for a reformation in the treatment of criminals as regards cleanliness, the ventilation and warming of the jails, and the providing of decent clothing, and for the introduction of some degree of moral discipline."[2]

The most important publication of this society bearing on the state prison, was the Third Annual Report published in 1852. This stated that the state prison was so crowded that thirty cells were occupied by two or more prisoners, and that conversation subversive to the discipline of the prison, and contrary to the fundamental theories of the Pennsylvania system, took place freely among prisoners in adjoining cells. It was further reported that the south wing of the prison was very inadequately heated, a number of prisoners having suffered from frozen hands

[1] *Constitution of the New Jersey Prison Reform Association,* Trenton, 1849, pp. 3–4. See Documents, Part II, pp. 485–8.

[2] *Memorial of the New Jersey Prison Reform Association to the Senate and General Assembly in Relation to the Improvement of County Jails,* Trenton, January 25, 1850, pp. 5–6. See Documents, Part II, pp. 636–8.

and feet during the last winter.[1]   The committee insisted upon the great need for a "House of Refuge" for juvenile delinquents, and for civic associations and philanthropic individuals to care for discharged prisoners and to secure for them honest employment.[2]

The committee on the "House of Refuge" pointed out the urgent necessity for an institution for juvenile delinquents where habits of activity and honest labor might be acquired.   It called attention to the fact that New Jersey was far behind her neighboring states in this respect.   Boston had been operating a successful juvenile reformatory for twenty-five years.   Delaware was erecting its third institution of this type at a cost of $250,-000, and New York and Pennsylvania also were provided with satisfactory reform schools for delinquent minors.[3]

As far as any printed evidence is available, the report of 1852 was the last one published by the Prison Reform Association. The only reason that can be assigned for its having passed out of existence is that Louis Dwight, the moving spirit in the Boston Prison Discipline Society, died in the latter part of 1853, and with him perished both the national organization and most of the state societies fostered by it.   It was many years before another equally important private association for prison reform existed in the state of New Jersey.

b. *Reform within the State Prison.*

However, all the movements toward penal reform did not originate outside of the state prison and its officials.   In his report for February 6, 1838, Mr. Joseph A. Yard, Keeper of the state prison, made at the request of the legislature an interesting investigation as to the degree of education possessed by the inmates of the state prison.   He found that of the 135 prisoners in the institution, 12 could read, write, and cipher and had studied

[1] This situation was remedied by the act of March 25, 1852, appropriating $5,000 to provide for better heating of the south wing.

[2] *Third Annual Report of the New Jersey Prison Reform Association,* Trenton, 1852, pp. 5-7.   See Documents, Part II, pp. 488-90.

[3] Ibid., pp. 17-19.

geography and grammar; 25 could read, write, and cipher; 24 could read and write; 30 could read only; 13 could spell simple words; 18 knew the alphabet; and 13 were even ignorant of the alphabet. In drawing his conclusions from his investigations, the Keeper made an eloquent attempt to correlate illiteracy and crime, and to urge the preventive and therapeutic values of education.[1]

In 1842 the legislature was induced to make an appropriation of $100 for a prison library, and 300 books were provided through this initial appropriation.[2] A decade later, the library, through further appropriations and private contributions, had reached a total of 1,000 volumes.

The act of March 4, 1847, provided an important improvement of the physical equipment of the prison by appropriating $5,000 for the erection of a suitable building for a kitchen, bakery, laundry, and storeroom.[3] Hitherto all the cooking and washing has been conducted in the halls and empty cells of the wings erected in 1836. Seven years later, in 1854, $15,000 was appropriated for equipping a prison hospital [4] and this hospital was not abandoned until after the present one was erected in 1895–7, when it was transformed into the long-hoped-for chapel.

A permanent moral instructor and teacher was provided for the prison by the Act of February 9, 1848. The moral instructor of the state prison, though usually handicapped by certain unscientific theological presuppositions, which have opposed a rational conception of crime and its treatment and prevention, has generally been a force for the betterment of prison discipline. A particularly good illustration of the enlightened views of the moral instructors during the middle of the last century is the report of the Rev. Samuel S. Starr, submitted in 1851. Rev. Mr. Starr was also Secretary of, and a moving figure in, the New Jersey Prison Reform Association, and his views on penology are, thus, an excellent illustration of the more intelligent theo-

---

[1] *Votes of the Assembly,* 62d General Assembly, 1837–8, pp. 442–5. See Documents, Part II, pp. 482–4.

[2] Ibid., 67th General Assembly, 1842, pp. 164–5.

[3] *Acts of the 71st Legislature,* 1847, pp. 173–4.

[4] *Acts of the 78th Legislature,* 1854, pp. 376–7.

logical opinions on crime and its punishment in this period. He thus summed up in the above mentioned report his views upon reformation as the chief purpose of the penal system:

"That day of the world is past in which it has been soberly supposed, and by Christian writers, too, that a criminal, because he is a criminal, is forever to be abandoned and shunned as a hopeless outcast from the world. Nothing can be weaker or more false than that sickly sentimentality which would sympathize more with the culprit than with the community whose rights he has injured, and whose safety he has wickedly invaded. At the same time, to reclaim the erring and draw back the lost to the ways of virtue, is always a work which claims the earnest sympathy of every Christian citizen. This is due to society, as truly and directly as to the guilty individual. It must be remembered that the inmates of our prisons are soon again to be free men, and to be actively mingling with the busy scenes of the world; and just in proportion as they can be made to understand the folly of dishonesty and violence, will be the prospect that society will be no further harmed by their crimes." [1]

The next agitation for reform in prison administration and discipline which interested the officers of the state prison was the attempt to prevent minors from being sent to the state prison with its inadequate provisions for reformation and education. In their reports of 1852 and 1853, the board of inspectors strongly urged the advisability of sending minors and first termers to the county jails or workhouses.[2] This agitation came at the same time that the New Jersey Prison Reform Association was making its "drive" for a reformatory to receive minors and petty offenders, but both movements were equally unsuccessful.

With the exception of Doctor Coleman's criticisms of the psychopathic effects of the system of solitary confinement, the nature and results of which have been outlined above, the prison officials took no further significant part in prison reform until the close of the "fifties," when they joined in the general attack upon the Pennsylvania system which brought it to a close in New Jersey.

[1] *Journal of the Senate,* 75th Session, 1851, p. 38.
[2] *Journal of the Senate,* 76th Session, 1852, Appendix, p. 170. Ibid., 77th Session, 1853, Appendix, p. 74.

8 P

c. *Politics and Prison Administration.*

Another important movement towards penal reform, which began in this period was that which was designed to effect the removal of the administration of the state prison from political influences. While the insidious influence of politics in the administration of the prison system of New Jersey had been dwelt upon by the citizens' associations in their reports for a score of years, one of the first cases of a frank recognition of this evil by the public authorities themselves, came in the report of the special committee on Governor Price's message of 1857 in which he advocated the abandonment of the system of solitary confinement in New Jersey. In its report, this committee, in defending the Pennsylvania system, maintained that it was more the incompetence of a political administration of the prison system, than the defects of the system of solitary confinement, which had caused its downfall. The office of keeper of the state prison being a part of the spoils system, the keeper was obliged to conduct his office with a primary view to insuring his reappointment and to waste considerable time in electioneering. The short terms of the officers and their selection as a reward for political services rather than for proved efficiency in prison administration all conspired to demoralize any movement towards bettering the administration of the state prison. The committee summarized their opinion in regard to the pernicious influence of politics upon administrative efficiency in the state prison, in the following paragraph:

"The greatest evil, however, which your committee considers to exist, is the political character of the Prison and the mutations of government to which it is liable from the frequent changes of party. The great qualification which seems now to be taken into consideration, is the peculiar political tenents of the Keeper, and not the fitness or ability which is requisite for an office in which so much depends upon its executive. While, however, the appointing power remains with the Legislature, your committee cannot hope for any radical reformation, and they therefore consider that it should be entrusted to the Chancellor and the Judges of the Supreme Court, as being further removed from political influences, and where a discrimination could be exercised, which is impossible in a popular body. The first questions which are now asked when an election occurs is to what party does the present incumbent belong? How long has he held the office, and how near has the prison been self-supporting? Not in what manner has he proved himself competent to fill the position. Under the present system, for at least three months in the year, the attention of the incumbent is bent upon securing his re-election, which cannot but in every way prove detrimental to the interests of the prison."[1]

The same note was sounded in the message of Governor William A. Newell in 1860, in which he frankly declared that politics was the most dangerous and powerful obstacle to efficient prison administration, and strongly urged that some method be devised of keeping the administration of the state prison free from political influences.[2] This movement was continued for a decade, especially by Governor Marcus L. Ward, and culminated in the report of the Legislative Committee of 1868, and in the comprehensive report of the Commission on Prison Discipline of 1869.[3]

d. *The Attempt to Establish a Juvenile Reformatory, 1850–1853.*

A promising movement for the improvement of the penal system of New Jersey during this period, which has already been mentioned and which came very near to succeeding, was the agitation for a "House of Refuge," or, in other words, for a reformatory for delinquent minors and petty offenders. The relation of the Prison Reform Association and the prison officials to this movement has already been pointed out. The pressure in this direction came very near to succeeding. In the session of the legislature of 1850 an appropriation of $15,000 was made for the erection of such a "House of Refuge."[4] A site was selected for the reformatory at Kingston, near Princeton, the foundations were laid and the walls partially erected, but the erection of the institution was made a political issue and with its defeat the institution was abandoned and the site and the partially constructed building were sold in 1853, much to the

[1] *Votes of the Assembly,* 81st General Assembly, 1857, p. 658.
[2] *Appendix to the Journal of the Senate,* 1860, p. 11.
[3] See Documents, Part II, pp. 508–14; 521–2.
[4] *Acts of the 74th Legislature,* 1850, pp. 125–127.

chagrin of the advocates of prison reform.[1] The following
excerpt from a letter of Samuel Starr to Louis Dwight illustrates the humiliation felt by the enlightened citizens of New
Jersey over this political scandal:

"As a Jerseyman, I am ashamed to say that the last Legislature appointed
Commissioners to sell the grounds purchased and the wall erected for a
House of Refuge. . . . It really makes us sick at heart. We have some
faint hope that it may be purchased and reserved for its intended purpose."[2]

The fact that the politicians were able to carry the day against
such a group of representative citizens as the Prison Reform Association is a fair indication of the sinister power of politics
in the "fifties" and an excellent proof that there was much need
for the attacks which were later made upon political influences
in prison administration.

III. SUMMARY.

The chief results of the experience of New Jersey with the
Pennsylvania system of solitary confinement may now be summarized. No one has ever doubted that the system was a failure
as tried out by New Jersey between 1836 and 1860. The causes
for its failure were two-fold; first, the defects inherent in the
system, even when perfectly administered, and secondly, those
added by the imperfect conduct of the system in New Jersey.
The inherent defects of the Pennsylvania system were alleged
to be: the failure of the system to effect any reformation unless
a very large number of attendants was furnished so that
adequate individual attention might be given to each prisoner;

[1] *Twenty-fifth Annual Report of the Prison Discipline Society of Boston,*
1850, p. 59. Ibid., 26th Annual Report, p. 10. Ibid., 28th Annual Report,
1853, p. 16. E. C. Wines, *Prisons and Child Saving Institutions,* 1879, pp.
155–6. The documents bearing on this abortive effort at Kingston are to be
found in the messages of the Governor, 1851, pp. 21–4; 1853, pp. 17–18; in
the *Minutes of the Assembly,* 1851, pp. 503, 804, and in the Appendix to the
House Journal, 1852, pp. 405–9. See Documents, Part II, pp. 569–79.
[2] *Twenty-seventh Annual Report of the Prison Discipline Society of Boston,* 1852, p. 129.

the pernicious mental and nervous effects of segregation and isolation, which directly opposed the fundamental gregarious instinct of the human race; the evil physical effects of the limited possibilities for adequate muscular exercise; and, finally, its lack of adaptation to the organization of a productive system of prison industry.

The additional disadvantages under which the system had to operate in New Jersey have already been set forth. They were: the failure to extend the capacity of the prison so as to prevent overcrowding and the necessity of violating the principle of solitary confinement by the sheer compulsion of physical circumstances; and the paralyzing of efficient prison administration, whatever the system, by the ruinous interference of politics with the selection and tenure of the prison officials, and with the conduct of the prison industries.

In spite of the fact that the Pennsylvania system, so unfairly tested in New Jersey, proved as complete a failure as the congregate system had proved by 1836 there was no such thoroughgoing investigation of the situation as had taken place in 1830, nor any clean sweeping away of old obstructions and the initiation of a completely new situation as had happened in 1833–1836. Governor Charles S. Olden, in his message of 1861, strongly advised the building of a new prison in the eastern part of the state, which should be constructed on the plan of the Auburn-Wethersfield type, so that the merits of the two contending systems might be tried out and the virtues of both adopted, to the exclusion of their defects.[1] Nothing came of his suggestions, however, and New Jersey, by building the congregate workshops, abandoned the Pennsylvania system and adopted the Auburn type of administration without really determining upon any fixed policy or attempting any thorough plan of reconstructing the prison system. In fact, some of the prison reports as late as 1868, seem to indicate that the officials were scarcely aware

[1] *Annual Message of the Governor,* 1861, pp. 11–12. The Governor showed how false had been the opinions expressed between 1833–1840 as to the deterrent value of the Pennsylvania system by pointing out that from 1830 to 1860 crime had increased much more rapidly than the population.

that there had been a change of prison systems in 1858–60. The haphazard and slovenly attitude taken in 1858–60, coupled with the difficulties and stresses of the Civil War, make it easy to understand why a decade later the investigation of 1869 revealed the fact that the prison was in as distressing a condition as it had been ten years earlier when the Pennsylvania system was abandoned.

NEW JERSEY AND THE AUBURN SYSTEM, 1860-1885

CHAPTER IV

NEW JERSEY AND THE AUBURN SYSTEM, 1860–1885.

I. NEW JERSEY AND THE AUBURN SYSTEM DURING THE DECADE OF THE CIVIL WAR.

1. GENERAL TENDENCIES OF THE PERIOD.

Except for matters of analytical convenience there is no valid reason for dividing the history of the state prison of New Jersey into different periods after 1858–1860, when the Auburn system was adopted. Since 1860 the same general system of associated work by day and solitary confinement by night has been followed in theory, if not entirely in practice. Likewise, the period from 1860 to 1917, or at least to 1911, has been uniformly character-

ized by the absence of any sweeping changes in the method of
prison discipline and administration and by the failure to adopt
any radically different attitude towards the problem of criminality and the function of imprisonment. Further, the changes and
advances which have been achieved have been sporadic and
piece-meal, and by their tardy and reluctant enactment they have
usually been foredoomed to failure due to the changes in conditions during the period of agitation.

However, for the sake of convenience in aiding an assimilation
of the facts concerning this long period of more than a half century, it seems wise to divide this era into at least three sections.
The first division logically ends with the abolition of the old
system of contract labor in 1884. The next period may correctly be said to extend to 1911, when the second attempt was
made to rid the state prison of contract labor and when there
began a period of unprecedented activity in reform legislation.
The third and final division includes these new developments
since 1911.

While there was no sweeping away of old systems in New
Jersey in 1858–60, this period really initiated a new era in the
history of New Jersey prisons. The periods of the original
state prison, 1797–1833, and of the Pennsylvania system, 1836–
1860, were really periods of bold originality and experimentation in systems of prison administration. The era from 1860
to the present time, on the other hand, has been one of com-
promise, and of forced alterations of old and outgrown institutions and systems. The history of the prison system in New Jersey in the last half century has been essentially one of continual
stress and agitation centering about attempts to solve by tardy
and improvised methods serious difficulties which could only be
met by a bold sweeping aside of antiquated obstructions and
making a new start upon a clean slate.

The period of the decade of the Civil War in the history of
New Jersey prisons was essentially one in which half-way measures were taken to convert the solitary system of confinement
into the Auburn system of congregate workshops. Most of
the evils which had brought about the downfall of the Pennsyl-

vania system were inherited by the new order of things after 1860 and yet no adequate provision was made to eliminate the serious defects which had stood out so clearly in the criticisms of the old system during the decade of the "fifties." Consequently, it is not strange to find that this make-shift and hybrid system broke down in 1869 and necessitated another partial reconstruction of the New Jersey prison system.

In looking over the general developments of the prison system in this decade, its history may be organized about the attempts to reconstruct the industrial system; the endeavor to lift prison administration out of politics; the provision of a new wing for men and of a separate wing for women prisoners; the successful agitation for the establishment of a reform school for delinquent boys at Jamesburg, and, above all, the report of the famous Commission of 1869 on prison discipline.

2. CHANGES IN THE LEGAL BASIS OF THE ADMINISTRATION OF THE STATE PRISON.

There were several noteworthy legal changes and advances between 1860 and 1869 which related to the state prison. The act of April 14, 1868, provided for the first system of commutation of prison sentence for good behavior ever introduced in the New Jersey state prison.[1]

The defects in the industrial administration of the state prison led to the creation of a new industrial manager for the prison by the act of March 26, 1869, the keeper thus being relieved of the duty of supervising the industry of the prison which had been imposed upon him since 1798. The "supervisor" of prison industries, thus created, remained the chief industrial officer of the prison until the office was theoretically abolished by the law of April 20, 1914. The supervisor along with the comptroller and the state treasurer constituted a board for the supervision of prison industries.[2] The law of March 26,

---

[1] *Acts of the 92nd Legislature,* 1868, pp. 981–82.
[2] *Acts of the 93rd Legislature,* 1869, pp. 772–3.

1869, also provided for the general organization of the administration of the state prison, but it was little more than a slight revision of the act of April 16, 1846.[1]

The remaining laws of any significance during this period were those of 1860, 1868, and 1869 appropriating funds to construct two new wings for men, new congregate workshops, and a separate wing for women.

3. THE INDUSTRIAL ADMINISTRATION OF THE STATE PRISON.

In spite of the rather promising reconstruction of prison industry made possible by the building of the new workshop in 1860–61, the abnormal conditions created by the first years of the Civil War dealt a hard blow to the finances of the prison. During the greater part of 1861, the most of the convicts in the state prison were idle, though there was a tendency later in the year to get readjusted to new conditions. Whereas the prison had earned a surplus exclusive of salaries of over $1,000 in 1859, the first year of the new workshop erected by the contractors, but two years later, owing to the effect of the war, it sustained a loss against maintenance of $8,000, exclusive of salaries amounting to over $16,000.[2] However, the depletion of the supply of free labor by the war and the gradual readjustment of the prison to abnormal conditions tended to reduce the deficit of the first year of the war, and in his report for the year 1862 the keeper stated that the prison was more than meeting the expenses of maintenance exclusive of salaries, and asked for the construction of more workshops, those already in existence only allowing him to employ 250 out of the 408 available prisoners.[3] The keeper's request was not granted, and as late as 1868, it was maintained that there were only half enough workshops provided for the available prisoners.[4]

[1] *Acts of the 93rd Legislature*, 1869, pp. 771ff.
[2] *Annual Report of the State Prison of New Jersey*, 1861, pp. 19, 26–7.
[3] Ibid., 1862, pp. 19, 20, 30–31. The gain over maintenance was $577.34, and salaries aggregated $19,425.
[4] Ibid., 1868, pp. 407–8.

The actual nature of the prison industries, as well as the manner of handling the labor of the prisoners, was considerably changed after the adoption of the congregate workshops in 1858–60 and the system of leasing contract labor that accompanied it. While chair-making had been by far the most profitable industry during the period of solitary confinement, after 1860 shoe-making (cordwaining) superseded it as the most remunerative of the prison industries. This work was practically all done under the control of contractors who leased the labor of the convicts. This was the first extensive adoption of the lease system in the state prison. From 1861 to 1865 one firm alone, Bigelow and Trask of New York, leased the labor of 250 convicts for 31 cents per day and employed them at making shoes. In 1865, $21,361 out of the total income from the prison industries was derived from the leasing of convict labor.[1]

The distribution of the industrial population of the prison in this period, as well as the income derived from convict labor, is readily apparent in the statistical tables presented in the annual reports of the state prison. In 1862 the gain on the operation of the industries of the prison was distributed as follows:

Shoe-making (cordwaining) on contract	$13,890.87
Chair-making	$ 3,282.57
Weaving	$ 685.11
Sundries	$ 2,375.02
Total	$20,233.57

The gain over maintenance in this year was $577.34 and the appropriation for salaries amounted to $19,425.[2]

The situation in 1864 as regards the gain from the operation of the industries was the following:

Convict labor, leased (250 at shoe-making)	$28,933.80
Chair-making	$ 2,430.72
Weaving	$ 1,300.90
Sundries	$ 1,527.15

[1] Ibid. 1862, p. 18; Ibid., 1865, in *Legislative Documents,* 1866, p. 798. See Documents, Part II, pp. 493–6.

[2] Ibid., 1862, pp. 30–31.

Shoe-making (in cells) ....$ 807.47
Interest ....$ 114.15
                                                 ──────────
          Total....................................$35,114.19

In this year the loss over maintenance cost was $5,114.07 and the appropriation for salaries was $24,829.16, making a total loss of $29,943.23.[1]

All in all, the industries of the state prison during the Civil War period were far from satisfactory and it was not until a large appropriation was made for additional workshops on April 12, 1869, that anything like an efficient physical basis for the economic management of the prison was provided. The method of handling the prison industries throughout this period, as has been pointed out, was that of the "lease" variety of the contract system, which had been generally adopted with the building of the workshops. The necessity for an efficient financial and industrial superintendent for the prison industries to relieve the keeper of these burdens was made evident by the provision for a supervisor of industries and a board of industrial supervisors in the law of March 26, 1869.[2]

4. PRISON BETTERMENT AND PRISON REFORM MOVEMENTS.

a. *The Movement Against Political Influences.*

The struggle which was begun in the "fifties" against political influences in the prison was revived about the close of the Civil War. In their annual report for 1865 the inspectors contended that the keeper of the state prison should be appointed for a series of years and that his appointment should be lifted clear from political considerations.[3] In their report for the following year the inspectors repeated the suggestion and recommended that the justices of the supreme court appoint the in-

---

[1] Ibid., 1864, pp. 16–17, 24–5.
[2] *Acts of the 93rd Legislature,* 1869, pp. 772–3, 774–8.
[3] *Annual Report of the State Prison of New Jersey,* 1865, in *Legislative Documents,* 1866, p. 799.

spectors and that the inspectors, thus selected, be given the power
to appoint the prison officers.[1] In his message of January 14,
1868, Governor Marcus L. Ward vigorously seconded the suggestions of the board of inspectors and insisted that partisan
politics should be discarded as a part of the system of prison
management.[2] He repeated practically the same opinions in his
message of the following year.[3] The report of the joint committee of the legislature on the management of the state prison
in 1868–1869 was essentially little more than a vigorous attack
upon the detrimental effect of politics upon efficient prison administration.[4] That this agitation for the elimination of politics
from prison administration had some immediate effect is to be
seen in the fact that the newly created supervisor of prison industries was to be appointed by a board consisting of the governor, the chancellor, the chief justice, and the attorney general of the state.[5]

b. *Improvement of the Physical Equipment of the State
Prison.*

The architectural phases of the history of New Jersey prisons
during this period centered around the agitation for the provision of a separate wing for women and the building of two
new wings and new workshops for the men.

It was pointed out above how the Pennsylvania system was
practically crowded out of existence in New Jersey by the growth
of the prison population and the failure to provide additional
cell room. When the prison was constructed in 1835–1836 provision had been made for 192 cells, but a part of these were
used for cooking, baking, washing, and storing purposes until

[1] Ibid., 1866, in *Legislative Documents,* 1867, p. 1061.
[2] *Annual Message of the Governor,* 1868, p. 12.
[3] Ibid., 1869, p. 14.
[4] *Legislative Documents,* 1869, pp. 321-7. See Documents, Part II, pp.
508-14.
[5] *Acts of the 93rd Legislature,* 1869, pp. 772-3, 774-8. The supervisor was
put back into the spoils system by the act of April 2, 1885.

after the erection of a separate building for these purposes in 1847. Even after 1847, however, it seems that there were never more than 180 cells uniformly available for occupation. By 1860, at the close of the existence of the theoretical application of the system of solitary confinement, there were 346 prisoners to be confined in these 180 cells. To remedy this situation, the legislature, after many years of petitioning on the part of the prison officials and prison reformers, passed the acts of March 22, 1860, and February 16, 1861, appropriating about $20,000 for the erection of a new wing now known as "wing number 3," with a capacity of 132 cells and located midway between the two radiating wings erected in 1835–6. The new congregate workshops were also erected out of this appropriation.[1]

In his annual report for 1865, the moral instructor of the prison pointed out the bad influence upon prison discipline which was produced by the contiguity of male and female prisoners and emphasized the need of a separate wing for women. His suggestions were taken up by the other prison officials and the law of April 16, 1868 provided an appropriation of $6,000 for building a separate wing for women.[2] Apparently, however, little was done on the new wing for women until the further appropriation of $9,700 for this purpose in April, 1869.[3]

The growth of the criminal population so crowded the prison that the capacity of "wing number 3" was soon outgrown and provision had to be made for still further extending the cell facilities for men. In their report of 1866 the inspectors pointed out that the prison was then so crowded that two and three prisoners had to be placed in cells which were originally intended for but one.[4] The prison physician in his report for the same

---

[1] *Acts of the 84th Legislature,* 1860, pp. 600–601; *Acts of the 85th Legislature,* 1861, p. 29. See the drawing opposite page 128.

[2] *Acts of the 92nd Legislature,* 1868, p. 1043.

[3] *Annual Report of the State Prison,* 1865, in *Legislative Documents,* 1866, p. 804. *Acts of the 93d Legislature,* 1869, p. 1055.

[4] *Annual Report of the State Prison,* 1866, in *Legislative Documents,* 1867, p. 1059.

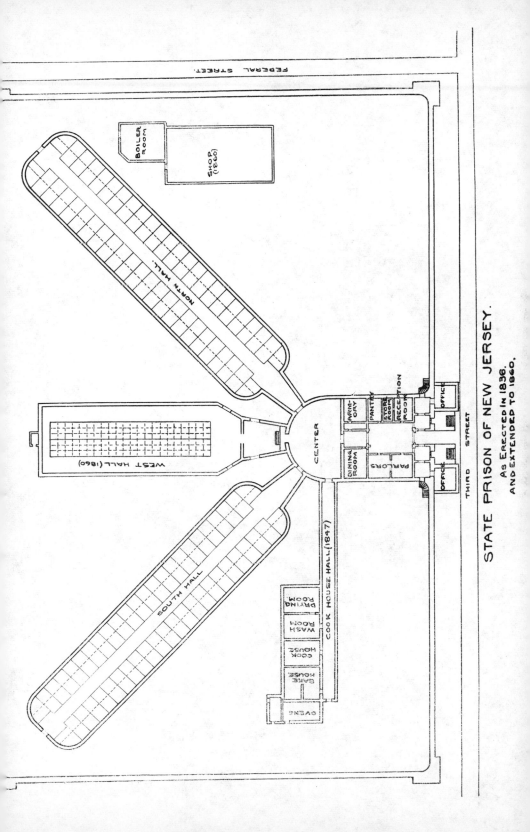

STATE PRISON OF NEW JERSEY.

As Erected in 1836.
And Extended to 1860.

year corroborated the statements of the inspectors.[1] This situation grew more and more serious until by 1869 there were 468 prisoners to be confined in 176 cells constructed in 1835–6, in addition to 132 confined in the new wing built in 1860–61.[2] This intolerable condition led to the appropriation of $50,000 in 1869, of $75,000 in 1871, and of $28,700 in 1872, to build a new wing for men and to extend the system of workshops, which were as inadequate to the needs of the prison population as the available cell room.[3]

It was also during this period that the agitation of a half century began for a chapel. Owing to the system of solitary confinement, the prison constructed in 1833 made no provision for congregate religious instruction. When the system of solitary confinement was abandoned at the beginning of the "sixties," the prison was not equipped with anything which would serve as a chapel.[4] The moral instructor in his report for 1865 stressed the urgent need for a chapel if any effective management of religious services was to be hoped for in the state prison. His request, like that of his successors for nearly a half century to follow, met with no response at the hands of the legislature, and it was not until near the beginning of the present century that the state prison of New Jersey was provided with even the miserably inadequate room which has since served as a chapel.[5]

c. *General Trends and Movements in Prison Reform.*

There were several important movements for prison reform during this period, among the most important of which was the provision of a state reform school for juvenile offenders. It

[1] Ibid., 1065.
[2] *Report of the Commission on Prison Discipline,* 1869, in *Legislative Documents,* 1869, pp. 333–4.
[3] *Acts of the 93d Legislature,* 1869, pp. 1446–7; *Acts of the 95th Legislature,* 1871, pp. 76–7; *Acts of the 96th Legislature,* 1872, pp. 75–6.
[4] See Documents, Part II, pp. 522–3, 610.
[5] The act of April 2, 1869, provided for the building of a chapel, but this provision was never carried into execution.

has already been pointed out how the earlier movement in this direction was stifled by political influences in the early "fifties." The urgent necessity for such an institution enlisted the vigorous support of Governor Joel Parker, to whom more than to anyone else, the state reform school for boys at Jamesburg owes its origin. In his annual message of January 12, 1864, he pointed out in the following words his conception of the need for a juvenile reformatory:

"Some place other than the State Prison should be provided for the incarceration of youth. In many instances the disgrace of confinement in the Penitentiary, and the evil communications which unavoidably attend the least contact with hardened offenders, prevent reformation. The object of imprisonment is to reform as well as to punish, and the State owes it to the youthful criminal to place him in circumstances that will tend to soften his pliant nature, rather than render him more obdurate." [1]

The Governor's championing of the necessity for a reform school was effective and an act was passed on April 6, 1865, "to Establish and Organize the State Reform School for Juvenile Offenders." [2]

Another step towards prison reform was the law of March 30, 1865, which provided a moral instructor for the state prison at a salary of $1,000 per year, who was to give his entire time to the spiritual welfare of the prisoners, the moral instructor provided by the act of February 9, 1848, having devoted only a part of his attention to the prisoners. [3]

A still more significant movement toward better discipline in the state prison was that which originated the system of a commutation of sentence for good behavior. This was very strongly recommended by the board of inspectors in their report for 1866. [4] These suggestions of the inspectors, which were seconded by the other prison officials and public authorities, resulted in the act of April 14, 1868, which established for the first

[1] *Annual Message of the Governor*, 1864, pp. 11–12.
[2] *Acts of the 89th Legislature*, 1865, pp. 886–893.
[3] Ibid., p. 702.
[4] *Annual Report of the State Prison*, 1866, in *Legislative Documents*, 1867, p. 1057.

time the commutation system in the state of New Jersey. It was provided that for each month of faithful labor a convict was to have his sentence reduced by two days; for each month of good deportment a further reduction of two days was to be allowed, and for every month of apparent effort at self improvement a reward of one day's reduction of sentence was provided, thus making it possible to earn five days' reduction of sentence by each month of perfect conduct.[1] This act was reproduced with no important change in the law of April 2, 1869.[2]

Another noteworthy phase of the growth of enlightenment in regard to penal institutions in this period was the frequent insistence by public authorities, prison officials, and private philanthropists that reformation was the chief purpose of imprisonment. It was in great part the recognition of the failure of the state prison as an institution for reforming offenders that produced the agitation leading to the establishment of the reform schools for boys and girls in New Jersey in 1865 and 1871, and to the vigorous but unsuccessful agitation in the decade of the "seventies" for an intermediate prison, or, in other words, for a reformatory for adult delinquents. The reformatory purpose of imprisonment was clearly expressed by the board of inspectors of the state prison in their annual report of 1866:

"When our laws cease mainly to regard the criminal as the enemy of society, to be restrained; and begin to recognize in him one of 'like passions' with us, who has fallen to a lower moral level through adverse surroundings, and whom we may lift up, then we will begin to fulfill in this respect that higher law which makes every man 'his brother's keeper.'"[3]

While this expression of opinion by the inspectors, which was only one of many such declarations during this period, perhaps

[1] *Acts of the 92nd Legislature,* 1868, pp. 981–982.
[2] *Acts of the 93rd Legislature,* 1869, pp. 1476–7.
[3] *Annual Report of the State Prison,* 1866, in *Legislative Documents,* 1867, p. 1061. Cf. also annual Message of Governor Parker, 1864, pp. 11–12; Moral Instructor's report, 1867, *Legislative Documents,* 1868, pp. 843–7; *Annual Message of Governor Ward,* 1868, *Legislative Documents,* 1868, p. 13; *Report of Commission on Prison Discipline,* 1869, pp. 13ff.

failed to comprehend the influence of heredity in criminal causation, their attitude was so far in advance of the penal codes and institutions of the time that it merits notice.

d. *The Report of the Commission on Prison Discipline in 1869.*

The general failure of the Auburn system in New Jersey during the period of the Civil War, along with the growing impetus of the movement for prison reform, culminated in the appointment by the Legislature in 1868 of a *Commission* to examine the various types of prison administration and management in the United States and to report on desirable improvements in the prison system of New Jersey. The report of this commission, which was submitted on January 22, 1869, is unquestionably one of the most important and enlightened documents that has yet appeared in the history of the penal institutions of the state of New Jersey.[1] The superior nature of this report was to a large degree due to the intelligent individuals who served as members of this commission. They were Daniel Haines, George F. Fort, and Samuel Allinson,[2] the first two of them ex-Governors, and all prominent citizens of New Jersey and leaders of their generation in prison reform in that state.[3]

The commission reported that they had carefully examined the penal institutions of Pennsylvania, Massachusetts, Connecticut, and New York.

They introduced their practical discussion of conditions in New Jersey by the significant remark that it was not difficult to make suggestions as to possible improvements in New Jersey's penal system, as almost any change would be an improvement.[4]

They pointed out very clearly that the downfall of the Pennsylvania system in New Jersey had been in large part due

[1] See Documents, Part II, pp. 514–37.

[2] Allinson is unquestionably the leading figure in the history of prison reform in New Jersey. His multifarious activities in this field may be ascertained by consulting the index to this volume.

[3] A certain touch of literary interest is given to this report by the fact that Richard Watson Gilder, as a member of the staff of the *Newark Advertiser,* aided Mr. Allinson in getting the act passed which created this Commission of 1869, and through his paper gave its work wide publicity. See *Letters of Richard Watson Gilder,* pp. 41–42.

[4] Report cited, p. 4.

to the failure to give it a just and proper trial. The failure to make additions to the prison in order to keep pace with the growth of the prison population caused the practical abandonment of the essential features of the Pennsylvania system long before it was abandoned in law or theory. The remainder of their criticisms was chiefly devoted to a convincing demonstration of the fact that administrative incompetence and legislative apathy were paving the way for as complete a failure of the newly adopted Auburn system.[1]

They pointed out, in the first place, the disturbing of prison discipline which came as a result of the archaic system of confining male and female prisoners in contiguity in adjoining cells, thus inviting the most corrupting conversation. They also called attention to a case of child-bearing by a woman inmate who had been confined in the institution for years. The commission failed however to point out that, from the very system of separate confinement of male and female prisoners, illegitimacy in the prison was more likely to have been due to the erring conduct of the prison officials or the official visitors than to the sins of the male convicts. This evil, the commission explained, would be done away with when the new women's wing, then in process of construction, was finished.[2]

There was found to be little or no attention paid to reformation in the prison. Even the system of commutation, which had been legally provided by the law of the previous year, had not been applied. The commission urged that steps be taken to see that this valuable instrument in effecting reformation was immediately put into operation.[3]

The most cruel and barbarous punishments were discovered in the state prison. Prisoners were strapped to the floor of their cells for three weeks at a time without being released for any purpose. That relic of the Spanish inquisition, suspension by the hands, was frequently employed. The commission expressed the opinion that many of the deaths in the state prison, which were attributed to other causes, had in reality resulted from the cruel punishments inflicted. They made it plain, however, as the Committee of 1830 had in their report, that, in their opinion,

[1] Ibid., pp. 4ff.   [2] Ibid., pp. 5–6.   [3] Ibid., pp. 6, 11ff.

it was the general system rather than individual depravity, either on the part of the officials or the convicts, which rendered necessary these severe punishments. The serious overcrowding of the prison, there being 468 prisoners to 176 cells even after the 132 new cells of "wing number 3" had been filled, made adequate discipline almost impossible with the available force of guards. Again, and fully as important, the pernicious influence of politics in the selection and tenure of the prison officials, and the short terms of the keepers and inspectors, made impossible any approach to a formulation and execution of a consistent policy of prison administration.[1] The commission thus expressed themselves regarding the detrimental influence of carrying over the "spoils" system into prison administration:

"Such being the present system of the Prison, the evils of it are quite obvious.

And the first to be noticed is the short term of office of the Keeper and Inspectors. Their annual appointment almost necessarily implies an annual change. In practice, it is a change with every change of policical party power in the State. From long usage, these offices have been regarded as the spoils of victory. They are consequently bestowed as the rewards of party. Proper qualifications may be sought for, but they are frequently subordinated to the capacity in party tactics and success in controlling votes. Political influences secure the appointment of the Keeper, and on the principle of "like master like man", his deputies are often selected for like qualifications. Hence, it is not surprising that pot house heroes should sometimes be found in the capacity of Assistant Keepers; and that where the strictest rules of sobriety ought to prevail, the excited manner and fetid breath of the officer should betray the use of the bottle.

The annual appointment, should it fall upon the best of men, diminishes if not destroys, by the shortness of the term, the hope of success."[2]

The economic conditions of the state prison were stated to be as unsatisfactory as its disciplinary aspects. The prison was proving an annual loss to the state of about $100,000. The contract system had not proved much of a success since its application on a large scale after 1860. Here again the insidious effect of politics upon the administration of the prison showed itself in preventing sound administration or broad policy in the economic administration of the prison.[3]

[1] Ibid., pp. 5, 7f., 9f.   [2] Ibid., p. 9.   [3] Ibid., pp. 9f.

The commission made a number of most important recommendations. As was pointed out above, it urged the immediate application of the system of rewards for good conduct which had been provided by the law of 1868. It further pointed out the very great need for an agent to look after discharged prisoners and secure for them honest employment, so that they would not be compelled by economic necessity to drift back into a life of crime. The commission insisted upon the wisdom of erecting an "intermediate prison," namely, a reformatory for adult delinquents. It also made clear the necessity for establishing a reform school for girls such as had recently been opened for boys at Jamesburg. Again, it was recommended that the county jails be so remodelled in architecture and administration that they would be used only as places of detention for those charged with crime, and would be fit to receive persons who might be innocent of all crime.[1]

In the appendix to their report the commission presented a summary of the "Irish" system of prison administration and discipline, which they held might be worthy of the consideration of New Jersey, and they drew up a proposed system of grading and meriting for adoption in the state prison. This system was designed to apply a rational mode of earning privileges, of lessening terms of imprisonment, and of achieving ultimate freedom by good behavior on the part of the convicts.[2]

The commission thus summed up its chief recommendations:

"To recapitulate: the system of prison discipline recommended is the *State Prison* under a proper and efficient government for the punishment of those convicted of the higher crimes. The *House of Correction* as an intermediate prison for those found guilty of offences of lesser turpitude; the *Boys' State Reform School;* a *State Reformatory for Girls;* and the *County and Municipal Jails* as places of detention."[3]

The advanced nature of this report becomes apparent when one reflects that it took New Jersey nearly half a century even partially to realize the reforms recommended. It would be hazardous to hold that "the proper and efficient government" of the

[1] Ibid., pp. 11 ff.
[2] Ibid., pp. 47–58. See Documents, Part II, pp. 535-7.
[3] Ibid., p. 24. This important report is preserved in the *Legislative Documents,* 1869, pp. 331ff.

state prison has yet been attained. And certainly the jails have not been transformed into places of detention only. Attention may now be directed to a brief consideration of the practical results which grew out of the recommendations made by this memorable commission.

II. New Jersey and the Auburn System from the Report of the Commission, 1869, to the Abolition of Contract Labor in 1884.

1. General Tendencies of the Period.

It is not easy to find, in the history of the state prison between 1869 and 1885, anything that can be recognized as a general tendency. The period was not one of marked development, but of experimentation, usually futile, in attempts to adjust the industrial situation to the hampering laws and external conditions of the time. It was also a period of futile agitation and criticism directed against the management of the prison. The only substantial achievement of the period under consideration was the legislative authorization, in 1871, of the long-deferred project for the establishment of a state industrial school for girls.

Several of the recommendations of the Prison Discipline Commission of 1869—especially those relating to the industrial reorganization of the state prison, the revival and strengthening of the law granting commutation for good behavior and the provision of additional room to relieve the overcrowded condition of the prison—were promptly carried into effect by the Legislature, but the most important recommendation of the Commission urging the establishment of a reformatory for adult first offenders under thirty years of age, was disregarded, notwithstanding persistent agitation therefor by the prison officials, public authorities and philanthropic citizens, culminating in the report of the Commissioners on "the prison system of New Jersey and on an intermediate prison", in 1878.

Aside from the above mentioned agitation for a reformatory and the brief description of the tendencies in prison industry, the chief features in the general development in the state prison between 1869 and 1885 were the investigation of the charges of cruel punishment in 1878, and the agitation against convict labor between 1879 and 1884.

As the investigation of alleged cruelties will be taken up in detail in the consideration of the development of prison reform in this period, it will suffice here simply to remark in passing that a very distressing situation was revealed, which showed that the recommendations of the Commission of 1869, as regards modification of punishment, had been given little consideration.[1]

The period from 1875 to 1885 was one characterized by widespread labor agitation throughout the country. The Knights of Labor, founded in 1869, became very powerful by the latter part of the following decade, and for a time exerted a remarkable influence on American industry and politics.[2]

This growth of agitation on the part of the labor element had an important effect upon the industrial development of the New Jersey state prison, as it ultimately led to the abolition of the "lease" form of contract labor in the prison.

2. LEGAL CHANGES AND DEVELOPMENTS.

The penal code, which had been previously systematized in the act of April 16, 1846, and supplemented by various successive acts, was worked over into a systematic form in the act of March 27, 1874.[3] However, the only significant feature of this revision was the insignificance of the changes therein, as compared with the code of thirty years earlier. The same background of primitive jurisprudence characterized it as had marked the earlier codes of 1796, 1829, and 1846. Many of the laws prescribing penalties for crimes had not even been changed in their wording since first enacted in 1796. The development of

[1] *Legislative Documents,* 1878, Documents 35 and 36. See below pp. 150f.
[2] See Ely, *The Labor Movement in America,* pp. 75–91. Hollander and Barnett, *Studies in America Trade Unionism,* pp. 353–380.
[3] *Revision of the Statutes of New Jersey,* 1877, pp. 224ff.

a more complicated series of social and economic relations than had existed in 1796, naturally necessitated the extension of the list of criminal acts, but there was practically no change in the theory or practice of prescribing punishment. For the acts which had been branded as criminal in 1796 almost identical penalties were prescribed in 1874, with the exception that, as in 1846, the death penalty for a second conviction of any major crime, which had been prescribed in 1796 and 1829, was commuted to a sentence of imprisonment for not to exceed double the period of imprisonment exacted for the first offence.[1] The law against "false prophets" was still retained,[2] as well as the equally archaic and irrational method of arbitrarily prescribing punishment without any accurate appraisal of the social damage inflicted by the crime, or without any regard to the individual offender. For instance, it was decreed that to steal money or property to the value of $19.99 would entail a maximum penalty of a fine of $100 and imprisonment for three months in a jail or penitentiary, while to take $20.01 would involve a maximum penalty of a fine of $500 and imprisonment for ten years in the state prison.[3] However, these primitive and irrational juristic conceptions were universal at the time and still persist to a large degree.

The revision of the constitution of New Jersey in 1875 provided for a change in the mode of appointment and in the tenure of the principal keeper of the state prison, as previously regulated by the constitution adopted in 1844. Instead of being appointed for one year by the joint meeting of the senate and assembly, it was provided that "the keeper of the state prison shall be nominated by the governor and appointed by him with the advice and consent of the senate." [4] He was to hold office on good behavior for five years. The appointment of the inspectors was no longer provided for by the constitution, but was fixed by the act

[1] Ibid., p. 262.
[2] Ibid., p. 238.
[3] Ibid., p. 250.
[4] *Revised Constitution*, 1875, Art. VII, Sec. ii, par. 4.

for the government and regulation of the state prison of April 21, 1876.[1] The lengthening of the term of the keeper was a distinct improvement, the ridiculously short tenure of one year having always been a serious obstacle to the formation and execution of a consistent and rational policy of prison administration.[2]

The legal basis of the administration of the state prison, which had been regulated up to this time by the act of April 16, 1846, with subsequent amendments, including the acts of March 26, and April 2, 1869, was reconstructed by the act of April 21, 1876.[3] This act, with minor subsequent amendments, formed the legal foundation of prison administration in New Jersey until the sweeping act of April 20, 1914.

The act of 1876 followed the precedent of the law of March 26, 1869, in providing for a supervisor of the state prison, appointed for three years by a majority of a board consisting of the governor, the chancellor, the chief justice and the attorney-general of the state. The supervisor was designed to be the general industrial manager and financial agent of the prison, except that the keeper was to regulate all activities connected with the domestic administration of the prison.[4] A board of inspectors, as hitherto, was provided, which consisted of the comptroller of the state, the state treasurer, and three others to be appointed for a term of three years by a joint session of the legislature. This board was to exercise control over the determination of the general policy of the prison, over the administration, and over the repairs made, and was to report to the governor the success or failure of the management at any given time.[5] The

[1] *Revision of the Statutes of New Jersey*, 1877, pp. 1111ff.

[2] *Report of Commission on Prison Discipline*, 1869, pp. 9–10. See Documents, Part II, pp. 521–2.

[3] *Revision of the Statutes of New Jersey*, 1877, pp. 1111ff.

[4] Ibid., pp. 1111–1115. The supervisor was put back into the spoils system by the act of April 2, 1885, which provided for his appointment for five years by the joint session of the legislature, *Acts of the 109th Legislature*, 1885, pp. 198–200.

[5] *Revision of the Statutes of New Jersey*, 1877, pp. 1111–1114.

principal keeper, appointed, as provided in the constitution of 1875, by the governor for a term of five years, was to be the chief executive and disciplinary officer of the prison.[1] It was enacted that the punishment in the prison was not to exceed confinement in a cell on bread and water for six days unless the inspectors ordered a more severe punishment in an individual case. Corporal punishment was forbidden.[2] The good behavior clause for reducing the sentence, as provided for in the acts of April 14, 1868, and April 2, 1869, was retained in the law of 1876, it being provided that if a convict were recommitted to the prison he was to serve out on his new sentence the time which had been remitted to him for good behavior during his previous term.[3]

The remaining legal changes of importance during this period related to the economic administration of the prison. The first of these was the act of March 25, 1881, which grew out of the agitation of organized labor against convict labor, and out of the suggestion of the Commission of 1879 that prison labor be as much diversified as was practicable. This act decreed that not more than one hundred convicts were to be employed in any one industry under the contract system.[4]

The next act touching the prison industrial organization was the act of February 21, 1884, which marked a definite victory for the labor group. It definitely provided that thereafter it should be unlawful to contract for the labor of any inmate of the state prison, a reformatory, a penitentiary, or a county jail.[5] This was followed by the act of April 18, 1884, which decreed that, as far as possible, the inmates of the prison, penitentiaries, reformatories and county jails should be employed on work for use in state institutions. Those who could not be so employed were to be put at work on the "piece-price" system or the "public account" system.[6]

[1] Ibid., pp. 1115–16.
[2] Ibid., p. 1118. But see the evidence in the Mott case as to the enforcement of this law. Document No. 36 in *Legislative Documents* for 1878.
[3] Ibid., p. 1119.
[4] *Acts of the 105th Legislature*, 1881, pp. 230–231.
[5] *Acts of the 108th Legislature*, 1884, pp. 21–22.
[6] Ibid., pp. 230–232.

The vicious aspect of this legislation was not the apparent abolition of the contract system. Such a step would have been a wise departure if the contract system had been superseded by an efficient application of the state use system. However, as will be explained in greater detail below, in treating the economic development of the prison, this law did not in any sense abolish contract labor. It simply replaced it by a subterfuge known as the "piece-price" system, which actually continued the contract system with all its bad features, and upon such a basis that both the state and free labor were the sole losers and the contractors the only ones who were benefited thereby.[1]

3. THE INDUSTRIAL PHASES OF THE ADMINISTRATION OF THE STATE PRISON.

The industrial developments at the state prison between 1869 and 1885 began with the appropriation of $50,000 in 1869, followed in 1871–2 by appropriations of $118,000 for an extension of the prison workshops and the building of a new wing.[2] This action grew out of the report of the Commission on Prison Discipline of 1869 which had so definitely called the attention of the legislature to the serious economic loss sustained by the state on account of the inefficient industrial administration of the state prison.[3]

Another very important innovation, already mentioned, which grew out of the recommendation of the above-mentioned commission that the state take steps to put the management of the prison on a sounder financial basis was the creation, on March 26, 1869, of a supervisor of prison industries and finances. The supervisor, together with the comptroller, the state treasurer and the board of inspectors, was to constitute a board of supervisors of

---

[1] Cf. *Annual Report of State Prison,* 1884, passim; 1885, pp. 8, 25; 1886, p. 12; 1887, p. 9; 1888, pp. 9–10.

[2] See above p. 129 and note. The total expenditures in improving and extending the physical equipment of the prison from 1869 to 1874 were $280,000. *Annual Report of the State Prison,* 1874, p. 9.

[3] Report cited, pp. 9f.

the industries of the state prison, which was to have general control over the industries and finances of the prison, immediately supervised and administered by the supervisor alone.[1]

The new workshops erected out of the appropriations of 1869, 1871 and 1872 were highly praised, and, together with the more effective industrial administration of the prison, proved a great aid in restoring the institution to a reasonably satisfactory financial situation. Governor Randolph pointed out in his annual message for 1871 that the annual deficit in conducting the state prison, exclusive of official salaries, had been reduced from over $50,000 to less than $3,500.[2] The joint committee of the legislature on the accounts of the state prison also expressed itself in an enthusiastic manner over the contribution of the new workshop to the prosperity of the state prison.[3]

By 1872 the increased industrial capacity and efficiency of the prison resulted in a gain of about $28,500 over the expenses of maintenance, exclusive of the salaries of the officials. As the salary item amounted to $47,780, the net loss sustained by the prison was less than $20,000, which was gratifying, as it was only about one-fifth what it had been in the years following the close of the Civil War.[4] During the years 1873-4 the prison apparently attained the highest degree of industrial prosperity which it had reached since 1837 and 1848, if not in its whole history. In 1874 it practically earned all of its expenses including the salaries of the officers, the net gain over maintenance

[1] *Acts of the 93rd Legislature*, 1869, pp. 772-8.

[2] *Annual Message of the Governor*, 1871, p. 13. The annual loss involved in the industrial income of the state prison as compared with the expenses of maintenance, and not including salaries, from 1865 to 1870, was as follows: 1865, $13,476; 1866, $50,983; 1867, $56,105; 1868, $55,977; 1869, $61,074; 1870, $3,410. In 1871 there was a net gain over maintenance exclusive of salaries of $40,609; in 1872 the gain was $28,478; and in 1874 the gain was $45,234.

[3] *Annual Report of the State Prison*, 1870, in *Legislative Documents*, 1871, p. 448.

[4] *Annual Report of the State Prison*, 1872, pp. 14-15. Cf. *Legislative Documents*, 1869, p. 337.

being $45,234 and the salaries $49,437.[1] This financial success has not even been approximated since. The supervisor reported the renewal of large contracts on an even greater scale, and stated that nearly $11,000 was being expended in erecting an addition to the workshops.[2] Everything seemed to point toward the dawn of an era of unequalled prosperity for the state prison. Shoe-making under the lease system was the chief industry of the prison at this time. In 1873 Bigelow and Howe were leasing the labor of 400 men for shoe-making.[3]

The promising outlook for better financial conditions at the state prison was soon destroyed by circumstances and forces which arose out of the general economic and social conditions of the country, namely, the "panic" of 1873–5 and the agitation of the new labor organizations, particularly the Knights of Labor, against convict labor.

The first manifestations of the panic must have had little effect upon the industries of the prison, as the report of the prosperity of the institution in 1873–4 proves. Its effect was apparent, however, by 1875, for in that year there was a loss of $23,650 in addition to the salaries of officials amounting to $47,230.[4] In the year 1876 the total loss sustained by the prison including the official salaries was still greater, totalling $92,045.[5] During 1877 the prison recovered to some degree from the shock of the panic, the total loss for this year being $57,535 or about $34,-500 less than in the previous year.[6] From this time until 1884, when the industries were again partially disorganized by the termination of the old contract system, the annual loss varied from about $50,000 to $70,000. After 1884 an even greater financial and industrial depression was the rule, as may be seen,

---

[1] *Annual Report of State Prison,* 1873, pp. 23, 26. Ibid., 1874, pp. 7, 19–23. *Annual Message of the Governor,* 1875, p. 9.
[2] *Annual Report of the State Prison,* 1874, p. 8.
[3] Ibid., 1873, pp. 16, 20.
[4] Ibid., 1875, pp. 9, 23.
[5] Ibid., 1876, p. 16.
[6] Ibid., 1877, p. 3.

by examining the annual reports giving the financial loss sustained by the prison.[1]

The industries of the prison had scarcely begun to recover from the effect of the panic of 1873–5 when they were faced by an even more serious difficulty, namely, the warfare against contract convict labor which was conducted by the newly formed labor organizations, chiefly the Knights of Labor. This organization was founded by Uriah S. Stephens of Philadelphia in 1869, and was led by him and Terence V. Powderly of Scranton, Pennsylvania. It had by 1880 become a very powerful organization, but fell into discredit by the domination of the more violent element in the organization in the St. Louis and Chicago Strikes of 1886. The Knights of Labor were superseded shortly after this time by the American Federation of Labor, an organization with much broader aims which adopted a more tolerant and conciliatory attitude towards the problem of the adjustment of the conflict between capital and labor. It was inevitable that the labor organizations would detect the menace of contract prison labor to free labor, though there is little doubt that they overestimated the danger when looked at from a general standpoint.[2]

The first definite evidence that labor agitation against contract convict labor was beginning to affect the industry of the prison is to be found in the report of the supervisor of the state prison for 1877, in which that official devoted considerable space to a refutation of the claim of the labor organizations that convict labor was a serious menace to free labor.[3]

More conclusive evidence of the effect of the agitation against the contracting of convict labor was revealed by the necessity

[1] The total loss, including salaries, for some of these years was: 1878, $61,730; 1879, $68,452; 1880, $47,360; 1881, $68,888; 1882, $61,163; 1883, $60,766; 1884, $69,934; 1885, $87,837; 1895, $113,326; 1906, $117,021; 1916, $233,694.

[2] Ely, *The Labor Movement in America*, pp. 75–91, 151, 185–6; Hollander and Barnett, *Studies in American Trade Unionism*, pp. 353–380.

[3] *Annual Report of the State Prison*, 1877, pp. 6–8.

which was felt by the Legislature of appointing a Commission on Prison Labor in 1879 to report on the situation and make recommendations. That the agitation was somewhat general may be seen by the fact that the New Jersey commission met with similar commissions from Massachusetts and Connecticut.[1]

The essential conclusions of this commission may be summarized as follows: Prison labor must be hard, continuous, healthy, reformatory, mechanical and productive. Convict labor cannot seriously compete with free labor unless the employment of prisoners is concentrated upon a few trades, and this should be avoided. The state use system cannot be successfully employed as long as politics dominate prison administration and prevent the ordinary efficiency of the business world from penetrating into the prison; until politics can be ousted from prison management the contract system is undoubtedly the best.[2]

The commission recommended a diversification of prison industries and the adoption of a scheme for securing the division of labor among prisons of different states. To meet the local difficulties it urged that the state arsenal, namely, the original state prison, be obtained and reconverted into a prison to relieve the crowded condition of the state prison, and further suggested that a reformatory be erected to fit petty offenders and young prisoners to return to society, a task for which the state prison was utterly unadapted.[3]

The effect of the commission's advice may be seen in the law of March 25, 1881, described above, which forbade contracting for the labor of more than one hundred prisoners in any one industry.[4]

That this law seriously disturbed the industry of the prison appears from the complaint of the prison officials and their vigorous request for more shops and better equipment if the

[1] See Documents, Part II, pp. 497–503.
[2] Report cited, pp. 4–5, 44–7. Document No. 37 in *Legislative Documents* for 1880.
[3] Ibid., p. 49.
[4] *Acts of the 105th Legislature, 1881*, pp. 230–231.

legislature expected to have the law carried out, and intended the prison to approach a self-sustaining condition.[1]

The report of the Commission of 1879 and the law of 1881 were but the prelude to more vigorous legislative action and more sweeping legal changes. The law of 1881 did not placate the labor organizations, and in 1883 a Special Committee from the assembly was appointed to investigate the general problem of contract labor for prisoners. After carrying on an extensive correspondence and hearing a large amount of testimony the committee held a final meeting on December 11, 1883, and recommended the abolition of the leasing of convict labor and the introduction of the "piece-price" system.[2] In 1884 there were passed, in part as a result of the recommendation of the above committee, the laws forbidding the further employment of the contract system and prescribing the adoption of the *state use, piece-price,* and *public account* systems.[3]

The "state use" system meant the transformation of the prison industries so as to make exclusively products to be used in state institutions. The "piece-price" system, whatever the intention of the framers of the law of April, 1884, was but an ingenious subterfuge which allowed the continuance of contract labor under a different name and in a manner distinctly more favorable to the contractors than the old system. The contractors furnished the raw material and then agreed to take the finished product at a certain price per piece provided that it was made according to the specifications imposed by the contractors. The prison officials were theoretically supposed to supervise the industrial operations, but in fact the contractors continued to supply the industrial instructors. The chief difference as to the duties of the prison officials caused by the introduction of the "piece-price" system

[1] *Annual Report of the State Prison,* 1881, pp. 6, 17, 29–30; Ibid., 1882, pp. 3, 6, 10, 26.

[2] *Report of the Special Committee of the General Assembly of 1883 on Contract Prison Labor,* Document No. 39 in *Legislative Documents* for 1884. John H. Murphy, William E. Ross, Peter Forman, Frank L. Sheldon, and Nelson M. Lewis were the members of this Committee.

[3] *Acts of the 108th Legislature,* 1884, pp. 21–22, 230–232. See Documents, Part II, pp. 504–7.

was that whereas under the old system they merely had to preserve discipline, under the "piece-price" system they were compelled to enforce discipline and also to "speed up" the prisoners
in their industrial activities. In the "public account" system, the
prison furnished the raw material, supervised the industry, and
then sold the products to the highest bidders. The "state use"
and "public account" systems, then, if adopted would have definitely put an end to the contract system, while the "piece-price"
system allowed its continuance, in fact, if not in name.[1]

Under the new "piece-price" system the contractors had a
great advantage as compared with the older contract system. In
the old system they had to assume full control of the industrial
operations, and waste or slovenly work meant loss to them and
not to the state. Now they were relieved of all of the responsibility in urging the prisoners to greater activity, and could require
high standards of excellence in manufacture upon the pain of
refusing the products. The state, then, had to assume all the
loss entailed by waste and careless work, while the contractors
were proportionately benefitted. The state was inevitably the
loser by the new system.

Again the change, which was made ostensibly to aid free labor
was, in reality, much more detrimental to free labor than the
old contract system, for the contractor paid less for each unit of
productive labor and thus cheapened still more convict labor. The
cheapness of convict labor and the element of unfair competition
involved therein was, of course, the main cause of labor agitation against it. Further, the new system operated against free
laborers, in so far as they were tax payers, by its creation of a
greater deficit in prison finances, which had to be met by additional taxes. Thus, the only one to be benefitted by the "piece-
price" system was the contractor. These considerations, together
with the fact that no attempt was made to introduce the "state
use" or "public account" systems, which would actually have

[1] Cf. *Annual Report of State Prison,* 1911, pp. 28ff., for a good discussion
by the prison supervisor of the different systems of prison industry in vogue
in New Jersey since 1876. See Documents, Part II, pp. 541–2.

done away with the contract system, inclines one to the strong
suspicion that the apparently insurmountable difficulty in getting
rid of the contract system was the political and financial influence
of the contractors. If so, these laws of 1884 were among the
cleverest in the history of political chicanery, for they not
only effectively silenced labor agitation without benefitting the
laborer, but also entrenched the contractors more firmly and
more favorably than ever.

The prison officials were not slow to detect the lack of logic
and business sense in this law, as far as it was supposed to aid
the state and free labor, and they ruthlessly exposed its glaring
weaknesses and inconsistencies. However, their opposition may
in part have come from the fact that this new system disturbed
the prison routine and threw more burdens upon the official
force.[1]

But whether the law substituting the "piece-price" for the contract system was a piece of indescribable legislative stupidity in
an honest but mistaken effort to aid labor, or a bit of shrewd political chicanery, certain it is that the change was most detrimental
to the industry and finances of the prison. The consideration of
this, however, belongs more properly with a history of prison
industry from 1884 to 1911, when another and equally unsuccessful attempt was made to rid the state of the contract system,
as practiced under the "piece-price" subterfuge.

The industrial distribution of the population of the state prison
during the period when the agitation against contract labor was
the sharpest may be ascertained from the condition in 1882. In
that year the labor of the 370 convicts productively employed was
leased to the following firms at the described rates.[2]

William McKnight,	Making shoes ....100 men @ 60c. per day.
Downs and Finch,	Laundry............... 80 men @ 50c. per day.
" " "	Making shirts .... 80 men @ 50c. per day.
" " "	Making collars .... 20 men @ 50c. per day.
" " "	Making boxes .... 20 men @ 50c. per day.
Wells Whip Co.,	Making whips .... 40 men @ 50c. per day.
John Tobin,	Making rubber goods.. 30 men @ 50c. per day.

[1] See Documents, Part II, pp. 543-7.
[2] *Annual Report of the State Prison,* 1882, p. 6.

The total income from this leased convict labor during the year was $67,546. The supervisor stated that there were 100 more men available for employment if he could be provided with adequate shop room.[1]

Thus, the industrial and financial history of the prison from 1869 to 1884 began and ended with a period of great financial depression, while for a brief space of two years in the first quarter of that period the prison reached the highest point of prosperity that it has attained since the first half of the nineteenth century.

4. PRISON DISCIPLINE AND PRISON REFORM.

a. *Discipline and Punishment.*

The last and, of course, the most important aspect of prison history during this period, was the movements and circumstances connected with the attempt to improve the management, discipline, equipment, and reformatory functions of the state prison. The survey may begin with the discussions and investigations centering about the problem of discipline and punishment.

It would seem that the official investigation of the state prison by the Commission of 1869 had been accompanied by newspaper revelations and considerable public excitement, for in the annual report of the state prison for 1869 the supervisor protested against any movement to take all disciplinary powers from the keeper, and the keeper, David P. Hennion, referred to the situation as follows:

"I am induced to call attention to this matter (the fact that punishments were worse in some other prisons,) because the public mind has recently been excited by reports in a respectable newspaper that the most cruel and inhuman punishments were indulged in, and myself held up to public odium in terms better suited to savage than to civilized life."[2]

[1] Ibid., pp. 6–7. This was provided by the large shop building erected in 1885.
[2] Report cited, in *Legislative Documents,* for 1869, pp. 240–41. The keeper failed to demonstrate, however, that the language of the newspaper was not well suited to the subject under discussion.

Little more was heard about the punishments inflicted in the state prison until the notorious investigation of the charges against Keeper Mott in 1878. While this investigation revealed, as will be seen, a very serious and scandalous situation, it was not without its extenuating circumstances, as far as the prison officials were concerned. To house and control 850 prisoners in 515 poorly ventilated cells without resorting to inhumanities in maintaining discipline would have called for a type of prison administrator not common then or now. The prison officials had called attention to the crowded condition of the prison for years, and could not be held responsible for the existing conditions.

The scandal of 1878 was brought to a crisis by the death of an unruly convict, Jacob Snook, who died, as the prison authorities claimed, of "meningitis" after having been "stretched" on the prison "stretcher" for about a quarter of an hour.[1]

The press took up the matter and the legislature was compelled to appoint a Committee to investigate the charges of cruelty made against the keeper, General Gershom Mott. This committee rendered its report in 1878, but the apologetic and evasive tone of this report convinces one that it did not approach the level of candor and accuracy attained by the investigating committees of 1830 and 1869. It reads like an attempt to shield and protect an individual who had long been prominent in military and political circles.[2]

The committee reported that charges of inhuman treatment had been made against General Mott, alleging that he had made use of such illegal and barbarous methods and instruments of punishment as the gag, paddle, douches, and the stretcher. The committee denied that any extensive use had been made of the first three of these. As to the stretcher, this was a device for drawing a convict up to a bar above his head after his

---

[1] Document No. 35 in *Legislative Documents,* 1878, pp. 4–5.

[2] Cf. Document No. 36 in *Legislative Documents,* 1878, passim. See also Wm. E. Sackett, *The Modern Battles of Trenton,* Vol I, pp. 157–8. This work, while one-sided, superficial and highly prejudiced, throws much interesting light on politics and civic administration in New Jersey from 1868 to 1894.

feet had been chained to the floor. As a matter of fact, it was practically identical in mechanical principles and physiological effects to the "rack" used in the Spanish Inquisition. The committee stated that General Mott had found this device in the prison and had used it, thinking that it was an entirely legal procedure. While there was no doubt that Snook died on the stretcher, the committee denied that there was any possibility that the intensity of the physical suffering could have caused his death. They did recommend, however, that the stretcher either be abolished altogether or used only in the presence of the keeper.[1]

The committee further admitted that alcohol had been poured on epileptics and then set on fire to detect "shamming," but they failed to find anything to condemn in this primitive but probably effective method of diagnosis.[2]

The committee summarized their conclusions by stating that they found the prison "well conducted and administered," and contended that the keeper needed more power rather than less in maintaining the discipline of the prison.[3] That the committee could render this decision in the face of the admission that medieval and wholly illegal punishments were being freely practiced is significant.

However, one is not left to the gracious apologies of this committee, as the testimony in the Mott case is preserved in a considerable volume listed as "Document No. 36" in the *Legislative Documents* for 1878. From this one may draw the facts in the case which seem to be substantially the following.[4] General Mott was a strict military disciplinarian and a very competent administrator, but displayed not the slightest evidence of possessing any real understanding of, or sympathy with, the prisoners

---

[1] Report cited, in *Legislative Documents*, 1878, Document No. 35, passim.
[2] Ibid., p. 6.
[3] Ibid., pp. 5–6.
[4] The best statement of the case from Mott's standpoint is to be found in the brief of the evidence in the case prepared by his counsel, Frederick Kingman. The only copy of this document, known to the writer, is to be found in the State Library at Trenton.

entrusted to his care. He had a violent temper and put unhesitating obedience above all other considerations in prison administration, not being at all averse to employing an unpardonable degree of cruelty to accomplish this end.

General Mott was not abashed by the investigation and continued to enlighten the citizens of New Jersey as to proper penal concepts and methods in his annual reports until he retired from office in 1881.[1]

It is characteristic of the usual inconsistencies in prison administration that about this time, some person, probably the moral instructor, placed a placard in one of the cell corridors, for the edification and spiritual guidance of the prisoners, which contained the following exhortation: "See that thou each day conduct thyself as though Jesus were here!"

b. *Commutation of Sentence for Good Behavior.*

The attempt, begun in 1868–9, to induce good discipline by the system of rewards and commutation of sentence for good behavior proved nearly as great a failure as the attempt to prevent barbarities in punishment. The law of 1868 which introduced this enlightened system of commutation for good behavior was not put into operation at first, as the court of pardons refused to honor its provisions.[2] After the criticism of the action of this court by the Commission of 1869, and the reënactment of the law in this same year, however, it seems that for a few years some attempt was made to carry out the provisions of this law. It was stated in the annual reports of the prison for 1869–1872 that the new commutation law was working well.[3] After that one hears less about it until the report of the Commission on the management of the prison system in New Jersey in 1878 stated

[1] See especially Document No. 66 in *Legislative Documents* for 1881, p. 29.

[2] *Annual Report of the State Prison,* 1868, in *Legislative Documents* for 1869, p. 401. *Report of Commission on Prison Discipline, January 22, 1869,* pp. 13–14.

[3] Reports cited, 1869, in *Legislative Documents,* 1870, p. 214; 1870, in *Legislative Documents,* 1871, p. 442; *Annual Message of the Governor,* 1873, p. 22–3.

that the law had never been effectively executed.[1]   The clerical force at the prison, which was either indolent or overworked, automatically advanced to each convict the maximum amount of "good time" which he could earn by perfect conduct, rather than taking the trouble to keep a record of the deportment of each convict.   Therefore, the law had little or no influence in promoting good behavior, as the convict received his good time allowance practically regardless of his demeanor.[2]

Another movement to improve the penal procedure of the state, which was likewise fruitless, during this period was the attempt to secure some adequate provision for the reëmployment of discharged convicts who had given evidence of a serious desire to reform and become law-abiding citizens.   It was pointed out very clearly that the social and industrial ostracism which followed a term in the state prison was one of the chief obstacles to the reclamation of the criminals and one of the chief incentives to recidivism.   In addition to the constant reiteration of this defect in penal procedure by the prison officials in their annual reports, a speedy solution of the problem was urged by Governor Randolph in 1872; by Governor Parker in 1873; and by Governor McClellan in 1881.[3]   However, aside from private aid given by charitable individuals and associations, their admonitions accomplished nothing.

c. *Attempts at Differentiation in the Treatment of Criminals.*

Of the efforts to provide for a greater degree of classification and differentiation in the treatment of delinquents in this period only one was successful, namely, that which culminated in the establishment of the State Industrial School for Girls at Trenton in 1871.[4]

[1] *Report of the Commission on the Prison System of New Jersey and on an Intermediate Prison*, 1878, pp. 8–9.
[2] Ibid.
[3] *Annual Messages of the Governors*, 1872, p. 9; 1873, p. 23; 1881, pp. 12–13.
[4] *Acts of the 95th Legislature*, 1871, pp. 78–83.

The Commission on Prison Discipline of 1869 had, as has already been pointed out, recommended a reform school for delinquent girls like that provided for boys at Jamesburg, and reformatories for delinquent adults of both sexes whose criminal record hardly justified incarceration in the state prison. Agitation was in progress for the provision of all three of these institutions, but only the first one was secured at this time.

The greatest volume of agitation for the reformatory for men came in the years between 1876 and 1879. The need for this institution was reëmphasized by the prison officials in these years, and especially by Governor George B. McClellan, who was an ardent advocate of a better penal system for New Jersey.[1]

This agitation culminated in the appointment of a Commission on the Prison System of New Jersey and on an Intermediate Prison or Reformatory, which submitted its report on February 23, 1878.[2] Besides reporting on the condition of the jails, as furnishing evidence of the need of a reformatory, the commission showed how the state prison was proving a complete failure as a reformatory institution. It especially criticized the severe punishments inflicted, which had been condoned by the legislative committee of the same year, and the failure properly to enforce the law granting commutation for good behavior. It emphasized the importance of reformatories as a part of the system of penal and correctional institutions of any state, and referred enthusiastically to the great success which had been attained by the recently opened reformatory in Elmira in New York State, which was under the able supervision of Z. R. Brockway. The commission was particularly impressed by the semi-indeterminate sentence, employed in commitments to Elmira.[3] This reference to Elmira is significant, as this institution exerted almost as great an influence upon the development of reformatories in the United States as the Auburn Prison had upon the shaping of the penal institutions of the country, and through the recom-

[1] *Annual Message of the Governor,* 1879, p. 23; 1881, p. 12.
[2] See Documents, Part II, pp. 599–611.
[3] Report cited, pp. 10–14.

mendations of the commission of 1890 it became the model for the reformatory at Rahway.

The commission summarized its main conclusions and recommendations as follows: The county jails should be used only as places for detaining those awaiting trial. All persons convicted of serious crimes should be sent to the state prion. In the administration of the state prison the law allowing commutation should be strictly enforced on the basis of a careful record of the conduct of each individual convict. Also there should be some officer attached to the state prison who should be solely occupied with securing employment for discharged prisoners. It was further urged that the physical equipment of the state prison be improved by the addition of a chapel and a lecture room. The commission was most emphatic, however, in its recommendation that a house of correction or state reformatory be erected, to which petty offenders and young "first termers" might be sent with some hope that they might be reformed and returned as safe members of society. Equally significant, was the commission's recommendation that a State Board of Charities be appointed to have a centralized advisory power over the penal and correctional institutions supported by public funds. Such a board, it was argued, would be able to exert a continuous supervision over these institutions and maintain a consistent policy, something which was impossible for the sporadic committees of investigation to accomplish. The commission thus expressed itself with respect to the value of a State Board of Charities:

"Several of our sister commonwealths have derived much benefit from the appointment of a State Board of Charities for the purpose of examining into the conditions and practices of the various penal and charitable institutions of their respective States. They report to the Governor or Legislature annually, making such suggestions as they deem proper, with reference to the more economical or efficient working of these institutions, and the harmonious accomplishment of the beneficent purposes of the State. The appointment of such a Board, consisting of five or six judicious and philanthropic citizens, to serve without compensation, (their necessary expenses, of course, being paid) would, we think, result in much good. Various evils have come to the knowledge of this commission which such a Board might have corrected or prevented."[1]

[1] The Department of Charities and Corrections was not created until 1905.

To aid the legislature the commission drafted a law to provide for a state reformatory along the lines that they deemed most desirable.[1]

The recommendations made by the commission, as usual, came to naught, and New Jersey remained without a state reformatory until 1901.

The need of a separate prison and reformatory for delinquent females was often presented in this period, but the agitation produced no significant results until the report of the joint committee of the legislature on a female prison and reformatory in 1886. Though this committee rendered a report strongly urging the erection of such an institution and the legislature passed a resolution supporting this report, nothing came of the movement and a reformatory for women was not provided until 1913.[2]

d. *Politics and Prison Administration.*

The laudable movement to oust politics from prison management, which had been reflected in the laws of 1869 and 1876 regulating the administration of the state prison, received a serious reverse about the close of the period under consideration. The act of April 2, 1885, put the supervisor, the most important financial officer of the prison, back into politics by giving his appointment to the joint session of the legislature instead of vesting it, as before, in a board made up of the governor, chancellor, chief justice, and attorney general.[3] The influence of politics in partially stifling the investigation of punishments in 1878, and in shaping the prison labor laws of 1884, has already been sufficiently dwelt upon. In general it may be said that the

[1] Report cited, pp. 15–22.
[2] Report cited, Document 39 in *Legislative Documents,* 1887. *Acts of the 110th Legislature,* 1886, p. 419. This report will be analyzed in greater detail in considering the movements for reform in the next period to be studied. See below, pp. 193f., 305.
[3] *Acts of the 109th Legislature,* 1885, pp. 198–200.

outlook as regards the elimination of the insidious influence of politics from the administration of the prison was much less promising in 1885 than it had been twenty-five years earlier when the new prison system was adopted.

e. *Attempts to Improve the Physical Equipment of the State Prison.*

In concluding this survey of the chief characteristics of the special phases of the development of the prison system in New Jersey from 1869 to 1885, attention may be directed to a consideration of the main attempts to improve the physical equipment of the state prison.

It has been pointed out that, at the time of the report of the Commission on Prison Discipline in 1869, the state prison was seriously overcrowded, there being 600 prisoners to 308 cells.[1] Between 1868 and 1872, $168,000 were appropriated to construct a separate block of cells for women, to add a new wing of cells for men, now known as the "east wing," and to erect a more extensive system of workshops.[2] The new wings were finished and occupied in 1872 and their construction was the occasion of much satisfaction to the prison officials.[3]

However, the accommodations afforded by these new wings were not sufficient to meet the requirements of a decade earlier, and by the time they were opened there were in the state prison about 100 more prisoners than could be confined in solitude at night, according to the law of the state. Consequently, it is not strange that only four years later, in January, 1877, Governor Bedle, in his annual message, called attention to the serious overcrowding of the state prison and the urgent necessity for providing another addition to the cell blocks.[4] The principal

---

[1] Report cited, p. 5.
[2] *Acts of the 92nd Legislature*, 1868, p. 1043; *Acts of the 93rd Legislature,* 1869, pp. 1055, 1446–7; *Acts of the 95th Legislature,* 1871, pp. 76–7; *Acts of the 96th Legislature,* 1872, pp. 75–6.
[3] *Annual Report of State Prison,* 1872, p. 23.
[4] *Annual Message of the Governor,* January 6, 1877, p. 11.

keeper, in his report for 1876, gave a definite statement of the situation. There were at that time 829 convicts confined in 515 cells. One hundred and twenty-two cells had to accommodate three prisoners each, and two convicts were confined in each of 58 cells. In addition, the cook house, the bakery, the wash house and the provisions for ventilation and sewerage constructed in 1836 and 1847, were antiquated and inadequate. Moreover, a new graveyard was needed as it had long been impossible to bury a prisoner without disturbing the skeleton of one previously interred.[1] To meet this distressing situation the legislature appropriated $100,000 on March 8, 1877, for a new interior for the old north wing built in 1835–6, and a new burial ground.[2] This alteration was promptly completed but, as the keeper pointed out, it was antiquated before it was finished, for with the added accommodations provided it would give but 698 cells, while there were 873 prisoners confined.[3] Nothing was done at this time to improve the antiquated cooking, baking and washing facilities at the prison which were erected in 1847. A gas plant for lighting the prison with gas light was provided after many years of agitation by the appropriation of $12,000 for this purpose on March 3, 1874.[4]

The inadequate nature of the new additions naturally led to a continuance of the requests for further alteration of the prison. During the next few years, however, these requests and recommendations did not center about the attempt to obtain new buildings, but rather were devoted to the most determined effort yet made to have the original state prison, erected in 1798, reconverted into a part of the prison after having been used as the state arsenal since 1837. This action had been recommended as early as 1859, and at this time even the powerful support of Governor McClellan was enlisted, but the agitation came to naught and the prison labored along with its overcrowded cells until

[1] *Annual Report of State Prison,* 1876, pp. 29–30.
[2] *Acts of the 101st Legislature,* 1877, pp. 82–3.
[3] *Annual Report of the State Prison,* 1877, pp. 32–3.
[4] *Acts of the 98th Legislature,* 1874, pp. 20–21.

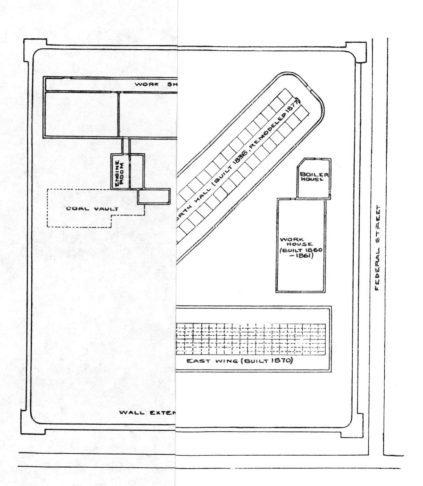

WORK SH...

ENGINE ROOM

COAL VAULT

...RTH HALL (BUILT 1836, REMODELED 1877)

BOILER HOUSE

WORK HOUSE (BUILT 1860 -1861)

EAST WING (BUILT 1870)

WALL EXTEN...

FEDERAL STREET

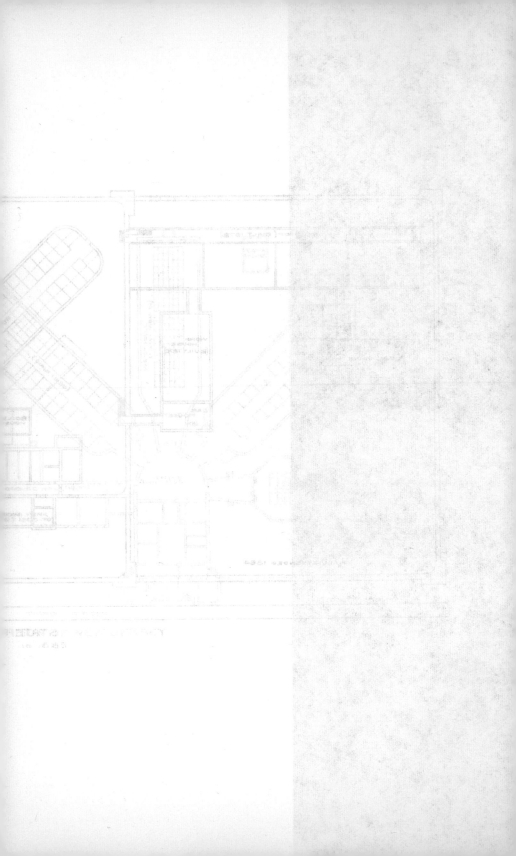

1895, when 1,026 prisoners were confined in 706 cells, a state law prescribing solitary confinement at night, notwithstanding.[1]

The need of an adequate chapel and assembly room, which had been repeatedly requested at intervals since the erection of the state prison in the "thirties," was reiterated annually by the several officers of the state prison and by most of the governors in their annual messages. The act passed on April 2, 1869, appropriating $50,000 for an addition to the prison was designed to provide a chapel, but this provision was not carried out.[2] The recommendations of the public authorities from 1869 to 1885 that a chaped be built was likewise ignored, and it was not until 1897, just sixty years after the erection of the prison, that it was provided with a chapel. The one then supplied was miserably inadequate, as it had a seating capacity of less than 275 while there were nearly 1,200 prisoners confined.[3]

Whatever the value one may assign to religious influences in the reformation of criminals, certain it is that there was little chance for any effective conduct of religious services without a chapel. It was necessary to repeat the service four times, once for each wing, and none of the services were particularly effective, as the prisoners slept or amused themselves in their cells during their progress.[4] In his annual report for 1871 the moral instructor reported that for the moral betterment of the prisoners the Apostolic Creed was repeated every Sunday in each of the four wings of the prison.[5] When one reflects that in the last forty-five years criminal psychiatry has progressed from "free will" and the Apostolic Creed to the Binet-Simon test, and the modern analysis of the neuroses, there seems to be cause for optimism as to the possibility of improving penal procedure.

That the provision for interesting literature in the prison library was rather inadequate during this period may be gathered

[1] *Annual Messages of the Governor,* 1879, pp. 23–4; 1881, p. 11. *Annual Report of the State Prison,* 1895, p. 28.

[2] *Annual Report of the State Prison,* 1871, p. 12. See drawing opposite page 158 for a summary description of the architectural changes during this period.

[3] *Annual Report of the State Prison,* 1897, pp. 27, 49–50.

[4] See Documents, Part II, pp. 522–3, 610.

[5] Ibid., 1871, p. 23.

from the report of the moral instructor in 1875 that "frequent calls are made for books of the highest religious order, such as Baxter's *Call to the Unconverted;* Baxter's *Saints' Everlasting Rest;* Doddridge's *Rise and Progress of Religion in the Soul;* and Guthrie's *Way of Life.*" [1]

5. SUMMARY OF THE PERIOD, *1869–1885.*

The results achieved by New Jersey in its state prison under the Auburn system of congregate work by day and solitary confinement by night, during the first twenty-five years of its existence, may now be summarized. It should be kept in mind, however, that these results have little or no significance in judging of the efficacy of the Auburn system as an abstraction. As was the case with the Pennsylvania system in New Jersey, the trial of the Auburn system in that state was accompanied with so many defects in administration that its success or failure has little bearing in forming an opinion of the virtues of the system when thoroughly and efficiently administered.

There was no attempt during this period to make a sweeping change or a radical departure in organizing a new system of penal procedure. Even the adoption of the Auburn system had been prepared for years before 1859–60 by the violation of the Pennsylvania system of solitary confinement, and many officials in the penal system were scarcely aware that any drastic change in penal methods had been contemplated or accomplished. All advances during this period in the improvement of the state prison and its administration were made by reluctant piece-meal legislation forced by years of agitation and appeal.

As to the physical equipment of the state prison, while many additions were made, they did not keep pace with the growth of the prison population and needs. Therefore, the physical aspects of the state prison in 1885 were relatively little better adapted to the existing situation than was the case in 1860.

The economic aspects of the administration of the state prison were very variable during this period. In 1862–5 and 1872–4

[1] Ibid., 1875, p. 27.

the income from prison industry was gratifying, but the business depression after the Civil War and the blow from the panic of 1873–5, together with the disruption of the industrial system of the prison by the labor laws of 1881 and 1884, served to make the industrial phase of the conduct of the prison as unprofitable and unpromising in 1885 as it had been at the outbreak of the Civil War.

The interference of the spoils system in politics with the effective administration of the state prison was as great in 1885 as it had been a quarter of a century before, and there was even less evidence at the close of the period of any determined effort to curb this serious evil. The laudable tendency towards reform in this regard from 1868–1876, which had resulted in the lengthening of the terms of the prison officers and in the appointment of some of them by partially non-partisan boards, had disappeared by 1885.

In the field of prison reform and the growth of a more rational system of penal procedure, some notable advances were made during this period. Especially important was the increased tendency to provide for a greater degree of classification and differentiation in the treatment of offenders. Up to 1865 there had been no differentiation except that provided by the state prison in 1798 between: (a) those convicted of serious crimes and (b) those awaiting trial or detained as punishment for minor offences. The reform schools opened in this period at Jamesburg and Trenton provided for a differentiated treatment of juvenile delinquents of both sexes in institutions that gave some promise of effecting reformation instead of increasing the mental and moral degradation of the individual offender. While the agitation for similar institutions for the less serious types of adult delinquents accomplished no immediate and practical results at this time, it gave an impetus to a movement which was brought to a successful conclusion many years later.

The function of the prison system in effecting reformation was clearly defined and consistently maintained during this period by several public commissions and by self-constituted pri-

11 P

vate associations for prison reform. It was also pointed out many times that no system of reformation could be regarded as complete which did not take into account the needs of the discharged convicts and an earnest but unsuccessful effort was made to have enacted an appropriate law to this effect.

The most notable improvements in prison management were the appointment of a supervisor of prison industries, the lengthening of the tenure of the prison officials, and the adoption, if not the enforcement, of a crude system of rewards and credits designed to earn a reduction of sentence through good behavior.

On the other hand, the investigation of 1878 revealed the fact that the punishments employed to maintain discipline were as barbarous as they had been in 1830. The failure to act on these revelations indicates that this situation was uncorrected at the time and continued so for some years.

All in all, the condition of the state prison and of penal administration in New Jersey in 1885 was such that it must have forced the intelligent students of crime and penology to recognize that, after a quarter of a century of the trial of the third prison system adopted by New Jersey, the state was still far from the attainment of a satisfactory system, and, even worse, that there were few signs that such a condition was likely to be reached in the immediate future. Yet there had been sufficient improvement in certain ways, so that the future might be contemplated without producing sentiments of complete discouragement.

CHAPTER V

THE STATE PRISON OF NEW JERSEY, 1885-1911

*(THE SECOND QUARTER CENTURY OF
THE AUBURN SYSTEM IN NEW JERSEY)*

CHAPTER V

THE STATE PRISON OF NEW JERSEY, 1885–1911.

I. General Tendencies of the Period.

In looking over the period as a whole the chief developments of interest and importance were the attempts to get adjusted to the new system of industrial administration which was forced upon the prison in 1884–5; the tardy provision of additional cell wings to meet the pressing needs of the greatly overcrowded prison; the origin of a crude but promising system of paroling prisoners; the establishment of an advanced type of reformatory for delinquent male adults at Rahway; the provision of a commissioner of charities and corrections, and the establishment of a prison school system.

The new "piece-price" system of industrial administration has never proved a success in New Jersey. It was opposed by the prison officials, in part, no doubt, because in rendering them responsible for the quality and quantity of the output, it imposed upon them many additional burdens and, in part, owing to the fact that they clearly perceived most of the false premises involved in the new system.[1] It was decidedly a poorly devised

[1] *Annual Report of the State Prison,* 1884, pp. 6–7, 18–19; Ibid., 1885, pp. 5–8, 25; Ibid., 1886, p. 12.

system for a state prison. The continual shifting of the industrial population, with the discharge of prisoners, made difficult the attainment of any high degree of excellence or uniformity in the production of prison made goods, and naturally led to the rejection of many articles. Moreover, the burden of the supervision of the prison industries was thrown, in part, upon the officials of the prison without any provision or opportunity for a proportional increase in revenue. The added duties and responsibilities of the administrative force of the prison made necessary the addition of more guards, and from 1885 to the present time the item of salaries has tended to be about equal to the total cost of maintaining the convicts. Even more important in adding to the annual deficit of the prison was the greatly decreased revenue from the labor of the convicts during the first years of the "piece-price" system. In 1885 the total loss sustained by the prison rose to $87,835 and has steadily increased until at present it has reached about a quarter of a million dollars annually, thus having grown much more rapidly than the increase in the prison population.[1] The law of 1910 allowing the employment of prisoners outside the prison has apparently opened the way for the development of new and remunerative modes of utilizing prison labor in a manner which should not only be profitable in a pecuniary sense, but also will be generally beneficial to the health of the prisoners.[2] The law of 1911, at the extreme end of the period under consideration, was designed to do away with the contract system altogether and to introduce the "state use" system, but at the beginning of 1917, after a period of six years, only twenty prisoners were so employed within the prison walls.[3]

The overcrowding of the prison remained the most serious problem in prison management as it had been for the previous half-century. Though half a million dollars were spent in im-

[1] *Annual Report of the State Prison,* 1885, p. 5; Ibid., 1916, p. 27.
[2] *Acts of the 134th Legislature,* 1910, p. 360.
[3] *Acts of the 135th Legislature,* 1911, pp. 769ff. *Annual Report of the State Prison,* 1916, p. 24.

proving the physical equipment of the prison between 1885 and 1911, there were, at the close of this period, about 1,400 prisoners to be confined at night in about 1,250 cells.[1] So overcrowded did the prison become at times that the "phenomenal clemency" of the court of pardons almost equalled that of the "forties," when, as a result of the overcrowded condition of the prison, a life sentence meant imprisonment for from five to eight years. Up to 1905, when a very extensive addition was made to the prison, the court of pardons was forced to liberate from 10 to 15 per cent. of the prisoners annually.[2] The law of April 11, 1910, and its amendments allowing the removal of a part of the inmates to the prison farms and road camps has provided a partial solution of the problem of the lack of cell room in the prison.[3]

The most important general developments in prison reform during this period were the adoption of a parole system in 1889–91, the establishment of the state reformatory for adult male delinquents at Rahway in 1901, the creation of a commissioner of charities and corrections in 1905, and the first legal provision for the formation of a pathetically inadequate prison school system in 1907. The powerful agitation for a reformatory for women at the beginning of the period subsided until its revival in 1903, and not until 1913 was such an institution provided for New Jersey. As these progressive achievements in penal reform will be discussed in detail later, it will not be necessary at this point to do more than indicate their nature.

Not the least among the notable aspects of the history of the prison during this era was the good fortune of New Jersey in having for twenty years the services of two exceptionally able principal keepers, John H. Patterson (1886–1896), and George O.

[1] *Annual Report of the State Prison*, 1911, pp. 12–13.
[2] Ibid., 1887, p. 6; Ibid., 1890, pp. 30–31, 57.
[3] *Acts of the 134th Legislature*, 1910, pp. 360; *Annual Report of the State Prison*, 1916, p. 20.

Osborne (1902–1912). These men, by their intelligent handling of the antiquated equipment provided, were able to secure results which made the system tolerable, whereas it would probably have proved unendurable under the direction of less able and energetic men.

While in the earlier periods most of the improvements had come as a result of influences extraneous to the prison officials, such as the investigations and recommendations of specially appointed committees, the advances made from 1885 to 1911 were to a considerable degree due to the energy of these two men. Mr. Patterson secured the adoption of a workable parole law; established a successful night school; abolished the archaic and humiliating custom of sending out discharged convicts in coarse suits of uniform design, which made the ex-convict as easily detected as though he retained his stripes; and strongly urged the provision of an indeterminate sentence law, the adoption of a system of pecuniary rewards for industrious convicts and of systematic aid to discharged prisoners and the use of the Bertillon system of identifying criminals. Mr. Osborne, whose accession as keeper was described as having "brought in a new and better order of things" in prison administration, succeeded in doing away with those relics of barbarism—the convict's stripes, the short haircut, and the lock-step. The fact that both of these men held office for two full terms indicates that the spoils system is likely to be balked when conspicuous ability is opposed to the principle of rotation in office.

II. Legal Developments in Prison Administration.

The developments in the legal basis of the administration of the prison from 1885 to 1911 were not epoch-making. There was no systematic reorganization of the legal basis of the administration of the state prison until 1914, and most of the acts passed in this period were provisions for additions to the physical equipment of the prison, for minor changes in the method of appointment of the prison officials, or piece-meal and sporadic attempts to realize a more perfect system of prison discipline and administration.

The act of April 30, 1887, was in reality the conclusion of the labor laws of 1884. It provided that all goods made in the state prison should be legibly stamped "Manufactured in the New Jersey State Prison." [1] The law was undoubtedly intended as a "sop" to the labor party, which had been cheated out of all the benefits of the act of February 21, 1884, by the subsequent act of April 18th of the same year.

In 1889, chiefly through the efforts of keeper John H. Patterson, the state of New Jersey adopted a parole law. It provided that all prisoners, except "second termers" and those convicted of murder, manslaughter, sodomy, rape, arson, burglary, or robbery, who had served out half their sentence, might be paroled upon the recommendation of the prison officials. [2] The attorney-general, however, questioned the constitutionality of this act, [3] and another law was passed on April 16, 1891, which decreed that the court of pardons might allow qualified convicts to be at large under such conditions as the court might see fit to impose. The court was given authority to revoke the parole if its terms were violated, and the violator of the parole was compelled to serve out on his sentence the time that had elapsed while he had been out on parole. [4] This law of 1891 was re-enacted in 1898 with no significant changes. [5] This same act, that of June 14, 1898, also conferred the parole power upon a parole board composed of the principal keeper of the state prison and the board of inspectors. [6] From this time onward there has existed in New Jersey the rather curious and awkward situation of having the power of paroling prisoners vested in two separate and distinct boards, each with different personnel and standards and not always working in harmony. The court of pardons,

---

[1] *Acts of the 111th Legislature,* 1887, p. 242.

[2] *Acts of the 113th Legislature,* 1889, pp. 445–446. This act of May 13, 1889, vested the parole power in the principal keeper and the board of inspectors.

[3] *Annual Report of the State Prison,* 1890, pp. 22–3.

[4] *Acts of the 115th Legislature,* 1891, pp. 426–427. The court of pardons, then as now, consisted of the governor, the chancellor, and the lay judges of the court of errors and appeals.

[5] *Acts of the 122nd Legislature,* 1898, p. 927–8.

[6] Ibid., pp. 925–6.

however, has always paroled more convicts than the boards of parole. The parole board created by the act of June 14, 1898, was replaced by the board of inspectors of the state prison, according to the act of April 15, 1914,[1] but the court of pardons retained its parole power, paroling in 1916 334 prisoners as compared with 124 paroled by the board of inspectors.[2] The Act of May 11, 1905, provided for a parole officer to assist the paroled prisoners and to investigate their conduct. It was enacted that the keeper of the state prison should appoint as a parole officer either a member of the board of inspectors or a deputy keeper. The parole officer, thus appointed, was to endeavor to find employment for paroled prisoners; to keep a personal record of the conduct of each paroled prisoner; and to revoke the parole and cause the return to the state prison of those who should violate the terms of their parole.[3] This act of 1905, as amended in 1915, has remained the basis of the legal provision for the very inadequate surveillance of paroled prisoners.[4]

Another important act in 1905 was that of March 25th which created a commissioner of charities and corrections. This new official was given general powers of inspection and investigation over the several state institutions; was authorized to prepare plans for the building and alteration of state institutions; and was given power to call a general advisory board to confer in regard to the condition of the charitable, penal, and reformatory institutions of the state.[5] While this was a most important step toward providing for that highly essential element of the coördination of the management of the whole system of charitable, penal, reformatory, and correctional institutions in the state, the act was very inadequate, in that it failed to provide for a well qualified non-partisan supervisory board, such as had been urged by the Commission of 1878.

[1] *Acts of the 138th Legislature*, 1914, pp. 429–32. The parole act of 1898 was amended in 1911, 1912, and 1913; see below, pp. 209–10, 212, 213–14.
[2] *Annual Reports of the State Prison*, 1916, p. 45.
[3] *Acts of the 129th Legislature*, 1905, p. 455. *Compiled Statutes of New Jersey*, 1911, pp. 4925–6.
[4] *Annual Report of the State Prison*, 1916, pp. 45–7.
[5] *Acts of the 129th Legislature*, 1905, pp. 92–3.

According to the provisions of an act of April 4, 1906, electrocution was substituted for hanging as the method employed in New Jersey for executing the death penalty.[1] Hitherto the death penalty had been inflicted by the sheriffs of the several counties at the county jails.

The first publicly authorized prison school was established by a law of April 15, 1907, which created a prison school board. This board was to consist of the principal keeper, two members of the board of inspectors, and the moral instructors of the prison, and was to exercise general control over the new prison school. It was provided that the salaried teachers must hold state teachers' certificates and that the head teacher could not be an inmate of the prison. Associate teachers might be recruited from competent inmates. The course of study was to be equivalent to the elementary education offered in the public schools and all inmates approved by the keeper might enter the school.[2]

A law of March 29, 1910, made an extremely feeble and crude attempt to satisfy the agitation for some adequate provision for the needs of discharged prisoners, which had been in progress for nearly half a century. It was provided that convicts, who had given evidence by their personal record while incarcerated that they were industrious and desirous of self-reformation, might receive a maximum sum of $25 from the board of inspectors when discharged. Unworthy convicts were to receive only the $5 prescribed by earlier laws, and between these two extremes the amount paid upon discharge might be graduated according to the record of the individual prisoner concerned.[3]

Another act of 1910, that of April 11th, provided that henceforth it would be legal to employ convicts, sentenced to the state

[1] *Acts of the 130th Legislature*, 1906, pp. 112–115.
[2] *Acts of the 131st Legislature*, 1907, pp. 123–125.
[3] *Acts of the 134th Legislature*, 1910, pp. 76–7. The benefits of this law have been suspended by the recent action of the board of inspectors, who have reduced all payments on discharge to $5 since they began to pay the convicts wages of 2½ cents per day in July, 1917.

prison, in work outside the prison walls, if their labor was properly supervised by officials from the state prison.[1]   This law, with subsequent amendments, thus gave a legal sanction to the important innovations in prison labor in New Jersey since that time, which have tended more and more to extend the opportunity to employ the prisoners in outside work, such as road construction and the reclamation of the soil.[2]

Such were the main legal developments in regard to prison reform.   There was in this period no general reorganization of the legal basis of the administrative system of the state prison.   There were, however, some changes worthy of note in this respect.   A law of March 22, 1888, provided for the employment of a second moral instructor, and from this time on the prison was provided with a Catholic chaplain.[3]   The act of April 20, 1889, took the appointment of the supervisor of the state prison from the joint session of the legislature and vested it in the governor with the consent of the senate.[4]   The appointment of the board of inspectors was also vested in the governor and the senate by the act of May 17, 1894.   An attempt to make this board non-partisan by making it bi-partisan appeared in the provision that of the six inspectors not more than three should belong to either major political party, and that this equality should thereafter be maintained between the two parties.   Of course, it must not be forgotten that a vast gulf may exist between a bi-partisan and a non-partisan board.   Along with these changes the same act provided that the tenure of the inspectors should be increased from three to five years.[5]

In addition to these legal changes directly connected with the state prison and its administration, the penal code of 1874 and its subsequent amendments were worked over and finally sys-

---

[1] Ibid., p. 360.
[2] *Annual Report of the State Prison,* 1916, pp. 6–10.
[3] *Acts of the 112th Legislature,* 1888, pp. 197–8.
[4] *Acts of the 113th Legislature,* 1889, pp. 323–324.
[5] *Acts of the 118th Legislature,* 1894, pp. 396–7.   This law of 1894 also provided that the subordinate officers of the state prison should be equally divided between the two major political parties.   The Constitution of 1897 retained the provision of the Constitution of 1875 that the principal keeper should be appointed for a term of five years by the governor with the consent of the Senate.

tematized in the act of June 14, 1898.[1] From the standpoint of the student of historical jurisprudence there was little advance in the juristic premises involved in this code, as compared with those embodied in the code of 1796 and its subsequent revisions down to 1898. They all belonged to, and reflected, the same era of theological and metaphysical juristic conceptions, or, rather, misconceptions. There was little trace in the code of 1898 of that sociological jurisprudence, which is now gaining ground with such rapidity as to make its final realization a foregone conclusion.

This code still retained as its basic premise the assumption that punishment should be abstractly prescribed according to the crime without any primary regard to the individual criminal, and that the seriousness of the crime could be accurately and arbitrarily discovered according to a graduated pecuniary scale. The grotesque dividing line between petit and grand larceny was still retained,[2] as well as the ancient statute, which dates as far back as the Pauline Epistles and the Theodosian Code of 438, prescribing punishment for "false prophets." [3] The maximum of a double sentence for second offences remained as it had been in the codes of 1846 and 1874.[4]

The only important innovations introduced by the code of 1898 were the general assimilation or reduction of all crimes except treason, murder, manslaughter, and arson, to two fundamental categories: misdemeanors and high misdemeanors, and the general reduction in the length of sentence to imprisonment. For a misdemeanor, a maximum penalty of a fine of $1,000 or three years' imprisonment, or both, was prescribed; while for a high misdemeanor there was provided a maximum of a fine of $2,000 or seven years imprisonment, or both.[5]

[1] *Compiled Statutes of New Jersey,* 1911, Vol. II, pp. 1739ff.

[2] Ibid., p. 1793.

[3] Ibid., p. 1770. This curious anachronism decreed that: "All impostors in religion, such as pretend to personate Jesus Christ, or suffer their followers to worship or pay them divine honors, or who terrify, delude, or abuse the people by false denunciation of judgments, shall be guilty of a misdemeanor."

[4] Ibid., p. 1812.

[5] Ibid. More severe punishment was specifically prescribed for a few particularly serious high misdemeanors.

There were both good and bad features in this change. In so far as it provided for an even greater degree of standardization and mechanical administration in the treatment of crimes and criminals than had been required in the codes of 1796, 1829, 1846, and 1874, it was to that degree more dangerous than these earlier codes. On the other hand, to the extent that it lessened the prescribed terms of imprisonment for criminal action, its effect was good, in so far as it related to those convicts who possess capacity for reformation. However, even as regards the reduction of sentences, its provisions were likely to be more conducive to evil than to good, for it made possible a quicker return to society of those classes of criminals whose character and criminal record require their permanent segregation. All in all, it would be most difficult to discover any intelligent student of criminology, penology, and sociological jurisprudence who would have the courage to maintain that this penal code of 1898 was in any way suitable to furnish the juristic basis of a rational and scientific system of penal, reformatory, and correctional institutions and administration. Of course, some of the crudities of this code are circumvented by the recent progressive legislation in regard to the indeterminate sentence and the parole and probation systems. However, the difficulties inherent in penal administration itself are sufficient to demand that no extra burden be imposed by an archaic and antiquated system of criminal jurisprudence.[1]

III. The Industrial Administration of the State Prison.

There were no radical changes or improvements in the industrial phases of the administration of the state prison of New Jersey between 1885 and 1911. The period, from an industrial standpoint, was essentially one in which the prison authorities

---

[1] This whole subject of the necessity of revolutionizing the existing criminal law to square with the premises of modern penology and criminology is best presented by Raymond Saleilles in *The Individualization of Punishment*, Cf. Also C. A. Ellwood, *The Sociological Foundations of Law*, in the *Green Bag*, Vol. XXII, pp. 575–81, and Roscoe Pound, *The Need of a Sociological Jurisprudence*, in the *Green Bag*, Vol. XIX, pp. 607ff.

became partially adjusted, though under protest, to the new "piece-price" system of contracting for the work of the employees. The abolition of the old system of contract labor disrupted the industrial system of the prison, and it never recovered from the blow. Though the prison had been a heavy loss to the state between 1875 and 1884, the deficit grew much larger after 1885. With the exception of a brief period of relative prosperity between 1898 and 1901, the annual deficit of the state prison increased steadily and more rapidly than the increase in the prison population until, by 1911, it had reached the serious total of $178,585.[1]

In tracing the industrial history of the prison from 1885 to 1911, the first step is to examine the comment of the prison officials upon the introduction of the new "piece-price" system, always bearing in mind the fact that anything which breaks up the routine of an institution, or imposes extra burdens on the official force, is likely to meet with disapproval whatever its virtues.

As early as the annual report for 1884, before the new system was fairly installed, the prison officials launched a violent attack upon the new organization of prison labor. There is no evidence that there was any serious thought given to the problem as to whether the "state use" or the "public account" systems might prove profitable. It seemed to be generally agreed by the authorities that the "piece-price" system was the lesser of three evils.[2] It was insisted that the legislature had ousted the old industrial system without making any adequate provision for installing the new. The legislature was urged immediately to enact the laws and make the appropriations which would be

---

[1] The total annual loss sustained by the state prison during some of these years, including official salaries, was as follows:—1885, $87,835; 1886, $88,865; 1887, $95,215; 1888, $98,725; 1889, $95,910; 1890, $97,890; 1891, $89,110; 1892, $83,635; 1893, $104,645; 1894, $113,326; 1896, $127,780; 1897, $132,980; 1898, $106,585; 1899, $93,940; 1900, $113,180; 1901, $112,100; 1902, $126.065; 1903, $132,820; 1904, $140,725; 1905, $136,525; 1906, $117,020; 1907, $114,225; 1908, $153,270; 1909, $163,490; 1910, $173,625; 1911, $178,585.

[2] *Annual Report of the State Prison,* 1884, pp. 6–7, 32–4.

necessary to execute any wholesale reorganization of the prison industry, such as was contemplated by the laws of February and April, 1884.[1] In addition, there was no provision made for a scientifically planned schedule of prices, and the prison authorities were compelled to resort to the expensive procedure of building up a satisfactory schedule of prices by the process of "trial and error." The officials were agreed that the new system would afford no advantage to free labor, but would constitute merely a serious blow to the already precarious condition of the prison industries.[2] Even the moral instructor protested against the radical changes in the industrial basis of the administration of the prison, on the ground that the probable failure of the new system would be likely to induce idleness, and hence, the mental, moral, and physical degeneration of the prisoners.[3]

The tenor of the report of 1885 was identical with that of 1884. The supervisor pointed out that the new "piece-price" system was in no way a better protection to free labor than the older method of contracting for convict labor, and correctly insisted that the only one to profit by the change was the contractor, who could throw the burden of supervising and expediting the prison industry on the state and could set high standards which the state must live up to at its own expense. He further stated that the first full year's trial of the "piece-price" system had demonstrated that it was not more than three-fifths as productive as the old contract system.[4] Only one official defended the new system. This was Keeper Laverty, who, in his report of the previous year, had presented a competent and effective criticism of the new system. His argument in support of the prospective success of the "piece-price" system was the naive assertion that the convicts would be likely to work much harder when they knew that the state was to profit by their additional industry. There is no evidence of any manifestation of this tender

[1] Ibid., pp. 18–19, 34.
[2] Ibid., passim.
[3] Ibid., pp. 37–8.
[4] Ibid., 1885, pp. 8, 25.

solicitude for the welfare of the state on the part of the prisoners. In fact, they would probably have worked better for the contractors, as the contractors gave an occasional gratuity to the convicts, while from 1860 to 1911 the state generally abandoned this policy.[1]

The supervisor, in his annual report for 1886, stated that the "piece-price" system had proved a failure, as compared with the older contract system, according to the ratio of .399 to .625.[2] In his report for the following year the supervisor tersely summarized the conventional arguments directed against the "piece-price" system by the prison officials at frequent intervals until its legal abolition in 1911. He said, in part:

"The second year's experience in working the prisoners under what is known as the 'piece-price' plan seems to afford no element of hope that, either as a revenue measure, or as a preventive of undue competition with honest labor, it will ever be even as potent as the contract system which it supplanted.

"In its practical workings, it is but a modification of the old system, possessing all its evils and none of its advantages. The working of the convicts is precisely similar under both systems, with the exception that under 'piece-price' plan the state is responsible for both quantity and quality of product, whereas, under the old plan, it was responsible for neither; the contractor assuming that risk."[3]

While the opposition of the prison officials to the new "piece-price" system was based on sound reasoning and a clear perception of the futile and disastrous nature of the change, it must not be forgotten that their disgust with the new system doubtless went far to prevent them from making an earnest and energetic effort to give it a fair trial, and, if possible, to make it a success. The new industrial system, then, was foredoomed to failure both on account of its own inherent weaknesses, and because the prison officials had from the beginning committed themselves to a belief in its insuperable defects.[4]

[1] Ibid., p. 39; see below, p. 179.
[2] Ibid., 1886, p. 12.
[3] Ibid., 1887, p. 9.
[4] See Documents, Part II, pp. 543-7.

12 P

Not only was the industry of the prison hampered during this period by the defects in the fundamental basis of the system of industrial administration, but it was also clogged and encumbered by the lack of proper and adequate physical equipment. Throughout the period the prison officials complained of the lack of adequate shop room and mechanical equipment, which prevented a complete utilization of the available labor force of the prison. On May 10, 1885, an appropriation of $15,000 was made to provide for more shop room, but this addition was soon outgrown. In 1893 the joint committee of the legislature complained of the serious lack of cell and shop room and repeated the time-worn suggestion that the state arsenal be reconverted into a part of the state prison.[1] In his report for 1896 the supervisor complained that from the lack of contracts and diversified equipment it was impossible to employ in any way more than 571 out of the 1,023 prisoners confined, and that only 365 could be utilized in the shops.[2] In 1897 the old cook-house, bakery, and storehouse were converted into a shop. More than a decade later, in 1909, the supervisor stated that out of 1,394 prisoners confined in the state prison only 821 were gainfully employed.[3] Though 1896 and 1909 were to some extent abnormal years, when the prison, as well as the country in general, was recovering from the effects of the industrial depressions of 1893 and 1907, there is an abundance of evidence that throughout this period the lack of adequate physical equipment was as serious an impediment to a successful administration of the industrial operations of the prison as the scarcity of cell room was to the maintenance of effective discipline.[4]

An attempt to stimulate the convicts to additional industry through a system of pecuniary rewards for increased production

---

[1] *Annual Report of the State Prison*, 1893, p. 6.
[2] Ibid., 1896, p. 18.
[3] Ibid., 1909, p. 24.
[4] For instance, in 1903, a normal year in general industry, only 578 out of 1,087 prisoners were gainfully employed. *Annual Report of the State Prison*, 1903, p. 18. See also *Annual Report of the State Charities Aid Association*, 1890, pp. 11–15, and Report of the *Special Committee on the Investigation of the State Prison*, 1890, p. 4.

was advocated by the prison officials throughout this period. In his annual report for 1891, Keeper Patterson urged the importance of granting the especially industrious convicts some financial reward for overwork so as to promote greater industry and give the convict something with which to get adjusted to life when discharged.[1] The supervisor, in his report for the same year, pointed to the existence of a law directing the keeper of the prison to pay industrious convicts a part of their surplus earnings, but complained that nothing could be done to carry out this law, as there was no appropriation provided for the purpose. He urged an appropriation of $2,000 to meet this expense.[2] This recommendation was repeated at frequent intervals throughout this period, but the state took no action upon the matter. However, the supervisor, in his annual report for 1908, stated that in that year the contractors had advanced $5,625 as gratuities to industrious convicts, and asserted that this practice of thus inciting the convicts to greater industry had been in vogue for some time.[3]

While there was no such high crest of prosperity, even for a few years, as was experienced in 1872–4, there were three brief periods from 1885 to 1911 when the receipts were unusually high. The first of these periods came in 1891–2, in the prosperous years just preceding the panic of 1893; the second was experienced from 1898 to 1901, after business had fully recovered from this depression; and the third appeared in 1906–7, just previous to the depression of 1907. In the second and the most conspicuous of these periods of relative prosperity, it was reported in 1899 that the revenue from the prison industries during that year had reached the total of $105,833, the greatest in the history of the institution up to that time. Even in this year, however, but 665 out of 1,216 prisoners were gainfully

[1] *Annual Report of the State Prison,* 1891, p. 20.
[2] Ibid., pp. 35–6. The Supervisor undoubtedly referred to the law of April 21, 1876, which provided that each prisoner should have the benefit of all excess labor, provided that the income from his labor was greater than the cost of his maintenance.
[3] Ibid., 1908, p. 23.

employed, and the expenses of the prison administration had so greatly increased that the net loss, including salaries, sustained by the prison in this year was $93,940.[1] This analysis of the situation in 1899 proves how very unsatisfactory was the condition of the prison industries and finances during this period, even in the most productive year of this quarter of a century's experience with the "piece-price" system. It must be remembered, of course, that the difficulty was not entirely with the industrial system; the inherent defects of the system were intensified by the partially valid opposition and condemnation of the prison officials, by the influence of politics in the contracting transactions, and by the inadequate physical equipment and commercial connections and organization of the industry of the state prison. But whatever may have been the chief factors contributing to the failure of the "piece-price" system in New Jersey, there can be no doubt that the failure was real, and it was the recognition of this fact that led in 1911 to the law commanding the abolition of the "piece-price" system and all other forms of private contracting for prison labor in the state.[2]

The general nature of the specific industrial operations of the prison during this period may be gathered from the following summaries of the industrial distribution of the population of the prison in four typical years, 1893, 1903, 1908, and 1911.

In 1893 out of a total of 940 prisoners confined, 534 were employed in productive labor under the "piece-price" system; 201 were engaged in the general domestic activities of the prison; and 205 were incapacitated for labor or unemployed for other reasons. The 534 productively employed were distributed as follows:[3]

On hosiery contract 95
On shoe contract 86
On mats and matting contract 74
On brush contract 82

[1] *Annual Report of the State Prison,* 1899, pp. 7–8, 15, 19.
[2] *Acts of the 135th Legislature,* 1911, pp. 769ff.
[3] *Annual Report of the State Prison,* 1893, pp. 15–16.

On shirt contract 83
On pants contract 95
On block contract 19

Total 534

The total earnings from the above labor for the year were $101,813.[1]

Ten years later, in 1903, there existed the following distribution of the prison population and industries: Out of an average population of 1,167 prisoners, 667 were gainfully employed by contractors on the "piece-price" system; 329 were engaged in the domestic activities of the prison; 136 were unemployed from physical incapacity or other reasons; and 35 were in the hospital, either sick or as attendants. The following contractors employed the 667 gainfully employed prisoners:[2]

Thomas H. Lynn & Sons ..mats and matting ....earnings, $24,605.75
Oppenheim and Co. ....trousers ....earnings, $16,365.82
George Rendell ....shoes ....earnings, $12,446.89
John Tobin ....brushes ....earnings, $8,818.51
F. Coit Johnson ....sacks ....earnings, $2,892.69
John Tobin ....blocks ....earnings, $2,418.20
John H. Cook ....brooms ....earnings, $4,428.57

Total earnings $71,976.43

In 1908, a typical year in the period immediately preceding the theoretical abolition of the "piece-price" system, the industrial distribution of the contracts was the following:[3]

Rancocas Mills ....mats and matting ....earnings, $22,737.21
Oppenheim and Co. ....pants and waistbands ......earnings, $11,737.93
George Rendell ....shoes......................earnings, $15,350.48
Edwin E. Gnichtel ....brushes and blocks ....earnings, $7,470.40
Trenton Mfg. Co. ....shirts ....earnings, $7,147.37
J. M. Schwerin ....handkerchiefs ....earnings, $13,345.45
John J. Cook ....brooms ....earnings, $9,831.23

Total earnings $87,620.07

[1] Ibid.
[2] Ibid., 1903, pp. 15–16, 19, 24–25.
[3] Ibid., 1908, p. 21.

In 1911, when the "Osborne Bill" was enacted, which ordered the abolition of the contract system in all its forms, the following contracts were in force, which were giving employment to about 850 men, and were to expire on the indicated dates.[1]

October   1, 1913....The Crescent Garment Co.,. .Shirts ....100 men.
January   1, 1914....Oppenheim and Co.,..........Trousers ....100 men.
  "   "   "   ...   "   "   "   ....Waist bands.... 50 men.
  "   "   "   ....Trenton Whisk Broom Co.,. .Brooms ....100 men.
February 1, 1914....W. S. Rendell................Shoes, cartons...125 men.
  "   "   "   ....Rancocas Mills ....Mats ....100 men.
  "   "   "   ...   "   "   ....Matting .... 75 men.
March   1, 1914....Mercer Brush Co.,...........Brushes, brooms 100 men.
  "   "   "   ....J. Schwerin ....Petticoats ......100 men.

IV. MOVEMENTS FOR PRISON BETTERMENT AND PRISON REFORM.

I. THE IMPROVEMENT OF THE PHYSICAL EQUIPMENT OF THE STATE PRISON.

In summarizing the efforts made between 1885 and 1911 to better the condition of the prison system in New Jersey, it seems wisest to begin with the attempts to improve the physical equipment of the prison, as one can only understand the difficulties of maintaining discipline and achieving reformation during this period when he is conversant with the impediments to effective administration which grew out of the archaic, inconvenient, and outgrown physical or architectural equipment placed at the disposal of the principal keeper of the prison and his deputies.

The appropriation in 1877 of $100,000 for the rebuilding of the old north wing had provided a total of 700 cells, but there were more than 870 prisoners confined before this addition was available.[2] The next addition was made by the appropriation of $20,000 in 1884 for an extension of the prison walls to the arsenal building, thus providing more yard room.[3]

[1] *Annual Report of the State Prison,* 1911, pp. 30, 33-4.
[2] Ibid., 1877, p. 32.
[3] Ibid., 1884, pp. 29-30.

No more additions were made to the cell room available until 1895, in spite of the serious overcrowding of the prison and the annual complaints of the prison officials over this condition. An appropriation of $100,000, made in 1890, to add a new wing, chapel, and hospital, was never made available, greatly to the disgust of the keeper and supervisor of the prison.[1] By 1895 the situation had become so serious as to compel action. For five years there had been an average of over 1,000 prisoners confined in 700 cells, though the old state law forbidding congregate confinement was still formally in force.[2]

This overcrowding not only hampered the prison discipline and depressed the prison industry and finances, but it also gave rise to a scandalous use of the pardoning power by the court of pardons. From 1885 to 1895 an average of ten per cent. of the prison population was pardoned annually. In 1886, eighty pardons were granted to relieve the prison of overcrowding.[3] During the next year, 1887, with an average convict population of 893, 398 were discharged, and 102 were pardoned.[4] In 1890 the board of inspectors reported that in spite of the "phenomenal clemency" of the court of pardons, which had pardoned more than ten per cent. of the prison population, there were still about 300 more prisoners than available cells.[5] It was stated by a competent investigator in 1890 that as great a percentage of those pardoned as of those discharged were returned as recidivists, thus indicating that little intelligent discrimination was exercised by the prison officials or the court of pardons in granting pardons to convicts.[6] It was in part the clearly perceived evils of this procedure of indiscriminate pardoning which led to the agitation for, and the enactment of, a parole law in 1889 and 1891.[7]

[1] Ibid., 1891, pp. 20–21, 36; 1892, p. 24; 1893, p. 722. *Acts of the 114th Legislature,* 1890, pp. 245–7.
[2] *Annual Report of the State Prison,* 1889, p. 3; 1890, pp. 30–33, 57; 1894, p. 28. *Annual Report of the State Charities Aid Association,* 1890, p. 12.
[3] *Annual Report of the State Prison,* 1886, pp. 11, 13.
[4] Ibid., 1887, p. 6.
[5] Ibid., 1890, pp. 30–31, 57.
[6] Daniel R. Foster, "Our Present Prison System" in *Annual Report of the State Charities Aid Association,* 1890, p. 12.
[7] *Annual Report of the State Prison,* 1892, p. 91.

The pressure of official complaints and of public opinion was too great for the legislature to resist and the act of March 25, 1895, appropriated $150,000 for additional cell room, hospital facilities and other much needed additions.[1] But this appropriation, welcome and indispensable as it was, came more than a decade too late. It provided for the building of "wing number 6," containing 200 more cells, making a total of 906, but for several years the average population of the prison had been in excess of 1,000. Thus, like its predecessors, this addition to the prison was antiquated and outgrown before it had been put into operation.[2]

With the exception of the $14,000 addition to the women's wing in 1899, the prison remained in this perennial state of overcrowding until, by 1904, the average annual population had reached about 1,100, which had to be confined at night in 900 cells.[3] To meet this situation, the legislature made an appropriation of $250,000 on May 31st, 1905, for the building of a new cell wing to replace the old "wing number 3." [4] However, instead of tearing down "wing number 3," built in 1860, and erecting the new "wing number 7" in its place, or, as was suggested, building it directly across Third Street from the prison, the awkward and irrational procedure was adopted of tearing down the wall from the entrance to the prison to the corner of Federal and Third Streets and erecting the new wing immediately adjoining the street. This huge new wing looming up in this position completely destroyed the symmetry of the prison architecture and also tended to crowd the already depleted yard room. This was the most extensive addition which has ever been made to the state prison, and it cost much more than the entire state prison when erected in 1833–6. This expensive new wing, which was thoroughly modern in every respect, though resembling a great steel cage, provided 350 new cells. It was completed on September 10, 1907, and for the first time since 1840 made

[1] *Acts of the 119th Legislature*, March 25, 1895, pp. 654–6.
[2] *Annual Report of the State Prison*, 1896, pp. 11–12. Ibid., 1897, p. 27.
[3] Ibid., 1904, p. 8.
[4] *Acts of the 129th Legislature*, May 31, 1905, pp. 181–2.

possible the strict observance of the law requiring solitary confinement by night.[1]

Adequate though this new and expensive cell block might have been to the needs of 1907, those who believed that this addition had forever solved the problem of providing sufficient cell room were doomed to serious disappointment, for five years later, in 1912, Keeper Madden complained that the prison was again seriously overcrowded, there being 1,460 prisoners to be confined in about 1,200 cells, thus necessitating the confinement of two men in cells having a floor space of five by seven feet.[2] Had it not been for the development of road and farm work which took many of the prisoners from the prison building altogether; the provision of reformatories for adult male and female delinquents in 1901 and 1913; and the greater use of the parole system, there cannot be the slightest doubt that a much more extensive addition to the state prison than that provided in 1905 would have been forced upon the legislature within another decade.[3]

An extensive addition to the workshops erected in 1860 and 1870–72 was provided by the appropriation of March 10, 1885, setting aside $15,000, plus the residue of the appropriation of $20,000 in the previous year for extending the prison walls, to construct the necessary extension of the shop facilities.[4] In 1897 the shop facilities were still further improved by the conversion of the abandoned cookhouse, bakery, and storeroom into a shop building.[5]

In addition to the need for more cell and shop room, it was pointed out in tracing the architectural history of the prison from 1869 to 1885, that there were repeated and insistent requests on the part of the prison officials for adequate cooking, baking, and hospital facilities, the existing ones having been constructed a

[1] *Annual Report of the State Prison,* 1907, p. 12.
[2] Ibid., 1912, p. 42.
[3] By 1914 the total number of those sentenced to state prison, and of those confined at Rahway and Clinton Farms, averaged over 2,000.
[4] *Acts of the 109th Legislature,* 1885, pp. 67–68.
[5] This alteration was begun in 1895 and finished in 1897.

half-century before.[1] Aside from a makeshift which converted part of an old whip-shop, erected in 1861, into a new cookhouse, nothing was done to provide for these needs until a part of the appropriation of 1895 was used for this purpose. At this time the prison was provided with a new cookhouse, bakery, cold-storage warehouse, laundry, and a hospital with accommodations for forty patients.[2]

There was no dining hall provided, however, to go with the new culinary facilities. The original prison, constructed on the principle of continual solitary confinement, had, of course, provided no dining hall. Under the Pennsylvania system the convicts received their food individually in their cells. When the Auburn system was adopted in 1858–1861, there was no provision for an adequate dining hall and the provision in the act of April 2, 1869, for the addition of a dining hall and chapel was never carried into execution. To the present day the convicts confined in the state prison at Trenton, in spite of a half century of protests from both convicts and prison officials, are still served through that hopelessly archaic, expensive, unpalatable, and unhygienic method of receiving their food in their individual cells.

But the most astonishing of all the architectural additions during this period was the provision of a chapel for the prison in 1897. The appropriation of $100,000, made in 1890 for a new wing, hospital, and chapel, was never available.[3] However, the extensive additions made to the prison out of the appropriation of 1895 at last provided the state prison with a chapel, after such a structure had been requested almost annually for sixty years by the moral instructors of the prison and had even been urged by many successive governors in their annual messages. The new chapel was opened on October 21, 1897, with appropriate celebration.[4] However, the moral instructors were "thankful for small favors," as the chapel thus provided had a

---

[1] *Annual Report of the State Prison,* 1876, pp. 29–30.
[2] Ibid., 1896, pp. 11–12; Ibid., 1897, p. 7; Ibid., 1898, p. 7.
[3] *Acts of the 114th Legislature,* 1890, pp. 245–7; *Annual Report of the State Prison,* 1891, pp. 20–21; 1893, p. 7.
[4] Ibid., 1897, pp. 27, 49–50.

seating capacity of less than 275, while the prison population at that time totalled over 1,100.[1] New Jersey has not yet provided its state prison with an adequate chapel or assembly hall.[2]

The acts of March 30, 1906, granted an appropriation for constructing a joint residence for the principal keeper and for the resident physician, the keeper having previously resided, since 1836, in the left half of the central building of the prison. This provision of a separate residence for the principal keeper came only as a result of appeals from the prison authorities extending over more than a generation.[3]

A death house was erected in 1907 to provide facilities for carrying out the provisions of the law prescribing electrocution as the method of inflicting the death penalty.[4]

2. IMPROVEMENTS IN PRISON DISCIPLINE.

As regards the discipline in the state prison during this period, it seems that there was a very considerable advance over the situation which had existed from 1860 to 1885. This improvement was to a very great degree due to the superior ability of Keepers J. H. Patterson and G. O. Osborne, who served during twenty out of the twenty-five years of this period. Both were highly enlightened men with relatively modern views regarding penal administration. Mr. Patterson was, perhaps, somewhat more severe in his discipline than was necessary, while Mr. Osborne erred to an equal extent on the side of leniency. However, they were much the best keepers that the prison has had under the sixty years of the Auburn system. Keepers Patterson and Osborne, while good disciplinarians, were not vindictive, and were apparently judicious in their selection and administering of punishment, though the former would seem, from his own statement, to have had recourse to some of the less severe methods

[1] Ibid., p. 27.
[2] *Preliminary Report of the Prison Inquiry Commission*, 1917, pp. 7–8.
[3] *Acts of the 130th Legislature*, 1906, pp. 81–82.
[4] Consult the drawing opposite page 186 for the ground plan of the state prison as it now stands. There have been no important additions since 1907.

of the old regime. In his report for 1890, Keeper Patterson stated:

"I have had little difficulty in maintaining good discipline, the mode of confinement being in dark cells on bread and water. The old methods of punishment which were in vogue some years ago in this prison have been abolished. Ball and chain is sometimes necessary, but at the date of this report none are adorned with that ornament." [1]

About 1893 there had evidently been some "press agent" exposures concerning the methods of punishment at the state prison, for Mr. Patterson clearly stated the necessity of taking a firm stand in regard to prison punishments. He insisted that the keeper must not let his conduct be guided by a desire for unnecessary harshness or by maudlin sentimentality.[2] But he fully understood the vital truth that good conduct could be created more effectively by stimulating the better inpulses of the convicts rather than by beating them into surly submission. He repeatedly urged the provision of a system of rewards, pecuniary and otherwise, for industry and good deportment, and to secure the aid of education in improving discipline he established the first night school in the state prison.[3]

Mr. Samuel S. Moore, keeper from 1886 to 1902, boasted of his ability to maintain good discipline without inflicting severe punishment, and maintained that he never went beyond prescribing six days' confinement in a dark cell on bread and water.[4] That Mr. Moore's success may not have been as striking as he reports, is apparent from the statement of the moral instructor that the appointment of George O. Osborne, as the next keeper, brought in a "new and better order of things" in prison discipline.[5]

Keeper Osborne stated that he never resorted to a more severe mode of punishment than confinement in a light and well-

[1] *Annual Report of the State Prison,* 1890, p. 20.
[2] Ibid., 1893, pp. 20–21.
[3] Ibid., 1887, p. 6; 1890, p. 24; 1891, pp. 17–20; 1892, pp. 92–3.
[4] Ibid., 1896, p. 27; 1898, p. 32; 1900, p. 29; 1901, p. 31.
[5] Ibid., 1902, p. 60.

ventilated cell for six days on bread and water. He asserted that he was able to maintain good discipline without the use of severe or cruel methods of punishment. In 1906 he asserted that there had been no escapes or outbreaks in the five years of his administration. Up to 1912, then, the evil of severe punishments as a general policy in prison administration seems to have been, in part, overcome.[1]

The efforts of various sorts to make the principle of reformation an integral part of the penal procedure were frequent, and, to some extent, effective during this period. Keeper Patterson, from the beginning of his term, was an ardent advocate of the adoption of a parole law for the benefit of the less hardened criminals who had given evidence of a desire to reform. He was able to get such a law passed in 1889, but it was declared unconstitutional by the attorney general. However, another parole law was passed in 1891 and that immediately went into operation and proved a moderate success from the first.[2] By 1902 only 36 out of the 488 prisoners, who had been paroled since 1891, had been returned to the prison. The law of 1905, which created a parole agent, provided for a feeble approximation to an adequate inspection of the conduct of paroled prisoners.[3]

In addition to being an effective advocate of the parole system, Keeper Patterson, as early as 1890, advocated the adoption of an indeterminate sentence law, in order to secure the permanent segregation of degenerates and recidivists of the worst sort and prevent the propagation of this class. He repeated this suggestion for several years, but with no direct effect.[4] The state prison of New Jersey has never been aided by a real indeterminate sentence law; the maximum and minimum sentence laws of April 21, 1911, and April 15, 1914, being but a step towards the

---

[1] Ibid., 1906, p. 49; 1907, p. 44; 1909, p. 38; 1910, p. 39.
[2] Ibid., 1890, pp. 22–3; 1891, p. 16; 1892, p. 91; 1893, p. 19; 1896, p. 28; 1899, p. 32; 1902, p. 39; 1906, p. 48; 1907, p. 50; 1910, pp. 41–2.
[3] *Acts of the 129th Legislature,* 1905, p. 455.
[4] *Annual Report of the State Prison,* 1890, pp. 24–5; 1893, p. 18.

real indeterminate sentence, which is more nearly provided for in commitments to Rahway and Clinton Farms.[1]

Another reform movement, which was supported by Keeper Patterson, was that designed to provide aid for discharged convicts, so as to prevent them from being forced back into crime from the sheer pressure of economic necessity. This agitation was continued throughout the period, but, aside from encouraging some private action in this respect, it had no practical results beyond the feeble law of 1910 providing a maximum payment of $25 to discharged convicts.[2] Mr. Patterson's attempt to secure aid for the discharged convicts by giving them their surplus earnings when discharged also was without avail.[3] When one takes into consideration all these reform measures which were either initiated or assisted by Keeper Patterson, one will quite agree with Mr. Daniel R. Foster, of the State Charities Aid Association, in declaring that he was one of those rare prison administrators who "understands that he is not only employed in keeping prisoners, but in working out a great sociological problem."[4]

The religious and educational forces making for reformation in the state prison were strengthened during this period. A second moral instructor was provided by the act of March 22, 1888, and a Catholic chaplain was duly appointed.[5] By 1904 regular Hebrew services, which had been held at intervals since 1892, were instituted,[6] and the law of March 31, 1911, authorized the appointment of three moral instructors, stipulating that their ag-

[1] Inmates of these reformatories cannot normally be detained longer than the legal maximum sentence prescribed for their offence.
[2] *Annual Report of the State Prison*, 1892, p. 93; 1893, p. 18; 1894, pp. 14-15; 1896, pp. 29-30; 1900, pp. 29-30; 1906, pp. 33-4.
[3] Ibid., 1890, p. 24; 1892, pp. 92-3; 1894, p. 16.
[4] *Annual Report of the State Charities Aid Association*, 1890, pp. 13-14. For a good statement of Patterson's views see *Annual Report of State Prison*, 1890, pp. 18ff.; 1891, pp. 16ff. There is, however, a persistent tradition at the state prison that these fairly enlightened reports were written by William A. Hall, financial clerk of the prison. See Documents, Part II, pp. 549-58.
[5] *Acts of the 112th Legislature*, 1888, pp. 197-8. *Annual Report of State Prison*, 1888, p. 30.
[6] *Annual Report of State Prison*, 1904, p. 32.

gregate salaries should not exceed $3,000.[1] A Hebrew chaplain was accordingly appointed in 1912.[2] In 1906 Maude Ballington Booth, of the Salvation Army, began to hold quarterly meetings in the prison, and the prison officials commented favorably upon the result of her labors in the institution in this and subsequent years.[3] The new chapel, cramped and inadequate as it was, offered the first opportunity that had even been presented in the prison of holding effective religious services.[4]

The extension of educational advantages in the prison in this period was not less marked than the improvement of the facilities for the exercise of religion. The first night school of any significance in the history of the prison was established by Keeper Patterson in 1887, twenty years before any legal provision was made for a prison school system.[5] By 1888 one hundred and thirty were enrolled in the school, and it had a successful existence for a number of years, in spite of a lack of proper assembly and instruction rooms and without any state support.[6] The prison school apparently lapsed under the administration of Keeper Moore, but it was revived again in 1903 by Moral Instructors Maddock and Fish.[7] Finally, the act of April 15, 1907, provided for a prison school, to be supported by the state, and created a prison school board to take charge of this work.[8] This important innovation in the reformatory work of the prison has never proved a success, and by 1911 but three hundred and eighty-two were enrolled; this number never at any one time, and the yearly expenses totalled only $1,319.[9] The chief cause for the failure of the state prison school has been the lack of physical equipment. No adequate and appropriate school room

[1] *Acts of the 135th Legislature,* 1911, pp. 127–8.

[2] *Annual Report of State Prison,* 1912, pp. 51–3.

[3] Ibid., 1906, p. 49; 1911, p. 55; Ibid., 1914, p. 45. She also aided discharged convicts to find employment, Ibid., 1907, p. 71; Ibid., 1914, p. 49.

[4] Ibid., 1897, pp. 49–50.

[5] Ibid., 1887, p. 6. Some instruction had earlier been provided by energetic moral instructors; see *Appendix to the Senate Journal,* 1852, p. 177.

[6] *Annual Report of the State Prison,* 1888, p. 12; 1890, p. 18; 1891, p. 16.

[7] Ibid., 1903, pp. 49–50; 1904, pp. 32–3.

[8] *Acts of the 131st Legislature,* 1907, pp. 123–125.

[9] *Annual Report of the State Prison,* 1911, pp. 61–62. The condition of the prison school was even less promising in 1916, but some progressive steps were taken in 1917.

has ever been provided, and the textbooks and other teaching equipment have been scanty and antiquated. In addition, enough teachers have never been provided to have made the school a success, if there had been available adequate physical equipment, and most of the recent keepers have been indifferent to the matter of prison education.

The prison library had also grown until, by 1908, 3,000 volumes had accumulated, and there was reported to be a continual circulation of over 1,000 volumes.[1]

An effort to provide a better psychological setting for efforts at reformation was evident in the abolition of the more barbarous stigmata of prison life, which had long been a source of personal humiliation to the convicts without affording any proportional benefits to society.

Up to 1891 it had been the custom to give the discharged prisoners a coarse suit of clothes of uniform and easily distinguishable pattern and color, so that it was as easy to recognize a discharged criminal as it would have been if he had retained his stripes. This primitive obstacle to reformation and the recovery of self-respect was temporarily abolished in 1891, when suits of varied patterns were provided for discharged convicts.[2]

The prison stripes, the short haircut, and the lock step were retained until 1903. In 1902 the newly appointed keeper, Mr. George O. Osborne, attended the National Prison Congress at Philadelphia and was astonished to find that New Jersey was among the few states which still retained these vestiges of penal barbarism. He strongly recommended their immediate abolition.[3] In his report for 1903 he was able to state that they had been done away with.[4]

---

[1] Ibid., 1908, p. 8. At present there are about 7,000 volumes in the prison library.

[2] *Annual Report of the State Prison*, 1891, p. 31. It appears, however, that this reform was not continued, for only a few years ago the suits given to prisoners were of a uniform and easily distinguishable color and pattern. At present the problem appears to be solved through the giving of decent suits of varied patterns.

[3] *Annual Report of the State Prison*, 1903, pp. 41-2.

[4] Ibid., p. 30.

3. THE AGITATION FOR THE ESTABLISHMENT OF REFORMATORIES.

There were vigorous movements for the establishment of reformatories for adult delinquents during this period. They were in reality but a continuation of the agitation in this direction which had been in progress for more than a quarter of a century.

The supervisor of the state prison in his annual report for 1886, discussed the problem of remedying the overcrowding of the prison and stated that an intermediate prison or reformatory would be by far the best remedy for the situation. He pointed out that, of the 900 prisoners in the state prison, 570 were under thirty years of age and most of them "first termers." [1] The agitation for a state reformatory for adult male delinquents continued, aided, in part, by the crowded condition of the state prison, until on March 28, 1895, an act was passed, based chiefly on the recommendations of the Reformatory Commission of 1890, providing for the erection of a reformatory for "first termers" under thirty years of age who had not been convicted of particularly serious crimes. [2] The reformatory was built at Rahway and was opened on August 5, 1901. [3]

Agitation for a reformatory for women was also vigorous during this period, but its success was longer delayed. In 1886 the legislature appointed a joint committee "on a Female Prison and Reformatory." This committee submitted its report in 1887. It stated that it had examined the three most advanced reformatories for women in the United States—those at Indianapolis, Indiana, at Sherborn, Massachusetts, and at Hudson, New York. It especially praised the system of classification, grading, and promotion of inmates which was employed at Sherborn. The committee presented its conclusions in the following words:

[1] Ibid., 1886, p. 11.
[2] *Acts of the 119th Legislature*, 1895, pp. 715–730. See Documents, Part II, pp. 611–18.
[3] *First Annual Report of the Commissioners of the New Jersey State Reformatory*, 1901, p. 5.

13 P

"In view of the fact that so many women and girls are annually committed to our county jails and penetentiaries at an enormous expense to the taxpayers—an expense which is largely increasing each year, without any possibility of their reformation—and because of the success of the institutions named in reforming this class of females (eighty per cent. of those committed to their care, according to statistics, being thoroughly reformed), we, your committee, recommend that a similar institution be erected in this state, and that an appropriation of seventy-five thousand dollars be made and a commission appointed to supervise the erection of such an institution."[1]

The legislature passed a joint resolution approving of the recommendations of the committee, but the matter went no further at this time.[2] It may be that the agitation for a reformatory for women abated to some extent on account of the excellent administration of the women's wing of the state prison by Mrs. John H. Patterson from 1886 to 1896, which, according to the opinion of the moral instructor, rendered a separate prison for women unnecessary.[3] About the beginning of the present century the agitation was vigorously resumed by the Federation of Women's Clubs of New Jersey and by other reform associations, notably the State Charities Aid Association. As a result, Governor Murphy appointed a commission in 1903, which reported in favor of a reformatory for women on the cottage plan.[4] This agitation was kept up until a law was passed creating such an institution on April 1, 1910.[5] The institution was located at Clinton Farms, in Hunterdon County, and was formally opened on May 26, 1913.[6]

The origin of these institutions, aside from their concrete aid in handling the delinquent population of New Jersey, was significant as marking a further recognition of that vital process of differentiation and classification in the study and treatment of delinquents. They completed the step, initiated by the origin of

[1] Report cited, Document No. 39 in *Legislative Documents*, 1887, pp. 6–7. See Documents, Part II, pp. 621–5.

[2] *Acts of the 110th Legislature*, 1886, p. 419.

[3] *Annual Report of the State Prison*, 1890, p. 62.

[4] *First Annual Report of the Board of Managers of the New Jersey Reformatory for Women at Clinton*, 1913, p. 6. See Documents, Part II, pp. 625–31.

[5] *Acts of the 134th Legislature*, 1910, pp. 101–109.

[6] *First Annual Report of the Board of Managers of the New Jersey State Reformatory for Women at Clinton*, p. 7.

the reform schools at Jamesburg and Trenton, of providing for a differentiation of the various classes of delinquents according to the seriousness of their offences and their relative potentialities for reformation.

Other important institutions which originated in this period, and which provided for a scientifically differentiated treatment of classes which had once been confined in the state prison when guilty of criminal conduct, were the Institution for Feeble-Minded Women at Vineland, opened in 1898, and the Village for Epileptics, opened at Skillman in the same year. These institutions, together with the previously established state hospitals for the insane at Trenton (1848) and Morris Plains (1876), and the colonies for feeble-minded males, opened in 1916, furnish a system for scientifically classifying and differentiating the mentally abnormal and subnormal classes and for providing them with specialized treatment. The next essential step is to see that proper provision is made for the transfer of members of these classes from prisons and reformatories to these special institutions.

Another important departure in the field of social reform was the creation of the *State Board of Children's Guardians,* by the act of March 24, 1899, which was designed to provide private non-institutional care for those dependent children who had hitherto been cared for in public almshouses. While this board was at first connected with the correctional institutions of the state only in the most indirect manner, it was brought into immediate relation with them through the juvenile court act of March 14, 1910, which authorized the courts to commit juvenile delinquents to the care and custody of the State Board of Children's Guardians.[1]

4. THE CREATION OF THE COMMISSIONER OF CHARITIES AND CORRECTIONS.

The remaining significant advances toward a better system of penal, reformatory and correctional institutions which occurred

[1] On the work of the State Board of Children's Guardians see the statistics published as an appendix to the *Report of the Prison Inquiry Commission,* 1917.

during this period were the establishment of the *State Charities Aid and Prison Reform Association* in 1886[1] and the creation of a *Commissioner of Charities and Corrections* in 1905. These organizations or departments are a most important force making for a better and more scientific treatment of the delinquent population. By exerting a constant supervision over the institutions which deal with the delinquents, they are able to maintain a steady pressure upon the public authorities to secure reform legislation. It is to permanent bodies such as these that New Jersey must primarily look for the successful solution of the problem of penal reform in the future. The sporadic investigating committees and commissions usually come into being only when a situation has been distressing for a considerable period of time, a state of affairs which could never exist if these permanent bodies of inspection and supervision were alert and vested with sufficient legal powers to carry their ideas into execution.

The creation of the commissioner of charities and corrections, an official who had been asked for in New Jersey as early as 1878, arose largely out of a campaign of education carried on by the State Charities Aid Association between 1900 and 1905. The eighteenth annual report of this Association, that for 1903, contained an exhaustive report by the veteran penologist, Frederick H. Wines, giving a history of the organization of centralized boards of supervision and of control over penal, reformatory, correctional, and charitable institutions in the different commonwealths of the United States. This report, along with its accompanying agitation, produced the law of March 25, 1905, creating the commissioner of charities and corrections of New Jersey.[2] The political leaders, however, in shaping the legislation creating this office, and in making the original appointment, converted it into a political sinecure. The commissioner was given practically no decisive executive powers, and the

[1] Its original designation was The State Charities Aid Association. Its amalgamation with the Prison Reform Association was a later development, which took place in 1904.

[2] *Acts of the 129th Legislature*, 1905, pp. 92-3.

office has remained chiefly one of inspection, criticism, and recommendation.

5. POLITICS AND PRISON ADMINISTRATION.

Finally, as to the attempts during this period to remove politics from prison administration, it can scarcely be said that anything was accomplished. The act of May 17, 1894, which prescribed that henceforth the board of inspectors and the subordinate officers of the state prison should be equally divided between the two major political parties, might have been regarded by some as making for a *non-partisan* penal administration, but in reality it simply provided for a *bi-partisan* administration. There is nothing in a bi-partisan administration which furnishes any guarantee whatsoever of greater efficiency than would be the case in a strictly partisan management.

It may add a greater degree of concreteness and personal interest briefly to summarize the political affiliations of the chief officers connected with the administration of the state prison in recent years and to indicate in some cases the nature of their previous occupation, as bearing upon their preparation for holding responsible positions in penal institutions and administration.

Attention may first be directed to the occupants of the office of principal keeper of the state prison since 1873.

Charles Wilson, keeper from 1873 to 1876, was the Republican leader of Camden county. He was appointed during the administration of Governor Joel Parker, a Democrat, but at this time the joint session of the legislature, which was Republican in its majority, elected the keeper.

General Gershom Mott was keeper from 1876 to 1881. He served with honor in the Mexican and Civil Wars. His only important positions in public life had been collector of the port of Lamberton and state treasurer. He was one of the most prominent Democrats of New Jersey and was appointed keeper by Governor J. D. Bedle, also a Democrat.

Patrick H. Laverty held the office of keeper from 1881 to 1886. His occupation was that of a merchant and an active politician. He had held the office of sheriff of Hudson county. He was probably the best campaign manager in the Democratic party in New Jersey at that time. He was appointed by Governor G. C. Ludlow, Democrat.

John H. Patterson, principal keeper for two terms, from 1886 to 1896, was by occupation a prosperous farmer and shipper. He was a very prominent Democrat, having previously served as sheriff of Monmouth county and as doorkeeper of the House of Representatives at Washington. He was appointed by Governor Leon Abbett, Democrat.

Samuel S. Moore, keeper from 1896 to 1902, was the first Republican keeper for a quarter of a century. His only technical experience had been as an accountant and postmaster, but for 25 years he had been a prominent member of the Union county Republican committee. He had held the offices of postmaster and overseer of the poor at Elizabeth and collector of Union county. He was appointed by Governor J. W. Griggs, Republican.

George O. Osborne, keeper from 1902 to 1912, was a Republican who for years had held appointive positions as warden of almshouses and hospitals in Hudson county. He was appointed by Governor Franklin Murphy, Republican.

Thomas B. Madden, keeper from 1912 to 1916, was a Democrat. His son, Dr. Walter Madden, was sheriff of and a leading Democratic politician of Mercer county. He had spent most of his life as a subordinate officer at the state prison. He was appointed by Governor Wilson, Democrat.

Richard P. Hughes, a Florence banker, was appointed to fill the interim caused by Keeper Madden's death. He was a member of the Democratic state committee and was appointed by Governor Fielder, Democrat.

The present keeper, Mr. James H. Mulheron, has for years been a leading figure in the politics of Mercer county. He has served as a Republican member of the legislature of New Jersey in addition to acting for many years as chairman of the Mercer county Republican committee. He was appointed early in 1917 by Governor Walter E. Edge, Republican.

In the selection of the supervisor of prison industries practically the same situation as regards political considerations in determining appointments has existed since 1885.

Charles B. Moore, supervisor from 1885 to 1888, was a Democrat, appointed by the joint session of a Democratic legislature.

The same circumstances prevailed with respect to the appointment of Henry L. Butler, supervisor from 1888 to 1891.

James M. Seymour, supervisor from 1891 to 1894, was a prominent Democrat, appointed by Governor Leon Abbett, Democrat.

Major E. J. Anderson, who held the office from 1894 to his death in 1905, was a very prominent Republican and was for years a member of the Republican state committee and of the Mercer county Republican committee. He was appointed by Governor G. T. Werts, a Democrat, in 1894, and was reappointed by Republican governors in 1897 and 1900. The appointment of Major Anderson was the only deviation from the series of strict partisan appointments of the chief officers of the state prison since 1885.

Samuel W. Kirkbride, supervisor from 1906 to 1912, was a prominent Republican, at one time a member of the Assembly. He was appointed by Governor E. C. Stokes, Republican, and reappointed by Governor J. F. Fort, Republican.

J. P. McCormack, the present supervisor (fiscal agent since 1914), was a prominent Hudson county Democratic leader. He was appointed by Governor Wilson, Democrat.[1]

It has been considered unwise to attempt to include a summary of the political connections of the inspectors of the state

[1] This information is taken chiefly from the biographical sketches in the successive volumes of the *Legislative Manual of New Jersey,* substantiated by evidence from local biographical volumes. No attempt has been made in this analysis to go beyond the objective facts.

prison during this period. Such a treatment would require an assignment of space quite out of proportion to the importance of the subject.

For a third of a century, therefore, political considerations have governed the choice of the most prominent officials connected with the state prison. While this system has brought into office some capable men, the majority of the political appointees have been men of mediocre ability and poorly prepared for the duties of their office. The "spoils system," thus, stands self-condemned as a *general method* for the selection of officials who must fill a position requiring high intelligence, unusual tact and judgment, extensive technical knowledge, and thorough special preparation.

6. THE DEPENDENCY AND CRIMES COMMISSION OF 1908.

A significant movement in the history of attempts at penal reform in New Jersey was the appointment of a Commission on Dependency and Crime, according to the act of April 9, 1908, which authorized the Governor to appoint a commission of nine persons to investigate in all their aspects the causes of dependency and criminality. It was specifically enacted that,

"The said Commission shall investigate the causes of dependency and criminality, and make inquiry for the purpose of ascertaining to what extent excessive use of alcoholic drinks or narcotics, diet, lack of home training, immigration, the present penal system, conditions of population, and unhealthful tenement house conditions, are contributory causes. The Commission shall also consider such other factors as, in its judgment, contribute to the increase of the defective and criminal classes, and shall recommend to the Governor the best methods, in its opinion, of alleviating these conditions and eliminating the causes thereof."[1]

To facilitate the desirable division of labor and specialization, the Commission divided itself into a number of special com-

[1] *Acts of the 132nd Legislature,* 1908, pp. 209–210.

mittees among which were apportioned the various subdivisions of the general field under investigation.[1]

The Commission accumulated a considerable body of important literature, a large part of which was never published and little of which was even given a proper amount of publicity. While its investigations are somewhat aside from the main center of interest of a sketch of the history of penal and reformatory institutions, it should be emphasized in passing that the general assumptions underlying the creation and the investigations of this Commission were of the utmost importance and significance as indicating a recognition of the fact that diagnosis and prophylaxis are quite as important in dealing with social pathology as they have long been recognized to be in handling the problems of individual pathology.[2]

The following constitute the most important recommendations relating to penal reform. The Commission urged that there be created a State Board of Charities and Corrections, presided over by a Commissioner of Charities, who must be an expert on the problems of charity and correction. This board was to have control over all the penal, reformatory, and correctional institutions of the state, as well as over the charitable institutions, and was designed to bring into existence that co-ordination of administration which had not been produced by the creation of the semi-powerless office of Commissioner of Charities and Corrections in 1905. The Commission favored abolition of the antiquated and unhealthy state prison plant and the construction of a new

---

[1] Alcohol and Narcotics—Rev. Ernest A. Boom, Chairman. The Present Penal System—Benjamin Murphy, Jr., Chairman. Unhealthy Tenement House Conditions—Edward A. Ransom, Jr., Chairman. Diet and Lack of Home Training—Mrs. Emily E. Williamson, Chairman. Laws Affecting Criminality and Dependency—M. T. Barrett, Chairman. Amusements and Their Relation to the Causes of Criminality—Mrs. Caroline B. Alexander, Chairman. *Report of the Chairman of the Committee on Narcotics of the Dependency and Crime Commission of the State of New Jersey,* Trenton, 1909, pp. 9–10.

[2] See Documents, Part II, pp. 558–65.

prison on a healthy site. They urged a more thorough application of the civil service system at the state prison and strongly condemned the contract system of administering the industrial operations of the prison. Finally, they recommended that the overcrowding of the women's wing of the state prison be remedied by the erection of the long-desired reformatory for women.[1]

With the exception of some slight influence upon the abolition of contract labor in the prison in 1911, and the passage of the law for the establishment of the state reformatory for women at Clinton Farms in 1910, there is little evidence that the many valuable suggestions of this Commission left any permanent impression upon the legislation with respect to the penal institutions of the state.

V. SUMMARY OF THE PERIOD.

One is now in a position to summarize the main characteristics and accomplishments of the second twenty-five years of the Auburn system of penal administration in New Jersey. The period was characterized in general, like that from 1860 to 1885, by "piece-meal" legislation, forced by serious pressure of circumstances and designed to make the existing system of prison administration endurable. There was in no sense any attempt at a sweeping transformation, which alone could have brought permanent improvement.

In the matter of legal development, with the exception of the adoption of the parole law in 1889–91, nothing of first-rate importance took place until the extreme end of the period, when a prison school was established and a law passed permitting the extra-mural employment of those serving a state prison sentence. Of the legal enactments indirectly related to the state prison, the most important was the creation of a commissioner of charities and corrections in 1905. The revision of the penal code in 1898 involved no such infusion of broad sociological principles into criminal jurisprudence as is needed to make the criminal code a valuable accessory to prison reform in New Jersey.

[1] *Report of the Dependency and Crimes Commission,* 1908, pp. 2–5, 16–19, 22.

In its industrial aspects, this period coincides exactly with the trial and failure of the "piece-price" system of contracting for the products of prison labor. The system was a failure chiefly on account of its own inherent defects, but two general industrial depressions, the opposition of the prison officials to this industrial system, the lack of adequate physical equipment in the way of shop facilities, and the interference of political considerations with industrial management were all strong contributing factors in its downfall.

It was in the department of the improvement and modernization of penal procedure that the greatest results were accomplished in New Jersey during this period. From the standpoint of prison architecture the capacity of the prison was almost doubled, at a cost practically equal to the total appropriations for prison architecture before 1885. But at the close of the period the prison population had outgrown these additions and the institution was again assuming its customary condition of demoralizing and unhygienic overcrowding. The savage punishments of the previous period were at least in part abolished, as well as the humiliating aspects of prison discipline, the prison stripes, the lock step, and the short hair cut. Among the most important developments of the reformatory function of penal administration were the adoption of a parole law, the provision of better religious and educational facilities, the establishment of a reformatory for adult male delinquents, and the enactment of a law creating a similar institution for delinquent females. A permanent semi-official organization for inspecting and criticizing the penal institutions of the state appeared with the origin of the State Charities Aid Association in 1886. A feeble attempt to realize the much needed coördination of the management of the penal, reformatory, correctional, and charitable institutions of the state was evident in the creation of the weak department of charities and correction in 1905, and a real provision for the centralized administration of these institutions was urged without positive results by the Dependency and Crimes Commission of 1908.

THE NEW JERSEY STATE PRISON, 1911-1917

(THE AUBURN SYSTEM
AT THE PRESENT TIME)

CHAPTER VI

THE NEW JERSEY STATE PRISON, 1911–1917.

I. The General Tendencies and Characteristics of the Period.

The history of the state prison since 1911 has differed radically in its general characteristics from that of any previous era since 1858–60, if not since 1830–37. For the first time since the beginning of the Civil War period there has been an attempt at sweeping transformations in the legal and industrial bases of the administration of the prison.

In the first place, the period has been one of unparalleled activity in reform legislation designed to improve the industrial system, the management and discipline of the institution, the facilities for the reformation of the individual, and the general organization of the government of the prison and its newly created appendages. While much of this advanced legislation has never been put into effective execution, because of a conflict of jurisdiction between authorities and the lack of the pressure of public opinion, the legal basis has been provided for at least a partial reformation of the state prison system.

The industrial foundations of the prison administration have been put on a more satisfactory legal basis, but the new era has scarcely been more than initiated in the industrial realm. The "piece-price" and all other systems of contracting for the labor of prisoners were abolished by the act of 1911 and the "state use" and "public account" systems substituted, the latter to be employed only when the possibilities of the former had been exhausted. However, the contract system has been extended by special acts conferring additional "periods of grace," and at the beginning of the fiscal year 1917 nearly six hundred convicts were still employed by the contract system, while only about twenty were actually engaged according to the "state use" system within the prison walls.

While the industrial changes within the prison walls have, thus, not been extensive, there has been a most notable and salutary innovation in the form of a very considerable transfer of prison industry outside the prison. This was allowed by the act of April 11, 1910, and its subsequent amendments. Practical action according to this law was taken in 1913, when two prison road camps were established to make possible the employment of convicts in the improvement of the state highways, and a prison farm of 1,000 acres was acquired at Leesburg. Since that time a third road camp has been established. The outlook for a better organization of prison industry is more promising in the department of extra-mural activities than within the prison itself. This outdoor employment of the prisoners promises to be advantageous from the standpoint of both revenue and hygiene, and, very likely, from that of reformation as well. Centralized control of the labor and industry of the state penal, reformatory and correctional institutions was provided by the creation of the Prison Labor Commission in 1911. Finally, provision has been made in law if not in fact for the payment of a small sum to the dependent families of inmates of the state prison.

From the standpoint of improving the administrative and reformatory functions of the prison, equally important legal provisions have been made. A step towards an indeterminate sentence law was enacted in the maximum and minimum sentence law of 1911 and its amendment in 1914. A better organization of the parole system was provided in the act of 1914 and the subsequent amendments, but the archaic and illogical system of dividing the parole powers is still retained. The honor system has been introduced to some extent in the discipline of the prisoners employed outside the prison walls. A crude beginning towards legal provision for a system of rewards for superior industry has been made, though it has received no extensive application. Finally, and most important of all, the law of 1914 laid the legal foundations for an authoritative and responsible government of the state prison by vesting it solely in the board of inspectors. Though this law may not secure an effective administration of the state prison, at least the people of New Jersey can, from this time on, know whom to hold responsible for the failures.

It will be apparent, however, that most of these reform measures were either designed for application among those employed outside the prison or have not been vigorously enforced.

II. Prison Legislation.

The first law relating to the state prison during this period was that of March 31, 1911, authorizing the appointment of a third moral instructor, or, in other words, the addition of a Hebrew chaplain.[1]

The act of April 21, 1911, constituted an approach to an indeterminate sentence law for the New Jersey state prison. It provided that a maximum and minimum sentence should be fixed by the court imposing sentence. When a prisoner should have completed the time prescribed as his minimum sentence he was to be regarded as eligible to parole if his prison record seemed to justify such action. Those with bad prison records might be kept until the expiration of their maximum sentence.[2] As a substitute for an indeterminate sentence this act provided for a speedy release of those who were amenable to rapid reformation, but it failed to detain indefinitely those degenerate recidivists who require permanent segregation. It thus was unsuccessful in fulfilling a most important function of the indeterminate sen-

[1] *Acts of the 135th Legislature,* 1911, pp. 127–8.
[2] Ibid., pp. 356–8.

14 P

tence. Probably the most vigorous supporter of the maximum and minimum sentence law of 1911 was Aloys M. Fish, the Catholic chaplain of the prison at that time.[1]

The law of April 27, 1911, provided for the erection of a separate hospital for the criminal insane on the grounds of the state hospital at Trenton and for the transfer of the criminal insane to this institution when it was finished.[2] Though this provision should have provided for the disposition of the criminal insane the keeper of the state prison complained, in 1916, of the demoralizing effect upon prison discipline of the presence of insane inmates in the state prison, thus indicating that the work begun by Dorothea Dix in the "forties" has not yet been brought to a successful conclusion.[3]

But the most important of all acts passed during the session of 1911 was that of June 7, known as the "Osborne Bill," framed and sponsored by Senator Harry V. Osborne and Superintendent Frank Moore of Rahway Reformatory, which abolished contract labor and created a Prison Labor Commission. This law decreed that there should be no more contracting for prison labor, except in cases where the state or some subdivision of the state should be the second party to the contract.[4] It directed that all prisoners who were physically able to do so should be daily employed except on Sunday and legal holidays for not to exceed eight hours per day.[5] It was ordered that their labor should be expended in the production of goods to be used by the state and state institutions, or by some subdivision of the state and its local public institutions.[6] The act, however, went much further than merely to provide for the administration of the labor of the state prison. It created a central board of control over the industry of all the penal, reformatory, and correctional institutions of the state. This board, designated as the *Prison*

[1] *Annual Report of the State Prison,* 1911, p. 59.
[2] *Acts of the 135th Legislature,* 1911, pp. 548-9.
[3] *Annual Report of the State Prison,* 1916, p. 41.
[4] *Acts of the 135th Legislature,* 1911, p. 769.
[5] Ibid., p. 769.
[6] Ibid., p. 769.

Labor Commission, was to be composed of the commissioner of charities and corrections of the state, the keeper of the state prison, the superintendent of the reformatory at Rahway, and two other members appointed by the governor for a term of five years.[1] It was decreed that the industry of all of the aforesaid penal, reformatory, and correctional institutions should be directed towards producing commodities for the use of the state and its subdivisions.[2] The commission was given power to determine the cost and selling prices of all prison-made goods.[3] In addition to prescribing the state use system as the basis of the industrial organization of the above institutions, the act provided that the public account system might be utilized to supplement the state use system in disposing of surplus agricultural products, it having been provided that mechanical industry among the inmates of the institution should be supplemented by a development of "agricultural, horticultural, and floricultural pursuits."[4] State institutions were expressly forbidden to buy supplies not made in state institutions without the consent of the prison labor commission, and this consent could be granted only when the necessary articles were not produced by the labor of inmates of state institutions.[5] It was directed that due precaution be taken to insure that convict labor would not interfere with free labor.[6] It was enacted that, as a means of offering a pecuniary reward to industrious convicts and of aiding their families, a sum not to exceed 50 cents per day should be paid to the dependent families of inmates of the state prison and the state reformatory.[7]

Such were the chief terms of the sweeping act which abolished the legal basis for contract labor in the state prison of New Jersey. However, beyond the employment of convicts on road and

[1] Ibid., pp. 769-70.
[2] Ibid., p. 770.
[3] Ibid., p. 772.
[4] Ibid., p. 772.
[5] Ibid., p. 773.
[6] Ibid., p. 774.
[7] Ibid., p. 774. This clause has never been systematically executed.

farm work its provisions have never been carried out, though a considerable start in this direction has been made by the reformatory at Rahway. The act was not supplemented by the necessary appropriations for working capital with which to install the new state use system, and the influence of the contractors has been strong in retaining the contract system.[1]

The law of March 13, 1912, allowed the transfer of inmates of Rahway over thirty years of age to the state prison.[2]

The most important act of the session of 1912 was relative to the extra-mural employment of inmates of the state prison. This provided that the boards of freeholders of the counties could utilize the labor of county prisoners on county highways, and that the state commissioner of public roads might make use of the labor of the inmates of the state prison in building and repairing the state highways. The prison labor commission was to retain general control of the convicts so employed, and the discipline and custody of the prisoners were to be vested in the officers of the state prison.[3]

The act of April 1, 1912, permitted the pensioning of incapacitated employees of the state prison who possessed a record of twenty years of faithful service.[4]

Finally, the law of April 12, 1912, supplemented the parole act of June 14, 1898, by decreeing that all prisoners not previously convicted of felony, and who had served two-thirds of their sentence were eligible to apply for parole.[5]

Most of the acts relating to the state prison which were passed by the session of 1913 concerned the industrial organization of the prison.

The act of April 3, 1913, authorized the board of inspectors, upon a requisition of the prison labor commission, to transfer

---

[1] *Annual Report of the State Prison*, 1914, p. 16; *Preliminary Report of the Prison Inquiry Commission*, 1917, p. 10; Cf. C. L. Stonaker, *Prison Labor Reform in New Jersey*, in *Prison Labor*, edited by Whitin and Lichtenberger, 1913, pp. 154f.

[2] *Acts of the 136th Legislature*, 1912, p. 90.

[3] Ibid., p. 361.

[4] Ibid., p. 564.

[5] Ibid., pp. 769–70.

any number of prisoners requested from the state prison to lands acquired for agricultural purposes, to quarries, and to other points essential in the preparation of road building materials. The transferred prisoners were to remain in the custody of the prison officials, and were to receive the usual benefit of the law prescribing commutation of sentence for good behavior.[1]

The Act of April 9, 1913, authorized the prison labor commission to purchase as much land as it deemed wise for agricultural and quarrying purposes; to equip it with buildings, tools, and implements; and to transfer the needed prisoners to this land.[2]

The act of June 7, 1911, had allowed the completion of the existing contracts for the labor of the inmates of the state prison, but had forbidden the making of any new contracts. Those interested in perpetuating the contract system in the state prison secured the passage of the act of April 14, 1913, which allowed the extension and renewal of contracts for prison labor until provision was made for the employment of the prisoners according to the state use system.[3] As no appropriation was made for supplying the equipment needed for the installing of the state use system in the prison, this law, for all practical purposes, meant the suspension of the law of June 7, 1911.[4]

Another important act passed provided for the creation of a new parole board of April 14, 1913. This board was to be composed of the principal keeper, the resident physician, and the moral instructor of the state prison. It was authorized to parole all prisoners with a good record who had served one-third of their sentence, or, if life prisoners, had served fifteen years. The board was to exercise its own discretion as to whether such a prisoner could be released with safety to society. The term of parole, if its conditions were not violated, was to extend to the time set for the expiration of the sentence, the good time allowance being deducted. The paroled prisoners were to

[1] *Acts of the 137th Legislature,* 1913, p. 483–4.
[2] Ibid., pp. 589–90.
[3] Ibid., p. 789.
[4] *Annual Report of the State Prison,* 1914, p. 16.

remain under the custody of the keeper of the prison and subject to the inspection of the parole agent. If a paroled prisoner should violate the terms of his parole he was to be returned to the prison and compelled to serve out his sentence without any deduction of the time when out on parole.[1]

No year has even been more productive of important prison legislation in New Jersey than 1914.

An act of April 14, 1914, appropriated $10,000 for the equipment of the state prison farm at Leesburg.[2]

A law of April 15, 1914, amended the law of 1911 prescribing a maximum and minimum sentence, and transferred the parole power to the board of inspectors. It provided that for each person convicted a maximum and minimum sentence should be prescribed, the maximum to be the legal maximum prescribed in the penal code, and the minimum equal to from one year to two-thirds of the maximum term, at the discretion of the court. It was further provided that at each monthly meeting of the board of inspectors the principal keeper should submit to them a list of the prisoners who had served out their minimum sentence. The board of inspectors was authorized to parole such of these prisoners as, by their personal record and through a personal hearing before the board of inspectors, could convince the board of "their ability and purpose to live at liberty without violating the law." It was stipulated, however, that no prisoner could be paroled until suitable employment had been found for him. Such prisoners as had served their minimum sentence, but could not convince the board of their ability to be paroled with safety, might be re-examined at periods of from six to twelve months and could then be paroled, if their record justified such action. Paroled prisoners were to remain under surveillance of the parole agent until the expiration of their maximum sentence, unless pardoned.[3] The parole act of April 14, 1913, with which this act of 1914 conflicted, was repealed on April 20, 1914, but the parole power was not taken from the

[1] *Acts of the 137th Legislature,* 1913, pp. 765-7.
[2] *Acts of the 138th Legislature,* 1914, pp. 318-19.
[3] Ibid., pp. 429-32.

board of pardons.[1] This act of April 15, 1914, is the basis of the present parole system of the state prison of New Jersey.

The act of April 20, 1914, amended the act of June 7, 1911, and reconstructed the Prison Labor Commission. Hereafter, the prison labor commission was to be composed of the commissioner of charities and correction, a member of the board of inspectors of the state prison, a member of the governing commission of the state reformatory at Rahway, and three citizens to be appointed by the governor for a term of three years. The commission was directed to secure the most profitable employment possible of the inmates of penal, correctional, and reformatory institutions in "agricultural, horticultural, and floricultural pursuits." The law

[1] Ibid., p. 564. See below, p. 230 note.
The court of pardons originally had no connection with the parole power, as it originated at a period when such a procedure as paroling prisoners was unheard of in New Jersey. The constitution of New Jersey, adopted in 1844, in Article V, Section X, provided that the governor, chancellor, and the six judges of the court of appeals and errors were to constitute a board having the power to remit fines and forfeitures and to grant pardons. The act creating an actual court of pardons was passed on January 18, 1853, and stated that the above mentioned officers should meet at Trenton on the third day of every regular term of the court of appeals and errors and at such other times as the governor might direct. They were to constitute a court of pardons and had the power to commute the death penalty to a term of imprisonment. A majority of the court was to determine the action taken.. (Elmer–Nixon, *Digest*, 1868, p. 665.) The act of March 20, 1857, granted the court the power to pardon offences and to remit fines and forfeitures in any case. (Ibid., p. 665.) The above legal regulations were carried over unchanged in the revision of 1877. (*Revised Statutes*, 1877, p. 794.) The act of March 17, 1881, gave the person convicted the power to be heard by the court in person or by counsel. (*Supplement to the Revision of 1877*, p. 783.) The parole power was given to the court of pardons by the act of April 16, 1891. (*General Statutes of New Jersey*, 1895, p. 2419.) This power was retained by the act of June 14, 1898. (*Acts of the 122nd Legislature*, 1898, pp. 927–8.) While subsequent acts have given the parole power also to the variously created parole boards and, finally, to the board of inspectors of the state prison, the court of pardons still holds the parole power and exercises it more freely, and, apparently, more indiscriminately than the board of inspectors. (*Annual Report of the State Prison*, 1916, pp. 45–7.) The difficulty which has been encountered in trying to abolish the paroling powers of the court of pardons may in part be explained by the liberal allowance paid to the lay members of the court when sitting in this capacity. The court of pardons is at present made up of the governor, the chancellor, and the lay judges of the court of errors and appeals.

also directed the adoption of a wage system for the inmates of the state prison and the reformatory at Rahway, prescribing that the wages were to be used for the care of the dependents of the prisoners, for the benefit of the prisoners after release, and, up to $25, to reimburse the state for the cost of trying the individual.[1]

But by far the most important of all the acts relating to the state prison which were passed during 1914, and, for that matter, the most important act which had been passed regulating the government of the state prison since 1798, was that of April 20, 1914. Up to 1914 there had never been provided a centralized and authoritative control over the state prison, since the act of 1798 had been amended almost a century ago, so as to deprive the inspectors of their plenary powers over the state prison. The last systematization of the legal basis of the organization of the state prison had been the law of 1876, which itself had little more than restated the provisions of the acts of 1846 and 1869 and their amendments. By 1914 the creation of various commissions and boards had hopelessly confused the administration of the prison. In that year the State Charities Aid and Prison Reform Association of New Jersey, aided by some of the ablest lawyers in the state, undertook to frame a clear, concise, compact, and logical act to provide for the government of the state prison.[2] This act, with a few minor alterations, was passed on April 20, 1914, and provided the state with a generally satisfactory legal basis for the administration of the state prison, though it failed to provide for a proper co-ordination of the government of the prison and other reformatory and correctional institutions and did not, as interpreted, remove the paralyzing conflict of jurisdiction between the inspectors and the Prison Labor Commission in regard to the control of the prison industries.

[1] *Acts of the 138th Legislature,* 1914, pp. 562-4. This payment of wages was never put in force at the state prison until in the summer of 1917, and then its benefits were practically abrogated by the rules of the inspectors ordering a reduction of the payment upon discharge from $25 to $5.

[2] *The New Jersey Review of Charities and Corrections,* January, 1914, pp. 1-3.

The act was described as one "defining the state prison and providing for the government and regulation thereof, and providing for the control and management of persons committed thereto." [1]   The act declared that the state prison "shall be taken to include the present existing prison in the city of Trenton, and any and all State farms, camps, quarries or grounds where convicts sentenced to the State Prison may be kept, housed, or employed." [2]

It was enacted that the "exclusive management" of the state prison should be vested in a board of inspectors, consisting of six members appointed by the governor with the consent of the senate for a term of six years, three members always to be from each major political party.[3]   The inspectors were to receive a salary of $500 per year and their expenses, and were required to hold monthly meetings at the state prison and other special meetings upon the call of the president of the board or of three of its members.[4]   The board of inspectors was vested with full authority to make all rules and regulations for the government of the prison and for the control of all officials and employees thereof.[5]   The board was further authorized to control the general policy of the state prison, to determine the number of officers and subordinates to be employed, and to fix their compensation.[6]

The keeper, appointed, as provided by the constitution of 1897, by the governor and the senate for a term of five years, was designated as the chief executive officer of the prison.   While this law could not prescribe the mode of appointing the keeper it could and did define and limit his powers.   It was provided that the keeper should be responsible to the board of inspectors for the "conduct and management of the state prison, under such rules and regulations as they shall from time to time provide." [7]

---

[1] *Acts of the 138th Legislature*, 1914, p. 565.
[2] Ibid.
[3] Ibid.
[4] Ibid., pp. 565–6.
[5] Ibid., p. 566.
[6] Ibid.
[7] Ibid., p. 567.

The keeper was authorized to appoint the subordinate officials and employees of the prison, subject to the approval of the board of inspectors.[1] It was, then, clearly and expressly stated that in all matters of administration and management of the prison, the keeper of the prison was on all points subordinate to the board of inspectors.

The act decreed that the office of supervisor, created in 1869, should be abolished, and that the supervisor should be superseded by a steward or *Fiscal Agent,* who should be the purchasing agent of the prison and perform such other duties as might be required by the inspectors.[2] The prison labor commission had taken over many of the original functions of the supervisor, and it was logical that, having relinquished many of his industrial duties, the supervisor should be replaced by another officer whose duties were generally limited to a control of the domestic economics and finances of the prison.

All of the acts passed in 1915 which concerned the state prison were of minor importance.

An act of April 8, 1915, permitted the principal keeper to serve meals to the board of inspectors or the court of pardons at the expense of the state.[3] The laws forbidding this procedure had been passed years before when it was alleged that the keeper was trying to establish his reputation as a "good fellow" with the board of inspectors at the expense of the state.[4]

The act of April 6, 1915, allowed the board of inspectors to use as much as was necessary of the appropriation of $20,000 to improve the equipment of the state prison farm at Leesburg.[5]

The law of April 12, 1915, allowed the transfer of female inmates of the penal, reformatory, and correctional institutions of the state from one institution to another, subject to the general

[1] Ibid.
[2] Ibid.
[3] *Acts of the 139th Legislature,* 1915, p. 457.
[4] See *Acts of the 79th Legislature,* 1855, pp. 647–8; *Acts of the 100th Legislature,* 1876, p. 262.
[5] *Acts of the 139th Legislature,* 1915, pp. 327–8.

laws governing commitments to these institutions. It was designed to facilitate desirable transfers between the state prison, the reformatory for women at Clinton, and the state home for girls at Trenton.[1]

The act of April 14, 1915, designated the official visitors of the prison and gave the board of inspectors the right to decide upon the other visitors and to determine the rules governing their admission.[2]

Finally, the act of April 23, 1915, decreed that the parole agent should be one of the deputies of the state prison, appointed by the principal keeper, with the approval of the board of inspectors. It was directed that the parole officer should make a personal investigation of the conduct of every paroled prisoner and that paroled prisoners should make periodic reports of their whereabouts. If any prisoner should violate the terms of his parole the board of inspectors were authorized to revoke the parole and cause the return of the violator to the prison.[3] If the parole power had been taken from the court of pardons, this act of 1915, together with that of April 15, 1914, would constitute a fairly adequate system for the state prison, though one parole officer can never be adequate to the task of inspecting the conduct of more than one thousand paroled prisoners.[4]

Nothing of special significance was enacted by the legislature of 1916 in regard to the state prison.

An act of March 21, 1916, amended the act of June 7, 1911, regulating the labor of the prison. It provided that when requested by the proper authorities the state treasurer should pay to the various state institutions the sums appropriated for their working capital to be applied under bond. It further directed that in determining the wages to be paid to prisoners, the maximum wage should be the difference between the cost of maintaining the prisoner and the proceeds from the sale of his manu-

[1] Ibid., pp. 474–5.
[2] Ibid., pp. 536–7.
[3] Ibid., pp. 743–4.
[4] See below, p. 230 note.

factured products. It also called for a monthly statement of the accounts of each institution.[1]

An act of March 29, 1916, ordered that the death penalty be retained for murder in the first degree, unless the jury should fix the penalty at life imprisonment.[2]

3. PRISON INDUSTRY.

While the changes in the legislation regulating prison labor have been more sweeping in the period between 1911 and 1917 than in any other period of equal length since 1858–61 and 1881–4, the actual changes in the industrial organization of the prison have been much less thorough-going than the governing legislation would indicate.

The Osborne Bill of June 7, 1911, described in detail above, in treating the legislation during this period which related to the state prison, abolished contract labor from a legal standpoint as completely as the law of February 21, 1884. But in the same way that the act of April 18, 1884, allowed a perpetuation of the contract system through the subterfuge of the "piece-price" system, so the law of April 14, 1913, permitted the continuation of the "piece-price" system by allowing the existing contracts to be extended. Again, in the same way that the "piece-price" system was a benefit to the contractor in 1884, as compared with the older contract system, so the extension of the existing contracts, allowed by the law of 1913, was advantageous to the contractors as compared with the former practice of renewing contracts. By obtaining the privilege of extending contracts upon the terms agreed upon years before, the contractors were able to profit by the very considerable rise in the cost of labor and of raw material in the last few years, while the prison suffered a corresponding loss.[3] At the same

[1] *Acts of the 140th Legislature*, 1916, pp. 511–12. The actual wages paid to the prisoners since July, 1917, when payment began, have been 2½ cents per day.

[2] Ibid., p. 576.

[3] *Annual Report of the State Prison*, 1916, p. 5; see above, p. 182.

time it can scarcely be denied that the granting of the privilege of extending the contracts was the wisest thing which could have been done under the circumstances, until some provision had been made by the state for working capital.

When the contract system was legally abolished in 1911, with the exception that the existing contracts might be carried out, the legislature made no adequate appropriation for working capital wherewith to install the "state use" system.[1] Therefore, it was not surprising that even those opposed to the contract system should advise its continuance until the state should have made provision for the real and business-like adoption of the "state use" system. At the same time, it is not difficult to fix the responsibility in a general way for this evasion of the law abolishing contract labor and for the failure to adopt the "state use" system. It is clear that the responsibility rests chiefly upon the legislature which decreed a change without making any provision for its successful execution either as to adequate funds, or with respect to clearly defined administrative powers and agencies.

The following paragraphs summarize briefly the chief phases of the conflict of jurisdiction, which has done so much to paralyze the efforts to introduce the state-use system in New Jersey:

When, after strong opposition, the bill to abolish the contracts and to provide for the state-use system was finally passed in June, 1911, the opposition attempted to win over Governor Wilson to a veto of the proposed measure. The Governor gave a public hearing on the bill and indicated at that time that he was heartily in favor of throwing out all contracts. He later signed the bill and his subsequent actions likewise plainly revealed the fact that he was strongly in favor of the change.

He appointed the members of the new Prison Labor Commission and urged them to make a study of the situation and find a way to employ the prisoners in some other manner than through contracts. Although no appropriation had been provided for this commission, several members at their own ex-

[1] Ibid., 1911, pp. 31–2; 1912, p. 30; 1913, pp. 11–13; 1914, p. 16.

pense toured about the country to gather information on the subject.

Their first report was made in December, 1912. The commission first recommended the purchase of from 1,000 to 2,000 acres of unimproved land in Cumberland county, an option for which had been obtained by the commission by their personal word that they would undertake to secure the money from the next Legislature. Next, it recommended the purchase of a farm along the Delaware river where a ledge of trap rock was found. Here a quarry might be opened where crushed stone for road building could be obtained.

The commission suggested that some legislation be provided to relieve the keeper at the prison from personal liability for escapes of prisoners employed on the farm or the proposed quarry and road work, and the custody of such prisoners be placed with the Prison Labor Commission. In short, this commission believed that all the prisoners available for outside work could be removed from the prison.

For those prisoners who must be kept at the prison, in addition to the work in upkeep, the commission suggested manufactures on state account to include shoes, clothing, underclothing, socks, stockings, blankets, brooms, brushes, mats, mattresses and beds. It also urged that a school be established at the farm.

The Legislature of 1913 provided $21,000 for the purchase of the farm near Leesburg, for which purchase an option had been secured, and the commission in its second annual report announced that in the previous August a tract of 1,009 acres had been secured. At the time of the report, forty prisoners were on the farm clearing land for spring farming. They were living in the remodeled farm house and were repairing the existing buildings for use. Clay deposits were announced as having been found on the land suitable for brick-making, and the commission proposed making brick at once for permanent structures on the farm. It is interesting to note that the clay yet remains undisturbed and all buildings so far have been constructed of wood. The report of road building included the description of the opening of the Andover Road Camp in Sussex county with 30 prisoners and the Rocky Hill Road Camp with 15 prisoners, both under the control of the State Highway Department. The report contained numerous suggestions for the future and urged the purchase of another tract of land in Cumberland county.

Meanwhile the Legislature was besieged by factions working in diverse direction on the whole subject of the prison and prison labor, and it was apparent that the then existing Board of Prison Inspectors were not in spirit with the program of the reform element. Subsequent events indicated that they were doing all they could quietly to show the whole matter of farm, road and state-use labor to be an impossible undertaking.

The Legislature by joint resolution in 1912 provided for a Convict Labor Commission. It was to be non-partisan and to consist of eight members. Yet the specifications were: two Republican members of the legislature, the Commissioner of Charities and Correction, the Secretary of the State Board of Health, the Commissioner of Roads, the Keeper of the Prison, and two representatives of the Federation of Labor. The Governor by this resolution was to "instruct said commission to formulate a comprehensive plan for the initiation and use of the labor of all convicts on the public roads, in public parks, in forestry and in such other ways to the public benefit, not in competition with free labor, as may suggest themselves, and to report said plan together with recommendations."

As was the case with the Prison Labor Commission of the previous year, this Convict Labor Commission was not provided with an appropriation, and it evidently did nothing of importance other than to submit a perfunctory report in March of the following year, which report was filed away and soon forgotten.

This Convict Labor Commission in this report endorsed the program of the Prison Labor Commission and urged the extension of out-door work for convicts, and recommended a similar program for the counties in handling the county jail population.

In view of the reports of these two commissions, and the report of the Inspectors for the preceding year, and with the knowledge that the keeper, Mr. Madden, was fighting for his alleged constitutional rights to ignore everybody both inspectors and commissions, the State Charities Aid and Prison Reform Association in the summer of 1913 undertook to clear the atmosphere by planning legislation that would definitely fix responsibility and the result was the passage on April 20, 1914, of the new state prison law which was designed to settle the whole question of authority by placing the entire management of the prison and the prisoners under the control of the Inspectors. This naturally required a change in the law relating to the Prison Labor Commission, which, up to that time, had been managing the farm, while the State Commissioner of Roads was employing the prisoners in the camps, and Keeper Madden was holding strongly to his responsibility for the safe-guarding of all prisoners by placing numerous guards at the camps and on the farm.[1]

In 1914, the original Prison Labor Commission was abolished and the new Prison Labor Commission came in under the new law. This new commission has made three annual reports, published as the third, fourth and fifth annual reports. It is generally known that there were many difficulties to be overcome, and much friction was encountered, for the Inspectors appeared to adhere to their general policy of antipathy to every movement seeking to abolish the contracts that were running on under a practically indefinite extension. The knitting shop for state use purposes was set up at the prison, and the Rahway reformatory went ahead in state use manufactures. The Prison Labor Commission found at Rahway that honest and earnest support of all their efforts, which never seemed obtainable by them at the prison.

Just as the Inspectors were beginning to realize that they must accept as permanent the farm and road work program, and just as Keeper Madden was "coming into line" and generally agreeing with the new situation, his death occurred in April, 1916. Mr. Richard P. Hughes, a banker of Florence, was appointed to fill the unexpired term, and he came to the prison without prison experience or knowledge of the complicated situation. He met

[1] See above, pp. 215–218.

a cold reception at the hands of the Inspectors, and his short term of service was beset with many difficulties which resulted in turmoil at its close.

In his final message to the Legislature, Governor Fielder severely criticized the prison conditions and offered some suggestions including the recommendation of other governors regarding the return of the State Arsenal grounds to prison use. Upon the subject of prison labor he said: "I am not satisfied that it is wise to discontinue the making of prison labor contracts", and this was followed by his reasons for such a reactionary statement. He then concluded: "If, however, the Legislature believes that these contracts should be terminated, it must do more than pass a law to that effect. It must provide ample funds to enable the prison authorities to set up other branches of work for the prisoners."

The subject of wages to prisoners, which was provided for in the 1911 act, had been one of the chief causes of unrest among the prisoners and was one of the underlying causes for the disturbances which soon followed the statements made by Governor Fielder in his message discussing that phase of the prison problem. This message was delivered on January 9, 1917, and when Governor Edge made his inaugural address on the 16th, he also spoke of the unsatisfactory conditions at the prison, and concluded with these words:

"In brief, there is necessity for harmonizing the conflicting opinions and views upon this question and obtaining speedy legislative action for the purpose not only of solving the prison reform problem, but, also, of reorganizing and placing on a sound business basis the management and care of public institutions of a charitable and correctional nature."[1]

But whatever the causes for the difficulties in ousting the contract system and for the failure of the "state use" system, there

[1] This summary has been based upon manuscript and documentary material placed at the disposal of the writer by Mr. C. L. Stonaker. A more detailed analysis of the work of the Prison Labor Commission, and of the conflict of jurisdiction, is to be found in the treatment of Prison Labor in New Jersey by Mr. Paul Kennaday, which is published an an appendix to the *Report of the Prison Inquiry Commission,* 1917.

can be no doubt of the reality of the failure of this proposed organization of the industry of the state prison. The first attempt to make a feeble beginning of the "state use" system did not come until 1915, when a small knitting plant was installed which would not employ more than 25 operators. Even this feeble "infant industry" was paralyzed by a conflict of powers between the Board of Inspectors and the Prison Labor Commission, which resulted in a ruinous schedule of prices.[1] In other words, after six years, the industrial situation, in its general aspects, within the prison walls was, until the summer of 1917, in practically the same condition as it was before the passage of the law of June 7, 1911.

Strange as it may seem, therefore, it is to the law of 1910 and subsequent laws permitting the employment of prison labor in extra-mural occupations, rather than to the formidable appearing and well-meaning law of 1911, that one must look for the legal basis of the most sweeping changes in the industrial organization of the prisoners since 1911. The condition of industry within the prison has remained practically unchanged, but a very great transformation has been accomplished by transferring a considerable number of prisoners to centers of employment outside the prison walls. In this development the year 1913 was truly epoch-making. On June 23, 1913, the first prison road camp was opened at Andover in Sussex County. On September 2, 1913, a second road camp was organized at Rocky Hill in Mercer County. On September 15, 1913, a state prison farm of 1,000 acres was obtained near Leesburg in Cumberland County.[2] Two years later a third road camp was opened in Salem County to work on the Elmer-Malaga road.[3]

These new avenues of employing the convict labor of the state, while they have not resulted in any considerable financial gain, have been very beneficial in a hygienic and reformatory sense, and have served to relieve the overcrowded condition of the state prison. Even in a financial sense these extra-mural in-

---

[1] *Annual Report of the State Prison,* 1916, pp. 1–3.

[2] Ibid., 1914, pp. 7–8. Cf. *Annual Report of the State Charities Aid and Prison Reform Association,* 1915, pp. 21–4.

[3] *Annual Report of the State Prison,* 1915.

dustrial centers have proved much more satisfactory than have the prison industries within the walls since 1874. The road camps in 1916 nearly met their expenses, including the salaries of the deputies detailed to retain them in custody and maintain discipline, while within the prison the gross expenses were almost exactly treble the receipts.[1] Even the state farm, while it has been a heavy loss as yet, possesses promises for the future. It consisted at the outset mainly of waste land, and when this shall have been reclaimed and put under cultivation, or sold, the farm may become a paying proposition. The increased value of the reclaimed land has not as yet appeared in the balance sheet.[2]

The present state of the prison industry and finances is revealed by the report of the state prison of 1916. In this year the total disbursements, including salaries, were $349,866, and the total receipts $116,172, leaving a net loss of $233,694.[3] The industrial distribution of the prison population for 1916 was as follows:[4]

State use system (knitting)	20
Farm work	112
Road work	103
Making men's suits	4
Making men's shoes	4
Printing	2
Identification bureau	2
Bedding and dresses	20
Prison purposes	252
Piece-price or contract	592
Incapacitated for labor	114
Total	1,225

[1] *Annual Report of the State Prison,* 1916, pp. 27, 30–32.

[2] Ibid., pp. 6, 8–9, 30–31. The buying of this waste land for a prison farm was doubtless a survival from the treadmill stage of prison industry which stressed the element of labor rather than income or useful training.

[3] The total loss in 1911 was $178,586; 1912, $184,525; 1913, $187,024; 1914, $236,909; 1915, $253,415; 1916, $233,694.

[4] *Annual Report of the State Prison,* 1916, p. 24. This was the situation on October 31, 1916. In October, 1917, the total prison population was 1,051. Of this number 294 were employed in extra-mural activities; 256 were engaged as domestics; 103 were incapacitated for continuous labor; and 398 were still employed on the "piece-price" contracts.

The prison farm was the greatest relative loss of any of the prison industries, the total expense being $25,466 and the total receipts only $6,894.[1] It must be remembered, however, that much of the labor expended on the farm in reclaiming land was not considered in the balance sheet. Within the prison walls the loss was relatively about as great, the expenditures for maintenance and salaries being more than three times as large as the receipts from the prison industries.[2] The road camps approached the nearest to being a financial success. Camp No. 1 at Andover sustained a loss of $2,129, as compared with a revenue of $10,935. Camp No. 2 at Rocky Hill lost only $423 and received a revenue of $11,683. Camp No. 3 on the Elmer-Malaga road sustained a net loss of $2,875 and had a revenue of $8,222.[3] There seems some hope, then, that the road-making industry may prove a method whereby a part of the prison population can meet its expenses.

Very limited application has been made of the provision of the law of April 20, 1914, permitting the payment of wages to industrious prisoners. No real application was made of the authorization until the summer of 1917, when two and one-half cents per day were paid, and even then its benefits were practically eliminated by reducing the amount paid on discharge from $25 to $5, the loss of this $20 being practically equal to the wages for three years, the average term of prisoners before parole.

IV. The Attempts to Improve Penal Administration,
1911–17.

1. CONDITION OF THE PHYSICAL EQUIPMENT.

There was little done during this period to provide an architectural basis for better prison administration. With the exception of the wings built and reconstructed by the appropriations of

[1] *Annual Report of the State Prison,* 1916, pp. 30–31
[2] Ibid., pp. 22–28.
[3] Ibid., p. 32.

PLATE III. The New Jersey State Prison, 1917.

1895 and 1905 and accommodating about 500 convicts, the physical equipment for housing convicts in the state prison remains hopelessly antiquated and very unhealthy.[1] But even these partially unhygienic quarters were seriously overcrowded by 1911. In 1912, Keeper Madden called attention to the fact that the brief respite from overcrowding which the prison had enjoyed for a few years after 1907, when the new cell block was opened, had then passed. He pointed out the fact that he was compelled to confine an average prison population of 1,460 in about 1,200 cells, nearly half of which had been constructed in the decade of the Civil War, or before.[2] He also made it plain that the yard room was as cramped as the cell facilities. The men employed in the prison shops and housed at night in the crowded conditions just described, where two men occupied a cell with a floor space of five by seven feet, had but a half-hour for exercise on Saturday afternoon because of the limited yard room available.[3] The only thing which has saved New Jersey from being compelled to add a new and expensive cell block has been the gradual migration of the prison population outside the walls through the opening up of road camps and the prison farm, and a more liberal use of the parole system. At the close of 1916 there were confined in the state prison about 1,000 prisoners, something like half of whom could be housed in relatively modern cells.[4]

2. IMPROVEMENTS IN PENAL ADMINISTRATION.

The very essential reformatory function of penal procedure has been notably advanced in New Jersey since 1911, but is still far from satisfactory.

The maximum and minimum sentence laws of April 21, 1911, and April 15, 1914, provided for the "minimum" aspects of an indeterminate sentence system, but failed entirely in providing

---

[1] *Annual Report of the State Prison*, 1912, p. 43; 1916, pp. 40–41; *Preliminary Report of the Prison Inquiry Commission*, 1917, pp. 5–6.

[2] Ibid., 1912, pp. 8, 42.

[3] Ibid., pp. 42–3.

[4] *Annual Report of the State Prison*, 1916, p. 20.

for an adequate "maximum," which, of course, should be nothing short of the natural life of such degenerate recidivists as require permanent segregation.

The parole system in New Jersey is far from adequate and properly centralized. It should be vested wholly in one competent board of parole, probably, as provided in the law of 1914, in the board of inspectors. This power should no longer be shared by the court of pardons, which should be limited wholly to the pardoning function.[1] Again, as Keeper Osborne pointed out in his last annual report, that of 1911, there is a great need for a more extensive and scientific system of grading and meriting in the state prison, so that the parole board will have more reliable data at hand upon which to render intelligent decision as to cases worthy of parole.[2] There is little evidence that any such mechanism has been provided, and the action of the parole boards and the court of pardons has continued to be largely a matter of routine and haphazard judgments. No parole board should be asked to grant a decision in a case of application for parole until it is furnished with an adequate record of the personal history of the applicant, of his conduct while in prison, and of the results of a rigid neurological and psychiatric examination of the individual prisoner in question. Furthermore, it is painfully obvious that one parole agent or officer is not sufficient to exercise any adequate supervision of the conduct of all the paroled prisoners, which on October 31, 1916, numbered 1,251. While care must be taken to avoid so rigid a supervision as to approximate inquisitorial interference with those who are making an honest attempt at personal reformation, it is equally essential that steps be taken so that the parole does not practically mean discharge from the prison.[3]

[1] The parole and pardoning machinery of New Jersey has been recently further complicated by the law of March 16, 1914, which authorizes a sentencing judge to recall a prisoner, reopen his case, and, if the judge desires to do so, resentence or discharge the prisoner.

[2] *Annual Report of the State Prison*, 1911, pp. 10–11.

[3] These needs in regard to a transformation of the parole system at the state prison are clearly indicated in the Annual Report of the *State Charities Aid and Prison Reform Association*, 1916, pp. 33–4. Cf. *Preliminary Report of the Prison Inquiry Commission*, 1917, p. 12.

The opening of the reformatory for women at Clinton Farms in 1913 completed the list of institutions necessary for even the most elementary differentiation and treatment of the delinquent population of the state. The lack of mandatory provision for the commitment of the proper classes to these institutions, however, is a serious omission and gives too wide a leeway to arbitrariness or carelessness on the part of the judiciary.

In the provision for the religious and educational facilities at the state prison nothing of importance has taken place since 1911, except the addition of a third or Hebrew moral instructor in 1912. The prison school, created by the act of 1907, has been in continuous operation since that date, but has been fatally hampered by a lack of teachers, proper school rooms, and other facilties needed for any adequate organization of the educational system of such an institution as the state prison.[1]

The necessity for the establishment of a modern and scientific psychopathic clinic at the state prison for the neurological and psychiatric examination and classification of those confined in, and those admitted to, the institution was recommended in an able statement by Keeper Hughes in 1916.[2] To attempt to handle the problem of criminality without providing for a complete utilization of the advances in modern abnormal psychology, such as the Binet-Simon and other tests for feeble-mindedness and even more important, the Freudian analysis of the neuroses and the psychoses, is equivalent to attempting to practice modern medicine without making any application of the discoveries of Morton, Lister, Koch, or Pasteur. The Binet-Simon test and the Freudian theory of the neuroses are rocks upon which the old theological dogmas of "free will" and the "free moral agent" have been hopelessly disintegrated. The psychopathic clinic, recently established at Sing Sing Prison in New York State under the direction of Dr. Bernard Glueck, is an indication of what is

[1] *Preliminary Report of the Prison Inquiry Commission,* 1917, p. 5.
[2] *Annual Report of the State Prison,* 1916, pp. 41–2.

likely to be the most notable advance in criminology and penology in the next quarter of a century.[1]

As regards the legal basis of the management of the state prison, there is little doubt that the law of 1914, vesting the full control of the state prison and all its appendages in the board of inspectors, is adequate to handle the local situation, once the conflict of jurisdiction with the Prison Labor Commission is adjusted. What is needed is to end the legal quibbling over the constitutionality and intent of the act and secure its complete operation. It will then be possible to place full responsibility for all failures in management, in so far as these are not the direct result of the inadequate and archaic physical equipment at the disposal of the board of inspectors.

3. GENERAL MOVEMENTS FOR PENAL REFORM.

Until practically the close of this period there were no general public commissions for the improvement of the penal situation in New Jersey after the Commission on Dependency and Crime of 1908 had completed its work. Most of the reform legislation was secured as the result of the agitation by public spirited individuals and by such private reform associations as the State Charities Aid and Prison Reform Association of New Jersey. In January, 1917, there was appointed, as a result of the resolution of the Legislature on the 22nd of that month, a Prison Inquiry Commission of five persons, which was authorized to "investigate into the conditions of the penal, reformatory, and correctional institutions of this State, and also into what is known as the 'State Use System,' and the employment of prisoners on roads, prison farms, or in other capacities."

It was further resolved that "The Commission shall report to the present session of the Legislature the results of its research, and with such recommendations as it may deem advisable."

[1] Cf. Coriat, *Abnormal Psychology;* Goddard, *Feeble-Mindedness,* and *The Criminal Imbecile;* Healy, *Mental Conflicts and Misconduct;* Glueck, *Forensic Psychiatry;* Brill, *Psychoanalysis;* Adler, *The Neurotic Constitution;* Pfister, *The Psycholanalytical Method;* Hitschmann, *Freud's Theories of the Neuroses;* and Jones, *Papers on Psychoanalysis.*

The Commission presented its "Preliminary Report" on February 12, 1917, and requested an extension of time before submitting its final conclusions and recommendations. This request was granted by the Legislature and the Commission was directed to report on or before January 1, 1918.

V. GENERAL SUMMARY.

The attempts of New Jersey to establish a successful state prison system have now been passed in review. It has been shown that all of these attempts have unquestionably been failures. A number of influences have contributed to this general result. The legislature has been apathetic and reluctant to enact the necessary legislation. When the essential legislation has been tardily enacted, the prison officials have generally, for one cause or another, failed to execute the laws. Political considerations have also interfered in withholding necessary legislation, in determining the selection of prison officials, and in the shaping of prison industry in the interest of contractors with political connections rather than in the interests of the state. But all of these factors are but symptoms of a more *fundamental disorder in the social mind.* Society does not permit "slip-shod" methods or personal favoritism in those realms and phases of activity where the interests of society are clearly understood to be vitally involved. The fundamental difficulty in the past has been that society has not understood the nature of the causation of crime and has believed that its interests were at an end when the prison gates were closed upon the offender and the revenge of society was thereby inflicted. When it can be made clear that the interests of the community extend to securing the ultimate reformation or permanent segregation of the offender, then society will no longer permit inefficiency and corruption to dominate the administration of the penal system. The cause, then, of the failure of the prison system of New Jersey, in common with that of practically every other state in the country, is simply one manifestation of the indescribable tardiness of the evolution of social intelligence and the almost unbelievable inertia in the public mind.

This does not mean that society must await the slow and costly method of allowing itself to be further enlightened solely by the tedious process of trial and error, but it does mean that permanent reform of penal methods can only come when accompanied by a program of public education as to the need and justification of such action.

CHAPTER VII

THE ORIGIN AND DEVELOPMENT OF THE STATE HOME FOR BOYS AT JAMESBURG

CHAPTER VII

THE ORIGIN AND DEVELOPMENT OF THE STATE HOME FOR BOYS AT JAMESBURG.

I. General Tendencies in the Development of the Institution.
II. The Legal History of the State Home for Boys.
III. The Chief Phases of the Industrial History.
IV. General Survey of the Development of the Management, Administration, and Physical Equipment.

I. GENERAL TENDENCIES IN THE DEVELOPMENT OF THE INSTITUTION.

The State Home for Boys, or, as it was called before 1900, the State Reform School for Juvenile Offenders, which was founded in 1865 and opened in 1867, chiefly through the efforts of Governor Joel Parker and other liberal and enlightened public and private philanthropists and reformers, marked an important stage in the development of penal, correctional, and reformatory institutions in the state of New Jersey. It was the second great step in that fundamental process of the differentiated treatment of the delinquent and defective classes, upon which the whole hope of future progress in the reform and scientific administration of penal, reformatory and correctional institutions depends. The first had been the building of a state prison, which had provided for a differentiation between the treatment of those convicted of serious crimes and those either awaiting trial or convicted of minor offences. Now, for the first time, an institution was provided which would allow of the segregation and relatively scientific treatment of that large class of delinquent minors who had previously been confined in the depressing and non-reformatory environment of the state prison or the even more demoralizing surroundings of the county jails, or had been allowed to remain at liberty to the danger and detriment of the community and the individual delinquent. Of course, it did not provide for the proper investigation, classification, and differentiation of the causes of juvenile delinquency and the proper treatment of each special type according to the needs in the case, but, as far as it went, the establishment of the institution at Jamesburg and the corresponding one at Trenton for delinquent girls, constituted a new epoch in the history of New Jersey penology.

An adequate account of the origin of the State Home for Boys goes back far beyond 1865, when it was legally established. Even as early as during the period of the first state prison, there were frequent complaints regarding the impropriety of sending young first termers and minor offenders to the state prison.[1] The famous committee of 1830 on prison discipline had complained of the disastrous effects of committing the young offenders to the prison, and had dwelt at length upon the cruel punishment often meted out to the boys in the prison, and the New Jersey Howard Society in 1833–4 made an eloquent appeal for the provision of an institution for the reformation of criminals under eighteen years of age.[2] From 1830 to 1850 there were frequent demands for the provision of an institution for delinquent minors, or, as it was called at that time, a "House of Refuge." It was one of the chief aims of the Prison Reform Association of 1849–52 to provide a juvenile reformatory for New Jersey.[3] By 1850 the agitation had become so vigorous that an act was passed authorizing the construction of a "House of Refuge" at Kingston.[4] Work was begun on this institution, and it was partially completed when, unfortunately, its construction was made a political issue and it was abandoned, greatly to the disgust of the advocates of prison reform in New Jersey.[5]

[1] *Votes of the Assembly,* 42nd Assembly, 1817, pp. 36, 80–81, 176–7.

[2] Report cited, in *Votes of the Assembly,* 54th General Assembly, 1830, pp. 179–80. *Ninth Annual Report of the Boston Prison Discipline Society* 1834, p. 85.

[3] *Constitution of the Prison Reform Association of New Jersey,* 1849, p. 3. *Memorial of the Prison Reform Association of New Jersey to the Senate and General Assembly,* January 25, 1850, pp. 5–6; *Annual Report of the Prison Reform Association of New Jersey,* 1852, p. 4. See Documents, Part II, pp. 485–8.

[4] *Acts of the 74th Legislature,* 1850, pp. 125–7.

[5] *Minutes of the Assembly,* 1851, pp. 463–72, 496–502. *Appendix to the Senate Journal,* 1852, pp. 405–9. 27th *Annual Report of the Prison Discipline Society of Boston,* 1852, p. 129. See Documents, Part II, pp. 569–79.

The need for such an institution, however, was so great that the agitation begun in the "fifties" never entirely subsided, and in 1864 the matter was taken up by Governor Joel Parker, who vigorously recommended the immediate provision of a suitable reformatory for juvenile delinquents.[1] The legislature acted on the governor's suggestions, and, by the resolution of March 29, 1864, created a Commission on the Reform of Juvenile Offenders and on an appropriate institution for their treatment.[2]

The commission made an elaborate investigation of the existing institutions for the reform of juvenile delinquents in the United States and Europe. They presented a voluminous report summarizing their results, and this report, in addition to being an excellent source of information as to the development of institutions of this sort at the time of the Civil War, was also one of the chief agencies in inducing the legislature to pass the act of April 6, 1865, creating the State Reform School at Jamesburg. The proposals submitted by these commissioners were, in fact, the basis for the drafting of the act.[3]

In its report the commission gave the following reasons for selecting the farm school as preferable to the "house of refuge" type of institution:

"Our reasons for preferring the farm school to the house of refuge are, briefly, that the former develops the bodily and mental powers naturally and healthfully; the varied influences of agricultural life being far more elevating and ennobling than those of the workshop. But above all do we prefer it because of its freedom from that ignominious restraint of grate and lock which sickens the heart of many refuge boys and impels them to risk their lives in efforts at escape though surrounded by comforts, advantages and opportunities unknown to them before."[4]

The circular sent by this commission to the different counties in New Jersey, as well as to the keeper of the state prison, revealed the serious need of such an institution and also made clear

[1] *Annual Message of the Governor,* 1864, pp. 11–12. See above, p. 130.
[2] *Acts of the 88th Legislature,* 1864, p. 773.
[3] *Acts of the 89th Legislature,* 1865, pp. 886–893. *Report of the Commissioners on the Reform of Juvenile Offenders,* in *Legislative Documents of the State of New Jersey,* 1865, Document No. 13. See Documents, Part II, pp. 579–88.
[4] Report cited, p. 10.

how little the limited capacity of the Reform School was able to deal with the problem of juvenile delinquency in New Jersey.[1]

In their report for 1866, the board of trustees of the new State Reform School thus described the main phases of the origin of the institution:

"The trustees of the State Reform School for Juvenile Offenders respectfully report that immediately on the passage and approval of the law of March 21, 1866, placing additional means at their disposal, the Board proceeded to the selection of a farm, and shortly after purchased one of 490 acres in Middlesex County, lying about two miles from Jamesburg, on the high land east of the village.

"In this purchase we think the requirements of the law have been complied with. The location is central and of convenient access from all parts of the State, by the Camden and Amboy and Freehold Railroads, the latter of which crosses the former at Jamesburg, and connects with the Trenton and New Brunswick Railroad at Monmouth Junction, while its extension from Freehold to Squakum will connect it with the marl region, and with the Delaware and Raritan Bay Road.

"The site is elevated and healthy, and commands a fine view of distant hills in almost every direction.

"The buildings can be abundantly supplied with pure water by a hydraulic ram which has been in use for a number of years.

"The soil is good and varies from heavy loam adapted to potatoes, wheat and grass to light truck land, the former of which predominates.

"After considerable thought and consultation with persons experienced with similar institutions, especially with Acting Commissioner G. E. Howe of the Ohio Reform School, the trustees agreed upon a plan for building which was approved by the Board of Control.

"Attempts were made to have it executed by contract, but the offers were at prices which were beyond the means at our command. We at length concluded to reduce the size of the proposed building and to erect it by employing mechanics under the supervision of a competent builder. We have, therefore, put up a brick building, 65 x 37 feet, three stories high, with a shallow basement cemented for kitchen, dining-room, etc. It is now covered with a substantial slate roof, the floors are laid, and the inside work is going on. A tower on the West front contains the principal stairway and will be valuable for ventilation.

"The building is expected to be ready for occupancy in the early Spring. It is calculated to accommodate the superintendent, and other officers, and 50 inmates. The trustees propose, as soon as necessary arrangements can be made, to have smaller buildings, each with its class or family of 30 boys, and a judicious man and his wife as the paternal caretakers; the several families to be united in chapel and in a common graded school."[2]

[1] Ibid., p. 41–44.
[2] Report cited, in *Legislative Documents of the State of New Jersey*, 1867, pp. 414, 415. See photograph of the original building opposite page 256.

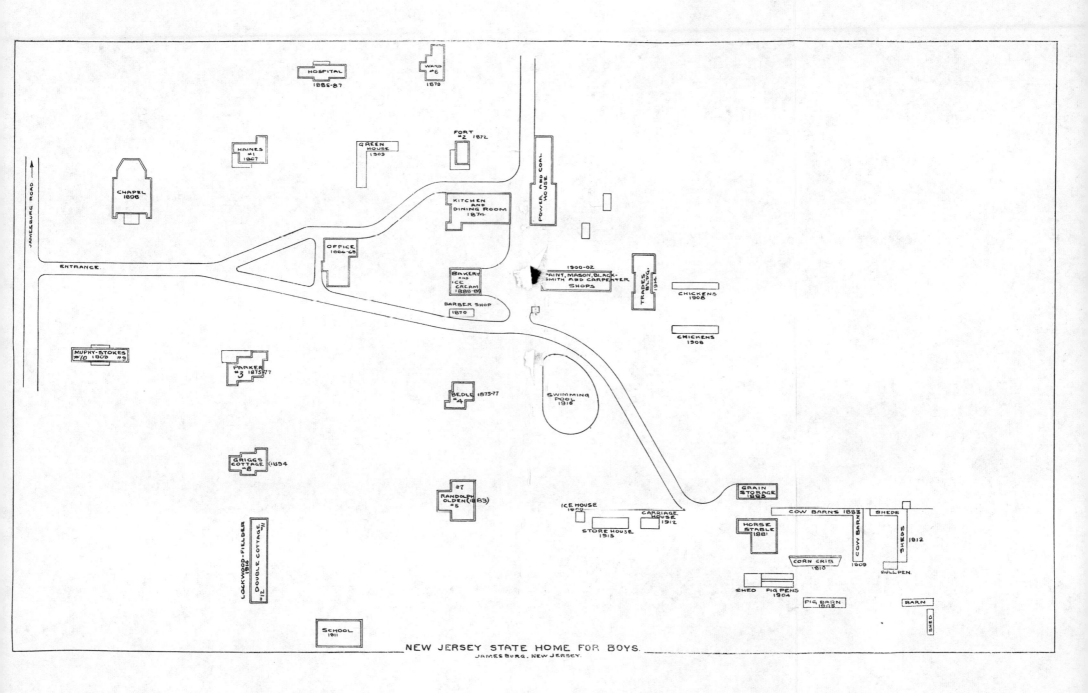

NEW JERSEY STATE HOME FOR BOYS.
JAMESBURG, NEW JERSEY.

The School was thus to be organized on what was known as the "family" basis, namely, its organization into groups or "families," each in the control of a subordinate officer of the institution, and housed in separate dwellings. It was thus designed to avoid, as far as possible, the main external characteristics of the conventional prison or reformatory.

While inmates were received by the 20th of June, 1867, the institution was not formally opened until October 29th of that year, when it was duly celebrated by various addresses expressing optimistic hopes for the future.[1]

From the beginning it was intended that a system of grades, credits and honors would be established which would make it possible to induce each inmate to make efforts toward good conduct, and personal reformation.[2]

The annual report of the Reform School for 1875, a decade after its organization, gives one a clear notion of the general operations of the institution after it became fairly well established as a working institution. At this time the average number of inmates for the year was 186. Since the opening of the school 603 boys had been committed to the institution and 411 had been indentured or discharged. The average age of the 69 committed during the year 1875 was twelve years, ten months, and twenty-three days. Practically all of those committed were those who had been guilty of burglary or theft in some of their various forms. The total expenses were $27,457, plus farm products used, to the value of $3,225. In addition to these products of the farm which were used in the institution, a revenue of $1,417 was realized from the sale of farm produce. The superintendent of the institution reported a satisfactory condition of the discipline and urged a more extensive develop-

[1] *Third Annual Report of the New Jersey State Reform School for Juvenile Offenders,* 1867, in *Legislative Documents of the State of New Jersey,* 1868, Document No. 3, pp. 77ff., 85ff.

[2] *Fourth Annual Report of the New Jersey State Reform School for Juvenile Offenders,* 1868, in *Legislative Documents of the State of New Jersey,* 1869, Document No. 30, pp. 1221ff.

16 P

ment of the family system so that not more than 25 boys would have to be grouped together in any family organization.[1]

By 1879 the population of the Reform School had so increased that the average number confined during the year was 270. Since the school had been opened, 947 had been committed, and 677 discharged or released. During that year the total receipts from the industries were $17,000, while the total expenses were $43,000, thus leaving the net expenses of the school $26,000.

In 1880 a controversy between two competitors for the labor of the boys in the institution at Jamesburg and the trustees revealed a scandalous prevalence of the practice of leasing the labor of the inmates to contractors. However, nothing was done at the time to eliminate the evil.[2]

A more general investigation of the management of the institution was conducted by a joint committee of the legislature in 1886, which showed very clearly that the Reform School had drifted into a mechanically conducted institution, which in no way approximated the substitute for home and family life that had been aimed at by the founders of the institution. The recommendations of the committee doubtless had some temporary influence in bettering the management of the school, but there can be no doubt that this investigation of 1886 uncovered what has always been the weakest spot in the administration of the institution at Jamesburg, in common with most schools of its kind.[3]

These investigations of 1880 and 1886 disclosed the chief difficulties encountered by the institution throughout its history, namely, to provide labor for the inmates which shall at the same time be productive and educational and to avoid a mechanical and repressive routine in discipline and administration. It can scarcely be said that the success of the institution in solving these major problems has ever been more than modest,

[1] Report cited, in *Legislative Documents of the State of New Jersey,* 1876, Document No. 17.

[2] *Report of the Committee of the Assembly,* 1880, Document No. 37, in *Legislative Documents* for 1880.

[3] *Report of the Committee on the State Reform School,* 1886, Document No. 42 in *Legislative Documents* for 1886. See Documents, Part II, pp. 588–92.

though the responsibility has probably been due as much to the lack of funds as to the absence of vision on the part of the management.[1]

In describing the general nature of the development of the institution at Jamesburg it is not necessary to deal specifically with the various phases of its growth which will be covered more thoroughly in an account of its legal, industrial and administrative history. It will suffice to state that it has tended to drift along in a mechanical and routine manner, providing a much better place for the reception of juvenile offenders than the demoralizing state prison and county jails to which they were previously sent, but never attaining anything like the family type of organization or the reformatory influence which it was supposed to bring into the penal and correctional system of New Jersey.

II. THE LEGAL HISTORY OF THE STATE HOME FOR BOYS.

The State Home for Boys was organized by the act of April 6, 1865, which provided that a reform school should be established for the reformation of delinquent boys between eight and sixteen years of age. A board of control, consisting of the governor, the chancellor, and the chief justice of the state, were to appoint six trustees who were to have immediate charge of the institution. These trustes were to be appointed for a term of three years, and in such a manner that two should terminate their office and two new ones be appointed each year. The trustees were given the authority to purchase the necessary land and erect the essential buildings for the reform school and make rules for its administration, subject to the supervision of the board of control. The main purpose of the institution was set forth in section seven of this act as follows:

[1] Mr. W. P. Letchworth, writing in 1883, confirmed the general impression of the situation as later presented by the committee of 1886. He remarked that while the children were always happy, they were especially happy to leave at the expiration of their commitment! *Industrial Training of Children in Houses of Refuge*, Albany, 1883, p. 22.

"They (the trustees) shall cause the boys under their charge to be instructed in piety and morality, and in such branches of useful knowledge as are adapted to their age and capacity, and in some regular course of labor, either mechanical, manufacturing, agricultural or a combination of these as is best suited to their age, strength, disposition, and capacity, and in such other arts and trades as may seem best adapted to secure the reformation, amendment and future benefit of the boys."

The trustees of the school were further empowered to apprentice or indenture inmates until they became twenty-one years of age, making proper stipulation for the education of those so bound out.   One of the trustees was to visit the institution semi-monthly and to make reports, and an annual report was to be prepared by them on the condition of the institution.   The chief executive officer, or superintendent, of the institution and necessary subordinate officers, in addition to the superintendent, were to be appointed by the trustees.   Those committed to the Reform School were to be kept there until twenty-one years of age, unless otherwise legally discharged.[1]

This act was supplemented by the act of April 13, 1867.   By this law magistrates were given the authority to use their discretion in committing to the Reform School boys under sixteen charged with or convicted of any crime except murder and manslaughter.   If a boy should prove incorrigible the superintendent was empowered to return him to the jail from whence he had been transferred.   Provision was also made for committing to the school habitually vagrant, disorderly or incorrigible boys upon the complaint of their parents or guardians.[2]

An act of April 2, 1868, provided for the personal liability of each boy committed, or of his parents or guardians, for his maintenance while in the Reform School, unless the trustees remitted this liability.[3]

A law of March 27, 1872, provided that upon complaint of any citizen, a justice of the supreme court might at his discre-

[1] *Acts of the 89th Legislature,* 1865, pp. 886–893.
[2] *General Statutes of New Jersey,* 1895, Vol. III, pp. 2722–2724.
[3] Ibid., 2724.

tion transfer to the Reform School any boy under sixteen who had been sentenced to the county jail or the state prison.[1]

An act of March 6, 1877, authorized the majority of the board of trustees to release unfit inmates of the Reform School when their permanent interest as well as the good of the institution seemed to demand such release.[2]

By a law of May 23, 1890, it was provided that while the boys should be normally retained in the institution until twenty-one years of age, the trustees might release as a reward for good conduct any inmate who had served three years in the institution.[3]

By an act of May 25, 1894, the appointment of the trustees of the State Reform School at Jamesburg was taken from the governor, the chancellor and the chief justice of the state and given to the governor, subject to the consent of the senate. The term of office and the number of the trustees were not changed, but it was provided that the board of trustees should be bi-partisan, not more than three being allowed to belong to the same political party.[4]

The present legal basis for the administration of the State Reform School for boys at Jamesburg was provided by the act of March 22, 1900, which collected, condensed, and organized the previous existing legislation on this subject. The name was changed from "The State Reform School for Juvenile Offenders" to "The State Home for Boys." The general control of the institution was placed in the hands of a board of six trustees, appointed according to the same provisions as those of the law of May 25, 1894; namely, for three years by the governor, with the consent of the senate. The superintendent and other subordinate officers were to be appointed by the trustees, and were to have the immediate control of the institution. Boys between eight and sixteen years of age were to be committed at

[1] Ibid., 2726.
[2] Ibid., 2727.
[3] Ibid., 2725.
[4] Ibid., 2726

the discretion of the court, if convicted of any crime except murder or manslaughter, or upon the complaint of parents or guardians. In general, inmates were to be discharged or paroled by the trustees whenever the interests of the individual and the state, as interpreted by the trustees, so demanded. The trustees were also given the power at any time to release unsatisfactory or unfit inmates. Unless discharged or paroled, all inmates were to be retained until they were twenty-one years of age. Parents or guardians, if financially able, might be compelled to pay the expenses of maintenance.[1]

III. The Chief Phases of the Industrial History of the State Home for Boys.

For about a decade after the foundation of the State Reform School for Juvenile Offenders, the chief industry carried on at the institution was agriculture. The school had been located on a large farm of 490 acres, and the farming operations served to employ about all of the relatively small number of inmates in the earlier years.[2]

But though the institution originated as primarily an agricultural institution, additional industries were soon introduced. The first important industry added was that of brick and tile-making. By 1879 the boys at the school were making annually 150,000 bricks and 25,000 tiles.[3]

The first provision for inside mechanical industry at the school came with the offer, in 1875, of Downs and Finch, a shirt-making firm, to lease the labor of a large number of boys for the making and laundrying of shirts, if adequate shop room would be provided by the school authorities. Accordingly, an appropriation of $20,000 was secured for a shop in 1876.[4] However,

[1] *Acts of the 124th Legislature,* 1900, pp. 176–189; *Compiled Statutes of New Jersey,* 1911, Vol. IV, pp. 4880–4887.

[2] *Second Annual Report of the New Jersey State Reform School for Juvenile Offenders,* 1866, in *Legislative Documents,* 1867, pp. 414–15.

[3] *Fifteenth Annual Report of the New Jersey State Reform School for Juvenile Offenders,* 1879, pp. 7–8, 20.

[4] *Acts of the 100th Legislature,* 1876, pp. 23–4.

Downs and Finch never secured any extensive service from the new shops, as will appear from the following account of the notable controversy between them and the trustees.

In 1880 occurred the first public investigation of the conduct of the institution. On January 27th of that year Messrs. Downs and Finch presented a memorial to the legislature in which they complained of unfair and dishonest conduct on the part of the board of trustees of the Reform School. These gentlemen stated that in 1875 they had begun to contract for the labor of the boys in the Reform School at ironing shirts. In 1877 they entered into an agreement with the trustees to employ the labor of more boys in the manufacture of shirts, and, accordingly, installed $2,000 worth of shirt-making machines in the shops of the Reform School. In the meantime, it was alleged, the trustees made a secret and covert contract with Rothschild and Gutman, a New York shirt-making firm, for the use of the labor of the boys in making shirts. Downs and Finch were then brusquely ordered to remove their machines from the school shops, which they did at a loss of $1,500. The ironing contract between Downs and Finch and the Reform School was continued, but very soon the school began to iron shirts for Rothschild and Gutman and to neglect the work sent by Downs and Finch. As a result, it was asserted by the latter firm that they lost over $10,000 in cancelled orders. Downs and Finch stated that they had never been able to get any satisfactory explanation from the trustees in regard to why they had taken such action, and insinuated that Rothschild and Gutman had made it "worth while" to the trustees to give them preference.[1]

A committee of the legislature was appointed to investigate the charges contained in the memorial. A mass of testimony was taken,[2] and from this testimony the committee submitted the following report:

[1] *Report of the Committee of the House of Assembly on the Reform School for Boys, Concerning the Financial and Industrial Management of the said Institution*, Document No. 37 in *Legislative Documents*, 1880, pp. 19–21.

[2] Ibid.; about 175 pages of testimony were taken.

"After duly hearing counsel and weighing the evidence submitted, your Committee are unanimously of the opinion that the statements in the said memorial which reflect upon the conduct of the trustees are not sustained. It is apparent that the trustees have acted honorably, and with a view to promote the welfare of the youth committed to their care."[1]

A perusal of the evidence leads one to suspect that the exoneration was not as complete as the committee stated, and Downs and Finch hardly seem to have received entirely fair treatment, though there is little probability that the trustees indulged in anything more than arbitrariness. But whether Downs and Finch or Rothschild and Gutman were legally entitled to the labor of the inmates of the Reform School, it is readily apparent that the trustees were morally wrong in either case, as the labor of the boys should never have been contracted for by any firm.

But regardless of the moral phases of the whole controversy and of the particular firm which was legally entitled to the labor of the boys, there can be no doubt that the venture was a financial success for the school and the making of shirts soon became its most profitable industry. By 1879 the leasing of labor made possible by the new shop had produced a revenue of over $33,000 and in 1879 alone brought in an income of $12,883.26.[2]

The industrial development of the institution proceeded without any particularly noteworthy innovations down to the close of the century.

The industrial condition of the institution at that time, together with the then existing instruction in useful trades, is amply summarized in the following selection from the report of the superintendent for the year 1900:

"Some idea of the industries of the institution may be formed from the following:

"The school farm contains 490 acres. After deducting for the campus and grounds occupied by the buildings and woodland, we have about 400 acres for cultivation. For five years past we have worked a farm of about 160 acres belonging to Richard Conover. We have employed no extra labor

[1] Ibid., p. 4.
[2] *Fifteenth Annual Report of the New Jersey State Reform School for Juvenile Offenders*, 1879, p. 20.

to conduct this. Besides this, a portion of each year about fifteen able-bodied boys worked in the brickyard, the results of which will be shown in the table relating to the brickyard.

"In the trades the boys have been instructed as follows:

"In sloyd, 121 boys have received instruction during the year, 29 completed the work, and 49 more have completed it. In the carpenter shop 126 have received instruction during the year, 2 having been in the shop the whole year. There are 6 now employed.

"In the mason department 9 have received instruction during the year, 2 during the whole year, and 8 are now employed. In the blacksmith shop there were 4 received instruction during the year; 2 are now employed.

"In the paint shop one boy has been under instruction for 2 years, 1 for 1 year, and 1 for 9 months. There are now 3 in the department.

"In the shoemaking department 13 have been under instruction during the year and an average of 19 have been employed.

"In the bakery 4 have received instruction during the year; 2 are now employed.

"In the printing office 2 have been under instruction for a year or over; total of 6 during the year.

"In the entire department 4 have received instruction in electric wiring, 4 in firing the boilers, 8 in running the engines, 5 in steam-fitting, and 2 in caring for cold-storage machinery.

"In band music, 63 have been under instruction during the year, 7 for one year, 10 for six months. In the drum corps 14 have received instruction. The making of clothes, and the sewing for the institution, besides the domestic work, is done by the boys under a head in each department.

"An average of about 85 boys are employed a portion of their time in brush-making. From this number boys are taken for lessons in sloyd work. With the separation of some of the larger boys whom we are obliged to excuse from school during the summer, all of these attend school three and one-half hours a day. Our schools are in session fifty weeks in a year."[1]

The system of contracting for the labor of the boys had declined somewhat by the close of the century, but as late as 1908 the Commission on Dependency and Crime found that it was still employed on a considerable scale and they recommended its abolition.[2] This was achieved by the law of June 7, 1911.

The present industrial situation at the State Home for Boys is described in detail in the last annual report. The summary of the industrial organization in 1916, which is given below, presents the picture of an economic organization which is far

[1] *The Thirty-sixth Annual Report of the New Jersey Home for Boys,* 1900, Document No. 37, *Legislative Documents* for 1900, Vol. IV.
[2] *Report of the Dependency and Crimes Commission,* 1908, p. 19.

removed from the simple agricultural establishment of 1867, but which has as yet made little progress towards furnishing an adequate industrial training for the boys committed to the institution:

"*Industries.*—The several industrial departments are maintained for the express instruction of the inmates. As they grow efficient they do much in making and repairing articles for the use in the Home.

"The class in carpentry, in which there are seven boys, make such pieces of furniture as are needed in the dining-room and cottages, also make the necessary repairs in and about the building, and assist in the erection of any new work or buildings we may be putting up or remodeling.

"The class in masonry, bricklaying and concreting, composed of twelve boys, lay the concrete walks, make concrete blocks, and make necessary repairs in buildings to the walls and assist in bricklaying and plastering.

"Six boys compose the class in blacksmithing. They not only shoe the horses and mules, thirty-five in number, but also keep the farm utensils and vehicles in repair. The scroll and other iron work embellishing the arch at the entrance to the institution grounds was made by them.

"The class in sloyd is composed of eleven boys, who keep in repair pieces of furniture for use in the departments of the institution.

"The printing class of twelve boys publish our weekly paper, *The Advance,* and do the necessary job printing for the institution.

"The class in plumbing and tinsmithing, composed of seven boys, are useful in making necessary repairs in plumbing, and in the making of tinware for the dining-rooms and kitchens, and in the installation of plumbing, etc.

"The class in painting, composed of nine boys, not only paint the interior and exterior of the buildings—omitting the roofs, which are not considered safe work—but also do the decorating and paper hanging, and are taught freehand drawing, lettering and sign painting. They paint all our carriages and other vehicles, including farm machinery.

"In the tailoring and sewing class sixty-five boys are employed making the clothing worn by the boys and sewing the household linen such as sheets, towels and other necessary articles in use in the Home.

"The shoes worn by boys in the Home are made by the twenty-five boys who work in the shoe shop, and the cobbling is also done by them. The suspenders worn by the boys are made by them, as is also the harness for the horses and mules.

"Eighteen boys compose a class who do the laundering for the institution, including that of the officers and teachers.

"In housework 115 boys are engaged. They are chiefly small boys. There are twelve cottages with two groups in each, one group working in the morning and the other in the afternoon. They not only do the housework, but also do the mending of the wearing apparel of the boys and of the household linen and bedding in the cottages.

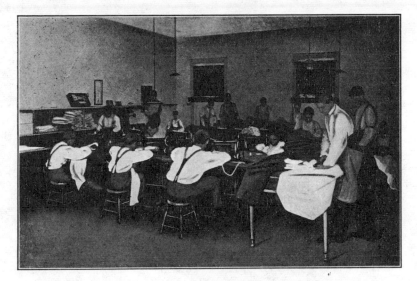

The Tailor Shop.

The Shoe Shop.

PLATE IV. Industry at the State Home for Boys.

"In the bakery there are seven boys employed. Under the direction of the baker they do the baking for the institution; not only the bread, but also the pastry, cakes, etc.

"In the class in cooking, not only the boy's kitchen, but also in the officers' kitchen, where the cooking is done for the teachers and employees, thirteen boys are engaged, under the instruction of the matron. Twenty-eight boys are engaged in dining-room work and waiting on tables.

"The class of eleven engaged in the power house do the work in connection with the firing of boilers, keep the power house clean, and, under the direction of the chief engineer, assist in all the necessary electrical work and the installing of steam and water pipes.

"In each cottage there are one or more boys who do the barbering, hair cutting and shaving.

"In the class of floriculture the boys, nine in number, have an opportunity to become familiar with the growing of plants and flowers and the care of trees, lawns, greenhouses and flower beds.

"There are two boys in the class in poultry raising. There are incubators in this department, and the class take part in all the work done in the plant.

"In agriculture and trucking, the class of thirty-two boys do the plowing and cultivation of the crops. They also do the work necessary to produce the vegetables consumed in the institution. They prune and spray the trees and small fruits, drive the teams in the hauling of coal and supplies from the railroad station, and do all the necessary work upon the farm.

"The class in dairy work and caring for the stock is composed of fourteen boys, who do the milking, keep the herd of Guernsey cows clean, washing, currying and rubbing them, and keep the barns, pig pens and the premises clean.

"Seven boys compose a class who are engaged in storeroom work, who, under the direction of the storekeeper, weigh out the supplies and deliver them to the various departments; also keep the storeroom clean and in order.

"The band is composed of forty-seven boys. A certain number compose the band which furnishes the music daily, at entertainments and at other times when called upon. The others practice preparatory to taking up the places of those in the regular band leaving the institution. All are under instruction daily." [1]

Though an appropriation of $20,000 was made for a trade school in 1913, it is readily apparent from the above account of the employment of the 400 boys uniformly employed out of the average of 573 inmates for the year, that there is little real manual and industrial training provided for, beyond what is incidental to carrying on the general activities involved in the maintenance and administration of the institution. In part,

[1] *The Fifty-second Annual Report of the New Jersey State Home for Boys,* 1916, pp. 10–12.

any thorough industrial training is rendered impossible by the practice of paroling or indenturing the boys after about a year in the institution, if their conduct justifies such action. Again, the appropriations for the maintenance and administration of the institution are so scanty that all the boys must be kept at work in the necessary activities of the school, and neither time nor money and equipment are available to allow the installation of a systematic course of industrial training. Thus, the industrial training, which probably should be most emphasized in such an institution, falls far below the level of efficiency that is attained in the graded school at the institution.

IV. GENERAL SURVEY OF THE DEVELOPMENT OF THE MANAGE-
MENT, ADMINISTRATION, AND PHYSICAL EQUIPMENT
OF THE STATE HOME FOR BOYS.

As has been pointed out above, the institution was definitely planned and erected on the "cottage" or "family" plan in preference to the congregate "house of refuge" system of management, which had been proposed in 1850–52.[1] It was also the plan to stimulate efforts at reformation and good conduct by a system of grades and credits.[2] How far this original attempt to establish a flexible domestic system of management failed, when the population and the problems of administration began to increase, is revealed by the report of the Investigating Committee of 1886, which conducted the first thorough investigation of the management of the institution. This report is especially interesting as revealing the condition of the management after about twenty years of the existence of the school.

The committee found that the management of the Reform School had drifted into a mechanical routine institution, and at that time made little approach to offering a substitute for a home for delinquent boys. The committee stated that the life of the

[1] *Report of the Commissioners on the Reform of Juvenile Offenders, in Legislative Documents of the State of New Jersey,* 1865, Document No. 13, p. 10.
[2] *Fourth Annual Report of the New Jersey State Reform School for Juvenile Offenders,* 1868, in *Legislative Documents,* 1869, pp. 1221f.

boys at the Reform School was "hard, routine, and monotonous," and that there was no adequate provision for any approach to home life or for means of effecting individual reformation. In short, the school had become an "institution" pure and simple.[1]

The committee submitted its recommendations in which the emphasis was put upon measures needed to effect an improvement and, if possible, a reformation of the boys sent to Jamesburg. Specifically, it was urged that more opportunities be provided for play; that the educational facilities be greatly extended, and that there be more thorough industrial and moral training so that the boys discharged would both desire to live better lives, and would be prepared to do so.[2]

That the recommendation of the committee may have had some effect is apparent from the message of Governor Green in 1888, in which he warmly commended the excellence of the new methods of management of the institution.[3]

This investigation of 1886 is mainly significant as illustrating the chief defect of the institution during its whole history down to the present day, namely, the almost inevitable tendency to drop back into the rut of monotonous routine and mechanical administration, which, next to a life of crime, constitute about the worst surroundings to which children can be consigned.

The next important investigation of the institution, that of 1902, centered about the financial operation of the institution rather than around the disciplinary aspects of its management. This investigation was precipitated by J. M. Mortimer, the book-keeper of the institution, who absconded with $4,000 of the funds of the Home. About $3,000 of this amount, which was unlawfully appropriated by Mortimer, was a fund which had been collected by the superintendent, Ira Otterson, from those who had taken indentured children from the institution, and had been held in trust by him without having ever been entered

[1] *Report of the Committee of the Senate and the Assembly on the State Reform School at Jamesburg,* 1886, Document No. 42, in *Legislative Documents* for 1886, Vol. III, passim. See Documents, Part II, pp. 588–92.
[2] Ibid.
[3] *Annual Message of the Governor,* 1888, pp. 21–3.

on the books of the institution.[1]   The remaining amount was obtained by duplicating vouchers.   While Mr. Otterson was exonerated from any charge of intentional dishonesty, it was generally agreed that his careless methods of keeping the accounts had made possible the defalcation.   He was asked to resign, and a new and more scientific method of accounting was adopted.[2]

There is little evidence that the system of discipline and management at the State Home for Boys at Jamesburg has escaped to any great extent from the monotonous routine which the committee of 1886 discovered was in existence thirty years ago.   The following schedule from a recent report gives the daily routine at the institution from April 1st to October 1st.   From October to April the boys rise a half-hour later and retire a half-hour earlier: [3]

DAILY ROUTINE FROM APRIL I TO OCTOBER I.

Rise	5:45 A. M.
Breakfast	6:30 A. M.
Detail for work	7:30 A. M.
School call	7:45 A. M.
Recess	9:15 A. M.
Recall	9:30 A. M.
School, shops and all work closes	11:00 A. M.
Dinner	11:45 A. M.
Detail for work	12:45 P. M.
School call	1:00 P. M.
Recess	2:15 P. M.
Recall	2:30 P. M.
School, shops and all work closes	4:00 P. M.
Drill, or singing exercise	4:30 P. M.
Supper	6:00 P. M.
Devotions	7:30 P. M.
Boys retire	7:45 P. M.

While the "family" system is carried out roughly by the distribution of the boys among the twelve cottages of the institu-

[1] *Supplemental Report of the Trustees of the New Jersey Home for Boys,* 1902, in the *Annual Report* for 1902, pp. 7–8; Document No. 42 in *Legislative Documents,* 1902, Vol. IV.

[2] Ibid.

[3] *The Forty-ninth Annual Report of the State Home for Boys,* 1913, p. 39.   The routine remains unchanged at the present time.

tion, there is no approximation to real family life, chiefly because trained, competent, and enthusiastic house-masters are not provided. The state has adopted the crude expedient of putting the boys in the cottages under the control of the various mechanics at the institution, who are at night transformed into house-masters or "leaders of the family." There can be little doubt that a wide gap often exists between the qualifications of a competent blacksmith, carpenter, mason, or shoemaker, and those of a trained house-master, who is fitted to organize and direct all the social life of from twenty-five to fifty boys.

As far as academic instruction is concerned, the educational facilities at the school will rank well with those which would be at the disposal of the boys if they were at liberty and free to attend the public schools of the cities and villages of the state. As was pointed out above in dealing with the industrial phases of the history of the school, there is almost a total absence of any provision for adequate industrial training, beyond participation in those activities which are carried on as a part of the ordinary routine of maintenance, in agricultural and manufacturing pursuits, and in domestic services. Adequate buildings have been supplied for a trade school, but equipment, stock, and instruction have never been systematically provided. It is doubtful, however, if any systematic system of industrial training would be possible, if adequate facilities were provided, as long as the general policy is pursued of paroling boys after having been at the institution for about one year.

The system of grades and credits, which was early introduced, is followed today under what is known as the "badge" system— a badge representing one month of perfect deportment. The earning of at least eight badges is made the basis for the determination of the fitness of the boys for indenture or parole. A rather mild system of deprivation is adopted, as the reverse of the merit or badge system, in promoting good discipline, though corporal punishment is resorted to in extreme cases of incorrigibilty. In general, a tendency towards mechanical administration and routine, with an absence of proper industrial training and of real social and family life, rather than cruel treatment, has been the chief defect in the management of the State Home for Boys. The generally unsympathetic attitude of the management in the past is reflected in the harsh rules as to unnecessary silence, and in the general failure to provide for an adequate organization of the social life of the boys.

The physical equipment of the institution is relatively adequate, the main defect being a constant lack of funds to carry on the necessary repairs. In an architectural sense the State Home for Boys has grown from the original building erected in 1886, now used as an administration building and capable of housing fifty boys, to an institution comprising nine cottages, three of which are double, an administration building, an excellent chapel, an adequate infirmary, an imposing new school building, and adequate shops, including one large building originally designed as a trade school. An appropriation was made by the Legislature in 1917 for an assembly hall and gymnasium, which should satisfy all the immediate architectural needs of the institution. The total valuation of the physical equipment of the institution is rated as $510,637.[1]

As to the future of the State Home for Boys it seems that the institution, itself one of the first products of that principle of scientific differentiation in the treatment of the delinquent and the defective, which has been the basic fact in all progress in correctional and reformatory institutions and upon which all hope for further progress must be founded, is now faced with the problem of further differentiation within itself. It should not be forgotten that the institution was originally founded, and doubtless should continue as one designed to deal with those delinquent minors who cannot be successfully and properly dealt with by non-institutional methods, or in truancy schools or parental homes, and yet are not sufficiently incorrigible or old enough to be treated in the reformatory, or so mentally abnormal as to be most fitly transferred to one of the institutions

[1] *The Fifty-second Annual Report of the State Home for Boys,* 1916, pp. 7, 11-12. See ground plan of the institution and its growth opposite page 240.

The Original Building.

Murphy-Stokes Double Cottage.

PLATE V. Views of the State Home for Boys at Jamesburg.

provided for the treatment of the psychopathic classes. Hence, it is apparent that those who do not belong to the class most properly dealt with in this institution should be transferred elsewhere, in order that, on the one hand, they may be more effectively handled, and, on the other, that they will not interfere with the properly specialized treatment of those for whom the State Home for Boys is most appropriately designed. This necessary improvement would require the transfer of the older and more incorrigible inmates to the state reformatory at Rahway, and the application of the principles and practices of probation, truancy and parental schools to those whose record as to conduct and intelligence gives hope that they may be speedily reformed and returned to society as normal and law-abiding individuals. It would further require that those who were revealed by the highly scientific modern tests as to mentality to be markedly defective should be removed to the proper institutions for permanent segregation and prevention of propagation. Of course, before any of these steps can be taken, provision must be made for a rigid psychiatric classification of the inmates, something which is totally lacking at present.[1]

Some of the short-comings of the institution were very clearly pointed out in the Annual Report of the New Jersey State Charities Aid and Prison Reform Association for 1914, a section from which is worthy of quotation:

"But the material side of this institution is not all. What are its results in training and developing boys? And how can better results be secured?

"The law requires this institution to retain control over all boys committed until each reaches his majority at 21 years of age. Many old boys of criminal heart and vicious experience are returned from long periods of parole because of this old law instead of being committed elsewhere. The law should be changed so that boys of 16 or upwards cannot enter this institution, either

---

[1] An important step towards the development of an adequate system of caring for juvenile delinquents outside of institutions such as Jamesburg was taken by the law of March 14, 1910, which authorized the courts to commit juvenile delinquents to the care and custody of the *State Board of Children's Guardians,* a body created by the act of March 24, 1899. See *Acts of the 123rd Legislature,* 1899, pp. 362–4; Ibid., *134th Legislature,* 1910, pp. 28–9.

from the courts or from parole. There should be a time limit for all paroled boys.

"We are beginning to believe that it is an injustice to brand boys with a criminal record so that they are prevented in after life from securing positions of trust and responsibility. The United States Navy and the United States Army will not knowingly accept men who have a record of imprisonment in an industrial school for boys. Civil service laws, national, state and municipal, exclude them upon such a record, and this exclusion of men because of a youthful record in an institution makes it necessar᛫ that we should be most cautious about committing juveniles to state reformatories. The movement, therefore, for special schools in cities, truancy schools, parental homes and the like, must be fostered and encouraged. Our probation work must be extended and improved. Every effort must be made to prevent the commitment of boys to the State Home at Jamesburg. Many boys are committed to Jamesburg from counties in this state simply because there is a lack of proper probation and truancy supervision in rural communities and the smaller cities of the state. The population could be reduced materially if the same probation work that is employed in Essex and Hudson County were employed throughout the state. This is demonstrated by the fact that where probation work is well done the commitments to Jamesburg are reduced to a minimum. Finally, the enforcement of parental responsibility by legal methods must be insisted upon. When parents are compelled to pay for the support of their boys at the state institution they will be more particular in preventing the commitment of their children. When counties are required to defray the cost of care of boys committed to Jamesburg more interest will be taken in juvenile court and probation work.

"Efforts should be continually made to make this institution a training school of a high type. It should not be an institution for old boys of deliberate criminal minds and vicious habits, neither should it be a convenient place to send boys who lack only a proper home environment and proper parental control." [1]

That the institution has made some progress in the direction in which its proper future activities lie is indicated by the last annual report of the above mentioned organization which states:

"Instead of a prison for boys committed by the courts, which is practically what this institution was originally, and what it has been in practice during past years, the institution has become under its new management virtually a training school for boys needing vigorous discipline." [2]

What remains to be done is, in the first place, to see that the institution is no longer hampered by the presence of those classes

[1] Report cited, pp. 23-4.
[2] *Annual Report of the New Jersey State Charities Aid and Prison Reform Association*, 1916, p. 35.

Entrance to the Grounds.

Military Drill.

PLATE VI. Views of the State Home for Boys at Jamesburg.

of inmates who cannot be properly dealt with in such an institution and who greatly hinder the adequate provision for those who properly belong therein. In the second place, the discipline and routine must be so modified that Jamesburg will no longer be merely an excellent "institution," but will approximate to a much greater degree than it does now the home or family care of which its inmates have been deprived. It is in this psychological aspect that the school at Jamesburg has failed, rather than in provision for the material needs of the boys. The recent appointment of Superintendent Charles H. Edmond, a man of long training in dealing with the problems of juvenile delinquency, may go far towards introducing a new order of things at the State Home for Boys.

Attention may now be turned to a brief consideration of the origin and development of the corresponding institution for the care of delinquent minors of the female sex—the State Industrial School for Girls, at Trenton, changed in name by the law of 1900 to the State Home for Girls.

THE ORIGIN AND DEVELOPMENT OF THE STATE HOME FOR GIRLS AT TRENTON

CHAPTER VIII

THE ORIGIN AND DEVELOPMENT OF THE STATE HOME FOR GIRLS AT TRENTON

I. Outline of the Development of the Institution.
II. Legal and Administrative History and Organization.
III. Architectural Development.
IV. Industrial History.
V. Present Condition.

I. OUTLINE OF THE DEVELOPMENT OF THE STATE INDUSTRIAL SCHOOL FOR GIRLS (THE STATE HOME FOR GIRLS) AT TRENTON.

The establishment of the State Reform School for boys naturally led to the provision of a similar institution for the care of wayward girls. Some idea of the need for such an institution may be seen from the fact that in 1870 there were in the state prison four girls between eleven and fourteen years of age, to say nothing of the much larger number confined in the generally worse county jails.[1] The agitation which preceded the establishment of the boys' school had also advocated the establishment of a reform school for girls, and it has already been pointed out that the noted Committee on Prison Discipline of 1869 urged the provision of a state reform school for girls on the lines of the one already established for boys at Jamesburg. The obvious need of this institution for the care of female juvenile delinquents was met by the act of April 4, 1871, which legally established the institution.[2]

The first annual report of the new State Industrial School for Girls in 1871, stated that a temporary location had been rented at Pine Grove, in the city of Trenton. A proper committee was authorized to provide a suitable permanent location and was

[1] *Annual Report of the State Prison*, 1870, in *Legislative Documents*, 1871, pp. 422–3.
[2] *Acts of the 95th Legislature*, 1871, pp. 78–83.

(263)

engaged in this quest.   It was reported that an experienced matron, the ex-matron of the Massachusetts State Industrial School for Girls, had been temporarily secured in order to initiate a scientific administration from the beginning.   Samuel Allinson, a member of the Commission on Prison Discipline of 1869, acted as president of the board of trustees of the institution, thus insuring an intelligent and enlightened general policy for the institution.[1]   No inmates were received until 1872.

The second annual report, that of 1872, stated that the institution had been opened in its temporary quarters at Pine Grove with accommodations for forty inmates.   However, but seventeen inmates were committed in the first year, and the trustees, well aware of the large number of female juvenile delinquents who should have been committed, endeavored to give publicity to the work of the institution and encourage the magistrates to avail themselves of the opportunity to commit to the institution those delinquents who were being sent to the demoralizing jails or allowed to remain at liberty.[2]

The third annual report, that for 1873, is important in that it describes the acquisition of the permanent quarters for the institution.   It was stated that a suitable location had been discovered and purchased at Ewing, one and one-half miles northwest of the State House at Trenton.   A tract of eighty acres had been purchased for $12,000.   The procedure of the State Reform School at Jamesburg was followed, in that the family or cottage system of organization and administration was adopted in preference to the more institutionalized large scale congregate scheme, though, as at Jamesburg, the original building was much too large for a family cottage.   It was planned to settle the inmates in families of thirty-five to forty girls in cottages on the grounds under the direction of sub-matrons.   This attempt at a "family" basis for management and administration was successfully carried out during the first years when the population was small.   When the number of inmates increased, however, instead of erecting new buildings for an extension of the cottage and

[1] Report cited, Document No. 11, in *Legislative Documents,* 1872.
[2] Report cited, Document No. 13, in *Legislative Documents* for 1873.

family system, additions were made to the original building until
it became a large rambling affair, housing 126 girls and approaching very closely the "House of Refuge" it had originally been
planned to avoid. Not until 1898 was the "family" system restored in part. "Needle work" constituted the main industry of
the institution during the early years of its existence. Twenty-
five had been committed by 1873 and at the close of the year there
were nineteen inmates.[1]

The details of the development of the institution need not
receive special analysis at this point, as they illustrate nothing
of particular significance beyond demonstrating the difficulty of
obtaining adequate legislative assistance even for a rationally
constituted and conducted institution. Its history has been that
of the conventional institution of its kind. The problems of
management have been more difficult than at Jamesburg, owing
to the fact that the delinquent girl is more difficult to handle by
routine methods than the delinquent boy. Considering the
period in which it originated, it was scientifically designed and
planned and has, in general, been conducted in a relatively intelligent manner, in view of the limited equipment and funds
available.[2]

A thoroughgoing public investigation of the State Home for
Girls was conducted by a committee of the legislature in 1900.
This committee found that the chief shortcomings in the management and administration of the institution were due to the
defects in the legal basis of its organization and administration.
The committee pointed out the following deficiencies in the
administration of the institution: (1) the powers of the lady
managers were not clearly stated; (2) no information was
sent to the school in regard to the personal history of the
girls committed, in most cases the sole comment in the commitment papers being that the particular girl was a "fit subject"
for the care of the institution; (3) there were no uniform pro-

---

[1] Report cited, Document No. 17, in *Legislative Documents,* 1874.
[2] The Annual Reports are readily accessible in the *Legislative Documents,*
and the non-serial documents are listed in Miss Hasse's Index, pp. 488–490.

visions as to commitment to the institution, this being left to the discretion of magistrates; (4) the trustees had no power to discharge an inmate until she had reached the age of twenty-one, regardless of the degree of reformation earlier attained; (5) the management had no power to parole inmates; (6) girls could be legally committed at the ridiculously early age of seven years.[1]

The exposure of these serious defects in the legal aspects of the organization of the institution led to the reorganization of the laws governing the school in the act of March 23, 1900, which, with the radical amendments of 1914, is the basis of the present organization. In addition to removing the legal obstacles to an effective administration, the law of 1900 also eliminated to some extent the penal stigmata of commitment by changing the name of the institution from "The State Industrial School for Girls" to "The State Home for Girls."

The State Home for Girls was one of the institutions investigated by the Commission on Dependency and Crime of 1908. While the Commission admitted that abuses had undoubtedly existed in the matter of administering corporal punishment and in the use of solitary confinement in dark cells, it found the general management of the institution to be highly satisfactory and worthy of commendation. The Commission recommended that corporal punishment and the employment of solitary confinement in dark cells as a method of enforcing discipline be abolished and that a reformatory for women be constructed which would relieve the institution of its overcrowding and of the older girls.[2]

Another investigation of the management of the institution took place in 1914, which attracted more attention and was accompanied by more bitter controversy than the investigations of 1900 and 1908. This investigation, which was begun in the early months of 1914, was precipitated by a letter sent to Joseph

---

[1] *Report of the Committee on the Industrial School for Girls,* 1900, in *Minutes of the Assembly,* 1900, pp. 452-4. See Documents, Part II, pp. 593-5.
[2] *Report of the Dependency and Crimes Commission,* 1908, pp. 17-19. *The New Jersey Review of Charities and Corrections,* December, 1908, p. 284.

P. Byers, State Commissioner of Charities and Corrections, by a minority of the trustees or board of managers of the institution, complaining of the management of the institution and asking the Commissioner to acquaint the Governor with the conditions which were alleged to exist. The Governor, accordingly, appointed as a committe of investigation, Commissioner Byers, Robert Williams, and Albert I. Grayton. The charges against the administration and management of the institution which were presented by the minority of the board of managers were the following: [1]

"The lack of a well-balanced trained office force.

"The lack of a proper filing system.

"The practice or policy of former presidents and secretaries signing vouchers in blank and leaving them with the clerks to fill in.

"The insertion of names on the petty cash and pay rolls after signature without notifying the signers.

"The lack of adequate information concerning the state of the annual appropriations, resulting in the home overdrawing its account to an amount not definitely known to us, as three sets of figures have been furnished, but not exceeding $3,000, we believe.

"The failure on the part of the proper officers and the treasurer to supply this information when requested and the lack of knowledge of this fact on his part.

"The lack of proper system in keeping and checking supplies.

"The lack of adequate records of girls in the homes and those paroled, and the failure to compile and keep such records; the failure to keep proper records of wages due to girls on parole and the lack of knowledge of amounts due and general failure of vigilance in their collection.

"The general doubt and confusion that exists in the home in reference to all records and the many and troublesome mistakes made on the records.

"The failure to secure definite information by letter within a reasonable time or to secure proper action towards carrying out recommendations made and formulated by the board.

"The failure to submit to the undersigned after repeated requests a properly itemized and analyzed budget.

"The lack of proper methods and knowledge as to the distribution of the annual appropriation, and the failure to have prepared and submitted a logical budget properly itemized and rigidly to be adhered to.

"The failure to inform the board on matters of discipline and the general policies and practices in relation thereto.

[1] The information regarding this investigation has been drawn chiefly from contemporary newspapers and from manuscript material placed at the disposal of the writer by C. L. Stonaker, the Secretary of the State Charities Aid Association of New Jersey.

"The failure to inform the board in regrading and reclassification of certain of the office positions.

"The high cost per capita in maintaining the institution and the generally unsatisfactory results attained.

"The failure on the part of the board itself to transact business according to parliamentary order and system, and its failure and neglect to observe the provisions of the old by-laws."

The charges, then, in the main grew out of friction within the board of managers and centered chiefly around the charge of unscientific and unbusinesslike administration, a condition not unlike that revealed by the investigation at the Boys' Home in 1902.

The investigation itself aroused a very considerable amount of personal controversy, but out of the whole matter came some very sound recommendations by the committee of investigation. The following were the more important of these recommendations:

"ADMINISTRATIVE CHANGES.

"A new board of managers of five members, at least three of whom shall be women.

"Elimination of all salaries to board members.

"The term of office or employment of all officers and employees at the home to terminate thirty days after the organization of the new board, provided that nothing shall disqualify any such officer or employee for reappointment.

"Selection of new superintendent by the board, with power of removal for cause.

"Selection of all assistant officers and employees by the superintendent, subject to approval by the board.

"Fixing all salaries by the board.

"The direct responsibility of the superintendent to the board for the administration of the home in all its departments, including inmates and officers.

"Monthly reports by the treasurer to the board.

"Closer cooperation between trustees and the superintendent.

FINANCIAL SUGGESTIONS.

"Reorganization of bookkeeping so that at all meetings of trustees an intelligent account is presented showing the exact situation regarding appropriations, expenditures and requirements.

"Monthly statement by comptroller showing balances of appropriations.

"A readjustment of the State's method of business so that the bills incurred during the fiscal year shall be paid from the appropriations of that year.

"The amount of bills rendered to be stated in affidavits attached thereto.

"Insurance of buildings, etc., to be handled by one of the State departments.

"The board should see that all bills are examined and checked by them before payment.

"The payment of schedules should be a part of every regular meeting, and all schedules should be voted by the board.

IMPROVEMENT OF DISCIPLINE.

"Segregation of inmates into groups of about twenty-five in separate cottages; for new girls, for mentally deficient, for return girls, for negroes, for very young girls, for older girls, and for more incorrigible girls.

"A disciplinary building.

"A reception cottage, where new girls can be kept under observation for classification purposes.

"Deprivation of privileges as a means of punishment and a uniform marking system established. Conversation at meals to be permitted to all inmates and prohibited only as punishment for disorder or disobedience.

"The transfer of feeble-minded girls of the custodial type to the State Home for Feeble-Minded Women.

"Provision for continuing under State's control girls whose degree of mental irresponsibility is such that they should have protection during the child-bearing period.

"Reduction of the age-limit for the commitment of girls from 19 to 17 years.

"Provision for transfer of old and difficult girls to the State Reformatory for Women, on the initiative of the Board of Trustees.

"Accurate and comprehensive records of all discipline administered with a summary to be submitted to the Trustees by the Superintendent monthly."

The report of the investigating committee issued in important practical results for the Legislature passed the act of April 17, 1914, which embodied many of the above recommendations submitted by the committee.[1] It would be rather hazardous to state, however, that the reforms contemplated in the law have all been put into execution, though there can be no doubt that the management of the administration has improved since 1914.

II. LEGAL AND ADMINISTRATIVE HISTORY AND ORGANIZATION.

The State Industrial School for Girls was legally established by the act of April 4, 1871. The general outlines of its organ-

[1] *Acts of the 138th Legislature,* 1914, pp. 479–481.

ization showed that it was obviously modelled on the law of 1865 establishing the State Reform School for Juvenile Offenders. The following are the chief provisions of this act.

It enacted that an industrial school be established in New Jersey for the reformation of such girls between the ages of seven and sixteen years as might be committed to it in the manner provided by law. The general control was vested in a board consisting of the governor, the chancellor, and the chief justice of the state, who were to appoint six trustees for a term of three years, who were to have immediate control over the management of the institution. The actual management was vested in the trustees and six lady managers appointed by the trustees, who were to be associated with the trustees in determining the policy of the institution. The trustees were to make the general by-laws and rules for the institution and to appoint a superintendent and such other subordinate officers as might be necessary. The superintendent and the matron were to constitute the chief executive and disciplinary officers of the industrial school. The purpose of the administration and management of the institution was set forth in the following section:

"That the said trustees and lady managers shall cause the girls who are under their charge to be instructed in piety and morality and in such branches of useful knowledge as may be adapted to their age and capacity; also in some regular course of labor, either mechanical, manufacturing or horticultural, or a combination of these; and especially in such domestic household labor and duties as shall be best suited to their age, strength, disposition and capacity, and in such other arts, trades and employments as may seem to the trustees best adapted to preserve their health, secure their reformation, and administer to their future benefit, and in binding out inmates, scrupulous regard shall be had to the moral religious character of those to whom it is proposed to bind them."

The trustees were given the power to indenture the inmates until they were eighteen years of age, providing that proper stipulation was made as to the treatment and education of those thus bound out.[1]

[1] *Acts of the 95th Legislature*, 1871, pp. 78–83; *General Statutes of New Jersey*, 1895, Vol. III, pp. 2728–2730.

By the act of March 5, 1872, the judges of the supreme court were given the authority to commit to the institution girls accused or convicted of crime or vagrancy.[1]

According to the act of March 2, 1877, the trustees were given the power to release unfit inmates at their discretion.[2]

By the act of March 18, 1881, the judges of the supreme court and the court of common pleas were given the authority to commit to the industrial school girls under sixteen who were sentenced to jail.[3]

The law of April 18, 1889, provided that the trustees should be appointed by the governor with consent of the senate, the term of office to be as before.[4]

The present legal basis of the organization of the state industrial school for girls was provided by the law of March 23, 1900, with the sweeping amendments of 1914. The name of the institution was changed in 1900 from the "State Industrial School for Girls" to the "State Home for Girls."

It was provided that the general control should be vested in nine trustees, five men and four women, holding office for a term of three years and appointed by the governor with the consent of the senate. They were to have the power to make rules and regulations for the institution and to determine its general policy. They were to appoint the superintendent and other subordinate officers, these to have the immediate control of the management of the institution, subject to the supervision of the trustees.

As to commitment, it was provided that normally the inmates were to be detained until they were 21, though they might be discharged or paroled by the trustees at their discretion when the interests of the individual and the state required. The proper judicial officers were empowered to commit to the institution girls between the ages of ten and sixteen who had been convicted

[1] Ibid., p. 2730.
[2] Ibid.
[3] Ibid., pp. 2730–2731.
[4] Ibid., p. 2731.

of crime or disorderly conduct or who were stated to be incorrigible by their parents or guardians. By the law of 1905 the maximum age was raised to nineteen. The obvious intent of the provisions as to commitment was that the female offenders might be sent to the industrial school rather than to prison or to jail. It was provided that the inmates, together with their parents or guardians, should be personally liable for the expenses of maintenance unless released from this liability by the trustees.[1]

The recommendations made by the Byers investigating committee of 1914 led to a radical revision of the organizing law of 1900. The act of April 17, 1914, amended in a sweeping manner the law of 1900 and furnishes the basis for the present government of the State Home for Girls.

It was enacted that there should be five trustees to act as the general governing body of the institution, three of the trustees to be women. These trustees were to be appointed for a term of five years by the governor with the consent of the senate, the tenure of the first incumbents being so arranged that the term of one trustee would expire each year. It was provided that the trustees should meet annually on the second Tuesday in March and elect a president, a vice-president, a secretary, and a treasurer. The treasurer was required to give a bond for a sum not to exceed $5,000 and to deposit all moneys received in such banks as the trustees should specify.

As to the duties and powers of the trustees it was decreed that they should make the by-laws for their own procedure; draw up the general rules for the government and regulation of the institution; provide employment for the inmates and indenture, parole, discharge, and remand them; appoint a superintendent, as chief executive officer, and provide for the appointment of a resident woman physician and such other officers as they deemed necessary; remove the said superintendent for cause, and fix the salaries of all officers. It was specified that the trustees themselves were to receive no compensation beyond their expenses in performing their assigned duties.

[1] *Acts of the 124th Legislature,* 1900, pp. 481–492.

PLATE VII. General View of the State Home for Girls at Trenton.

The superintendent was empowered to appoint all subordinate officers, determine their duties, and remove them for cause, all these acts to be performed with the approval of the trustees. It was further enacted that the superintendent "shall have charge and custody of the girls, and shall discipline, govern, instruct, employ, and endeavor to reform them, in such manner, as, while preserving their health, will secure the formation, as far as possible, of moral, religious, and industrious habits, and qualify them for regular trades and employments." [1]

III. Architectural Development.

The architectural development of the institution has not been characterized by any circumstances of particular significance, aside from explaining the slow development of the cottage or family system of administration. The original building erected in 1872 at a cost of $23,330 and known as the Murphy-Fielder Cottage, with successive additions, served to house the inmates until the building of the Stokes Jr. Cottage in 1891. As a result, the cottage or family system was rendered practically impossible of application when the population of the institution began to increase. By the close of the century about 130 girls were housed in the building. In 1898, however, a resolute attempt was made to reintroduce the family system. The execution of this determination was facilitated by the erection of Voorhees Cottage in 1900–1, and by the addition of three more cottages since that time—Stokes in 1904–5, Fort in 1908–10, and Wilson in 1912. An assembly hall was provided in 1909 and a small but well equipped infirmary in 1915. A separate school building has never been provided. The present physical equipment is valued at $303,765. The transformation of the original building into an industrial building, the erection of a school building, and the provision of two or more smaller cottages are much needed architectural additions to the physical equipment of the school. [2]

[1] *Acts of the 138th Legislature,* 1914, pp. 479–81.
[2] See grounds and buildings, plan, opposite page 274.

18 P

IV. Industrial History.

The industrial history of the State Home for Girls is neither extensive nor important. Little has ever been done to furnish equipment for installing a system of industrial training. The industrial activities have been limited to work on the institution farm, the care of the grounds, and the general domestic activities incidental to the maintenance of the institution, such as sewing, cooking, baking, and laundering. While a thorough mastery of all phases of domestic activity would constitute a most valuable training for the average inmate of the Home, it has been difficult to provide for a sufficient rotation of employment so that the girls would be thoroughly trained in all the domestic branches. It would seem that the proposed transformation of the original building into a trade school is an indispensible preliminary to a satisfactory industrial organization of the institution. As in all institutions for juvenile delinquents, the matter of training and reformation should take precedence over productivity and financial revenue.

V. Present Condition of the State Home for Girls.

The outstanding features of the present organization and management of the institution may be gathered from the last annual report of the institution.

The chief defects in the institution at present are the antiquated and inadequate equipment and the insufficiency of its administrative force rather than the lack of a proper conception of the functions and methods of a correctional institution for delinquent girls.[1]

The last annual report of the institution, 1916, makes an vigorous plea for additions to the building equipment and to the administrative force. There seemed to be a most inexcusable

[1] *Annual Report of New Jersey State Charities Aid and Prison Reform Association,* 1916, p. 36.

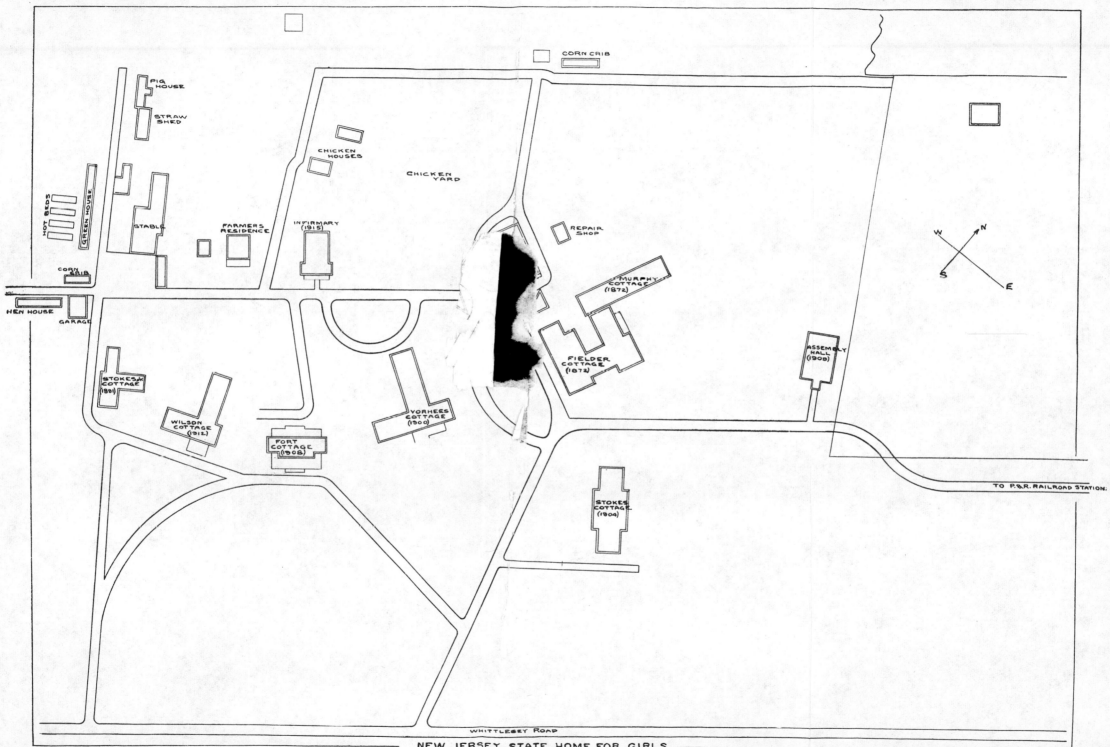

PIG HOUSE

STRAW SHED

CORN CRIB

CHICKEN HOUSES

CHICKEN YARD

CORN CRIB

HOT BEDS

GREEN HOUSE

STABLE

HEN HOUSE

GARAGE

FARMERS RESIDENCE

INFIRMARY (1915)

REPAIR SHOP

MURPHY COTTAGE (1872)

FIELDER COTTAGE (1872)

ASSEMBLY HALL (1908)

STOKES Jr. COTTAGE (1891)

WILSON COTTAGE (1912)

FORT COTTAGE (1908)

VORHEES COTTAGE (1900)

STOKES COTTAGE (1804)

TO P.&R. RAILROAD STATION.

WHITTLESEY ROAD

W N S E

NEW JERSEY STATE HOME FOR GIRLS
TRENTON, NEW JERSEY.

lack of provision for a sufficient number of officers and teachers, it being reported by the superintendent that they were compelled to work fourteen hours each day with no holiday, even having been compelled to relinquish their previous luxury of one holiday each month.[1]

The total number of inmates in the institution in October, 1916, was 227. The Binet-Simon psychological test was administered to the inmates during the year and revealed the somewhat disconcerting fact that of 258 inmates tested, but 36 were normal, 98 being borderline cases and 125 positively defective.[2] These statistics reveal the fact, then, that about half of the inmates of the Home for Girls at Trenton do not belong at all in that institution, but rather at Vineland, or some other institution for custodial care of the mentally sub-normal.

In addition to the materials for use at the institution, which are produced on the farm and by the other industries of the Home, the annual expenses of maintenance are at present about $70,000, of which about $20,000 are appropriated for salaries.[3]

The chief features of the organization and administration of the institution at present may best be derived from the following selections from the superintendent's report for 1916:

"1. *Recreation.*

"Trained Playground Worker.—We have secured a trained playground worker and have fine work to show through her training. On July 4th we had a field day, going out on the grounds immediately after breakfast and remaining out until bedtime, eating the two meals in true picnic fashion. A group of friends came in to play a match with the girls; the opponents consisted of two priests and two Protestant clergymen, one State House official, one newspaper man, and three laymen, and the girls won, perhaps through the gallantry of our guests, but all enjoyed themselves. In addition to the ball games, there was basketball, running, jumping, and tennis.

"Folk Dances.—On Labor Day we had the folk dances of all nations danced in appropriate costume, the national hymn of each country being sung by the school, one girl holding up the national flag that all might be able to identify the particular one. All the other holidays have been properly observed.

[1] Report cited, 1916, pp. 5–8.
[2] Ibid., p. 13.
[3] Ibid., pp. 8, 15.

"*2. Industries.*

"Farm Work.—Our farm has done well, both in the way of raising produce and in training our girls. We have put up, with our own labor, an overhead irrigation plant, covering a little more than an acre, and now will erect more as we find it needed.

"Road Making.—We have done some road making, the Department of Roads kindly marking out the plans for us. As soon as this year's appropriation is available we hope to finish this work, as through grading of the Philadelphia & Reading Road quantities of soil are at our disposal.

"Dressmaking.—We are particularly proud of our sewing-rooms, where excellent dressmaking has been done. Many girls who are not interested in general housework, take kindly to dressmaking, and can support themselves in this way.

"Shampooing.—Girls have been taught scalp treatment and shampooing, and keep up their practice by taking care of each other.

"Extra Work.—During the year, besides the absolutely necessary sewing, a gymnasium suit has been made for each girl in the Home. Three hundred rugs have been woven from the cuttings of our garments. These rugs have been placed at the side of the beds, adding to the general comfort.

"*3. Differentiated Treatment of Inmates.*

"Grouping of Girls.—We are reorganizing our girls into five groups:

"The School Group, which takes in our little girls under school age, has school two sessions a day and help with the industrial work as they would do in their own homes, with plenty of time for recreation. To see them on their roller skates, or exercising with jumping ropes, swings, tetering see-saws, playing ball, besides their gym work, one realizes what a well-balanced life they have.

"The Academic Group are the girls who are beyond the school age, but have intelligence and ambition sufficient to continue their studies. These girls have one session a day under a competent teacher, and spend the other half day in industrial work of a kind that will fit them for self-support on the outside, such as dressmaking or housework. For this special line, the Administration Building should be equipped to teach girls home making, and those going out should graduate from this building; but this calls for a special instructress who would have to receive a proper salary, which we hope we shall have.

"The Industrial Group consists of girls over sixteen who have no inclination for studies. These girls will be delegated to the different houses to take care of the general housework, so as to release the girls who have school work to attend to.

"The Manual Group is now working at chair caning, rug weaving and farm work, but we hope in addition to this they will be taught brush making, cobbling, etc., with the view of eventually transferring many of them to other institutions, as they should not be allowed to go outside without proper supervision.

"The Observation Group consists of new girls and girls incapable of doing any work well, but who may be interested in different kinds of work and can be kept busy, although some of the work may not have much commercial value, save as a means of keeping them pleasantly occupied. After awhile girls can be moved from this group into one of the others. To carry all this out we must have at least three or four additional teachers. The greater number of our girls will go outside, many will marry and will be the mothers of coming generations. As they are now the wards of the State, it is the duty of the State to equip them to develop their best powers and save their children from entering the State institutions.

"4. *Avoidance of Institutional Treatment When Possible and Desirable.*

"Placing Little Girls.—Will it not be possible to secure a fund which will enable us to place most of our little girls in individual homes, where they may be assimilated and thus avoid being institutionalized? We ought not to place more than one girl in any home. The understanding should be that the girl will attend school regularly, and to assure this the school report should be in constant evidence. A payment of ten dollars a month should open many good homes to us, and this would be better for the girl and cheaper for the State. Girls in institutions will swap experiences and are inclined to play to the gallery. In a good home the danger of this is largely removed."[1]

In looking forward into the future of the institution two important changes seem to be indicated. The first was pointed out in the last paragraph from the report of the superintendent which was just quoted, namely, to avoid institutional commitment when it is for the best interests of the individuals and the community. It would seem that such procedure would be wise in all cases where the record of the girl indicated that anything short of institutional treatment would be likely to effect the desired correction and reformation.[2] The second change, is to weed out from the institution those mentally so sub-normal as to possess no possibility of leading a normal independent existence, and put them in the proper institutions. Valuable suggestions as to how to carry out this step are presented in the annual report of the State Charities Aid Association for 1913. These suggestions, which are quoted in part below, would, of course, apply with equal or greater force to the Boys' Home at Jamesburg:

[1] Ibid., pp. 8–10. The Superintendent is Mrs. Elizabeth V. H. Mansell, who has had a long and generally successful career as head of the institution.

[2] This is in part made possible by the act of March 14, 1910, referred to above, allowing the courts to commit juvenile delinquents to the custody of the *State Board of Children's Guardians.*

"A STATE PROGRAM FOR DEFECTIVE DELINQUENTS.

"One practical plan would be to change our laws relating to commitment so that commitments shall be without a time limit and shall be to existing institutions with authority on the part of the managers of such institutions to make suitable investigations regarding the social environment from which the person came and his present physical, mental and moral condition. Upon that showing the managers of such institutions would then have power to transfer, segregate or otherwise adjust the person to such treatment as seems wise.

"A simpler plan would be to secure an observation clinic for each institution, or a state central psychopathic hospital and laboratory. All admissions should be to such a clinic for observation and study and then a proper classification and placing based upon such a study. To illustrate: The Jamesburg School for Boys now has a population of 500 on a farm tract of 600 acres. There is ample room to place on a remote portion of that farm away from the present colony such a laboratory, or the investigation could be made at some point within the present colony and then segregation be made to the remote institution on that farm tract.

"There is such an opportunity afforded likewise at the Village for Epileptics at Skillman, at the Home for the Feeble-Minded at Vineland and on the new farm tract now opening for use of the State Prison and its population. A similar segregated group could be planned for at the Woman's Reformatory at Clinton. Because of the congested space at the State Home for Girls, all that could be done there would be a separation in a cottage within the same group of cottages.

"The problem of juvenile delinquency and a study of the defective type of juvenile delinquents must rest upon the future policy regarding commitments of juvenile delinquents, whether defective or not. The Jamesburg colony of 500 acres should not be increased, unless it be as a separate group placed at the other end of the farm tract. Either a new institution must be created by the state or some form of county or municipal plants must be established. We have laws authorizing the establishment of such institutions by the counties, by the cities, or by the school boards, and we have laws permitting the placing of our juveniles in private institutions.

"Essex County and Hudson County, and possibly Mercer County, might be induced to finance a plan of county administration, but to get any county action in such counties as Sussex or Warren, Cape May or Ocean, is so improbable as to be not worthy of much thought.

"The juvenile defective delinquents are found in the scattered communities of the rural sections of our state as well as in the congested districts of our factory cities. How to know them when found and what disposition to make of them when found must be for New Jersey at the outset a state problem, and for a beginning of this work with hopes of development it would seem most practical to start it by establishing a staff of investigators under the direction of the Commissioner of Charities. Whatever the plan, the preliminary investigation and the tests to be made must be done by persons of training and experience. We cannot hope to train our judges to do this work. We may secure probation officers with training to make these tests. We may develop the idea and feel our way towards a logical solution of the question by establishing a well equipped research bureau in connection with the office of the Commissioner of Charities, giving that official power with his staff of experts to make the investigations and to determine upon the treatment.

"A parental school in connection with a board of education could be used as the first sifting process, and normal children of recoverable type could be returned thence to their homes and the regular schools. Those found subnormal in such parental schools could then be turned over to the experts of the Commissioner for future disposition. Only one or two cities in this state could probably finance such a parental school. Newark has one now, but there is no work in that school other than the usual reformatory methods of the past with some attempts at modern educational development. There should be a trained expert there to make the tests. But, should the larger cities of the state be encouraged to develop the parental school, the adjoining school districts and possibly all of a county could board their uncertain cases in such a parental school at the expense of the several school districts."[1]

All of this is in keeping with the proposition strictly adhered to by the writer that only in a careful scientific differentiation and classification of delinquents and specialized treatment of each class can there be found any rational way out of the problems of correction and reformation. This general position seems unassailable, the immediate measures to be taken to realize this condition must be the result of careful thought and proper adjustment to special circumstances and localities.[2]

[1] Report cited, pp. 29–31.
[2] A valuable summary of the legal provisions for the care of delinquent children in New Jersey is to be found in *A Guide to the Laws of New Jersey Relating to Children,* issued by the New Jersey Child Labor and Welfare Committee, 1917, especially pp. 16–19, 28–33.

CHAPTER IX

THE ORIGIN AND DEVELOPMENT OF THE STATE REFORMATORY AT RAHWAY

CHAPTER IX

THE ORIGIN AND DEVELOPMENT OF THE STATE REFORMA-TORY AT RAHWAY.

I. Legal and Administrative History and Organization.
II. General Survey of the Development of the State Reformatory at Rahway.

I. LEGAL AND ADMINISTRATIVE HISTORY AND ORGANIZATION.

While the state reformatory for men at Rahway has been in existence for less than twenty years, attempts had been made to provide such an institution for New Jersey over a period of more than half a century. It was not until March 28, 1895, however, that the decisive step was taken in this direction. On that date an act was passed creating a state reformatory. It was then enacted that,

"Whereas it is deemed advisable that there shall be a state reformatory in this state for the custody and confinement of criminals between the ages of 16 and 30 who have not been previously sentenced to state prison in this or any other state or country, and of persons convicted for the first time of a crime not involving moral turpitude,"

the governor was to appoint six commissioners to build an "intermediate prison." [1] These commissioners were directed to buy for their purposes as much as was needed of the Edgar Farm in Union county at a price not to exceed $10,000, to appoint an architect, and to advertise for and open bids for the building of the said reformatory.[2]

The new institution was to be designated as "The New Jersey State Reformatory." [3] When it had been built and made ready for occupancy, it was enacted that the six commissioners above

[1] *Acts of the 119th Legislature,* 1895, pp. 715–730; *General Statutes of New Jersey,* 1895, Vol. III, p. 3164.
[2] Ibid.
[3] Ibid., p. 3165.

mentioned were to be converted into a board of managers and were to hold office for three years.[1] The managers were authorized to appoint a warden for a term of five years, who was to be the chief executive officer of the reformatory.[2] The warden was empowered to appoint his subordinate officers, subject to the approval of the managers.[3] The board of managers was vested with the general authority to make the rules and regulations for the management of the institution, and they were to have charge of the grounds, the construction of shops, and the purchase of large quantities of supplies.[4] The warden was to be the head disciplinary official in the reformatory and was to have immediate direction of the prison industries, which were to be conducted, as in the state prison, on the "piece-price" or the "public account" system.[5] The courts were empowered, but not commanded, to commit to the institution the classes of inmates specified in the enacting clause.[6] It was provided that the keeper of the state prison might send to the reformatory as many properly qualified prisoners of those classes as the board of managers and the warden of the reformatory requested.[7] The same provisions for good conduct were enacted as had been created by the acts of 1868, 1869, and 1876 for the state prison.[8]

However, this organizing law of 1895 never regulated the administration of the reformatory. In the same year that the reformatory was opened, 1901, the law of 1895 was replaced by a new act, that of March 21, 1901, providing for the regulation of the institution. The same name—"The New Jersey State Reformatory"—was retained. The general control of the institution was vested in a board of eight commissioners appointed by the governor for a term of four years, it being stipulated

[1] Ibid., p. 3165.
[2] Ibid., p. 3166.
[3] Ibid.
[4] Ibid., p. 3167.
[5] Ibid., pp. 3168-9.
[6] Ibid., p. 3169.
[7] Ibid.
[8] Ibid., p. 3170.

that not more than four should belong to the same political party.[1] The commissioners were authorized to regulate the general policy of the institution and to appoint a superintendent for a term of 5 years and to fix the salaries and determine the number of subordinate officers.[2] The superintendent was to be chief disciplinary and executive officer, to have charge of the industries of the reformatory, and to appoint his subordinate officers with the consent of the commissioners.[3] The provisions as to industrial administration, commitment, and transfer were practically the same as those of the law of 1895.[4] An imperfect substitute for an indeterminate sentence was enacted, which provided that the period of confinement could not be longer than the legal maximum prescribed for the crime.[5] The commissioners were authorized to determine the procedure and provide the rules governing the parole of inmates.[6] They were further empowered to grant final discharge to inmates upon the recommendation of the superintendent.[7]

The remaining legal changes of significance, since the law of 1901 was enacted, have been those connected with the industrial administration of the institution. The reformatory was affected by the law of June 7, 1911, abolishing contract labor, as well as by the subsequent laws permitting extra-mural industries and reconstructing the Prison Labor Commission. Moreover, the reformatory at Rahway has been the one institution which has made a conscientious effort, though hampered by legislative apathy, to carry out the provisions of the law of 1911 and introduce the "state use" system as the basis of industrial organization.

[1] *Acts of the 125th Legislature*, 1901, pp. 231–238; *Compiled Statutes of New Jersey*, 1911, Vol. IV, p. 4929.
[2] Ibid.
[3] Ibid., pp. 4929–30.
[4] Ibid., pp. 4930–31.
[5] Ibid., p. 4931.
[6] Ibid., p. 4932.
[7] Ibid.

II. General Survey of the Development of the State Reformatory at Rahway.

While the New Jersey State Reformatory at Rahway was not opened until August 5, 1901, its history really goes back far into the previous century. The need of an institution for young "first termers" was frequently emphasized in the "forties," [1] and the unsuccessful attempt to erect the "House of Refuge" at Kingston in 1850–52 was an effort, which narrowly escaped success, to provide an institution which would have combined the characteristics of the Jamesburg and Rahway institutions. [2] The need of a reformatory or "intermediate prison," as it was most frequently called down to 1895, was strongly stressed in the able report of the Commission on Prison Discipline of 1869. [3] A more vigorous attempt to found a reformatory came at the close of the "seventies," when, in 1878, a commission was appointed to report on the desirability of an "intermediate prison" for New Jersey. [4] Though this commission strongly urged the immediate provision of a reformatory, and drafted an act to establish such an institution, and its request was warmly seconded by Governor McClellan in his annual messages, no practical results ensued. [5] However, the agitation was continued by public authorities, prison officials, and by the newly organized State Charities Aid Association. [6]

This agitation, together with the serious overcrowding of the state prison and the need of some proper institution to which to send the larger and more unruly boys from Jamesburg, led to

[1] Cf. *Constitution of New Jersey Prison Reform Association,* 1849, p. 3.

[2] *Annual Message of the Governor,* 1851, pp. 21–4; *Minutes of the Assembly,* 1851, pp. 463–72, 496–502, 804; *Appendix to the Senate Journal,* 1852, pp. 405–9; *Annual Message of Governor,* 1853, pp. 17–18. See Documents, Part II, pp. 569–79.

[3] Report cited, pp. 21–2; see Documents, Part II, pp. 531–3.

[4] *Report of the Commissioners on the Prison System of New Jersey and on an Intermediate Prison,* 1878, pp. 10–15. See Documents, Part II, pp. 599–611.

[5] *Annual Message of the Governor,* 1879, p. 23; 1881, p. 12.

[6] Cf. *Annual Reports of the Association,* 1887–1895.

the passage of an act in 1889 authorizing the appointment of
commissioners to examine the most advanced types of reformatories in the country and to make a report to the legislature embodying the results of their investigations and accompanied by
their recommendations.[1]   The members of this commission were
Charlton T. Lewis, Patrick Farrell, David M. Chambers, Ira
Otterson, and Robert W. Elliot.

The commissioners investigated the three most widely known
and successful reformatories in the United States, namely, those
at Elmira, N. Y., at Huntington, Pa., and at Concord, Mass.[2]

While the commission was deeply impressed with the honor
system applied at Concord,[3] it concluded:

"That on the whole, the best institution and system now in operation in
any State of the Union as an intermediate reformatory is the institution
known as the New York State Reformatory at Elmira, and the system of
government and discipline there practiced."[4]

Having thus decided upon the Elmira institution as the type
to be adopted, the commission stated that the most available site
for such an institution, which was owned by the state, was the
Edgar farm in Union County near the city of Rahway.[5]
Actually, the Edgar farm was a most unsuitable site for the reformatory, as it was nothing more than an abandoned clay-pit
and brick-yard which had been thrown on the hands of the
state as the result of some political and financial chicanery.   Only
the energy of Superintendent Moore has transformed the site
from a forbidding swamp to relatively healthy and well-graded
grounds.   Plans for the new reformatory were drawn up by J.
R. Thomas, and it was estimated that the new institution would
not cost more than $300,000.[6]

[1] *Report of the Commissioners to Establish the New Jersey Reformatory*,
April 9, 1890, Document No. 20, in *Legislative Documents*, 1890.   This report
is also contained in *Votes of the Assembly*, 1890, pp. 783–91.   See Documents, Part II, pp. 611–618.
[2] Report cited, p. 6.
[3] Ibid., p. 8.
[4] Ibid., p. 6.
[5] Ibid., p. 6.
[6] Ibid., pp. 6, 13–14.

The commissioners drafted a bill to be introduced, in order legally to authorize the erection of the reformatory,[1] but no decisive action was taken until Governor George T. Werts took up the matter in his annual message for 1894 and vigorously recommended that immediate action be taken to carry into effect the recommendations of the commission of 1890.[2] The result of the Governor's activity and of private agitation led by Charlton T. Lewis was apparent in the act of March 28, 1895, establishing the state reformatory at Rahway.[3] The close relation that the act of 1895 bore to the agitation of 1890 is evident from the fact that this act was little, if anything, more than a combination of the act of 1889, creating the commission of 1890, and the law which this commission drafted to accompany its report.[4]

Thus, with the establishment of a reformatory organized according to the system in use at Elmira, New Jersey had modelled both her penal and her reformatory institutions after those of the neighboring state of New York, the state prison of New Jersey having been conducted according to the Auburn system since 1860. The only unfortunate phase of the origin of Rahway was the fact that those who built the institution were never able to rid themselves of the idea that it was an "intermediate prison." The fact that the institution was viewed as primarily a "prison" for the less hardened criminals is apparent in the frequent use of the term "intermediate prison" in this act of 1895 as being synonymous with the proposed "reformatory," and this view was given objective expression in the complete adoption of the prison type of architecture in constructing the institution.[5]

[1] Ibid., pp. 15–18.
[2] *Annual Message of the Governor,* 1894, pp. 4–5.
[3] *Acts of the 119th Legislature,* 1895, pp. 715–730.
[4] *Report of the Commissioners to Establish the New Jersey Reformatory,* 1890, pp. 5–6, 15–18; *General Statutes of New Jersey,* Vol. III, p. 3164.
[5] Probably next to the adoption of a prison design the greatest amount of poor judgment that was exhibited in the construction of the reformatory centered around the building of the immense dome which is larger than that

Plate VIII.   The New Jersey Reformatory for Men at Rahway.

But whatever may have been the views of the legislature and the architects as to the nature of the institution, it is plain that by 1901 those in control of the reformatory recognized its real function. The following quotation from the First Annual Report of the Commissioners of the New Jersey State Reformatory demonstrates that from the opening of Rahway the purposes of a reformatory have been clearly recognized: [1]

"The Reformatory principle denies the correctness of the old idea that so much punishment should be meted out for so much crime. The civilized world no longer believes in that idea. The new theory and practice has enacted into law a better purpose as the object of criminal treatment. Society is to be protected from the criminal first of all, but this protection is to be through the reformation of the criminal rather than through his incarceration as a punishment. Through these new methods the wrongdoer is returned to society when there is a strong and reasonable probability that it is safe to do so, without regard to punishment, whether little or much, and without regard to the particular crime for which he may have been imprisoned. Whenever any prisoner will live at liberty, without prejudice to the welfare of his fellow men, then he is entitled to liberty, and, what is just as important, not until then.

"The Reformatory, therefore, has been established for the purpose of reforming those who have been improperly formed as to habits and character, or neglected physically, intellectually, or morally. It must begin where the parent, the church, and society have failed. Its design, in brief, is to give everyone within it a chance, by good conduct and his own efforts to rehabilitate himself; to give proper schooling; to teach industrious and honest habits, and by all possible means to advance his material, mental and moral habits." [2]

This excellent statement of the fundamental functions and purposes of a reformatory makes it certain that New Jersey will

of the capitol at Washington. The many thousand dollars expended in the construction of this relatively useless portion of the reformatory plant have been sorely needed since for the erection of shops and other indispensible adjuncts to the efficient operation of the institution. The physical plant at present represents an investment of $1,325,000. For the details of the architectural development see the diagram of the grounds and buildings opposite page 294.

[1] These same advanced ideas on criminal and penal jurisprudence had been expressed in the *Report of the Commissioners to Establish the New Jersey Reformatory*, 1890, pp. 9-10.

[2] Report cited, pp. 6-7, Document No. 46, in *Legislative Documents* for 1901, Vol. V.

19 P

never need to restate the theoretical premises on which its reformatory was established, however varied may be the experiments which are necessary in order that this general aim may be realized. When one grasps the fundamental assumptions involved in the above statement of the premises of modern penology and criminology, it is scarcely possible to be convinced that two so widely different views of crime, punishment, and reformation, as the above and those contained in the revised penal code of 1898, could have been issued in the same state within a period of three years. From the standpoint of the intellectual evolution of humanity they are separated by two centuries.

This report further outlined the general policy of administration and discipline, as it existed in the opening year of the institution. It was stated that the discipline which had been introduced was of a semi-military character.[1] To improve discipline and stimulate personal efforts at reformation, a system of grading and meriting, which had been notoriously lacking in the state prison, was adopted. This important innovation was described as follows:

"Each prisoner, on entering, is placed in the middle grade, and is given 5 credit marks each day for good behavior, diligence in work and progress in school. For a perfect record he is given a bonus at stated times so that in six months he may earn the 1,000 credit marks which will entitle him to enter the first grade. Six months of perfect record in the first grade entitles him to a parole, when suitable occupation will be found for him, and he will be allowed to leave the institution and go at large. Six months of perfect record while on parole will entitle him to an absolute discharge."[2]

Every person committed to the institution was given a rigid physical and mental examination to enable him to receive a properly differentiated treatment.[3]

By the close of the next year 193 inmates had been received,[4] and at the time of making the annual report for 1906 the daily

[1] Ibid., p. 7.
[2] Ibid.
[3] Ibid.
[4] *Second Annual Report of the New Jersey Reformatory,* 1902, p. 8.

PLATE IX. Military Drill at the Rahway Reformatory.

average of inmates was 398.5.[1] In that year the expenses of
the institution were $141,670.50, with an income of $95,430,
thus making a net loss of $46,240, or a per capita cost of
$116.03,[2] as compared with a per capita cost of $171.31 for the
state prison during that same year.[3] Many of the inmates were
employed in improving the physical equipment of the reformatory; work on the reformatory farm furnished work for a number of others; and mechanical industry conducted on the contract system had been introduced on a moderate scale.[4]

In 1910 the system of grading and meriting was varied by
the new superintendent, Dr. Frank Moore. He replaced the
unit system, based on credits, by one based on days, as more
intelligible to the inmates and more conducive to promoting
efforts at reformation. A suitable reward was provided for skill,
scholarship, and industry, as well as for deportment. A careful daily record has been kept of the deportment, scholarship,
and general proficiency of each inmate. Six months of perfect conduct insure the advancement of the inmate into the
"first class," and six months of perfect record in the first class
secures eligibility for application for parole. In no other institution of the state has the grading and meriting system been
as systematically applied as at Rahway. A "bankruptcy court"
was provided for those with bad reformatory records who
avowed a strong determination to reform. It was asserted that
these new rules had proved a great success in bettering the discipline and in promoting efforts at reformation.[5] Dr. Moore
stated that he followed, as far as the law would permit, the
laudable procedure of making the apparent reformation of the
individual the test of release from the institution.[6]

The superintendent stated that the rational policy had been
adopted of making the life in the reformatory as much like that

[1] *Sixth Annual Report of the New Jersey Reformatory,* 1906, p. 12.
[2] Ibid.
[3] *Annual Report of the State Prison,* 1906, p. 16.
[4] *Sixth Annual Report of the New Jersey Reformatory,* 1906, pp. 17–18, 25ff.
[5] *Tenth Annual Report of the New Jersey Reformatory,* 1910, p. 11, Document No. 15, in *Legislative Documents,* 1910, Vol. II.
[6] Ibid., p. 11.

of the outside world as was possible, to the end that the person discharged from the institution might be the more able to adjust himself to a normal and independent existence.[1] One cannot but reflect upon how different this conception is from that of the conventional ideas upon penology which assert that a prison should be as different from normal life as possible, in order that the prisoner may feel more severely the revenge of society, but never take into consideration the fact that this treatment makes the offender still less able to lead a normal life than when he was committed. To further the ability of the inmates to live a normal life when released, the honor system was introduced as far as practicable in prison government.[2]

Another important innovation introduced under Dr. Moore's direction, in 1910, was a rigid mental examination of those committed to the institution, which revealed the startling but vital information that about 50 per cent. were subnormal.[3] It is such investigations as these which cause one to lose faith in the efficacy of the Apostolic Creed in remedying all the mental and moral defects of the criminal population.

Dr. Moore reported that all the evidence available pointed to the fact that about 65 per cent. of those discharged from the reformatory were permanently reformed.[4]

Since 1909 the reformatory has been under the direction of Dr. Moore, who brought to the office a trained mind and disciplinary powers and experience acquired through many years of service in school administration. During this period there have been few institutions of this type in the country which have been as well managed with the equipment at hand. Dr. Moore's success at Rahway has been a convincing demonstration that a man of intellectual attainments is not necessarily by that fact alone disqualified to serve as the administrative head of a penal or reformatory institution. While much of the credit

[1] Ibid., p.   12.
[2] Ibid., pp. 13–14.
[3] Ibid., p.   15.
[4] Ibid., p.   17.

for the attainment of the present high standards of management at Rahway is due to the personal energy and sound judgment of the superintendent, there can be no doubt that his success has been facilitated through the aid of an exceptionally able Board of Commissioners, among the members of which the veteran philanthropist and penologist, Decatur M. Sawyer of Montclair, has been the most active.

The annual report of the superintendent for 1914 was important in that it showed that the excellent work at the reformatory was being utilized in conducting a program of public education as to advanced methods of treating criminals. Illustrated lectures were given in all the counties of the state upon the methods of reformation employed at Rahway. Dr. Moore thus gave evidence of the fact that he recognized the very important truth that the very best management of a penal or reformatory institution is to a great extent a failure, unless it is accompanied by an attempt to lift the general intelligence of the community, in regard to these matters, up to a level approximating that held by the officers of the institution.[1]

Another important innovation in 1914 was the establishment of a tentative form of inmate self-government. This was described as follows:

"One of the new features of the year has been the adoption of a plan of self-government. During the summer just passed there was organized a council composed of thirty of the inmates elected by the inmates themselves. The duty of this counsel is to assist in the discipline of the institution. They give particular attention to keeping order on the tiers, and to suppressing conversation with regard to crime and to preventing profanity. They have elected their own president and secretary, and meet twice a week. All new inmates after they have been addressed by the Superintendent are taken into the council meeting and given advice by the President of the Council as to how they may best conduct themselves while in the Reformatory and as to what is the spirit of the inmates and the desire of the council to lend them help whenever it can. The power has been given to the council not to administer punishment in any way, but to deprive inmates whose influence is harmful from the privileges of the yard and from entertainments."[2]

[1] *Fourteenth Annual Report of the New Jersey Reformatory,* 1914, pp. 8-9. Cf. Ibid., 1916, p. 7.

[2] Ibid., pp. 9-10. See below, p. 295, for the results of this trial of the system of self-government.

It was reported that in this year the new trade school shops, providing for the operation of some eleven important trades, had been completed and the superintendent urged an adequate assignment of work to the inmates so that the "state use" system could be put into effective and extensive operation. He also suggested the advisability of finding out-of-door employment for qualified inmates in road making and allied occupations.[1]

Another important recommendation made by the superintendent in his report for 1914 was that when an inmate had been honorably discharged from the reformatory, he should be automatically restored to citizenship.[2]

But the most sweeping, and probably the most important, recommendation was that the Rahway plant be abandoned as a reformatory and be turned over to the state for future use as the state prison. Dr. Moore pointed out the fact that the reformatory was constructed when such an institution was viewed as essentially a prison, and that as a result its architecture was distinctly unfavorable to the successful administration of a reformatory conducted along advanced lines. He further claimed that the Reformatory building would make an ideal state prison, while a new reformatory could be erected in another district where a more extensive development of the agricultural industry would be possible, and according to a type of architecture adapted to the aims and methods of a modern reformatory.[3] While these suggestions have not yet been accepted, the trend of intelligent sentiment in the state has been towards the approval of this proposal as the only way of solving in a rational manner the architectural weaknesses of both the state prison and the reformatory.

Finally, both the board of commissioners and the parole officers complained that two parole officers were entirely inadequate to the task of investigating the conduct of over six hundred paroled prisoners.[4] When one reads this complaint he can

[1] Ibid., pp. 10–11.
[2] Ibid., p. 12.
[3] Ibid., pp. 13–14.
[4] Ibid., pp. 5, 16.

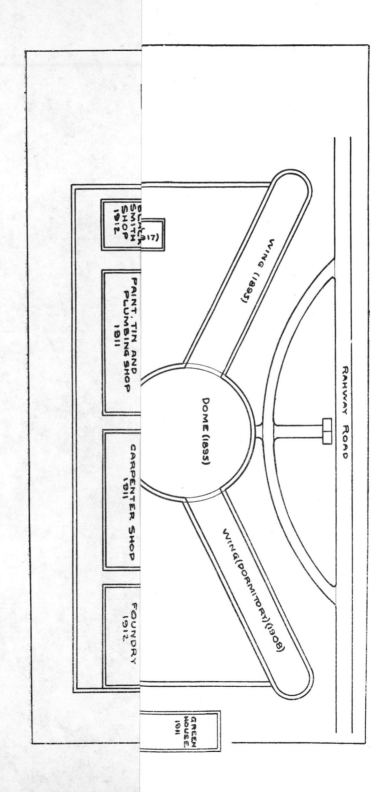

BLACK
SMITH
SHOP
1912

(1917)

PAINT, TIN AND
PLUMBING SHOP
1911

CARPENTER SHOP
1911

FOUNDRY
1912

WING (1895)

DOME (1895)

WING (DORMITORY) (1908)

RAHWAY ROAD

GREEN
HOUSE
1911

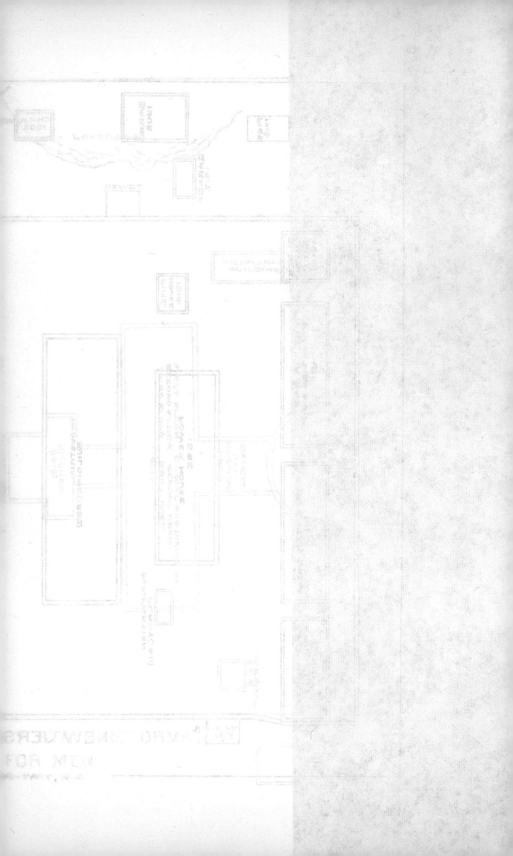

scarcely avoid reflecting upon what must be the condition of the supervision over those paroled from the state prison, where one officer is supposed to "follow up" over twelve hundred paroled prisoners.[1]

The report of 1915 was particularly significant in two respects. In the first place, it described the first real introduction of the "state use" system as the basis for the organization and administration of the industries of the reformatory.[2] But even more interesting was the account given therein of the trial and abandonment of the plan of self-government, the establishment of which, in 1913, was described in the report of the previous year. After a year of experiment with the new system, its continuance was rejected by the vote of an overwhelming majority of the inmates. Both the institution authorities and the inmates were convinced that the scheme had degenerated into an ingenious duplicate of the conventional ward politics of the average municipality, and that fair and equitable administration was much more likely to be received from the public authorities than from the governing council of the inmates. However, it would be unwise to judge of the general value of the system of self-government in penal and reformatory institutions by the experience of Rahway. As far as administrative problems are concerned, self-government is rather a remedy for incompetent and unfair government by public authorities than something which is likely to be desired by those who are efficiently and equitably governed from above. But more fundamental than this is the problem as to whether the best system of administration from outside can fit the inmate for a life of liberty in society as well as a moderate experience with self-government while in an institution. It would seem that those who are not able to govern themselves while in an institution are likely to encounter difficulties in self-government when released. The solution of this perplexing problem can be left, however, to the respective

[1] *Annual Report of the State Prison,* 1916, p. 45.
[2] *Fifteenth Annual Report of the New Jersey Reformatory,* 1915, pp. 10-12.

adherents to the divergent views of Dr. Moore and Thomas Mott Osborne.[1]

The physical equipment of the Rahway reformatory, in its general aspects, is adequate but not appropriate. As Superintendent Moore has pointed out for several years, it was built as a prison and not as a reformatory, and while it is adequate to house the inmates, its whole construction is opposed to the modern idea of what a reformatory should be in its architectural aspects. Its transformation into the state prison, then, would confer as great an advantage upon the inmates of the reformatory as upon the inmates of the present state prison.[2] Pending this change the most pressing need at present is for a new storage building and adequate officers' quarters, a number of the officers now being compelled to sleep in the reformatory barn.[3]

The industrial equipment and organization of the reformatory is probably its weakest point, though the officers have made the utmost of the limited opportunities presented to them, and the industrial organization of the institution is far more efficient than that of any other state institution. In the early years of the existence of the reformatory the inmates were employed in erecting the buildings, in managing the reformatory farm, and the remainder on contracts in the shops. Superintendent Moore was one of the most ardent advocates of the law of June 7, 1911, abolishing contract labor, and aided Senator, now Judge Osborne, in drafting the above bill. Owing to the lack of legislative action in appropriating funds wherewith to install the "state use" system, it was not systematically introduced until 1915. In the interval some additional shops were erected to be held in readiness for the action of the legislature in providing working capital. At present Rahway has made far greater progress in organizing its industries in an efficient manner on the "state use" system than any of the other penal, reformatory, or correctional institutions.

[1] Ibid., pp. 8–10.
[2] *Sixteenth Annual Report of the New Jersey Reformatory,* 1916, pp. 10–11.
[3] Ibid., pp. 11–12.

Print Shop.

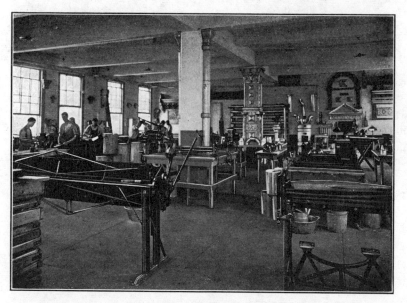

Tinsmith Shop.

PLATE X. Industries at the Rahway Reformatory.

During the first full year of this new system orders to the value of $21,420 were filled in manufacturing tinware, furniture, beds, iron castings, printing work, shoes, and clothing.[1]   But, as Superintendent Moore clearly pointed out, in spite of these promising beginnings, New Jersey has only been "playing" at introducing a systematic application of the "state use" system in the reformatory.   But $5,000 was appropriated in 1916 for working capital, whereas, for example, the state penitentiary of Ohio carried a capital stock of about $216,000.   This scanty provision of working capital has greatly hampered the industries of the institution by preventing the accumulation of stock and the prompt filling of orders.   As has been the case with the state prison, there has been in the last few years a development of extra-mural industries at Rahway.   A number of inmates have been employed in building roads near the city of Rahway, and others on the large and well cultivated reformatory farm which produced a net gain of $23,293 in the last year.[2]   During the present year, 1917, in addition to caring for the large farm at Rahway, the reformatory has been cultivating two extensive farms at Annandale, in Hunterdon county.   This development of agricultural activities under the direction of Mr. E. S. Hoover has proved a decided success, producing a profit of about $10,000, and doubtless forecasts more extensive operations in this direction.

In the matter of the work that the institution is accomplishing towards the reformation of the inmates, there seems no doubt that almost everything is being done in this respect which is possible with the equipment and funds available.   The unsatisfactory nature of the general architecture has been sufficiently emphasized above.   The educational facilities are adequate, and the commissioners boasted in their last report that the reformatory school was perhaps the best in the country.[3]   A personal investigation of the school system by the writer convinced him that this claim on the part of the commissioners was justified by the facts.   It is certain that the personnel and training of the teach-

[1] Ibid., pp. 7–8.
[2] Ibid., pp. 8–9, 34.
[3] Ibid., p. 5.

ing staff, and the degree of educational efficiency attained, are greatly in advance of what are generally reached in the public schools of the state.

The attempt is made to provide at least the rudiments of a general cultural education, as well as a more intensive and specialized industrial education, though the latter is carried on more according to the productivity than the strict trade school method. As far as possible, the educational system is adapted to the individual needs of the inmates.[1] The provision for religious exercises is ample, there being provided a Protestant and a Catholic chaplain.[2]

The parole system at Rahway has been brought up to a high level of efficiency, due in a large part to the energy of the veteran parole officer, Charles S. Moore. The only defect in the system is the lack of a sufficient parole force to permit a thorough administration of institutional and office duties, and at the same time to allow of an adequate supervision of those on parole.[3] During the last year Superintendent Moore made a careful statistical study of the results revealed by the working of the parole system in the year 1916. He found that of the 950 on parole, 93, or about 10 per cent., were returned for a violation of the parole.[4] A careful statistical analysis of this 10 per cent. revealed the following facts regarding them.[5]

Feeble-minded	50%
Previously committed to juvenile institution (66% feeble-minded)	43%
Arrested five times or more	30%
In Reformatory less than 15 mos.	70%
Went home when paroled	57%
Worked in trade shops while in reformatory	65%
Went out to work at same trade	5%

From these facts Dr. Moore made the following deductions regarding the working of the parole system, and concerning the

[1] Ibid., pp. 19–22.
[2] Ibid., pp. 25–8.
[3] Ibid., pp. 17–18.
[4] Ibid., p. 12.
[5] Ibid., p. 13.

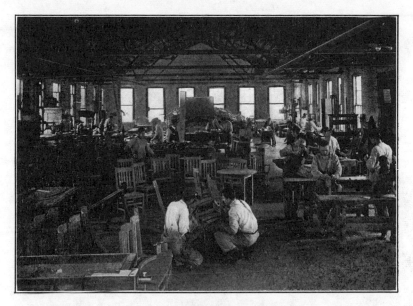

Cabinet-Making Shop.

A Classroom at the Reformatory School.

PLATE XI. Industrial and Academic Education at Rahway.

problems of reformation in general: (1) permanent segregation and humane confinement must be provided for those who
are not amenable to reformatory influences; (2) before committing an offender, the magistrate should acquaint himself with
the personal record and mental traits of the convicted person,
and those with marked and persistent criminal tendencies should
be sent to the state prison, or if feeble-minded to the proper
custodial institution for such classes; (3) an attempt must be
made to transform the homes of those paroled or discharged,
if these homes are not conducive to right living; (4) the inmates of the reformatory must be taught a trade and an effort
must be made to get the labor unions to admit paroled and discharged inmates as apprentices; (5) those committed must be
retained in the institution long enough to allow the reformatory
influences to have some opportunity to operate.[1]

The changes, then, which, according to some of the best
opinion in the state, are most needed in the reformatory, are:
first, a relinquishment of the present site and plant, and the
erection of a new plant modelled on the most advanced ideas of
reformatory architecture, so that the management will not be
hampered by defects in the physical equipment; and, second,
an adequate provision of working capital which will allow a
thorough and business-like reconstruction of the industries on
the "state use" system, both in mechanical industries within
the institution, and in outdoor activities on a reformatory farm,
or in road building and allied industries. In general, it is most
essential that the present theory and practice at Rahway be converted into a general system of reformatory procedure and be
made a part of the general attitude of the community towards
the offenders so that it will not remain chiefly dependent upon
the present enlightened board of commissioners or upon the personal energy and ability of the superintendent and be likely to
perish with their departure.

[1] Ibid., pp. 13–16.

THE ORIGIN AND DEVELOPMENT OF THE STATE REFORMATORY FOR WOMEN AT CLINTON FARMS

CHAPTER X

THE ORIGIN AND DEVELOPMENT OF THE STATE REFORMA-
TORY FOR WOMEN AT CLINTON FARMS.

I. The Legal Organization and Administration.
II. General Survey of the Foundation and Development of New Jersey State
Reformatory for Women.

I. THE LEGAL ORGANIZATION AND ADMINISTRATION OF THE STATE REFORMATORY FOR WOMEN AT CLINTON FARMS.

After a period of agitation lasting over half a century, a law was finally passed on April 1, 1910, establishing a reformatory for women at Clinton.[1] It was enacted that the name of the institution should be "The New Jersey State Reformatory for Women." [2] The general control over the administration and policies of the institution was vested in a board of six commissioners appointed by the governor, with the consent of the senate, for a term of three years.[3] The commissioners were to receive no salary. The board of commissioners was authorized to appoint as the chief executive and disciplinary officer, a superintendent, to hold office during good behavior at the pleasure of the board, and to determine the number of subordinate officers and fix their salaries.[4] It was provided that the superintendent should appoint and remove the subordinate officers subject to the approval of the commissioners.[5] As to commitment, it was provided that all women convicted of other than capital crimes, over the age of seventeen, might be committed to the reformatory by the courts, and that all such female inmates of the state prison

---

[1] *Acts of the 134th Legislature*, 1910, pp. 101–109; *Compiled Statutes of New Jersey*, 1911, Vol. IV, pp. 4933ff.

[2] Ibid., p. 4933.

[3] Ibid., p. 4934.

[4] Ibid.

[5] Ibid., p. 4935.

might be transferred to the reformatory.[1] It was specified that
the commitment was to be indeterminate, limited only by the
maximum legal penalty for the particular offence for which the
individual was committed.[2] The commissioners were authorized to draw up the rules to govern the discharge and parole of
inmates, it being specified that the commissioners, upon the recommendation of the superintendent, should have the power to discharged paroled prisoners.[3]

The act of February 5, 1913, slightly changed this organizing
law of 1910 by authorizing the governor to appoint two additional commissioners for a term of three years, thus increasing
the membership of the board of commissioners to eight.[4]

There can, thus, be no doubt that the state reformatory for
women originated under better legal auspices than any of the
other penal, reformatory and correctional institutions of the
state. Its modern and flexible legal organization was doubtless
due to the fact that the institution originated so recently that it
was able to avoid being burdened with the paralyzing traditional
criminal and penal jurisprudence.

2. General Survey of the Foundation and Development of the New Jersey State Reformatory for Women.

While the reformatory for women at Clinton has had so short
a period of existence that it can hardly be said to have a history,
like the reformatory for men at Rahway, the story of its origin
covers the greater part of a century. As there was little thought
of providing separate institutions for the treatment of male and
female delinquents in New Jersey before the period of the Civil
War, the requests for the provision of a reformatory or intermediate prison for the younger and less hardened convicts,
which go back to the first quarter of the nineteenth century, ap-

[1] Ibid., p. 4936.
[2] Ibid., p. 4937.
[3] Ibid.
[4] *Acts of the 137th Legislature,* 1913, p. 15.

plied to a reformatory for women as well as for men. Therefore, the attempts made to provide a reformatory in 1849–52, and in 1869, may be regarded as in part efforts to furnish New Jersey with a reformatory for female first offenders. By the "seventies," however, there was little thought of providing a single reformatory for both men and women, and the agitation was then divided into attempts to establish separate reformatories for male and female delinquents. It was generally understood that both were required, but the larger number of male delinquents produced a greater volume of pressure for a reformatory for men, and the establishment of Rahway thus preceded Clinton Farms by a decade.

The advocates of penal reform in New Jersey came near to a successful agitation for a reformatory for women in 1886, when a joint committee of the legislature was appointed "on a Female Prison and Reformatory." This committee visited the most advanced and successful reformatories for women then in existence, namely, at Indianapolis, Indiana; at Sherborn, Massachusetts, and at Hudson, New York.[1] In its report, it eloquently urged the erection in New Jersey of an institution of this type.[2] The legislature passed a resolution approving the report of the committee, but never took any further action.[3]

After 1886 the agitation for a reformatory for women died out to a certain degree, in all probability due to the fact that in that year Mrs. John H. Patterson began her ten years' service as matron of the female ward of the state prison, and proved so competent an administrator that the necessity of a reformatory for women was greatly lessened.[4] An expenditure of $14,000 in improving the women's wing of the state prison in 1899 also

---

[1] *Report of the Joint Committee on a Female Prison and Reformatory,* 1886, p. 3; Document No. 39, in *Legislative Documents* for 1887. See Documents, Part II, pp. 621–5.

[2] *Ibid.,* pp. 6–7.

[3] *Acts of the 110th Legislature,* 1886, p. 419.

[4] *Annual Report of the State Prison,* 1890, p. 62. See also the *Report of the Special Committee of the Legislature on the State Prison,* 1890, Document, 27, in *Legislative Documents,* 1890.

20 P

operated to postpone any crisis in the efforts to provide a reformatory for women.

By 1903, however, the Federation of Women's Clubs of New Jersey and various reform associations, particularly the State Charities Aid Association, induced Governor Murphy to appoint a commission on a reformatory for women. This commission reported strongly in favor of a reformatory on the cottage plan, but nothing definite resulted from their report beyond a resolution of the Legislature in 1904 requesting the Commission to prepare another report on the same subject. This supplemental report repeated the request of the report of the year before for the immediate establishment of a reformatory for women.[1] Though neither of these reports succeeded in their immediate aims, they served to give impetus to the agitation. In 1907 a bill to establish a reformatory for women passed the Assembly, but failed of passage in the Senate. The demand for the erection of a women's reformatory was also advanced in vigorous terms by the Commission on Dependency and Crime of 1908.[2] By 1910 the pressure of public opinion was too great for the Legislature to resist and the advocates of the institution secured the passage of the law of April 1, 1910, establishing the reformatory for women.[3] Throughout the decade of agitation preceding the final success, Mrs. Caroline B. Alexander-Wittpenn was the leader in organizing the sentiment in favor of the erection of the institution, and since its establishment she has been, as president of the board of commissioners, most energetic in getting the reformatory organized and equipped as a working institution.

While there is no doubt that New Jersey has lost greatly by not being provided earlier with this indispensible adjunct to any complete system of institutions for dealing with the delinquent population, the late origin of the reformatory for women was

[1] The reports of 1903 and 1904 are printed as Document No. 57 in the *Legislative Documents* for 1904, Vol. V. See Documents, Part II, pp. 625–31.

[2] *Report of the Dependency and Crimes Commission,* 1908, p. 17; *New Jersey Review of Charities and Corrections,* December, 1908, p. 284.

[3] *First Annual Report of the Board of Managers of the New Jersey State Reformatory for Women at Clinton,* 1913, pp. 5–8. This first report gives a short sketch of the origin of the institution.

Stowe Cottage.

Paddock Cottage.

PLATE XII. Views of the New Jersey Reformatory for Women.

not without its beneficial and compensating aspects. If it had originated in 1886, when such an institution was thought of as synonymous with a "female prison," the institution would now have fastened on it the burden of an outgrown set of traditions concerning crime and its treatment, of an archaic type of administration, and of an even more antiquated physical equipment than Rahway is hampered with at present. There cannot be the slightest doubt that within a decade the reformatory for women in New Jersey will be a more advanced and successful institution than would have been the case if it had originated thirty years ago.

A picturesque and salubrious site for the reformatory was selected at Clinton, in the hills of Hunterdon County, where a farm of 346 acres was purchased. A competent superintendent was secured in the person of Miss May Caughey, formerly of the House of Refuge for Girls at Darlington, Pennsylvania.[1]

The first inmates were received in January, 1913, and the institution was formally opened on May 26, 1913.[2]

In the beginning the institution was conducted on the theory that all inmates must be submitted to a rigid psychological test, and, as far as possible, receive the specialized treatment which their individual cases should require, but the important psychological tests have, of late, not gone beyond the Binet-Simon test for sub-normal mentality. Frequent visits by a competent psychiatrist are indispensible.[3]

It has been the policy of the institution to adapt its education to fitting the inmates for competent domestics. As the superintendent expressed this aim:

"To summarize our general work here, our aim is to make the women feel the importance and necessity of doing good housework in all its branches."[4]

The honor system of institutional government has been followed in the main since the opening of the institution.[5]

[1] Ibid., p. 7. Miss Caughey was succeeded by Miss Helen M. Hamilton in 1917.
[2] Ibid.
[3] Ibid., pp. 8–9; *Second Annual Report,* 1914, p. 6; 1915, p. 10.
[4] *Annual Report,* 1914, p. 7.
[5] Ibid., pp. 8–9; Ibid., 1915, pp. 12–13.

The third annual report, that for 1915, sets forth the aims and ideals of the institution as they had been formulated after two years' experience with the problems which must be faced by the institution. The board of managers thus describe the two fundamental ideals of their institution:

"First, to return to society, individuals transformed from a menace into an acquisition, and secondly, to contribute our quota to a study of the whole question of the delinquent girl, second but yet valuable." [1]

The assertion that the reformatory idea is kept continually in the foreground is also well stated by the superintendent:

"The work of every reformatory institution should be two-fold; to train the women in the institution to useful and helpful work, and to prepare them to again take their places in the world, better able to cope with the difficulties, social and economic, than before. Unless the majority of women can be returned to the world to lead successful lives, they ought not to be in a reformatory, but in some custodial institution." [2]

Especially significant is the careful administration of the parole system:

"No girl is paroled from Clinton Farms until the Managers are convinced of three things, that the girl intends to make a new start, that she has learned to make an honest living, that she is placed in surroundings which will help her upwards and not downwards." [3]

Sympathetic personal training for future liberty and guidance when on parole are furnished by the institution authorities. [4]

The chief defect in the system of management has been the lack of a scientific system of grading and meriting. The institution has been conducted mainly as an overgrown family. This semi-domestic procedure has succeeded admirably, owing to the tact and ability of the superintendent and the active interest of the commissioners, but it will be entirely inadequate to handle

[1] Report cited, p. 3.
[2] Ibid., p. 9.
[3] Ibid., p. 5.
[4] Ibid., p. 10.

PLATE XIII. Chapel at New Jersey Reformatory for Women.

the situation when the population has increased, as it is likely to do when the advantages of the institution are fully realized and utilized by the courts.

While the site selected for the reformatory was admirable, even if slightly inaccessible, the physical equipment was rather primitive at the outset, and has never been brought up to the needs of the institution. At first, the inmates were housed in three farm buildings, which were located on the grounds purchased by the state for the reformatory. Stowe Cottage, a separate building for the negro inmates, was erected in 1914, and has proved adequate as yet for the housing of the colored population. Paddock Cottage is nearing completion, and this will provide an infirmary and an administration building, together with housing facilities for a number of inmates. A chapel has been erected through the generosity of Mrs. Wittpenn. Adequate farm buildings for the scientific exploitation of the agricultural resources of the reformatory farm have not been provided as yet.[1]

The industries at the reformatory at Clinton Farms have never been developed beyond those which are incidental to the general problems of maintenance, including the cultivation of the reformatory farm and the domestic activities of the institution. While one may agree with the managing authorities that domestic training is an exceedingly valuable type of discipline for the inmates, there is little doubt that more extensive facilities should be provided for the development of real and varied industrial training, including both the mechanical and clerical branches.

The following extract from the Report of the Secretary of the State Charities Aid and Prison Reform Association for 1915 presents the impression made by the reformatory at Clinton upon a trained and experienced observer of penal and reformatory institutions:

"The Board of Managers of the New Jersey State Reformatory for Women, better known as 'Clinton Farms,' has succeeded in developing an almost ideal custodial and training institution for women. When one considers that throughout the United States so little has been done by the public,

[1] See plan of grounds and buildings opposite page 310.

through city, county or municipal effort, for the correction and reformation of women who have committed criminal acts, the work at Clinton Farms is far in advance of any modern effort undertaken elsewhere. This is due to the fact that the institution is a new one, and advantages have been taken of the errors and mistakes made in other states and other commmunities.

. . . .

"With this situation in New Jersey clearly understood, a visit to Clinton Farms is a revelation; it cannot help but appeal even to the superficial observer. Here is a farm house remodeled into a comfortable, home-like house, with rugs on the floor, a fire in the grate in the living room where there are rocking-chairs, curtains at the windows, and a canary and other household pets. There are rooms, clean and neat in their appointments, where the women sleep. There are no clanging steel or iron doors except the two in the basement for the temporary confinement of the women who develop a nervous tendency to temporarily rebel at authority. If it were not for the fact that these women feel that they are under sentence of the court and deprived of their liberty they would be more satisfied with their lot; however, the fact that one person is under the control of another prevents any sort of institution, however well equipped and planned, from being satisfactory to the inmates. There are no indications from the dress of these women that they are different from others. They wear khaki bloomers while at work in the laundry and at various outdoor occupations, but within the house they dress in neat garments and live very nearly a normal life. The new cottage for the colored women is a distinct division of Clinton Farms. It is located a quarter of a mile, at least, from the main farmhouse. It is also provided with neat rooms, one for each of the women, a very attractive sitting room and a large veranda for fresh-air purposes, a neatly appointed dining-room and an admirable kitchen. That this kitchen has been given good opportunity for service is indicated by the large and varied assortment of fruit and vegetables in glass jars that have been 'put up' during the summer and fall by these women. In another farmhouse, further down the hill from the main farmhouse, a group of women having been living, almost from the beginning of the institution, practically by themselves without guard.

"These are the selected and trustworthy women who fully appreciate the opportunity of living in a condition of the least possible supervision and restraint. It is a far cry from the old institutional management of cells and strict supervision to the comparative freedom and opportunity for self-expression afforded the women offenders in New Jersey by this new type of institution at Clinton Farms. All the routine of housework is performed with the thought of its educational and training values. In addition to this, many opportunities are afforded for the development of the women, mentally and physically, in outdoor occupations, in the garden, around the barns in the care of livestock, and in the cultivation of crops on the farm. There are a round of interesting features from the early spring ploughing and planting, through the cultivation period up to the time of harvest and the gathering of the varied crops. It is a slow work, of course, to take these

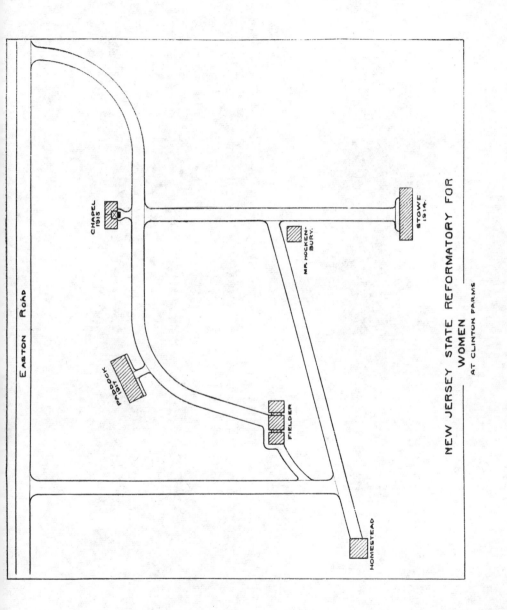

EASTON ROAD

CHAPEL 1915

PADDOCK 1911

FIELDER

MR. HOCKEN-BURY.

STOWE 1914.

HOMESTEAD

NEW JERSEY STATE REFORMATORY FOR WOMEN

AT CLINTON FARMS

women from all the unhappy and unfortunate training of previous years, transfer them to this farm colony and develop them under all these advantages of comparative freedom, varied activity and the inspiration that comes from plenty of open-air work on a farm, which at Clinton Farms happens to be admirably located, possessing as it does some very attractive scenic possibilities. While it is, of course, too soon to assert that this method is restoring women to normal social life, the experience of the three years at Clinton Farms has given enough concrete examples to satisfy the Board of Managers that the present program has great possibilities in the future." [1]

While, to one who has followed closely the history of the penal institutions of New Jersey, this description may seem almost as idyllic as Rousseau's picture of the life of man in the state of nature, there can be no doubt that at Clinton Farms a glimpse has been caught of at least the *spirit* of the reformatory of the future. It is most essential to see to it that its facilities are made available for a greater number of delinquent girls and that its resources are increased in keeping with the intelligence of its management and in proportion to the scope of its activities.

[1] C. L. Stonaker, in the report cited, pp. 26–8.

A BRIEF SURVEY OF THE DEVELOPMENT OF THE COUNTY PENAL INSTITUTIONS: JAILS AND WORKHOUSES

CHAPTER XI

A BRIEF SURVEY OF THE DEVELOPMENT OF THE COUNTY
PENAL INSTITUTIONS: JAILS AND WORKHOUSES.

I. THE LEGAL AND ADMINISTRATIVE HISTORY OF THE NEW JERSEY COUNTY JAIL SYSTEM AND THE COUNTY WORKHOUSES.

I. THE COUNTY JAILS.

There were no radical changes made in the basis of the organization and administration of the county jails of New Jersey after the adoption of the state constitution, 1776. The laws that were adopted between 1776 and 1800 to regulate the administration of the county jails were obviously modelled after those of 1683, 1710, 1714 and 1748 vesting the financial control of the jails in the board of chosen freeholders, and the administration of the jails in the sheriff of the county.

The constitution adopted in 1776 declared that the sheriff should be elected annually by the qualified voters of his county, and that he might hold office for three years in succession, after which three years had to elapse before he would again be eligible to hold the position.[1]

The acts of October 8, 1778, and March 18, 1796, vested the control of the jails in the sheriff of the county. It was enacted that,

[1] *Constitution of the State of New Jersey,* 1776, Sec. XIII.

"The sheriff of each county in this state shall have the custody, rule, keeping, and charge of the gaol or gaols within such county, and of all prisoners in such gaol or goals; and shall be responsible for the conduct of any keeper, whom he shall appoint for the same.

"It shall be the duty of the sheriffs and gaolers to receive from constables and other officers, all persons who shall be apprehended by such constables or officers for offences against this state; and if any sheriff or gaoler refuse to receive any such offenders, he shall be adjudged to be guilty of a misdemeanor and, on conviction, shall be fined at the discretion of the court." [1]

It was further decreed that the prisoners in the jails might have anything to eat, drink, or wear that they might send for and receive from outside, and the sheriff was directed to keep the debtors and convicted criminals in separate compartments. [2]

The fees to be received by the sheriff for administering the county jail were regulated by the general "Fees Act" of June 13, 1799. This provided that the sheriff should receive ten cents per day for "victualling a prisoner," twenty-five cents for receiving a prisoner, and twelve cents for discharging a prisoner. [3]

The general financial control of the board of chosen freeholders over the building and repairing of county jails, first bestowed by the laws of 1710 and 1714, was confirmed by the law of February 13, 1798, which decreed that,

"It shall be the duty of every board of chosen freeholders, at their stated annual meeting, or at any other meeting duly held for the purpose, to vote, grant, and raise such sum or sums of money for the building, purchasing, and repairing of poorhouses, gaols, courthouses, and bridges. . . . All which moneys, so raised, shall be applied, paid, and expended under the direction and management of the said corporation." [4]

The chief innovation introduced by the law of 1798 was that it eliminated the justices of the peace from the county board and incorporated the freeholders alone.

[1] Act of March 18, 1796, in *The Laws of New Jersey, Revised and Published under the Authority of the Legislature by Joseph Justice*, Trenton, 1821, pp. 238–9.

[2] Ibid., p. 240.

[3] Ibid., pp. 488–9.

[4] Ibid., p. 318; Cf. Elmer, *The Constitution and Government of the Province and State of New Jersey*, in *Collections of the New Jersey Historical Society*, Vol. VII, p. 18.

These laws, passed in the closing years of the eighteenth century, remained the legal basis for the administration of the jail system for more than half a century with no changes whatever, and are, in all fundamental aspects, the legal foundation of the present jail system. The new constitution, adopted in 1844, incorporated the provisions of the constitution of 1776 regarding the election and tenure of the sheriff.[1] The revision of 1846 retained unchanged the laws of October 8, 1778, and March 18, 1796, vesting the control of the jails in the sheriff; the laws of February 18, 1795, and June 13, 1799, prescribing the fees to be received by sheriffs for the administration of the jails; and the act of February 13, 1798, authorizing the board of chosen freeholders to assume the financial control of the county jails.[2]

The first important variation in this legal basis of the administration of the state prison came in the law of February 27, 1857, but this was not a general act but rather a special law for the benefit of two populous counties which contemplated the erection of a more elaborate and modern type of county jail and workhouse. This act provided that in Essex and Hudson counties the control of the county jails should be taken from the sheriff and vested in the board of chosen freeholders. The freeholders were authorized to appoint a jailor for a term of five years, who was also to be the master of the workhouses, which, it was contemplated, would be erected as a part of the penal system of these counties. It was further provided that the court might sentence a prisoner to the workhouses in these counties at hard labor instead of sending him to the state prison. Courts in other counties were also authorized to send prisoners to these counties, with the consent of the freeholders of Essex and Hudson counties, and under such conditions as the freeholders might impose.[3]

The revision of 1876-7, while keeping the same general organizing acts that were incorporated in the revision of 1846,

---

[1] *Constitution of the State of New Jersey*, 1844, Art. VII, Sec. ii., par. 7.
[2] Elmer-Nixon, *Digest of the Laws of New Jersey*, 2nd Ed., 1855, pp. 101, 269, 751.
[3] *Acts of the 81st Legislature*, 1857, pp. 40ff.

added a few innovations. The act of April 20, 1876, gave the freeholders the power to fix the price of "victualing the prisoners" in the county jails, provided that they did not exceed the legal allowance for this purpose in any county.[1] The law of April 21, 1876, authorized the board of chosen freeholders to remit sentences in the county jail for good behavior, up to one-sixth of the sentence, though a discharge by the board in advance of the expiration of the sentence of the court was required to be countersigned by the presiding judge of the court of common pleas.[2]

A feeble attempt was made in 1880 to provide a legal basis for the solution of the perennial problem of idleness in the county jails. It was enacted that the jailor might employ at "reasonable labor" all prisoners confined in the county jails for fines or non-payment of costs.[3] This provision was extended to all jail inmates by the law of May 6, 1889.[4]

The first really significant departure from the original laws of the eighteenth century defining the organization of the county jails was the act of March 3, 1887, which authorized the board of chosen freeholders in any county to assume the control of the county jails, if a majority of the board desired to do so. In all counties where they did so assume the control, the freeholders were vested with the power to appoint a warden or keeper of the jail and to make the general rules for the conduct of the jail. In case a workhouse was a part of the county jail system in any county the keeper of the jail was also to act as master of the workhouse.[5]

The act of March 21, 1888, attempted to eliminate the evil of promiscuous herding of prisoners of all ages in the county jails. It provided that there must be separate compartments provided for the confinement of all persons under sixteen years of age who were detained in county jails. No person under sixteen was

[1] *Acts of the 100th Legislature*, 1876, p. 230.
[2] Ibid., pp. 381–2.
[3] *Acts of the 104th Legislature*, 1880, p. 82.
[4] *Acts of the 113th Legislature*, 1889, p. 349.
[5] *Acts of the 111th Legislature*, 1887, pp. 42–4.

to be confined more than twenty-four hours in any jail where there was no provision for separate confinement.[1]

The law of May 25, 1894, partially abrogated the law of March 3, 1887, by declaring that the sheriff of the county should assume charge of all jails in first class counties.[2]   By the act of March 23, 1900, this provision was extended to all counties having a population of less than 125,000, the sheriffs being vested with the control of the jails in all such counties, but in all counties the sheriff was authorized to order the freeholders to assume the duty of administering the jails.[3]

In 1894, a decision was given in a test case that finally ended all discussions regarding the right of custody of jails and prisons:

"The office of sheriff, with its common-law duties, having been continued by the colonial and state constitutions, and a part of such duties being the custody of the county jails and of the prisoners confined therein, such parts of this act as provide that the charge and keeping of county jails and custody of the prisoners therein be transferred from the sheriffs to the boards of chosen freeholders, are unconstitutional and void."[4]

Laws that attempted to give the custody to boards of freeholders were repealed, and subsequently other laws have been enacted to enable some counties to take over the jail management, but, in the face of this decision just quoted, such laws apparently cannot stand. The sheriff still must assume custody of prisoners and must assume the responsibility of jail control, and it is doubtful if a law permitting that official to ask to be relieved will stand a test in court.

The laws of 1894 and 1900, having thus brought the jails back into the custody of the sheriff,[5] and the act of 1798 vesting the financial control of the building and repairing of jails in the board of chosen freeholders having been retained without any

[1] *Acts of the 112th Legislature*, 1888, pp. 188–9.
[2] *Acts of the 118th Legislature*, 1894, pp. 378, 534–5, 597.
[3] *Acts of the 124th Legislature*, 1900, p. 474.
[4] Virtue *vs.* Board of Chosen Freeholders, 67 L. 139, 50 A. 360.
[5] The amended constitutions of 1876 and 1897 provided that the sheriff should be elected by general vote of the county for a term of three years.

significant changes, it is correct to state that the legal basis of the administration of the county jails is not fundamentally different from that with which the state entered upon the nineteenth century.

2. WORKHOUSES.

The present legal basis of the administration of the workhouse system in New Jersey even more closely resembles the colonial practice and traditions than the legal organization of the county jails of the present day.

The first state act regulating workhouses was that of February 20, 1799. According to this law it was enacted,

"That the board of chosen freeholders of every county in this state are hereby authorized, whenever they may think proper, to build or purchase a workhouse, at such place in the county, as the said corporation shall think fit."

The board of chosen freeholders were to have general charge of the workhouse and determine its general policy and frame the rules for its administration. They were also empowered to appoint a fit person for master of the workhouse and such other officers as might be necessary. Every person sentenced to imprisonment at hard labor for less than six months was to be sent to a workhouse. The freeholders were directed to supply raw materials for the workhouse and to keep an account of the expenses of maintenance, raw material used, and earnings, and were ordered to turn over the proceeds into the general treasury of the county. Finally, this law authorized two or more counties to unite in building or purchasing a joint workhouse.[1]

The general resemblance of this act of 1799 to the original workhouse act of 1748 is readily apparent.[2] This law has never been altered, as the basis of the workhouse system of New Jersey, to the present day. A slight addition was made by the act of

[1] *Laws of the State of New Jersey, Revised and Published under the Authority of the Legislature by Joseph Justice,* Trenton, 1821, pp. 443–5.
[2] See above, pp. 5of.

March 4, 1847, which allowed the board of freeholders to convert as much of the county jail into a workhouse as they desired.[1]

II. GENERAL OUTLINE OF THE DEVELOPMENT OF THE JAIL AND WORKHOUSE SYSTEMS OF NEW JERSEY SINCE THE COLONIAL PERIOD.

1. THE JAIL SYSTEM.

There were no radical changes in either the legal or the administrative basis of the jail system of New Jersey after the adoption
of the state government. The Constitution of 1776 continued
the office of sheriff as the chief executive officer of the county,
and the acts of October 8, 1778, and March 18, 1796, confirmed
the colonial practice by vesting the administration of the jails in
the sheriffs. Again, the act of February 18, 1798, reënacted the
provisions of the laws of 1710 and 1714 giving to the boards of
chosen freeholders the financial powers over the building and repairing of jails and courthouses.

There is no evidence that there was any change in the conventional notion of the nature of a jail or in the method of jail administration after 1776. The jails built in the latter part of the
eighteenth century and in the first quarter of the next century
were usually constructed in a more substantial manner than the
rough frame buildings of the colonial period, being in the main
constructed of stone or brick, probably because of the notorious
experience of the colonial period with jail burning. But this
aspect of greater permanence was the only advance in jail architecture. There was little or no provision for any proper degree
of classification, differentiation, or segregation of the different
classes of criminals and the reports of contemporary investigating committees indicate that in many cases the sheriffs did not
carry out the provisions of the laws of 1778 and 1796 which

---

[1] *Acts of the 71st Legislature,* 1847, p. 175; *General Statutes of New Jersey,*
1895, pp. 1838–40; *Compiled Statutes of New Jersey,* 1911, pp. 2952–2955.

directed the sheriff to keep the debtors and convicted criminals in separate compartments. Many of the jails were nothing more than dungeons in the basements of the courthouses and were thus both demoralizing and extremely unhealthy.

The one great improvement, as regards the conditions in the jails, which took place at the extreme end of the eighteenth century, came not as a result of any direct improvement of the jails, but indirectly through the erection of a state prison, in 1797. This allowed a separation of the more vicious criminals from those convicted of minor offences and those detained for trial or as witnesses, it being enacted that all persons sentenced to imprisonment for more than six months should be sent to the state prison at Lamberton (Trenton). However, this did not provide for the elimination of what is conventionally deemed to be the worst type of criminals, for all persons condemned to death were kept in the jails until their execution by the sheriffs. Not until the beginning of the twentieth century was the death penalty inflicted by state officials in the state prison. But in spite of its shortcomings, however, the erection of the state prison lifted a great burden from the administration of the county jails, though the state officials complained that there had been too great a shifting of the load upon the state, and for years urged that no person be sent to the state prison for a term of less than one year.

In addition to the general defects inherent in the jail system, such as idleness, indiscriminate huddling together of all classes of prisoners, filthiness, and complete lack of instruction in educational and religious matters, a particularly serious situation developed in regard to the imprisonment of debtors in the county jails, New Jersey adhering, up to 1846, to the barbarous and irrational practice of confining debtors in the jails.[1] This evil, in a large degree, brought into being the *New Jersey Howard Society* in the early "thirties," which was named after the famous Englishman who had done so much to improve the condition of debtors in the jails and prisons of England.[2] It was in part due to their efforts, supported by the New Jersey representatives of

[1] See Documents, Part II, pp. 635–6.
[2] *Ninth Annual Report of the Boston Prison Discipline Society,* 1834, p. 85.

the Boston Prison Discipline Society, that the laws of April 15th and April 16th, 1846, were passed which abolished imprisonment for debt in practically all cases not involving fraud.

The lack of any religious instruction in the jails was a serious shock to many of the citizens of the state and the *New Jersey Prison Instruction Society* was organized in 1832–3 to provide facilities for preaching the gospel in the jails and the state prison.[1]

Another extremely important movement for the improvement of the jails of New Jersey was that which centered around the efforts of Dorothea Dix in the "forties" to secure some adequate provision for the care of the insane, who were at that time confined in the almshouses and jails, and often treated in the most cruel and revolting manner. The famous *Memorial* of Miss Dix to the legislature in 1845 revealed in a graphic manner the depressing situation which existed and was very instrumental in arousing sentiment for the establishment of a state hospital for the insane at Trenton in 1848.[2]

The best source for the condition of the county jails in the middle of the nineteenth century is the reports and memorials of the *New Jersey Prison Reform Association* which flourished from 1849 to 1852. The best summary of the situation is presented in the Memorial of the Association to the Legislature on January 25, 1850, relative to the improvement of the county jails. From a detailed examination of the different county jails the committee declared that "there is, throughout the state, with hardly an exception, a defective system of management in our county jails, resulting in increased moral degradation to the criminal, serious expense to the counties, and injury to the community at large." [3] The committee found that there were four conspicu-

[1] *Eighth Annual Report*, 1833, pp. 95–102. See Documents, Part II, pp. 480–2.

[2] *Memorial of Dorothea L. Dix to the New Jersey Legislature on the Insane in the New Jersey County Jails, Almshouses, and State Penitentiary*, January, 1845, pp. 5–23.

[3] *Memorial of the New Jersey Prison Reform Association, to the Senate and General Assembly in Relation to the Improvement of County Jails*, January 25, 1850, p. 3. See Documents, Part II, pp. 636–8. One should also consult the Annual Reports of the Prison Reform Association from 1850–1852.

ous evils in the existing jail system. In the first place, there was an almost complete lack of employment for those confined. Though the law of 1799 authorized the freeholders to erect workhouses, only one county had made the slightest approach to availing itself of this legal provision.[1] In the second place, there was no proper classification of prisoners as to age, sex, and degree of criminality. In some cases even the sexes were not separated. The committee concluded that "this promiscuous association cannot but lead to moral pollution."[2] In the third place, there was little attention paid to the cleanliness and comfort of the inmates of the jails. While a few of the jails were kept in a condition of moderate cleanliness, the majority of them were in a condition of "loathsome filthiness."[3] Finally, there was no approximation to a rational system of "moral discipline." The committee saw little hope for the reformation of offenders when every prisoner "was shut up in common with a crowd of degraded beings like himself, in a cold and filthy cell, with scarcely clothes enough for decency, not even straw to lie upon, no occupation but that of imparting or learning lessons of vice—without books—without a word of good advice, and almost without hope."[4]

The general situation was summarized as follows:

"It cannot but be evident to the most casual observer that our jails, with their promiscuous intercourse, their idleness, their scenes of drunkenness, and, your memorialists regret to add, their loathsome filthiness, cannot be otherwise than sources of great moral evil to the community."[5]

The committee presented their recommendations in the following paragraph:

"Let then wise, well-considered, and judicious enactments be passed, that shall provide for the strict enforcement of *hard labor,* for the proper separation of the hardened criminal from those younger in vice, and from those merely committed for trial, as also the sexes; for a reformation in the treat-

[1] *Memorial* cited, p. 4.
[2] Ibid., pp. 4–5.
[3] Ibid., p. 5.
[4] Ibid.
[5] Ibid.

ment of criminals as regards cleanliness, the ventilation and warming of the jails, and the providing of decent clothing, and for the introduction of some degree of moral discipline." [1]

In short, this report was an effective demonstration of the fact that the jails of New Jersey had made no advance over those of a century earlier and were a failure at every point except as a partial protection to society. Even in this respect, it is scarcely probable that their net result was beneficial, for the increased demoralization of the inmates no doubt more than offset the protective value of their temporary detention apart from society.

That the protests of the memorialists of 1850 availed little in improving the jail situation in their state is apparent from the following letter sent by a leader of the New Jersey Bar to E. C. Wines and T. W. Dwight, and included by them in their report on the penal situation in America in 1867:

"A distinguished member of the bar of New Jersey writes to us in the following strain about the jails of that state: 'You ask me to add a paragraph concerning our county jails. This I can hardly do without feeling my indignation rise. I regard the outrages which are committed through these institutions as disgraceful and oppressive. They are not constructed properly. I have never been able to see by what right a person is deprived of the light and air of heaven, when he is committed only for trial; especially when, in nearly one-half of the cases of such commitment, there is not even an indictment found, and when, even if the accused is indicted, there is no conviction. Such persons are confined only to answer, and not as a punishment. There is no law justifying the privation of air and light, a comfortable bed, books to read, and other like reasonable comfort. Persons who have never before been charged with crime, and only now with a small offence, not able at present to give bail, are thrust into jail; subjected to dirt, vermin, offensive air and darkness; without a chair or table in the room; fed like a felon behind the bars; associated with the depraved and disgusting criminal; eating, sleeping and living with the wicked and profane: the whole suffering and degradation far heavier to bear than the penalty of the offence charged, which would only be a small fine, if convicted at all, which may not be the case. Oh! what a burning shame! There is no law for such treatment. Inexperienced youth, male and female, and respectable men and women, are sometimes obliged to be put into the sheriff's custody for a day or two, or longer, and they suffer such outrages as those described above, without any redress.

[1] Ibid., pp. 5–6.

" 'There should be more variety in the cells. There should be comfortable rooms, made secure, but not dark cells only. There should be more discrimination in the treatment of persons in jail. There should be an eye to the prevention of crime in the jailor. The jail, which generally is only preliminary as it were to the state prison, is a far greater punishment than confinement in the prison. Mercer county jail is notoriously bad. Several grand juries have presented it.' " [1]

This distressing condition of the county jails did not escape the vigilant Commission on Prison Discipline of 1869. In an appendix to their justly famous report they presented a detailed summary of the existing conditions in the county jails, dealing with both the physical equipment and the condition of management and administration.

In general, the commission found that there was no employment nor any instruction provided for the inmates. The physical condition of the jails was very poor, as a rule, though there were a few new jails, but these were rarely, if ever, designed according to the dictates of scientific penology, and while architectural ornaments they were very poor jails. [2]

In the matter of industries no employment was provided in more than two jails. Essex county had by far the best developed industrial organization and leased the labor of the inmates of the jail to contractors for 35 cents per day. They were employed in making leather novelties, scissors, and mail bags. Morris county also provided a workshop in connection with the jail and furnished employment for the inmates in making chair bottoms, hoops, and baskets. Hudson county was just erecting its well-known workhouse at Snake Hill. No employment was furnished to the inmates of any of the remaining county jails. [3]

The food provided in the jails was generally fair in both quantity and quality; only in Somerset county was it described as positively bad. [4]

[1] Wines and Dwight, *Report on the Prisons and Reformatories of the United States and Canada*, 1867, pp. 314–15.
[2] *Report of the Commissioners to Examine the Various Systems of Prison Discipline and Propose an Improved Plan*, Trenton, 1869, Appendix A, pp. 27–42.
[3] Ibid.
[4] Ibid.

PLATE XIV.   Relics of Barbarism in the New Jersey Jails.

No systematic instruction was provided in any jail in the state. In a few there were occasional preaching services and in Mercer county instruction was given to the children by an attendant.[1]

The physical equipment of the county jails varied greatly, some jails, such as those of Mercer, Salem, and Cumberland counties, were relatively new and modern, while others, notably those of Bergen, Burlington, Morris, Somerset, and Warren counties were hopelessly antiquated, and in some cases almost uninhabitable. Even the new jails were not scientifically constructed as penal institutions.[2]

The average population of the jails in 1868–9 also varied greatly, ranging from 106 in Essex, 87 in Hudson, 32 in Middlesex, and 30 in Sussex, to 5 in Cumberland, 4 in Hunterdon, 3 in Atlantic, 2 in Ocean, and 1 in Cape May[3]

The facilities for the segregation of the different classes of individuals confined in the jails were generally very limited. Some jails, such as those in Hudson and Essex counties, provided for the separation of debtors and witnesses, or for the segregation of the accused and the convicted, but in most of the jails the only provision for classification and segregation was a separation of sexes, and even this elementary differentiation was scarcely provided in Sussex, Gloucester, and Ocean counties.[4]

The commissioners found that the punishment consisted chiefly of confinement in damp and filthy dungeons, with some employment of the ball and chain, but, as a whole, the punishments inflicted were scarcely as serious or depressing as the more fundamental mistakes and failures of the whole jail system as a type of penal administration.[5]

The next important source of information regarding the condition of the jails of New Jersey is the report of the Commissioners on the Prison System of New Jersey and on an Intermediate Prison, in 1878. The commissioners reported that they

[1] Ibid.
[2] Ibid.
[3] Ibid.
[4] Ibid.
[5] Ibid.

had found some evidence of an improvement in the condition of the county jails as a result of the recommendations of the commission of 1869.[1] They found the same variation in physical equipment that had existed in 1869, but in most of the jails the sanitary provisions were tolerable. In all cases the commissioners found that the food served was adequate. The industrial situation, however, was as bad as possible. Only in Essex and Hudson counties, which had recently constructed workhouses, was there any systematic employment of the inmates of the county penal institutions. The commissioners concluded that the most fundamental defect in the contemporary jail system was "the indiscriminate mingling together of the prisoners in enforced idleness, with little effort to give them instruction, religious or moral or literary."[2] "Moral contamination and degeneration" could not but result from such a situation.[3] The commissioners, following the precedent established by the commission of 1869, strongly recommended that the jails be entirely transformed into places of detention for the accused and be abandoned as penal institutions.[4]

Since the establishment of the New Jersey State Charities Aid Association in 1886 the reports of this association have been the chief source of information regarding the condition of the county jails. The first extensive report by the Association on the county jails was presented in 1889. The standing committee of the Association on jails and station-houses submitted a detailed report on the structure and management of the most important jails. The worst defects of the system were found to be idleness, overcrowding, and a lack of the proper provisions for the segregation of the widely varied classes detained within the walls of the jails. In spite of the law passed on March 21, 1888, directing that separate quarters be provided in all jails for inmates under 16 years of age, the committee found that in many cases this pro-

[1] *Report of the Commissioners on the Prison System of New Jersey and on an Intermediate Prison,* 1878, p. 3. See Documents, Part II, pp. 599–611.
[2] Ibid., p. 3.
[3] Ibid., p. 4.
[4] Ibid., p. 15.

vision had not been complied with. Another serious abuse was the indiscriminate "huddling" of the detained witnesses with those accused and those convicted of crime. While few of the jails were scientifically constructed, the physical condition of the jails was condemned as bad only in the cases of those in Morris, Burlington, Essex, and Passaic counties. Only two jails, those of Union and Passaic counties, provided any employment for the inmates, and in Union county this merely consisted in working on the county buildings. Only in Passaic county were the inmates of the jail systematically employed. Here the men were consistently employed on road work and in breaking stone, and the women in sewing and cooking. The example of Passaic county was recommended to the thoughtful consideration of the freeholders of the other counties.[1] The committee thus summarized its findings:

"The detailed report attached will give a fair idea of the structure and management. Overcrowding and idleness are the greatest evils to be overcome. The general methods of detaining witnesses should receive especial attention; on no account should they be placed in cells with criminals.

"Your committee through the secretary has sent copies of the law requiring the separate confinement of persons under sixteen years of age to the chairman of the Board of Chosen Freeholders of the several counties that have not complied with its terms.

"We particularly commend the requiring of more work from prisoners, such as repairing the public roads, breaking stone, etc., for men not employed in the building.

"Women should be employed in the sewing-room when not needed in the kitchen and laundry. Idleness is the greatest evil to be overcome in prison life. We call your especial attention to the report on this subject from the Passaic county jail."[2]

In short, forty years after the famous Memorial of the Prison Reform Association very little advance had been made towards the transformation of the jails into a rationally conducted depart-

---

[1] *Annual Report of the State Charities Aid Association of New Jersey,* 1889, Document No. 39, in the *Legislative Documents* for 1890, pp. 12ff.

[2] Ibid., p. 8. Thomas S. Crane, Charlton T. Lewis, Mrs. Z. K. Rangborn, and Mrs. B. Williamson, Jr., were the members of this committee on jails and station houses.

ment of the penal administration of the state, and no determined move had been made towards adopting the advice of the Commission on Prison Discipline of 1869 relative to converting the jails into institutions solely for the detention of those accused of crime.

The next significant detailed report on the county jails, which was published by the State Charities Aid Association, appeared in 1901. This report is important chiefly as demonstrating that practically nothing had been done towards remedying the abuses which had been pointed out so clearly in 1889. The same general defects of uniform idleness and lack of provision for differentiation, classification, and segregation of inmates were as painfully apparent in 1901 as they had been a decade before. In spite of the law of 1888, the condition of minors in some of the jails was particularly distressing. As in 1889, there was nowhere, except in the jail of Passaic county, an attempt at a systematic employment of inmates. Elsewhere, the inmates of jails were either wholly unemployed or merely engaged a portion of the time in the domestic activities of the jails. The courts were also severely criticized for failing to sentence enough of those convicted for minor offences to the workhouses of Hudson, Essex, and Mercer counties.[1] The report contained an interesting statistical summary of the jail population and it is worthy of note that in 1901 the average jail population was 985 males, 144 females, and 49 juvenile inmates, making a total of 1,178.[2] This number was approximately equal to the average annual population of the state prison at that time.

The general situation in the county jails of New Jersey during recent years is best revealed in the reports of the State Charities Aid and Prison Reform Association of New Jersey since 1913. These are based upon the investigations of the Secretary of the Association, Mr. C. L. Stonaker, who has been particularly active in agitating for jail reform during his occupancy of the office.

[1] *Annual Report of the State Charities Aid Association,* 1901, Document No. 29, in *Legislative Documents* for 1901, pp. 94–123, especially pp. 29–31.
[2] Ibid., p. 94.

The physical equipment of the jails may be briefly summarized as follows: The county jail of Atlantic county at May's Landing is a comparatively modern jail with at least elementary provisions for the segregation of inmates.[1] Bergen county built a new jail at Hackensack in 1912 at a cost of $250,000, but so much money was lavished upon externals and upon the cage construction that it was crowded almost as soon as it was opened for the reception of inmates.[2] The Burlington county jail at Mount Holly is an exceedingly antiquated structure more than a century old.[3] The Camden county jail at Camden is a relatively modern structure with moderate provisions for segregation.[4] The jail of Cape May county at Cape May Court House is entirely adequate for the needs of that sparsely populated county.[5] The Cumberland county jail at Bridgeton was erected in 1897 and is adequate to the needs of the county.[6] The Essex county jail at Newark is sufficient to provide for the jail population, especially since the addition of a new wing in 1914 at a cost of $18,900.[7] The Gloucester county jail at Woodbury, while small, and erected in 1877, meets the needs of the county.[8] The Hudson county jail at Jersey City has long been recognized as inadequate to the needs of this populous county and a new jail has been planned for some time, but has not yet been provided.[9] The Hunterdon county jail at Flemington is one of the antique jails of the State, having been erected in 1826.[10] Mercer county has one of the best jails in the state, having erected a new one at Trenton in 1913–14, at a cost of $150,000.[11] Middlesex county has long possessed an obsolete jail at New Brunswick, but is now erecting a

[1] *Annual Report of the State Charities Aid and Prison Reform Association of New Jersey*, 1913, p. 42.

[2] Ibid., pp. 42–3. Ibid., 1914, p. 44.

[3] Ibid., 1913, p. 43.

[4] Ibid.

[5] Ibid.

[6] Ibid.

[7] Ibid., pp. 43–4; Ibid., 1914, p. 46.

[8] Ibid., 1913, p. 44.

[9] Ibid., p. 44; Ibid., 1914, pp. 46–7; Ibid., 1916, p. 39.

[10] Ibid., 1913, p. 44.

[11] Ibid., p. 45.

new jail and a county workhouse.[1]   Monmouth county has a
modern jail structure at Freehold.[2]   The Morris county jail at
Morristown, erected in 1826, is one of the oldest and worst constructed jails in the state.[3]   The Ocean County jail at Tom's
River, though built in 1850, is adequate to needs of the small jail
population.[4]   The Passaic county jail at Paterson, erected in
1854, is an extremely antiquated and poorly constructed jail, and
the situation is particularly serious in view of the size of the jail
population in this county.[5]   Salem county has an old jail at
Salem which was erected in 1866, but the recent practice of employing the inmates of the county jail on road work has relieved
the pressure on the old jail.[6]   Somerset county has a good new
jail at Somerville, and thus no longer enjoys the distinction that
it possessed in 1850 and 1869 of having the worst jail in the
state.[7]   Sussex county has a well-equipped jail located at New-
ton.[8]   Union county enjoys the distinction of having the cleanest
and best disciplined jail in the state, located at Elizabeth.[9]   Warren county erected a new jail built on the cage plan in 1913–14.[10]
Thus, as far as physical equipment is concerned, the New Jersey
jails are in a fair condition, only Burlington, Hudson, Hunterdon, Morris, and Passaic counties being in serious need of new
jail structures.

With respect to employment, the situation is much less satisfactory.   Only in Bergen, Salem, and Sussex counties is there
any systematic attempt to provide employment for the inmates
of the county jails beyond participation in the general domestic
activities of the institution.   In Bergen county the inmates of the

[1] Ibid., p. 45; Ibid., 1916, p. 40.
[2] Ibid., 1913, p. 45.
[3] Ibid., p. 45.
[4] Ibid., p. 46.
[5] Ibid., p. 46.   Ibid., 1914, p. 49.
[6] Ibid., 1913, p. 46.   Ibid., 1915, pp. 53-4.   Ibid., 1916, p. 42.
[7] Ibid., 1913, p. 46.
[8] Ibid., p. 46.
[9] Ibid., p. 47.   Ibid., 1916, p. 42.
[10] Ibid., 1913, p. 47.   Ibid., 1914, p. 50.

Colonial Jail at Perth Amboy, Erected in 1766.

Burlington County Jail, Erected in 1810.

Bergen County Jail, Erected in 1912.

PLATE XV. The Evolution of Jail Architecture in New Jersey.

jails are employed to some extent on the county farm.[1] In Salem and Sussex counties they are utilized in repairing the roads of the counties.[2] Obviously, then, the industrial situation in the jails today is in most cases as primitive and undeveloped as it was when the Memorialists of 1850 addressed their appeal to the Legislature for the provision of "hard labor" in the county jails.

No intelligent student of the subject denies that the solution of the jail question in New Jersey, as in other states, consists in abandoning them as places of punishment and in retaining them solely as places for the detention of those awaiting trial. The pentitentiary or workhouse is the only rational penal institution for those sentenced to imprisonment for short terms. The desirability of this fundamental differentiation in the county penal institutions was completely recognized by the noted Commission on Prison Discipline in 1869, which recommended in an unqualified manner the provision of county workhouses and the transformation of the jails into places for detaining the accused. This opinion has been shared by every important investigating committee on the penal institutions of the state since that time, including the Commission of 1878 and the Commission on Dependency and Crime of 1908. Ever since its organization the State Charities Aid Association of New Jersey has labored strenuously for the employment of the jails solely as places of detention for the accused; those convicted to be sent to the workhouses. But in spite of the general recognition of the necessity of this departure, only Essex county has even approximated its realization, by employing the jail mainly for the purpose of the detention of the accused and sending the condemned to the penitentiary or workhouse at Caldwell.

2. THE WORKHOUSE SYSTEM.

Legal provision for the development of a workhouse system in the state of New Jersey was early provided when the act of February 20, 1799, continued the precedent established by the colo-

---

[1] Ibid., 1916, p. 38.
[2] Ibid., 1914, p. 49. Ibid., 1915, pp. 53-4. Ibid., 1916, p. 42.

nial law of 1748 in authorizing the board of chosen freeholders to erect or purchase workhouses in each county.[1]   In addition to this general law of 1799, the act of November 22, 1808, authorized Trenton to erect a jail and workhouse,[2] and similar authority was conferred upon Burlington by the act of February 2, 1813.[3] Again, a general act of March 4, 1847, empowered the boards of chosen freeholders to convert as great a portion of the county jail structures into workhouses as they saw fit.

However, ample as were these legal provisions, they were scarcely exploited by the freeholders of the counties. The Memorialists of the New Jersey Prison Reform Association in 1850 reported that during the first half of the nineteenth century but one county had taken any advantage of these acts, and in this case only in a "half-hearted" manner.[4]   Not until Hudson county erected its noted workhouse or penitentiary at Snake Hill in 1869 was there any thoroughgoing attempt on the part of any county in the state to avail itself of the provisions of the law of 1799.[5] Essex county followed the example of Hudson and began erecting its workhouse at Caldwell in 1873.[6] The next step in the development of the workhouse system of the state came in the construction of a similar institution in Mercer county near Trenton in 1892. These three workhouses in Hudson, Essex, and Mercer counties are the only institutions of their kind that have as yet been constructed in the state. A municipal workhouse was provided by the city of Camden in 1913–14,[7] and in 1916 bonds were issued by the citizens of Middlesex county for $60,000 to construct a county workhouse.[8] Thus, the state is as far from pro-

[1] *The Laws of the State of New Jersey, Revised and Published by Joseph Justice,* Trenton, 1821, pp. 443–4.
[2] Ibid., pp. 538–9.
[3] Ibid., pp. 558–9.
[4] *Memorial* cited, p. 4.
[5] *Report of the Commissioners to Examine the Various Systems of Prison Discipline and Propose an Improved Plan,* 1869, p. 28.
[6] *Annual Report of the New Jersey State Charities Aid and Prison Reform Association,* 1915, p. 58.
[7] Ibid., 1914, p. 45.
[8] Ibid., 1916, p. 40.

viding the necessary system of county workhouses for the confinement of those sentenced to short terms of imprisonment as it is from abolishing imprisonment from the county jails and transforming them into institutions for detention only.

Even the three county workhouses now in operation in the state are not in any sense highly developed industrial institutions, though their relatively elementary industrial equipment is a great advance over the system of uniform idleness in vogue in the county jails. The Mercer county workhouse located at Moore Station, about twelve miles from Trenton, is chiefly a quarry site. Though there is a slight development of agricultural activities, the chief occupation is the breaking and crushing of stone.[1] The Hudson county workhouse, located at what was formerly known as Snake Hill, now changed to Laurel Hill, is also primarily a quarry site where the inmates are employed in crushing stone, and in road work. In addition there is some development of agricultural industry on reclaimed lands.[2] Essex county has provided a more diversified industrial organization at its workhouse located at North Caldwell. While, as in Hudson and Mercer counties, the basic industry is the quarrying and crushing of stone, there has been a considerable development of agricultural industry and the employment of prisoners in building roads. The women inmates are engaged in making clothing for the inmates of the workhouse and other county institutions. Two rather notable innovations have been recently introduced, namely, a modest night school and an elementary system of wage-payment for the inmates.[3]

While it would obviously be impossible for the less populous counties to support separate county workhouses, it would be highly practicable for a number of counties to unite in the support of a joint workhouse and thus relieve the jails of their demoralizing idleness and needless expense, to say nothing of the

[1] *Annual Report of the New Jersey State Charities Aid and Prison Reform Association,* 1915, pp. 59–60.

[2] Ibid., pp. 60–61.

[3] Ibid., pp. 61–2.

probable deterrent effect of a well-equipped workhouse system in causing a marked decline in the volume of petty crimes.[1]

[1] For a detailed statistical statement of the present situation, as to the condition of jails and workhouses in New Jersey, see the report on this subject by Mr. Philip Klein, published as an appendix to the *Report of the New Jersey Prison Inquiry Commission,* 1917.

PART II

DOCUMENTARY

CHAPTER I

DOCUMENTS RELATING TO THE
COLONIAL PERIOD

CHAPTER I

DOCUMENTS RELATING TO THE COLONIAL PERIOD.

I. THE PENAL CODES OF THE COLONIAL PERIOD.

1. THE CONNECTICUT ANTECEDENTS OF THE EAST JERSEY CRIMINAL CODE OF 1668.

Many of the settlers in East Jersey were Puritans who had come from New Haven Colony, Connecticut. Naturally they brought with them the harsh Puritanical criminal code for which Connecticut has been notorious. The following documents constitute the original criminal codes of Connecticut, the first one being enacted in 1642, and the second, which embodied the first, with the additions indicated below, was adopted in 1650. A comparison of the Connecticut codes with the code of East Jersey will readily convince the reader of the genetic relationship between them.

CAPITALL LAWES ESTABLISHED BY THE GENERALL COURT,
THE FIRST OF DECEMBER, 1642.

1. Yf any man after legall conuiction shall haue or worship any other God but the Lord God, he shall be put to death. Deu: 13. 6, & 17. 2: Ex: 22. 20.

2. Yf any man or woman be a witch (that is) hath or consulteth wth a familiar spirit, they shall be put to death. Ex: 22. 18: Lev: 20. 27: Deu: 18. 10, 11.

(341)

3. Yf any prson shall blaspheme the name of God the Father, Son or Holy Goste, wth direct, expres, prsumptuous, or high-handed blasphemy, or shall curse God in the like manner, he shall be put to death. Leu: 24. 15, 16.

4. Yf any Prson shall comitt any willfull murther, wch is manslaughter comitted vppon mallice, hatred or cruelty, not in a mans necessary and just defence, nor by mere casualty against his will, he shall be put to death. Ex: 21. 12, 13, 14: Num: 35. 30, 31.

5. Yf any person shall slay another through guile, either by poysonings or other such divillishe practice, he shall be put to death. Ex: 21. 14.

6. Yf any man or woman shall ly wth any beast or bruit creature, by carnall copulation, they shall surely be put to death, and the beast shall be slayne and buried. Leu: 20. 15, 16.

7. Yf any man lye wth mankynd as he lyeth wth a woman both of them haue comitted abomination, they both shall surely be put to death. Leu: 20. 13.

8. Yf any prson comitteth adultery wth a married or espoused wife, the adulterer and the adulteres shall surely be put to death. Le: 20. 10 & 18. 20: Deu: 22. 23, 24.

9. Yf any man shall forcebly and wthout consent rauishe any mayd or woman that is lawfully maried or contracted, he shall be put to death. Deu: 22. 25.

10. Yf any man stealeth a man or mankind, he shall be put to death. Ex: 21. 16.

11. Yf any man rise vp by false witnesse, wittingly and of purpose to take away any mans life, he shall be putt to death. Deu: 19. 16, 18, 19.

12. If any man shall conspire or attempte any inuasion, insurrection or rebellion against the Comonwelth, he shall be put to death.[1]

CAPITALL LAWES, 1650.

(Of the Capital Laws, fourteen in number, the first twelve agree, word for word, with those adopted in Dec., 1642, and recorded on page (92) of Vol. I (p. 77, ante.). It has not been thought necessary to repeat them here. The others follow:)

(13.) 13. If any Childe or Children aboue sixteene yeares old and of sufficient vnderstanding, shall Curse or smite theire naturall father or mother, hee or they shall bee put to death, vnless it can bee sufficiently testified that the Parents haue beene very vnchristianly negligent in the education of such Children, or so prouoake them by extreame and cruell correction that they haue beene forced therevnto to preserue themselues from death (or) maiming. Exo: xxi: 17; Levit: xx (9); Exo: xxi. 15.

14. If a man haue a stubborne and rebellious sonne of sufficient yeares and vnderstanding, viz: sixteene yeares of age, wch will not obey the voice of his father or the voice of his mother, and that when they haue chastened

---

[1] *The Public Records of the Colony of Connecticut,* edited by J. H. Trumbull, Hartford, 1850; pp. 77–78.

him, will not hearken vnto them, then may his Father and Mother, being his naturall parents, lay hold on him and bring him to the Magistrates assembled in Courte, and testifie vnto them that theire sonne is stubborne and rebellious and will not obey theire voice and chastisement, but liues in sundry notorious crimes, such a Sonne shall bee put to death. Deut: xxi. 20, 21.

It is allso ordered by this Courte and authority thereof, that whatsoeuer Childe or Servant, within these Libberties, shall bee convicted of any Stubborne or Rebellious Carriage against their Parents (14.) or Governours, wch is a forerunner of the aforementioned euills, the Gouernor or any two Magistrates haue libberty and power from this Courte to committ such person or persons to the howse of Correction, and there to remaine vunder hard labour and severe punnishmt so long as the Courte or the maior parte of the Magistrates shall judge meete.

And whereas frequent experience giues in sad euidence, &c.

(This provision is precisely as enacted in Dec., 1642, and follows immediately after the twelve capital laws recorded on page 78.) [1]

2. THE ORIGINAL CRIMINAL CODE OF THE PROVINCE OF EAST JERSEY, 1668.

ACTS passed and assented unto by the Governor, Council and Burgesses of the General Assembly, of the Province of New Cæsarea, or New Jersey, the 30th day of May, Anno Domini, 1668.

CAPITAL LAWS.

Punishment for burning houses.   *Be it enacted* by the authority aforesaid, that if any person or persons whatsoever shall maliciously, wittingly, or willingly, set on fire any dwelling house, out house, store house, barn or stable, or any other kind of house or houses, corn, hay, fencing, wood, flax or any other combustible matter, to the prejudice and damage of his neighbour, or any other person or persons whatsoever, shall be committed to prison without bail or mainprize, and make full satisfaction, and if he or they are not able to make satisfaction, for the damages sustain'd by such willful and malicious act, then to stand to the mercy of the court whether to be try'd for life, or to suffer some other corporal punishment, as the court shall judge, all circumstances being first duly examin'd and considered of.

Punishment for murder.   ITEM. If any person or persons shall wittingly or willingly, by lying in wait, poison, or any other way commit willful murder, they shall be put to death.

and false witness.   ITEM. If any person or persons shall willingly and maliciously rise up to bear false witness, or purpose to take away a man's life, they shall be put to death.

[1] Capital Laws of the Code of 1650 in Connecticut. *Public Records of Connecticut,* edited by J. H. Trumbull, Hartford, 1850; p. 515.

Buggery.   ITEM. If any man or woman shall lye with any beast or brute creature by carnall copulation, they shall be put to death; and the beast shall be slain and burnt.

Sodomy.   ITEM. If any man lyeth with mankind, as he lyeth with a woman, they both shall be put to death; except the one party were forced, or under fourteen years of age, in which case he shall be punished according to the discretion of the court.

ITEM. If any man shall willfully or forcibly steal away any mankind he shall be put to death.

Burglary.   ITEM. If any person within this Province shall commit burglary, by breaking open any dwelling house, store house, ware house, out house or barn, or any other house whatsoever, or that shall rob any person in the field or highways; he or they so offending shall for the first offence be punished by being burnt in the hand with the letter T, and make full satisfaction of the goods stolen, or the damages that are done; and for the second time of offending in the like nature, besides the making of restitution, to be branded in the forehead with the letter R. And for the third offence to be put to death as incorrigible.

Stealing.   ITEM. If any persons or persons within this Province shall be found stealing, or proved to have stolen any goods, money or cattle, or any other beast of what kind so ever, shall make treble restitution for the first offence, and the like for the second and third offence; with such further increase of punishment as the court shall see cause; and if incorrigible to be punished with death. And in case they are not able to make restitution for the first, second and third offence; they shall be sold that satisfaction may be made: but in case any person be disabled through poverty, or any other ways, to make restitution in kind, or the value thereof, as well concerning the law of burglary as to this of theft, he or they so offending, shall be liable to such corporal punishment as the court shall think fit to inflict upon them; and notwithstanding restitution shall be made of all or so much of the goods so stolen as can be found discovered, in whose hands or custody soever they be found.

ITEM. If any person be found to be a witch, either male or female, they shall be put to death.

Conspiracy.   ITEM. If any man conspire, or publicly attempt to invade or surprise any town or towns, fort or forts, within this Province, he shall be put to death.

Undutiful   ITEM. If any child or children above sixteen years of age, and children.   of sufficient understanding, shall smite or curse their natural father or mother, except provoked thereunto, and forced for their safe preservation from death or maiming, upon the complaint or proof of the said father or mother, or either of them (and not otherwise) they shall be put to death.

Rapes.   ITEM. If any man shall force a maid or married woman, he shall be put to death, or severely punish'd according to the discretion of the court.

Adultery.   ITEM. If any person or persons shall commit adultery, they shall be divorced, corporally punished or banished, either or all of them, all circumstances being first duly examined and considered of, as the court shall judge.

Night walking and revelling. ITEM. For the better preventing disorders and misdemeanors in your persons and others, *Be it also enacted* by this present General Assembly, that if any person or persons shall be abroad from the usual place of their abode, and found in night walking, drinking in any tapp-house, or any other house or place at unseasonable times, after nine of the clock at night, and not about their lawful occasions, or cannot give a good account of their being absent from their own place of abode at that time of the night, if required of them, shall be secured by the constable or some other officer, till the morning, to be brought before a justice of the peace or magistrate, to be examined, and if they cannot give them a satisfactory account of their being out, at such unseasonable times, he or they shall be bound over to the next court, and receive such punishment as the justices upon the bench shall see cause to inflict upon them.

Whereas the meeting of the Governor and his Council with the Burgesses or Deputies for the country, are called the General Assembly of the Lords **Meeting of Assembly;** Proprietors, according to the Concessions, it is enacted that the said General Assembly are to meet on the first Tuesday in November next, and so to continue their meeting yearly on the said day, until they shall see cause to alter the said time of meeting, and the deputies of each town to be chosen the first day of January according to the **and time when chosen.** Concessions; and for the absence of any deputy of the said towns, he shall be liable to pay forty shillings for every days absence, as a fine to the country, unless upon his or their reasons given for their absence, the General Assembly shall see cause to remit the same, referring all extraordinary occasions of calling the General Assembly together, at any other time or times to our Governor and his Council as they shall see cause, and as the necessity and weighty affairs of the Province shall require.

30 £ levied. *It is enacted* by the authority aforesaid, That a rate of thirty pounds be levied upon the country, for the defraying of publick charges, and this rate equally proportioned to each town. That is to say five pounds for each town to be paid in manner as followeth, Winter wheat at five shillings a bushel, Summer wheat at four shilling and six-pence. Pease at three shillings and six-pence. Indian corn at three shillings. Rye at four shillings. Barley at four shillings. Beef at two-pence half-penny. Pork at three-pence half-penny a pound. And this rate to be paid at or before the next general court, into the hands and custody of Mr. Jacob Mollins of Elizabeth Town, which we desire of him to take into his hands for the use of the Province, and when received to disburse and pay to Capt. Bollen, the sum of twenty pounds, and the rest as he shall have order to improve for our use.

For the preventing of unlawful marriages, it is ordered and enacted by the same authority, that no person or persons, son, daughter, maid or servant, shall be married without the consent of his or their parents, masters or overseers, and three times published in and at some publick meeting, or kirk, where the party or parties have their most usual abode; or set up in writing their purposes of marriage, on some publick house where they live and there at least to abide for the space of fourteen days before marriage, which is to be performed in some publick place, if possible may be, and none but some approved minister or justice of the peace within this Province, or some chief officer, where such are not, shall be allowed to marry or admit of any to join in marriage, in their presence, and under the penalty of twenty pounds for acting contrary hereunto, and to be put out of their office, according to the liberty of conscience granted by the Lords Proprietors in their Concessions: *Always provided,* That it is and may be lawful for the Governor to grant his license, under his hand and seal, to any person or persons that are at their own disposing, or to any other under the tuition of their parents, masters or overseers, to join in matrimony; *provided* that the parents, masters or overseers are present and consenting thereunto, or that their consent be attested by some publick officer, and presented to the Governor before the granting thereof, and the others to clear themselves by oath or certificate.

Concerning pounds, *It is enacted* by the same authority, that every plantation within this Province, do make and maintain a good and sufficient pound for all sorts of cattle, within a quarter of a year after publication of this act; and if any trespass or damage be done by horses, cattle, sheep or swine of any kind whatsoever, in any man's corn, hay, flax or any other fruits, when the fence is sufficient, they shall pay all damage whatsoever; but in case there be no fence, or not a sufficient fence, then he that owns the defective fence or fences whatsoever, shall bear the damages and the cattle shall be free. *And be it further enacted* that every town shall chuse and appoint two of the freeholders to be the viewers of their fence or fences, from time to time as need shall require. It is also enacted, that if any person or persons shall at any time break up the pound, shall pay a fine of five pounds; twenty shillings thereof to be paid to the informer, and the remainder to the use of the publick.

Concerning fugitives, *It is enacted* by the same authority, that every apprentice and servant that shall depart and absent themselves from their masters or dames, without leave first obtain'd, shall be judged by the court to double the time of such their absence, by future, service over and above other damages and costs which master and dame shall sustain by such unlawful departure.

And it is also enacted, that whosoever shall be proved to have transported, or to have contrived the transportation of any such apprentice or servant, shall be fined five pounds, and all such damages as the court shall judge, and that the master or dame can make appear, and if not able, to be left to the judgment of the court.

And it is also enacted, that every inhabitant that shall harbour or entertain any such apprentice or servant, and knowing that he hath absented himself from his service, upon proof thereof, shall forfeit to the master or dame ten shillings for every days entertainment or concealment, and if not able to satisfy, then to be liable to the judgment of the court.

For the better supporting and upholding the lawful authority established in this Province, by the Lords Proprietors and their successors, or by any other person in authority under them, and for the encouragement of the same, it is ordered and enacted by this present General Assembly, that if any person or persons whatsoever shall abuse, contemn or resist the lawful authority, settled and appointed in this Province, either in words or actions, as the Governor, justices of the peace, magistrate, or any other inferior officer or officers in the execution of his or their respective offices, or at any other time: *Provided,* that such as are in authority do not abuse any man, but only defend themselves, shall be liable to such fine or corporal punishment, as the court after due examination of the fact shall determine.

Concerning fornication, *It is enacted* by the authority aforesaid, that if any man commit fornication, with any single woman, they shall be punished by enjoining marriage, fine, corporal punishment, either of which according to the discretion of the court; and the parties so offending shall put in good security for the discharging of the town or parish from any charge by such unlawful birth.

Concerning that beastly vice drunkenness, *It is hereby enacted,* that if any person be found to be drunk, he shall pay one shilling fine for the first time, two shillings for the second, and for the third time, and for every time after two shillings and six-pence, and such as have nothing to pay, shall suffer corporal punishment, and for those that are unruly and disturbers of the peace, they shall be put in the stocks, until they are sober, or during the pleasure of the officer in chief in the place where he is drunk.

Concerning swearing, *It is enacted* by the aforesaid authority, that if any person or persons shall profanely take the name of God in vain, by swearing or cursing, he or they shall pay for every such offence one shilling, half to the informer, and the other half to the country.

Concerning taking away of a man's life, *It is enacted* by this present General Assembly, that no man's life shall be taken away under any pretence but by virtue of some law established in this province, that it be proved by the mouth of two or three sufficient witnesses.[1]

3. THE ORIGINAL QUAKER CRIMINAL CODE OF WEST JERSEY, 1681.

The Original Quaker Criminal Code of West Jersey was drawn up by the Proprietors in 1676–7, and later enacted as the Criminal Code of West Jersey by the General Assembly, meeting in Burlington in November, 1681.

[1] Aaron Leaming and Jacob Spicer,—*The Grants, Concessions, and Original Constitutions of the Province of New Jersey,* (reprint of 1881); pp. 78–84.

THE CHARTER OR FUNDAMENTAL LAWS, OF WEST NEW JERSEY, AGREED UPON.

Chapter XIII.

THAT THESE FOLLOWING CONCESSIONS ARE THE COMMON LAW, OR FUNDAMENTAL RIGHTS, OF THE PROVINCE OF WEST JERSEY.

Charter or Fundamental Laws.   THAT the common law or fundamental rights and privileges of West New Jersey, are individually agreed upon by the Proprietors and freeholders thereof, to be the foundation of the government, which is not to be altered by the Legislative authority, or free Assembly hereafter mentioned and constituted, but that the said Legislative authority is constituted according to these fundamentals, to make such laws as agree with, and maintain the said fundamentals, and to make no laws that in the least contradict, differ or vary from the said fundamentals, under what pretence or alligation soever.

Chapter XIV.

BUT if it so happen that any person or persons of the said General Assembly, shall therein designedly, willfully, and maliciously, move or excite any to move, any matter or thing whatsoever, that contradicts or any ways subverts, any fundamentals of the said laws in the Constitution of the government of this Province, it being proved by seven honest and reputable persons, he or they shall be proceeded against as traitors to the said government.
. . .

Chapter XVI.

THAT no men, nor number of men upon earth, hath power or authority to rule over men's consciences in religious matters, therefore it is consented, agreed and ordained, that no person or persons whatsoever within the said Province, at any time or times hereafter, shall be any ways upon any pretence whatsoever, called in question, or in the least punished or hurt, either in person, estate, or priviledge, for the sake of his opinion, judgment, faith or worship towards God in matters of religion. But that all and every such persons, and persons, may from time to time, and at all times, freely and fully have, and enjoy his and their judgments, and the exercises of their consciences in matters of religious worship throughout all the said Province.

Chapter XVII.

THAT no Proprietor, freeholder or inhabitant of the said Province of West Jersey, shall be deprived or condemned of life, limb, liberty, estate, property or any ways hurt in his or their privileges, freedoms or franchises, upon any account whatsoever, without a due tryal, and judgment passed by twelve good and lawful men of his neighbourhood first had: And that in all causes to be tryed, and in all tryals, the person or persons, arraigned may except against any of the said neighbourhood, without any reason rendered, (not exceeding thirty five) and in case of any valid reason alleged, against every person nominated for that service.

Chapter XVIII.

AND that no Proprietor, freeholder, freedenison, or inhabitant in the said Province, shall be attached, arrested or imprisoned, for or by reason of any debt, duty, or thing whatsoever (cases felonious, criminal and treasonable excepted) before he or she have personal summon or summons, left at his or her last dwelling place, if in the said Province, by some legal authorized officer, constituted and appointed for that purpose, to appear in some court of judicature for the said Province, with a full and plain account of the cause or thing in demand, as also the name or names of the person or persons at whose suit, and the court where he is to appear, and that he hath at least fourteen days time to appear and answer the said suit, if he or she live or inhabit within forty miles English of the said court, and if at a further distance, to have for every twenty miles, two days time more, for his and their appearance, and so proportionably for a longer distance of place.

Chapter XIX.

THAT there shall be in every court, three justices or commissioners, who shall sit with the twelve men of the neighbourhood, with them to hear all causes, and to assist the said twelve men of the neighbourhood in case of law; and that they the said justices shall pronounce such judgment as they shall receive from, and be directed by the said twelve men, in whom only the judgment resides, and not otherwise.

And in case of their neglect and refusal, that then one of the twelve, by consent of the rest, pronounce their own judgment as the justices should have done.

And if any judgment shall be past, in any case civil or criminal, by any other person or persons, or any other way, then according to this agreement and appointment, it shall be held null and void, and such person or persons so presuming to give judgment, shall be severely fin'd, and upon complaint made to the General Assembly, by them be declared incapable of any office or trust within this Province.

Chapter XX.

THAT in all matters, civil and criminal, proof is to be made by the solemn and plain averment, of at least two honest and reputable persons; and in case that any person or persons shall bear false witness, and bring in his or their evidence, contrary to the truth of the matter as shall be made plainly to appear, that then every such person or persons, shall in civil causes, suffer the penalty which would be due to the person or persons he or they bear witness against. And in case any witness or witnesses, on the behalf of any person or persons, indicted in a criminal cause, shall be found to have born false witness for fear, gain, malice or favour, and thereby hinder the due execution of the law, and deprive the suffering person or persons of their due satisfaction, that then and in all other cases of false evidence, such person or persons, shall be first severely fined, and next that he or they shall forever be disabled from being admitted in evidence, or into any publick office, employment, or service within this Province.

Chapter XXI.

THAT all and every person and persons whatsoever, who shall prosecute or prefer any indictment or information against others for any personal injuries, or matter criminal, or shall prosecute for any other criminal cause, (treason, murther, and felony, only excepted) shall and may be master of his own process, and have full power to forgive and remit the person or persons offending against him or herself only, as well before as after judgment, and condemnation, and pardon and remit the sentence, fine and punishment of the person or persons offending, be it personal or other whatsoever.

Chapter XXII.

THAT the tryals of all causes, civil and criminal, shall be heard and decided by the virdict or judgment of twelve honest men of the neighbourhood, only to be summoned and presented by the sheriff of that division, or propriety where the fact or trespass is committed; and that no person or persons shall be compelled to fee any attorney or counciler to plead his cause, but that all persons have free liberty to plead his own cause, if he please: And that no person or persons imprisoned upon any account whatsoever within this Province, shall be obliged to pay any fees to the officer or officers of the said prison, either when committed or discharged.

Chapter XXIII.

THAT in all publick courts of justice for tryals of causes, civil or criminal, any person or persons, inhabitants of the said Province may freely come into, and attend the said courts, and hear and be present, at all or any such tryals as shall be there had or passed, that justice may not be done in a corner nor in any covery manner, being intended and resolved, by the help of the Lord, and by these our Concessions and Fundamentals, that all and every person and persons inhabiting the said Province, shall, as far as in us lies, be free from oppression and slavery. . . .

Chapter XXXI.

ALL such person or persons as shall be upon tryal found guilty of murder, or treason, the sentence and way of execution thereof, is left to the General

Assembly to determine as they in the wisdom of the Lᴏʀᴅ shall judge meet and expedient.[1]

II. Tʜᴇ Cʀᴇᴀᴛɪᴏɴ ᴏꜰ ᴛʜᴇ Cᴏᴜɴᴛʏ Jᴀɪʟ Sʏꜱᴛᴇᴍ ᴏꜰ Cᴏʟᴏɴɪᴀʟ Nᴇᴡ Jᴇʀꜱᴇʏ.

1. Tʜᴇ Aᴄᴛ ᴏꜰ 1714, ᴀᴜᴛʜᴏʀɪᴢɪɴɢ ᴛʜᴇ ʙᴏᴀʀᴅꜱ ᴏꜰ ᴄʜᴏꜱᴇɴ ꜰʀᴇᴇ-ʜᴏʟᴅᴇʀꜱ ᴛᴏ ʙᴜɪʟᴅ ᴀɴᴅ ʀᴇᴘᴀɪʀ ᴄᴏᴜɴᴛʏ ᴊᴀɪʟꜱ ᴀɴᴅ ᴄᴏᴜʀᴛ ʜᴏᴜꜱᴇꜱ.

The law of 1714, given below, has furnished the basis of the procedure in building and repairing jails in New Jersey from the beginning of the 18th century to the present time.

An Act for raising of Money for building and repairing of Gaols and Court-Houses within each respective County of this Province.

Sec. 1. Wʜᴇʀᴇᴀꜱ Gaols and Court-Houses are absolutely necessary for the administration of Justice, and putting the Laws in Execution.

Bᴇ ɪᴛ ᴇɴᴀᴄᴛᴇᴅ, by the Governor, Council and General Assembly, and by the Authority of the same, That the Inhabitants of each Town and Precinct, within each County, shall assemble and meet together on the second *Tuesday* in *March,* yearly and every Year, at the most publick Place of each respective Town and Precinct, and, by the Majority of Voices, chuse two Freeholders for every such Town and Precinct for the ensuing Year; which Freeholders, so chosen, or the major Part of them, together with all the Justices of Peace of each respective County, or any three of them (one whereof being of the *Quorum*) shall meet together, *{The Inhabitants of each Town to meet yearly, and chuse two Freeholders, who, or the major Part of them, with the Justices, &c., shall meet.}*

(For the County of *Bergen,* near to the *Dutch Church,* by *Hackensack* River. For the County of *Essex,* at *Newark.* For the County of *Middlesex,* at *Perth Amboy.* For the County of *Somerset,* at the most convenient Place of the County, which shall be agreed upon by the major Part of the Freeholders that inhabit there. For the County of *Monmouth,* at *Shrewsbury.* For the County of *Burlington,* at *Burlington.* For the County of *Glouces-*

---

[1] *The Concessions and Agreements of the Proprietors, Freeholders, and Inhabitants of the Province of West New Jersey, in America,* 1676–7, from Leaming and Spicer, pp. 393–404.

This code in the *Concessions and Agreements* was enacted as law for the province of West Jersey by the General Assembly in November, 1681. In addition to the above enactments, it was at that time decreed that *"all persons to be committed to prison for criminal causes, shall be compelled to work for their bread, during the time of their commitment, in such work as they shall be able to perform."* Leaming and Spicer, p. 434. This was probably the legal origin in America of imprisonment at hard labor.

ter, at *Gloucester.* For the County of *Salem,* at *Salem.* For the County of *Cape-May,* near to the Prison there) And agree upon such Sum and Sums of Money, as shall be needful for Repairing such Gaols and Court-Houses as are already built, and for building such as are wanting, *viz.* In the County of *Bergen,* near to the *Dutch* Church, by *Hackensack* River. In *Essex,* at *Newark.* In *Middlesex,* at *Perth Amboy.* In *Somerset,* at the most convenient Place where the Freeholders, Inhabitants, shall agree upon. In *Monmouth,* near the House of *John Okeson,* of *Freehold.* In *Burlington* County, at the Town of *Burlington.* In *Salem* County, at the Town of *Salem.* In *Gloucester,* at the Town of *Gloucester.* In *Cape-May* County, near the present Prison there. And shall appoint Assessors and Collectors; which said Assessors, so named, for each Town and Precinct, shall meet together at the Places above-mentioned within each County, on or before the fourth *Tuesday* in *March,* yearly, to assess the Inhabitants within each Town and County equally, and make a fair List of the said Assessments, and deliver the same to the respective Collectors, at or before the first *Tuesday* in *April,* yearly; which Collector shall deliver a true Copy thereof to the Constable of each Town and Precinct, who are hereby required immediately, on the Receipt thereof, to give Notice to the several Inhabitants within their respective Districts, of the Sums they are to pay, which Sums shall be paid to each Collector at or before the fourth *Tuesday* in *May,* yearly. And upon Nonpayment, the Collectors are hereby required to deliver a List of the Delinquents to any one Justice of the Peace of the County where the Default is, who is hereby required forthwith to issue his Warrant or Warrants to the several Constables, commanding them to levy the same by Distress on the Goods and Chattels of each Delinquent, and expose the same to sale, and to pay their respective Sums to the Collector or Collectors, at or before the second *Tuesday* in June, *yearly,* and return the Overplus, if any be, to the Owner, deducting *Twelve Pence* to himself for each Distress, and *Six Pence* to the Justice, for the Warrant.

2. AND BE IT ENACTED, by the Authority aforesaid, That the Justices, and Freeholders appointed and elected as aforesaid, are hereby required to appoint Managers, to do and see done such Things and Works as they shall agree upon to be done and performed; which said Managers are hereby authorized and impowered to draw Warrants on the Collectors respectively, for Payment of the Work and Materials needful in building and Repairing Gaols and Court-Houses, as aforesaid, not exceeding the Sum or Sums appointed by the Justices and Freeholders aforesaid, for that Purpose, which Warrants the Collectors are hereby required to answer and pay. And all the Assessors, Collectors and Man-

---

Note, This clause relating to raising Money is alter'd, See Chap. 31. 77.

Freeholders, &c., so met, to agree what Money is necessary, to build and repair Gaols, and Court-Houses, &c.

And to appoint Assessors and Collectors, which Assessors shall meet, &c., and assess the Inhabitants, &c.

Collectors to give Notice to the Inhabitants, and to collect the Money assessed, &c.

Those who neglect, to be levied on by Distress, &c.

Justices and Freeholders to appoint Managers, who may draw on the Collectors for Payment of the Work.

agers, shall be accountable to the said Justices and Freeholders, when called thereunto: the Allowance for their Pains and Trouble, shall be, for the Assessors, *Four Pence per Pound;* the Collectors, *Four Pence per Pound;* the Constables (for giving Notice of the Sums and Time of Payment) *Two Pence per Pound;* the Managers, *Ten Pence per pound.*

3. AND BE IT ENACTED, by the Authority aforesaid, That if any Person or Persons appointed or elected, as aforesaid, shall neglect or refuse to act, do and perform, whatsoever is required of them by this Act, such Person or Persons, so neglecting or refusing, shall forfeit the Sum of *Twenty Shillings* for each Offense, to be levied by Distress of each Defaulter's Goods and Chattels, as aforesaid, to be applied towards building and repairing the respective Gaols and Court-Houses. And, in case of Death, Absence or Refusal, of any Person or Persons nominated and appointed, as aforesaid, any three Justices of the Peace, one being of the *Quorum,* shall appoint a Person or Persons in his or their Stead, and who shall, in Case of Neglect or Refusal, also be liable to all the Penalties above-mentioned.

Any Person appointed, &c., neglecting or refusing, to forfeit 20 s. &c.

In case of Death, &c., any three Justices (Quorum unum) to appoint another.

4. AND BE IT ENACTED, by the authority aforesaid, That if the Inhabitants of any Town or Precinct, shall neglect to meet and chuse Freeholders, as aforesaid, then it shall and may be lawful, for the Justices (at their next Court of Quarter Sessions) to appoint two Freeholders residing in such Town or Precinct that shall so neglect or refuse, as aforesaid, and who shall, in Case of Neglect or Refusal, also be liable to the Penalties above-men-tioned, any Thing contain'd herein to the contrary notwith-standing.

5. AND BE IT ENACTED, by the Authority aforesaid, That the Act, entituled, *An Act for building and repairing Gaols and Court-Houses within this Province,* made in the Month of *January,* One Thousand Seven Hundred and Nine, in the Eighth Year of Her Majesty's Reign, be, and is hereby repealed, and every Clause and Thing therein contained, to all Intents, Constructions and Purposes. And whereas there was, by Virtue of that Act of Assembly hereby repealed, an Assessment made, and Part of the Money collected, and expended, towards the building a Gaol in the County of *Monmouth;*

6. BE IT THEREFORE ENACTED, by the Authority aforesaid, That the Justices and Freeholders aforesaid, shall, and are hereby impowered to examine and compute the Money so collected and expended, and raise so much over and above the Sum they determine to raise on their County of *Monmouth* aforesaid, for the Building a Court-House and Gaol, by the Directions of this Act, as was collected and expended by Virtue of the Act hereby repealed, and the Persons that have paid their former Assessments, as aforesaid, are hereby empowered to stop the Sum so

paid by them, out of their Proportions of the Assessment which shall be made, as aforesaid, and the Collector or Collectors are hereby required to allow the same.

Justices and Freeholders neglecting to meet, any three Justices to appoint a further Time, &c.

7. AND BE IT FURTHER ENACTED, by the Authority aforesaid, That if any of the Justices and Freeholders aforesaid, shall neglect or refuse to meet at the Time or Times, appointed by this Act, or refuse to do what is required of them, then any three of the Justices in each respective County (one being of the *Quorum*) shall appoint such Time or Times, as they shall think proper, to meet and act as aforesaid and every Person neglecting or refusing to meet and act, at such Time and Times so appointed, provided publick Notice be put up by the said Justices in Writing eight Days before, in some publick Place in each respective Town or Precinct, shall be liable to the penalties before mentioned in this Act, as if they had neglected or refused to meet and act at the Time or Times before mentioned in this Act.[1]

2. TYPICAL ADVERTISEMENTS FOR JAIL-BREAKERS IN COLONIAL NEW JERSEY.

Whereas *Joseph Robins* of the County of Monmouth, Yeoman, being in custody of William Nicholls, Esq., High Sheriff of the said County, did on Tuesday, the 19th of this Instant, in the night, break the Goal of the said County, and an escape from the said Sheriff did make: The said Sheriff doth hereby promise *ten pounds* for a reward, besides reasonable charges, to any person or persons that shall take up, and so secure the said *Joseph Robins,* that he may have him again, he being a Tall slender man, thin faced, bottle-nosed, light lank hair, and about thirty years of age.

WILLIAM NICHOLLS.[2]

Freehold, in Monmouth
County, Aug. 23, 1729.

—*The Pennsylvania Gazette,* the 4th of the 7th Month, 1729.

Broke out of the Goal at Salem, and *ran-a-way,* the two following Persons, viz:

James Mac Peters, of middling stature, wears brown short curled Hair, is Pock-fretten, and of a sandy complexion: He had on an old Broadcloth Coat, a black Jacket patch'd, a narrow brimm'd Hat, and Leather Breeches. Also,

Henry Robinson, a Tall pale-fac'd Man, wears dark brown Hair; had on a Frize Coat, a red jacket fac'd with black, a large brimm'd Hat and a pair of light Plush Breeches.

---

[1] Bradford—*The Acts of the General Assembly of New Jersey,* 1703–1730; pp. 42–44.
[2] *New Jersey Archives,* Vol. XI, page 187.

They have a Wallet with Linen and other things in it.

Whoever takes them up, or either of them, and secures them so that *John Hunt,* High Sheriff of *Salem,* may have them again, shall have *three pounds* Reward for each, and reasonable charges paid.

By JOHN HUNT, Sheriff.[1]

Salem, April 9, 1737.

—*The American Weekly Mercury,* April 7–14, 1737.

Broke out of the Goal of *Burlington* in *New Jersey,* a certain man, named John Crues, of middle Stature, hollow-mouth'd (that is) his Nose and Chin inclined to meet, a Weaver by Trade, but pretends to be a Quaker-Preacher; he took with him two Coats, one a light colour'd Camblet or Duroy, the other a brown homespun Stuff, both very plain, a Searsucker Jacket and Breeches, and a pair of patch'd leather Breeches, two fine Shirts, and a half worn Beaver Hat, thread Stockings, and peek'd toe'd Shoes, his Garters have his name wove at full length; he had also with him a pair of Saddle Bags. He's suppos'd to be gone to *New-England* near *Boston,* to Preach again where he has Preach'd before.

Whoever takes up and secures the said Man, in any Prison, giving notice to *Charles Tonkin,* Under Sheriff of *Burlington* aforesaid, shall have *three pounds* Proclamation Money as a Reward, paid by me

CHARLES TONKIN, Sub.-Sheriff.[2]

Aug. 4, 1737.

—*The Pennsylvania Gazette,* Aug. 4–11, 1737.

EIGHTY DOLLARS *Reward*

Essex County   Two Persons escaped from Jonathan Hampton, High
New-Jersey. *ss.*   Sheriff of Essex County, as they were going to Baskin-
                Ridge, where they lived, to get Bail for the Actions they were then taken upon, not known to the Sheriff to be for Felony and Foergery, as they since appear to be, which the Persons then knew, viz: WILLIAM HAMILTON for Sheep-stealing, at the Camp on Staten-Island, born in Ireland, about 50 years old, a lusty, dirty, slouching Butcher, much sun-burnt, wears a cut wig, seldom combed; has an impudent Boy his Son, about 14 Years old, with him; he had several other Actions against him, for which Sylvester Cole became special Bail, and unless he is soon taken, must pay the Debts and Costs. His Wife and Children are since gone to him.

John Barclay, for forgery, born in Ireland, about 50 Years of age, a short chunkey Fellow of sandy complexion, full of Palaver when drunk (which is as often as he can), talks thick and quick, is a Clothier by Trade. They both went to the southward last Spring, were at Pequea last July, and would have been taken there if one Andrew M'Gown had not helped them to escape,

---

[1] *New Jersey Archives,* Vol. XI, p. 493.
[2] *New Jersey Archives,* Vol. XI, pp. 507–508.

and secreted them, well knowing they had left me, as above; M'Gown lately went from Baskin-Ridge also.

Barclay's Wife and some of her Children went in the stage to Philadelphia and Lancaster about two Months ago; she is exceeding much Pock-marked, very brown, named Catherine, about 40 Years of age, but looks much older, a very neat little women. It is thought they are somewhere between Pequea and Will's Creek, but most likely about Sasquehannah; but if they are further southward, even to Carolina, it is hoped they will be apprehended, as such Villains ought not to be countenanced. Whoever apprehends and secures them, so that I may have them again, or brings them to me, or my Goal keeper, shall have for Hamilton Fifty Dollars, and for Barclay Thirty Dollars, and all reasonable Charges, paid by

JONATHAN HAMPTON, Sheriff.

N. B. A Letter sent by Post, will immediately come to me.[1]

TEN DOLLARS Reward.

Made his escape from Trenton Goal, on Saturday night, the 27th of August, one James Bray, about 5 Feet 9 Inches high, has had Small-pox, has a Blemish in one eye, black Hair, lately cut short, is much inclined to drink strong liquors: Had on, when he went away, a red or Scarlet Coat, with a black Cape, the Cuffs of the Coat torn off, old Leather Breeches, mended with white Thread, coarse white Shirt, light blue Yarn Stockings, old Shoes, with Strings, an old Castor Hat, born in the County of Hunterdon, in West Jersey, and is about 30 Years of Age. Whoever takes up the said James Bray, and secures him in any Goal, shall be paid the above Reward by me.

GEORGE BROWN, Goaler.

N. B. All Masters of Vessels are forbid to carry him off, at their Peril.[2]

—*The Pennsylvania Gazette*, No. 1810, September 1, 1763.

III. THE WORK-HOUSE SYSTEM OF COLONIAL NEW JERSEY.

I. THE ACT OF 1748, ORGANIZING THE WORK-HOUSE SYSTEM OF NEW JERSEY.

This Act of 1748 stands in much the same relation to the development of the work-house system of New Jersey that the laws of 1710, 14 stand to the development of the jail system. The Act of 1748 was re-enacted, with slight changes, on February 20, 1799, and the Act of 1799 has remained the basis of the New Jersey Work-House System down to the present day.

---

[1] *New Jersey Archives*, Vol. XXIV, pp. 110–111.
[2] *New Jersey Archives*, Vol. XXIV, pp. 226–227.

AN ACT *to enable the Inhabitants of the County of* MIDDLESEX *to build a Work-House and a House of Correction within the said County, and to make Rules and Orders for the Government of the same.*

Sect. I. WHEREAS divers of the Inhabitants of the County of *Middlesex,* have humbly certified to the General Assembly by their Petition, that the Numbers of poor People have of late years very much increased within the said County, and that for the better Regulation and Government of the said County, it is highly necessary that a Poor-House shall be erected within the same, for the Maintenance and Employment of such Poor Persons as may become chargeable to the several Cities and Townships, within the said County, and for the educating and bringing up poor Children in some honest and industrious Way; as also a Work-House and House of Correction for setting to Work and punishing all Vagrants, Vagabonds, and Pilferers, and all idle and disorderly Persons, Servants and Slaves, within the Limits of the said County, Therefore for the Encouragement of Honesty and Industry and depressing of Vice and Immorality. *Preamble.*

2. BE IT ENACTED by the Governor, Council and General Assembly of this Colony, and it is hereby enacted by the Authority of the same, that in some convenient Time after the Publication of this Act, it shall and may be lawful for the Justices of the Peace of the said County, or any three of them, (one being of the *Quorum*) to issue a Warrant under their Hands and Seal, directed to the Constables of the said County, commanding them forthwith to summons all the Justices of the Peace of the said County,' as also all the Freeholders of the said County which are chosen by Virtue of an Act of Assembly of this Colony, entitled *An Act for raising of Money for building and repairing of Gaols, and Court-Houses within each respective County of this Province,* to meet at the Court-House within the City of *Perth-Amboy,* at a certain Time in the said Warrant prefixed, not less than ten Days from the issuing of the said Warrant. *Any three Justices empowered to summon the Justices and Freeholders chosen, &c.*

3. AND BE IT FURTHER ENACTED by the Authority aforesaid, that if the said Justices and Freeholders of the said County so assembled and met together, by Virtue of the Warrant aforesaid, or the Major part of the said Justices so met, and the Major part of all the Freeholders of the said County so chosen as aforesaid, shall think it expedient and necessary to build a Poor-House and Work-House, or House of Correction, within the said County, that then and in each Case it shall and may be lawful for them to agree and fix upon a certain Sum of Money to be raised within the said County for the building, finishing and maintaining a Poor-House and Work-House, or House of Correction, some where near or adjacent to the Court-House in the said City of *Perth-Amboy.* And the said Sum or Sums of Money so agreed *The Justices, or the major part of them & the Freeholders, agreeing to build a Work-House, may raise Money for that purpose.*

upon by the said Justices and Freeholders, or the major part of
the said Justices and the major part of all the said Freeholders
of the said County, shall be raised and collected in the same manner and form within the said County, as all publick County Money
is by the Laws of this Colony ordered to be raised and collected.

4. AND BE IT FURTHER ENACTED by the Authority aforesaid, That
from and after the Publication of this Act, there shall and may
be a Corporation to continue forever, for and within the County
of *Middlesex,* which Corporation shall consist of the Justices of
the Peace of the said County, for the Time being, and of the
Freeholders of the said County, chosen as aforesaid, for the Time
being, and they the said Justices and Freeholders shall forever
hereafter, in Name and Fact, be one Body Politick and Corporate
in Law to all Intents and Purposes, and shall have a perpetual
Succession, and shall be called by the name of *The Overseers and
Trustees of the Poor, and Managers of the Workhouse of the
County of* Middlesex: And the said Corporation shall be enabled
to plead, prosecute and sue, and to be sued and impleaded by that
name, in all Courts and Places of Judicature within this Colony,
and by that Name shall and may, without Licence in Mortmain,
purchase, take or receive any Lands, Tenements or Hereditaments,
of the Gift, Alienation or Devise of any Person or Persons having
a Right, and not being otherwise disabled, to grant, alien or devise the same. And the said Corporation is hereby, without further Licence, enabled to take, receive, transfer and grant the
same, and any Goods and Chattels whatsoever, in, to or for the
Use and Benefit of the Corporation aforesaid.

5. AND BE IT FURTHER ENACTED by the Authority aforesaid, That
the said Corporation or the Majority of them, assembled and met
together, shall by the Plurality of Voices of the Trustees then
present, have power to chuse a Treasurer, and all such other
Officers and Servants as shall be thought needful to be employed
in and about the Premises, and them, or any of them, from Time
to Time to Remove or Discharge as they shall see Cause; and
upon the Death or Removal of any of them, to chuse and appoint
others in their Places, and to make and give such reasonable
Allowances to them or any of them, out of the Stock or Revenue
belonging to the said Corporation as they shall think fit.

6. AND for the better regulating and well-governing of the said
Poor-House, and Work-House and House of Correction, and of
all persons concerned therein and Dependant upon the same, BE
IT FURTHER ENACTED by the Authority aforesaid, That a General
Meeting of the said Overseers and Trustees shall be held once in
Six Months at least, at the Court-House in the City of *Perth
Amboy,* which said General Meeting or Assembly, shall consist
of at least, Eleven of the said Corporation; at all which Meetings
or Assemblies, there shall be one of the Judges of the Inferior

Court of Pleas for the said County, for the Time being, and also the major Part of all the Freeholders of the said County, chosen as aforesaid; and at all which said Meetings or Assemblies, all and every one of the said Overseers and Trustees, Officer and Officers of the said Corporation, for the Time being, are hereby enjoined to appear and be present, and not to depart from the same without the Licence or Leave of the said Overseer or Trustees, or the major Part of them then assembled. And it shall and may be lawful for the said Trustees or the major Part of them, to adjourn any such Meeting or Assembly to such Time and Place within the said City of *Perth Amboy,* as shall be thought fit by the major Part of the Trustees then present.

How they may adjourn.

7. AND BE IT FURTHER ENACTED by the Authority aforesaid, That the said Corporation at any Meeting or Assembly, by the Votes of the major Part of them then present, shall have Power and Authority to make and appoint a Common Seal or Seals, for the Use of the said Corporation, and to make and ordain Rules, Orders and Ordinances for and concerning the better Governing the said Corporation, and the Poor of any of the Cities or Townships within the said County, or any Trade that shall be set on Foot by the said Corporation for employing the said Poor, and other the Ends and Purposes by this Act intended; and also to constitute and appoint such and so many Committees, to consist of such Number of the Trustees as shall be thought fit, for the more easy and effectual Execution of the several Trusts and Purposes by this Act reposed and vested in the said Corporation. AND ALSO that it shall and may be lawful for the said Committees to provide such Materials and Things as they shall judge necessary, for the setting to Work the Poor aforesaid, of what Age or Sex soever they be; and shall have hereby Power and Authority (at their Discretion) to compel such idle or poor people, begging or seeking Relief, who do not betake themselves to some lawful Employment, or who do or shall hereafter seek and receive Alms of any of the Cities or Townships within the said County, or who ought to be maintained or provided for by any of the said Cities or Townships, to dwell, inhabit and to work in the said Work-House; And also to set to work all persons sent to the said House of Correction, to do all such Work as they shall think them able and fit for; and to receive, provide for, and detain and keep in the Service of the said Corporation, and to set to work until the Age of Fourteen Years, any Poor Child or Children belonging to any City or Township within the said County, who are or shall be, or whose Father or Mother, or other Relation or Person, with whom they shall dwell, are or shall then be maintained by any of the said Cities or Townships as aforesaid, or begging Relief, or which by any of the Laws now in Force or hereafter to be in Force, ought to be maintained or provided for by the said County:

Have Power to appoint a Seal and make Rules, Orders,

And to appoint Committees.

They to provide Materials and set the People to work.

And to set to work Persons sent to the House of Correction.

And poor children till 14.

And after they shall have attained their said age of Fourteen Years or sooner, the said Corporation, by Indenture under their Common Seal, shall have Power, and are hereby required and authorized to bind and put forth such Child or Children Apprentices to any honest Person or Persons within this Colony, who are willing to receive such Child or Children, for any Number of Years not exceeding Seven Years, as they shall think convenient, which Indenture or Indentures shall be binding to such Child or Children: And the Justices of the Peace for such County, City, Town or Place where the Masters or Mistresses of such Apprentices shall live, shall have the like authority over them, as by any Law now in Force, in that part of *Great Britain* called *England,* the Justices of the Peace there have over Apprentices.

To bind them out not more than 7 Years.

Justices Power over such Apprentices.

8. AND BE IT FURTHER ENACTED by the Authority aforesaid, That the said Overseers and Trustees assembled as aforesaid, shall from Time to Time have, and are hereby empowered and authorized to appoint a Committee, to consist of five of the said Trustees at least, who (or any three of them, one of the Justices of the Peace of the said County being always one) shall from Time to Time, or any Time till the next Meeting or Assembly, have power to oversee and take Care of the said Workhouse and Persons belonging thereto, and to inflict such Correction and Punishment as to them shall seem reasonable, on any Person or Persons within the said Work-House, or House of Correction, who shall be so set to work and shall not conform to such Rules, Orders and Ordinances made or to be made as aforesaid, or shall misbehave in the same.

A Committee to oversee the Workhouse.

9. AND BE IT FURTHER ENACTED by the Authority aforesaid, That the said Corporation, shall take Care and provide for the Maintenance of all the Poor belonging to any of the Cities and Townships within the said County committed to their Care, of what Age or Sex soever they be, who are or ought to be by Law, relieved and provided for by the said Cities and Townships. And in order thereunto the said Overseers and Trustees, or Committee thereof, appointed for that Purpose, shall have full Power to command and require the Constables of the several Cities and Townships within the said County, so oft as they shall think proper, from Time to Time to examine, search and see what Poor Persons there are come into, inhabitating or residing within the said Cities and Townships, and make Report thereof to the said Overseers or Committee at their next Meeting. And if any of the said Constables shall in any Thing neglect or refuse the Duty required of him by this Act, he or they shall be liable to be fined to the Use of the Poor of the said Corporation, a Sum not exceeding *Ten Shillings* for each Offence, to be recovered as by this Act is directed.

Corporation to search after and provide for the Poor.

In what Constables to obey the Corporation.

Penalty on neglect or refusal.

10. AND BE IT FURTHER ENACTED by the Authority aforesaid, That it shall, and may be lawful for the said Overseers and Trustees at their Meeting or Assembly, by the Votes of the major Part of the said Justices present, and of the major Part of all the Freeholders of the said County, chosen as aforesaid, from Time to Time, to set down and ascertain what Sum or Sums of Money shall be needful for the Maintenance and Employment of the Poor of the said Workhouse, or House of Correction, or other Poor within the Care of the said Corporation, and to proportion and allot what each City, Township, Precinct or District within the said County, shall pay for and towards the same, which shall be according to the Number of Poor Persons such City, Township, Precinct or District shall have in the said Poor or Workhouse, or committed to the Care of the said Corporation, to the Intent that no other Levy or Assessment may be made for any other Maintenance or Allowance, to or for any such Poor; which Sum or Sums of Money shall be assessed, levyed and raised in such Manner and Form, as by the Laws of this Colony is or shall be appointed and directed for the Support and Maintenance of the Poor of any other County within this Colony, and when raised and received shall be paid to the Treasurer of the Corporation aforesaid, for the use aforesaid and for no other. *How the Trustees to ascertain what shall be paid for the Support of the Poor and how the money to be raised.*

11. PROVIDED ALWAYS, That such Poor in any of the said Cities, Townships or Precincts, as shall not be sent to the said Workhouse, or committed to the Care of the said Corporation, shall be maintained in such Manner as is already provided for by Law. *Poor not committed to said Corporation, how to be maintained.*

12. PROVIDED ALSO, That if any Person or Persons shall find him or themselves to be unequally taxed or assessed, he or they may appeal to the next General Quarter Sessions of the Peace, to be held for the said County after such Assessment made and demanded, and the Justices of the Peace at such Sessions, shall and hereby have full Power and Authority to hear the same and to make such Order therein as to them shall seem just and reasonable, which Order shall be final. *Persons unequally taxed may appeal to the Sessions.*

13. PROVIDED ALSO, that no Constable or Constables of the said Cities or Townships, shall be liable to pay towards any Assessment which shall be made for any of the said Rates during the Time of his or their continuing in that Office. *Constables not to be taxed while in Office.*

14. AND BE IT FURTHER ENACTED by the Authority aforesaid, that the Treasurer of the said Corporation, for the Time being, and all other Officers belonging to the said Workhouse, or House of Correction, shall from Time to Time accompt to the said Corporation for such Sums of Money, Stock and other Things belonging to the said Corporation, Work-House, or House of Correction, as shall come to his or their respective Hands, or be under his or their respective Care, upon every reasonably Warning and *Treasurers and other Officers to accompt to the Corporation.*

Notice thereof to them respectively given, and shall pay or deliver over such Money and other Things as shall be found in their Hands, to any succeeding Treasurer, or other Officer or Officers which may be appointed by the said Corporation as aforesaid, who shall give Receipts for the same. And if any

Penalty on refusal or neglect.

Treasurer, or other Officer, belonging to the said Corporation, shall refuse or neglect to accompt and pay or deliver as aforesaid, such Person shall and may be prosecuted by Order of the said Trustees for the same, in Manner by this Act directed.

Penalties how to be recovered and applyed.

15. AND BE IT FURTHER ENACTED by the Authority aforesaid, that all Penalties and Forfeitures shall be levied in the usual Manner, by distress and sale of the Offenders Goods and Chattels, by Warrants under the Hands and Seals of any of the Justices of the Peace of the said County, for the Time being; and being so levied shall be paid to the Treasurer aforesaid, to be applyed to and for such Uses and Purposes as the said Poor Rates are hereby directed to be applyed, restoring the Overplus, if any be, the Charges deducted.

Justices to send Rogues &c. to the House of Correction &c. then to the Place of their last Settlement.

16. AND BE IT FURTHER ENACTED by the Authority aforesaid, that it shall and may be lawful for the Justices of the Peace of the said County, or any of them, and for the Justices of the Peace of any of the Cities within the said County, or any of them, and they are hereby required to apprehend, or cause to be apprehended, by any of the Constables or other Officers of the said Cities or County, all Rogues, Vagrants, Vagabonds and sturdy Beggars, and other idle and disorderly Persons, which shall be found wandering or misbehaving themselves within the said Cities or County, and cause them to be set to work to hard Labour for any Time, not exceeding the space of one Month from the Time of such Apprehension: And in Case it shall appear upon Examination, that any such Person or Persons hath obtained any legal Settlement elsewhere within this Colony, or within the Province of *New-York* or *Pennsylvania,* then every such Person or Persons shall be sent to the Place or Places of his, her or their last legal Settlement by such Order, and in such Manner, as by the Laws of this Colony other Persons, likely to become chargeable are or ought to be sent.

Who are liable to be sent to the House of Correction.

17. AND BE IT FURTHER ENACTED by the Authority aforesaid, that all Persons able in body, and not having wherewithal otherwise to maintain themselves, or use loitring, and refuse to work for the usual and common Wages, all Servants who shall run away from their Masters or Mistresses, all idle Persons wandering abroad and begging, and all Persons using any subtle Craft to trick honest People, or practicing any unlawful Games or Plays, shall by this Act be liable to the Pains and Penalties hereby prescribed.

18. AND BE IT FURTHER ENACTED by the Authority aforesaid, that if any Person or Persons so apprehended as aforesaid, shall refuse to be examined upon his, her or their Oaths before such Justice or Justices of the Peace, touching the Place or Places of his, her or their Birth or Settlement, or being so examined, shall knowingly give any false or unsatisfactory Account thereof, such Person or Persons so refusing or being detected of such falsity as aforesaid, before any Justice or Justices of the Peace in a summary way, shall be deemed Rogues and Vagabonds, and shall be punished in such manner as Rogues and Vagabonds are directed by this Act to be punished; of which Punishment the Justice or Justices of the Peace who shall take such Examination, shall apprise and inform the Person so examined before the Examination taken as aforesaid. *(Persons refusing to be examined, &c. to be deemed vagabonds.)*

19. AND BE IT FURTHER ENACTED by the Authority aforesaid, that it shall and may be lawful for the said Justices, or any of them, to commit to the said Work-House, to hard Labour, all or any white Servant or Servants, Slave or Slaves, which may or shall be brought before him or them, by their Masters or Mistresses, or others, Inhabitants of the said County, for any Misdemeanor, or rude or disorderly behaviour committed within the said Cities or County, and to order such rude and disorderly Servant or Slave to receive the Correction of the House, as shall be thought reasonable by the said Justice, not exceeding Thirty Lashes for any One Offence. *(Servants or Slaves how to be committed to the Work House &c.)*

20. AND BE IT FURTHER ENACTED by the Authority aforesaid, that it shall and may be lawful for any two of the Justices of the Peace of the said Cities or County, to commit to the said House of Correction to hard Labour, any Person or Persons who shall be convicted before them of pilfering or stealing within the said Cities or County, under the value of *Twenty Shillings,* (Provided such Crime or Crimes be not above the degree of *Petit Larceny*) and to order such Person or Persons to have the Correction of the House, in such Manner as the Nature of the Offence may require, Provided the said Punishment shall not exceed Thirty nine Lashes for any one Offence. *(Two Justices may commit for theft under Petty Larceny and order Correction.)*

21. PROVIDED ALWAYS, That if the Person or Persons accused, shall make it his, her or their request to be tryed by the Course of the Common Law, he, she or they shall be remanded by the said Magistrates to Gaol, there to be kept for that Purpose. *(Persons desiring to be try'd by the Common Law how to be dealt with.)*

22. AND BE IT FURTHER ENACTED by the Authority aforesaid, that in Case any Person or Persons so committed by any of the said Justices of the Peace, to the House of Correction as aforesaid, shall, before the Time be expired for which he, she or they shall be so committed, voluntarily break out and make his, her or their escape from the said House of Correction, he, she or they shall, for every such Offence, be whipped at the Discretion of any two *(Persons Breaking out and escaping from the Work-House, their punishment.)*

Justices of the said County, not exceeding Thirty nine Lashes for any one Offence, and shall be again committed by the said Justices to the House of Correction to hard Labour, for any Time not exceeding six Months.

How the Corporation may receive Persons from other Counties.

23. AND BE IT FURTHER ENACTED by the Authority aforesaid, that the said Corporation hereby constituted (or a committee by them appointed) shall have and hereby hath full Power and Authority (at their own Will and Pleasure, and for such Time or Times as they shall think Proper) to agree for, receive, employ and set to work, any Rogues, Vagabonds, idle and disorderly Persons, Servants and Slaves, of any City, Borough, Township, Precinct or Liberty within any County of the *Eastern* Division of *New-Jersey,* and such Persons after they shall be so received, are hereby in all respects made subject to, and shall be ordered and governed by the said Corporation, in such sort and manner as any other such Persons there.

24. PROVIDED ALWAYS, that every such City, Borough, Township, Precinct or Liberty within the several Counties as aforesaid, so making use of the said Work-House, or House of Correction, as aforesaid, shall first pay, or secure to be paid, to the Treasurer of the said Corporation, such Sum or Sums of Money as shall be so agreed for.

Persons received from other Counties into the Work-House not to entitle them to a Settlement.

25. PROVIDED ALSO, that the receiving, working or continuance of any Person or Persons not belonging to the said County of *Middlesex,* in the said Work-House, or House of Correction, shall not be deemed or construed to be any Settlement within the said County for such Person or Persons, but he, she or they, when discharged from the said Work-House or House of Correction, shall return or be sent to the same City, Borough, Township, Precinct or Liberty where they were before settled, or from whence they were sent to the same Work-House, or House of Correction: any Law, Usage or Custom to the contrary hereof in any wise notwithstanding.

Corporation empowered to Hire or purchase a House till one shall be built.

26. AND BE IT FURTHER ENACTED by the Authority aforesaid, that until such Time as a Work-House, or House of Correction, shall be built and prepared within the said City of *Perth-Amboy,* it shall and may be lawful for the said Corporation to hire or purchase, and make use of any other House within the said City, (which they, or the Majority of them as aforesaid, shall think fit and convenient for a Poor-House, Work-House, and House of Correction) in manner and form as is by this Act prescribed.[1]

[1] Allinson, *The Acts of the General Assembly of New Jersey,* 1702–1776; pp. 179ff.

DOCUMENTS RELATING TO THE ORIGINAL STATE PRISON OF NEW JERSEY, 1797-1836

CHAPTER II

DOCUMENTS RELATING TO THE ORIGINAL STATE PRISON OF
NEW JERSEY, 1797–1836.

I. The Origin and Organization of the Original State Prison of New
   Jersey.
   1. The Act of March 1, 1797, Authorizing the Erection of a State
      Prison in New Jersey.
   2. Description of the Physical Equipment of the First State Prison
      of New Jersey.
   3. The Legal and Administrative Basis of the Original Prison System
      of New Jersey.
   4. Contemporary Description of the Management and Administration
      of the Original State Prison of New Jersey in the First Years
      of its Existence.
II. Prison Management and Industries in New Jersey from 1800 to 1836.
   1. Report of the Board of Inspectors of 1811 Relative to the Need
      of a Prison Sales Agent.
   2. Report of the Joint Committee of the Legislature of 1816 in Re-
      gard to the Confusion Arising from the Original System of
      Accounting Employed at the State Prison.
   3. Memorial of the Inspectors of the State Prison in 1818.
   4. Report of the Joint Committee to Settle the Accounts of the State
      Prison in 1822 with Respect to the System of Prison Accounting.
   5. Prison Finances and Industry in 1825.
   6. Prison Industry and Prison Management in 1826.
   7. The Report of the Famous Prison Investigating Committee of 1830.

I. The Origin and Organization of the Original State Prison of New Jersey.

1. The Act of March 1, 1797, Authorizing the Erection of a State Prison in New Jersey.

An Act for erecting a State Prison.

Sect. 1. BE IT ENACTED by the Council and General Assembly of
this State, and it is hereby enacted upon authority of the same:
That Jonathan Doan be, and he is hereby appointed agent to
superintend the building of a state prison for the purpose of
confining and employing persons convicted under the law for the
punishment of crimes.

Agent ap-
pointed to
build a State
Prison.

Of whom to
purchase land.

2. *And be it enacted,* that the said agent shall contract for and purchase a tract or lot of land of Peter Hunt situate at Lamberton in the County of Burlington, being the eastermost lot of the said Hunt, containing about six acres and a half acre, at any price not exceeding forty-five pounds per acre, and procure a

Deed; to
whom given.

deed for the same to be given to the Governor of this State and his successors in office, for the time being, for the use of the State. And the said agent shall cause the said deed to be recorded and deposited in the office of the secretary of this State;

And moneys
to be drawn
to pay for the
same.

and the said agent is hereby authorized to draw so much of the public moneys as shall be necessary for the payment of such purchase from the treasurer of this State who is hereby required to pay the same to the said agent, taking his receipt therefor, which sum shall be allowed in the statement of the accounts of the said treasurer.

Description of
the building.

3. *And be it enacted,* that the said agent shall, as soon as may be, cause suitable buildings for the purpose aforesaid to be erected; the house for the keeper of the said prison to be forty-eight feet by forty-two feet, two stories high, besides the ground story or cellar; the wings on each side to be sufficient to accommodate such number of prisoners as will probably be confined therein (not exceeding forty) with arches over the rooms intended for confinement, and two cells in a separate building for solitary confinement, and a yard of three hundred feet by two hundred and fifty feet, to be enclosed with a stone wall not less than twelve feet above the ground.

4. *And be it enacted,* that the said agent shall, as often as may be necessary, draw on the treasurer for any sum or sums of money requisite for the purpose of erecting and completing the said state prison, not exceeding in the whole the sum of five

Moneys to be
drawn from
the treasurer.

thousand pounds; and shall keep a fair account of all the moneys by him received, and of his disbursements thereof, which, with proper vouchers for the same, together with an account of his time and expenses, he shall lay before the Legislature at their next sitting for their approbation and allowance.

Agent to give
security to the
treasurer.

5. *And be it enacted,* that the said agent shall, previous to his drawing any money out of the treasury, enter into bond to the treasurer of this State, with two sufficient sureties, to be approved of by him, in the sum of five thousand pounds, conditioned for the faithful discharge of the duties and services required of him by this act, and that the moneys he is hereby authorized to draw shall be solely appropriated to the uses and purposes in this act expressed.[1]

A. Passed at Trenton, March 1, 1797.

[1] *Acts of the Twenty-first General Assembly of the State of New Jersey,* March 1, 1797; pp. 189–90.

2. DESCRIPTION OF THE PHYSICAL EQUIPMENT OF THE FIRST STATE PRISON OF NEW JERSEY.

Mr. Marsh, from the Joint Committee appointed to enquire into the state of the penitentiary house and to settle the accounts of Jonathan Doan, made the following report:

That they have examined the said buildings: The keeper's house consisting of four rooms on a floor, besides the hall, cellar and piazza. The rooms on the first floor are finished and convenient for the purposes intended; two of which are designed for the keeper, the other two for the inspectors and clerks. The upper rooms are not finished. The cellar or ground story, is divided into a kitchen or cooking room, a baking room, a dining room that will admit of about sixty persons dining at once, and two store rooms, all very convenient.

The left wing of the said building, intended for the confinement and employment of male prisoners, is completed, or nearly so; the ground story of which is divided into a long hall, a washing room, a work shop, a pump room containing the well of water. The second or middle story is divided into two work shops or rooms, an infirmary, a long hall and a temporary cell, all secured with iron doors, with bars and locks, and arched overhead. The third or upper story is divided into two lodging rooms of confinement, which will contain about fifteen persons each, a lodging room for the under keepers, two halls and a temporary cell, all secured with iron grated doors, bars and locks, also arched overhead.

The right wing, designed for the confinement and employment of females, is not yet finished; the walls of which are nearly up; the cellar or ground story of which is divided into a cellar, a washing room and one other working room, a hall and stair case. The third or upper story is divided into two lodging rooms of confinement, a hall and stair case. The yard is enclosed with a stone wall agreeably to the directions of the law, with a partition wall of the same height dividing the apartment designed for the males from that of the females; there is besides the well above mentioned two other wells of water, one for the use of the famale prisoners, the other near the place where permanent cells are to be built.

The whole of the work, as far as your committee could judge, appears to be well done and the regulations established by the board of directors appear to be judicious and well calculated to promote the intentions of the institution, and the methods made use of by the keeper of the house as to the treatment of the prisoners, keeping their accounts, diet, &c. meets the approbation of your committee; but the said prisoners are not yet employed at any manufactoring business owing, as it is said, to the prevalence of the sickness in Philadelphia, which has prevented procuring proper materials.

And Your committee further report that we have examined the accounts of Jonathan Doan and find the said Jonathan Doan has drawn from the treasury the sum of £4852 0 3, and received for sundry refuse materials sold £5 10 8½, making £4857 10 11½, and that he has expended the sum of

£5244 5 8, including the sum of £494 4 2, reported to be due him on the 4th day of November last, and that a balance is now due to him of £386 14 8½ and a further sum of £195 13 1 for 250 days' attendance, superintending the work and expenses.

And your committee further report that the said Jonathan Doan has made several contracts for materials not yet paid for, which, with his estimate for finishing the said building, will amount to about £1400 more; which is stated as follows, viz:

STATE PRISON
to
JONATHAN DOAN,   *Dr.*

To balance due him, reported last year, ...	£494	4 2
To amount of his account per vouchers examined from No. 1 to 95, ...	4750	1 6
	£5244	5 8
Credit—by cash drawn out of the treasury, .. £4852 0 3 ⎫ By refuse sold at vendue, ... 5 10 8½ ⎬	4857	10 11½
	£386	14 8½
Jonathan Doan's expenses, 250 days as super- intending the State Prison at 14s, ... £175 0 0 ⎫ Expenses of procuring materials, ... 20 13 1½ ⎬	195	13 1½
	£582	7 10
Estimated expense yet wanted, ...	1400	0 0
	£1982	7 10

By order of the Committee.

DANIEL MARSH

SILAS CONDICT

November 5, 1798.

Which report was read and ordered a second reading.[1]

[1] *Journal of the Legislative Council of the State of New Jersey*, November 5, 1798; pp. 16–17.

3. THE LEGAL AND ADMINISTRATIVE BASIS OF THE ORIGINAL PRISON SYSTEM OF NEW JERSEY.

An Act making provision for carrying into effect, the "Act for the punishment of crimes."

Passed the 15th of February, 1798.

1. BE IT ENACTED *by the Council and General Assembly of this state, and it is hereby enacted by the authority of the same,* That every person sentenced to hard labor and imprisonment, agreeably to the directions of the "Act for the punishment of crimes," for a longer time than six months, shall, within twenty days after his or her conviction, be transported, at the expense of the state, to the state prison, by the sheriff of the county, where such conviction may be had, or his lawful deputy, and there delivered into the custody of the keeper of said prison, with a copy of the sentence of the court ordering such punishment, together with the costs of prosecution against such offender, certified under the hand and seal of the clerk of said court, to be there safely kept until the term of his or her confinement shall have expired, and until the fine or fines, and costs of prosecution shall be paid, or until he or she shall be discharged by due course of law; for which service the said sheriff or his deputy shall receive the sum of ten cents per mile going to, and ten cents per mile returning from, the said prison, to be calculated from the gaol of the county, in which the conviction was had, for his time and expenses, together with all reasonable expenses for sustaining, transporting and securing such offender while on his way to the said prison; all which sums shall be certified by two or more of the inspectors hereinafter mentioned, and paid on their order by the treasurer of this state, out of any moneys in his hands belonging to the state. *Provided always, and be it enacted,* That every person sentenced to imprisonment, agreeably to the act aforesaid, for any time not exceeding six months, shall be confined in the common gaol of the county, where the conviction was had, there to be safely kept until the term of his or her confinement shall have expired, and until fine or fines, and costs of prosecution shall be paid, or until he or she shall be discharged by due course of law.

Persons sentenced to hard labor for a longer time than six months, to be sent to the state prison.

2. *And be it enacted,* That every person, sentenced to hard labor and imprisonment as aforesaid, shall be separately washed, cleansed and lodged, and shall continue in such separate lodging, until it shall be certified by some physician, that he or she is fit to be received among the other prisoners; and the clothes, in which the said person shall then be clothed, shall either be burnt, baked, fumigated, or carefully laid by, at the discretion of any

When to be received among the other prisoners.

two of the inspectors appointed as hereinafter mentioned, until the expiration of the term of confinement of such offender, to be then returned to him or her.

Offenders, how to be clothed, fed, and employed

3. *And be it enacted,* That all such offenders shall, at the expense of the state, during the term of their confinement, be clothed in habits of coarse materials, uniform in color and make, and the males shall have their hair cut short once every month, and their beards close shaven at least once in every week, and all the said offenders shall, during the said term, be sustained upon inferior food, at the discretion of the said inspectors, and shall be kept, as far as may be consistent with their sex, age, health and ability, to labor of the hardest and most servile kind, in which the work is least liable to be spoiled by ignorance, neglect or obstinancy, and where the materials are not easily embezzled or destroyed; and if the work to be performed is of such a nature as may require previous instruction, proper persons for that purpose, to whom a suitable allowance shall be made, shall be provided by order of any two of the said inspectors, during the time of which labor the said offenders shall be kept separate and apart from each other, if the nature of their several employments will admit thereof, and where the nature of such employment requires two or more to work together, the keeper of the said prison, or one of his deputies, shall, if possible, be constantly present.

Hours of labor.

4. *And be it enacted,* That such offender, unless prevented by ill health, shall be employed in work every day in the year, except Sundays, and the hours of work of each day shall be as many as the season of the year will permit, but not exceeding eight hours in the months of November, December, and January, nine hours in the months of February and October, and ten hours in the rest of the year; and when in each day such hours of work are passed, the working tools, implements and materials, or such of them as will admit of daily removal, shall be removed to places proper for their safe custody until the hour of labor shall return.

Stock and materials, working tools and implements, clothing and diet, for offenders, how to be procured.

5. *And be it enacted,* That the keeper of the said prison shall, from time to time, with the approbation of any two of the inspectors, appointed as hereinafter mentioned, provide a sufficient quantity of stock and materials, working tools and implements for such offenders; for the expense of which, the said inspectors, or any two of them, shall be, and they are hereby authorized to draw orders, to be countersigned by the auditor of the state, on the treasurer of the state, if necessary, specifying in such orders the quantity and nature of the materials, tools or implements wanted; which orders the said treasurer is hereby required to discharge out of the moneys in his hands; for which materials, tools and implements, when received, the said keeper shall be accountable; and the said keeper shall, with the approbation of

any two of the said inspectors, have power to make contracts with any persons whatever for the clothing, diet and all other necessaries for the maintenance and support of such offenders, and for the implements and materials of any kind of manufacture, trade or labor, in which such offenders shall be employed, and for the sale of such goods, wares and merchandise, as shall be there wrought and manufactured; and the said keeper shall cause all accounts concerning the maintenance of such offenders to be entered regularly in a book or books, and shall also keep separate accounts of the stock and materials so wrought, manufactured, sold and disposed of, and the moneys for which the same shall be sold, and when sold and to whom, in books to be provided for those purposes; all which books and accounts shall be at all times open for the examination of the said inspectors, and shall be regularly laid before them, at their quarterly or other meetings, as hereinafter is directed, for their approbation and allowance; and an abstract of the expenditures and receipts of moneys, the account of labor, the purchase of raw materials, and sale of articles manufactured, shall be laid before the legislature at their annual meeting, and at such other times as the legislature shall direct and require.[1]

The keeper of the state prison to keep an account of the expenditures and receipts of moneys, &c., and lay the same before the legislature.

6. *And be it enacted,* That if the said inspectors, at their quarterly or other meetings, shall suspect any fraudulent or improper charges, or any omissions in any such accounts, they may examine upon oath or affirmation, the said keeper, or his deputy, or any of his assistants, or servants, or any persons of whom any necessaries, stock, materials, or other things, have been purchased for the use of the said prison, or any persons, to whom any stock or materials, wrought or manufactured therein, have been sold, or any of the offenders confined in such prison, or any other person or persons, concerning any of the articles contained in such accounts, or any omission thereout.

In what cases it shall be the duty of the inspectors to examine the said keeper, or other persons relative to his accounts.

7. *And be it enacted,* That in order to encourage industry, as an evidence of reformation, separate accounts shall be opened in the said books for all persons sentenced to hard labor and imprisonment, in which such persons shall be charged with the expenses of their clothing and subsistence and such proportionable part of the expenses of the raw materials, upon which they shall be employed, as the inspectors, at their quarterly or other meetings, shall think just, and shall be credited with the sum or sums, from time to time received by reason of their labor, and if the same shall be found to exceed their expenses, one half of the said excess shall be laid out in decent raiment for such

Separate accounts to be opened against the offenders respectively.

[1] That part of this section, which directs that the orders of the inspectors shall be countersigned by the auditor, was repealed the 6th of November, 1798, by the fourth section of the act for the safe keeping of the books and papers of the auditor's office.

persons at their discharge, or otherwise applied to their use and benefit, as the said inspectors shall, upon such occasions, direct; and if such offender, at the end or other determination of his term of confinement, shall labor under any acute or dangerous distemper, he shall not be discharged, unless at his own request, until he can be safely discharged.

8. *And be it enacted,* That no person whatever, except the keeper, his deputy, assistants or servants, the said inspectors, officers and ministers of justice, counsellors or attorneys at law, employed by a prisoner, ministers of the gospel, or persons producing a written license, signed by one of the said inspectors, shall be permitted to enter within the walls, where such offenders shall be confined; and that the doors of all the lodging rooms and cells in the said prison shall be locked, and all lights extinguished at the hour of nine, and one or more watchmen shall patrol the said prison, at least twice in every hour, until the return of time of labor in the morning of the next day.

9. *And be it enacted,* That the walls of the cells and apartments in the said prison, shall be whitewashed with lime and water, at least twice in every year, and the floors of the said cells and apartments shall be washed once every week, or oftener, if the said inspectors shall so direct, by one or more of the said prisoners, in rotation, who, at the discretion of the said keeper, shall have an extra allowance of diet for so doing; and the said prisoners shall be allowed to walk and air themselves for such stated time as their health may require, and the said keeper shall permit; and if proper employment can be found, such prisoners may also be permitted with the approbation of two of the said inspectors, to work in the yard, providing such working and airing be in the presence or within the view of the said keeper, or his deputy or assistants.

10. *And be it enacted,* That one or more of the apartments in the said prison shall be fitted up as an infirmary; and in case any offender, being sick, shall, upon examination by a physician, be found to require it, he or she shall be removed to the infirmary, and his or her name shall be entered in a book to be kept for that purpose, and when such physician shall report to the said keeper, that the said offender is in a proper condition to quit the infirmary and return to his or her employment, such report shall be entered by the said keeper in a book to be kept for that purpose, and the said keeper shall order him or her back to his or her former labor, so far as the same shall be consistent with his or her state of health.

11. *And be it enacted,* That the keeper of the said prison shall have power to punish all such offenders guilty of assaults within said prison, when no dangerous wound or bruise is given, profane cursing or swearing, or indecent behavior, idleness or negligence in work, or wilful mismanagement of it, or disobedience to the

orders and regulations hereinafter directed to be made, by confining such offenders in the cells or dungeons of the said prison, and by keeping them upon bread and water only, for any time not exceeding two days; and if any such prisoner shall be guilty of any offense within the said prison, which the said keeper is not hereby authorized to punish, or for which he shall think the said punishment is not sufficient, by reason of the enormity of the offense, he shall report the same to two of the inspectors, who, if upon inquiry they shall think fit, shall order such offender to be punished by close confinement in the said cells or dungeons, with bread and water for sustenance, for any time not exceeding six days.

12. *And be it enacted,* That it shall be lawful for the said inspectors to appoint a suitable person to be keeper of the said prison, who shall be liable to be removed by the said inspectors, when occasion may require; in which case another shall, from time to time, be appointed in like manner, who shall receive as a full compensation for his services, in lieu of all fees and gratuities, by reason or under colour of the said office, so much by the year, as the said inspectors, at the time of appointment shall direct, to be paid, in quarterly payments, by orders drawn on the treasurer of the state by any two of the said inspectors; and also five per centum on the sales of all articles manufactured by the said offenders; and such keeper shall have power, with the approbation of the inspectors aforesaid, to appoint a deputy, and also a suitable number of assistants, at such reasonable allowance as the said inspectors shall think just and proper; which allowances shall be paid, quarterly, in like manner; and before said keeper shall exercise any part of said office, he shall give bond to the treasurer of the state, with two sufficient sureties, to be approved of by the said treasurer, in the sum of one thousand dollars, upon condition, that he, his deputy, and assistants, shall well and faithfully perform the trusts and duties in them reposed; which bond, the due execution thereof being proved before, and certified by, any one of the justices of the supreme court, or any one of the judges of the county, wherein it may be executed, shall be recorded in the office of the secretary of state, and copies thereof, legally exemplified by the said secretary, shall be legal evidence in the courts of law in any suit against such keeper or his sureties.

Inspectors to appoint a keeper of the State Prison, who shall be allowed an annual salary.

By whom a deputy and assistants shall be appointed.

Keeper to give security to the treasurer before he enters on the duties of his office.

13. *And be it enacted,* That at the first joint meeting of the legislature after passing this act, eight suitable persons shall be chosen as inspectors of the said prison, who shall continue in office for one year, and until others are chosen in their stead, and at the first joint meeting, which shall happen after every annuall meeting of the legislature thereafter, the said inspectors shall be re-elected, or others chosen in their stead, who shall

Eight inspectors to be annually appointed by the legislature.

likewise continue in office for one year, and until others are appointed in their stead; and if any vacancy shall happen by the death, removal, resignation, or other inability of any of the inspectors, in the recess of the legislature, it shall and may be lawful for the person, administering the government, to appoint a person or persons to fill such vacancy until the next joint meeting of the legislature.

14. Executed.

Inspectors when to attend and their powers and duties.

15. *And be it enacted,* That such inspectors, five of whom shall be a quorum, shall meet once in three months, in an apartment to be provided for that purpose in the said prison, and may be specially convened by the two acting inspectors, who shall continue such for such time as shall be directed by a majority of said inspectors when met together; and the acting inspectors shall attend at the said prison at least once in every week, and shall examine into and inspect the management of said prison, and the conduct of the said keeper, his deputy and assistants, so far as respects the offenders employed at hard labor and the directions of this act, and shall do and perform the several matters and things herein before directed by them to be performed.

The board of inspectors to make orders and regulations for the government of the prison.

Penalty on the keeper, his deputy, or assistants, for obstructing the inspectors in the exercise of their powers and duties.

16. *And be it enacted,* That the board of inspectors, at their quarterly or other meetings, shall make such orders and regulations for the purpose of carrying this act into execution, and for the good government of the said prison, not repugnant to the laws of the state, as they shall deem necessary; and such orders and regulations shall be hung up in at least six of the most conspicuous places in the said prison; and if the said keeper, his deputy, or any of his assistants, shall obstruct or resist the said inspectors, or any of them, in the exercise of the powers and duties vested in them by this act, such person shall forfeit and pay the sum of thirty dollars, to be recovered by any one of the inspectors, in any court having cognizance of the same, and applied to the use of the said prison, and moreover shall be liable to be removed in manner aforesaid from his office or employment in the said prison.

Powers of the sheriffs and their deputies in conveying offenders to the State Prison.

17. *And be it enacted,* That the sheriffs of the several counties in this state, and their lawful deputies, during the time that they or either of them shall, agreeably to the directions of this act, be employed in conveying to the said prison any person or persons sentenced to hard labor and imprisonment as aforesaid, shall have the same power and authority to secure him, her or them in any gaol of this state, and to demand the assistance of any sheriff, gaoler, or other person within the State, in securing all such offenders, as if such sheriff were in his own proper county; and all sheriffs, gaolers, and other persons aforesaid, shall be aiding and assisting such sheriff, or his lawful deputy, under the same penalties as if such officer was in his proper county.

18. *And be it enacted,* That any constable or other person, who shall take up and convey to the said prison any offender, who shall escape from his confinement, shall be allowed mileage, going and returning, at the rate of ten cents per mile, and such additional sum as the said inspectors shall think reasonable for the necessary expenses incurred, to be paid by the treasurer of the State, on orders drawn by the said inspectors, or any two of them.

Allowance for taking up offenders, who have escaped.

19. *And be it enacted,* That if any keeper or other person whatsoever shall introduce into, or give away, barter or sell, within the said prison, any vinous, spirituous, or fermented liquirs, excepting only such as the keeper shall make use of in his own family, or such as may be required for any prisoner in the state of ill health, and for such purpose prescribed by an attending physician, and delivered into the hands of such physician, or other person appointed to receive them, every person so offending shall forfeit and pay the sum of thirty dollars, to be recovered and applied in the manner hereinbefore directed.

No spirituous liquors to be given or sold in the prison.

20. *And be it enacted,* That the costs of prosecution against any person, sentenced to hard labor and imprisonment, shall be paid by the inspectors, out of the first moneys arising from the net profits of the labor of such offenders.

Costs of prosecution against persons sentenced to hard labor, how to be paid.

21. *And be it enacted,* That the inspectors of the said prison shall and may, from time to time, employ a physician to attend such prisoners, who shall receive a compensation for the services by him to be performed, to be determined by the said inspectors.

Physician to be employed.

22. *And be it enacted,* That when funds shall be in the hands of the inspectors of said prison sufficient to discharge any of the expenses, which are by this act directed to be discharged by the treasurer of the State, it shall and may be lawful for the said inspectors to discharge the said expenses out of any moneys so in their hands, and insert the same in their accounts, to be laid before the legislature.[1]

Funds to be applied for paying expenses.

4. CONTEMPORARY DESCRIPTION OF THE MANAGEMENT AND ADMINISTRATION OF THE ORIGINAL STATE PRISON OF NEW JERSEY IN THE FIRST YEARS OF ITS EXISTENCE.

In 1804, a committee was appointed by the Legislature to inquire into the system of management in vogue in the newly established State Prison. The unusually systematic report of

[1] *Acts of the 22nd General Assembly of the State of New Jersey, 2nd Sitting, February 15, 1798,* pp. 280ff.

this committee gives an admirable and exhaustive picture of the industries and management of the first State Prison in New Jersey at about the period when it had just become established as a working institution. This report furnishes one of the best contemporary descriptions of the congregate system of prison administration at the opening of the last century.

WEDNESDAY, February 22.

Half-past nine o'clock. The House met.

The committee appointed to enquire into the regulations of the State Prison, also to take into consideration the petition of Doctor Jeremiah Woolsey, praying a compensation for extra service, report,

That they have visited the Prison, stated certain queries to the Inspectors and received their answers, which documents we present to the House; from examining said papers, are of opinion the business is conducted with propriety.

The committee likewise report, that after examining the petition of Doctor Jeremiah Woolsey, and the documents attending the same, are of opinion that no farther allowance ought to be granted said petitioner for past service.

By order of the Committee,

ISRAEL DAY.

Which report was read, and agreed to by the House; and the following Documents accompanying the same, ordered to be printed with the Report in the Minutes of this House.

To the Queries proposed by a Committee of the Legislature on Monday, February 13th, 1804, The Keeper, and Inspectors of the State Prison, give the following answers, viz.

Query 1. How many Keepers and their salaries?
Answer.   1 Principal Keeper, salary, dolls., ... 600 per. ann.
          1 Clerk, ... 400 do.
          1 Assistant Keeper, ... 350 do.
          1 Do. .... 350 do.
          1 Do. .... 250 do.
          1 Do. .... 200 do.

Query 2. What number of prisoners generally?
Answer. Sixty-nine.

Query 3. How many employed, and at what?
Answer. Cutting nails, ... 10.
         Heading nails, ... 23.
         Making wrought nails, ... 4.

Turning grindstones & attending Nailors, ... 3.
Black-smith, ... 1.
Shoemaking, ... 7.
Coopering, ... 2.
Cooking, ... 2.
Tayloring, ... 2.
Weaving, ... 2.
Washing and sawing wood, ... 4.
Spinning, ... 1. Wom.

      Employed, ... 61.

Sick, ... 4. }
Old men not able to work, .. 4. } Unemployed, ... 8.

      Total, ... 69.

Query 4. What quantity of work is considered as a days work, at each particular branch?

Answer. A days work will vary considerably according to the season of the year, and the quality of the work, but is supposed to average nearly follows, viz.

A Days Work.

	d.		lb.		
Nail-cutting.	20 Nails,	....	200.		
	12 do.	....	180.		
	10 do.	....	160.		
	8 do.	....	140.		Allowed the prisoners for
	6 do.	....	110.		cutting nails and brads, 3s
	4 do.	....	72.		per day.
	3 do.	....	50.		
Brad-cutting.	12 Brads,	....	130.		
	10 do.	....	115.		
	8 do.	....	100.		
	6 do.	....	80.		

                                      Allowed for heading.

Heading Nails.	20 Nails,	80.		
	12 do.	70.		
5s per 100 Wt.				
	10 do.	60.	6s	do.
	8 do.	60.	7s	do.
	6 do.	40.	8s4	do.
	4 do.	25.	14s	do.
	3 do.	16.	18s	do.
Making Wrought Nails	10 & 12	13.	3d½	per lb.
	8 do.	10.	4d	do.
	6 do.	8.	5d	do.

A Days work.

Shoe-making, Mens calf skin ....⎫
shoe lined, &c. ....⎬ 1 pair 3s9 per pair.
Mens coarse do. ....1½ do 2s6 do.
Womens slippers, ...2 do 2s6 do.
Bootees, ... ½ do 7s6 do.

Coopering, 4 Nail kegs 11d per keg.

Note. The staves of which all the Nail kegs are made, are taken out of the cord wood that is purchased for the use of the prison.

A Days work.

Weaving, Plainwork such as linen, linsey, &c. from 5 to 8 yds... 8d per yard.
Rag carpents, 6 to 10 do. ....8d do.
Double work such as Bedtick, Diaper, &c. 5 to 7 do...10d do.

Spinning, Flax-yarn, ¾ a days work, at 2s6 per lb.
Tow, do. 1 do. 1/6 do.

Note. Sundry other work, allowed for by the day, according to the nature of the business; and in proportion to the abilities of the performer, such as Cooking, Tayloring, Black-smith, Carpenter work, Washing, Sawing wood, Scrubbing and cleaning the rooms, white-washing, mending clothes, &c. from 2s, 2s6, 2s9, to 3s per day.

Query 5. The nature of contracts for materials, whether on credit, and how long?
Answer. Materials are purchased on the most advantageous and convenient terms, sometimes for cash, and sometimes on sixty days credit.

Query 6. The nature of contracts for the sale of Manufactures whether on credit, and how long?
Answer. The Manufactured articles are sold, some for cash, and some at sixty, or ninety days credit, according to the nature, quality, and quantity of the sale.

Query 7. How much per week is each prisoner charged for his board?
Answer. 20 cents per day, or dol. 1,40 per week.

Note. In the above sum of one dollar and forty cents per week, it is contemplated they should pay for fire wood in their bedrooms, lamp light, bed cloathes, the expence of cooking, Kitchen furniture, such as knives, forks, spoons, dishes, plates, pans, &c. &c. besides their provisions.

Query 8. How much for cloathing?
Answer. Cloathes are charged for in proportion to the price and quality of cloth, that can be procured for that purpose, general as follows, viz.

1 upper jacket made of blue cloth, ...dolls. 2 80
1 Under do.   do. 2 00
1 Pair Trowsers,   do. 2 50
1 Pair do.   linen, ... 1 25
1 Shirt,   from 1 50 to 1 67
1 Pair shoes,   generally 1 50
1 Pair stockings,   from 50 cents to............. 1 00

Query 9. What sum is allowed each prisoner for each particular Manufacture?

Answer. See answer to Query 4.

Query 10. How much allowed for a Physician?

Answer. Sixty dollars per annum, he finding Medicine.

Query 11. What kind and quality of food allowed?

Answer. For breakfast and supper, they have Indian meal made into mush *quantum sufficit,* with 1-2 gill of molasses to each man per meal. For dinner they are allowed 1-2lb. coin'd beef or 3-4lb. of veal, or other fresh meat, made into soup, with vegetables, (say) potatoes, turnips, cabbage, &c. together with 10 oz. rye bread to each man.

Note. For variety and economy, they are fed one or two days in the week, for dinner, on smoaked herring, and bread.

Query 12. What are the particular internal regulations, so far as relates to hours of work, rest, meals, &c?

Answer. Every day in the year (if in health) except Sundays, they work from sun rise, until within three quarters of an hour of sun set, allowing half an hour for breakfast, one hour in winter, and one hour and a half in summer for dinner, and half an hour for supper.

Hours of Rest.

They are locked up in their rooms every evening at sun set, after which time they do no kind of work, they generally go to sleep at nine o'clock at night, or sooner if they will, and there continue until sun rise next morning.

Hours for Meals.

In winter breakfast at 8, dinner at 12, and supper at 4. In summer breakfast at 7, dinner at 12, and supper at 6, or nearly so according to the season.

Query 13. What are the particular duties of the Keepers, by night, and by day?

Answer. Principal Keeper see the Law, page 272.
Clerk needs no explanation.

1. Assistant Keeper to superintend the different manufactories, keep order amongst the men, keep them to their work, weigh and take an account of their work daily, render an account of their work quarterly to the Clerk, or oftener if required, weigh the Nails, and see them put in kegs, weigh the Iron when it comes to the Prison, &c. &c. such is his duty by day, and at night, take his regular tour of watch.

2. Assistant to unlock the prison rooms, and let out the prisoners every morning, lock them up at night, and through the course of the day superintend the internal affairs of the Prison, such as examining the rooms, to see that the grates, floors or walls, have not been cut, or injured by the Prisoners, examine the cells, and those that are confined there, give out their provisions, ring the bell, and attend them while at meals, ring the bell to warn them to work, call for and deliver anything that may be wanted through the main door, &c. &c. and take his regular tour of watch by night.

3. Assistant to watch all day in the Prison yard, and take his regular tour of watch at night.

4. Assistant to do. all the out door work, such as carting Iron, Nails, or anything that may be wanted, to and from the Prison, go of errands, attend the outside gates, when Iron, wood, Nails, &c. are going through, take care of the horse, attend in the Prison yard at meal times, or any other time that occasion may require, and take a tour of watch at night if necessary.

Query 14. What alterations (if any) they may judge necessary in the existing Laws, so far as relates to the power of the Inspectors, or for enforcing obedience in the Prisoners, &c?

Answer. The Law is already sufficient to enforce obedience in the Prisoners, but in our opinion the Inspectors ought to have power invested in them, to remit costs, and discharge invalids, &c. without troubling the Governor and Council.

Query 15. What price each particular Manufacture are sold at?
Answer.

CUT NAILS.

By the ton & upward.		By the keg.	
d	cents.	d	cents.
3 Nails,	12½ per lb.	3 Nails,	14 per lb.
4 do.	12	4 do.	13
6 do.	11	6 do.	12
8 do.	9	8 do.	10
10 do.	9	10 do.	10
12 do.	9	12 do.	10
20 do.	8½	10 do.	8½

CUT BRADS.
are sold at the same price as Nails.

Wrought Nails whole sale.   Retail.
   d   cents.   d   cents.

  12 ⎫   12 ⎫
  10 ⎬ 13 per lb.   10 ⎬ 14 per lb.
   8 ⎭   8 ⎭

   6 15   6 16

Mens calf skin shoes, dolls., ... 1 67 per single pair
Mens coarse, do. .... 1 50 do.
Womens slippers, ... 1 12 do.
Bootees, .·................................ 4 50 do.
Fire buckets, ... 4   do.
Chip hats, from 50 cents to 1   per hat.
Rush-bottomed chairs, ... 3 50 per ½ doz.

Query 16. What number of Negroes, and how many were free and how many slaves?

Answer. Twenty Negroes.
    12 of which were free.
     8 slaves.
      ——
    20

Query 17. What number of Foreigners and their nation?

Answer. Six Foreigners,
    of which are   1 German.
               1 Englishman.
               1 West Indian.
               3 Irishman.

    Total 6

Query 18. What is the present situation of the ground belonging to the State, near the Prison, and what it would probably rent for per year?

Answer. It now lies waste, the fence being much out of repair, and in its present state, we do not think it would rent at any sum. Yet in our opinion it may be managed so as to benefit the State, (i e) by repairing the fence, manuring and tilling the ground and raising potatoes, corn, &c. for the use of the State Prison.

The above answers to the several queries proposed, is submitted to the Committee.

           HENRY BELLERJEAU,
               Keeper of the State Prison.
           MOORE FURMAN,
               President of the Board of Inspectors.[1]

[1] *Votes and Proceedings of the Twenty-eighth General Assembly of the State of New Jersey*, February 22, 1804, pp. 147–155.

II. Prison Management and Industries in New Jersey from 1800 to 1836.

1. Report of the Board of Inspectors of 1811, Relative to the Need of a Prison Sales Agent.

The Speaker presented to the house the following letter from the President of the Board of Inspectors of the State Prison.

To the Honorable the Legislature of the State of New Jersey, now in session.
Gentlemen,
    The inspectors of the state-prison beg leave to suggest the propriety of repealing the per centage on sales to the keeper for his services, which possibly might hereafter prevent litigation. The law alluded to is in Paterson's edition, 12th section of the state-prison law.—The reason is this, The keeper has for many years past been allowed a salary for his services, giving up the per centage pointed out in the law. But in case of the Keeper's death, possibly his representatives might demand the per centage, exclusive of the salary—and if the entry made in their minute book should be lost, or by some means could not be produced to rebut such a demand, they have their doubts whether or not the state would be exonerated from payment.
    The inspectors also suggest the propriety of their having authority by law to appoint an agent or agents, to dispose of their nails at distant places.
    There will most probably be on hand by April or May next, two hundred tons of nails—and without adopting some plan more than heretofore, they fear too large an amount will be continued on hand.
    But by having agents at distant places most probably considerable quantities might be disposed of; and likely often to more advantage, than when sold at the prison.
    All which is respectfully submitted.
    By order of the Board,
        I am, gentlemen, your humble servant,
                PETER GORDON, President of the Board.[1]
    February 15, 1811.

2. Report of the Joint Committee of the Legislature of 1816 in Regard to the Confusion Arising from the Original System of Accounting Employed at the State Prison.

When the State Prison management was organized in 1798, the practice was instituted of charging each prisoner for the ex-

[1] *Votes and Proceedings of the Thirty-fifth General Assembly of the State of New Jersey,* February 15, 1811; pp. 508–509.

penses of maintenance, clothing, heat, light and service, and then balancing against this total the proceeds from the income of the labor of each individual prisoner. According to law, the inspectors were authorized to retain in prison all prisoners who had not paid with their labor the expenses of conviction and the total cost of their support while in prison. As the industrial provisions in the original prison were extremely crude and generally unproductive, it was very difficult for many of the prisoners to earn a sum which was equal to that which was charged against them for the expenses of conviction and maintenance. As a result, the very limits of the physical capacity of the prison compelled the inspectors to discharge the prisoners in spite of the fact that a heavy balance against them existed on the prison books. This accumulation of bad accounts against individual prisoners was a source of great confusion in the prison accounting, and the following report is but one of many successive protests against this awkward system of administering the finances of the prison.

Mr. Parker, from the joint committee appointed at the last sitting, on the subject of the State Prison, made the following report:—

That the materials and stock of the Institution on the 1 October, 1814, amount to 25,349 02
And there was received from the Treasury during the year ending 1 October, 1815, the sum of 4,087 46

Making altogether, ... 29,436 48
That the stock and materials on hand the 1 Oct., 1815, as stated (per account marked A) to amount to .. 25,439 96
To which is added iron, not included in that account, as per certificate of the Inspectors, dated 31 January last, ... 1,068 56

Making the whole stock and materials on 1 October, 1815, ... 26,508 52

And by which a loss appears to have accrued of $2,927 96

The loss thus incurred appears to have arisen on the following items of profit and loss, viz:

25 P

Articles of Loss.

Weaving account, ...	171 92
Cordwainers, ...	38 30
Prison repairs, ...	238 46
Prisoners discharged, &c.	1,218 40
Salaries of Keeper and assistants, Inspectors, &c.	3,380 00
Incidental expenses, ...	483 68
Screw factory, ...	12 22

————— 5,542 98

Articles of Gain.

Nailery, ...	1,380 81
Cooperage, ...	120 19
Clothing Account, ...	108 53
Provision Account, ...	928 42
Interest, ...	77 07

————— 2,615 02

Amount of loss as above stated, ... $2,927 96

That the loss on the operations of the prison for the year ending 1 October, 1814, was $2,344.14 making an increased loss during the last year of $588.82.

It will be remarked that a large item of loss is the amount due by prisoners discharged, amounting during the year past to $1,218 40. A part of the amount due from prisoners consists of the costs of prosecution and conviction, which by law the inspectors are bound to pay on receipt of the offender, and which are charged to his account; and these costs are at times greatly extended by the circumstance of the prisoner's being convicted on several separate indictments. The inspectors consider themselves bound by law to discharge prisoners at the expiration of the term for which they are committed, upon a representation of their good behaviour from the keeper, notwithstanding their being in debt—and as many are committed for short terms, and cannot so soon earn these expenses, over and above their subsistence; and others committed for longer terms are, from decrepitude and other causes unable to earn their living—an apparent loss arises to the institution, which in fact does not accrue upon its own operations, but by its paying the expense of convicting offenders committed to it.

It is to be remarked also, that this item of loss varies in different years, from the accidental cause of the sentences expiring in one year being more numerous than in others. And that the loss the last year from this item, exceeds that of the year preceding the sum of $465.19; and also that the amount due from infirm prisoners is not carried to the debit of the profit and loss account until their discharge or death—by which means a loss which has accrued and been increasing for several years, appears as if it arose during the year in which the discharge or death takes place. In the year to end the 1 October, 1816, one instance of this kind will occur, wherein the debit of an old and decrepit convict is nearly $600 for his subsistence during

10 years confinement; but the whole of which without examination, would appear to be the loss of one year.

The item of incidental expences has been greater the last year than usual, owing to the purchase of a horse and several other articles of extraordinary expence: and the manufacture of nails, a considerable source of profit, has been the last year less productive than in the year 1814, by the sum of nearly 700 dollars. This last is stated to the committee to have arisen from the circumstance that the iron and nail rods used had been greatly enhanced in price, while the manufactured article could not be sold at a correspondent advance. The committee submit for the information of the Legislature, all the statements handed them relating to the concerns of the State Prison, together with a comparative statement of the profit and loss during the two past years.[1]

JN. FRELINGHUYSEN,
Chairman of Committee from Council.
JAMES PARKER,
GEO. HOLCOMBE.

3. MEMORIAL OF THE INSPECTORS OF THE STATE PRISON IN 1818.

On February 3, 1818, the Board of Inspectors of the State Prison presented the following important memorial to the Legislature. This memorial is significant in three different ways. In the first place, it points out how nail-making, the most important original industry of the State Prison, was destroyed by the flooding of the American market with English cut-nails after 1816. In the second place, it repeated the protest of the joint committee of 1816 against the awkward system of accounting employed at the State Prison. Finally, it is especially significant as indicating a trend of opinion toward the abandonment of the congregate system of prison management and the institution of the system of solitary confinement. The recommendations of the inspectors relative to solitary confinement of the more serious types of criminals, which were embodied in the law of 1820, marked the first experiment in New Jersey with what came to be known as the Pennsylvania System of solitary confinement.

TUESDAY, February 3.
Ten o'clock the House met.
The Speaker laid before the House, the following memorial from the Inspectors of the State Prison.

[1] *Votes and Proceedings of the Fortieth General Assembly of the State of New Jersey,* February 13, 1816; pp. 236–239.

To the Honorable, the Legislature of the State of New Jersey.

The memorial of the Inspectors of the New Jersey State Prison, respectfully represents.

That this institution is at present laboring under very great disadvantages, which they would respectfully make known to your honorable body, hoping and trusting that you, as the immediate guardians of the good citizens of this state, would make such alterations and amendments as your honorable body in your wisdom may think proper.

1st. The inspectors would inform the Legislature that from present appearances the manufacture of nails, which is the principal article now made in this institution, and which has hitherto been a very productive employment for the men, has become latterly instead of producing a profit to this institution, by reason of the great reduction in the price of that article, so much so that if sales could be made to the extent of there being manufactured, there would nett but a very small advance from the first cost of the iron of which they are manufactured; but we have with pain and disappointment, to state, that the article of nails has the last year increased on our hands to an alarming extent, as will be seen by the following statement:

On the 1st of October, 1816, there were on hand...... 963 kegs
On the 1st of October, 1817, do ....1784 do.

                                                        ————
                                                         821

Thus it will appear that there were 821 kegs, or upwards of 41 tons manufactured in one year, ending 30th September, 1817, more than were sold in the same space of time.

The Inspectors would candidly acknowledge, that they have no reason to calculate on a greater sale of nails the present year, than the former one, but on the contrary, believe that our sales will be more limited from a variety of causes; the principal one, is that a number of manufacturers of that article, in the vicinity of our large cities, are selling their nails at a less price than this institution can possibly manufacture them, even in some instances at the prime cost of the iron. This may arise in part from a great quantity of cut nails having been imported from England in the last year, and we have no reason to suppose a stop will be put to the importation.

2d. In order to meet the current expenses of this Institution, to pay for the articles of iron, fuel, &c., the Inspectors, from the very limited sale of nails, have been obliged to make large drafts on the Treasurer of this State, the last year, and they feel confident that the drafts on the Treasurer the ensuing year must be much larger, as from the increased number of prisoners, and the manufacture of nails being the only article of consequence, under the present mode of punishment they can employ the prisoners at, the quantity on hand will be every year increasing over and above the sales, consequently a much larger amount of monied capital will be necessary to carry on the business, which capital will be laying invested in cut nails on hand, which cannot be disposed of in the opinion of the Inspectors at a forced sale, for the first cost of the iron of which they were made.

Note.—The amount of money drawn from the Treasurer the last year exclusively for the payment of iron, was about the sum of eight thousand dollars, and for the current year the Inspectors would suppose the sum of ten thousand dollars at least will be necessary to conduct the business of the Institution under the present regulations.

3d. The Inspectors have now under their charge, one hundred and twelve prisoners in the Prison, who are employed in the following manner:

- 30 men cutting and heading nails,
- 10 do. making wrought nails,
- 6 Shoemakers,
- 8 Weavers,
- 19 Men spinning,
- 8 do. in gun-shop.

And the remainder of the men and women in different occupations, as tailors, basket makers, coopers, blacksmiths, &c., &c., which small employments are carried on to as great an extent as circumstances will admit, so that the Inspectors feeling themselves bound to keep the men at labor, they have employed as few men in the manufacture of cut nails as they possibly can.

4th. In the internal concerns of the prison we would again most respectfully invite the attention of your honorable body, to a circumstance calling for the interposition of the Legislature, to wit, excessive bills of cost, charged to prisoners, as frequent cases occur, wherein prisoners have several large bills of costs charged to them, which in the first instance this Institution is obliged to pay, without ever receiving any remuneration by the prisoners' labor, or by any other means, whereby the Institution becomes greatly the sufferer.

The Inspectors having in the foregoing hasty remarks, shewn your honorable body into what a situation we are placed by reason of the many inconveniences under which we labor, would proceed most respectfully to recommend such alterations in the laws as justice and sound policy should dictate, and

1st. Would again call your attention to short terms of imprisonment. This we can truly say has been exceedingly against the interest of this Institution, which this board had the honor to represent to your honors last year.— We would therefore recommend that no prisoner be sent to this prison on any occasion for a less term than one year, but that such other punishment should be inflicted on persons for small crimes, as the Legislature in their wisdom may think expedient,

2d. To the revival of a supplement of the act entitled "An act making provision for the carrying into effect the act for the punishment of crimes," passed March 1, 1804, and repealed by an act passed February 16, 1816.

Your honorable body will discover by examining the several acts, that the former gave the inspectors discretionary powers in certain cases; and the act passed February 16, 1816, to repeal the former and which repeal places the power in the Governor and Council. The Inspectors would state their reason for wishing the act of March 1, 1804, revived; first, that the court of pardons sits but twice in a year, to wit, in May and November; secondly, that frequent cases occur that the prisoners' times expire soon after the sitting of the Court, who are unable to pay the balance of cost, &c., consequently the Inspectors are obliged to keep the men in confinement, frequently at a great expense to the state, until the meeting of the next court.

3d. It having become manifest to the Inspectors, and must certainly have become more or less so to your honors, that from the present mode of punishment little or no good can be expected, as to the reformation of the persons in confinement, or as a terror to those without, from the very trifling or probably nothing of punishment and the probable chance of effecting their escape. To make the punishment more commensurate to the crimes committed, the inspectors would again call the attention of the Legislature to the subject of erecting a sufficient number of cells for the purpose of confining the most abandoned, and for such as may commit capital offences, separate and apart from each other. This with due deference to your honors, would we conceive be the most effectual means of lessening the number of convicts sent for high crimes, as the circumstance of separate confinement would soon get abroad among that class of society, which would no doubt prevent a number from violating our most excellent laws, and would ultimately, we have no doubt, be the means of bringing about a reformation in those who should unhappily become the subjects of such a mode of punishment.

ELLETT TUCKER,
President of the Board of Inspectors.
HON. EBENEZER ELMER,
Speaker of the House of Assembly.

January 30th, 1818.[1]

4. REPORT OF THE JOINT COMMITTEE TO SETTLE THE ACCOUNTS OF THE STATE PRISON IN 1822 WITH RESPECT TO THE SYSTEM OF PRISON ACCOUNTING.

The following report is a vigorous condemnation of the system of accounting, referred to above, whereby an individual account was opened with each prisoner, balancing his expenses of maintenance against the proceeds from his labor:

The joint committee appointed to settle the accounts of the state prison, Respectfully Report—

That they have carefully examined the accounts and vouchers submitted to them by the keeper and inspectors, and the books kept at the prison, and

---

[1] *Votes and Proceedings of the Forty-second General Assembly of the State of New Jersey,* February 3, 1818; pp. 130–136.

believe them to be accurately stated and balanced. They report herewith the statement exhibited, with the remarks of the inspectors.

Your committee however are of opinion, that these accounts do not exhibit the actual annual expense of the institution to the state, and that it is impossible they should, so long as the existing laws on the subject remain unaltered. The principal source of error appears to result from charging the prisoners (as well those sentenced to hard labor as those confined in the cells) with the daily sums of twenty cents each for their board, and additional sums for costs, clothing, &c. agreeably to the provisions of the 7th section of an Act making provision for carrying into effect the act for the punishment of crimes. These charges accumulate a heavy balance against almost every prisoner sentenced to labor, and must necessarily have that effect against those in the cells. The total amount of these balances is stated this year at fourteen thousand three hundred and seventy dollars forty cents, being two thousand nine hundred and sixteen dollars seventy-seven cents more than the amount stated last year, and of course increasing the stock on hand the last mentioned sum. But a very small proportion of these balances are ever paid, and it is believed nearly the whole amount now due may be considered as a bad debt. In calculating the actual profit and loss, this item must therefore be struck from the account.

There is also stated to be due the institution, from sundry persons, the sum of ten thousand six hundred seventy-nine dollars forty-nine cents, including sixteen hundred ninety-three dollars, thirty-six cents, charged to the state for repairing and cleaning arms. This sum, it appears, has been accumulating several years, and many of the debts are lost by death and insolvency. The inspectors, at the request of the committee, have made an estimate of those that may be considered as desperate, amounting in the whole to seventeen hundred and six dollars eleven cents, besides four hundred and six dollars twenty-one cents due on notes of prisoners discharged, the recovery of which is considered doubtful; leaving eight thousand two hundred twenty-four dollars and seventy-seven cents, to be estimated as good debts.

In order, therefore, to ascertain the true loss of the institution for the year ending on the first of October last, your committee have made up a general account, discarding on the one side the debts due from prisoners, and those due from individuals that are considered as lost, and on the other side the items in favor of fines, transportation and costs of prosecution, these last being included in the charges against prisoners. As these items have accumulated through a series of past years, they have deducted the amounts stated in the accounts of last year, from the amount of nett stock to begin with October 1, 1821. This account, marked A, your committee pray be received as part of their report. The actual loss to the state for the past year, appears from it to be the sum of six thousand five hundred and forty-two dollars forty-five cents.[1]

[1] *Votes and Proceedings of the Forty-Seventh General Assembly of the State of New Jersey*, November 12, 1822; pp. 76–77.

5. PRISON FINANCES AND INDUSTRY IN 1825.

The following report of the joint committee of the Legislature on the accounts of the State Prison, gives a brief and concise description of the industrial distribution of the prison population at the close of the first quarter of the 19th century:

Mr. Capner, from the joint-committee of Council and Assembly, appointed to settle the accounts of the state prison,

Reported, That they have examined the accounts and vouchers submitted to them by the keeper and inspectors, and compared the same with the books of the prison, and believe them to be substantially correct, as stated.

From the statements herewith submitted, taken to the first of January, 1825, it being the first three months after the settlement of the accounts last year, there is an apparent balance of ten thousand seven hundred and twenty-six dollars and two cents, against the prison, the greater part of which sum arises, not from any direct loss the institution has sustained, but from a depression in the value of the stock and a different mode of making the estimate, and other causes, which are exhibited in document No. 4, in which $8,552.40 are accounted for, leaving an actual loss of $2,173.63.

From the statement, as submitted to us, of nine months, as taken from the first day of January last to the first day of October, there appears a loss of $3,314.19; of this $783.29 are accounted for in amount paid for repairs of the prison, apprehending prisoners, &c. (See remarks in document No. 5) which leaves the real loss to the institution, for the last nine months, to be $2,530.90, including keepers' salaries and every other charge, except a proportion of the allowance to the inspectors, for their services, amounting to $124.50, for the last nine months, which will appear in the account of the next year.

The committee further report, that there were fifty-six convicts confined on the 30th day of September last, of which number thirty-six were white, and twenty blacks: nineteen were under the age of twenty-five, thirty-one between twenty-five and fifty, and six over fifty years. Forty-nine of them are Americans, one Englishman, five Irishman, and one Dutchman; and are employed—eight at weaving, three at spooling, seven at shoemaking, five at sawing stone, two at plaster pounding, two at spinning, one tailor, one cooper, one basketmaker, two smiths, one carpenter, two cooks, two at cutting wood, one at washing, two waiters, thirteen solitary, and three sick.

The committee lay before the House the report of the prisoners who have made their escape, and also some suggestions of the inspectors, as to the future arrangement and government of the prison.[1]

All which is respectfully submitted.

SILAS COOK,   THOMAS CAPNER,
WILLIAM EDGAR,   JAMES S. GREEN,
CHARLES CARSON,   GERSHOM MOTT,
JOHN TRAVERS.

6. PRISON INDUSTRY AND PRISON MANAGEMENT IN 1826.

The report of the joint committee of the Legislature on prison accounts, given below, is, in the first place, an excellent summary of the financial and industrial situation in 1826, but it is still more significant in that it admitted that the five years' trial of the system of solitary confinement in New Jersey had been an undoubted failure, and recommended strongly the adoption of the Auburn system of congregate work by day and solitary confinement by night. When the committee of 1833 so enthusiastically recommended that New Jersey adopt the Pennsylvania system of solitary confinement, they must have been profoundly ignorant of the result of New Jersey's previous experience with the system which they were recommending as "the most perfect type of prison administration ever devised by the mind of man."[2]

Mr. Kinsey, from the joint committee of Council and Assembly, appointed to settle the accounts of the state prison,

Reported, That they have examined the accounts, and have compared the vouchers produced to them by the keeper and inspectors of the prison with the books kept at the prison, and also with the stock account of the last year, and believe the statements made, and herewith submitted, to be substantially correct.

By these statements it appears, that the loss sustained by the operations of the prison during the last year is less than in former years. The amount of loss in the year ending the 30th September, 1826, being $3,975.07, from which sum should be deducted the sum of $220.04, expended in repairs done to the prison, and from the above sum deduct also the amount of keepers' salaries and inspectors' fees, being $3,025, and there will still remain a loss of $730.03, being the amount expended in addition to the proceeds of the labor of the prisoners for provisions, wood, clothing, &c., provided for the prisoners. By

[1] *Votes and Proceedings of the Fiftieth General Assembly of the State of New Jersey,* November 15, 1825; pp. 92–93.
[2] See below, pp. 436ff.

inspecting the treasurer's accounts, it will be found that there has been drawn from the treasury during the last year the sum of $1,654.89, to defray the costs of criminal prosecutions and the expense of transmitting convicts to the state prison.

The committee further report, that there were in the prison on the 30th day of September last, 65 convicts, who were employed in the following manner:—Shoemaking 8, weaving 14, spooling 6, attending sick and washing yarn 3, stone sawing 4, pounding plaster 2, basket-making 2, carpenter's work 1, spinning wool for prisoners' clothing 2, baking and cooking 3, gardening 1, tailoring 2, attending sick and sweeping rooms 1, and, in the cells, 16 sentenced to solitary confinement.—59 of the prisoners are American, 5 Irish, and 1 German;—8 are above the age of fifty years, 26 above the age of twenty-five years, and 2 under fifteen years,—36 of them are white, and 23 black, all men and boys—of the blacks, 6 are slaves.

The number of prisoners during the year have averaged 65, the keeping of whom have cost the state—

For provisions,	$1,154.00
Clothing,	489.64
Wood,	362.00
Incidental expenses,	465.55
Furniture,	58.30
Amounting to	$2,529.49

Making the expense of each convict,

For provisions,	$17.75
Clothing,	7.53
Wood,	5.56
Furniture,	.87
Other incidental charges,	7.16
Making an average to each person of	$38.87

To which, if we add the amount of keepers' and other officers' compensation, being $3,025, making an average expense on each person of $46.54, the whole amount of the cost of each prisoner will be about $85.45.

The following will show the profits of the labor done by the prisoners, and the comparative profit from the different kinds of labor:

14 weavers, with 6 persons employed at spooling, yielding a profit of	$475.93
8 shoemakers,	498.37
4 sawing stone,	246.80
2 pounding plaster,	195.12

The committee were led to believe, that, by judicious employment, the convicts may be made materially to reduce the present expense of the establishment; but, from the peculiar organization of the institution, it must be left to the experience and discretion of the inspectors to procure materials, and make the necessary arrangements respecting the labor and employment of the prisoners.

After a careful examination of the prison, the situation and employment of the prisoners, and the state of the finances, there appears to have been, by the management of the present inspectors, manifestly a progressive improvement.

On the subject of solitary confinement, there is a coincidence of opinion, that as the judgment or sentence for solitary confinement is executed in our prison, there is not that benefit and advantage derived, which was by many expected from the change made in our criminal code. The morals of the prisoners are not more, if as much improved, as if he was sentenced to hard labor; habits of industry he cannot acquire; his knowledge of the honest means of obtaining subsistence cannot be increased; and when his term expires he is unable to endure manual labor, if willing to perform it; and, without friends and without character, or the means of gaining an honest living, he is cast upon the world, and is soon induced again to commit some offence against the laws of society.

On a careful review of the different modes of punishment, there is a decided preference in favor of confinement at hard labor, under a suitable course of discipline, as being more effectual in displacing the evil propensities, and reclaiming the convict to habits of industry and usefulness; and if the reformation should not be complete, yet the wretch who is the object of punishment may be chastised and made better, and at the same time the public relieved from such of the burthen of his support. Solitary confinement at night would be some punishment, and, with a strict discipline in the yard or work-shop in the day, will enforce on the mind of the criminal a self-examination which must prove beneficial.

It will be observed, from the statements made, that the mode of employment of the prisoners has been changed from nail making to weaving and other labor, by reason of which the old nail factory articles are entirely useless, and will probably remain so. Those materials, together with a quantity of nails, which have been on hand many years, form a material item of the stock book account every year, and remain dead property and a loss to the state.

Your committee would therefore recommend the following resolution:—

Resolved, That a committee be appointed to inquire into the expediency of directing an immediate sale of such articles as are no longer useful to the institution.

SILAS COOK, } Committee from
JOHN MOORE WHITE, } Council.

CHARLES KINSEY,
JOHN T. McDOWELL,
WILLIAM STITES, } Committee from Assembly.
ELIAS P. SEELEY,
ISAIAH TOY,

Which report was read, and, together with the general statement and the accompanying documents, were ordered to lie on the table.[1]

7. THE REPORT OF THE FAMOUS PRISON INVESTIGATING COMMITTEE OF 1830.

The joint committee from the Legislature on the State Prison accounts, presented in 1830, in addition to their usual report on the finances and industry of the prison, a detailed and illuminating analysis and criticism of New Jersey's first system of State Prison administration.[2]

Mr. Hillard,' from joint committee, to settle the accounts of the State Prison, and to report what measures would be proper to be adopted as an amendment to our State Prison discipline, made the following report:

That they have carefully examined the accounts submitted, and have compared them so far as was considered necessary with the entries in the books, and with the vouchers.

They find the following to be the state of the monied concerns of the institution, as exhibited under each respective head.

PROVISION ACCOUNT.

The amount of provisions on hand on the 1st of October, 1828, as per inventory and valuation then made, was		$240.80
Amount expended from that time to the 30th September, 1829, was		1725 27¼
Making whole amount of provisions		$1966 07¼
From his sum is to be deducted amount sold by the keeper	103 97½	
Value of provisions on hand as per inventory	268 90	
		372 87½
Leaving amount expended for provisions for the whole year		$1593 19¾

CLOTHING ACCOUNT.

Amount on hand, 30th September, 1828, as per inventory	$240 51
Amount expended from that time to 30th Sept. 1829	536.27
Making the whole amount for clothing	$776 78

---

[1] *Votes and Proceedings of the Fifty-first General Assembly of the State of New Jersey,* December 5, 1826; pp. 132–135.

[2] See particularly, pp. 402ff.

From this is to be deducted amount received for
    clothing, made by the prisoners, &c. 41 66
Amount on hand, 1st Oct. 1829, as per inventory 227 95
                                                 269 61

Leaving whole amount expended for clothing for the year $507 17

INCIDENTAL ACCOUNT.

Amount of inventory, 1st October, 1828, ... $307 00½
Amount expended chargeable to this account 397 36½

Whole amount charged to this account $704 37
From which is to be deducted articles sold &c. 42 26¼
Amount of inventory, 1st Oct. 1829 .... 316 98
                                           359 24¼

Leaving amount chargeable to this account for the whole year.. $345 12¾

FURNITURE ACCOUNT.

Amount of inventory, 1st October, 1828 .... $893 36½
Amount expended up to 1st October, 1829 .... 199 88

Making whole amount $1093 24½
From which is to be deducted amount received on sale
    of ten plate stove, ... 8 00
Amount of inventory, 1st Oct. 1829 .... 1069 09
                                           1075 09

Leaving amount expended on this account for the year......... $18 15½

PRISON REPAIRS.

Amount of inventory, 1st October, 1828 .... 12 40
Amount expended up to 1st Oct. 1829 .... 70 37

                                           $82 72
From which deduct amount of inventory, 1st Oct. 1829 .... 16 83

Leaving amount chargeable to this account for the whole year... $65 94

FINAL ACCOUNT.

Amount of inventory, 1st October, 1828, ... $45 00½
Amount expended up to 1st October, 1829 .... 503 93½

                                           $548 93½

From which deduct 1¼ cords of wood at $4 .... $5
Amount of inventory, 1st Oct. 1829   30
                                                         ————   35 00

Leaving amount expended for the whole year $513 93½

NAIL FACTORY ACCOUNT.

Amount of inventory, 1st Oct. 1828 .... $532 29½
Amount expended, 1 pair bellows and freight on sundry articles   5 80

Making whole amount expended 538 09½

This account is to be credited with articles sold 28 19¾
Amount of inventory, 1st October 1829 ....   519 97
                                                         ————   548 16¾
Making a profit on this account for the year $10 07¼

COOPERAGE ACCOUNT.

Amount of inventory, Oct. 1st, 1829 .... $36 50
Amount expended, 500 hoop poles and porterage 5 87½

Making whole amount $42 37½

This account is credited with articles sold 26 30
Amount of inventory, Oct. 1, 1829 ....   31 81¼
                                                         ————   58 11¼

Making profit on this account for the year $15 73¾

PLAISTER ACCOUNT.

Amount of inventory, Oct. 1, 1828 .... $252 82½
Amount expended on this account for material, &c. 145 62½

Making whole amount 398 45
This am't. is to be credited with articles sold 642 47½
Amount of inventory, 1st Oct. 1829 ....   111 32½
                                                         ————   753 80

Making the profit on this account for the year $355 35

SUNDRY ACCOUNT.

Amount of inventory, Oct. 1, 1828 .... $94 95
Amount expended 25 05¾

Making in all the sum of $120 00¾

This account is credited with work done by prisoners   90 78¼
Amount of inventory, Oct. 1, 1829 .... 156 12
                         ————— $246 88¾
Making the profit on this account for the year 126 88

CORDWAINERS' ACCOUNT.

Amount of inventory, Oct. 1st 1828 .... $321 54½
Amount of purchases, chargeable to this account 675 12½

Making whole amount $996 67

This account is to be credited with articles sold 1813 26¼
Amount of inventory, Oct. 1, 1829 .... 289 44
                         ————— 2102 70¼
Making the profit on this account for the year 1106 03¼

WEAVING ACCOUNT.

Amount of inventory, Oct. 1st, 1828 .... 578 10
Amount expended on this account 469 67¾

Making in all $1047 77¾
This account is credited with articles sold 2201 90¼
Amount of inventory, 1st Oct. 1829 .... 554 79
                         ————— 2756 69¼

Making the profit, for the year, on this account $1708 91¼

STONE SAWING ACCOUNT.

Amount of inventory, Oct. 1, 1828 .... $50 00
Amount paid for carting, &c. 6 50

Making in all $56 50

This account is to be credited with sawing 35 82
Amount of inventory, 1st Oct. 1829 .... 50 00
                         ————— 85 82

Making profit on this account for the year $29 32

INTEREST ACCOUNT.

Amount paid chargeable to this account $11 11½

Amount credited to this account, being interest received, ... 86 79

Making a profit on this account $75 67½

PROFIT AND LOSS ACCOUNT.

Uncurrent notes on hand	$34 00
Paid for transcribing law	4 00
	$38 00

By the foregoing account, it appears that the amount received at the Prison, is, on the

Nail Factory account	$10 07¼
Cooperage account	15 37¾
Plaister account	355 35
Sundry account	126 88
Cordwainers' account	1106 03¼
Weaving account	1708 91¼
Stone sawing account	29 32
Interest account	75 67½
Making whole amount received $3427 98¼	

There has been expended on the

Provision account $1593 19¾	
Clothing account 507 17	
Incidental account 345 12¾	
Furniture account 18 15½	
Prison repairs 65 94	
Fuel account 513 93½	
Profit and loss account 38 00	
Making the whole amount expended	3081 52½
Which being deducted from amount received, makes the gain or profit of the prison	$346 46

The whole amount expended on account of the State Prison, from October 1st, 1828, to October 1st, 1829, is $8410 04¾	
To which add salary for principal keeper 800 00	
4 assistant keepers, at $400, ... 1600 00	
Clerk 500 00	
Guard 67 50	
Physician 75 00	
Chaplain 75 00	
	$3117 50

Making the whole amount expended during the year $11527 54¾	
Amount received during same period, including amount on hand as per different inventories	8750 50¾

Making the loss of the institution for the year ending October
1st, 1829, ... $2771 04

To ascertain the net gain over and above the expense of keeping
the prisoners, exclusive of salaries, there must be added to the
amount of profits, as before stated $346 46

For prison repairs, this not being properly chargeable to the expense of keeping prisoners 65 94

Counterfeit money received by former keeper, and charged to this
year's account 34 00

Paid for a copy of law, not part of prison expenses 4 00

Purchase made in 1828, and charged this year 140 00

Making the amount received over and above the expense for
keeping prisoners $590 85

By referring to the statement, as made by the committee, in the
year 1828, it will be found that the actual loss of the operations
of that year of the prison, exclusive of keepers' salaries, was.. $400 41½

To this add the amount gained this year, exclusive of salaries.... 590 85

Makes a difference in favor of the prison, between the past year
and the year preceding, of $991 26½

The foregoing account does not show the amount paid out of the
treasury for the cost of prosecution and transportation of
prisoners, which, by the treasurer's account, appears to amount
to $1759 52

To which add loss before stated 2771 04

Makes the actual loss of the institution for the year ending the
1st of October, 1829 .... $4530 56

From the accounts as presented by the inspectors, it is altogether impossible
to ascertain, with accuracy, the actual expenditures and receipts of the institution, so far as it regards the expenses and labor of the prisoners.

These accounts show the amount in value of articles on hand, on the first
of October, 1828; the amount of purchases, for one year, up to October first,
1829; the amount chargeable, or to be credited, to each particular account for
the year; and the amount, in value, of the articles on hand at the expiration
of the year. And these accounts are divided and subdivided into as many
heads as the ingenuity of book-keeping can suggest. The *same kind* of
articles are debited and credited under different heads or accounts. But in
all the variety, there is no *cash account* to be found; no account showing
at one view, the amount of money expended, and the amount of money
received, and for what the money was received and expended. It is by such
an account alone that it is possible, with accuracy, to show the true state of
the institution, as it regards its monied concerns.

There were confined in the prison, on the first day of October, 1829, ninety
prisoners. Of these, there were received, from the 1st of October, 1828, to

26 P

the 1st of October, 1829, forty-four. There are fifty-four white men, *not one white woman;* twenty-nine free negro men; two free negro women; three negro men, slaves; and two negro women, slaves. There are eighty-three Americans, three English and four Irish.

Seventy-nine are committed for the first offence; seven for the second; two for the third; and two for the fourth.

Sixteen are employed in shoe-making; twenty-six in weaving; thirteen in spooling; three as carpenters; one in basket-making; two in coopering; three as tailors; five in spinning; three in washing and attending cells; four in stone-sawing; one as a baker; two as cooks; two in sawing wood, &c. &c. Three are unable to work, and there are six in solitary confinement.

The committee have thought it necessary to make a new inventory of what are considered the standing articles in the prison, which inventory is herewith submitted, marked—Exhibit A. By comparing this inventory with the one, handed to the committee by the inspectors, there appears a difference of *nine hundred and seventeen dollars and fifty cents.* The inventory and appraisement made by the committee being so much less than the one made by the Inspectors.

All of which is respectfully submitted.

> A. Howell,   ⎫ Committee of Council.
> Amzi Dodd, ⎬

> Charles Hillard,   ⎫
> Littleton Kirkpatrick, ⎪ Committee of
> Ferdinand S. Schenck,   ⎬ Assembly.
> Isaac Hinchman,,   ⎭

The Committee appointed to settle the accounts of the State Prison, and to which was assigned the additional duty of reporting a system of Prison discipline, beg leave further to report:

That in order to make a thorough investigation into the affairs of the prison, so far as it regards the discipline of the same, and the manner in which its affairs have been conducted, the legislature, by resolution, empowered the committee to send for persons and papers.

By virtue of this authority, your committee have examined with great particularity into all the concerns of the institution, and have arranged the evidence under different heads.

The principal object has been to show the difficulty, under the present construction and arrangement of the buildings, shops and offices, to enforce a proper discipline, and also to point out the expenses attendant on the present arrangement.

1st. ON THE CONSTRUCTION.

The Guard Room is on the north-west corner of the building. It commands a view of neither the yard, the shops, the wings, or the walls of the prison; here the principal keeper, and the clerk, who acts as deputy, transact much of their business; and while they do this, they know nothing from actual observation, for the time being, of the conduct of the assistant keepers, or prisoners, in any part of the establishment. They might as well be placed in one of the solitary cells, so far as the inspection and control of the prison is concerned. The prisoners might rise upon the under keepers, in the shops; the prisoners, in the cells of either the north or south wing, might make their escape; the sentinel, on the wall, might sleep at his post, and the principal keeper and his deputy, in the guard room, be so far removed from hearing, and cut off from sight, as to know nothing of it. Instead of this, the guard room should command, from one position, the range of cells, the whole yard, the prisoners in the shops, under their respective officers, and the sentinel on the wall; then the principal keeper, from the guard room, or in his absence, his deputy, commands the whole establishment.

Again, the NIGHT ROOMS are not sufficiently numerous to separate the men. They are put two, three, and four, in a room; and the rooms are constructed, that the men can freely communicate from window to window, and from door to door, and from the building to the street. Besides all this, the halls, by the side of which the night rooms are arranged, are separated from the passage, leading to the room, where the watch is on duty, by solid doors, with complicated fastenings, and this passage, by other doors, from the guard room. Thus the prisoners, by the construction of the night rooms, are removed as far as possible from the inspection, or control of the subordinate officers. In consequence of this, we shall see in the progress of the report, how many plans of mischief are devised, and how many escapes are effected, from the arrangement and construction of the night rooms.

The SHOPS, too, and other places of labor, are scattered about, without form or unity of design; and the men are necessarily divided into small companies, so that it would require a much larger number of keepers, than are at present employed, to exercise a constant inspection of the men, without which there can be no thorough discipline. One of the buildings is divided into five small apartments, which would require as many officers, to keep a proper discipline; while in the whole of this building, with the present number of keepers, there can be but *one* officer. In the other apartments of this building, therefore, there may be traffic of the state's property, gambling, fighting, and other mischief, without detection.

The COOKERY, HOSPITAL and PLACE OF WORSHIP also, are inconvenient and concealed. The *cookery*, is directly under the center building, far removed from the observation of a keeper. From the front window of the cookery, the prisoners have been in the habit of passing and repassing things to persons in the street. This is a very natural and easy outlet for the shoes, belonging to the state, which are missing. The *hospital* is an old room, not well ventilated, and is so impregnated with the prison smell, that it would be likely to make a well person sick; and is so situated as not to be under inspection, or control, unless an officer is set apart for this duty; which cannot be done without an increase of officers. Finding this a convenient place of concealment, the prisoners under false pretences, leave their work, and get into it. The *chapel* is liable to similar objections. It is separated by four passages, and five doors, from the building, in which the prisoners are lodged; so that much time and labor are necessary in getting the prisoners into it. And besides, it is a small and uncomfortable place for the religious worship of so many men. It is in its size and character like the hospital. It is one of the old night rooms, used many years ago for the purpose of lodging the men, before the south wing was built.

The Sentinel's Box on the wall, is not well designed. It does not command the interior of the yard. There are many hiding places, where the men can screen themselves from the observation of the sentinel, behind the shops, and other buildings, and many prisoners prepare themselves, without his knowledge, or the knowledge of the men under whose particular care they are placed, for attempting to escape. Besides, the sentinel cannot command the north wall, on the north side; nor the west wall, on the west side; nor the south wall, on the south side. Discharged convicts, therefore, and persons ill disposed, can approach the prison from north, south, and west, without the knowledge of the sentinel, on the wall, and furnish prohibited articles, and implements of mischief, and escape, to the convicts. We dwell the longer on the construction of the prison, in this respect, because we shall see the consequences of it, in the progress of the report, in the very great number of escapes, which have taken place, since the prison was built. Thus we have seen, that the guard room, the night rooms, the shops, the cookery, hospital, chapel, and sentinel box are not properly constructed.

2d. ON THE DISCIPLINE OF THE PRISON AS CONNECTED WITH THE CONSTRUCTION.

In a prison, thus constructed, there can be no discipline. *The subordinate officers are not subordinate.* The principal keeper has no good position, from which to command his men. It would take him a long time to go around the prison, and look them all up. Instead of which, he should have a position, from which, he can, at once overlook officers as well as prisoners. This would effectually prevent those faults, which the keeper of the prison, in his official report to the committee, says, page 2. *"he found requiring a remedy 1st. great laxity on the part of the assistant keepers, in their duty; leaving the prisoners alone to the great neglect of their occupations, and the destruction of all system and order. 2d. the general prevalence of insubordination and the pre-existence of a perfect familiarity, and almost unrestrained intercourse among the prisoners, and between the prisoners and the assistant keepers; and 3d. the extensive indulgence of a system of traffic, between the prisoners and their keepers, in which articles made by them, and property over which they had no control, were exchanged with the keepers, for other commodities in a secret and covert manner."* How are these things to be prevented, if the principal keeper is to be shut up in a room, from which he can see nothing, that is done by officers or men. The great principle of unceasing inspection is lost sight of, and these deeds of darkness are done, because they can be done in the dark. The way to correct them is, to bring them out into open day, so that the principal keeper can at any moment, with a single glance of his eye, inspect the whole establishment.

In consequence, partly of the same defect in the construction of the buildings, *the convicts are idle and disorderly.* The shops are so divided and subdivided, that there are nearly twice as many separate apartments, for the convicts, as there are officers. The convicts, therefore, must necessarily, be left alone. This single disadvantage, would break up the discipline of the best prison in the world. The officers leave the shops, and the convicts of course leave their work. In such circumstances, what security can there possibly be, that the convicts shall be all the time profitably at work.

There are complaints not only, that the convicts are idle and disorderly in the shops, but they leave the shops, and go into the yard; and one witness testified that "he could not get them back, till they were sent for." The reason assigned by them for leaving the shops are from necessity; but in a well constructed prison, there is a water closet connected with every shop, which only one man can enter at a time, and which he can enter only from the shop, and this breaks up all necessity for leaving the shops, and all opportunity for false pretences, in regard to this thing, and leaves the keeper the command of his men; so that all, excepting one, at every moment of time, are under his eyes, and this one, who for a little time is removed from his observation, is in solitary, and it is known where he is.

As the prison is constructed, *there are various opportunities for combination in mischief, among the prisoners, which are broken up at once in a well constructed prison.* Much evidence is furnished to the committee by different witnesses, concerning a combination of men in the prison called the STAUNCH GANG. One witness says, *"they will lie, and swear to it; they will steal provision, and carry it off; they will lurk in the kitchen and steal other men's provisions; they will threaten each others lives; they will make dirks; they will lie, steal, and gamble; they will make their own cards. I gave one of the inspectors one pack, and sent one pack to a friend in the country, that he might see what can be done in the prison. They have rules by which they are bound to each other; one rule is, if a man tells any thing, they will fall a foul of him and beat him."*

Another witness was asked if he knew any thing about the STAUNCH GANG. He said there was such a GANG. *They would not tell of each other; if they did, they would beat the informer. He had known one to stab another. They consider him a traitor, who informs of their evil deeds. Such men are called snitch.*

Another witness says, the STAUNCH GANG, are persons *combined together to get away, and not to tell each others secrets.* "If any one tells of them they fall on him and beat him. There was a black man nearly killed in the weave shop. They took the stone coal and beat him on the head: and, it cut like a knife. He was nearly killed." Another witness, when asked about the staunch gang, said "he thought the state had better let them go, than be under such discipline. They have frequently drawn knives upon each other in the yard. In one instance one would have cut out the bowels of the other."

Much evidence has also been furnished to the committee, concerning the want of power to enforce discipline among the convicts, *in consequence of the manner in which the south wing is constructed where the convicts sleep.* One witness says the prisoners will steal oil to burn in the cells, and carry sticks and strings to the cells, that they may pass things, from one to the other, and from door to door.

Another witness was asked if the convicts could communicate with each other, after they were locked up at night. He said, *they could communicate with each other, twenty of them.* Witness says, that the convicts often worked in the cells, on the sabbath, making hats; he had caught them at it and put a stop to it; but he did expect they carried it on. He gave the name of the convict who made a complete ladder in the cells to scale the walls; with which it was done. Witness was asked if he heard any conversation among the men at night, he said "that it was impossible to prevent it; and the former keeper was opposed to it, in the way the men are kept; they would be generally talking about roguery." Witness then gave a particular account of the instruction he heard an experienced thief give one less experienced, about the best way of raising twenty dollars to begin with after he got out. The latter was a young convict who was soon to be discharged.

Another witness says, "the men are so much together, it is very much against the interest of the institution. They talk about what they have done, and what they will do, and how they may get out."

Another witness believes, "that the prisoners have had knowledge of the difficulties existing in the government of the prison. He has heard the prisoners talk about it in the cells. He has heard them talk about the change in the government of the prison, in the cells at night. He has heard the prisoners after they were locked up in the cells conversing with discharged prisoners, in the street. No longer ago than four weeks, two men came along and began to converse, and he stopped them."

Witness says further, "in the cells, one night, two of the prisoners fought, one bit the others finger, and a piece of the bone came out. They are put together old and young without regard to their crime. They lay their beds on the floor. They are single beds, but when there are three, they make them up all as one, and sleep altogether. They sometimes want to be separated, because they quarrel."

Another witness has often heard the prisoners talking from the south wing, with persons on the out side. He has caught them at it, late at night. They once shot an arrow attached to a string, into the street, and the string was found extending from the night room to the street—supposed to be for the purpose of drawing in something. Witness does not think, any thing more can be done for the benefit of the state, in that prison, than is now done.

Another witness speaking of putting three or four in a room, at night, and the things going on among the men, after they were locked up, concluded by saying, "as to that prison it is a mere burlesque on prisons."

Owing to the construction of the prison, it is very difficult, if not impossible, to prevent traffic with the prisoners, which is subversive of all discipline. In a properly constructed prison, it is the impression upon every mind, both of convict and assistant keeper, I am constantly under inspection. Every thing which I do will be seen. But there are so many hiding places in this prison, and so few facilities for inspection, that this seems, not at all, to be the impression, on the minds of either keeper or convict.

The principal keeper says, "when he became keeper of the prison, he found an extensive traffic between the prisoners and under keepers, particularly in the articles of straw hats and whip stalks. When asked to give a statement of the principal evils which he had discovered in the prison. He said the shoe shop was a place of resort for the keepers; some of the keepers told him, that another was in the habit of going into the kitchen, and spending some time there, while his men went at loose ends. He watched the keeper of whom this complaint was made, and found that it was so. Since this he has found it of little use to attempt to enforce any orders, and has had enough to do to get along any way." He then gave a particular account of some hats, sold by a convict to a keeper, and the price put upon them by the convict.

Another witness stated, "that convicts had made hats to sell, it was likely they had made other things: they would be taken out and sold. He believed one of the keepers had taken out things, and sold them for the convicts." This keeper afterwards acknowledged to the committee, that he had done so. Witness further says, "the convicts get tobacco, I do not know how they get it, the proceeds of hats, and other things might buy it. There are many ways they have in common." Witness could not watch his men so as to know, where they went. There were more of them to watch him. They might go out if they pleased, and if he saw them about the wagons which came into the yard, he would drive them away. Witness said, that some time last spring, one of the keepers sold articles for the convicts. He understood the principal keeper was opposed to it, but it was done. I believe it was done in both their times.

Another witness, testifies, "that one of the keepers told him, that the old convict who takes care of the cloth from the weave shop, is never without money; that he used to traffic in tobacco, buy it and sell it out again."

Another witness, a citizen of Trenton, thinks he has seen one of the keepers carry articles to a certain store, and exchange them for the convicts. The keeper and store keeper referred to, were both called, and acknowledged that it was so. Witness did not believe, that the traffic was confined to this keeper.

Another witness knows, "that many articles were made in the prison by the convicts, but he does not know how they got out."

Another witness, one of the keepers, says, "he has thrown tobacco on the ground for convicts." This was done to avoid an order which prohibits assistant keepers from giving them tobacco. Witness further says, "that his children have taken things from prisoners, and sold them, in exchange for other articles. He believes that all the keeper's children have done it.

Witness explains by saying, "that they went on the wall, and let down strings to take things up; that it has also been done through the basement store windows, in front of the house with convicts in the cookery." Many of these things, it would be very difficult, if not impossible to prevent, in the buildings as they are now constructed. There is no point of observation from which there can be a thorough supervision, by the principal keeper of the whole establishment; but on the contrary, very many hiding places, besides a guard room for the principal keeper, and his deputy, from which they can only look into the street, and see nothing that is done in the prison.

For the same reason, the discipline is interrupted by a knowledge in the prison, among the convicts, of almost everything that is done abroad. The principal keeper says, that "things which take place in town are known to the prisoners within twenty-four hours, which could not be known except from the keepers; there is such a familiarity between them that these things are all communicated." This familiarity, between keepers and convicts could soon be broken up, by the principal keeper, if he was faithful, if the construction was such, that he could from his office overlook the whole establishment, and see keepers and convicts at the same time.

Another witness said, that "it was too much the case, that there was a familiarity between the convicts and keepers. He says the convicts seem to know most every thing that is going on."

Another witness thinks "the convicts know what is going on in Trenton," and says "they will know within a month what is going on here today."

He says they have newspapers; "I have seen papers more than once; but did not see any one give them to the convicts." This is the great difficulty in this prison, almost anything may be done, (there are so many hiding places to do mischief,) and the responsible officer cannot see who does it.

Owing in part to the construction of the prison, the discipline is such, that riots are frequent, and it is difficult to prevent them; there are many places for concealment, and necessarily from the construction, frequent opportunities for combination, out of which these riots have grown. The principal keeper said, "he had lately had an attempt at riot, and there was another riot, since he had been there, in the weave shop. The keeper was absent from his shop contrary to the regulations of the prison. The rule is, that no keeper shall leave his shop till the relief comes. This rule is violated every day:" This is the testimony of the principal keeper. While the assistant keepers say, truly, in their defence, that there are more shops, and places of labor for them to oversee, than there are keepers; and they are obliged to go from one to the other; consequently an opportunity for riot is afforded when the keeper of a shop is absent.

Another witness testified, "that they had pretty severe riots. If any one tells of them, they fall on him and beat him. It has been done four or five times in a year." One of the inspectors testified, "that the prison had been in a regular state of insubordination, during the last year." Another witness, one of the contractors testified, "that he saw a very alarming riot at the prison. When I went to the door, said witness, there could not have been less than thirty convicts, between the two shops. One of the keepers was doing all that he could to suppress it; another threatened to fire upon them from the wall; another keeper came to the gate and called for a musket. He was as pale as death. There was some private difficulty, between the two convicts, and the others took sides. I heard one of the convicts swear, that he would not leave the yard, till he had been the death of the other." If the prison was so constructed as to separate the convicts at night, and admit of keeping them in their places, in the day time, under constant inspection, both from the keepers in the shops, and those in the guard room, these riots would be effectually prevented.

Again, the discipline of the prison is destroyed by the keepers sleeping at their posts, and as the prison is constructed, the safety of the prison has frequently been endangered at night. The principal keeper testifies, "that during the summer, he found the assistant keepers sleeping on their posts at night. They were called before the board of inspectors, and acknowledged that they had done so." The board notified them through the keeper, that they should expect them hereafter to do their duty. After this the assistant keepers locked the principal keeper out of the Hall, which led to the room, where they were on duty one week, which he attempted to enter several times, but could not. The assistant keeper alleged as a reason for doing this, that the safety of the prison was in danger from discharged convicts, who had formed the design of coming over the wall in the night; entering the passage, which leads to the room, where the watch is on duty; securing the watch, and releasing the prisoners. About this time, according to the testimony of both the assistant and principal keeper, two or more discharged convicts did actually come over the wall, in the night, into the yard; the dogs gave the alarm; the keepers were at once on duty; the ladder was found where they had scaled the wall; the alarm bell was rung; but the villains made their escape. The principal keeper supposes that their object was plunder, as some shoes were found which they had taken from the shop, near the place where they had scaled the wall. The assistant keepers suppose that their object was the release of the prisoners.

Not a great while after this, there was another alarm of a similar kind, when the principal keeper was not at home; but it was not satisfactorily ascertained, whether at this time, any person from without, came over the wall. The result of the whole was, that a different arrangement was made between the principal and the assistant keepers, by which the former was supplied with a key to open the door of the passage, leading to the night watch, and the night watch were supplied with a key, that they might secure themselves against the assaults of discharged convicts. This would seem reasonable, so far as the safety of the prison is endangered from discharged convicts; but it is not calculated to keep the night watch awake while on duty, because they are so securely locked, and concealed from observation, in a small room by themselves, that they might sleep on their posts, and still not be detected; for when the principal keeper comes to unlock the door of the passage leading to the watch room, the noise would be likely to awaken the night watch if he were asleep, so that the principal keeper would not know, whether he had been asleep or not.

There is another difficulty about the place where the night watch is on duty in this prison. If the watch is awake, he cannot see from the room where he is usually stationed, any part of the building, where the convicts are lodged. He must leave his station, and go out into the passage, and pass through one or two doors, before he comes to the only place where he can see the night rooms, and even then he must go into four stories, and peep over the tops of eight doors, before he can inspect forty cells, and after all, he can only see the doors, he cannot see the interior of the cells, nor know whether the convicts are there, or whether they have escaped through the roof or external walls into the yard.

In a prison, properly constructed, the place where the night watch is on duty, is not liable to such objections; because the principal keeper from his private apartment, at any moment, can look in upon him, and see that he is awake, without the knowledge of the night watch; and the night watch, from the open space in which he is placed, by changing his position, 30 feet, without passing through any door, can command the doors and windows of every night room in the building, and at the same time, if a convict gets out of his cell, he is not only exposed to the fire of the sentinel, but he is still in prison, for it is a prison within a prison. He has got out of one prison into another. He has got out of his cell, but he has gotten into a place, where he is exposed to the fire of the sentinel, and if the alarm is given, to the fire of the musketry of all the keepers in the guard room.

Not so in our state prison, the convicts may get out of their night rooms, into the open yard; thence unseen in the dark, over the yard wall into the street. The construction is, therefore, such, that the night watch may sleep at his post, and the convicts escape with impunity.

3d. OF ESCAPES.

To show, that this is not a representation, unsupported by facts, we have obtained information from the records of the prison, concerning the *escapes* which have actually been effected since the prison was built. This list is now before us, it contains the names of ONE HUNDRED AND EIGHT convicts, who have made their escape. This is more than one twelfth part of all who have been committed to the prison; a proof of the insecurity of the prison, so far as our knowledge extends in the history of prisons, without a parallel.

Of the whole number who thus escaped, *ten* escaped, *one* at a time, *sixteen, two* at a time, *twenty-one, three* at a time, *twenty-four, four* at a time, *five* at one time, *fourteen, seven* at a time, and *eighteen, nine* at a time. Total ONE HUNDRED AND EIGHT. Males *one hundred and three*, females *five.* One escaped by making a hole in the door, one by a false key, two, who were at work on the new cells, three by forcing the hall door, four, through the yard gate, four, in a manner not specified, five, through the grates without sawing, five, by sawing the grates, twenty-nine, by scaling the wall, and forty-nine through the roof, walls and doors of the main building. Total ONE HUNDRED AND EIGHT. Twenty-eight were re-taken the same day, twenty-five after more than one day, and in less than one year, six were gone, time not specified, two were gone one year, one two years, one three years, and fifty-five were never re-taken. Total ONE HUNDRED AND EIGHT. In these troubles one keeper was stabbed, three prisoners broke into a guard room, and got two guns with which they escaped, two prisoners were shot, but not killed, and one was shot dead.

The official document from the prison records from which these results are taken, is herewith submitted, marked A.

The amount paid in apprehending the above prisoners, was seven hundred and twenty-eight dollars and three cents.

4th. OF PUNISHMENT.

Notwithstanding the number of escapes from this prison, there does not appear to be any want of sufficiently severe punishments for misdemeanor.

Solitary confinement, on a scanty allowance of bread with cold water, is much used. The period of time not unfrequently extends to twenty and thirty days, and this too in the winter season in cells warmed by no fire. The suffering in these circumstances is intense; the convicts loose their flesh and strength and frequently their health; they are sometimes so far broken down, as to be unable to work, when they are discharged into the yard, and to require nearly as much time in the hospital, to recruit them, as they have had in the cells to break them down.

The committee saw a man in the hospital, last week, just taken from the cells, where he had been punished for misdemeanor about twenty days. He was prostrate upon the bed, emaciated and unable to work, and complained of much pain. The physician called the attention of the committee to his pulse, which he remarked was very feeble. The keeper thought it would be sometime before he would be able to work.

Besides punishments, in this mode, the records show, that chains are much used; sometimes with a fifty-six attached to them, and sometimes for the purpose of chaining the prisoner to the place where he is at work. A number of the prisoners, at the present time, have chains upon them, and the committee saw one, twelve or fourteen years of age, who had on, an iron neck yoke, with arms extending 18 or 20 inches each way from his head, which was said to be, not for punishment, but to prevent his getting through the grates.

The following list is furnished by the clerk of the prison, who has been there twenty years. It shows the number of prisoners, that is supposed to have died, in consequence of being severely punished, in the cells, for disobedience: William Thomas, Thomas Stewart, John O. Brien, William Bower, John Brown, Tunis Cole, Aaron Strattain, Thomas Somes, Pomp Cisco, and Peter Marks—10.

The documents from which this statement is taken is herewith submitted marked B.

If the prison were so constructed, as to separate the men at night and keep them perfectly still, and thus break up all such combinations, as that of the *staunch gang;* and if the shops were so constructed as to admit of a constant inspection, so as to keep the prisoners in their places, at their work in silence, there would be comparatively little need of severe punishment, because rebellion and villainy would be prevented in the very beginning.

5th. OF DEATHS.

The whole number of DEATHS, in the prison, including the ten above mentioned, is *forty-nine.*

The whole number of prisoners committed, is one thousand two hundred and six. The average number of prisoners, taking the whole period of time, is supposed to be fifty; which gives a bill of mortality of about three per cent. which is three per cent. less than that of the Walnut street prison, in Philadelphia, and about two per cent. more than that of the prisons at Auburn and Wethersfield.

The document *herewith* submitted, from which the above is taken is marked C.

6th. OF RECOMMITMENTS.

The RECOMMITMENTS, are out of ninety, the whole number, *seven* a second time; *two* a third time, and *two* a fourth time. CASES OF REFORMATION, we have heard of few, or none. At Auburn, out of six hundred, the whole number, the recommitments are, *seventeen* a second time, and from latest information, *none* a third. CASES OF REFORMATION, at Auburn, out of two hundred and six discharged convicts, ONE HUNDRED AND FORTY-SIX well authenticated.

7th. OF EXPENSES.

Some particulars in regard to the expenses and earnings of the New Jersey State Prison, as furnished from the treasury department, are as follows:

The expenses exceeding the earnings, in four years, from 1800,
    to 1803, inclusive, ... $21,776.29
In nine years, between 1810 and 1822, ... 58,651 33
In eight years from 1822 to 1829, inclusive, ... 46,425 44
Total loss, including the loss in the periods specified above, ... 164,963 81
Average loss to the state, annually, from September 1798 to
    September 1829, thirty-one years, ... 5,304 05

The official document from which these results are taken is herewith submitted, marked D.

How can these things be; they are not satisfactorily explained. According to the return of the committee from the prison, the food of the prisoners per day, costs .... 4 cents 8 mills
the clothing 1   5
incidental expenses 2   9
                                                            —   —
Total amount excluding pay of officers 9   2
Pay of officers for each man daily 9   4
                                                            —   —
Total expenses of each convict daily 18   6
                                                            —   —

Of the whole number of convicts, sixteen are employed in shoe making, each of whom, as an easy days work, is said to make one pair of coarse shoes per day. The price paid by contractors for making such shoes, is for each pair, thirty-three cents, the state to find shoe thread, &c.

When any part of the shoemakers are employed for the state, the shoes which they make are charged to the state, at one dollar and twenty-five cents a pair, for common shoes, and other work at a similar rate. Why then do not the shoemakers earn from twenty-five to thirty cents per day; and not as they are returned only eighteen cents and nine mills. If the returns are properly made, it must be because they are not furnished with work, and kept at it. When the committee visited the prison several shoe makers were sitting in idleness; because the contractors had not furnished them with work. One of the inspectors testified before the committee, as follows: "no longer ago than yesterday, I went to the prison, and the keeper of the shoe shop was not in his place I found only two of the men at work; as soon as I stept in, the convicts said "whist," and went to their places like a parcel of rabbits. I went round the prison, and when I came back, the keeper was in his place, and I gave him a piece of my mind." This business of the *shoe shop,* is the most important branch of business, *except one,* in the prison; that is the *weaving business.*

In the weaver's shop, thirty-nine hands are employed. This is a branch of business, in which most of the hands in the Baltimore penitentiary are employed, which has cleared for the state, over and above every expense, in the last eight years, upwards of *seventy thousand dollars.*

In the weavers shop, in the New Jersey state prison, thirty-nine hands are employed and twenty-six looms. The cheapest work done on these looms, is done for two and a half cents per yard, which is about half a cent less per yard, than is paid for the same kind of work, done for the same persons, in town. The task in winter is ten yards per day; but the average quantity of work done is supposed by the keeper, not to exceed nine yards in winter. Allowing it to be nine yards, this would give the earnings twenty-two and a half cents per day, at the lowest prices, in the shortest days. In the summer season, the task is fourteen yards per day. Suppose them in summer to fall short of their task, one yard per day, as in winter, and weave but thirteen yards; they would earn thirty-two and a half cents per day in summer. This is supposing the lowest prices for all the looms. But many of the looms weave cloth for three cents, and three and a half cents per yard, and the country looms for ten cents a yard. In such cases the business is much more advantageous, to the state, than in the cases above mentioned. But with the most favorable supposition to the weaving department, and the most unfavorable to the state, it appears, that the men, in the weave shops can earn, in winter, each twenty-two and a half cents a day, and in summer thirty-two and a half cents per day; or an average for the whole year of twenty-seven and a half cents per day. The ordinary days work, in town, for hired hands, is twenty yards, and the lowest price three cents per yard, by which a weaver in town, at the most moderate estimate in weaving the same goods, can earn sixty cents per day. But in the prison, according to the official returns to the committee, the weavers earn, but eighteen cents per day; or if the spoolers are included, they earn but twelve cents and a fraction. Thus in this most extensive branch of business, if the returns are correctly made, the men do not pay their part of the expenses by six cents and eight mills per day each. They earn twelve cents, and they cost eighteen cents and eight mills. Here, too, the explanation is the same, as in the shoe shop. The contractors do not supply work, or the overseer does not keep them at it. The principal keeper says, "that many hundred days are lost in consequence of the contractors not supplying work;" and one of the inspectors testified, "that he had been into the shop and found the over- seer asleep at his post." The same witness says, "the prisoners leave their shops when they choose, and things are pretty much out of sorts at the prison."

Besides weavers and shoe makers, it appears from the official returns, that TWO MEN were employed as coopers, and this department produced for the state, from the labor of these men, in the course of the year, *fifteen dollars and seventy-three cents.* FOUR were employed in sawing stone, and this department produced, for the labor of these *four men,* in the course of the year, twenty-nine dollars and thirty-two cents; THREE were employed as tailors, and FIVE in spinning; but the proceeds of their labor cannot be ascertained from the returns; TWENTY-NINE promiscuous hands, including all the above except the weavers and shoe makers, having their food and clothes found them, earned on an average, according to the official returns, *five cents* per day each. From the same returns, it appears that the whole number earned on an average *ten cents and four mills per day,* and cost *eighteen cents and eight* mills.

The committee would not express an opinion, whether these very un- favorable results, provided the returns are correctly made, are to be at- tributed, to which of the three following causes, in the greatest degree; to the construction of the prison, which admits of such combination in villainy, during the night, and such concealment in idleness, during the day: to the neglect of the overseers: or to the imperfection of the contracts, which do not make the contractors liable if the men in their employ are not supplied with work. All three, in the opinion of the committee, are evils demanding a speedy remedy.

That they are not necessary evils, subjecting the state to such heavy ex- penses, for the support of the prison, is evident from a comparison be- tween the State Prison in New Jersey, and the new State Prison in Con- necticut, in regard to their expenses and earnings during the last year.

The New Jersey prison had *ninety* prisoners; the Connecticut *one hundred and thirty-four.*

The expenses of the New Jersey prison were, ... $6,199 00
The expenses of the Connecticut prison were, ... 5,876 13

The expenses of the New Jersey prison for the support of ninety
  prisoners, exceed the expenses of the Connecticut prison for
  the support of one hundred and thirty-four prisoners, ... 322 87

The earnings of the New Jersey prison were, ... 3,427 98
The earnings of the Connecticut prison were, ... 9,105 54

The earnings of the Connecticut prison exceeded the earnings of
  the New Jersey prison, ... 5,677 56

And the *expenses* of the Connecticut prison are less than the expenses of the N. Jersey prison, ... 322 87

This is the view which the committee have taken of the expenses and
earnings of the prison.

The document from which the above results are taken, is herewith submitted, marked E.

Besides, among the official documents returned to the committee, it is
stated, that one hundred and thirty-three dollars and twenty-one cents, are
due from the state to the convicts for *overstint.* This, however, makes no
part of the trial balance sheet, as it ought, if it is due. The under keepers,
say it is due, the principal keeper, says it is not. From one sheet of the
official returns, it would appear to be due. From the other, on which the
other debts of the institution are stated, and the trial balance sheet, it appears not to be due.

One of the inspectors testifies, "that the accounts do not show exactly the
amount made or lost. He understood from the clerk, that there were outstanding bills not handed in. He coincides with the other witnesses, that
the inventory was taken generally by the keeper, and principally by copying
the old inventory, so that the state could not know from year to year what
is lost." Once in several years the inventory would be taken right. By this
mode of taking the inventory, it will be perceived, there would be a heavy
loss all at once, while the state would appear from year to year, not to be
loosing more than *five thousand dollars annually.*

OF THE FOOD, FUEL, NUMBER OF OFFICERS, LOCATION, AND REMEDY FOR EXISTING EVILS.

The principal articles of *food,* with the quantities and prices, during the
last year, were

273 cwt. 2 qrs. 17 lbs. of rye flour, from $1 62½ to 250 per cwt. $449 51
40 cwt. corn meal from $1 to 1 12½ per cwt. 43 12
Other flour and meal bought by the bushel and barrel 101 37

Total cost of bread stuff $594 00

6129 lbs. of beef from 3 to 3½ cts. per lb. 197 16
4352 do. pork from 4½ to 5 cents 206 61
1969 do. hogs heads from 2½ to 3 cents 48 10
7500 herring at $1 per thousand 7 50
1 beef's head   25
                                                      ─────────
Total cost of meat $459 62
1232 gallons of molasses from 28 to 40 cents per gallon 428 16½
178 bushels of potatoes from 23 to 33 cents per bushel 53 12½
                                                      ─────────
Total $481 29

RECAPITULATION.

Bread stuffs .... 44,699 lbs.   cost $594 01½
Meats .... 12,450 "   "   451 87½
Molasses .... 39,424 gills   "   428 16½
Potatoes .... 13,392 pints   "   53 12½
                                                               ─────────
                                                               $1527 18
Other and smaller articles of food 66 01½
                                                               ─────────
Total expense of food $1593 19½

The proportion of each article, which this would
    give to each man daily, estimating the num-
    ber of men at ninety, is .... 1 lb. 4 oz. 3–10 bread stuffs
                                              6 "   2–10 of meat
                                              1 gill 2–10 of molasses
                                              1 gill 6–10 of potatoes

It will be observed, that the molasses costs almost as much as the meat, and eight times as much as the vegetables. The committee are satisfied, that this is out of all just proportion. That the molasses should be diminished from one gill and 2–10 to ½ a gill, which would save on the molasses two hundred and thirty-nine dollars 76 cents annually. That the sum thus saved on the molasses, be expended for beef, so far as to make the ration of beef one half more than it now is. The allowance of beef the last year has been only three ounces to each man per day, the cost of which was one hundred and ninety-seven dollars, 16 cents. The change we recommend is, that out of the two hundred and twenty-nine dollars 70 cents, saved on molasses, one hundred and ninety-seven dollars 16 cents, be expended to purchase beef, which will give *six* ounces of beef instead of *three* ounces. This diminution of molasses, and increase of beef, will enable the men to work with more strength, and we shall still have forty-two dollars 60 cents saved on the molasses.

We recommend further, that the indian meal be diminished from 6 ounces and 6.10 per day to 4 ounces. The men, many of them, complain that they have too much mush and molasses. This will save forty-four dollars annually on the mush. That the money thus saved shall be expended for potatoes, which will increase the quantity of potatoes from one gill and 6.10 to three gills.

We recommend also, that the rye flour be diminished from 14 ounces and 9.10 to 12 ounces, which will save on this article one hundred and ten dollars; that thirty-eight dollars and forty cents of the sum thus saved be expended for potatoes, which will increase the allowance of potatoes to one pint, and that the remaining seventy-one dollars 60 cents saved on the rye flour, together with the forty-two dollars 60 cents saved on molasses, be expended for beef, which will increase the allowance of beef to eight ounces per day, by increasing the expenses of the state on the provisions nineteen dollars 24 cents annually.

Any two men in the weave shop, on the custom work, in consideration of this change and improvement, in the ration, may easily make up this deficiency, by the additional work performed. The ration when changed will stand thus per day, ¾ lb. rye flour, and ¼ lb. corn meal, ½ lb. beef, and 3 ounces of pork, 1 pint of potatoes, and ½ a gill of molasses, and the smaller items, salt, &c. amounting to $66.01½ unaltered.

This ration would nearly resemble the ration in those prisons where the men more than support themselves.

The *fuel* required in the prison, as it is now constructed, amounted last year to *one hundred and one cords and a half* of wood, twelve and a half tons of stone coal, and two hundred and ninety-four bushels of charcoal, at an expense of five hundred and twenty-three dollars 93 cents. Eight stoves are used to warm forty night rooms, while in a properly constructed prison, two stoves would warm one hundred and fifty. Twenty-two fires are used to warm the whole establishment, and as the prison is constructed, the committee do not see how any of these fires can be dispensed with. While in a well constructed prison, the committee are convinced from the returns of the new prison in Connecticut, that the number of fires required is so much less as to diminish the expense in the article of fuel more than three hundred dollars annually.

The *number of officers* required in this prison to promote a wholesome discipline, must be according to the testimony which the committee has received, seven, where there are now but three; that is an increase of four, at four hundred dollars per annum each. This would increase the expenses sixteen hundred dollars annually, while the present number of officers in a well constructed prison would secure a better discipline, than the number thus increased, in the old prison. The difference of expense then, in the old prison, and in a new and well constructed prison, as to the number of officers and the fuel, would be one thousand nine hundred dollars annually, or the interest of thirty-one thousand six hundred and fifty-six dollars, a sum sufficient to build a new prison.

27 P

The *location* is unfavorable for business. No man would think of selecting that as a good place for the transaction of a large business. If Trenton is the town for the prison, the present site is not the place for it. It is without natural advantages. It was put where it is because a man gave the land to build it on. It is estimated that the least difference between the expense of transacting the business of the prison where it is, and in town, would be three hundred dollars annually. The prison then, with its present location and construction, has physical disadvantages, viz: on the location, annually $300; on fuel $300; and on the number of officers $1600, which would make a difference of two thousand two hundred dollars annually between the old prison and a new one, which is the interest on thirty-five thousand dollars, a sum more than sufficient to build a new prison.

These considerations are entirely independent of the greater security, industry and more productive labor, which can be secured in a new prison; by breaking up, the traffic, combinations in villainy, attempts to escape, riots, fighting, gambling, making cards and counterfeit coin. The committee see no reason why these evils cannot be removed in New Jersey as well as in Connecticut, nor why the state prison in New Jersey like that in Connecticut, should not, instead of being an expense to the state of five thousand dollars annually, be a source of income of three thousand dollars annually.

The directors of the new prison in Connecticut say in their last report to the legislature, "We found a system in operation at the old prison, which had for ten years previous to its abandonment, occasioned to the state an expense of $84,634.05 over and above its earnings, which sum had been drawn from the treasury, being an average deficit of more than $8,400 per annum. We found the moral results of the system to be more unfortunate, than the pecuniary, and that all its tendencies were to debase and corrupt the convict. The new prison for the year ending on the first of April last, after defraying every expense for its management and support has earned to the state $3229.41; making a difference to the state between the old and new prison of $11,629.41 annually; an annuity more than sufficient, in three years, to cover the expense of building the new prison.

"The results of the experiment," say the directors, "are now before the public. We can truly say, they have exceeded our highest anticipations, both as it respects their moral and pecuniary character."

Your committee have yet to learn why such results cannot be realized in New Jersey, as well as in Connecticut.

Thus the committee, on the state prison, has endeavored to submit the facts, in the case now before them, in a full and impartial manner. These have produced, in the minds of the committee, an unanimous opinion, that the *construction* of the prison is *altogether wrong,* and does not admit of being *essentially corrected* in the old establishment. The *discipline in consequence, in great part, of the construction,* may be called *disorder* rather than discipline. The *escapes* have been, so far as our knowledge extends, without a parallel, *principally in consequence* of the *imperfection of the buildings.* The *punishments,* from the same disadvantages in construction, have been very severe, to prevent riots, insurrections, and escapes. The committee *greatly lament* the facts in evidence on this part of the subject. The *deaths* are more numerous, than they would be in a prison well constructed and well ventilated. *The re-commitments* are numerous in proportion to the number of convicts, 'and the *cases of reformation, few or none;* because the men are *associated together day and night for purposes of mutual corruption,* and this *cannot be prevented* in these buildings.

The expense of supporting the establishment is *very heavy,* and this too, in great part, *because the men cannot be kept at their business.*

The difficulties among the officers are greatly to be lamented. If the construction of the prison is such, that the prisoners provoke the under officers, because they do not stay in their places,. and mind their business, and the under officers provoke the principal keeper because *they* do not stay in *their* places and mind *their* business; *this is no sufficient excuse for passion, profane swearing, and wrangling among the officers; these things should have no place in this public institution, which has written over its door* "THE NEW JERSEY PENITENTIARY."

We have recommended an alteration in the food of the prisoners, for the purpose of giving them more health and strength to labour, without any considerable additional *expense* for food to the state; and we think, we have shown that there is a difference, necessarily, of *more than two thousand dollars a year,* in the expense of supporting the old prison, and a new one, in consequence of the quantity of fuel, and the number of officers required in the old prison, and the inconvenience of its location. In this connection, we think, we have shown, also, from the example of the state of Connecticut, *how the state of New Jersey can save,* in a few years, *by building a new prison, a sum more than sufficient to defray all the expenses of its construction.*

The committee, therefore, recommend, with entire unanimity, the building of a new prison, on the general plan of those at Auburn, in New York, and at Wethersfield, in Connecticut.

The committee beg leave to state to the legislature, that the Prison Discipline Society at Boston, has appropriated and expended in our state prison for the purpose of moral and religious instruction, the sum of two hundred and seventy-one dollars, in different sums and at different periods, which amount they recommend should be refunded to the society.

In concluding the report, the committee consider themselves bound to acknowledge, publicly, the great benefit and advantage which they have reieved from the Rev. Louis Dwight, the secretary of the prison discipline society of Boston.

His intimate acquaintance with every thing touching the subject of prison discipline, and the information which the committee has derived from him, have greatly facilitated the researches and examinations of the committee, and highly merit the thanks of the legislature.

A. Howell, ⎫
Amzi Dodd, ⎬ Committee of Council.

Charles Hillard, ⎫
Littleton Kirkpatrick, ⎪ Committee of
Ferdinand S. Schenck, ⎬ Assembly.
Isaac Hinchman, ⎭

DOCUMENT (B).

Showing the number of prisoners that is supposed to have died, in consequence of being severely punished in the cells for disobedience, &c.

William Thomas,	died	17 December, 1809.
Thomas Stewart,	"	23 July, 1811.
John O. Brian,	"	3 Sept. 1823.
William Bower	"	25 April, 1816.
John Brown	"	10 Sept. 1821.
Tunis Cole	"	22 August, 1822.
Aaron Stattain	"	20 Nov. 1827.
Thomas Somes	"	29 Nov. 1827.
Pomp Cisco	"	29 Sept. 1828.
Peter Marks	"	29 Feb. 1820.

DOCUMENT (D).

New Jersey Treasury Department,
Trenton, Jan. 30th, 1830.

To His Excellency Peter D. Vroom, Esq.:

Sir, in compliance with the request contained in your note of this morning, I herewith annex a statement showing the general as well as the annual operation of the New Jersey state prison, on this department, from 1797, the time the first appropriation was made for its erection, up to 1829, inclusive. The statement includes all expenses incurred in transportation of prisoners, costs of prosecution, erection of prison, officers salaries, &c. &c. by which it appears that the annual average loss is about five thousand dollars; the whole loss being $164,963.01. It will also appear by the statement, that in 1809, 1810, 1812, and 1813, there were balances in favour of the prison. These results did not arise from the operation of the prison in any of those years. It grew out of the sales of articles manufactured in former years. From the best information, that I have been able to obtain, I think myself safe in saying, that the prison has not supported itself in any one year since its erection.

I am with great respect, your obedient humble servant,

CHARLES PARKER.

STATEMENT AS FOLLOWS:

1797	Paid prison agent	....		$14,327 18
1798	do	do	....	13,545 92
1799	do	do	....	13,285 45
1800	do	keeper	.... $5,579 03	
1801	do	do	.... 5,079 27	
1802	do	do	.... 3,255 13	
1803	do	do	.... 7,862 86	
				21,776 29
1804	do	do	.... 3,179 38	
1805	do	do	.... 2,856 95	
				6,036 33
				$68,968 17
1805	do	do	.... $2,607 29	
1807	do	do	.... 1,884 65	
1808	do	do	.... 2,486 73	
				6,978 67
				$75,946 84

Cr.

1809	by received from keeper	....	5,146 21	
1810	" do	do	.... 8,910 50	
1812	" do	do	.... 1,264 84	
1813	" do	do	.... 738 25	
				16,059 80

Balance against the prison $59,887 04

Dr.

1811	to paid keeper	....	$7,443 34	
1814	" do do	....	4,135 50	
1815	" do do	....	3,980 00	
1816	" do do	....	6,354 55	
1817	" do do	....	8,770 75	
1818	" do do	....	9,859 24	
1819	" do do	....	6,065 61	
1820	" do do	....	1,872 50	
1821	" do do	....	10,169 84	
				58,651 33

1822	to do do	5,805 00	
	Transportation, &c.	1,678 49	
			7,483 49
1823	to paid keeper	3,725 00	
	Transportation, &c.	2,740 27	
			6,465 27
1824	to paid keeper	6,331 00	
	Transportation &c.	2,160 31	
			8,491 31
1825	" paid keeper, ...	3,350 00	
	Transportation	1,444 43	
			4,794 43
1826	" paid keeper	2,025 00	
	Transportation &c.	1,654 89	
			3,679 89
1827	" paid keeper	2,987 50	
	Transportation.	1,790 24	
			4,777 74
1828	" paid keeper	3,029 37	
	Transportation &c.	2,818 94	
			5,848 31
1829	" paid keeper	3,125 48	
	Transportation &c.	1,759 52	
			4,885 00

Total, ... $164,963 81

DOCUMENT (E)

New Jersey Prison—90 Prisoners, 1829.

Expenses.		Earnings.	
Provisions $1593.19¾		Nail Factory	$10.07½
Clothing	507.17	Cooper Shop	15.73¾
Incidentals	345.12½	Plaster	355.35
Furniture	18.15½	Sundry Account	126.88
Repairs	65.94	Shoe-Shop or Cordwainers	1106.93½
Fuel	513.93	Weaving Account	1708.91
Profit & loss act.	38.00	Stone Sawing Account ...	29.32
		Interest Account	75.67½
	$3081.50¾		
Pay of officers	3117.50		$3427.98
			3081.50
	$6499.00¾		
			$346.48

Connecticut Prison—134 Prisoners, 1829.

Expenses.		Earnings.	
Provision	1863.03	Smith's Shop	474.39
Clothing & Bedding	495.20	Cooper's Shop	1258.88
Fuel & Incidental expenses		Shoe Shop	3540.62
including the salary of the		Nail Shop	1771.64
officers	3378.78	Carpenter's Shop	1363.72
Hospital	139.12	Tailor's Shop	15.84
		Labour of Lumpers	40.35
	$5876.13		614.58

Earnings of Connecticut ...$9,105.54
Do.   N. Jersey 3,427.98

Difference 5,677.56
Expenses of N. Jersey, more than Connecticut $ 322.86½
Earnings of   do.   less than   do.   5,677.56

Which report was accepted; and the documents, together with a resolution submitted by the committee, recommending the construction of a new prison, Was ordered to lie on the table.[1]

[1] *Votes and Proceedings of the Fifty-fourth General Assembly of the State of New Jersey,* February 11, 1830; pp. 164–191.

DOCUMENTS RELATING TO NEW JERSEY'S EXPERIENCE WITH THE PENNSYLVANIA SYSTEM OF SOLITARY CONFINEMENT, AS A TYPE OF PRISON ADMINISTRATION, 1836-1860.

CHAPTER III

DOCUMENTS RELATING TO NEW JERSEY'S EXPERIENCE WITH
THE PENNSYLVANIA SYSTEM OF SOLITARY CON-
FINEMENT, AS A TYPE OF PRISON
ADMINISTRATION, 1836–1860.

I. The Reconstruction of the Prison System of New Jersey, 1830–1836.
   1. Annual Report of the New Jersey Prison Instruction Society, 1833, Relative to the Contemporary System of Prison Adminis-tration.
   2. The Report of the Joint Committee of 1833 on the Question of the Erection of a New State Prison.
   3. Report of the Board of Inspectors of 1837 on the New Prison System Established in 1836.
II. Prison Administration and Prison Industry in New Jersey Under the Pennsylvania System, 1836–1860.
   1. Report of the Board of Inspectors of the State Prison in 1840 Relative to the Industry and Management Under the New System of Prison Administration.
   2. The Effect of the Pennsylvania System of Solitary Confinement on the Health of Prisoners.
   3. Rules for Prison Administration in the Middle of the 19th Century.
   4. Prison Finances, 1836–1843.
   5. Prison Finances and Industry, 1844.
   6. Prison Finances and Industry, 1853.
   7. The Final Defense of the Pennsylvania System in New Jersey, 1857.
   8. The Collapse of the Pennsylvania System in New Jersey.
   9. The Establishment of the Auburn System of Prison Administra-tion in New Jersey.
III. Prison Reform Movements from 1833 to 1860.
   1. The New Jersey Prison Instruction Society.
   2. The Relation of Illiteracy to Crime, 1838.
   3. The New Jersey Prison Reform Association, 1849–1852.
   4. The New Jersey Prison Reform Association on the Defects of the State Prison.

I. THE RECONSTRUCTION OF THE PRISON SYSTEM OF NEW JERSEY, 1830–1836.

I. ANNUAL REPORT OF THE NEW JERSEY PRISON INSTRUCTION SOCIETY, 1833, RELATIVE TO THE CONTEMPORARY SYSTEMS OF PRISON ADMINISTRATION.

The New Jersey Prison Instruction Society was one of the
many important prison reform associations which flourished in

the United States from 1825–1850, and which were reflections
of a general European and American interest in the problems of
penal reform. The first annual report of this Society in 1833,
which is reprinted below, is one of the most illuminating and
informing sources of information regarding the early systems
of prison administration in the United States. In addition to
this general information, the report corroborates the opinion of
the prison investigating committee of 1830, relative to the hopeless failure of the congregate system of prison administration
in New Jersey.

ANNUAL REPORT, 1833.

*In this report will be briefly noticed the several systems of Prison discipline,
their effects on the health and character of the convicts, and the financial
concerns of the different systems.*

The old system of Prison discipline, in this country and in Europe, is, perhaps, too well known to need description in detail. Suffice it to say, that
convicts, in most cases, were sent to Prison, and shut up in crowded rooms,—
old and young, good, bad, and indifferent, together.

When labor in shops and yards has been a part of the discipline during
the day, the prisoners have been crowded together at night in lodging-rooms,
where the novice in crime has been trained to deeds of greater darkness, and
where all the inmates were strengthened in their combinations against order
and society. And in these institutions, where there should have been reform,
there were, in reality, unutterable abominations.

The reports of societies and individuals in England, between 1820 and 1830,
give details of wretchedness in their Prisons which called loudly for attention and reform; and these calls were heard by the government. They are
now successfully endeavoring to reform the Prisons and Jails throughout
the Empire.

In France, this class of institutions has been wofully passed by in former
years. Convicts were, in some cases, sent to Prisons like the Bastile, without
labor, or anything to cheer or reform, and consequently became insane; or
sickened and died, with none to "visit" them, or "care for their souls". In
other cases, nine hundred or a thousand were together in a Prison, without
moral and religious instruction, without proper separation and inspection,
and where employment was the only good feature in the system. But the
French government, like the British, has taken a course which will doubtless
lead to reform. The French commissioners have visited some of the Prisons
in the United States, as well as those in some other countries.

In Italy, most of the institutions of punishment are in a deplorable state.
In Sardinia, one prison has been noticed as filthy and wretched in the

extreme. Three hundred and sixty men were confined in one large room. They were chained down by the legs, at night, close, side by side.

Some of the old Prisons, and many of the Jails, in our own country, have been but little, if any, better than the mass in Europe.

Within these dreadful purlieus of natural and moral pollution, not only have criminals been combining and strengthening, in order to speed their way in villany, but even debtors, who previously knew no crime, have been brought to breathe the same contaminating air.

In this wretched state of things, what reasonable man can be surprised that hardened villains have been rapidly multiplying throughout the habitual globe? and that crime of every grade, from the slight aberrations of the child to the foulest deeds within the compas of human ability to perpetrate, are but too common on sea and land?

While the picture has been thus dark in the general, both in Europe and America, there have been some bright spots, even in former days. More than half a century ago, that man of noble spirit, the philanthropist HOWARD, much admired the neatness and order of the Prisons in Belgium. But the institution of this kind, which, above all others, in former years did honor to that country, was the Penitentiary at Ghent. It was mostly on the plan of the present Prison at Auburn, New York. Prisoners were committed, to remain from one to twenty years. They had separate cells for lodging at night, and joint labor by day.

Conversation was not allowed between the prisoners,—spirituous liquors were prohibited,—prayers were daily put up, and other divine services were engaged in on the Sabbath. About sixty years ago, Howard was present, and said of the prisoners,

"This company, of one hundred and ninety stout criminals, was governed with as much apparent ease as the most sober and well-disposed assembly in civil society."

Again it was visited and examined by another benevolent and intelligent individual in 1817. From the whole number of prisoners, then more than thirteen hundred, the number of sick did not exceed twenty-five; of those who were discharged, only about five per cent ever returned. Many instances had occurred, within the governor's recollection, wherein discharged convicts had set up for themselves in trades which they had learned in Prison; and some had done so in Ghent, and had flourished by those habits of industry which they had thus acquired.

At present there appears to be a general disposition in Europe, as in America, to improve the condition of Prisons. Associations are multiplying in the large cities and states, on both sides of the Atlantic, to investigate and spread information on this great and momentously important subject.

Several reformed Prisons in the United States demand our attention.

The State Prison at Auburn, New York, was commenced in 1816. In 1819, the legislature, alarmed at the progress of crime, and the condition of the old Penitentiaries, authorized an alteration in the plan of the Prison. After this arrangement, there were five hundred and fifty separate cells.

This was the first prison in this country on the plan of solitary confinement at night.

After this improvement, the first report of the Eastern Prison Discipline Society says:—

"It is not possible for us to describe the pleasure we feel in contemplating this noble institution,—after wading through the moral and material filth of many Prisons. We regard it as a model worthy of the world's imitation. The unremitted industry, the entire subordination and subdued feelings of the Prisoners, have probably no parallel among an equal number of convicts."

In 1826, an inquiry was instituted in relation to the conduct and character of convicts discharged from Auburn. In 1827, it brought fifty-two favorable cases: in 1828, it brought one hundred and twelve favorable cases: in 1829, letters were addressed to postmasters and sheriffs in all parts of the state of New York, and intelligence was received concerning two hundred and six, of whom one hundred and forty-six were reformed.

And further, concerning many of the one hundred and forty-six here mentioned, information had been received two and even three years in succession, giving them the same character, and some of them the character of decidedly pious men.

In 1830, the report of the Eastern Prison Discipline Society says again of Auburn Prison:—

"It maintains the same general character it has done during a course of years. Silence, industry and order reign throughout the establishment. The health, among a population of more than six hundred within the walls, is about equal to that of the most favored country villages in New England, and better than that of the city of Boston. The annual deaths during six previous years were one in seventy-one; and during 1830, they were less than one in one hundred. The moral influence is good, as might, indeed, be expected from the public worship, the Sabbath school, the reading and studying of the Bible, the solitude, the private admonition, the absence of temptation, the mild and wholesome discipline, and the daily acknowledgment of God. And the moral influence is proved to be good by numerous cases of reformation, and comparatively few of recommital. Such is the condition, on the whole, of this Prison, that those who hear much of it, and afterward visit it, go away, and say, the half was not told them; and thousands visit it from America and Europe as a model for imitation."

The average expense of building a Prison on the Auburn plan is reckoned to be two hundred and twenty dollars per cell.

In reference to the finances of that institution, after it was built, we have all the necessary facts in the case up to the present time.

During the first years of experiment, after the Prison was built on the new plan, fears were entertained that it would not support itself; and for its support ten thousand dollars were annually drawn from the state treasury.

For several years after the erection of the Prison, the agent purchased all the raw materials, caused them to be manufactured in the Prison, and sold them from the Prison stores on account of the state. Very serious losses resulted from this system; in consequence of which losses the legislature abolished the system, and adopted the plan of hiring by contract, which is now pursued with decided advantage.

The contractors furnish the materials, pay a certain fixed sum per diem for the labor of the convicts, and dispose of the articles manufactured exclusively on their own account. The results of this latter system have been highly encouraging.

At the close of 1828, the profit to the state, after deducting every expense during the year, was found to be three thousand three hundred and thirty-six dollars and ninety-seven cents. At the close of 1829, the earnings of the convicts, after paying the salaries of the officers, &c., was found to have exceeded the expenditures of the Prison to the amount of five thousand eight hundred and sixty-two dollars and sixty cents.

We have another important item of intelligence, on this subject, which the corresponding secretary of the New Jersey Prison Instruction Society has lately received. Under date of December 24, 1832, the chaplain of Auburn, Rev. B. C. Smith, thus closes his letter:—

"In conclusion, let me state one fact, which will be found in no report but that which is about to be made from this Prison to our legislature. In compliance with a law of the last session, our agent and keeper has built, during the last season, a block of two hundred and twenty cells, (probably the most perfect in the world,) estimated at about fifteen thousand dollars, wholly from the funds of the Prison, without drawing upon the state treasury for a dollar; and at the same time earned, in the ordinary operations of the Prison, during the year, more than three thousand dollars over and above all its expenditures. It may be necessary to explain, that money expended on the new cells is the accumulated overplus earnings for several years."

A new State Prison at Wethersfield, Connecticut, was commenced in the summer of 1826, and completed in 1828. It is built on the Auburn plan, and contained originally one hundred and thirty-six cells for males, besides a female department, a chapel, keeper's house, hospital, and offices for warden and guard. The original cost of this Prison, like that at Auburn, was about two hundred and twenty dollars per cell, including the wall and all the buildings; so that the first one hundred and thirty-six cells cost about thirty thousand dollars.

To say nothing about the expense in building either Prison, we may profitably consider the comparative finances of the old prison at Newgate, Connecticut, and the new one at Wethersfield.

Previous to 1826, the Newgate Prison had been occupied thirty-six years; and notwithstanding the number of prisoners was comparatively small, yet in no one of the thirty-six years did it support itself; but the average annual expense to the state, during the whole time, was near six thousand dollars.

In relation to the New Prison, the results have been most truly encouraging. From the very day in which the prisoners were removed from Newgate to Wethersfield, the pecuniary concerns began to wear a brighter aspect; and the prospects in this department have grown brighter and brighter to the present day. In 1832, the governor, in his message to the legislature of

Connecticut, stated that a revenue might hereafter be expected from the Prison to the state of ten thousand dollars annually.

We shall close this notice of Wethersfield Prison with an extract of a letter very recently received from the chaplain of said Prison, Rev. William Whittlesey. He says :—

"During the last year, the average number of convicts was about one hundred and eighty; and the earnings of these, above every expenditure of the Prison, were eight thousand seven hundred and thirteen dollars; whereas, in 1817, 1818, 1819, the average expense was twelve thousand one hundred and ninety-two dollars annually, above the earnings of the convicts; and then we had only about seventy-five for whom to provide. Accordingly, the difference is nearly twenty-one thousand dollars a year; and yet the great objection to building this Prison and changing the mode of discipline was its enormous expense to the state. This Prison has much more than paid for itself since its erection, a term of five years; but this is not all; indeed, it is but a small part of the benefit accruing from the change. The reformation of character, and, in many instances, the salvation of the souls of men, effected in consequence of the change in our Prison, is a good that cannot be valued in money."

In Pennsylvania great attention has been paid, during some years back, to the improvement of the penal code and Penitentiary system. The Old Walnut Street and Arch Street Prisons, in Philadelphia, during a too long course of years, had been most efficient schools of vice and places of un- utterable crime. To remedy evils like these, the legislature made provision for the erection of two new Penitentiaries, one at Philadelphia, the other at Pittsburg.

The original plan of these institutions was somewhat peculiar. The first design was, that the convict should be entirely solitary by day and night, without labor or instruction. After one hundred and fourteen cells had been built in the New Penitentiary at Philadelphia, the legislature arrested the work on the original plan, and passed a law providing for the introduction of labor into the New Prisons at Philadelphia and Pittsburg, and providing also for a religious teacher in the Philadelphia Penitentiary.

The last mentioned institution received some convicts in 1829; and at the close of 1830, there were fifty-four convicts in the Prison at work, each in his cell. January 1st, 1831, the inspectors stated the system of discipline to be "solitary confinement at labor, with instruction in morals and religion." The inspectors, physician and warden reported to the legislature that this discipline did not "produce insanity or bodily infirmity," but they highly ap- proved of solitary confinement day and night when thus modified.

The experiment was so far successful as to induce the legislature, in March, 1831, to appropriate one hundred and twenty thousand dollars, for the erec- tion of four hundred additional cells within the walls formerly built.

Provision was also made to raise one hundred and fifty thousand dollars, for erecting a new County Prison in the city of Philadelphia, on the plan of solitary confinement; said Prison to contain three hundred dormitories; thus providing that Walnut Street and Arch Street Prisons be not much longer used as places of wretchedness amid natural and moral death.

January, 1832, the inspectors, warden and physician report, a third time, favorably in relation to the New Penitentiary. Whether any definite inquiry had been instituted relative to the conduct of discharged convicts, as there has been at Auburn, does not appear; but the warden says:—

"Of the whole number discharged from the commencement of the establishment, twenty-one in all, we have received an unfavorable account of but one."

The physician at the same time says:—

"The health of the prisoners for this year has been generally good, though a few cases of severe indisposition have occurred. The confinement operates differently on different prisoners, increasing the health of some and lessening that of others."

After another year's experience, the warden again reports favorably, January, 1833, and says:—

"No prisoner whom we have discharged has been re-convicted; and the information from those who have left here has been generally satisfactory. It is a mistake to believe that the inmates of prisons are a set of outlaws and tiger-like beings,—lost to all good in this world, and without hope of a hereafter. Too many, indeed most of them,—on first conviction, are either neglected youth, thrown into the world without education, and without friends (often the victims of hard masters)—or ignorant men, the dupes of artful knaves who know how to elude detection. Neglect of early education, the use of ardent spirits, gambling and dealing in lottery tickets, are the most prominent causes of felony."

With regard to the New Prison at Pittsburg, so far as we have been able to obtain information, though erected at an immense expense, it seems indeed among the unfortunate institutions of the age. It was on the same plan, though not so happily constructed, as that at Philadelphia.

The cost of building on the plan adopted in Pennsylvania is, of course, much greater than that adopted in New York, and most other states. The prisoners in their solitary cells, during these three and a half years, have about supported themselves by their labor, without paying the salaries of their keepers.

The State Prison at Sing-Sing, New York, on the banks of the Hudson, has been in building and in operation about seven years. The main building, as lately finished, is five hundred feet long, and forty wide, five stories high, containing one thousand cells for solitary confinement at night, and where also in solitude the prisoners take their meals. The general plan of discipline is like that at Auburn, Wethersfield and Charlestown. There have been glorious results in the radical reform of prisoners. In December, 1831, the chaplain reported from his department; and though the report was encouraging, yet its author spoke with great care in relation to the number of cases of reform; but in speaking of these cases, he says:—

"It is worthy of remark, that not one of this hopeful number, in all my intercourse with them, has ever given the most remote intimation of a desire to be released from present punishment; nor am I aware that one has been released on account of any religious professions."

28 P

This officer at Sing-Sing, the Rev. Jonathan Dickerson, appears to have a wholesome distrust of the class of men with whom he has to deal, and to look for hypocrisy; and yet, from facts that have come to his knowledge, he thinks there is great reason and encouragement to be attentive and faithful to this class of men. In a recent communication to the New Jersey Prison Instruction Society, he says:—

"There have been cases where convicts, when discharged, have offered themselves to the people of God, and maintained a religious character; one of whom has since died, and in death as well as life was an ornament to the church of which he was a member. The cases of radical reformation have greatly increased during the last year. There are from fifty to eighty that have hopefully passed from death to life; and the greater part are marked cases. During the last season, scarce a week has passed without the occurrence of a new case."

Indeed, they are beginning to feel at this Prison, as at some others, that the best punishment for criminals is that repentance which leads them to look back upon their crimes with humble loathing and contribution of soul. This is the secret of the whole thing: the convict should be brought to feel as the keeper of Maryland State Prison says some of his prisoners felt, when they lately died with the cholera. Said he:—

"They rejoiced, in the hour of death, that they were ever brought to Prison."

And as it respects pecuniary concerns, it will be found in practice, as it might well be found in theory, that *economy* and *moral improvement* go hand in hand.

There are several other reformed Prisons within the United States which we might go on to describe; but suitable brevity in this report forbids it. We should especially be happy to detail the interesting features and results of the State Prison at Charlestown, Massachusetts. In this Prison, as in many others, the Sabbath school is deemed a very important part of the exercises on the Sabbath. About five hundred gentlemen, of different denominations, from Charlestown and Boston, teach in the Sabbath school alternately. These visits to the prisoners are said to have raised a great interest in behalf of this class of men.

The brief notices we have given, as well as others which might be given, all go to show the great truth, that if Prisons are commenced and carried on as they should be, instead of being places in which men are matured in crime, they may be indeed reformatory in their character; and instead of being a heavy tax on the state, they may *at least* support themselves.

A few facts like the following will show what an enormous expense the old Prisons have been to the several states.

Connecticut paid, for its then comparatively small number of prisoners, from 1791 to 1826, the sum of two hundred and four thousand four hundred and eighty dollars. New York paid for state prisoners, from 1796 to 1828, one million and eight hundred thousand dollars. Massachusetts, from 1805 to 1828, paid more than three hundred thousand dollars. From 1819 to 1825, the state of Pennsylvania paid, in six years, for merely one prison, that on Walnut Street, the sum of one hundred and seventy-nine thousand three hundred and seventy-three dollars and thirty cents, over and above the labor of the convicts. But we forbear to speak further of mismanagement abroad, and turn for a moment to view the prison concerns of New Jersey.

And here we may state at once, that, with reference to the past, there is but one wretched story to tell; and as to the future, there is but one dismal prospect, unless things shall take a turn for the better. These things are perhaps seen and felt by a large portion of the citizens of New Jersey; and if they are not seen and felt here, they are in other states, and other countries. It is a notorious fact, that the almost hopeless condition of the Penitentiary in this state is a theme of conversation and of writing, among men of information, from Maine to Georgia, from the Atlantic to the Mississippi, and not only in America, but Europe. The buildings are badly constructed and insecure. In the able report of the committee of six from the legislature, in January, 1830, regarding the insecurity of the Prison, they say:—

"We have obtained information, from the records of the Prison, concerning escapes which have actually been effected since the Prison was built. This list is now before us. It contains the names of one hundred and eight convicts who have made their escape. This is more than one-twelfth part of all who have been committed to the Prison,—a proof of the insecurity of the Prison, so far as our knowledge in the history of Prisons extends, without a parallel."

The moral condition, even so far as deeds have seen the light, has been too soul-sickening to be viewed with composure.

And, as in the case of other Prisons on the old plan of construction and discipline, the annual drafts upon the treasury of the state have been almost uninterrupted from the time the Penitentiary was built to the present year. The late state treasurer, Mr. Parker, after going through the whole range of the financial concerns of the establishment, from the time it was founded, in 1797, up to 1829, including more than thirty years, reported to Governor Vroom, January 1830, and says:—

"From the best information I have been able to obtain, I think myself safe in saying, that the Prison has not supported itself in any one year since its erection."

If there be no change in the Prison and Jails of this state, we have yet to learn what disposition will be made of that multitude of villains who are crowding in upon our territory from abroad.

This state is the great thoroughfare between the two greatest cities of the new world. In these two cities, the people are reforming their institutions for correction, improving their penal codes, and critically watching the conduct of delinquents of every class. As these cities are rapidly growing and improving, their vagrant population will scatter more and more into this state; and if there be no change for the better in the discipline of the vicious within our borders, the time is not far distant when the streets will be filled with rascals of every possible description; and no safety will remain to the honest citizen at his fireside or by the way.[1]

[1] Report cited, reprinted in the *Eighth Annual Report of the Boston Prison Discipline Society,* 1833; pp. 96–99.

2. THE REPORT OF THE JOINT COMMITTEE OF 1833 ON THE
QUESTION OF THE ERECTION OF A NEW STATE PRISON.

TUESDAY, January 15, 1833.

Mr. Kaighn from the Joint Committee appointed to enquire into the ex-
pedience of building a new State prison, made the following report, viz:

REPORT

*Of the Joint Committee of Council and Assembly on the erection of
a new State Prison.*

The Committee to whom were referred the joint resolution of the Council
and Assembly, on the subject of the erection of a New Penitentiary,

Report, That, in the consideration which, in the recess of the session they
have given to the several matters committed to them by these resolutions,
they have been animated in the performance of their duty by the early
notice which they received at the first sitting; and the prompt attention
which was given to that part of the late Governor's Message relating thereto.
And they cannot avoid expressing the additional gratification which they
have received, in the earnest and zealous response of the public sentiment
of the State, to these movements of its Legislature.

That the time has arrived when something must be done—when opinion
must be reduced to practice, and New Jersey brought to something like an
equality with her sister States, in the adaptation of the best means of punishment to offenders against her laws, and that her present (misnamed) Penitentiary is a standing reproach to the benevolence and enterprize of the State,
are conceded by all who have devoted to this subject any attention.

In accordance with the views entertained by some, that the present prison
might, by alterations, repairs and additions, be made to answer all necessary purposes, as a place of punishment, your committee early directed their
inquiries to this point, and a little observation and reflection satisfied them
that it cannot (without encountering an expense greater than would be required in the erection of a new Penitentiary) be made to answer any useful
purpose. It is an incongruous pile, without order or arrangement, heaped
together from time to time, according to various and conflicting plans, upon
which can be instituted no good system of penitentiary discipline; and which,
if continued, will annually present not only a comparative loss in its pecuniary
affairs, but a total failure in all the great purposes of human punishment.
There is one fact (though heretofore often expressed) we cannot fail to
repeat, that our prison, instead of deterring from the commission of crime,
has actually invited its perpetrators from other States; and that the number of our convicts is constantly increasing from this cause.

The late Governor in his last message states, "The experience of another
year satisfies me of the truth of the suggestion I had the honor to submit to
the Legislature at their last meeting, that the situation of our prison was

such as to invite to the commission of crime within our State. Its condition is well known to that class of offenders who are familiar with punishments. It offers to them all the allurements of that kind of society which they have long been accustomed to, freed from the restraints to which they would be obliged to submit in other places of confinement; and at the same time holds out a prospect of a speedy escape. To this may be attributed the great number of our convicts, and as long as it continues, we may expect our prison to be filled. Within the last three years, the number has increased from eighty-seven to one hundred and thirty, being an increase of fifty per cent."

These considerations should alarm us not only for ourselves, but from the appalling inference to be drawn from them, that we are by our system and means of punishment, contributing to the increase and propagation of crime.

To counteract these fearful consequences; to devise the best means to prevent crime, which is the great object of punishment, and to give to the policy of our State on this subject such a practical direction as will comport with the just and enlightened views of the age in which we live; and more especially in our own country, has been the sincere and undeviating effort of your committee, and they respectfully submit the reasons which have brought them to the conclusion presented.

The prevention of crime is effected by deterring men from its commission, and by the reformation of the offender. If the plan and discipline of a prison recommended by your committee make any approach to these great results, we shall feel amply rewarded, from the considerations, that we have been instrumental in advancing the cause of philanthropy in our native State.

There is much cause to fear, that the idea of cruelty has, in the minds of a portion of the community, constituted a necessary ingredient in their notions of punishment; and that the victims of crime should be considered as the reprobate children of the human family, whose only destiny should be, either an interminable separation from society, or if restored to it again, after their probation of punishment, to be consigned to the degradation and scorn of their fellow men. The intelligence and humanity of the present day have successfully combated these errors; and the power of society over its offending members, is now limited and restricted by all those rational deductions, which arise from the moral nature of man, his liability to err, and the just claims of that society in which he exists, and against which he has offended, for its peace and security. While a regard is had to these principles, we may fairly indulge the hope of a continual advancement of the system of penitentiary discipline, and the consequent moral improvement of society; in a disregard of them, is to be found the true cause of the failure of the prison system in New Jersey.

The system of prison discipline has probably been brought to greater perfection in the United States than in any other part of the world, and we are not therefore driven far in our researches for the best practical illustration of its true principles.

An act passed by the Legislature of the State of New York, in 1821, was perhaps the first, and most important in its introduction of an improved prison discipline. "This act subjected convicts wholly or partially to solitary confinement, according to their degree of depravity, and also requiring that each prisoner should be lodged in a separate cell."

The reform that has been introduced since the enactment of this statute consists, in the solitary confinement of the convicts, not only at night but during the time of taking their meals; of collective labor during the day, a collective and private moral and religious instruction, and a strict supervision, at all times, to prevent any communication amongst them. We are indebted to the prisons at Auburn and Wethersfield, for the best and most gratifying examples of these details. While these experiments were in progress, the State of Pennsylvania commenced the erection of her eastern penitentiary, which when fully completed and carried into effective operation upon the system adopted by its founders, we believe will exhibit one of the noblest and most enduring monuments of human charity. The system of this institution is that of "solitary confinement at labor, with instruction in labor, in morals and religion."

It differs from those institutions first named in two respects. In this, the labor and instruction of the convicts are solitary, in those they are collective.

An honest difference of opinion is entertained by many good men, as to the respective merits of these systems, and your committee would with great defference, submit the reasons which have swayed them in favour of the system of the Eastern Penitentiary of Pennsylvania.

It is found by experiment, indeed it is a part of the philosophy of our nature, that the most powerful agent in the work of individual reformation is *solitude.*

In this position the mind of man is necessarily cast upon itself; its powers, passions, habits and propensities are all before it.—The mass of his life is surveyed with a scrutiny that it never encountered before and conscious as in his prison house he must be, that escape is hopeless, he continues the unwelcome task of self examination, till his obduracy is subdued, his disposition humble and teachable, and he, prepared to receive with gladness such moral and religious instruction as may be best adapted to his circumstances. In the eloquent and emphatic language of another, "If any circumstances can be imagined, calculated to impress the warning, the encouragements, the threats or the hopes of religion upon the mind, it must surely be those of the convict in his cell, where he is unseen and unheard, and where nothing can reach him but the voice which must come to him as it were from the other world, telling him of things, which perhaps never before entered into his mind; telling him of God, of eternity, of future reward and future punishment, of suffering far greater than the mere physical endurances of the present life, and of joy infinitely beyond the pleasures he may have experienced. These instructions frequently discover to the guilty tenant of the cell, what seems often not to have occurred to him, the simple fact, that he has a spiritual nature, and that he is not the mere animal which his habits and hitherto uncontrolled propensities would indicate. And this is a discovery which alone may and does effect a great change in a man's whole character. He feels that he is a being superior to what he had thought himself, and that he is regarded as one having higher powers than he had supposed. This first step in the path of improvement is a prodigious one; a new ambition is awakened, and the encouragement of it is the principal thing now needed. This encouragement it is a part of the system to give."

Collective labour and instruction interrupt and in some degree paralize these individual and solitary efforts.

The association of convicts for any purpose, and under the strictest supervision, is attended with evil consequences.

There is a sympathy in crime which renders its subjects, when assembled together, at least complacent, if not bold; and it is believed, that the closest watchfulness of faithful supervisors has not been competent to detect and prevent all communication between them. That much has been effected in this way, cannot be denied, but is it not a defect in the system of collective labour and instruction, that this attendant evil is not only possible but probable?

Here at the least is a knowledge of faces, and no doubt of names and offences. Curiosity is excited, the social principle (one of the strongest in our nature) begins to operate, and ingenuity, with its infinite contrivances, is set to work to counteract the interdict of communication.

The solitude of the convict however, is only an exclusion from the society of his fellows, and those who may in any way weaken the force of the discipline under which he is placed. His cell is opened at all proper times for the visits of those, whose desire it is to do good and to communicate instruction.

In the language of the second report of the Inspectors of the Eastern Penitentiary of Pennsylvania, speaking of the solitary convict, "There, he can only read and hear what is calculated to make him industrious and virtuous."

But the plan of solitary labour and instruction has one advantage over the other, which claims in its behalf our peculiar regard; which is, that no convict is seen by another after he enters the prison walls, and he cannot know unless by previous knowledge, who are its inmates. He thus has presented to his mind the highest incentive to reformation. He is not surrounded by those who may thereafter proclaim his shame, and his once debased mind indulges the hope that he may yet live a new life of respectability and usefulness.

Although this penitentiary has been in operation, and this partially, but a few years, the history of its discharged inmates, exhibits many affecting and delightful instances of its salutary effects; and the intelligent and faithful warden in his report of last year, states "That of the whole number discharged from the commencement of the establishment, we have received an unfavourable account of but one."

Much reliance has been placed on the good effects produced by collecting or assembling the convicts together for public religious instruction.

Your committee would be among the last to undervalue this mode of instruction, but they ask with confidence if all the good anticipated from this course is not attained with more certainty and effect upon the plan of this Penitentiary? The desire for instruction is stimulated by the longing for social enjoyment, the attention is more exclusive, because less distracted, and he feels, deeply feels, when it is said to him, "Thou art the man."

But moral and religious instruction upon this plan is not alone communicated to the convicts privately in their cells. Such is the structure of the cells, that religious instruction may be communicated by the preaching of the gospel, the minister, for this purpose, standing in the corridor of the building and directing his voice through the halls of the cells. In the report referred to, the Warden states, that "during the past year service has been performed mostly once a week by the minister preaching in the corridor to all the convicts in the establishment without their being removed from their cells, or seeing or communicating with each other, and the various impressions thereby produced have been similar in appearance to those in any other assembly of the same number. In what manner can man be placed where the words of the gospel would be more impressive than in their situation? Sitting alone, without seeing or being seen by any human being, nothing to abstract their thoughts or divert them from the truths delivered to them, alone when they hear; and left alone when the minister has finished, to ponder and reflect."

Solitary confinement without a proper employment of the physical powers would be totally inconsistent with a healthy state of the mind or body, and would operate as the exercise of cruelty upon the convict.

To obviate this he is required to labour in his cell at some mechanical trade, it being either one with which he is already acquainted or one which he readily learns.

The facility with which he acquires a knowledge of, and the short time in which he is taught successfully to work at some mechanical occupation, ceases to surprise those, who consider the avidity with which he seeks to alleviate his solitude, and of course the devoted attention that he must necessarily pay to his business.

The Warden in the same report states, that "Every prisoner with four exceptions, who has been here even six months is now earning his maintenance." These exceptions were cases of sickness, infirmity and old age.

The severest punishment inflicted on the refractory convict is depriving him of his labour. The Inspectors in the same report state, "An opportunity of witnessing the effect of absolute solitude without labour, has occasionally been presented, when as a punishment to a sturdy and disorderly convict, the Warden has ordered the light of his cell to be closed. Little time has elapsed with the most hardy, before the prisoner has been found broken down in his spirit, and begging for his work and his Bible to beguile the tedium of absolute idleness in solitude.

That the system of Solitary labour and instruction is salutary in its effects upon the convicts has been shown. That its tendency must be to deter from crime is equally manifest. We seek to avoid that which we most dread, and if we can overbalance the love of crime, by the fear of its inevitable consequences, we have in a great measure attained the second grand principle in the administration of punishment.

In this respect the history of the Eastern Penitentiary is already fruitful in facts. In the report referred to, the Inspectors state, "great terror is known to have been impressed upon the minds of the convict community by this Institution; and the small number of prisoners sent from the Eastern district, including a vast majority of the population of the State; together with the careful manner in which it has been ascertained, that the most knowing rogues avoid committing those offences which would subject them to its discipline, may be regarded as powerful reasons for extending its operation to those penitentiary offences, not at present included within the statute."

The position of New Jersey peculiarly demands that she should hold out the most powerful repellant to the commission of crime within her limits. The dense population of the two cities, that skirt our borders, are prolific nurseries from which are constantly emanating the lawless adepts in crime; and the history of many of the inmates of our prison furnish abundant evidence, that there they received their first lessons in iniquity.

If your committee are opposed to collective instruction, they are equally so to collective labour, and for the same reasons. It may be said by some that various kinds of labour can alone be accomplished by the combined strength and skill of the convicts, and that the pecuniary profits resulting hence would be greatly increased. The answer to this objection (if it be one) is, that in its nature it is predicated of labour and profit alone, which here are to be considered as subsidiary to the great ends of punishment. The labour of the convict is simply a mean, dictated by the wisest benevolence, for the health of his moral and physical powers. If it did not tend to effect this, it should be abandoned as a part of the system. The objection converts a penitentiary into a manufactory. The best good of the convict and that of the society against which he has offended, are the high purposes aimed at, and should the labour and profit be lost, it would bear no comparison to the good proposed to be attained. But it has already been shown, by the experience of the Eastern Penitentiary, that a convict can in six months earn his maintenance. And its Warden in the report referred to, further states that "the short time we have been in operation, induces me to believe that the nett profits of a prison conducted on the plan of separate labour, will be greater than those which might result from joint labour." In the report of 1832 he states, "that the experience of another year has also tended to confirm the opinion that the prisoners can generally maintain themselves by their labour in solitude."

A part of your committee having, since the last adjournment, visited this penitentiary, acknowledge with unfeigned pleasure the gratification they experienced, in the exhibition of its structure, plan and discipline, enhanced as it was by the frankness with which all their enquiries were answered, and in the facilities afforded and attentions shown to them by its intelligent officers; and we feel that we cannot render a more acceptable service, in the performance of our duty, than in the exhibition of the effect of its discipline, as contained in the succinct and clear review of the same, since it has gone into operation, by the present Governor of Pennsylvania.

In his last message he states,

"Our Penitentiary system as immediately connected with the administration of criminal justice, is to be regarded as being of the first importance, in reference as well to the security of the persons and property, as to the general morals of our citizens; and so far as it regards the Eastern Penitentiary, the philanthropic advocates of penitentiary reform, may justly congratulate themselves upon the success with which their exertions have been crowned, in bringing so near to perfection, a system surrounded by so many difficulties.

The government of this prison has been conducted in regard as well to its economy, as its discipline, in a manner worthy of all commendation; and the experiment of the efficacy of solitary confinement with labour, so far as there has been an opportunity to test it, has exceeded the expectations of the most sanguine among its friends. On the 25th October, 1829, the first convict was received into the Eastern Penitentiary, and from thence until the first of November 1832, the whole number amounted to one hundred and thirty-two males and four females convicted of various offences. On the day last mentioned there remained in confinement ninety male and four female prisoners. The whole number discharged between the above dates by reason of the expiration of sentence was twenty-eight; nine died and five were pardoned. One fact in reference to this institution bears strong testimony in favor of its discipline. It appears that not a single convict discharged from this prison has ever been returned to it; which would seem to prove pretty clearly, either that a thorough reformation has been produced, or that a dread of a repetition of the unsocial manner of life, which had proved so irksome before has deterred from the commission of crimes within those limits of the State in which a conviction would ensure a sentence to the Eastern Penitentiary.

"The annual accounts of the prison are not closed, until the 30th of November. I have not therefore been able to ascertain with accuracy how far the earnings of the prisoners will be available to defray the expenses of the Institution. It is believed that for the present they will pay all except the salaries of the officers, and it is not doubted that as soon as the prison shall have been fully organized, the entire expenses will be defrayed out of the proceeds of the establishment. The experiment made in the Eastern Penitentiary, has demonstrated the fact, that solitary confinement with labour does not impair the health of those subject to that species of discipline. The prisoners work to more advantage; having no opportunity for conversation or amusement they eagerly desire employment. Here all communication is cut off, no one knows his fellow prisoner, no acquaintance is formed, no contamination takes place, the convict sees no one, holds communion with no one, except such as will give him good advice; he is placed in a situation, where he has every inducement to grow better, but little temptation to grow worse, here thought and reflection will crowd upon the mind, and prepare it for solemn impressions, and for moral and religious instruction.

"The discipline established in this position, the manner of the construction and arrangement of the building itself, and of the cells in which the prisoners are confined and employed, are admitted by all who have turned their attention to the subject of Penitentiary reform, to possess decided advantages over those of any other establishment, designed for similar objects in this or any other country. Foreigners, whose especial business it has been to visit the Penitentiaries in this country, generally for the purpose of acquiring information in reference to the subject of Penitentiary punishment, and its efficiency in producing reformation, in those subjected to its discipline, have with one voice, awarded the meed of merit to that established in the Eastern Penitentiary of Pennsylvania."

The plan, draft and estimates of a Penitentiary for New Jersey, herewith submitted, were drawn, at the request of your committee, by Mr. John Haviland of Philadelphia, after whose design, and under whose direction, the Eastern Penitentiary spoken of, and many valuable institutions of the like character in our country have been constructed, and to whose intelligence we are indebted for many valuable suggestions; and we cannot avoid expressing our conviction that every consideration of utility, economy and taste, requires, that the erection and completion of a Penitentiary contemplated by this State, should be under the direction and inspection of the designer and architect, aided as he must necessarily be by competent and responsible commissioners.

The plan submitted is substantially upon the principle (with several improvements) of the Eastern Penitentiary, varying, however in its application correspondent with a scale of reduction. It is plain, simple and economical, and susceptible of extension according to the increasing demands of the State, and this too, not only without marring its original design, but by carrying the same into complete effect.

A location near the site of the present Prison is strongly indicated from the abundance, quality of and facility in procuring building materials in its neighborhood, in the comparative ease with which water for the use of the Prison may be procured, and from its central position in the State.

The means necessary for the object contemplated, may be raised by tax in such annual proportions as will not materially affect the present rate of taxation; or they may be raised by a loan redeemable in a given time, at a small per cent—the effect of which would be scarcely perceived as a burden.

But we again repeat, New Jersey is prepared to act on this subject; the tardiness of legislation has provoked her jealousy, and roused her pride of character in behalf of this long neglected, but interesting department of her internal policy; and we indulge without fear, the just expectation, that it will be resumed and acted upon, in the same spirit of promptness and zeal with which it was committed, and that the present session will be coeval with the redemption of the character of our State from the severe but just imputations upon the system of Penitentiary discipline.

All of which is most respectfully submitted.

JOSEPH KAIGHN,   J. W. MILLER,
PETER I. CLARK,   WILLIAM R. ALLEN,
Committee of Council. CHARLES F. WILKINS,
BENJAMIN HAMILTON,
Committee of Assembly.

January 15th, 1833.

Gentlemen,—In compliance with your request, I have made the accompanying drawing, model and estimate, for your contemplated new State Penitentiary, designed for "solitary confinement with labor". Since the commencement of our extensive Eastern State Penitentiary, much valuable experience has been obtained and considerable improvements made in the desired properties of security, ventilation, light, warming and supervision of the cells, and location of the operative offices of the institution.

In designing the plan before you, the most approved features of our building has been adopted and its imperfections avoided.

In the estimate, I have calculated every feature of the design to be executed in the most substantial and approved manner, and the best materials of their several kinds, avoiding useless ornament, and employing members best calculated to perfect the desired properties of the institution. The value of labor and materials taken from the best information and experience.

It is a candid, fair, and full calculation, that can be depended upon and guaranteed, which your subscriber esteems it his duty to report in preference to one of a contracted character, which might lead to disappointment.

The whole plan will accommodate three hundred prisoners, and admit the erection of any one of the radiating blocks as circumstances may require from time to time, without interfering with each other.

Upon examining the general features and detail of the design, the practical and well informed warden will find it calculated to carry into execution all the desired objects of the institution.

ESTIMATE.

External Wall, ...	$14,000
Front building, containing the Culinary, Laundry, and Bathing Offices, Store Rooms, Keeper's Chambers, Observatory, Reservoir, Belfry, and other fire proof rooms, expressed in the plan:	15,000
Culvert, Sinks, Cast Iron Pipes, Covered Ways, Apparatus for cooking, warming, and raising water into the Reservoirs :.......	13,000
Block A containing 50 cells, ...	18,000
B 75	27,000
C 50	18,000
D. 75	27,000
E 50	18,000
300 Cells Total	$150,000

JOHN HAVILAND.

Philadelphia, January 15, 1833.[1]

[1] *Journal of the Proceedings of the Legislative Council of the State of New Jersey,* January 15, 1833; pp. 64-74.

3. REPORT OF THE BOARD OF INSPECTORS OF 1837 ON THE NEW PRISON SYSTEM ESTABLISHED IN 1836.

The advocates of prison reform in New Jersey were exceedingly optimistic regarding the results which they hoped to see achieved by the newly adopted system of solitary confinement. This report of the Board of Inspectors of 1837, in addition to presenting an interesting picture of the new system of prison administration, is also noteworthy as being perhaps the best expression of the satisfaction and optimism which characterized contemporary opinion regarding the remarkable virtues which were alleged to reside in the new system. The inspectors were so confident regarding what they conceived to be the superior excellence of the Pennsylvania system, that they predicted the speedy disappearance of all other types of prison administration.

To THE HONORABLE THE LEGISLATURE OF THE STATE OF NEW JERSEY:

The Inspectors of the new State Penitentiary in obedience to the requirements of section 1, article 1, of "an act for the regulation of the State Penitentiary," passed, March 15th, 1837; Respectfully ask leave to report:

That on the first day of October, 1836, (the commencement of the fiscal year) the whole number of prisoners remaining in confinement in the old penitentiary, amounted to 113, which number had increased to 120 on the 24th of the same month, when they were removed to the new state penitentiary, placed immediately in separate confinement, and put to labor, as soon as the several cells could be furnished and fitted up for that purpose; with the exception of about 17 men who were employed by the commissioner for the erection of the new penitentiary, under the authority of the act of 27th of February, 1833; and a few who were employed through the day, in cooking, baking, washing, &c. for the prisoners.

The law of March 15th, 1837, which prohibits the employing any convict, as cook, clerk, or servant, in the prison, rendered it necessary for the Board to authorize such alterations to be made as would enable the principal keeper to have the baking and washing done by two of the convicts, in the shops adjoining their cells; and also to sanction the employing three servants, one as cook for the prisoners, one as engineer, and one to do the out-door labor in the yard. Since that period, the Pennsylvania system of separate confinement with labor, and occasional religious and moral instruction, has been carried out as far as practicable, in the new state penitentiary; and has thus far more than realized our hopes and expectations.

The close of the year, on the 30th of September, 1837, found us with the number of prisoners in confinement here, increased to 141; exclusive of 17 who have been discharged by expiration of sentence, 17 by pardon from the Governor and Council, and one who died in the old prison, before his removal here; from which it will be seen, that the commitments to the new state penitentiary within the year, have amounted to 63.

Of those in confinement, on the 1st day of October, 1837, one was nine years old when received in prison, 22 between the ages of 10 and 20, 64 between 20 and 30, 35 between 30 and 40, 9 between 40 and 50, 9 between 50 and 60, and one 62 years of age; ninety-one of which are while males, one white female, forty-five colored males, and four colored females.

Seventy-one are natives of New Jersey, eight of Pennsylvania, six of Delaware, four of Maryland, one of Kentucky, one of Michigan, two of Virginia, one of Massachusetts, one of Vermont, two of Connecticut, fifteen of New York, one of Upper Canada, one of the Province of New Brunswick, one of the West Indies, Thirteen of England, eight of Ireland, one of Scotland, three of France, and one of Poland; of which, one was received in the year 1825, two in 1827, one in 1829, three in 1830, seven in 1831, four in 1832, ten in 1833, nine in 1834, twenty-seven in 1835, thirty-four in 1836, and forty-three in 1837. Of their crimes: 26 were committed for misdemeanors, 34 for burglary, 22 for larceny, 17 for grand larceny, 8 for assault and battery, 7 for assault and battery with intent to commit a rape, 2 for rape, 5 for burning, 2 for forgery, 3 for assault with intent to kill, 4 for manslaughter, 1 for polygamy, 1 for sodomy, 4 for passing counterfeit bills, 1 for attempting to poison, 1 for overdrawing with intent to defraud "The bank at Patterson," 1 for perjury, 1 for breaking jail, and 1 for receiving stolen goods.

Two of which were sentenced for 9 months, thirteen for 1 year, 1 day, one for 1 year 1 month, four for 1 year 6 months, twenty-two for 2 years, one for 2 years 2 days, twenty-seven for three years, one for 3 years 1 day, ten for 4 years, one for 4 years 6 months, fifteen for 5 years, four for 6 years, ten for 7 years, four for 8 years, twelve for ten years, one for 10 years 2 days, two for 12 years, seven for 15 years, two for 20 years, one for 21 years, and one for 24 years.

Of their commitment: 123 are committed for the first offence, 16 for the second, 1 for the third, and 1 for the fifth.

Of the whole number, 11 have been sent from the county of Bergen, 35 from Essex, 6 from Sussex, 10 from Morris, 7 from Warren, 4 from Somerset, 9 from Middlesex, 11 from Monmouth, 9 from Hunterdon, (including 5 from the city of Trenton,) 15 from Burlington, 17 from Gloucester, 4 from Salem, 1 from Passaic, 1 from Cape May, and 1 United States prisoner from the District of New Jersey.

No final escape has occurred during the year.

Of those now in confinement, as near as we can ascertain, 17 have had a good education, 89 can barely read and write, the remaining 35 can neither read nor write; of these one is partially insane, and one idiot; to whom it is earnestly, but respectfully requested, that executive clemency may be extended.

It will be perceived, by the account of the receipts and expenditures of the penitentiary for the year, that notwithstanding the difficulties attending the removal of the convicts; the loss of time in fitting up and furnishing the new cells for them to pursue their respective trades in; the alterations made at considerable loss of time, in consequence of the law of the fifteenth of March last; and in addition to this, the difficulties to be encountered, in common with the rest of the community, in the increased high price of every article furnished for the support of the convicts; the diminished demand for their labor, and the consequent diminished price paid for that labor, in some instances; still, the earnings of the prisoners, in the new state penitentiary, in the first year of its operations, have paid all the current expenses for the same period; including the salaries of all its officers, assistants and servants, amounting to four thousand six hundred and seven dollars, twenty-nine cents; and has a balance standing in favor of the labor of the convicts, after paying all its expenses, of over one thousand seven hundred dollars: and this too without an instance of oppression, within our knowledge; and with a milder system of treatment than could possibly be introduced into the old prison. We think that we may safely congratulate the Honorable the Legislature, in the pleasing prospect, that the new state Penitentiary, under proper and judicious management, is not likely hereafter to become a burden upon the community.

It will naturally be inquired, how has this been accomplished? We answer, by the conscientious fidelity with which, (as we believe) the principal Keeper has discharged his duty to the state; in the judicious and systematic arrangement and employment of the convicts, aided by experienced and intelligent mechanics as assistant keepers, men who know their duty, and who have performed it faithfully.

The great advantage of employing as assistant keepers, men who are capable of instructing the convicts placed under their particular care, in the different mechanical branches which have been introduced into the new penitentiary, has been strikingly apparent: and has certainly been attended with the most beneficial results during the past year; not only to the pecuniary interests of the institution, but to the peaceable and orderly conduct of the convicts generally; and the system, good order, and cleanliness, visible throughout the whole ranges of cells, may be attributed to a praiseworthy rivalry between the different assistant keepers, in regard to the cells of which they have the particular charge, and the responsibility which rests upon each of them to the Principal Keeper, of giving constant and unremitting attention and instruction to the convicts committed to their care. From the whole of our observations throughout the year, we are irresistibly led to the conclusion, that it has been owing to the practical knowledge and experience of the Principal Keeper and his assistants, in prison discipline, carried faithfully into every cell, that the new penitentiary has made so successful an effort in its infant state, to carry out the Pennsylvania system of separate confinement with labor and occasional instruction to an extent far beyond the hopes of its most ardent friends.

The masterly manner in which the clerk of the Institution has performed the laborious and perplexing duties of his office, coming, as it does, immediately before the honorable the committee on the accounts of the prison, requires no comment of ours; we would respectfully leave that duty for them to perform.

In closing this branch of our report, it is worthy of remark that there has not been a single complaint made to the Board, of neglect of duty or disobedience of orders, against any of the officers of the institution during the year. The law of the 15th of March has been our guide, and a strict observance of it, by the different officers, precluded the necessity of the Inspectors reporting any farther rules for the government of the prison.

In performance of the "further duties" enjoined upon the Board of Inspectors, we would respectfully state:

That an intercourse of two years and upwards, as Inspectors in the old prison, had long since convinced us of the immense, the incalculable evil to society, resulting from social, or promiscuous labor in that institution, and in all others conducted upon the same principle. We believe it to be beyond the power of human effort, to put a stop to the moral pestilence, where vice, in all its contaminating and seducing forms, is permitted to mingle together in the prison yard, or workshop, from day to day; where the novice in crime, or the unfortunate misguided victim of momentary passion, is placed, (often from necessity) in the same cell at night, or at the same work bench through the day, with the vilest felon. The pernicious effects of such associations are but too visible, in the alarming increase of crime throughout the country within the last fifteen years.

But we feel a peculiar pleasure in having it in our power, even in the infant state of the new penitentiary, to bear testimony to the beneficial effects of the Pennsylvania system, upon the minds and morals of many of the convicts, who had been sentenced to, and spent years in, the old prison, and who were removed here in October, 1836. We cannot forbear noticing, the striking contrast between their abandoned conduct exhibited there, and their orderly deportment after a year's confinement here. Our frequent visits to their cells, enable us to state from personal observation, the visible improvement in the whole tenor of their conduct. Some of the most hardened and vicious desperadoes in the old prison, the ringleaders in riot and disorder, whose ferocious looks spoke vengence to the keepers, and whose minds were occupied day and night in hatching plots for insurrection: and keeping the officers in a continual state of alarm; now, from the salutary restraints of the Pennsylvania system for one year, these very men show, (to all human appearance) a subdued temper, and yield to the firm persuasive, moral treatment, adopted in the new penitentiary: with but a few exceptions, every convict removed here who can read, bear unequivocal evidence of their improved condition, and almost to a man, regret that they ever were placed at social labor; dreading to meet again with their old associates in crime, after the expiration of their sentence.

This simple fact alone speaks volumes as to the vast superiority of separate confinement, with labor and instruction, in ameliorating the condition of the convict, over every other system of prison discipline that we have any knowledge of.

Amongst the numerous advantages of this system, the following might be mentioned. The isolated situation of the convict, affords the keeper the very best opportunity to study and know his disposition, his character and his propensities, and to regulate his treatment of him accordingly; besides, there is no means by which any of the convicts, in the adjoining cells, can interfere with, or operate against, this judicious course of treatment; add to this, the strict privation of intercourse, from every human being, except the officers in the daily discharge of their duties or the casual appearance of an "official visitor"; the unhappy man, cut off thus from the world, is thrown back upon himself, and sooner or later the "monitor" placed within will speak. In proof of this, we have witnessed, (in a visit to one of the cells but a few days since) the powerful athletic frame tremble in agony, and the big pearly drops steal down the manly cheek, whilst the conscience-stricken convict, in deep distress of mind, related to us his first departure from the path of duty, in "despising a mother's advice," and "disregarding a father's authority;" and this, the small commencement of a career of crime, which has terminated in the lonely cell of a prison.

In solitary confinement here, every prisoner who can read, has placed within his reach "the word of Life, which is able to make wise unto salvation;" and we have good reason to believe, that not a few of these unfortunate men, peruse it daily to advantage, as their orderly conduct abundantly testifies.

We have watched with deep solicitude, the conduct of those who have been committed to the new penitentiary within the past year, for the first offence, *who can read;* and thus far, both from the report of the principal and assistant keepers, and our own personal observation, we are inclined to think favorably. We know that the natural associate of solitude is reflection, and when a convict is once brought seriously to reflect upon his past conduct, with wholesome admonition, and the Bible for his constant companion, we would be deficient in charity, were we to consider his case as hopeless.

But when we turn to the moral desolation too glaring in those cells, where the miserable inmate has never been blessed with even the rudiments of moral culture; would you witness the stern severity of the Pennsylvania system of separate confinement with labor, in its most appalling form, you will find it there; where the unfortunate victim of neglected education, is placed by his violation of a law of which perchance he is ignorant; without one ray of hope glimmering upon his benighted mind, save the occasional instruction he receives from the keepers, the casual official visiters, who may chance to call upon him, or the distant voice of the minister of the Gospel, in his labor of love on the Sabbath afternoon; all else to him is one vast vacuum; the mind has nothing left to rest on for relief; labor and sleep are his only comforters; and in his distress of mind, he either sinks down into stupidity, an object more of pity than of punishment; or, reckless of life, in his narrow cell, he sets the majesty of the law at defiance, resists the authority of his

29 P

keepers, and subjects himself to the salutary restraints necessary to sustain good order in the institution.

Having stated facts, derived in a great measure from our own observation, we would respectfully submit the conclusions drawn from them. Convinced as we are of the superiority of the Pennsylvania system of separate confinement with labor combined, on the minds of the more enlightened convicts, we are well satisfied, that it cannot be considered as complete, until moral and religious instruction is carried daily into every cell in the new state penitentiary. We consider that the most benevolent feature in the system, is the moral reformation of the convict. But this cannot be effected, without the means to accomplish that end. And as, from the favorable operations of the Institution for the past year, we have reason to hope that (if prudently managed) it will hereafter sustain itself; we would respectfully suggest the appointment, (either by the Honorable the Legislature, or the board of inspectors) of a suitable person, with a reasonable compensation, *as a teacher,* to give daily instruction to those of the convicts who cannot read; and also to the whole of the convicts, in the duties which they owe to their Creator, to society, and to themselves; one who would lay sectarian feelings at the threshold of the prison, and enter upon his duties in this moral wilderness, with a persevering determination to impart, as far as in his power, useful instruction to those ignorant beings; nor consider his labors as completed until he had taught each convict to read, for himself, the glad tidings of salvation. We believe that instruction of this nature, and carried out in this way, would do more towards reclaiming, and reforming the convicts, than the most polished, and eloquent discourses, delivered publicly, at stated periods.

If you would reach those benighted, abandoned immortals, effectually, it must be done in their cells.

While on this subject, we would ask leave to call the attention of the Honorable the Legislature, to the deficiency of books of instruction, for the use of the convicts who can read. It is true that every prisoner who can read, is provided with a Bible in his cell; still, there are some meritorious prisoners, to whom a change of reading, (after the labors of the day) might be profitably extended. We are decidedly of the opinion, that a small amount might be appropriated to very great advantage, in the purchase of well selected moral and religious books, for the use of such prisoners, as by their good conduct and strict attention to business, might be considered as entitled to the use of them, as the reward of merit.

We lay the foregoing suggestions before the Honorable the Legislature, with much diffidence; yet we respectfully hope that where tens of thousands have been lavished, upon exterior decorations for the noble edifice, in which those unfortunate and misguided men are incarcerated; a sufficient amount of their own earnings, will be cheerfully appropriated, to afford them such moral and religious culture, as may, by the blessing of Divine Providence, fit them to mingle with society after the expiration of their sentences, improved in character, and determined to act the part of good citizens.

On the subject of pardons, we feel it our duty to offer a few remarks, and these shall be confined, chiefly, to those convictions which took place in the old prison.

It will be recollected, that the insecure state of that building, and the frequent escapes of convicts from it, had so emboldened the prisoners, that during the last year which it was occupied, great fears were justly entertained for the safety of the lives of the officers and guard. From occasional information given to some of the assistant keepers, by the better disposed convicts, the principal keeper was enabled to take timely measures to check and prevent several premeditated insurrections; which might, and in all probability would, have proved fatal to some of the keepers. It was hoped that the meritorious conduct of those convicts, would have been remembered favorably by the Honorable, the Governor and Council; and we humbly conceive that no injury would result to society now, by extending executive clemency to such of the convicts as had distinguished themselves, by their regard for the safety of the lives of the keepers and the welfare of the institution, at that trying period. When we consider also, the severity of separate confinement, compared with that of social labor, to which those convicts were sentenced to the old prison, we do cherish the hope that, where in addition to all this, sufficient evidence exists of moral reformation in those men, the period for which they were sentenced may be shortened by pardon.

As it respects the convictions to this prison, we are most decidedly of the opinion, that the hope of pardon operates unfavorably to the reformation of the convict. We believe, that every criminal sentenced here, should be made to understand distinctly, that the sentence of the court would be carried out in all its severity; for whilst the hope of a pardon remains, the unhappy man clings to it, often to his own injury: experience has shown us, that it renders the prisoner less liable to receive or retain good impressions, from the means of instruction placed within his reach; and has a tendency to harden the mind, against those admonitions which might, under a kind Providence, lay the foundation for repentance and reformation. The repeated solicitations made by convicts to the Inspectors on this subject, within the past year, incline us more and more to the belief, that except in cases where a prisoner has been sentenced upon circumstantial evidence, and positive proof of innocence has been afterwards obtained, the powers granted to the Governor and Council, by the 9th section of the Constitution, might be beneficially withheld from the convicts sentenced to this prison. In order to render punishment effectual, it must be certain.

The board of inspectors cannot but express their fears, that the sixth section of "A further supplement to the act for the punishment of crimes," passed March 15, 1837, will operate unfavorably to the interests and good order of this institution. We are well persuaded that no conviction here should be for a shorter period at least than one year. Were our county prisons constructed and arranged upon the plan of this prison, and all convictions for a shorter period than one year, at separate confinement and labor therein, our faith in the efficacy of this mode of punishment would almost lead us to the conclusion, that before the present generation passes away, many of these buildings would stand tenantless monuments, a terror to evil-doers.—We would fondly cherish a hope that those counties which are about to build new prisons, will make the experiment.

It will be seen, from the number of prisoners, (141) compared with the number of cells and shops finished, that there were but three vacant cells on the 1st of October. Hence the imperious necessity of an immediate appropriation, to finish the remaining cells in the upper story of the south wing. It is matter of sincere regret that those cells were left unfinished by the commissioner, as it must be done at an increased expense to the state, and interfere very much with the policy of the institution while finishing. We would respectfully solicit the earliest attention of the Honorable the Legislature, to this most necessary and important appropriation, as the increased number of prisoners which will necessarily be sent here under the law of March 15, 1837, will place it out of the power of the officers to carry the system of solitary confinement into operation for want of cells; and compel them from necessity, to have recourse to the old abominable system, which we hope may never be known here.

The employing the prisoners in such a way as to interfere as little as possible with mechanical labor out of the prison, has had its weight with the board, and they are happy to know that little, if any, prejudice exists against the manner in which they are employed.

It will be seen from the report of the Principal Keeper, and that of the Physician, to which we respectfully refer you, that the health of the prisoners has, during the past year, been unusually good. Our own observations lead us to the conclusion, that with the strict attention to cleanliness in every respect, which is at present maintained, and a due regard paid to those changes of food, which the confined situation of the convicts requires, and which they have always enjoyed; there is much less to apprehend from sickness, than where the whole inmates work and eat together, and are frequently crowded together at night.

Taking their own statements, they enjoy better health here than in the old prison, and although they consider the punishment of privation severe, they prefer their present situation. The fact that no death has occurred since their removal here in October, 1836, with an average of about 130 prisoners, speaks well for the health of the prison.

We cannot consider our duties as performed, without noticing, with feelings of grateful respect, the Christian spirit manifested by the ministers of the Gospel, in Trenton and its vicinity, to the inmates of the institution. Since it was first occupied, they have vied with each other in their attention to the immortal welfare of the prisoners on the Sabbath. "Verily they have their reward". And in connexion with this, we would express our thankful acknowledgments to those benevolent societies and individuals, who have favored the institution with books and tracts for the use of the prisoners.

In closing this report to the Honorable the Legislature, the board would respectfully invite their attention, while in the performance of their duties as "official visiters" to the new prison, to the manner in which some of our county prisons are kept. We believe that such might be done to ameliorate their condition, by making, as we have done, a strict enquiry from the sufferers themselves. The filthy condition of some, the brutal treatment received in others, and the want of discipline in most of them, is to be lamented. Whilst such a state of things exists in our county jails, we need not expect to attain that state of perfection in discipline here, which might naturally be hoped for, were prisoners from their apprehension to their removal here after sentence, kept in separate confinement and treated humanely. Our object in noticing it at this time, is to call public attention to the subject, and we trust we will not be considered as overstepping the bounds of official duty, in thus laying it before the representatives of the people of New Jersey.

We are sincerely desirous to see every obstacle to the prosperity of this infant institution, removed out of the way; considering, as we do, that the Pennsylvania system of separate confinement, with labor and instruction, adopted here, is likely, ere long, to be the only one known to civilized society. At this period of its existence here, it requires cautious, mild treatment. Our hope for its welfare is in the combined wisdom of an intelligent Legislature, every member of which is its particular guardian; who we doubt not will extend to it that fostering care, which, under a benign and gracious Providence, may render its salutary discipline signally instrumental in restoring to society many of those wanderers from the paths of virtue and of peace, reformed and amended, living monuments of the wisdom, benevolence, and humanity of its founders.[1]

> Respectfully submitted,
>
> MOSES WILLS,
> JOHN AARONSON
> JOHN TITUS
> ANDERSON LALOR.

JASON H. ROE, Secretary.
New Jersey Penitentiary, Nov. 6th, 1837.

II. PRISON ADMINISTRATION AND PRISON INDUSTRY IN NEW JERSEY UNDER THE PENNSYLVANIA SYSTEM, 1836–1860.

I. REPORT OF THE BOARD OF INSPECTORS OF THE STATE PRISON IN 1840 RELATIVE TO THE INDUSTRY AND MANAGEMENT UNDER THE NEW SYSTEM OF PRISON ADMINISTRATION.

The report of the inspectors in 1840 is significant as indicating a considerable decline in the optimism which had characterized the report of the inspectors in 1837.

[1] *Journal of the Legislative Council of the State of New Jersey,* 1838. Pages 71–80.

REPORT OF THE BOARD OF INSPECTORS OF THE STATE PRISON, FOR THE YEAR
ENDING SEPTEMBER 30, 1840.

To the Honorable the Legislature
of the State of New Jersey.

In conformity with the act of February, 1838, the Board of Inspectors of
the Prison respectfully REPORT:

That at the commencement of the year there were in the prison one hundred and sixty criminals, and that sixty-one have been received since,
making two hundred and twenty-one. Of these forty-three have been discharged upon the expiration of the terms of their sentences, twenty-four
have been pardoned by the Governor and Council, and two have died, amounting altogether to sixty-nine, and leaving in confinement on the 30th September, one hundred and fifty-two. Of these ninety-seven are white males, forty-
nine colored males, two white females and four colored females. When they
were received at the prison, one was nine years old, nineteen were between
ten and twenty, sixty-two between twenty and thirty, forty between thirty
and forty, eighteen between forty and fifty, eight between fifty and sixty,
three between sixty and seventy, and one between seventy and eighty.

Ninety-five are natives of New Jersey, eight of Pennsylvania, three of
Maryland, four of Virginia, four of Massachusetts, one of Vermont, one of
Connecticut, fourteen of New York, one of Upper Canada, ten of England,
nine of Ireland, one of Germany, and one of Wales. One was received in
the year 1830, three in 1831, one in 1832, two in 1833, two in 1834, three in
1835, two in 1836, eighteen in 1837, twenty-six in 1838, fifty-three in 1839,
and forty-one in 1840. Thirty-four were committed for the crime of burglary, thirty for larceny, ten for misdemeanors, eight for grand larceny, six
for assault and battery, one for attempt to commit a rape, one for assault
and battery with intent to commit a rape, three for rape, eight for burning,
four for forgery, ten for atrocious assault and battery, one for assault and
battery with intent to kill, two for assault with intent to rob, one for
atrocious assault and battery with intent to commit a rape, one for assault
and battery with intent to kill and murder, one for polygamy, one for Sodomy,
nine for passing counterfeit bills, three for breaking jail, six for horse-steal-
ing, five for manslaughter, one for atrocious assault and battery with intent
to kill, one for robbery, one for destroying a horse, one for an attempt to
poison, one for cutting timber, &c., one for breaking shop, and one for
murder in the second degree.

Four were sentenced for six months, one for nine months, thirteen for
one year, one for one year and one day, seven for one year and six months,
twenty-three for two years, two for two years and six months, twenty-three
for three years, seventeen for four years, one for four years and six
months, twenty-three for five years, five for six years, one for six years
and nine months, seven for seven years, four for eight years, one for nine
years, ten for ten years, two for twelve years, three for fifteen years, two for
twenty years, one for twenty-four years, and one for life.

One hundred and twenty-five were committed for the first offence, twenty-two for the second, three for the third, and two for the fourth.

Twenty-eight were sent from the County of Essex, thirteen from Bergen, three from Sussex, twelve from Morris, five from Warren, three from Somerset, eight from Middlesex, fifteen from Monmouth, five from Hunterdon, sixteen from Burlington, five from Gloucester, six from Salem, one from Cape May, thirteen from Passaic, two from Atlantic, four from Cumberland, eight from Mercer, two from borough of Elizabeth, two from the city of Trenton, and one from Hudson.

The schedule accompanying this report, contains the names of those who have been pardoned and discharged. We have adopted the plan of not reporting the names of these convicts, for the reasons mentioned in the report of last year, to prevent them from being printed and going before the public, to operate as a discouragement to their efforts to obtain an honest standing in society.

There have been but two deaths up to the date of this report; they were caused by consumption of the lungs. The general health of the prison has been as good as that of any previous year. For the particulars of the prisoners' health, we respectfully refer you to the physician's report, believing that there are evils peculiar to solitary confinement as it is here applied, and that the principal derangement of health is owing to insufficient warmth and bad ventilation, conditions in punishment that ought to be avoided.

From the keeper's report it will be perceived that the money operations of the prison have not been as favorable as could be wished, and it is proper to state that considerable losses have occurred in consequence of transactions last year entered into by the keeper, contrary to the advice of the Inspectors, as will be perceived by reference to their minutes. There is a falling short in the earnings, which is to be attributed mainly to the state of the times, there being less demand for convicts' labor than formerly. Two of the leading articles manufactured in the prison, *chair seats and shoes,* have accumulated in consequence of no sales having been effected to any considerable extent. What might have been done, had more pains been taken to procure a market, we are not warranted in asserting; but as the duty has heretofore devolved on the principal keeper, who is the financial agent of the prison, we think it important that your attention should be called to this part of the interest of the prison.

It has appeared to the board for some time past, that an out-of-door agent, one acquainted with the market and business transactions generally, who would act under direction of the Inspectors, in relation to the mechanical operations of the prison, as the manager of a manufacturing establishment, would be a highly important officer. The keeper then would have his own appropriate duties to perform. He would attend to all the requirements of the law, so far as discipline is concerned—would see that his assistants faithfully attended to their duties—visit the convicts—see that their situation is made as comfortable as the nature of their confinement admits—and attend to their moral improvement. As these two important branches of the keeper's office now stand, neither can be properly attended to; either the money interest, or the discipline must be neglected. We submit this to your honorable body as the conclusion drawn from careful observation.

On the subject of solitary confinement viewed in a moral light, the board have to report but few known changes for the better amongst the convicts. In one or two instances, when prisoners were received young, and for crimes the result of rash propensities, instead of pursuing that course of life after their liberation which had been anticipated from their good conduct while in prison, they have been guilty of crimes that evince a settled depravity. No prison is a school for perfect reformation; a man's self-esteem is debased by his sentence, and after he has served out his term, he feels that he has no place in society. The board undoubtingly believe that the solitary system is the best of all others, and if any desirable change is to be made in the convicts, it is to be looked for in this system alone. But they wish to convey the idea to your honorable body, that this system cannot, under any management, produce the unnatural results that have frequently been claimed by its advocates. As far as bad example, and the pernicious intercourse with veterans in crime are prevented, and the best opportunities afforded to convince the convict of his errors, no other system can be equal to that of solitary confinement.

The board are of the opinion, that many of the terms of sentences are too long. Ten years' confinement in our penitentiary would be a terrible punishment, and from the experience of the past, they doubt whether the best constitution could endure that term, without being seriously injured, if not completely destroyed. Some of the convicts sentenced to the old prison for long terms, are serving out their terms in this, much enfeebled in health. Their cases deserve some consideration.

According to the physician's report, there are twelve deranged prisoners in the prison, and more than half fit subjects for a lunatic asylum when they were received. The board feel that the admission of these persons into an institution that requires solitary confinement, quiet, and an orderly discipline, is subversive of all system, and that it is an evil that calls for redress. Our prison is no asylum for the insane. Solitary imprisonment instead of affording relief, is of a character to confirm the malady.

The moral condition of the convicts has been less the subject of attention during the past year, than any preceding time within this institution. Peculiar circumstances have occasioned this neglect.

The present keeper was unacquainted with the duties of his situation when he received his appointment, and having no knowledge of the convicts, he could not at once begin the discipline that was so zealously attended to by the former keeper. As he becomes more familiar with his situation, this important branch of his duty will be better understood. Of all systems of imprisonment our's calls for the most frequent, mildest—yet most guarded intercourse with the convicts. All the moral instruction comes through the keeper, and neglect of this important duty destroys the great object of the institution. As we have adopted the system of reformation, rather than of punishment, we ought to carry out the design by all the appliances that it demands.

The board would here acknowledge their obligations to the clergy of Trenton for the continued devotion to the interest of the prisoners—ever ready to minister to their wants, and anxious for their reformation.

A subject of the first importance to the institution, has already been laid before you—that of heating and ventilating the cells. The board cannot recommend this proposed alteration too strongly to your consideration.

No new rules for the regulation of the prison have been adopted by the board.

Respectfully submitted,

By order of the board of Inspectors.

J. S. McCULLY, Secretary.

Inspectors' Room,
New Jersey Penitentiary House,
November 13th, 1840.[1]

2. THE EFFECT OF THE PENNSYLVANIA SYSTEM OF SOLITARY CONFINEMENT ON THE HEALTH OF PRISONERS.

The Pennsylvania system in New Jersey did not lack critics after the first few years of its trial. The most effective onslaughts delivered against the new prison system were the annual reports of the prison physician, Dr. James B. Coleman. He pointed out with telling lucidity the harmful psychic and physical effects of solitary confinement, without adequate provision for association and exercise.

PHYSICIAN'S REPORT.

Gentlemen of the Board of Inspectors:

Since the last report, but little has occurred within the prison to make the year just closed essentially different from the past. Nearly the same amount of sickness, and the same kinds of diseases have been noticed amongst the prisoners. Two deaths have taken place, up to the thirtieth of September, and both from consumption of the lungs. The first was a prisoner on his second commitment, with diseased lungs on his admission—the other a negro of consumptive habit, in whom the disease was fatally developed in the prison.

---

[1] *Report of the Board of Inspectors of the State Prison, 1840, in Votes and Proceedings of the Sixty-fifth General Assembly, 1841; pp. 212–216.*

The effect of solitary confinement on the prisoners in this institution, is well determined, however different it may seem from what is reported of other similar establishments. As the punishment is carried out in this place, the result upon the convict is a diminished force of his organs generally; and particularly a weakening of the muscular fibre—obstructions of the lymphatic glands—and vitiated nervous action. The mind suffers in this state of the organs, and when absolute derangement does not take place, its powers are considerably weakened.

In this prison, as much attention is paid to the health of the convicts, as the nature of their confinement will admit. Wholesome food abundantly supplied—sufficient clothing—cleanliness—kind treatment—all tend to make their situation as comfortable as possible. When sickness requires a departure from the law, the convict has a nurse in his cell, or he has the privilege of taking the air in the yard. As far then as this mode of treatment extends, every opportunity is offered to make the system of punishment tolerable. But still the inroads that are made upon health, are a constant cause of complaint amongst the prisoners; and as they are making applications for pardon on this ground, more than any other, the physician is constantly solicited for certificates of health, under the belief that his statements will go far to induce the court to suppose a farther confinement will destroy the life of the petitioner. Some have been pardoned for this reason, who have died soon after they left the prison.

As the tendency of the present system is injurious to the health of the convict, such alterations ought to be made in the arrangements of the prison, as will insure the greatest degree of health, consistently with the plan of solitary confinement. Some change ought to be made in heating and ventilating the cells. This is imperiously demanded. Confinement in a small, unventilated room, will produce anywhere, and on almost any animal, the very effects that have been observed in our penitentiary. Some pathologists of Europe have lately been trying experiments on animals, to prove the effects of a deficiency of air and light, and the results of all their trials have been a development of tubercles in the lungs, and glandular obstructions—the very state of the organs that is produced in our prison. It was said in a former report, that *post mortem* examinations had shown excessive glandular obstructions; and also, that of all diseases, those of the chest were the most unmanageable.

The evils of bad ventilation ought to be seriously considered. One of the worst systems of heating is adopted in the prison, that of radiation from pipes. If a plan were devised for warming, without purifying an apartment, a more effectual mode could not be conceived. The same air may remain for days, excepting the occasional entry and escape from apertures that have not been made for the purpose; for, owing to a deficiency of heat from the pipes, the ventilators are kept closed in the winter by the convicts, or they suffer from cold. Heated air, as they cannot have fire-places or stoves in their cells, is the only plan that ought to be resorted to, and in it we have all that is desired for the most perfect degree of warmth and ventilation. Were the alteration made, one great cause of disease in the institution would be overcome; the men would always feel more able to attend to their work—their minds would be less depressed, and almost every benefit that attends good wholesome air out of doors, would be brought into the cells.

Another effect of the alteration, and one certainly worth consideration, would be the freedom from offensive odors that now fill almost every part of the establishment. The Eastern Penitentiary of Pennsylvania, and ours, are alike in this particular. The first breath that a stranger inhales, as he enters them, is felt, instinctively, to be unwholesome. The emanations from the prisoners, and the outlet pipes, are floating through the interior of the building, when there ought to be a strong current of air driving them out of doors. The Moyamensing Prison near Philadelphia, is warmed by hot air, and is without this nuisance—its atmosphere is perfectly pure, and at once tells the superiority of this plan of heating.

The plan that has been offered by your committee to the Legislature, embraces your views upon these particulars, and takes from me the necessity of mentioning it in detail. As it has been so often before you, and you are so fully impressed with its importance, you will doubtless strongly recommend its adoption by the Legislature.

Connected with this subject, we *again* call your attention to the mode of discharging the outlet pipes. If possible, let it be done from the outside of the walls—not within the cells, and those too used for the purposes of washing and baking: this arrangement is too offensive to be borne.

There are now amongst the one hundred and fifty-two prisoners, twelve deranged men: more than half of these were fit for a lunatic asylum when they were received. Such men are not proper subjects for the discipline of our penitentiary. They subvert all order, and call for more attention than can be given to them. Instead of receiving any benefit from their confinement, they become confirmed in their malady. The other cases of derangement have occurred in the prison, from masturbation, and from the nature of the confinement.

It is not necessary to particularise cases, and draw the nice distinctions between the different species of mental derangement. The difference between a sound mind, in which the faculties preserve their balance, and that wide departure from sanity, which is noticed by the common observer, is all that need be regarded when we investigate the influences of solitary confinement. If from a state of ordinary reason, we observe such changes as warrant us to believe that the prisoner has become diseased in his perceptive and reflective faculties, either by their increased or diminished action, or any irregularity in their operations, we can class him amongst the mentally deranged. The reported cases of mental derangement are to be understood in their most comprehensive sense.

The good effects resulting from a few of the prisoners being suffered to go into the yards for the benefit of the air, have been strongly marked. Could this treatment be extended to a greater number, and not interfere with the plan of separate imprisonment to a greater extent than it has done thus far, it would be of the utmost importance to their health.[1]

Very respecfully,
JAMES B. COLEMEN.

Trenton, November 13th, 1840.

PHYSICIAN'S REPORT.

Gentlemen of the Board of Inspectors:

Since the last medical report has been made to your board, there has been some change in the treatment of the prisoners, when diseased, as well as slight alterations in the cells, which have proved beneficial. To prevent the evils of solitary confinement, especially those which grow out of an abuse common to this system of punishment, when prisoners have shown evidence of that abuse, other convicts have been put with them in their cells, and the evil, in many cases, remedied. Cases of derangement of the mind have been prevented by this course. Those suffering from want of air have been turned into the yard for a few hours each day, and gained in health and strength rapidly. More pains have been taken to ventilate the cells than heretofore, and in proportion to the change of air, have the prisoners improved in health. The ventilation has been effected by raising the windows of the cells, the only plan that could be adopted under the present arrangement.

Another cause of better health in the establishment, is the rigid exaction of the labor of each convict. No man who can work is suffered to remain idle; and constant employment, occupying the mind and exercising the muscles, goes far to preserve the body in a constant state of vigour, that enables it to resist, in a degree, the influence of solitary confinement.

But two deaths have occurred during the past year, one from consumption of the lungs, caused by suffocation in smoke, the other from a diseased heart. Diarrhœas and dysenteries have prevailed in the house, as they have in the neighborhood. Many of the prisoners have been under treatment, some having these complaints in aggravated forms, but, fortunately, none have died. I must here acknowledge the services of Mr. Campbell, who, as apothecary and nurse, shows a judgment in his branch, and an attention to the sick, which make him a most valuable officer in the institution: to his care are many of the cures to be attributed.

Perhaps more license has been taken in prescribing tobacco to the prisoners, than the literal construction of the law regulating this matter admits. As an article of the *materia medica,* and the best remedy for those suffering under despondency in solitary confinement, I do not think its use ought to be withheld in the institution. Many cases have come under the notice of the keepers and physician of its certain utility. Had the prisoner been denied its use, and other circumstances had continued the same, derange-

---

[1] *Votes and Proceedings of the Sixty-fifth General Assembly of the State of New Jersey,* 1840; pp. 219–222.

ment of the mind, as former experience has proved, would have been the consequence.

The number of insane is less than at the time of the last report. The expiration of terms and pardons have relieved the institution in a measure of these convicts; and a better treatment, as before stated, has prevented the predisposed, in some instances, from losing their reason. Still there are five or six in the cells who ought to be transferred to a mad-house. If the same interest were attached to petty offenders that attends the murderer, our county courts would as often find crimes of a trifling nature the result of insanity, as cases that call for capital punishment; and the accused, instead of being sent to a penitentiary, would be confined in an asylum.

The opinions expressed heretofore on the effects of solitary confinement upon the system, are strengthened by every year's experience. The more rigidly the plan is carried out, the more the spirit of the law is observed, and the more its effects are visible upon the health of the convicts. A little more intercourse with each other, and a little more air in the yard, have the effect upon the mind and body that warmth has upon the thermometer, almost every degree of indulgence showing a corresponding rise in the health of the individual. That an opinion to the contrary should have been advocated at this time, when the influences that control the animal functions are so well understood, seems like a determination to disregard science in the support of a mistaken but favourite policy. The medical reports from this prison have been read with an interest that nothing but a candid exposure of facts can explain. These facts are nothing more than what medical science unhesitatingly acknowledges, and what every man's daily experience teaches. They are in accordance with the views of one who is acknowledged to be the best living writer on a subject of which this is a part. Mr. Combe, in his recently published Moral Philosophy, says:

"A difference of opinion exists among intelligent persons, whether the system of solitary confinement and solitary labor, pursued in the eastern penitentiary of Pennsylvania, or the system followed at Auburn, of social labour in silence, enforced by inspectors, and solitary confinement after working hours, is more conducive to the end of criminal legislation. The principles now stated lead to the following conclusions:

"The system of entire solitude weakens the whole nervous system. It withdraws external excitement from the animal propensities, but it operates in the same manner on the organs of the moral and intellectual faculties. Social life is to these powers what an open field is to the muscles; it is their theatre of action, and without action there can be no vigour. Solitude, even when combined with labour and the use of books, and an occasional visit from a religious instructor, leaves the moral faculties still in a passive state, and without the means of vigorous and active exercise. According to my views of the laws of physiology, the discipline of the Eastern Penitentiary reduces the tone of the *whole* nervous system to the level which is in harmony with solitude. The passions are weakened and subdued, but so are all the moral intellectual powers. The susceptibility of the nervous system is increased, because all organs become susceptible of impressions in proportion to their feebleness. A weak eye is pained by light which is agreeable to a sound one. Hence, it may be quite true, that religious admonitions will be more deeply felt by prisoners living in solitude than by those enjoying society; just as such instruction, when addressed to a patient recovering from a severe and debilitating illness, makes a more vivid impression than when delivered to the same individual in health; but the appearances of reformation founded on such impressions are deceitful. When the sentence is expired, the convict will return to society with all his mental powers, animal, moral, and intellectual, increased in *susceptibility,* but *lowered in strength.* The excitements that will then assail him will have their influence doubled by operating on an enfeebled system. If he meet old associates, and return to drinking and profanity, the animal propensities will be fearfully excited by the force of these temptations, while his enfeebled moral and intellectual powers will be capable of offering scarcely any resistance. If he be placed amid virtuous men, his higher faculties will feel acutely, but be still feeble in executing their own resolves. Convicts, after long confinement in solitude, shudder to encounter the turmoil of the world; they become excited as the day of liberation approaches, and feel bewildered when set at liberty. In short, this system is not founded on, or in harmony with a sound knowledge of the physiology of the brain, although it appeared to me to be well administered." He then adds:

These views are supported by the report of the physician to the New Jersey state prison, (in which solitary confinement, with labour, is enforced) addressed to the board of inspectors, November, 1839." After quoting some passages from the report that accord with his views, he sums up by saying, "There are advantages that go far to compensate the evils of solitude, but none to remove them." [1]

Respectfully submitted,
JAMES B. COLEMAN,
Physician to N. J. State Prison.

3. RULES FOR PRISON ADMINISTRATION IN THE MIDDLE OF THE 19TH CENTURY.

The following rules, governing the daily administration of the State Prison in 1853–4, are interesting as describing in detail the nature of the daily routine in existence during the last decade of the existence of the Pennsylvania system in New Jersey.

[1] *Votes and Proceedings of the Sixty-ninth General Assembly of the State of New Jersey,* 1841–42. Pages 189–192.

RULES FOR THE OFFICERS.

The deputy keepers shall be at the prison by sunrise in the morning, and continue on duty until sunset. During the winter season, such of them as shall not have been on duty during the night shall take their breakfast before coming in the morning; they shall so regulate their going to meals as to leave at least three at all times within the walls of the prison, and not absent themselves longer than necessary, at no time to exceed one hour, without the express permission of the principal keeper. There shall, at all times during the day, be at least one deputy keeper within each hall. At sunset, all the doors of the cells shall be securely bolted and locked, at which time the deputy keepers shall be dismissed from duty, except two of their number, who shall remain during the night within the prison, and shall have charge of the keys of the cells, which duty shall be done by all the deputy keepers alternately, under such regulations as they may agree upon, subject to the approval of the principal keeper.

2. The night watch shall be within the prison at 8 o'clock, P. M., and remain until sunrise; they shall patrol each hall as silently as possible at least once in each hour during the night, and shall examine the exterior walls of the cells and main building twice between ten o'clock P. M., and daylight. They shall receive the key of the front door from the deputy keepers, and shall not suffer any person to pass in or out while on duty, save only the members of the keeper's family and persons visiting them, none of whom, except the officers, shall be suffered to enter the centre room. They shall have no intercourse and hold no conversation with the prisoners, farther than is necessary to maintain order.

3. The doorkeeper shall be at the prison at sunrise to receive the key from the night watch, and shall continue on duty until sunset; during which time he shall not absent himself from the prison, without permission from the keeper; it shall be his duty to receive visitors and persons having business at the prison; he shall receive all materials brought to the prison to be manufactured, and take an account of the same in books provided for that purpose, and keep a correct register of the receiving and delivering of said goods, (excepting such as are manufactured for contractors;) he shall not suffer any person to enter the centre hall, excepting official visitors, without permission, and being attended by the keeper or one of his deputies.

4. The deputy keepers and all others passing in and out the cells, must shut and safely fasten the doors of the same.

5. All barter, trade and traffic, with the prisoners is strictly forbid; and no person shall be allowed to furnish them with tools or materials for making fancy, or any other, save only their regular work.

6. The deputy keepers, in their daily examination of the cells, shall see that they are properly cleansed, that no prisoner mutilate or deface the same, and that nothing be put upon the walls that would conceal an attempt to break out.

7. On sabbath, there shall at all times two deputy keepers remain in the prison, and during divine service there shall be three to attend alternately.

8. All rules and regulations heretofore adopted by the board shall be and remain in full force, (except such as are at variance herewith.)

9. The principal keeper is hereby directed to furnish each of the subordinate officers with a copy of these rules and to report any violations of the same that may come to his knowledge, at the next ensuing meeting of the board of inspectors.

10. Nothing in the foregoing rules and regulations shall be so construed as to relieve the officers of the prison from any of the duties imposed on them by law.

FOR VISITORS.

1. That no person will be allowed to visit the prison without the consent of the principal keeper, unless furnished with a permit from one of the keepers of the institution, always excepting the official visitors, who are privileged by law to visit the institution.

2. The hours for visiting shall be as follows; (excepting persons having business with the institution:) from the first day of October to the first day of April, between the hours of nine, A. M., and half past eleven, and from one to four o'clock, P. M.: from the first day of April to the first of October, between the hours of half past eight and half past eleven, A. M., and from one to five o'clock, P. M., excepting Saturday and Sunday, when no person will be admitted unless the occasion be of a business nature with the institution.

RULES TO BE OBSERVED BY PRISONERS.

1. They are to labor faithfully and diligently; to obey all orders promptly, and preserve unbroken silence.

2. They are not to exchange words with each other under any pretence, nor to communicate any intelligence to each other in writing; they are not to exchange looks or laugh with each other, or make use of any signs except such as are necessary to convey their wants to their keepers.

3. They must approach their keepers in the most respectful manner, and be brief in their communications; they are not to speak to them on ordinary topics, nor address them except when it becomes necessary in relation to their work or their wants.

4. They are not at any time or under any pretence (without leave) to speak to any person who does not belong to the institution, nor receive from them anything whatever without permission.

5. They are not to suffer their attention to be taken from their work to look at visitors.

6. No prisoner is wilfully or carelessly to injure his work, tools, wearing apparel, bedding, or anything belonging to the prison; nor will any prisoner be suffered to mark, injure, or in any way deface the walls or any part of his cell; nor will he be suffered to execute his work badly when he has the ability to do it well.

7. No prisoner shall receive or transmit any letter or paper, except under the inspection of the keeper, nor shall any prisoner hold any correspondence in the prison, nor converse with any person except the officers of the prison.

8. Each prisoner shall at all times keep his cell in order and cleanliness, as suited to the character of his work, and have especial care over his bed and bedding.

9. At the ringing of the bell at 9 o'clock, P. M., every prisoner must retire, and a profound silence must be observed from that time until the ringing of the bell in the morning, at which time every prisoner must immediately dress himself and prepare for breakfast.

10. Each bunk must be hung up every morning and kept hung up during the day.

11. Each cell must be swept up every morning.

12. Each cell must be scrubbed at least once every week.

13. No prisoner will be allowed to sleep with his clothes on.

14. Each prisoner must shave himself at least once a week, and particular attention is required to be paid to the cleanliness of his person.

15. If any prisoner becomes sick, or from any cause feels unable to work, he shall report himself to the keeper under whose charge he may be.

16. Any prisoner that defaces the above rules will be promptly punished.[1]

4. PRISON FINANCES, 1836–1843.

The following summary statement of the prison finances during the greater part of the first decade of the Pennsylvania system, indicates the fluctuating condition of prison finances during this period, and demonstrates that the new system of prison administration was scarcely as much of an economic success as had been predicted.

[1] *Annual Report of the State Prison,* January 20, 1854; *Journal of Senate,* 1854; pp. 37–41.

A STATEMENT,

Showing the amount drawn from the Treasury from the 1st October, 1835, to the 1st October, 1843, for salaries of the officers of the New Jersey State Prison, Prison repairs, improvements, appropriations for Heating Apparatus and for prison uses, together with the amount in the Treasurer's Report paid out for Prison Improvements, &c, not on Prison books, and the loss or gain to the State in each year, during the administration of Joseph A. Yard, John Voorhees, and Jacob B. Gaddis, as keepers of the New Jersey State Prison, respectively.[1]

Keeper of the Prison.	in the year.	Amount of Salaries of the Officers, &c, of the N. J. State Prison.	Amount of Prison repairs and Improvements, partly done by convict labor.	Amount of Appropriation for the Heating apparatus.	Amount of Appropriation for Prison uses.	Amount in the Treasurer's Report paid for prison improvements &c. not on the books of the prison.	Total Amount drawn from the Treasury in each year.	Gain in the operations of the prison for each year exclusive of salaries &c.	Loss in the operations of the prison for each year.	Surplus earnings being a revenue to State each year.	Prison loss to the State of New Jersey each year.
Joseph A. Yard	1836	$4333 55					$ 4333 55	$2981 44		$1741 41	$1352 11
do.	1837	4607 29					4607 29	6348 70		1541 74	
do.	1838	6192 49					6192 49	7734 23			
do.	1839	6659 55					6659 55	1075 39			5583 16
John Voorhees	1840	6416 30		$3000 00	$6000 00		12,416 30		$3466 89		15583 19
Jacob B. Gaddis	1841	6782 43	$2502 36		5000 00		17,284 79		1049 76		18334 55
do.	1842	6757 50	1760 98		books 100 00	$607 18	9225 56	4178 22			5047 34
do.	1843	6792 00	361 90				7153 90	2969 80			4184 10
							$ 67,873 43				

Total amount drawn from the Treasury for Prison purposes in the eight years, $ 67,873 43

Of which Joseph A. Yard, drew during his administration of four years,... 21,792 88
    John Vorhees.   " one year, ... 12,416 30
    Jacob B. Gaddis   " three years,.. 33,664 25

Total,...... $ 67,873 43

Sum Total drawn from the Treasury in the four first years $21,792 88
    "   "   "   "   four last years, 46,080 55

Total,.......$21,792 88
    do.   46,080 55

Making a difference between the four first and four last years of $24,287 67

[1] *Report of the Inspectors of the New Jersey State Prison. Minutes of the Votes and Proceedings of the Sixty-eighth General Assembly of the State of New Jersey,* February 9, 1844; p. 408.

5. PRISON FINANCES AND INDUSTRY, 1844.

The following statement of prison accounts for the year 1843–4, is noteworthy as illustrating both the methods of accounting, then in vogue, and the chief industrial operations of the prison at this time. It will be evident that chair-making was the most profitable industry, with cordwaining, or cobbling, second, and weaving, third. These were the chief and almost the only productive industries of the prison in 1844. Complicated industries, requiring the association and the active participation of any considerable number of men, were impossible under the Pennsylvania system of solitary confinement. Therefore, the industries in vogue from 1836 to 1860 were necessarily of that simple type which would allow of being carried on in the individual cells of the prisoners.

A STATEMENT, SHOWING THE OPERATION OF THE NEW JERSEY STATE PRISON, FROM THE 1ST OCTOBER, 1843, TO THE 30TH SEPTEMBER, 1844.[1]

Dr.			*Cr.*
	Dollars Cts		Dollars Cts
Furniture Account.			
To amount of inventory on 1st October, 1843,	8,362 32	By amount of credits since 1st October, 1843 ...	12 55
" amount of charges to 30th September, 1844,	1,616 31	" amount of inventory on 30th September, 1844	8,969 48
		Loss on this account, ...	996 60
	9,978 63		9,978 63

[1] *Votes and Proceedings of the Sixty-ninth General Assembly of the State of New Jersey,* 1845. Pages 250–255.

Dr.   *Cr.*

	Dollars Cts		Dollars Cts

Provision Account.

	Dollars Cts		Dollars Cts
To amount of inventory on 1st October, 1843,	400 96	By amount of credits since 1st October, 1843, ...	235 85
" amount of charges to 30th September, 1844,	4,689 46	" amount of inventory on 30th September, 1844, ...	564 48
		Loss on this account, ...	4,290 09
	5,090 42		5,090 42

Hospital Account.

To amount of inventory on 1st October, 1843,	59 59	By amount of credits since 1st October, 1843, ...	78
" amount of charges to 30th September, 1844,	178 28	" amount of inventory on 30th September, 1844, ...	76 22
		Loss on this account, ...	160 87
	237 87		237 87

Fuel Account.

To amount of inventory on 1st October, 1843,	101 48	By amount of credits since 1st October, 1843, ...	21 67
" amount of charges to 30th September, 1844,	1,647 07	" amount of inventory on 30th September, 1844, ...	237 68
		Loss on this account, ...	1,489 20
	1,748 55		1,748 55

Incidental Account.

To amount of charges during the year, ...	1,056 32	By amount of credits during the year, ...	72 40
		Loss on this account, ...	983 92
	1,056 32		1,056 32

Dr.   Cr.

Dollars Cts   Dollars Cts

Weaving Account.

To amount of inventory on 1st October, 1843, 891 87
" amount of charges to 30th September, 1844, 1,202 54
Gain on this account, ... 2,170 04

By amount of credits since 1st October, 1843, .. 3,385 13
" amount of inventory on 30th September, 1844, ... 879 32

4,264 45   4,264 45

Chair Making Account.

To amount of inventory on 1st October, 1843 6,272 26
" amount of charges to 30th September, 1844, 3,959 83
Gain on this account, ... 5,768 76

By amount of credits since 1st October, 1843, ... 9,075 58
" amount of inventory on 30th September, 1844, ... 6,925 27

16,000 85   16,000 85

Cordwainers' Account.

To amount of inventory on 1st October, 1843, 436 65
" amount of charges to 30th September, 1844, 363 51
Gain on this account, ... 3,817 18

By amount of credits since 1st October, 1843, ... 4,333 54
" amount of inventory on 30th September, 1844, ... 283 80

4,617 34   4,617 34

Sundries Account.

To amount of inventory on 1st October, 1843, 354 05
" amount of charges to 30th September, 1844, 27 91
Gain on this account 869 32

By amount of credits since 1st October, 1843, ... 1,059 93
" amount of inventory on 30th September, 1844, ... 191 35

1,251 28   1,251 28

Dr.   *Cr.*

Dollars Cts   Dollars Cts

Interest Account.

	Dollars Cts		Dollars Cts
To amount of charges to 30th September, 1844,	5 10	By amount of credits since 1st October, 1843, ...	10 13
Gain on this account, ...	5 03		
	10 13		10 13

Recapitulation.

Furniture account, per net loss,	996 60	Weaving account,	
Provision " " "	4,290 09	per net gain,	2,170 04
Hospital " " "	160 87	Chair making " " "	5,768 76
Fuel " " "	1,489 20	Cordwainers' " " "	3,817 18
Incidental " " "	983 92	Sundries " " "	869 32
Gain on the operations of prison for the year ending 30th September, 1844, ...	4,709 65	Interest " " "	5 03
	12,630 33		12,630 33

6. PRISON FINANCES AND INDUSTRY, 1853.

The following financial statement indicates that the industrial operations of the State Prison had not changed in character or in order of importance in the decade following the report of 1844, though the advances in mechanical weaving had, by competition, well-nigh ousted the system of hand-weaving carried on in the cells.

STATEMENT B.

A STATEMENT SHOWING THE OPERATIONS OF THE NEW JERSEY STATE PRISON
FROM 31ST DECEMBER, 1852, TO THE 31ST DECEMBER, 1853.[1]

Dr.   *Cr.*

	Dollars Cts		Dollars Cts

Chair Making Account.

Dr.		Cr.	
To amount of inventory, Dec. 31, 1852,	7,063 73	By amount of credits since Dec. 31, 1852,	18,943 19
" " of charges since that time,	6,380 31	" " of inventory Dec. 31, 1853,	6,163 07
Gain on this account, ...	11,662 22		
	25,106 26		25,106 26

Cordwainers' Account.

Dr.		Cr.	
To amount of charges since Dec. 31, 1852, ..	16,350 59	By amount of sales since Dec. 31, 1852,	21,732 89
Gain on this account, ...	6,200 01	" " of inventory Dec. 31, 1853,	817 71
	22,550 60		22,550 60

Weaving Account.

Dr.		Cr.	
To amount of inventory, Dec. 31, 1852,	1,341 77	By amount of sales since Dec. 31, 1852,	3,755 64
" " of charges since that time	2,698 87	" " of inventory Dec. 31, 1853,	1,138 33
Gain on this account, ...	853 33		
	4,893 97		4,893 97

Sundries Account.

Dr.		Cr.	
To amount of inventory, Dec. 31, 1852,	817 89	By amount of credits since Dec. 31, 1852,	915 01
Gain on this account, ...	416 94	" " of inventory since Dec. 31, 1853, ...	319 82
	1,234 83		1,234 83

[1] *Annual Report of the State Prison for the year* 1853; pp. 8–15.

Dr.   Cr.

	Dollars Cts		Dollars Cts

Furniture Account.

To amount of inventory, Dec. 31, 1852,	8,682 85	By amount of inventory Dec. 31, 1853,	9,412 54
" " of charges since that time	2,553 69	Loss on this account, ...	1,824 00
	11,236 54		11,236 54

Provision Account.

To amount of inventory, Dec. 31, 1852,	964 10	By amount of inventory Dec. 31, 1853,	659 03
" " of charges since that time,	8,809 12	" " of credits since that time, ...	256 57
		Loss on this account, ...	8,857 62
	9,773 22		9,773 22

Fuel Account.

To amount of inventory, Dec. 31, 1852,	929 58	By amount of inventory Dec. 31, 1853,	1,078 60
" " of charges since that time,	2,433 72	Loss on this account, ...	2,284 70
	3,363 30		3,363 30

Incidental Account.

| To amount of charges since Dec. 31, 1852, ... | 1,003 24 | Loss on this account, ... | 1,003 24 |
| | 1,003 24 | | 1,003 24 |

Dr. *Cr.*

	Dollars Cts		Dollars Cts

Discharged Convicts Account.

To amount of charges since Dec. 31, 1852, ...	320 22	Loss on this account, ...	320 22
	320 22		320 22

Overwork Account.

To amount of charges since Dec. 31, 1852, ...	591 54	Loss on this account, ...	591 54
	591 54		591 54

Hospital Account.

To amount of inventory, Dec. 31, 1852,	157 90	By amount of inventory Dec. 31, 1853,	158 56
" " of charges since that time,	413 47	Loss on this account, ...	412 81
	571 37		571 37

Interest Account.

To amount of charges since Dec. 31, 1852, ...	343 74	By amount of credits since Dec. 31, 1852,	209 90
		Loss on this account, ...	133 84
	343 74		343 74

Dr.   Cr.

	Dollars Cts		Dollars Cts
Recapitulation.			
Chair making account gain,	11,662 22	Furniture account, loss, ..	1,824 00
Cordwainers' " "	6,200 01	Provision " "	8,857 62
Weaving " "	853 33	Fuel " "	2,284 70
Sundries " "	416 94	Incidental " "	1,003 24
		Discharged convicts "	320 22
		Overwork account "	591 54
		Hospital " "	412 81
		Interest account "	133 84
		Balance, being amount of gain on the operations of the Prison, for the year ending Dec. 31, 1853, ...	3,704 53
	19,132 50		19,132 50

7. THE FINAL DEFENSE OF THE PENNSYLVANIA SYSTEM IN NEW JERSEY, 1857.

While the Pennsylvania system was freely criticised by individuals throughout its trial in the State of New Jersey, it was not until Governor Price, in 1857, called attention to the obvious economic and administrative failure of that system in New Jersey, that the public authorities of the State took any active part in the campaign against the system of solitary confinement. The following report of the Legislative Committee, appointed to consider the recommendations of the Governor as to a change in the system of prison administration, is of great interest in that it is probably the last serious defense of the system of solitary confinement, which was put forward by the public authorities of New Jersey. While one may not assent to the claims of this Committee relative to the virtues of the Pennsylvania system, one cannot avoid agreeing with the Committee that its failure in New Jersey was quite as much due to the local defects in management as to the general shortcomings of the system, considered as a type of prison administration.

REPORT.

The special committee, to whom was referred that portion of Governor Price's Message relative to Prison discipline, respectfully report:—

That owing to the limited time which has been afforded them, they have not been able to pursue their investigations to that extent which they would have desired, but after a careful examination of the two systems which have been adopted in this country, the congregate or separate, and the silent, they have arrived at the conclusion that the preference in all respects is to be awarded to the former; but while doing so they do not desire to be understood as endorsing that which has been pursued in our own State Institutions, for owing to the parsimonious appropriations of the State which have created the necessity of confining more than one in a cell in consequence of a lack of accommodation, and from other causes which will be hereafter enumerated, the separate system has not been fairly tested, and in fact the only institutions in which it has been carried to perfection in this country, are those of Pennsylvania, where since the year 1829 it has been in operation.

Great objections have been raised against this system, which your committee approved, because as it asserted it is solitary, and glowing pictures have been presented of the fearful effects of non-intercourse of the convict with his fellow man. Nothing however, can be more erroneous than this assertion, for the word separate does not necessarily convey the idea of solitude, for while the prisoners are separate at all times, it is only so far as regards their fellow convicts. In the Penitentiaries previously alluded to, they are visited by the overseers frequently during the day, and whenever the prisoner desires by the warden, the physician, the moral instructor and the schoolmaster; by the inspectors, clergymen of whatever denomination the prisoner may prefer, by the judges of the courts, the sheriffs and commissioners of the counties from which they are sent, by the committee of "the prison society", and any official person who may visit the prison. Thus he has a constant and beneficial intercourse.

If a reform is to be effected in a person who is being punished for violating the laws of God and man, it can only be done by operating on his self-respect, by teaching him that though for a while exiled from the society of those who have not so offended, it is within his power to regain the position which has lost. There are few, indeed, who, when left to the beneficial influences of meditation and reflection, shut out from the gaze and association of those who are more degraded than they, who do not experience regret at their evil course of life. Some do so from a recollection of their parents, their families, and their associations with honest men, and feel that their punishment is merited, regret the crimes which induced it.

If the convict is ignorant, he is taught to read and write; if he has lacked the means by which to gain a livelihood, he is instructed in a trade, so that when he goes out into the world, not only has he every incentive to pursue a virtuous life, which freedom from recognition by his fellow convicts gives, but he has the very means of subsistence placed in his hands by the power which punished him. Thus under this system is the great object of all punishment more fully obtained—reformation.

Says Dr. Given, an intelligent physician formerly connected with the Eastern Penitentiary of Pennsylvania:—

"Would not mature reflection lead us to believe—nay, have not years of experience proved—the entire safety of a system of imprisonment, the principles of which are to protect the young and less culpable offender from the demoralizing influences of association with the hardened and irreclaimable, by confining him to a separate cell; to furnish him with a trade the exercise of which will be sufficient for his support, to show him the temporal as well as eternal advantages of a moral and religious life; to protect him from vulgar curiosity, so that when discharged, qualified and determined to gain an honest livelihood, his best efforts may not be thwarted by the recognition and denunciation of a malicious fellow convict or the thoughtlessness of a visitor to the Institution in which he has been confined."

In the many and great advantages exhibited in this system over the congregate or silent, there are none more important than the facility which is afforded the overseer to become intimately acquainted with the peculiar disposition of the convict, and the opportunity to vary the minor details of discipline, so as more fully to compass the end desired—his reformation.— For it is as absurd to apply the same course of discipline to all convicts, as it would be for a physician to prescribe the same treatment for a number of persons laboring under different species of fevers.

It has been urged against the separate system, that it is prejudicial to health, and yet experience has shown that directly the reverse is the case. In the Pennsylvania penitentiaries, to which your committee refer as the most perfect of their kind, for many years the mortality has never exceeded, and seldom equalled one per cent.; which, when the usually dissipated course of life led by these persons is taken into consideration, is astonishingly low.

The great security which this system presents against escapes and insurrections, is also a great argument in its favor, as against that which is adopted in the Sing Sing, and Auburn, and Massachusetts penitentiaries, from the first of which, escapes are almost weekly, and in all of them insurrections frequent. In the Auburn and Massachusetts prisons two deplorable and unfortunate instances of revolt have lately occurred, which ease of concert among the prisoners greatly facilitated, and which under the separate system would be impossible.

The great defect which exists in the State Prison, is the limited accommodation for the number of convicts, which is continually increasing in a ratio with our population; your committee, therefore, consider that an imperative necessity exists for the erection of a new wing, and the creation of a hospital to which those who are so ill as to require greater and more constant attention than it would be possible to give in a cell, might be removed. This they conceive should receive as early an attention from the State as the condition of its finances will permit. They would also recommend that in the event of such erection, that to each cell upon the ground floor should be attached an enclosed yard of about ten feet by fifteen, in which the prisoners, under such regulations as might be considered proper, should be permitted to exercise.

The greatest evil, however, which your committee considers to exist, is the political character of the Prison and the mutations of government to which it is liable for the frequent changes of party. The great qualification which seems now to be taken into consideration, is the peculiar political tenets of the Keeper, and not the fitness or ability which is requisite for an office in which so much depends upon its executive. While however, the appointing power remains with the legislature, your committee cannot hope for any radical reformation, and they therefore consider that it should be entrusted to the Chancellor and the Judges of the Supreme Court, as being further removed from political influences, and where a discrimination could be exercised, which is impossible in a popular body. The first questions which are now asked when an election occurs, is, to what party does the present incumbent belong? How long has he held office, and how near has the prison been self-supporting? not in what manner has he proved himself competent to fill the position. Under the present system, for at least three months in the year, the attention of the incumbent is bent upon securing his re-election, which cannot but in every way prove detrimental to the interests of the prison.

That the separate is the best system, your committee consider that twenty-eight years of experience in the Pennsylvania prisons has conclusively shown, and a further evidence of its excellence is, that upon an examination by Commissioners, it has been adopted in France, Belgium, and several other European countries.

Your committee cannot conclude their report without expressing the great obligations they are under, to Mr. Halloway, Warden of the Eastern Penitentiary of Pennsylvania and its other officers, as also to the Hon. Richard Vaux, of Philadelphia, who for fifteen years has been one of its Inspectors, for his polite attentions and the valuable information which he imparted to them.[1]

> DANIEL HOLSMAN,
> J. C. THORNTON,
> JOHN P. HARKER,
> *Committee.*

8. THE COLLAPSE OF THE PENNSYLVANIA SYSTEM IN NEW JERSEY.

While the Committee of 1857 had been disposed to defend the Pennsylvania system, that of 1859 was unqualified in its con-

[1] *Minutes of the Votes and Proceedings of the Eighty-first General Assembly of the State of New Jersey*, March 4, 1857; pp. 655–659.

demnation of the system of solitary confinement, and recommended vigorously the appropriation of funds wherewith to establish the Auburn system of congregate work-shops for the daily employment of the prisoners, in accordance with the law of the previous year which legally authorized such action.

REPORT OF THE JOINT COMMITTEE ON STATE PRISON ACCOUNTS, TO WHOM WAS REFERRED THAT PART OF THE GOVERNOR'S MESSAGE RELATING TO THE STATE PRISON.

The Joint Committee on State Prison Accounts, to whom that part of the Governor's Message relating to the Prison was referred, beg leave to report—

That they have carefully considered the condition of the Prison, its capacity for accommodating in proper manner its inmates, and the system of employment now pursued, for the purpose of recommending to the legislature such improvements as, in the judgment of the committee, may seem necessary.

The Prison is now so full that the system of solitary confinement is, in practice, disregarded; many cells having two or more prisoners. The necessity for additional room is imperative, and your committee fully endorse the report of the Inspectors, in reference to this necessity, and would recommend an appropriation of *sixteen thousand dollars* for the purpose of building a new wing or lock-up, similar to the lock-up in the Albany Penitentiary.

The mode of working the prisoners, as at present pursued, is, in the judgment of the committee, detrimental to the interests of the State.

The fact that Pennsylvania and our own State only retain the solitary system, in connection with hard labor, is a strong argument in favor of a change.

The advantages of the work-house system are so obvious, that this committee does not consider it necessary to go into lengthy details.

With a well established system, it is the unanimous opinion of the committee, that the State Prison will afford an income sufficient to sustain itself, and in a few years reimburse the full amount now asked for.

It is stated, that the cost of keeping each prisoner is abouty twenty cents per day; your committee have assurances that contracts can be made for the labor of the prisoners at the rate of forty cents per day.

From this statement it will be perceived, that the committee are justified in recommending the work-house system, for its pecuniary advantages.

All experience proves that the health of the prisoner is materially affected by solitary confinement, and consequently the moral improvement so much desired, is entirely prevented.

Broken down in health, with all the better feelings of manhood crushed out, moral improvement is out of the question.

Your committee therefore unanimously recommend the establishment of a work-house system, and that the sum of *four thousand* dollars be appropriated to build the necessary work-shop.

Your committee also recommend that the Judiciary Committee be instructed to report a bill, giving the necessary legal power to carry this system into effect.

All of which is respectfully submitted.

JOHN R. AYRES,
ABM. EVERITT,
    Committee of Senate.
SAML. A. DOBBINS,
ANDREW McDOWELL,
AMZI CONDIT,
AUSTIN H. PATTERSON,
ISAAC LEIDA,
    Committee of the House of Assembly.[1]

9. THE ESTABLISHMENT OF THE AUBURN SYSTEM OF PRISON ADMINISTRATION IN NEW JERSEY.

While the Auburn system had been rejected in favor of the Pennsylvania system by the State of New Jersey in 1833–6, it ultimately ousted the Pennsylvania system and the Act of March 18, 1858, legally authorized the establishment of congregate work-shops for the industrial administration of the State Prison. These congregate work-shops, together with solitary confinement at night, were the distinguishing marks of the Auburn system, and this law of 1858, therefore, spelled the doom of the Pennsylvania system and marked the date of the legal introduction of the Auburn system of prison administration in the State of New Jersey.

AN ACT making an appropriation to the state prison.

Appropriation to be applied to the payment of debts.

1. BE IT ENACTED *by the Senate and General Assembly of the State of New Jersey,* That the sum of five thousand dollars be paid by the treasurer, out of the treasury, to the keeper of the state prison, to be applied to the payment of the debts now due and unpaid against the aforesaid institution; and also the further sum of five hundred dollars, to be expended under the

[1] *Appendix to the Journal of the Fifteenth Senate of the State of New Jersey,* 1859; pp. 351–353.

direction of the inspectors and keeper in the erection of workshops within the enclosure of the state prison.

Convicts to be employed in workshops.

2. *And be it enacted,* That the keeper of the state prison is hereby authorized from time to time to employ in said workshops, as many of the convicts in said prison as may be deemed expedient for the interests of the institution.

Statement of debts, &c. to be made to legislature.

3. *And be it enacted,* That an accurate and true account of the debts liquidated out of the money above appropriated, stating the amount of such debts respectively, for what purpose contracted, and to whom and when paid, shall be kept by the said keeper, and a true copy thereof annexed to his annual report to the legislature.

4. *And be it enacted,* That this act shall take effect immediately.

Approved March 18, 1858.[1]

III. PRISON REFORM MOVEMENTS FROM 1833 TO 1860.

1. THE NEW JERSEY PRISON INSTRUCTION SOCIETY.

One of the earliest prison reform associations in the State of New Jersey was the *Prison Instruction Society,* organized in 1833. The constitution of this Society, which is printed below, together with a list of the organizers of the Society, is interesting and illuminating as illustrating how the many prison reform movements which flourished at this time were, in a large degree, motivated by theological as well as by humane considerations.

CONSTITUTION OF THE NEW JERSEY PRISON INSTRUCTION SOCIETY.

ARTICLE 1. This Association adopts the name of "THE NEW JERSEY PRISON INSTRUCTION SOCIETY."

ART. 2. The chief object of this society shall be, to extend to the convicts in the Prisons of this state the benefits of the Sabbath school system of instruction, and also to furnish them with preaching.

ART. 3. In connection with the foregoing object, provision shall also be made for inquiring into the relative efficiency of different modes of Prison discipline, and of different methods of instruction.

ART. 4. The officers of the society shall be, a president, a vice-president, a corresponding secretary, a recording secretary, a treasurer, a librarian, and a superintendent of the Sabbath school.

[1] *Acts of the 82nd Legislature,* 1858; p. 453.

ART. 5. The president shall preside at all meetings: it shall be his duty to frequently visit the schools, and to have a general superintendence of the concerns of the society. In his absence the vice-president shall discharge his duties; and in the absence of both, a person selected for the occasion.

ART. 6. The corresponding secretary shall be charged with the execution of the third article of this constitution; the recording secretary with the preservation of the minutes.

ART. 7. The treasurer shall take charge of all moneys which may come into the possession of the society, by donation, or otherwise, and hold them subject to its order.

ART. 8. The librarian shall take charge of the books belonging to the library, subject to the order of the society.

ART. 9. The superintendent of the Sabbath school shall make provision for the due instruction of the school: it shall also be his duty to request clergymen of different denominations to visit the school and preach to the prisoners, whenever, in the opinion of the keeper, it can be done with convenience.

ART. 10. The Society shall meet annually, in Trenton, on the second Saturday of September, at which time the officers shall be chosen for the ensuing year: the society shall also meet on its own adjournments, and at the call of the presiding officer.

ART. 11. Those persons shall be considered members of the society who have become such by the adoption of this constitution, and such other persons as the society may elect.

> JOSEPH A. YARD, of Trenton, *President.*
> ALANSON SCOFIELD, of Princeton, *Vice-Pres.*
> JOHN MACLEAN, of Princeton, *Treasurer.*
> SAMUEL EVANS, *Librarian.*
> JOHN STUART, of Princeton, *Cor. Sec.*
> JOSEPH C. POTTS, of Trenton, *Rec. Sec.*
> JOHN STUART, *Superintendent of Sabbath School.*

Annual Meeting of the Prison Instruction Society in New Jersey, in the State House at Trenton, January 10, 1833.

Pursuant to public notice, the society convened this evening in the State House.

Most of the legislature, and many other persons, were present. At half past seven o'clock, the president, MR. JOSEPH A. YARD, took the chair, and the exercises were commenced with prayer.

The minutes of the last meeting, and the constitution, were read by the recording secretary, MR. JOSEPH C. POTTS.

The corresponding secretary, MR. JOHN STUART, reported on the advantages of the modern system of Prison discipline, as exemplified in other states, compared with that which preceded it, and which now exists in New Jersey.

On motion of STACY G. POTTS, ESQ., seconded by the speaker of the legislative assembly, JOHN P. JACKSON, ESQ., it was

Resolved, That the report of the corresponding secretary be adopted and published.

On motion of L. Q. C. ELMER, ESQ., seconded by Governor SOUTHARD, it was

Resolved, That the moral instruction of convicts forms a very important part of Prison discipline.

On motion of Professor MACLEAN, seconded by MR. J. STUART, it was

Resolved, That, in the opinion of this meeting, it is highly desirable that some provision should be made for affording suitable employment to the convicts discharged from our Prisons.

The addresses by the gentlemen who made and seconded the motions were listened to with great attention, and increased the interest previously felt in the objects of the society.[1]

2. THE RELATION OF ILLITERACY TO CRIME, 1838.

In 1838, Joseph A. Yard, keeper of the State Prison, furnished, at the request of the Legislature, a statement as to the education of the prisoners at that time confined in the institution. In spite of the keeper's somewhat naive attempt directly to correlate illiteracy and criminality, his report is interesting as indicating at least a vague comprehension of education as a prophylactic for crime.

Mr. Mairs presented the following Report from the Keeper of the State Prison:

To the Honorable
the Legislative Council
of the State of New Jersey.

GENTLEMEN,—In compliance with a Resolution, passed January (1837 or 1838,) requiring the Keeper of the New Jersey Penitentiary to furnish a statement of the amount of Education, to that of Crime, as exhibited in the cases and convictions to the New Jersey Prison.

Permit me to state, that of the number of prisoners now in confinement:

12 can read, write, cipher, and have studied grammar and geography.
25 can read, write and cipher.
24 can read and write.
30 can read only.
13 can spell.
18 know the alphabet.
13 do not know the alphabet.

[1] *Eighth Annual Report of the Boston Prison Discipline Society,* 1833; pp. 95–96, 101–102.

Making in all one hundred and thirty-five.
Of the above number fifty-one are blacks:
 9 of them do not know the alphabet.
12 of them do know their letters.
11 of them can spell.
13 of them can read.
 6 of them can read and write.
Of the whole number,
41 were convicted of burglary.
 5 for setting fire to property.
49 " grand larceny.
 6 " attempting to commit a rape.
15 " for atrocious assault and battery.
 2 " forgery.
 4 " manslaughter.
 1 " polygamy.
 1 " sodomy.
 3 " passing counterfeit money.
 1 " for attempting to poison.
 3 " receiving stolen goods.
 1 " turning switch on railroad.
 2 " putting obstructions on railroad.
 1 " bigamy.

The above statement is the result of careful investigation with each convict, which of itself, presents a scene in general, of the darkest ignorance, and as it is a subject intimately connected with a topic now agitating the community, the diffusion of general knowledge among the lower classes, I beg leave to make a few remarks deduced from the above document. That crime is the necessary concomitant of gross ignorance, is a fact which might long be dwelt upon, and admits no proof more striking than the entire want of education prevailing in this and all penitentiary institutions throughout the Union; but this as a first or principal cause I will leave to those worthy philanthropists to comment on, whose hearts never glowed with a holier flame; and endeavor to make a slight exposition of an abstract consequence, which is that when the ignorant mind becomes infatuated with crime, there is but little hope of recovery. Of the twelve men whom I have classed first and may be ranked as tolerably educated, I can say that I have hopes of most of them. The effect of education upon their minds developes itself plainly in their behaviour and general deportment; they are alive to all the sensations of shame and remorse, and deeply lament the prodigalities of the past. They are susceptible of religious impressions, and the fine feelings which it implants in their bosoms, enables them to reason, and draw the contrast between vice and virtue. Education has given them a taste for social happiness, the love of which makes them indignant and restless under shame and disgrace, and although religion should not administer its sanctifying aid, they may be allured from vice by the former. They do not discover that degree of wantonness and cupidity, common to the baser sort, but by an unfortunate chain of circumstances, have been as it were, imperceptibly whirled into the vortex of crime, from whence they would joyously return. To such men we do, and feel bound to, administer our gentlest sympathy, seeing they are susceptible of its impulse by a reciprocity of good behavior. And were a generous community to discover the same, education would prove triumphant, and they would become ornaments to society. Of those whose education, are very slight, reading, writing, &c., it may be observed that they discover a tractability, in proportion to the advantages received; but not having acquired a fondness for reading, their tastes are yet gross and vitiated, and discover but little susceptibility of fine feelings. Religious impressions may be made upon them, and that will be their only antidote. It is the only thing which in their present uncultivated state of mind can produce those reacting influences, shame and remorse. They are men of vigorous minds and bodies, and good natural capacities, and had they been a little further improved, might not only have avoided the road to infamy, but become worthy members of society. From a variety of circumstances their education has been neglected; but principally from the poverty of their parents, who were in many cases intemperate, and suffered their children to roam at large. About twenty out of the one hundred and thirty-five, said their parents were able to educate them. For such we feel the greatest pity, believing that it is in the power of a little wholesome legislation to arrest much of the calamity which awaits the future generation. Although these men of whom I have been speaking, seem to be enveloped in the darkest cloud of ignorance; yet they form a contrast with that class which I am now about to name, the grossly ignorant, which composes the majority of our number. Of these it may be remarked, that they possess a sagacity superior to the beast, and although they may have minds innate, yet it has never developed itself, for the want of education; but it is discoverable that there are grades among them, and these gradations exemplify themselves in proportion to the converse they have had with their superiors, and the families in which they have lived, very plainly showing that education might have had a sanctifying influence upon them. They possess but little susceptibility of any sort, and if they should ever reform, religion must be the cause, for education has not implanted in their bosoms, any charms of moral courage, to combat with the temptations which will daily beset them, and no shame to deter them from the disgrace of detection, and its consequent effects. These facts will, at first view, present to the mind a confutation of an opinion commonly current in our community, that the greater part of men, who get into prison are smart men. If the cunning of the fox, and the sagacity of the horse, may be called smartness, then the supposition is true; but if applied to men of literary acquirements or mental capacity, it is false in nine cases out of ten. The above exhibit, does also prove the strong intimacy existing between vice and ignorance; which should enkindle a holy zeal in every philanthropic bosom to press with renewed energy upon the minds of the community, the all important interests resulting from universal education.

All of which is respectfully submitted.[1]

JOSEPH A. YARD.

[1] *Report of Joseph A. Yard, Keeper of the State Prison,* February 6, 1838, pp. 442–445.

3. THE NEW JERSEY PRISON REFORM ASSOCIATION, 1849 TO 1852.

Of all the prison reform associations that flourished in New Jersey during the period of the existence of the Pennsylvania system in that State, the New Jersey Prison Reform Association was, during its brief period of existence, the most active and included among its members the most distinguished members of the New Jersey clergy, bar, and teaching profession. Its reports, covering a period from 1849 to 1852, are by far the best source of information extant regarding prison conditions in the middle of the 19th century. The constitution of the Society, which is here reprinted, presents the fundamental aims of the association. The New Jersey Prison Reform Association was organized chiefly under the inspiration of Louis Dwight, the energetic Secretary of the Prison Discipline Society of Boston, and the greatest figure in American penal reform during the first half of the 19th century. After Dwight's death, in 1852, the New Jersey Association, like the parent society of Boston, ceased its active and organized existence.

CONSTITUTION OF THE NEW JERSEY PRISON REFORM ASSOCIATION, Adopted at a Meeting held in the City of Trenton, April 19, 1849.

PRISON REFORM ASSOCIATION.

On partial and informal notice, a few friends of Prison Reformation held a meeting at the State House, in the City of Trenton, on the 20th of March, 1849.

CHIEF JUSTICE GREEN was called to the Chair, and TIMOTHY ABBOTT, ESQ., was appointed Secretary.

The objects of the meeting were brought forward and discussed at some length, after which, on motion, it was unanimously resolved that an adjourned meeting should be held on the 17th of April, for the purpose of a State organization, and that notice of such meeting be given in the Trenton newspapers, and through them in such other papers of the State as should be disposed to extend it.

Agreeably to such resolution, the adjourned meeting convened at 10 o'clock, when for want of time was, on motion of Judge Ogden, again adjourned to 7½ on the evening of the 19th.

The meeting was held according to adjournment, when there were present —the Governor of the State, several members of the Bench and Bar, with many citizens from different sections of the State.

Gov. HAINES was called to the Chair, and T. ABBOTT, ESQ., was chosen Secretary.

The following Constitution that had been previously prepared, was presented, and after some amendments, was unanimously adopted, in the form following:

CONSTITUTION.

Article I.

This society shall be called the NEW JERSEY PRISON REFORM ASSOCIATION.

Article II.

The leading essential designs contemplated in the organization are:

First.—The improvement of the prisons and jails of the State.

Secondly.—The physical, moral and religious improvement of prisoners therein, especially the improvement of juvenile offenders, and the provision of more ample and appropriate means than now exist in the State, for their proper punishment and reformation.

Thirdly.—The due encouragement of all such convicts on their discharge, as shall have conducted themselves well during their imprisonment, and who, on professed resolutions of amendment, desire aid in procuring by their labor the means of an honest livelihood, and in regaining the blessings of a reputable character.

Article III.

The Association shall hold its annual meeting in the City of Trenton, on the third Tuesday of January; and special meetings may be called by the President, or through the Secretary, at the request of any two members, at such time and place as may be designated; notice of any such meeting being duly published in not less than three newspapers of the state.

Article IV.

The officers of this Association shall be a President, two Vice-Presidents, a Secretary and Treasurer, whose duties shall be such as are ordinarily indicated by the titles which they respectively bear.

Article V.

Sec. 1.—There shall be a Central Executive Committee of five members, (embracing the principal Keeper and the Moral Instructor of the State Prison,) and an Executive Committee of five members in each county of the State; and through these several Committees, the benevolent designs of the Association shall be pursued.

Sec. 2.—The Central Committee shall have a general supervision over those interests of the State Prison convicts, which are contemplated in the second article of this Constitution. It shall be their duty to encourage and advance in every suitable manner the reformation of the prisoners; to ascertain who of those whose terms of sentence are near their expiration, desire the aid of this Association on their discharge; to recommend and aid such only as they have good grounds of confidence of believing will profit by the aid afforded; and then by information gained through the County Committees, or otherwise, to provide to the extent of their ability, the most suitable labor and the most secure homes for those who, in apparent good faith, accept the guardianship thus provided for their benefit. This Central Committee shall appoint one of its members its Secretary, whose duty it shall be to keep up a correspondence with a similar officer in each one of the County Committees, by way of gaining information, and in general of advancing the objects of the Association.

Sec. 3.—It shall be the duty of each County Executive Committee to visit the prison or prisons of their County, and with the consent of the constituted authorities to whose care by law the prison is committed, to examine all its arrangements, to note its excellencies and defects, to inquire into the mode of treatment and government adopted—whether a proper classification is maintained and with due regard to age and sex—whether especially, an adequate supervision is extended to young prisoners to prevent increased contamination by intercourse with older offenders, and to encourage their reformation—whether workshops or other means of productive labor are provided—and finally, to ascertain the full condition of the prison—what wants and defects exist, and whether they may not by legislative enactments, or by the exertions of voluntary benevolence, or by both combined, be corrected and supplied.

It shall be the further duty of each County Executive Committee to use their influence in behalf of such discharged convicts as on proper recommendations shall desire to be furnished with employment—to commend such convicts to the favorable regards of the benevolent and humane in their respective neighborhoods, so far as it may be proper and necessary to secure them occupation—and by correspondence through a Secretary with the Secretary of the Central Committee, furnish information for the benefit of convicts discharged from the State Penitentiary.

Sec. 4.—Each of these Committees may act independently in their mode of reaching the objects herein expressed, and may adopt their own by-laws and rules of operation. Reports of their proceedings with all the important information they may be able to collect, may be presented at any meeting of the Association; but it shall be their duty to make full reports at each annual meeting.

Article VI.

All the offices and appointments contemplated in this Constitution, shall be first filled at the time of its adoption, and after this all the Officers and Committees shall be elected at the annual meeting. But any vacancy occurring in any Committee before an annual meeting, may be supplied by the other members of such Committee.

Article VII.

Any person, by the payment of *one dollar,* shall become a member of this Association, and shall obligate himself to the payment of a like sum each year during his membership. Any person, by the payment of *ten dollars,* shall become a member for life.

Aricle VIII.

This Consitution may be altered only at an annual meeting of the Association, and by a vote of two-thirds of the members present at such meeting.

The following gentlemen were elected Officers for the ensuing year:
His Excellency, DANIEL HAINES, President.
The Hon. PETER D. VROOM,　　　　⎫
The Hon. JOSEPH C. HORNBLOWER, ⎬Vice Presidents.
REV. SAMUEL STARR, Secretary.　　⎭
TIMOTHY ABBOTT, ESQ., Treasurer.[1]

4. THE NEW JERSEY PRISON REFORM ASSOCIATION ON THE DEFECTS OF THE STATE PRISON.

The following section of the annual report of the New Jersey Prison Reform Association for 1852 is a typical example of the constructive criticism of contemporary penal institutions which was a dominant feature of the work of the Association.

NEW JERSEY PRISON REFORM ASSOCIATION, ANNUAL REPORT, 1852.

REPORT OF THE CENTRAL COMMITTEE.

The Central Committee respectfully report—that during the past year, every facility has been afforded them for performing their duty, in visiting the State Prison, and suggesting improvements in regard to it. We regret to have to report that no measures have yet been taken for the enlargement of the prison; in consequence of which, nearly thirty cells have two prisoners each—thus violating the very principle on which our Penitentiary discipline is based. The communication of prisoners with one another through several adjoining cells, cannot probably be effectually prevented without a change in the construction of the building; but the existence of such means of conversation, known to be a violation of the rules, is a constant source of injury to the convicts and to the discipline of the house.

[1] The only copies of the Reports and Documents of this Association known to the writer are in the Library of the New Jersey Historical Society at Newark, and in the State Library at Trenton.

But that which demands the most immediate attention, is the want of means of warming the southern wing of the building. In the northern wing steam has been substituted for hot water, and the cells are dry and comfortable; but the original method is still continued in the other wing, which gives to each cell no other heat than what is produced by hot water, running through a single iron pipe one and a half inches in diameter, which passes over the width of the cell; and even this heat has to be suspended for several hours every day, when the water is drawn off for the rekindling of the furnaces. The Committee found that the prisoners were not only unable to work during the severe weather of the present winter, but that several of them had been frosted in their hands and feet. The effect of this suffering on the dispositions of the prisoners, as well as in disabling them for their manual occupations may be readily imagined. The Committee earnestly second the recommendation, which they understand that the Inspectors will make to the Legislature, of an addition to, or change of the means of warming the southern wing, as a matter of absolute necessity, which no considerations ought to postpone for another winter.

In all other respects than that just referred to, we have found the condition of the prisoners to be what justice and humanity require—and we trust that strict discipline, united with moral instruction and kind treatment will continue to vindicate our penal system as the most efficient for the ends in view.

We should be glad if any testimony of ours, or of this Association, could have weight in promoting the separation of youthful offenders from the convicts of the State Prison, and placing them in such an institution as has been so appropriately name a "House of Refuge". We feel confident that all that is necessary to bring the Legislature to coincide with these views, is to become acquainted with the practical differences between the two establishments. The *prison* is intended to shut up each convict by himself, where he may neither receive nor communicate moral corruption from companions, and where he may learn to fear a repetition of his crime. But every one knows that these objects are not to be gained in the same way for the adult and the child. The very difference suggested by the terms *youth* and *manhood* implies that neither punishment nor reformation can be planned on the same scale for both. The youth may be both punished and reclaimed by gentler measures than the more hardened adult. Youth is the time for education, for apprenticeship, for moral impressions. These are afforded them in ways appropriate to their time of life, and character and sex, in a house conducted rather as a school or asylum than a place of ultimate punishment, whilst the confinement and discipline are so adapted as to make the inmates sensible that they are offenders. To know all these differences, the Prisons and the Refuges must both be visited; children in our solitary cells must be compared with children in the workshops and schoolrooms of the Refuge. Those who faithfully make this comparison will see, better than can be expressed on paper or by plans, the true wisdom and policy, as well as philanthropy, of a separate establishment and distinct system for juvenile offenders.

The Committee regret that they have nothing of consequence to report upon that important branch of their duties which concerns the rendering of aid to prisoners after their release, in finding industrious employment. In this matter they can do nothing, unless, through the County Committees, or other benevolent persons, they are informed of situations to which they may send such as they can recommend as hopefully reformed, and resolved to pursue an honest life. It surely will not be maintained that every man who has been sentenced to a prison—by nature of the offense, its circumstances, or his connection with it what it may—is, therefore, an utterly hopeless character, and so to be abandoned to a friendless and discarded life ever after. Yet such a abandonment must be the fate of a large number of those who are annually discharged, unless there can be found persons who are willing to confide in the testimony of those who have watched the whole course of a prisoner's conduct, and have some knowledge of his history, character, and capacity. There are so many occupations in which even a convict might be employed without any more risk than attends the employment of strangers who are commonly hired without any questions as to their history or knowledge of their character, that it does not seem to be expecting too much of those who make their business a source of philanthropy, to aid in this effort to give a chance to the released prisoner to recover his standing.[1]

In behalf of the Committee,

J. HALL.

[1] *Annual Report of the New Jersey Prison Reform Association*, 1852; pp. 5–7.

Chapter IV

DOCUMENTS RELATING TO NEW JERSEY'S
EXPERIENCE WITH THE AUBURN SYSTEM
OF PRISON ADMINISTRATION
FROM 1860 TO 1885.

CHAPTER IV

DOCUMENTS RELATING TO NEW JERSEY'S EXPERIENCE WITH
THE AUBURN SYSTEM OF PRISON ADMINISTRATION
FROM 1860 TO 1885.

I. PRISON INDUSTRY 1860 TO 1885.

1. THE INDUSTRIES OF THE STATE PRISON, 1865.

The following financial and industrial statement reveals the
distribution of prison industry and labor in the decade of the
Civil War. When the congregate work-shops were provided for
the State Prison in 1860–61, the practice was adopted of leasing
outright the labor of the prisoners to contractors. Therefore,
whereas in the first days of the original State Prison, nail-making
had been the chief source of income to the Prison, and in the
first years of the Pennsylvania system, chair-making had been the
most productive industry, so now, at the beginning of the Auburn
system, the chief revenue of the prison came from the lease of
the labor of the convicts, who were at this time employed by the
contractors mainly in the making of shoes.

EXHIBITING THE OPERATIONS OF THE INSTITUTION FROM THE 1ST DECEMBER, 1864, TO NOVEMBER 30TH, 1865.[1]

Chair Making.

Dr.			Cr.	
To amount of inventory.	Dolls. Cts.	By amount of credits.		Dolls. Cts.
December 1st, 1864, ...	1,096 54	Since December 1st, 1864,		11,097 73
Charges since that time,..	7,689 68	Inventory Nov. 30, 1865, .		3,774 96
Balance being gain, ...	6,086 47			
	14,872 69			14,872 69

Cordwaining.

Dr.			Cr.	
To amount of inventory,	Dolls. Cts.	By amount of credits.		Dolls. Cts.
Dec. 1st, 1861, ...	415 60	Since December 1st, 1864,		4,251 96
Charges since that time,..	3,182 05	Inventory November 30th,		
Balance being gain, ...	1,259 83	1865, ...		605 52
	4,857 48			4,857 48

Weaving.

Dr.			Cr.	
To amount of inventory,	Dolls. Cts.	By amount of credits.		Dolls. Cts.
December 1st, 1864, ...	729 92	Since December 1st, 1864,		1,831 51
Charges since that time,..	666 70	Inventory November 30th,		
Balance being gain, ...	561 19	1865, ...		124 30
	1,955 81			1,955 81

Sundries Account.

Dr.			Cr.	
To amount of charges.	Dolls. Cts.	By amount of credits.		Dolls. Cts.
Since December, 1864, ..	29 36	Since December 1st, 1864,		1,170 02
Balance being gain, ...	1,140 66			
	1,170 02			1,170 02

[1] *Annual Report of the State Prison*, 1865; pp. 812–815; in Legislative Documents for 1866.

Convict Labor Account.

Dr.			Cr.
To amount of charges.	Dolls. Cts.	By amount of credits.	Dolls. Cts.
Since December 1st, 1864,	10 65	Since December 1st, 1864,	21,372 28
Balance being given, ...	21,361 63		
	21,372 28		21,372 28

Provision.

Dr.			Cr.
To amount of inventory,	Dolls. Cts.	By amount of credits.	Dolls. Cts.
December 1st, 1864, ...	849 25	Since December 1st, 1864,	2,384 86
Charges since that time,..	28,088 31	Inventory Nov. 30th, 1865,	644 10
		Loss on this account, ...	25,908 60
	28,937 56		28,937 56

Overwork.

Dr.			Cr.
To amount of charges.	Dolls. Cts.		Dolls. Cts.
Since December 1st, 1864,	3 45	Loss on this account, ...	3 45
	3 45		3 45

Interest.

Dr.			Cr.
To amount of charges.	Dolls. Cts.		Dolls. Cts.
Since December 1st, 1864,	159 59	Loss on this account, ...	159 59

Furniture.

Dr.			Cr.
To amount of inventory,	Dolls. Cts.	By amount of credits.	Dolls. Cts.
December 1st, 1864, ...	16,579 31	Since December 1st, 1864,	7 28
Charges since that time,..	9,333 12	Inventory Nov. 30th, 1865,	18,853 38
		Loss on this account, ...	7,051 77
	25,912 43		25,912 43

Fuel.

Dr.					Cr.
To amount of charges.	Dolls.	Cts.	To amount of inventory,	Dolls.	Cts.
Since December 1st, 1864,	7,072	60	November 30th, 1865, ...	2,625	60
Inventory Dec. 1st, 1865,	3,034	35	Loss on this account, ...	7,481	95
	10,106	95		10,106	95

Hospital.

Dr.					Cr.
To amount of inventory,	Dolls.	Cts.	By amount of credits.	Dolls.	Cts.
December 1st, 1864, ...	570	84	Since December 1st, 1864,	61	92
Charges since that time			Inventory Nov. 30th, 1865,	746	20
for medicine, food for			Loss on this account, ...	1,967	97
sick, and tobacco, ...	2,205	25			
	2,776	09		2,776	09

Incidental.

Dr.					Cr.
To amount of charges.	Dolls.	Cts.		Dolls.	Cts.
Since December 1st, 1864,	767	08	Loss on this account, ...	767	08

Discharged Convicts.

Dr.					Cr.
To amount of charges.	Dolls.	Cts.		Dolls.	Cts.
Since December 1st, 1864,	546	05	Loss on this account, ...	546	05

Recapitulation of Statement B.

Dr.					Cr.
	Dolls.	Cts.		Dolls.	Cts.
Convict labor, ...	21,361	63	Provision, ...	25,908	60
Chairmaking, ...	6,086	47	Furniture, ...	7,051	77
Sundries, ...	1,140	66	Fuel, ...	7,481	95
Weaving, ...	561	19	Hospital, ...	7,967	97
Cordwaining, ...	1,259	83	Discharged convicts, ...	546	05
Balance being loss, ...	13,476	68	Incidental, ...	767	08
			Interest, ...	159	59
			Overwork, ...	3	45
	43,886	46		43,886	46

2. LABOR AGITATION AND PRISON LABOR IN THE "SEVENTIES."

The period of the "Seventies" is noteworthy in American social and economic history as marking the period of the first extensive development of labor agitation in this country. One of the chief objects for the attack of the labor unions was the system of contracting for the labor of prison inmates. This cheap prison labor was regarded by the labor agitators as a source of unfair competition with free labor. The situation became so pressing that, in 1878, a commission was appointed in the State of New Jersey to report regarding the agitation of labor unions against prison labor. The most important portions of the report of this commission rendered in 1879 are herewith reprinted.

REPORT OF THE COMMISSION ON PRISON LABOR OF THE STATE OF NEW JERSEY, 1879.

REPORT.

To His Excellency the Hon. George B. McClellan, Governor of the State of New Jersey:

SIR—The Legislature of this State, at its last session, adopted the following preamble and resolution, viz:

"WHEREAS, it is asserted and believed by large numbers of the citizens of this State that prison labor, as at present managed in the State Prisons and Pentitentiaries of this and other States, affects injuriously the welfare and means of living of masses of our mechanics and working men, by maintaining an unjust competition with their labor. Therefore,

"Be it Resolved by the Senate and General Assembly of the State of New Jersey, That the Governor be, and is hereby requested to appoint a Commission, to consist of five persons, who shall make a careful inquiry into the subject of prison labor, and whether it comes into competition with free labor, and if so, in what manner, to what extent, and what in their opinion is the best means of preventing such competition, and at the same time providing proper maintenance for the prisoners; that said commission shall receive for their services and necessary expenses such compensation as may be approved by the Governor, and that they shall report to the Governor on or before the meeting of the next session of the Legislature."

The Commission appointed by your Excellency, in pursuance of this resolution, respectfully report that, being deeply sensible of the importance of the inquiry entrusted to them, they have endeavored so far as the limited time allotted to them has permitted, to make it thorough and exhaustive.

32 P

They have carefully examined the labor system of our own State Prison, and those of other States, several of which have been visited by them, while the reports of nearly all have been placed at their disposal; they have obtained by correspondence with wardens or other officers of all the prisons of the United States, statistics and valuable information, which will be found in subsequent pages of this report, or tabulated in its Appendix.

They have also availed themselves of the researches and conclusions of similar Commissions in other States, and invited, personally, by letters and circulars, and through the public press, full and free expressions of opinion as to the difficulties in question, and suggestions as to the means of removing them from all persons who were interested in the subject in any way whatever.

Recognizing with the Legislature the impossibility of dealing with the subject of inquiry with relation to New Jersey alone, they have very gladly joined the Commissions appointed for a similar investigation by the Governor of Connecticut, and the Legislature of Massachusetts, whom they have met at Newport, at New Haven, and finally at New York City, where a number of gentlemen interested in the subject of prison management and reform, and in the trades most deeply affected by prison labor, were present, and gave their views at considerable length.

Among those who participated in the discussion at that time were the venerable Dr. E. C. Wines, the patriarch of prison reform in this country; Dr. Elisha Harris, the agent for discharged convicts of the State of New York; Prof. Francis Wayland, of Yale College, President of the State Prison Association, and Chairman of the Board of State Prison Directors of Connecticut; E. D. Cornell, Esq., President of the National Hat Finishers' Association; George J. Ferry, Esq., of Orange, N. J.; William D. Yocum, Esq., of New York City; Capt. Julius Ellendorf, of South Norwalk, Conn., and John Phillips and Chas. Thetford, Esqrs., of Brooklyn. Mr. Chas. D. Bigelow, President of the Bay State Shoe and Leather Company, and one of the largest, most experienced and successful of the employers of convict labor in the United States, was present also by invitation, and gave the Commissions the results of his experience very fully.

The Commission have also felt it their duty in comparing the workings of the contract and public account systems of prison labor, to visit the New York State Reformatory at Elmira, the most successful example of the latter known to them in this country; to correspond with the warden of the State Prison at Thomaston, Maine, where that system has been carried on for many years, and the master of the House of Correction at East Cambridge, Massachusetts, whose management of the labor of short-term convicts is such a brilliant financial success. Letters from these gentlemen, from John S. Perry, Esq., the veteran head of the great stove establishment of Perry & Co., now employing nearly one thousand convicts at Sing Sing Prison; from Andrew Dickey, Esq., the managing partner at Sing Sing of the same firm, and from leading shoe manufacturers and dealers in our own State, will be found at the close of the report.

After full consultation and discussion, the united Commissions, at their sessions in New York, agreed upon the following propositions:

(1.) The general purpose of incarceration is the protection of society by the punishment of crime; and, in carrying out this purpose, the reformation of the criminal should be kept constantly in view.

(2.) Partisan politics should be absolutely excluded from the management of penal and reformatory institutions.

(3.) The welfare of the State and prisoner both demand that he should be employed in productive labor.

(4.) The right of the State to make its Prisons self-supporting should be conceded, but it should not expect to make a profit out of the labor of the criminals, at the expense of their reformation, or to the injury of its industrial interests.

(5.) The product of convict labor, when compared with that of the entire mechanical industries of the nation, is insignificant, but its concentration upon a very few branches of industry may be seriously injurious to the citizens engaged in those branches.

(6.) The burden of the competition of convict labor should be distributed as widely and equally as possible.

(7.) The injury to any one branch of industry from prison labor may be reduced to very small proportions, by the greatest practicable diversity of employments in prison.

(8.) The proper diversity of employments in the prison should be secured by limiting the number of convicts to be employed in any one industry; such limitation should be adequate to secure the industrial interests of the country from serious injury, and to afford the convict a reasonable certainty of employment upon his release.

(9.) Where the contract system prevails, contracts for convict labor should be so drawn as to give the State absolute control of the discipline of the prisons; and the State should prescribe all rules governing contractors and their employees.

The conclusions the Commission have reached have been fully stated in the course of this report, and may be briefly resumed, as follows:

1. The *character* of convict labor is necessarily PENAL.

Prisoners are consigned to it as a punishment for crime, and the security of society—its very preservation—demands that crime should be punished so severely that the idle and vicious may be, in so far as is possible, deterred from committing it. This one hard fact meets the investigator at the beginning, and can never, for a moment, be lost sight of. The law must not be broken with impunity.

Therefore, prison labor must be HARD. The convict should do all the work he is capable of performing—as much at least as a free man of equal capacity could do, under the same restrictions.

It must be SAFE. There is no use of condemning the culprit to hard labor, unless he can be held securely to its performance. He must not escape from the penalty of his crime until he has finished it, and the nature of his work must have this always in view.

It must be HEALTHY. We have a right to punish by exacting work, and hard work, but we have no right to destroy the capacity for working. The convict should leave the prison in as good or better mental and physical health as when he entered it.

It should be REFORMATORY. The convict in most cases returns to the society he has injured at the close of his imprisonment. If he has merely been prevented from committing crime during his term by taking away his opportunity, without removing his inclination for it, one of the most important and essential of the objects of imprisonment will have been neglected. If his treatment has hardened, degraded or embittered him, the wholesome fear of punishment will have been counterbalanced by the desire for revenge. A hardened, brutalized convict, is a constant menace to society. Life and property are unsafe the moment he is at large. If the first object of prison labor is the prevention—by means of punishment— of crime, the next is the reform of the criminal. His labor should tend to elevate, rather than to degrade him.

He should, therefore, be employed in the higher grades of work, so far as is possible. The man who has learned a useful trade, is far on the way towards becoming a good citizen. The better the trade, the greater his proficiency in it, the easier it will be for him to find employment;—and employment to the discharged convict is the great instrument of his restoration. The man who has broken stones for years in prison, has in those years learned little which will be useful to him when he becomes free. But the firstrate workman in any good trade need very seldom be idle. Prison labor should therefore be MECHANICAL.

Finally: Prison labor must be PRODUCTIVE. To employ a prisoner in unproductive labor is barbarism in itself—a waste of strength and of money, unworthy of civilization. The able-bodied prisoner should earn his own support. He has no right to be kept in idleness, a burden upon honest labor. The commission of crime imposes upon society the obligation to punish the criminal—not to tax itself for the support he could earn. The idea of making a profit out of a convict's labor may be rejected, but the expenses of his trial, guarding and maintenance should be met by his labor as far as possible. The surplus proceeds of it may safely be given him, or applied to his imprisonment.

If he supports himself, it must be by working at something which can profitably be used or sold—in *productive labor.*

2. Prison labor, if productive, COMPETES with free labor, in the same branches, as all production is necessarily competitive. Every convict who makes any salable articles does work that a free laborer might do, and therefore competes with the latter. The duties of the prison, the most menial offices, cooking, washing, making and mending prisoners' clothing, the very sweeping of the floors, might be done by free men and women, and no doubt would be done very gladly by some of them. Convict labor does, then, compete with free labor, and that competition will be injurious whenever the supply of the kind of labor carried on in the prisons exceeds the demand.

3. The EXTENT of the competition of the convicts in the New Jersey prison with the free labor of the State is at present that of one shop of

three hundred and sixty-eight hands, working at one trade, the manufacture of shoes; which employs in the State over six thousand free workmen.

The LIMIT of that competition is the employment in any one trade of, not to exceed six hundred men, the whole available force of the prison, after taking out the sick and disabled, and those employed in the work of the prison.

The GOODS made in the prison are not sold in the State directly.

The AMOUNT of the goods produced in the prison by convict labor is too small, at present, to exert any serious injury upon the trade outside.

The DANGER of convict competition is in the concentration of convict labor in the prisons of the whole, or a greater part, of the country, upon a very few trades, which would be unwise, and should be carefully avoided.

4. The best means of preventing convict labor from becoming injurious to free labor are, first, to employ prisoners in the greatest number of trades than can be carried on advantageously in the prisons, and provide a proper maintenance for them; and, second, to reduce the number of convicts by providing an intermediary prison, or reformatory, where young prisoners, and those convicted of minor offences, could be taught trades, trained to habits of obedience, regularity and sobriety, separated from bad influences, and reformed, if possible.

No State, by itself, can protect its industries against convict or other competition. Trade, commerce and manufactures ignore State lines entirely, and if convicts were employed in manufacturing an article of general use in one State only, the goods thus produced, if better or cheaper than those made by free labor, would very soon find their way to all the other States, and compete with their labor in that branch of industry.

Any distribution of prison labor among the various industries of the country, to be equal, just and efficient, must be made by the joint action of all the States.

The system of contracting the labor of convicts, though liable to abuse, has been so limited and guarded in New Jersey as to prevent most of the evils complained of with regard to it in other States. The prison, the shops, the prisoners, and the contractor and his agents, are subject to the rules and discipline of the prison, no infringement of which is tolerated.

Though open to objection, the Commission agrees with the most intelligent and enlightened critics of the system, with Dr. Wines and Dr. Harris and Prof. Wayland, that so long as prisons are managed and controlled in the interest of partisan politics, its abolition would increase the prison expenses, demoralize and corrupt the prison officers, and bring no substantial benefit to the free workman.

The complaint that, under prison contracts, the convict learns no trade, or only a part of a trade, is not true in fact. The prisoners learn exactly the same parts of trades which are learned and practiced outside, and the sub-division and confinement to single branches of any trade, are carried out quite as thoroughly in the great factories as in the prisons.

Such are the conclusions of the Commission. It is not pleasant for its members, in closing their labors, to be obliged to state that in all the researches they have been able to make, for themselves, or which have been made by others, and laid before them; with all the aid they have received from manufacturers and employers of labor, from workingmen and trades-unions, represented by their ablest and most intelligent leaders; with all the light the most earnest and faithful of prison reformers and managers could give, they are now, as at first, confronted with the fact that the one remedy which might remove the ugly element of convict competition entirely, if it could once be fairly and equitably put in operation, is beyond the power of the State of New Jersey. What the Federal Government could do perfectly by a single enactment, had the States thought proper to relegate to it the necessary powers, is an impossibility for the strongest of them all, standing alone.

New Jersey can provide for the division of her prison labor among several industries, thus preventing, so far as in her lies, the extension of the evil; she can provide a reformatory for those of her convicts who are not hopelessly wedded to evil; she can put a stop to much of the terrible instruction and training to crime which goes on in her jails—the hotbeds of vice and immorality and debauchery; she can extend the powers and the sphere of her noble Reform School; but she cannot protect her free industries from the competition of the convicts of New York, and Massachusetts, and Maryland, and other States.

The evils, for the redress of which the Commission was created, are at this time, in its opinion, more imaginary than real. They have grown out of a financial and industrial depression almost without a parallel, and which is now happily passing away, and taking with it the injurious effects of overproduction and overtrading, which, rather than the labor of convicts, or the selection or manner of their employment, have distressed and burdened our laboring and manufacturing classes. Business is now reviving. The leading shoe-manufacturers in New Jersey are extending their business and advertising for hands to carry it on. And much of the agitation of the question in the past has sprung from the ignorant and interested efforts of demagogues, who have taken advantage of the general distress and depression to exalt their own importance and further their own selfish ends.

Such being the facts, the Commission believe that, to prevent possible interference in the future between free and convict labor, and to reduce to a minimum every just cause of complaint from honest industry, it is only necessary for them to recommend the following, rather as preventives of future evil, than as remedies for the present:

First. That the Supervisor and Inspectors be instructed to employ the convicts in the State Prison in as many different industries as the facilities at their disposal, and a due regard for the proper maintenance and support of the prison and prisoners, will admit.

Second. To enable this to be done, and for the urgent needs of the State Prison in other respects, hereinbefore mentioned, that the present State Arsenal and the grounds pertaining to it, be added to the prison and fitted for its uses.

Third. That in order to prevent the labor of the convicts in our State Prison from becoming injurious to free labor in future periods of depression—for it is only in periods of financial and industrial depression that the competitive labor of convicts can be injurious, or sensibly felt—the Legislature should empower the Governor to confer with the Executives of the other States, proposing the appointment of a Commission, to consist of two or more members from each State, to devise a plan by which the convict labor of all the States may be so distributed and employed among the various productive industries as to be just and fair to each one; and that the Governor be also empowered to appoint Commissioners to represent the State in such Commissions whenever the proposal shall have been accepted by a majority of the States in which convict labor is an important competing element.

Fourth. That the Legislature provide for the establishment of an *Intermediary Prison,* where convicts between the ages of sixteen and thirty years, sentenced to imprisonment for the first time, may be kept separate from old and hardened offenders, trained to useful occupations and regular habits, and, so far as possible, reformed.

Thus, your Excellency, the Commission have endeavored to discharge the responsible duty you have committed to them. Thanking you for the confidence you have reposed in them and for the countenance and assistance you have given them in their labors, they respectfully submit this report, with the testimony and statistics appended to it, for your consideration.[1]

EDWARD BETTLE,
W. R. MURPHY,
A. S. MEYRICK,
SAMUEL ALLINSON,
SANFORD B. HUNT.

3. THE DIVERSIFICATION OF PRISON LABOR IN NEW JERSEY.

An unmistakable outcome of the report of the commission on prison labor of 1879 was the law of March 25, 1881, which decreed that not more than one hundred prisoners could be leased to any contractor in any one branch of industry.

A Further Supplement to an act entitled "An act for the government and regulation of the state prison," approved April twenty-first, one thousand eight hundred and seventy-six.

1. BE IT ENACTED *by the Senate and General Assembly of* Section *the State of New Jersey,* That section four of an act entitled amended "An act for the government and regulation of the state prison," approved April twenty-first, one thousand eight hundred and

---

[1] *Report of the Commission on Prison Labor of the State of New Jersey,* 1879, in Document No. 37 of Legislative Documents, 1880; pp. 3–6; 44–50.

seventy-six, and which section, as amended by a supplement
approved March fourteenth, one thousand eight hundred and
seventy-eight, be amended as follows:

Proviso.
Provided, further, that nothing in section four shall be
deemed, taken or construed to authorize said supervisor or
board of inspectors, to contract with any person or corporation
to hire or contract out the labor of the prisoners, or any part
of them, exceeding one hundred persons in number, at any
time, in the prosecution or conduct of any special branch of
industry, trade or business or making or manufacturing goods,
wares or merchandise of any kind whatsoever.

2. *And be it enacted,* That this act shall take effect immediately.

Approved March 25, 1881.[1]

4. THE ABOLITION OF THE "LEASE" FORM OF THE CONTRACT SYSTEM OF PRISON LABOR, AND THE INTRODUCTION OF THE "PIECE-PRICE" SYSTEM.

It is evident that the law of 1881, ordering the diversification
of prison industries, did not conciliate the labor organizations.
To meet their continued agitation, the Legislature on February
21, 1884, passed an act abolishing contract labor in the State
Prison, as well as in all the other penal and correctional institutions of the State. However, by the Act of April 18, 1884, the
Legislature allowed the continuance of the contract system under
the subterfuge of the "piece-price" system.

An Act to abolish and prohibit the employment under contract of convicts and inmates of prisons, jails, penitentiaries and all public reformatory institutions in the state
of New Jersey.

Unlawful to
contract for
labor of
prisoners in
state prison.
1. BE IT ENACTED *by the Senate and General Assembly of
the State of New Jersey,* That it shall be unlawful for the
principal keeper, supervisor and board of inspectors of the
state prison of this state, in anywise to contract for the labor
of the prisoners confined in said prison or for any portion
thereof.

[1] *Acts of the One Hundred and Fifth Legislature of the State of New Jersey,* 1881;
pp. 230–231.

2. *And be it further enacted,* That it shall be unlawful for any keeper, warden, superintendent or other official, or member of any governing body or board of any prison, penitentiary, jail or public reformatory institution located within this state, in anywise to contract for the labor of the inmates of any such prison, penitentiary, jail or public reformatory institution.

3. *And be it further enacted,* That any principal or other keeper, supervisor, inspector, warden, superintendent or other officer, or any member of any governing body or board as aforesaid, who shall violate any of the provisions of the two preceding sections of this act, shall be deemed guilty of a misdemeanor, and on conviction thereof, shall be punished by a fine not exceeding two thousand dollars, or by imprisonment, at hard labor, in the state prison not exceeding two years, or both.

4. *And be it further enacted,* That all acts and parts of acts, whether general or special, inconsistent with the provisions of this act, be and the same are hereby repealed.

5. *And be it further enacted,* That this act shall be a public act, and shall take effect immediately.

Approved February 21, 1884.[1]

An Act to provide for the employment of the inmates of any prison, penitentiary, jail or public reformatory institution located within this state.

1. BE IT ENACTED *by the Senate and General Assembly of the State of New Jersey,* That the prisoners or persons confined or kept in any prison, penitentiary, jail or public reformatory institution located within this state, shall, so far as practicable in the judgment of the managers of such prison, penitentiary, jail or public reformatory institution, be employed in the manufacture or at work upon goods used in such institutions as are under state control, and all prisoners or persons not employed for said purpose shall be employed on what is commonly known as the "piece price plan", as the managing authorities of such prison, penitentiary, jail or public reformatory institution may be able to arrange for with parties desiring such labor, or they shall be employed under what is known as the "public account system"; and the revenue derived from any such employment in the state prison or any public reformatory institution shall be paid into the treasury of the state; and if derived from any penitentiary or jail in any county in this state, it shall be paid to the county collector of such county.

Marginal notes:

Unlawful to contract for labor of inmates of any prison, penitentiary, jail or public reformatory institution in this state. Penalty for violating the provisions of the two preceding sections.

Repealer.

Managers authorized to enable prisoners in the manufacture of goods used in state institutions.

Revenue to whom paid.

[1] *Acts of the One Hundred and Eighth Legislature of the State of New Jersey,* 1884; pp. 21–22.

Managers
authorized to
purchase tools,
stock, &c.

2. *And be it enacted,* That the authorities managing the state prison or any reformatory institution shall, with the assent of the governor, purchase any tools, machinery or stock necessary to carry out the provisions of this act, and the money necessary therefor shall be paid by the treasurer upon a warrant of the comptroller; and the authorities of any penitentiary or jail may, with the assent of the board of chosen freeholders of the county, purchase any tools, machinery or stock necessary to carry out the provisions of this act, and the county collector shall pay the expenses thereof by resolution of the board of chosen freeholders.

Authorities to
advertise bids
for labor of
prisoners or
sale of goods
manufactured.

3. *And be it enacted,* That the authorities of any prison, penitentiary, jail or public reformatory institution, before they shall make any agreement with any party or parties for the labor of the prisoners, or persons in their charge under the "piece price system", or before they shall dispose of any goods made in their institution under the "public account system", shall advertise in not less than four of the principal newspapers of the state for the space of three weeks once a week calling for public bids, so that there shall be a proper and just competition either for the labor of the prisoners or persons confined in such institutions or for the sale of goods; this advertising may be done before or after the goods are completed, and every effort shall be made to obtain current market prices for the same.

Act not to
be construed
to abridge
powers of
chosen free-
holders, &c.

4. *And be it enacted,* That nothing in this act contained shall be construed to in any way abridge the powers of any board of chosen freeholders in any county in this state to employ any persons confined in any penitentiary or jail in said county in any other capacity they may deem wise, except under the "contract system" now in use in the state prison, and the authorities of any reformatory institution are also authorized to apprentice any of the minors in their institution.

Parties em-
ploying pris-
oners may
place instruc-
tors.

5. *And be it enacted,* That any party or parties who may employ any portion of the prisoners or persons within the limit prescribed by law, shall have power to place one or more instructors, if necessary, in any prison, penitentiary, jail or public reformatory institution of the state, where their work is being done, the expenses or salary of said instructor or instructors to be paid by the party or parties so employing them; or if the work is done under the "public account system," that such instructor or instructors shall be paid by the state; such instructors shall in no wise interfere with the discipline or management of the prisoners, and shall be while so employed in the prison subject to all the rules and regulations made by its officers for its government.

6. *And be it enacted.* That all acts or parts of acts incon- Proviso.
sistent with the provisions of this act be and the same are
hereby repealed; *provided, however,* that no such prisoners Repealer.
or persons shall be employed at any trade where such employment is now prohibited by law; *and provided, further,* that Proviso.
no greater number of persons shall be employed in any business or occupation than is now provided by law.

7. *And be it enacted,* That this act shall be deemed and construed a public act, and shall take effect immediately.

Approved April 18, 1884.[1]

II. Prison Administration and Prison Reform, 1860–1885.

1. THE INTRODUCTION OF COMMUTATION OF SENTENCE FOR GOOD BEHAVIOR.

By the Act of April 14, 1868, the first system of commutation for good behavior was introduced into the administration
of the State Prison. While this provision was re-enacted in
the laws of 1869–1876, it never accomplished the end for which
it was intended, namely, the stimulation of efforts at self-improvement on the part of the prisoners. The commission on the
prison system of New Jersey, in 1878, found that the law had
never been faithfully carried into execution, it being the habit
automatically to advance to the prisoner the maximum amount
of good time allowed by law for perfect deportment, except in
cases of notorious incorrigibility.

A Supplement to the Act entitled "An Act for the governement and regulation of the state prison." Approved April 14, 1868.

WHEREAS, it is desirable to promote the permanent reformation of the convicts in the state prison by incitement to industry, good behavior and
self-improvement; therefore,

23. Sec. 1. From and after the passage of this act it shall be the duty
of the inspectors of the state prison to assign to one or more officers thereof
the keeping of a correct daily record of the conduct of each prisoner and

---

[1] *Acts of the One Hundred and Eighth Legislature of the State of New Jersey,* 1884;
pp. 230–232.

of his labor, whether satisfactory or otherwise, and it shall be the duty of the keeper to see that the said record is regularly made and preserved under his care.

24. Sec. 2. It shall be the duty of the said inspectors to make reports three times in each year from the said record of the conduct and labor of each prisoner; and said inspectors are hereby required to make and deliver a copy of the said reports to the secretary of state, on the Tuesday immediately previous to the meeting of the court of pardons, to be submitted to said court on the first day of their regular meeting, and afterwards filed in the office of said court.

25. Sec. 3. For every month of faithful performance of assigned labor by any convict, as shown by the said record, there may be remitted to him by the said court of pardons two days of the term for which he was sentenced; and for every month of continuous orderly deportment, two days; and for manifest effort at intellectual improvement and self-control, one day.[1]

2. POLITICS IN PRISON ADMINISTRATION IN THE PERIOD OF THE CIVIL WAR.

In 1868 a joint committee from the Legislature was appointed to investigate the admitted defects in the management of the State Prison. The report of this committee is one of the most telling arraignments of the demoralizing influence of political appointments upon the effective administration of public institutions, which exists in the public documents of the State of New Jersey.

REPORT OF THE JOINT COMMITTEE OF THE SENATE AND GENERAL ASSEMBLY, TO INQUIRE INTO THE MANAGEMENT OF THE NEW JERSEY STATE PRISON FOR THE YEAR 1867, APPOINTED BY CONCURRENT RESOLUTION PASSED MARCH, 1868.

REPORT.

The Joint Commitee of the Senate and House of Assembly, appointed under a concurrent resolution of the last Legislature, passed March, 1868, as follows, viz:

"Resolved, (Senate concurring), That a committee of three members on the part of the House and two from the Senate be appointed to inquire

---

[1] Acts of the 92d Legislature, 1868; pp. 981–982.

into and examine the management of the State Prison for the past year, and that said committee have power to send for persons and papers", beg leave to report—

That in pursuance of their appointment, they met in the City of Trenton to investigate certain claims preferred against the Keeper and Inspectors of the State Prison by a shoe manufacturer then working under articles of agreement with the Governor and Inspectors, and employing the convict labor of said prison in accordance with his contract. He claimed damages in the sum of ten thousand dollars ($10,000), for alleged losses sustained during the term of said contract, basing his claim upon certain allegations, prominent among which was the want of proper discipline, whereby the work was imperfectly performed, the hours of labor not properly adhered to and enforced, &c., &c. The Committee having power to send for persons and papers, in accordance with the terms of the resolution which created it, proceeded to take sworn testimony, and also documentary evidence bearing upon the case. After a laborious and thorough investigation, they were unanimously of the opinion that there exists no just ground for said claim for damages as preferred by the said claimant, he having failed to establish his case to the satisfaction of the committee. They therefore dismissed the complaint as unjust, and not warranted by the facts brought before them.

During the whole pendency of this investigation, your Committee was deeply and sensibly impressed with the necessity of a thorough and radical reform in our present system of Prison discipline. They are convinced that the most important aim and object of all penal discipline and restraint, the reformation of the offender, and his restoration to society as a useful member thereof, instead of a spoiler and a curse, is practically defeated by the fundamental and radical defects inherent to the vicious system that governs and controls our Prison organization. We allude more particularly to the evils consequent upon the intimate connection of the present system with the varying ascendency of political parties. We believe no intelligent man will deny that the evils, admitted and deplored by all, which underlie and vitiate our Prison management, are but the natural and legitimate outgrowth and consequence of that dangerous and fatal connection and control. Claiming the appointment of the Keeper and chief executive officers as the proper right and inheritance of that political party which the varying passions of the hour have placed in a temporary ascendency, the selection of those officers upon whose vigilance, fidelity and moral fitness the whole welfare of the institutions so largely depends, is but the expression of some real or fancied political necessity, the reward of some mere partisan, whose only merit may be a numerous grog-shop acquaintance, or a peculiar dexterity in the manipulation of fraudulent repeaters.

And as with the chief, so is it with the subordinates. The men who have the daily oversight and control of the Prison, whose influence, whether for evil or for good, is so constant, so direct and so powerful in its every-day economy and government, are, too often, the mere annual waifs thrown up by the changing sea of political excitement, without fitness, and careless or ignorant of any moral responsibility. Now, we do not wish to be misunderstood. Your Committee, composed of members of each political organization, distinctly and emphatically deny any personality of allusion, or any animadversion upon the appointees of any political party, now or in the past.

We make no such allusion—no such charge. We charge it upon the vicious *system* that has so long controlled our whole Prison organization, and upon which it is, in fact, founded. Its vices and defects are radical and inherent, and in a radical and fundamental change alone can there, in our judgment, by either hope or expectation of reform.

Nor in our State alone has this unwise alliance with politics wrought out and insured its disastrous consequences. In the State of New York, and elsewhere, its evils have long been felt and deplored. In the annual report of the Prison Association of New York, an institution chartered by the State, with ample powers, constant reference is had to the baneful influence of party politics upon the whole system of penal administration and reform, and long and strenuous have been the efforts to accomplish a complete and thorough divorce.

Alluding to the great mass of testimony adduced before its Committee, regarding the effects of this great evil upon the good administration and reformatory power of the New York State and County Prisons, the report holds the following language:—"If this evidence as summed up by the Commissioners, and spread, *in extenso,* before the public, does not cause this abomination, for it can be regarded as nothing less, to totter to its fall, it will be either because no credit is given to the testimony and opinion of men most competent from long experience and observation to form a correct judgment as to their operation and effect, or because the community will not read what is published on the subject, however weighty and startling it may be, or because the people are indifferent to the gravest abuses in one of the most important departments of the public administration." Nor have these efforts at reform been unavailing. In many of the New York prisons partisan politics are wholly ignored, and exercise no control in the appointment of either Inspectors, Wardens or Deputies. In the Erie County Penitentiary, containing an annual average of about 300 convicts, since the year 1863 political considerations have entered but little into the appointments. From even that incomplete emancipation the best results have followed, and, in the language of the report, it may now be classed among "the best penal institutions in the country." In the Monroe County Prison, near Rochester, with an average of 217 convicts, there is a complete freedom from political intermeddling. In the Albany Penitentiary, General Pillsbury, the present incumbent, has held the position of warden for 23 years continuously. When he assumed its duties, it was upon the distinct understanding that politics should be excluded from any influence upon the prison management and government. And the understanding has, to quote the words of the report, "been faithfully observed ever since by all the parties to it." As a proof, it may be stated that the majority of the appointing board has been about half the time of one political party, and half the time of the other; and yet Mr. Pillsbury has been eight times chosen to the office of Superintendent by a *unanimous vote.* In appointing his subordinates, the Superintendent never inquires into the party creed of any one who applies for a position in the prison, and, of course, he never removes an officer on any such grounds. He knows nothing of politics in the administration of the penitentiary. There are officers under him who have served eight, ten and twelve years; and he always retains a good officer just as long as he is willing to stay. He avows that, without being a politician, he has his own political views, that he holds them firmly and acts upon them conscientiously in the sphere to which they belong, but he declares that as a prison officer he ignores the whole thing. He attributes the success of the institution, in a great measure, to his utter repudiation of party politics from its government and administration, and believes that its history would have been very different had this influence, healthy and beneficient when confined to its proper sphere, but always pestilent and often disastrous when it reaches beyond that sphere, been permitted to obtain a controlling power over its affairs. This penitentiary is a model institution, and the great and marked success attending its administration is largely owing to the above causes. One remarkable fact may be stated here. The prison is weak and has no walls, yet with an average of more than 500 convicts, there have been but two or three attempts at escape in the whole history of the institution. There has never been an escape from the *inside:* the few instances above alluded to being from prisoners engaged on outside work.

Another serious evil resulting from partisan control, as exemplified in our present system, is the want of permanence in the appointments. It is almost impossible, as now chosen, that officers can be had possessing the proper and necessary qualifications. The changes are so constant and the tenure of office so precarious that the best men will not suffer themselves to be candidates; and even though they may haply possess the requisite ability, they will lack the necessary experience to render that ability useful and availing. Indeed, the evil effects of the shortness and insecurity of the tenure by which our prison officials hold their position, extend through every grade and class.

When the verdict of the November elections has been adverse to that political party to which they owe their appointment, the necessity of some other provision for the future becomes the immediate and constant care of each official. With their attention so naturally and inevitably engrossed by their own personal interests in the near event of their removal, the vigilance and sense of moral responsibility so indispensable to proper discipline become of but secondary consideration and importance. Nor does the evil end here. The convicts themselves, aware of the coming change, become more difficult to manage, are more prone to acts of insubordination, more eager in determined efforts to escape, and the discipline, as an unavoidable consequence, becomes relaxed, demoralized and inefficient. Nor is the lowest depth of this thoroughly faulty system yet sounded. The new officers are confronted with the low *morale* of the institution, adding materially to the difficulties attendant upon their want of experience and the grave responsibilities of the management and moral control of more than five hundred convicts.

The question can be asked, and with great force and pertinence, why the beneficial effects that attach to the permanency of appointments in the control of the State *Lunatic Asylum* should be deemed as of slight account, or wholly disregarded in the management of the *State Prison?* Or, what would be thought of that Board of Directors who should insist upon a strict accordance with their own political views as the one essential requisite in the qualifications of a bank president, in all other respects incompetent, and, who, perchance, could with difficulty define the difference between a dividend and a discount, a coupon or a clearing-house? Good behavior, and the possession of his faculties in a tolerable state of preservation, as a general rule, alone limit the permanence and continuance in office of the Superintendent and President of a lunatic asylum or a bank.

Now, if ability and experience are deemed virtues to be cherished, how much more are they to be prized in those who have to deal with the souls of sinful men, than in the more profitable investment of money, or even in the care of those unfortunates to whom God has, in His inscrutable wisdom, denied the gift of a sound reason, and from whom He, in His mercy, exacts no responsibility.

Indeed, the whole system seems to be an unalloyed *purity of evil.* We think it may be set down in all truth and soberness as an undeniable axiom, that politics and prisons are totally incompatible with each other. Whether regard is had to the great end of all prison discipline, the moral training and reformation of the convict, or to mere pecuniary considerations, the appointment to office of Inspectors, Keeper and subordinates, upon merely partisan grounds, and as a source of patronage to a dominant political party, will always and inevitably end in disappointment and disaster.

It is but maintaining a simple proposition to assert, that if these institutions are ever to become reformatory and self-sustaining, the management of our prisons, both as regards the welfare of society and the convict, *must* be trusted to men who have the aptitude and ability for that peculiar trust, who are conscientiously alive to the moral and religious responsibilities of their position, who are to be chosen without reference to their political opinions, and who are to be placed on the firm basis of an assured permanence, above the mutations of party.

Another matter of vital importance, in the judgment of your Committee, and to which they would respectfully invite the attention of the Legislature, is the limited power of the Inspectors. As now appointed, and as their duties are now construed, they are little more than mere clerks invested with some responsibility, but without the corresponding power to meet that responsibility. Over the heavy expenditure necessary for the proper maintenance of so large an institution they have almost no control. In many other prisons and almshouses in New York, Pennsylvania, and elsewhere, the disbursements of money for provisions, coal and other supplies, are under the direct control of the Board of Inspectors. We believe that the awarding of the various contracts necessary for the maintenance of the Prison to the lowest bidder, in fair competition, upon previous public notice by the Board, would remove a fruitful source of complaint, would insure a better performance at less pecuniary cost to the State, and would also enable the Keeper to divide his time and attention more thoroughly and systematically to that close, daily, vigilant oversight and care of the institution which is his peculiar sphere and duty and upon whose faithful discharge its successful operation so greatly depends. Under the present system the Inspectors' power and duties begin and end in the merely clerical office of seeing that the bills, incurred without their knowledge or assent, are properly receipted and correctly added up.

Your Committee would also call attention to the crowded condition of the prison. The want of proper cell accommodations and the enforced and inevitable herding of the convicts incident to that condition must and will prove destructive to proper reform and discipline. Men harden and grow worse by evil companionship, and young offenders, undergoing the penalty of a comparatively slight offense, become, by the very means intended for their reformation and restoration, the pupils and victims of men grown gray in every crime of the decalogue.

The necessity for prompt action is urgent, and your Committee would specially commend the consideration of increased accommodations, either by a new Prison or by enlargement of the present institution, to the serious and early attention of this Legislature.

Your Committee are aware that to insure that complete isolation and divorce from politics which is absolutely essential, in their judgment, to any practical scheme of reform, the cordial and thorough co-operation of both parties is demanded and must be accorded. The Constitution determines the mode and form of the appointment of Keeper and Inspectors. They are to be nominated and voted for by the Legislature, in joint meeting assembled. If that domination be made by the Legislature, it can hardly be hoped or expected that there can be a freedom from partisan bias, or that the usual caucus influence will fail, as they never yet have done, to exert a powerful control, and to lay their imperative obligations upon members. If, by common consent, the selection of the Keeper and five Inspectors was entrusted to the Supreme Court, with the distinct understanding that ability, aptitude for the task, and moral qualifications alone should be the governing requisites, to the total exclusion of political partisanship as an element of consideration, who can doubt we should have made most essential progress in that reformation of our present system which can alone make it subserve the true ends of a wise and Christian penal administration.

Such a selection would in no wise clash with the provisions and letter of the Constitution. The choice of the Supreme Court would supersede that of the caucus, and the Keeper and Inspectors so selected and nominated could then be voted for by joint ballot as at present.

If it were also understood that, while in compliance with the requirements of the Constitution, the election of those officers must be annually made, as

33 P

in the case of a sheriff, yet, except in the event of death, resignation, removal, neglect, incapacity or malfeasance, their term of office should be permanent, and last through good behavior or for a specified term of years, then, in the opinion of your Committee, the second and almost equally indispensable requisite in the successful management of the State Prison has been secured.

That a reformation of our present system, somewhat in the manner indicated, will commend itself to every intelligent mind, we cannot permit ourselves to doubt; nor does there exist any insupportable obstacle in its accomplishment.

All that is needed is the earnest co-operation of the good men and true of both parties, who prefer that the penal system of our noble State shall take its stand upon the true basis of an advanced and enlightened Christian sentiment, rather than that the pernicious and demoralizing effect of mere political partisanship shall longer be permitted to mar and dwarf its fair proportions, and make that a reproach and a failure which should be among the proudest monuments of our age and civilization.

Should legislation be needed to give a legal and permanent embodiment to these or other suggestions of a kindred nature, we would respectfully ask that a proper Committee of both Houses be appointed to draft such a bill as may most efficaciously carry out the desired end.

Your Committee would ask to be discharged from any further duty under the resolution creating it.[1]

> JOHN H. ANDERSON,
> EDWARD BETTLE,
>   Committee of Senate.
> JOHN H. WHELAN,
> BALTES PICKEL,
> JAMES PECK,
>   Committee of House of Assembly.

3. THE REPORT OF THE FAMOUS COMMISSION ON PRISON DISCIPLINE OF 1869.

By a joint resolution of April 9, 1868, three commissioners were appointed to examine the various systems of prison administration in the United States and suggest improvements in the New Jersey system. The report of these commissioners, submitted on January 22, 1869, is altogether the most important single document which has yet appeared in the history of prison reform in the State of New Jersey. It is, at the same time, both

[1] *Legislative Documents*, 1869; pp. 319–327.

an excellent commentary on prison administration in the United States at the close of the Civil War and a crushing indictment of the glaring weaknesses of the prison system in New Jersey after the first decade of its experience with the Auburn system. Most important perhaps of all phases of this extremely significant document were the recommendations submitted by the commissioners as to the improvement of the penal system of New Jersey. From that time to the present, no reform commission or committee in the State has done much more than to reiterate the chief recommendations of this commission of 1869. Ex-Governor Daniel Haines, the chairman of the commissioners, attained such a general reputation by this report that he was invited to be a prominent participator in the great Cincinnati Prison Congress of 1870.

REPORT OF THE COMMISSIONERS TO EXAMINE THE VARIOUS SYSTEMS OF PRISON DISCIPLINE, AND PROPOSE AN IMPROVED PLAN, APPOINTED BY JOINT RESOLUTION APPROVED APRIL 9, 1868.

To the Honorable the Senate and General Assembly of the State of New Jersey:

The subscribers, Commissioners appointed by the joint resolution of your honorable bodies approved April 9, 1868, "to examine into the system existing in the State Prison of this State and similar institutions of other States, and to report to the Legislature at its next regular session, by bill or otherwise, an improved plan for the government and discipline of the said prison, having special regard to economy and the reformation of criminals; and also to report such suggestions or measures bearing upon the subject as to them shall seem fit and proper," beg leave respectfully to report:

That soon after their appointment, the Commissioners entered upon the duties with which they were charged, and together made several visits to the State Prison of this State and carefully inspected its arrangements, plan, system and government, receiving from its officers all the facilities desired and all the information in their power to give. They also visited the Eastern Penitentiary of Pennsylvania, and the Philadelphia County Prison. In Massachusetts they examined the State Prison at Charlestown, the House of Correction and the County Prison at Boston, and the several corrective institutions on Deer Island; and also the Female Reformatory at Lancaster, in that state. In Connecticut they saw the State Prison at Wethersfield; in New York the Albany Penitentiary, the State Prison at Sing Sing, the several corrective and charitable institutions on Blackwell's and Randall's Islands, and the City Prison, known as the

Tombs. And they take great pleasure in expressing their grateful acknowledgments of the signal courtesy and kindness received from all the officers of those institutions.

Their thanks are especially due to Dr. Samuel G. Howe, the President, and Edwin Morton, Esq., Secretary of the Board of State Charities of Massachusetts, who kindly accompanied them to the prisons at and near the city of Boston; and to the Hon. Judge Russell, the Collector, and to Gen. Underwood, the Surveyor of the port of Boston, who put at their command a revenue cutter, and politely joined them in a delightful excursion to Deer Island, passing through the Boston Harbor, with its scenery of such historic and classic interest. Thanks are due, also to Frederick B. Sanborn, Esq., late Secretary of the State Board of Charities, for many valuable documents and communications; and to Gen. Amos Pilsbury, of the Albany Penitentiary, for communications and suggestions which his long and successful experience render exceedingly valuable. To Gen. James Bowen and Isaac Bell, Esq., officers of he Board of Corrections and Charities of New York, who politely attended them to the institutions under their charge, and fully explained the object and conduct of them, many thanks are due.

The Commissioners take pleasure also in acknowledging their indebtedness to the Hon. Theodore W. Dwight, Chairman of the Executive Committee, and the Rev. Dr. Wines, Secretary of the Prison Association of New York, for much valuable information, and especially for copies of their very able, interesting and exhaustive report on Prisons and Reformatories, made to the Legislature of New York in 1867, of which liberal use has been made in the preparation of this report.

To John S. Halloway, Esq., Warden, and Thomas H. Powell, Esq., Secretary of the Board of Inspectors of the Eastern Penitentiary of Pennsylvania, and to the Hon. Joseph R. Chandler, Inspector of the Moyamensing Prison, for their politeness and valuable information given, we are greatly indebted.

Under the comprehensive resolution requiring a report of an improved plan of discipline, the Commissioners deemed it proper to visit the several county jails of the State, some account of which will be found in the appendix to the report.

To suggest an improved system of government and discipline, is a work of no difficulty; for painful as it is to affirm, yet true it is, that almost any change in the present system would be an improvement. But to report such a system as will be approved, which in the conflict of opinions shall meet the general view, and supply what is requisite to the wants of the State, having reference to economy and reformation, this is labor, this is work indeed. Yet from the information derived from the inspection of the prisons of our own and of other States, from the knowledge gathered from the numerous volumes of reports and treatises submitted, and the valuable communications made by so many experienced officers and patrons of corrective institutions, the Commissioners entertain the hope that their conclusions may be received with some degree of favor, if not with entire approbation.

The great rule of legislation is, the consideration of the old law, the mischief and the remedy. So on a question of reformation, it is proper to examine the existing system, its evils, and the remedy for them. Such will be the order of this report.

Forty years ago what is now the State Arsenal was the New Jersey Penitentiary, where prisoners labored in association. The results were unsatisfactory, and a conviction pervaded the public mind, that the convicts went out more hardened criminals than they entered. The philanthropists of a neighboring State having, after careful consideration, arrived at the conclusion that convicts should be separately confined, induced their Legislature to establish a State Prison with that fundamental idea. The advantages claimed for the system were, that evil communication was prevented; that the prisoner could not in after life recognize the voice or features of even those who for years, had been separated from him by only a few inches of wall, and moreover, that from the meditations of his solitude, and the good influences brought to bear upon him, penitence would follow, and reformation be effected. Approval of this system seemed almost universal.

Dissatisfied with her own system, New Jersey resolved to adopt that of Pennsylvania.

And the State Penitentiary of this State was constructed "on the principle of separate confinement at hard labor, with the capacity of holding one hundred and fifty prisoners." It was commenced in 1833 and completed in 1838, with one hundred and ninety-two cells. For some years it was found adequate to all the objects for which it was designed, and seemed to confirm the views of the advocates of the separate system, and was self-sustaining.

But afterwards when, with the increasing population, the number of convicts multiplied, the accommodations became too limited, and the officers were compelled from time to time to depart from that system, and the departure was sanctioned by an act of 1859, which authorized the employment of the men in work-shops.

Notwithstanding the one hundred and thirty-two cells since constructed, all the cells that can be used for the purpose, are occupied—many by two, some by three, and others by four and even five inmates. The cells of the north and south wings are seven and a half feet by twelve feet in size, with twelve feet ceiling. The cells of the centre wing, four feet by seven, sufficient under any circumstances for one prisoner only.

There were in prison several times during the past year, and are now, more than six hundred. Of these, one hundred and thirty-two occupy the smaller cells, leaving at least four hundred and sixty-eight for the remainder. As sixteen of these remaining cells are required for other purposes than the ordinary confinement of prisoners, there remain but one hundred and seventy-six cells for four hundred and sixty-eight prisoners, and some of course are crowded.

There having been heretofore no separate cells for females, they had to be confined in the same range with the males, and communications through pipes and windows were maintained between them of the most corrupt and corrupting character. The want of good morals was exhibited in the person of a mulatto child eight months old, born of a colored woman who had been in the prison for several years. This is hoped and believed to be an exceptional case. But the Commissioners could learn of no investigation of the matter, nor of the punishment of any prisoner, nor removal of officer on account of it; showing a want of vigilance to detect, or an absence of a sense of the iniquity of the offence.

The cells for female convicts now nearly completed are designed to accommodate sixty, and are so arranged as to separate them entirely from the other parts of the prison, and to exclude all communication therewith, and so as to afford the means of exercise in the open air without exposure, by sight or sound, to the other prisoners. For the judicious arrangement and the construction of this range of cells, almost entirely by the labor of prisoners, much credit is due to the Keeper and Inspectors who had charge of it.

The government of the prison is committed to a Keeper and five Inspectors, who, by the constitution of the State are required to be appointed by the Legislature in joint meeting, to hold their offices for one year, and until their successors shall be qualified into office. The Keeper is authorized to appoint as many assistants and deputies as the Inspectors shall deem necessary and proper to enable him to execute the duties of his office.

The Inspectors appoint the physician annually. The Governor of the State, with the Inspectors, is authorized to employ a suitable person as a teacher and moral instructor, whose whole time is to be employed in that service. He instructs the prisoners in their cells in the primary branches of education, and in morals and religion; and preaches in each corridor, unseen by his audience, who are in their cells and out of his sight.

The library, as represented by its catalogue, consists of sixteen hundred and fifty volumes, a very large proportion of which have been lost or mutilated, and many destroyed by the recent fire. The appearance of those remaining gives evidence of having been much handled, if not carefully read. What effect upon the minds and morals of the readers they have had, is uncertain. It is to be feared not so much for good, as the influence for evil of the pictures of an exciting, inflammatory and, in some instances, of a lewd character which were exhibited on the walls of many of the cells and of the more public apartments. The presence of these demoralizing cuts from sensational periodicals, seems to have escaped the notice of all the officers, or failed to impress them with the sense of their impropriety. On the suggestion of the Commissioners to the late Keeper many of them were removed.

The prisoners work in shops, associated under the silent system, and take their meals in the cells, and are supplied with an abundance of plain and wholesome food.

The Commissioners have investigated and considered the subject of punishment of convicts both in our State Prison and County Jails, as well as in the penal institutions of other States.

Punishment of convicts, is thus provided for by law in this State, "If any Deputy Keeper shall report that any prisoner has violated any of the rules and regulations for the government of the prison, the Keeper shall have before him said prisoner and Deputy Keeper who charges him with such offence, and shall inquire into such charges, adjudge the case, and award such measure of punishment as he may deem proper, not exceeding close confinement in a dark cell, on bread and water, with a chain on the leg, or handcuffs, or both, for six days; and if in his opinion the convict should receive further punishment, he shall refer the case to the acting Inspectors, who shall order such further punishment as they shall think proper; provided, that corporal punishment shall in no case be inflicted." By this provision it will be perceived that severe or other forms of punishment than such as are herein defined are permitted in obstinate cases of disobedience to be inflicted by order of the acting Inspectors and according to their will, with a saving clause in reference to "corporal punishment." The inference is that punishment in its nature as severe, cruel and painful as corporal punishment, in the meaning of that term, shall not be prescribed. The observations made in the prisons of other States satisfied the Commissioners that the kind and degree of punishment defined by our statue, without discretionary power of further inflictions by either Keeper or Inspectors, is amply sufficient to control and subdue all refractory cases, unless there is defective management in the Prison.

Mr. Brockway, the Superintendent of Detroit, Michigan, House of Correction, says: "Coercive measures are only resorted to by unqualified officers." Where such institutions are properly managed, deprivation of privileges and such retributive punishments as it may be expedient to inflict are usually sufficient. General A. Pilsbury, the able, efficient and distinguished Chief of the Albany Penitentiary, who has for 40 years, or more, presided most successfully over penal institutions in New Hampshire, Connecticut and New York, assured the Commissioners that corporal or painful punishment was never necessary in a well regulated Prison, and that seventy-five per cent. of his men passed through their term without a harsh word. Mr. Haynes, the Warden of Massachusetts Prison, at Charlestown, Capt. Robbins of the House of Correction of South Boston, and others, were equally explicit on that point and agreed fully with General Pilsbury.

Such, the Commissioners regret to remark, has not been the practice in New Jersey. In one of their visits to our State Prison they found five men fastened in separate cells, prostrate and in a prone position, straps of strong leather passing around both wrists of each convict, and secured to iron rings in the floor, allowing very little movement of the person, obliging the condemned to void his excrements in his clothing and rendering the air of the cell nauseatingly offensive. One case, it was stated, required such punishment to be continued twenty-two, another ten, and a third six days. In some cases suspension by the hands or wrists is resorted to, tying culprits up with arms elevated above the head and allowing the feet scarcely to touch the floor. This is a painful infliction, and but few can bear it without danger. The cold shower bath is occasionally used at Sing Sing Prison, New York, but is considered so dangerous to life that it is only imposed under the supervision of the Prison Physician. Punishment by douche bath was formerly inflicted in our prison, but discontinued in 1848, by direction of the Governor then in office. It gratifies the Commissioners to state that Governor Ward has recently protested against the modes of punishment herein disclosed, and that they have been abandoned by the present Keeper and Inspectors. These practices of fastening down and tying up, to which females also have been subjected are obvious deviations from the letter and spirit of our statute upon the subject; for while it allows *other* punishments than those defined to be inflicted in *certain cases,* it disallows, in *all cases,* "corporal punishment." If the practices named are not *corporal punishment,* to what species of punishment would they belong? The executive officers referred to very properly forbade their further continuance, in pursuance of their duty to see the laws faithfully executed.

The inquiry may very prperly be made, what is the effect upon the personal health of the subject of such punishments?

Confining the body for a long time in the same posture tends to weaken the whole system and unfits it to perform its proper functions by impairing vital action. The injurious effect upon the brain and lungs from such inflictions is patent. The protracted inhalation of foul and noxious gases in a close and imperfectly ventilated room, without attention to personal cleanliness, is of itself highly injurious and might be in certain cases positively and rapidly fatal. Carbonic acid and sulphuretted hydrogen gases with other impure exhalations soon fill the atmosphere of the prisoner's cell, and being inhaled during respiration, deprive the blood of its due supply of oxygen and speedily renders it unfit for the support of animal life. It is a question whether deaths occurring in prisons may not be traceable, in many cases, to such methods of subduing refractory convicts. Humanity even to criminals is characteristic of the present age, and human life is too sacred to be subjected to an *experimentum crusis* by incompetent officials to rectify their own mismanagement. Suspending the body in the manner stated with the arms elevated, if long continued, produces a congested condition of the blood-vessels of the lungs, which is highly injurious to health and is promotive of fatal diseases both of the heart and lungs.

Permanent injury to health is not the object of criminal punishment. The public security and the reformation of the convict should be kept steadily in view in all controlling measures which may be instituted by the government in his case. With a qualified Keeper or Warden, and proper Assistants to carry out the regulations of discipline, punishments of any kind would rarely be needed. Deprivation of privileges, confinement to a dark cell, or a restricted diet would be entirely effectual.

The industries of the prison have been boot and shoe making, under contractors at forty cents per day for long days, and thirty cents for the short days of the three winter months, and the manufacture of chains, also under contractors, and the making and seating cane chair bottoms, cordwaining and weaving under the management of the Keeper. There are now unemployed three hundred prisoners.

The destruction by fire of the workshops for chains in July last, has interrupted that branch of business, and swelled the number of those not employed. The other branches continue, but not with sufficiently remunerating results.

The Prison for many years has not been self-sustaining, the salaries of the officers and per diem of the Inspectors has always, except the first few years after its erection, been charged on the State Treasury. Latterly large appropriations have also been made to meet the current expenses; in March, 1863, there was appropriated to pay its indebtedness the sum of $5,000; in February, 1866, $20,000; in March, 1867, $75,000, and in April, 1868, the further sum of $75,000, being for the last three years an average expense to the State by direct appropriation of over $56,000. Add to this sum $36,495 for the salaries of officers and per diem of the Inspectors, together with the charges for repairs, and it will be found to be an annual charge upon the State Treasury of more than $100,000.

The report of the Keeper and Inspectors for the year just past, exhibits about the same financial result, showing that the Prison in the last four years has cost the State more than four hundred thousand dollars.

Such being the present system of the Prison, the evils of it are quite obvious.

And the first to be noticed is the short term of office of the Keeper and Inspectors. Their annual appointment almost necessarily implies an annual change. In practice, it is a change with every change of political party power in the State. From long usage these officers have been regarded as the spoils of victory. They are consequently bestowed as the rewards of party. Proper qualifications may be sought for, but they are frequently subordinated to the capacity in party tactics and success in controlling votes. Political influences secure the appointment of the Keeper, and on the principle of "like master like man," his deputies are often selected for like qualifications. Hence, it is not surprising that pot-house heroes should sometimes be found in in the capacity of Assistant Keepers; and that where the strictest rules of sobriety ought to prevail, the excited manner and fetid breath of the officer should betray the use of the bottle.

The annual appointment, should it fall upon the best of men, diminishes if not destroys, by the shortness of the term, the hope of success.

A man must possess extraordinary talents, and unusual fitness for the place, and have, indeed, the gift of "discerning spirits" who in one year could fully comprehend the duties of the office and become familiar with the workings of such an institution, and the art of governing such a class of men. It is safe to affirm that very few men could, in one year become fitted fully for the station. As a poet must, so a ·Keeper may, be born; but in this department, especially, is it generally found that practice alone can make perfect.

The policy of other States seems to be based on this principle and proves its truth conclusively.

In Massachusetts, the Warden of the State Prison at Charlestown, holds his office during good behaviour, and with the experience of eleven years service, has become an adept in his profession.

The Master of the House of Correction, in South Boston, has been an officer of that institution for forty-four years, and its Master for thirty-five years.

The Superintendent of the Albany Penitentiary has been connected with the government of prisoners for more than forty-four years; and although his office is triennial, the Mayor and Recorder of the city, and Supervisors of the county of Albany, who in joint meeting constitute the appointing power, have so esteemed the thorough practical experience and eminent success of General Pilsbury, that his reappointment is regarded as indispensable to the welfare of the Prison. Excepting one term, in which he was voluntarily in another field, he has held the position since 1845.

The Wardens and Keepers of the Prisons of Pennsylvania hold their office during good behavior; and a change is seldom made, and is always regarded as undesirable.

As an almost necessary consequence of the frequent change of officers, another evil is found in the want of discipline. Every new officer is subjected to a severe ordeal. The prisoners are every ready and quick to test his capacity to govern, his patience to endure annoyances, his power to resist temptation to passion, his firmness and ability to restrain insubordination. If on such trial he is found wanting, disorder follows, work is neglected, materials spoiled; and as in a recent instance, the authority of the officers is defied and insurrection threatened.

Such insubordination is seriously felt in the demoralization of the prisoners, and the interruption of the government of the whole Prison.

A revolt, if only partially successful, necessarily diminishes the authority of the Keeper and his Assistants. Reformation, one of the great objects of imprisonment, becomes a failure.

Another mischief, resulting, chiefly, from the short term and inexperience of the Keeper, is the small earnings of the prisoners.

The continual change of officers almost necessarily requires the resort to the contract system.

Should a Keeper, quite competent to his station, arrange for working the prisoners under his own management, and be successful in the effort; his successor may be wholly incompetent, and cause great loss to the State. If the labor is let to others and there is no unfair combination of bidders to lessen the price, yet the contractor will insist upon a large margin of profits to meet the fluctuations of trade. The wages allowed for any one year may be very excessive or very inadequate for the year following.

Few manufacturers would be willing to contract for labor outside of the Prison for four or five years in advance, unless at a very low rate.

The mode of giving moral instruction is clearly defective. In the personal private interviews of the Moral Instructor with the prisoner, it would be proper, and as it should be, were there but one prisoner in a cell; but when two or three are together there can be but little private conference and counsel.

The labor in preaching is multiplied by the number of corridors. As only one can be used at a time, the sermon or lecture must be preached in each.

The power of sympathy between the speaker and his audience is greatly diminished, if not wholly lost, by reason of being hidden the one from the other.

What might be expected as the result of the efforts of the best of preachers who should be concealed from his hearers?

If a screen were stretched before every pulpit, how many converts might be expected? How much attention from the audience? What zeal would animate the speaker? In such case it might well be asked, Is not this a mockery of religious service?

Yet in the prison, the preaching in the corridors promises little more. Little benefit can be reasonably hoped for to men out of sight of the speaker and of all the officers, some of whom in the cells more remote, are beyond the reach of his voice. It is not surprising, therefore, that some amuse themselves with games; that some disturb the speaker by loud laughing and talking; that others scoff, and many are listless.

Were they in separate confinement, in pursuance of the original plan, a prisoner, being alone, might, for the sake of variety listen to the sacred admonitions, but associated as they are now, very little benefit is to be expected, and less is realized.

The remaining, and more important inquiry is, What remedy is to be found for these evils?

In seeking a solution of the question, we must remember that the great object of imprisoning men is the protection of society from their depredations. By confinement, they are deprived of the power—by reformation, of the will, to injure others. Confinement is usually temporary, reformation permanent, and when thorough, continues through life. Hence, while imprisonment is a present necessity, it may be made the instrument of greater good; the means of convincing the convict of the folly as well as the iniquity of his course, and of returning to society an honest and useful citizen, in the person of one who before was distrusted and feared because of his power and disposition to do evil.

But imprisonment does not necessarily produce reformation. It may and often has the effect of hardening and exasperating, rendering the bad worse, the novice in crime a confirmed villain.

Through a system of reformatory agencies, planned in wisdom and maintained with consistent, uniform patience and forbearance, great good has been done to the prisoner and to the public.

Of these agencies, the first in importance and in power, is the thorough inculcation of the principles of morals and religion. If the heart and conscience are not affected, all measures of reformation are unreliable. Penitence may be sincere, but temporary, and such as will be repented of. With the temptation renewed, the habit and disposition to evil may return. Hence the necessity and value of moral and religious instruction by the use of the Scriptures, and of religious books and tracts, the preaching of the Gospel and the counsels of the Moral Instructor.

Next to moral and religious training, comes secular education. As Dr. Wines properly remarks: "Education quickens the intellect, gives new ideas, supplies food for thought, inspires self-respect, supports pride of character, excites ambition, opens new fields of labor, and offers opportunities for social and personal improvement."

Another agency is the formation of habits of industry. Idleness is the parent of vice. To it may be traced much of the crime for which convicts suffer. Labor, honorable, systematic and persistent, is a means of support not only, but an auxiliary to virtue as well.

It is therefore of primary importance that a habit of patient, persevering industry be inculcated.

Without such habit, the discharged convict will naturally seek the haunts of vice, and soon become again involved in crime, and with increased desire and power for evil continue his depredations on society.

But with such habit, rendered agreeable by continuance, the means of support are supplied, self-reliance and self-respect are fostered and the temptations to evil diminished.

With the habit of industry and as the means of insuring the certainty of self-support, some useful trade should be taught. With the capacity to engage in skilled labor, to compete with a toiling multitude outside, he is inspired with hope, and, with the consciousness of his ability to provide against want; and if he have the desire to live honestly, he has the power so to do.

Without such habit and such capacity, whatever may be the purposes of his mind, he will probably return to his former course of iniquity.

Most convicts are without trade or any regular business. Many without any certain means of support, some from disability, or the want of instruction, some from idleness. Yet these, with proper training, may become industrious, self-supporting citizens.

The highest order of charity, is that which enables one to provide for himself. Benevolence, therefore, as well as economy demands such instruction. If the labor of the prisoner should be entirely unproductive of pecuniary profits, it is nevertheless indispensable as the means of reformation.

Another efficient instrument in the process of reformation, is hope. If a convict is without this, if he feels that there is a warfare between him and the public, that they are his enemies, and that he has the right to quarter upon them when he can; if his feeling are those of the lad recently arraigned, who, when asked, "Whose boy are you?" in the bitterness of his soul, and with tears coming down his cheeks, replied, "I'm nobody's boy," then there is no hope for him, and but little hope of him. But if he can be convinced that he is the victim, not of the law, but of his own folly; that the officers of justice are seeking his reformation as well as the safety of the public; that while he will be required to observe all the rules of the prison, he will be treated with kindness, hope will dawn upon him and he will soon see that good conduct will secure kind treatment, and he may enter upon a course of reform.

With most men kindness will do more to subdue than severity. "A soft word turneth away wrath," but angry words excite enmity and a spirit of resistance. While every rule should be strictly enforced, and implicit obedience required, the mode of enforcing may be so gentle as to win a ready obedience.

A system of rewards properly devised and sustained, will also be found a great power for good.

Attendance on some of the religious services and at the Sabbath School may be made a privilege.

Lectures or instruction on interesting subjects or connected with the simpler branches of science and arts, may be made rewards of good conduct— the privation of the privilege of hearing them, a punishment.

A pecuniary allowance for good conduct and faithful labor would tend to secure order and industry. If, for example, an account be kept with each convict of his expenses and his earnings, and he allowed a percentage of the profits, to be paid to his family if he desire, or to himself when discharged, and some part of it for proper articles during his confinement, it would be a great incentive to good conduct, and his increased industry would be profitable to the institution. An allowance for overwork, if properly arranged, would induce industry, and if made to depend on proper deportment, would have its influence in restraining from disorder.

The commutation system, where it has been fairly tried, has been found to be a very efficient auxilliary in the reformation of prisoners. Our act of 1868, was designed to provide for it. But either from some defects of its provisions, or misapprehension of them, it has failed. The statement in the appendix exhibits the time earned by the prisoners under the incentive of the act, and the hope of an earlier discharge. The disappointment arising from the failure to give effect to that law was very great, and very discouraging to those who had resolved to merit its reward.

The great heart of the community has no vengence to wreak upon its prostrate criminals. Its object is to protect the public and reform the offender. Toward the latter point a wise prison keeper will make all the appliances at his command concentrate. His first object will be to secure the hearty co-operation of the convicts, which can only be done by winning their affectionate respect and confidence. To recognize and encourage their efforts at self-control and reformation will be among his most delightful duties. The system which does not acknowledge these efforts by appropriate rewards is radically unjust and doomed to failure. In every prison, offences of various kinds will occur which must be noticed. It is an important question how they are to be noticed. Severe punishments have been fully tried. The lash, the thumb-screw, the underground dungeon, and other brutal exercises of power have had their day. And what a day! Who ever was softened or reformed through their ministrations? They have passed. But the same animus which prompted them may show itself in the frequency and severity of allowed punishments, or in those of a degrading character, or in harsh, stinging words. These, too, should give place to Christian kindness, and to wise, moral agencies, and results will be attained impossible to brute force, or harsh, unloving treatment. The moral of the fable of Phoebus and Œolus is true today; the warmth of the sun effects what the rude blasts cannot do.

The course adopted in the best regulated prisons is to encourage good behavior by appropriate rewards, and to discourage misconduct by deprivation of privileges.

First, and most effective in the class of rewards, is the abatement of a certain portion of the term of sentence of each convict whose deportment shall, by an impartial daily record, be shown to be satisfactory. Under the appellation of "Commutation acts," this system has been adopted in eighteen States, (see Appendix B,) and the results, wherever it has been fairly tried, have proved beneficial. Gideon Haynes, the admirable Warden of the State Prison at Charlestown, says of it: "I think it is the most important step in prison discipline that has been taken in this country in the last forty years." A warden of the Michigan State Prison says: "Of prisoners discharged last year, more than ninety per cent. conducted themselves with such propriety as to secure the whole of their 'good time'."

This system places within the power of the prisoner a means of shortening his term of confinement by the adoption of a line of conduct which his own best judgment approves. If he enters upon and continues this course, his labor will be steady and of better quality, and the standard character of the prison products will be raised. A contractor can well afford to pay more for his time; or, if employed for the State, its interest are advanced. The expense of keeping him is lessened, for the needless waste of food, of implements and of materials ceases, and he keeps himself by adhering to the prison rules. The habit of good conduct, in its various phases, strengthened by continuance through months or years of confinement, and enforced by the moral and religious instruction he will receive, we may trust, with some degree of confidence, will not be abandoned on his release. As the object of this whole arrangement is the reformation of the convict, it is believed that if that end is not attained, the time he has passed should, in whole or in part, be forfeited by subsequent misconduct.

In the last printed report of the State Prison, being for 1867, we find the following statement under the head of "Statistics of Prisoners." "There have been discharged as follows: By expiration of sentence, 132; pardoned one day off to restore to citizenship, 7; pardoned for other reasons, 188." Notwithstanding this great exodus, the number remaining in confinement the 30th day of November, 1867, was 550, being about 240 more than the cells in use can properly accommodate. During the last year upwards of 130 were pardoned; yet there are now in the prison 607 convicts. With such an overflowing prison, a liberal use of the pardoning power must have seemed to the excellent members of our Court of Pardons as an indispensable act of humanity. But for these liberations the number now confined would probably have exceeded 700. And yet this relief produces a feverish excitement in every cell, where each man longs for freedom, and labors for a continual presentation of his case to the court with urgent reasons for his release. Crimes are covered up; falsehood and deceit take the place of penitence and frank confession. That hopes thus fostered are a hindrance to any valid reformation, reason and experience alike demonstrate. Can we not give a new and better direction to the convict's hopes and efforts by opening to him a path by which he can *earn* his liberation? Lord Brougham well observes: "Every mitigation of a convict's sentence, in treatment, diet included, or duration of punishment, must be earned by the convict himself." When, after trial and conviction by an impartial jury, a sentence, in accordance with the requirements of law and the principles of justice, is solemnly pronounced in open court by the judge, we think a belief should impress the mind, not only of the culprit, but of the community, that the *sentence will be carried out*. This execution of judgment is essential to the maintenance of the proper respect and dignity of the tribunal. But courts, as individuals, are fallible, and erroneous testimony, or a misconception of facts, may consign an innocent man to prison. Circumstances may come to light after a trial which will extenuate the offence, or show an absence of criminal intent. To save the State, therefore, from the stigma of inflicting unjust punishment all governments lodge, *somewhere,* the power of pardon. It is a grave error, however, to suppose that this merciful and wise provision is designed to enable the pardoning power, in whomsoever vested, to sit as a court of general jail delivery, and try the criminal's case anew, upon his own statement, without the introduction of any opposing testimony, or the argument of adverse counsel. The difficulties, we may say the *dangers,* of our position, claim the earnest attention of the Legislature. Except under the influence of those reasons which prompted the establishment of the pardoning power, crime, it seems to us, should be repressed by giving stability to the administration of justice. To this end a large increase of our prison accommodation seems necessary.

An agency, either official or voluntary, for providing employment and giving counsel and encouragement to discharged convicts would contribute greatly to their reformation.

As in this state there is no Prison Association or other voluntary organization for such purpose, we greatly need a State agent for discharged prisoners. Such agent should have an office in the Prison, and should visit in their cells those convicts whose term of sentence have nearly expired; should make himself acquainted with their character and capabilities and learn their wishes as to their future employment.

It should be his duty to acquire knowledge of individuals and establishments where laborers are wanted; and not only to aid the released prisoner in procuring employment, but also awaken a sympathetic interest on the part of the employer, which will prompt to efforts for the permanent reformation of his previously erring fellow man.

Such agents are employed in Philadelphia and New York, and their influence is of a most beneficent character. Of the varied and important services of the agent in Dublin, mention is made in an article on Irish convict system. (Appendix D.) Here however, as well as elsewhere in connection with prisoners, the officers' heart must be in his work.

In our own state it is doubtless true, as in others, which we visited, that a large proportion of the convicts have come to their present position through the influence more or less direct, of intemperate appetites and habits. The experience of centuries, demonstrates the fact, that violations of laws human and divine, are closely connected with the use of intoxicating drinks.

Such is the uniform testimony of all the prison officers to whom we spoke on the subject. As it is wiser and easier to prevent than to punish crime, it seems to the Commissioners, that the serious consideration of the Legislature ought earnestly to be directed to the best means of repressing intemperance.

In considering the remedy to be applied, the first, and in the judgment of the Commissioners, the most important and the most efficient, means of establishing an improved plan will be found in the extension of the term of office of the Keeper and Inspectors.

This can be effectually done only by an amendment of the Constitution of the State. Yet if the political parties would agree upon some mode of selecting persons best qualified for the places, without regard to their political creed and continue in office during good behavior, those who prove themselves to be worthy, there would be some hope of reformation. Without some such arrangement generously made, and faithfuly adhered to, there is little hope of improvement.

It is of no consequence how perfect may be the system, if there is a want of proper officers to sustain it. *"Principia non homines"* may be the correct rule in civil polity; but *"Principia nec non homines"* is the true rule in morals and reform.

This evil of continual change is not the fault of the mode of appointment, but of the usage of party discipline. Under the first Constitution of the State, the Legislature, in joint meeting, appointed all the State officers, executive and judicial.

The experience of more than sixty years proved their ability and their desire to exercise the power to the best interests of the State, and to the satisfaction of their constituents, and that success usually attended their efforts.

It may not be inappropriate here to suggest that the Inspectors of the State Prison should be selected from the first and best class of citizens; men of the highest character for integrity, and who like the Managers of the Lunatic Asylum, and Trustees of the Reform School, would give their time and influence and discharge the duty for the love of it, and for the cause of justice and humanity. Under the government of competent officers, proper discipline may be maintained, the earnings of the prison increased, and the reformation of the prisoners promoted. And while the contract system is continued, proper persons will be sought in the contractors and in their instructors; men, who, while properly striving to make due profits for themselves, will do justice to the State, and learn and act upon the principle that their own interest can be better promoted by the maintenance of good order and by aiding in the reformation of the prisoners.

But it is to be hoped that the contract system will not long be continued. It is prejudicial to the management of the prison. Its tendency is to create disorder, and hinder reformation. It militates directly against the financial prosperity of the institution, as well as against its discipline.

In some of the prisons we visited, this system is regarded with favor. Under the management of their experienced and accomplished officers, and a happy selection of contractors it has been comparatively successful. But in the judgment of the Commissioners it is to be resorted to in this State, only as a necessity, and should be discontinued when that necessity is removed.

The direct consequence of that system is, to place the prisoners during hours of labor almost entirely under the control of men, who are not officially responsible; men who see in the convicts only so much machinery for making money; men whose only recommendation to the positions they hold, is that they were the lowest bidders.

The instructors employed by the contractors are equally irresponsible; not usually selected with reference to their moral character, and with no desire to aid in reformation; men often so devoid of principle as to smuggle into the shops contraband articles for sale, at exorbitant prices, or to bestow upon their favorites causing jealousy and discontent.

It is not unusual with such men, while favoring some, to wreak their vengence upon other prisoners, by causing unmerited punishment.

The transmission of mischievous messages from one part of the prison to another, and to and from persons outside is no uncommon occurrence.

The contractors in making their bargains claim consideration for every contingency, and especially for the disadvantages arising from want of proper discipline, and the consequent imperfection of the work; and in this State, and in this condition of the prison, they will not contract for such prices as will be remunerative. The truth of this is seen in the existing contracts 40 cents for long days, 30 cents for short.

Whilst in the prison at Charlestown, the price is from 75 cents to 107 cents, averaging 93 cents per day for each man.

In New Hampshire, the contract price for one quarter of the men at boots and shoes is 70 cents; three-fourths at manufacturing bedsteads, 90 cents per day.

The earnings of those prisons and of others are a surplus of all expenses.

In that at Wethersfield, although the contract price for labor was fixed several years since, when the prices of labor and supplies were much lower than during the last year or two, yet the earnings paid all the expenses of the prison, including the salaries of officers, and the wages of the Watchmen and Assistants, with a balance of net gain of $1,706.33.

In the Albany Penitentiary, for the year ending December, 1867, the earnings exceeded all expenses of the institution, including salary and wages by $21,346.04.

In the Massachusetts State Prison at Charleston, for the same year, the net gain was $22,346.16.

Notwithstanding the low price of labor in our prison, large claims are made and allowed for lost time of the convicts, by reason of absence from sickness or under punishment, and also for defective work, and injured materials. Besides this, the contractors are furnished without charge, with

34 P

yard room, and sometimes with shop room, and with other appliances for their work.

The history of prisons shows that contractors who understand their business, and will conduct it properly, have usually reaped large, and, in many instances, immense profits from the labor. They are expected, of course, to make the best bargains they can for themselves, but it is not unusual for competing tradesmen to combine in securing the contracts on their own terms, and to the great prejudice of the State.

It is urged in favor of this system that no one man is competent to the government of the prison, the employment of the prisoners, the purchase of materials, and the sale of the products. But experience proves this position to be untenable.

In Wethersfield, General Pilsbury, when acting as warden there during a part of the time managed the entire labor of the prison. During another part of the time, about half the labor was let to contractors. In his testimony before the commissioners of New York he said: "In a financial point of view, the management of the labor by myself was most successful." In the Clinton Prison of New York the system of contracts was abolished, and the labor performed under the officers. The result was that, instead of being an annual charge on the State Treasury of $30,000, its income exceeded all expenses by about $3,000.

In Thomaston, Maine, under the management of the warden, the profits of the prison labor exceeded all expenses, including salaries and wages.

Mr. Cordier, of the Wisconsin State Prison, says: "Our average number of convicts was 110, of whom only 63 could be employed on productive labor. Their earnings amounted to $25,727.54, showing that the 63 men earned $1.36 per day each." He adds, "If the labor of the .convicts had been let to contractors, at say sixty cents a day (a high figure), they would have earned only $11,340, supposing them to have lost no time from sickness or other causes; and the State would have sacrificed in one year $14,387.34."

In Illinois, where the plan is to lease the labor of the prison at a bonus, or annual rent, the lessee, in a few years, amassed a very large fortune.

In Kentucky, the keeper, instead of a salary, had for compensation one-half of the net profits; and a large sum of money was annually paid into the treasury of the State. In one year, with an average of less than 150 prisoners, the clear profits were $30,000.

In our own prison the labor on chair bottoms, under the management of the officers, averaged 50 cents per day to each man, while in the shoe department 40 cents and 30 cents were agreed for.

If the evidence of such men and such statistics are of any value, it is evident that one man may accomplish even all this. With the aid of competent assistants, and, if need be, of a commercial agent for purchase and sale, there is no reason why the industries of the prison may not be conducted on State account. If by reason of the fluctuations of trade loss is to be incurred, the State is as able to sustain it as an individual contractor;

if gain is the consequence, the State will have the benefit of it. If there is a loss under the contract system, the State usually is the loser, either by allowance made to the contractor, or by failure to fulfil.

Another and a serious objection to the contract system is that under it a prisoner is seldom instructed in all the branches of a trade. He can sooner be taught one branch and become more perfect in it, and the interest of the contractor is to continue him in that branch as a specialty. In the shoe department, for example, the man who is kept at driving pegs can never learn to fit the sole. He who is wholly employed in stitching uppers, can never learn to put on the heel. This, it is true, may be stipulated against in the contract, and the competent prisoner be permitted to go through several or all the branches. But it is found to be difficult to enforce such contract, and it is always embarrassing.

Without such knowledge of the trade the discharged convict must seek employment where laborers are needed for his special branch, and his chances of employment are diminished proportionately.

To remove the disadvantages of the present mode of giving moral and religious instruction, a chapel is requisite. In it the prisoners could be assembled on the Sabbath for regular religious services, and for Sabbath school instruction, and during the week for daily worship. There, lectures of a religious, moral, and intellectual character could be delivered to the improvement of the prisoners, and to the advantage of the prison, by the effects upon their conduct and efforts to reform.

If it be objected that it will not be safe to assemble the convicts in such a place, it may be replied that there is less danger from men so collected, without offensive instruments, than from half this number in the shops armed with hammers, sledges and knives, &c.

The same rule of silence may be enforced more effectually in a chapel, where silence is the order of the hearers than in the shops where the hum and clatter of tools and machinery drown the noise of talking, and give opportunity of indulgence.

In the erection of a chapel, arrangements could be made for a mess room. By this, much labor in serving the meals in the cells, would be saved; less provisions would be wasted, the noisesome odors and accumulation of dirt incident to that mode would be prevented, and the cells and prison less infested with vermin. It is proper to state, that the mode of serving food to prisoners is a debatable question among experienced Keepers.

But the prison is overcharged with convicts, there being an average of about six hundred, with accommodations for only about three hundred, besides those who will soon occupy the new cells for females.

The only remedy for this evil is the addition of more wings to the present building, or the construction of an entire new one.

On due reflection and careful examination of the subject, the Commissioners respectfully recommend the construction of a new prison in such part of the State as will furnish most of the requisites of such an institution. The chief of such requisites are ease of access, facilities of transportation, sources of supply at reasonable rates of materials for construction, and articles of consumption. There should be salubrity of situation, an absence of stagnant water, and of sources of miasma, with means of furnishing healthful and remunerative employment for the prisoners. Such a site may be found on Snake Hill in the county of Hudson, where the Chosen Freeholders of that county are erecting a County Work House. This is on the east bank of the Hackensack river, where materials and supplies can, except during a few weeks in winter, be furnished by vessels. Here is a great mass of trap rock, the supply of which seems to be inexhaustible, and its demand for paving unlimited.

This will afford employment to all who have any degree of muscular force; heavy work for the strong, light work for the feeble, requiring but little experience in the work, yet yielding the profits of skilled labor.

It is quite possible that an arrangement can be made with the authorities of that county to place the work-house now in construction and its grounds under the control of the State. Other sites, it is thought, may be obtained on the Hudson River, in the county of Bergen, accessible to craft of almost any size at all seasons of the year.

There the palisades afford salubrious sites, with an ample supply of trap rock, and all the advantages of the vicinity of a large city for sales and purchases.

In the construction of a building sufficient to accommodate three or four hundred prisoners, with each a cell at night, plain and neat, without unnecessary ornament, and with sufficient strength to prevent escapes, will be found a remedy for the crowded condition of the State prison.

To this building may be given the name of the "House of Correction," for the reason among others, that many, who through the waywardness of youth or want of experience, have been betrayed into crime, may be saved from the stigma of having been an inmate of the State Prison, and thereby encouraged to efforts of reformation; and that it is intermediate between the place of detention and the penitentiary.

To this House of Correction may be committed males, convicted of offences of lesser turpitude. To classify such offences by the names by which they are known in the law, would not be expedient, nor meet the thing desired. To provide that all guilty of felony shall be committed to the State Prison, would require the punishment there of petit larceny, a felony at common law. To declare that all guilty of misdemeanor be committed to the House of Correction, would be to punish there, those convicted of perjuries, libels, conspiracies and atrocious assaults, which are misdemeanors at common law. Homicide may be committed under circumstances of less turpitude than attend some cases of larceny. To say, that all guilty of Homicide must be punished in the State Prison, and all of larceny in the House of Correction would not meet the exigencies of the case.

It is deemed better to classify the convicts by the terms of their sentence, leaving it with the Courts, as it is now, to fix the term. Or to submit it to the discretion of the Courts to commit to the State Prison or to the House of Correction, as in their judgment may be expedient.

If all whose term of punishment shall be for three years or less were committed to the House of Correction it would reduce the number to be punished in the State Prison about one half, and give a cell to each prisoner at night, and when not in the workshops or on other duty.

The plan of associated labor with solitary confinement at night, which seems at this time to be most adapted to the wants and circumstances of this State may be continued.

The House of Correction may be under the government of a Warden and Board of Managers, to be appointed as are the Trustees of the Reform School for juvenile delinquents, by the Board of Control, consisting of the Governor, Chancellor and Chief Justice.

It is indispensible to the reformation of prisoners that there should be an entire separation of the sexes, that they be kept beyond the sight and hearing of each other, and it is eminently proper that the females should be under the charge of the matron and her female assistants. The new range of cells now about completed, will furnish room for all females who may be convicted of offences for which the punishment must be by imprisonment. If with the increase of population, and the consequent increase of crime, more room will be required for this class, additions can be made to it, or a workhouse be constructed or procured from one of the counties for that purpose.

It may be of interest for us here to state, that in the female department of the House of Correction, at South Boston, we saw forty-two sewing machines in active operation, at clothier's work, and tended by as many women. About an equal number were employed at finishing work with the needle. Capt. Robbins assured us that their average earnings were from 75 to 80 cents per day. Six years ago the average earnings of the females were but about *five cents* per day. If Massachusetts can thus improve, why may not New Jersey? Truly muscle may be turned to some account if there be but brains to work it.

With the establishment of a Reformatory for girls, it is believed that no further provision will be required for females at present. Such Reformatory Institution is greatly needed, and the want of it has been painfully felt for some time past, and the Commissioners respectfully recommend it as a part of their system of discipline and reform.

Under the plan proposed, the county jails may and should be kept as places of detention only, for persons awaiting trial or transportation after conviction; but (excepting for vagrants and disorderly persons) never as places of punishment.

Vagrants and disorderly persons who are usually committed for short terms may be confined in those jails, for the first and second offence. The greater number of this class are the victims of intemperance, and with many of them, the routine is, commitment for ten or twenty days,[1] just

---

[1] We found one woman had been committed to prison in Boston thirty-seven times. One in New York more than a hundred times. On third offence a term of two or three years, under proper discipline, might have benefitted the individual. It would have saved trouble, and expense to the community.

long enough to recover from the effects of their debauch; then a discharge, with increased appetite, then a "glorious treat," and another commitment.

After the warning of a second conviction such persons should, as in Massachusetts, be sent to the House of Correction, where by a longer term, they may be enabled with the aid of proper appliances, to conquer their taste for strong drink, or other evil propensity, and by their labor, do something towards reimbursing the counties or cities for the charges incurred on their behalf.

In the county jails accommodations should be provided for each person in a separate apartment. These apartments, and all apartments and cells of every prison should be clean, well ventilated and healthful. The objects of imprisonment are threefold, the security of the public from further depredations, the deterring from crime, and the reformation of offenders. Apartments, cold and damp, with fetid atmosphere may accomplish the first two of these objects by shortening life, but will not tend to reformation. The law demands justice, but not cruelty, and its officers have no right to employ machinery or provide apartments which become implements of torture. Yet nothing can be more cruel or unjust than the impairing of the constitution and the destruction of life by means of the foul air or a damp, narrow, ill-ventilated cell.

To the county jails, to which persons are committed before indictment, while they are presumed by law to be innocent; persons detained as witnesses or for some other cause are these remarks especially applicable. The purest man in the community may be charged with crime, and for want of friends at hand to become his bail, or for the want or neglect of a magistrate to take it, he must be committed.

To thrust any such into a cell, in darkness and dirt, infested with vermin and with fetid atmosphere, is repugnant to every feeling of humanity.

To require such to associate with convicted felons, with depraved and disgusting criminals, inexperienced youth with hardened rogues is a violation not only of law but of the dearest rights of the citizen.

Some of the county jails, as will be seen by the report of them in the Appendix, need reform, and all need supervision. In many of them abuses occur of which the public are ignorant. Those who cause the abuses endeavor to conceal them. The complaint of those who suffer are seldom heard or heeded. Whether such abuses arise from ignorance or wilfulness, there should be a more efficient power to correct them. To wait till the Court shall assemble and the Grand Jury may presentment, and then till the Board of Freeholders take action on the subject, in many instances will afford no relief. There should be an official Inspector of the Jails, with power to suggest improvements, and to report the defects of the prisons and of their management, and to call a meeting of the Board of Chosen Freeholders for prompt relief, and to report annually to the Governor or Legislature.[1]

[1] To these duties might be added, at least for a single year, a thorough investigation and report upon the county and township poor houses, or arrangements for the poor. Should the care of the destitute be humane and considerate, as it is in many cases, it would be a satisfaction to the Legislature and the people of the State to know it. Should deficiencies appear they could meet their appropriate remedy.

To recapitulate: The system of prison discipline recommended is the State Prison under a proper and efficient government for the punishment of those convicted of the higher crimes. The House of Correction as an intermediate prison for those found guilty of offences of lesser turpitude; The Boys State Reform School; a State Reformatory for Girls, and the county and municipal jails as places of detention.

All of which is respectfully submitted.

DAN. HAINES,
GEO. F. FORT,
SAMUEL ALLINSON.

Trenton, Jan. 22, 1869.

APPENDIX E.

SUGGESTIONS FOR IMPROVED DISCIPLINE OF STATE PRISON.

The details of prison management, as to the mode of confinement, diet, labor, instruction, privileges, shortening of confinement in different classes by good marks, &c., &c., should be determined, under the control of general statute laws, by the Keeper and Board of Inspectors. Of course such large powers should be committed only to men of tried integrity, of practical ability and wise humanity, who protecting on the one hand the interests of the community, would labor on the other to bless the hundreds of immortal beings entrusted to their charge. The following plan, substantially the Irish system, is therefore merely proposed for consideration. If approved, its essential features might be adopted in the House or Houses of Correction, the establishment of which has been urged as a relief to both State and County Prisons.

First, or Penal Stage for Male Convicts. Eight months of close cellular confinement, except one or two hours of school, in successive classes each day, and an opportunity of Scripture reading or worship. These privileges to be withheld if abused. The first four months on as low diet as is consistent with good health and at oakum picking, or some analagous employment. This moiety to be shortened to three months by good conduct and industry. The last four months (also reducible to three months) to be at other cell labor, the convict may understand or readily be taught.

Second Stage. Associate confinement during the day, in cells at night. The "mark system" to be adopted, being three marks each for satisfactory conduct, school and labor, nine marks per month. Enter in third class. In two months if eighteen marks are attained, advance to the second class. Here six months are spent, and fifty-four marks are required before reaching the first class. Each advance to be marked by some added privilege in diet or liberty, and by an increase of gratuity to be placed to their credit, say in third class five cents per week, in second class ten cents, and in first class twenty cents. In the first class those with a sentence of three years might remain for six months, and till they get fifty-four marks; five to ten years men nine months, eighty marks being required; those over ten years, twelve months and one hundred and eight marks. The prisoner is now passed on to the advanced or A class, where it is proposed that the principal part of long sentences shall be spent. As the men by their proper deportment have earned their way up, their privileges should be greater than those ordinarily allowed in our prison, and a gratuity of forty cents per week might be credited to them. The mark system being still enforced, his gaining month by month, the requisite nine marks will entitle him to the register of A 1, A 2, A 3, &c. His continuance here to be in proportion to his length of sentence and his register. Misconduct, in any stage to arrest progress, or cause degradation.

Third Stage. Intermediate Class. The convicts, by the steady discipline to which they have been subjected, and to which they have yielded their assent, will have now attained a far more hopeful standing than that generally reached by our prisoners at the time of their unconditional discharge.

It is proposed to test their fitness for freedom, before conferring upon them that great boon. An appropriate plan for this would be to furnish some kind of employment in workshops under steady control and surveillance. Shops might be erected on ground adjoining the prison. There should be a "moral confinement" to the place, but very little, if any, prison restraint of bolts and bars. The men should feel that they are trusted and the community that they are worthy of trust. An agricultural or horticultural colony might doubtless be established by the Inspectors with advantage when a suitable class is prepared. A gratuity of one dollar per week might be allowed the men in this class, with permission to spend one-fourth for themselves or one-half for their families.

Fourth Stage. Conditional liberty. For the convicts who have earned all the requisite marks and advances it is now proposed to remit as follows:

From a three years' sentence, remit, one-sixth.

From a four to six years' sentence, remit, one-fifth.

From a six to fifteen years' sentence, remit, one-fourth.

From fifteen and upwards, one-third.

The conditions of the liberation might be a monthly report by the convict, in person or by letter to the Keeper of the State Prison or an agent for discharged prisoners, stating his residence and mode of life. Should this report be regularly made, and the Keeper or Agent be satisfied of his own knowledge, or on suitable evidence that the man has lived an orderly life from his discharge until the expiration of his full term, the fact should be stated to the Governor, who might be authorized to grant a certificate and restore his right of citizenship. The gratuities standing to his credit might be paid to him on the expiration of his sentence, or at the time of his discharge, if the Keeper or Inspectors are satisfied it will be to his benefit or that of his family.

A plan for the discipline of female prisoners might be adopted similar in its aims and suited to their needs, the intermediate stage to be passed in a Refuge, from whence they might be restored to society.

Whilst the Commissioners have no special desire for the adoption of the various details above suggested, they do feel a strong conviction that the principle which underlies them is correct, and that an increase of the privileges of a convict, or the shortening of his sentence, should be by some fixed rule and dependent upon his observance of the prison rules, and the faithful performance of assigned duty.[1]

[1] Report cited, in *Legislative Documents,* 1869;   pp. 331ff.

CHAPTERS V AND VI

DOCUMENTS RELATING TO THE HISTORY OF
THE STATE PRISON OF NEW JERSEY FROM
1885 TO THE PRESENT TIME.

CHAPTERS V AND VI

DOCUMENTS RELATING TO THE HISTORY OF THE STATE PRISON OF NEW JERSEY FROM 1885 TO THE PRESENT TIME.

I. PRISON INDUSTRY AFTER 1885.

1. SURVEY OF THE CHANGES IN THE ADMINISTRATION OF PRISON LABOR, 1885 TO 1911.

After the passage of the Act of June 7, 1911, abolishing the "piece-price" variety of the contract system, which was introduced by the Act of 1884, Supervisor Kirkbride, in his annual report for 1911, presented a brief survey of the different methods of administering prison labor from the time of the employment of the leasing system to the legal abolition of all forms of contract labor by the Act of 1911.

In 1876 the labor of the Prison was employed under what was termed convict labor; that is to say, contractors bid a certain sum for the employment of each prisoner, they furnishing the machinery, employing instructors to instruct the men in their work, paying for the fuel required to be used and the men necessary to guard and look after the discipline; the entire responsibility of production rested upon the party making the contract. At that time there were no restrictions upon the number of men to be employed on any one industry. At the session of the Legislature in 1881 the act of 1876 was amended to prohibit the employment of more than one hundred prisoners on any special branch of industry. In 1884 an act was

(541)

passed providing, as a means of reducing the alleged competition with free labor, two methods of employment of the convicts, one termed piece-price, that is to say, the bidder to pay a certain sum per piece, gross, pound or otherwise, the other, the public account system, that is to say, the State purchase the machinery, tools, equipment and materials, employ instructors to instruct and manufacture the goods and sell them at public auction. The managing authorities carefully considered the relative benefits to be derived by the State, as well as the question of competition, and unanimously reached the conclusion that the piece-price system was the best of the two, and in accordance with such conclusion it was adopted in 1885 under this system. The contractor was required to furnish the machinery, the material necessary to manufacture the various articles and the employment of instructors to instruct the men in their work. This system is still in operation and the various industries employed are for the manufacture of pantaloons, waist bands, shirts, men's drawers, children's turned shoes, brooms, whisk brooms, cocoa mats, matting, brushes and brush blocks.

At the session of the Legislature of 1911 a radical change in the employment of the labor was adopted by the passage of a law, Chapter 372, Laws of 1911, approved June 7th, 1911, which creates a Board composed of the Commissioner of Charities and Corrections, the Keeper of the State Prison, the Superintendent of Rahway Reformatory and two others, to be appointed by the Governor, by and with the advice of the Senate, to regulate the employment of convict labor. This act provides that the labor shall be employed in agricultural, horticultural and floricultural pursuits, and in the manufacture of such articles as they may be capable of producing for the various institutions and State departments, and all excess productions resulting from such industries shall be disposed of by public sale. This law further prohibits the making of contracts for convict labor, but stipulates that this shall not apply to existing contracts prior to the passage and approval of this act, but also provides that the Board of Inspectors of the State Prison and the Commissioners of the New Jersey Reformatory at Rahway are authorized, subject to the approval of the Commissioner of Charities and Corrections, to pay to the wife, children or parents of any inmates of their respective institutions who, by reason of the imprisonment of such inmate, were made dependent upon public or private charity for their support a sum not exceeding fifty cents a day for each working day that such inmate was employed at productive labor, and that the said Inspectors and Commissioners were authorized to avail themselves of the services of any organized bureau of associated charities or charity organization situate in the district where said dependents may reside to distribute an expenditure for the relief of said dependents' families a sum not to exceed in any one year five per cent. of the value of the goods or articles manufactured or produced by the labor of said inmate.[1]

[1] *Annual Report of the Supervisor of the State Prison,* 1911; *New Jersey Legislative Documents,* 1911, vol. II, pp. 28–31.

2. RECEPTION OF THE "PIECE-PRICE" SYSTEM BY THE STATE PRISON OFFICIALS.

The prison officials were bitterly opposed to the abolition of the lease system and the introduction of the new "piece-price" system. Perhaps the best criticism of the new "piece-price" system was contained in the annual report of P. H. Laverty, the Principal Keeper of the State Prison in 1884.

But by far the most important matter I desire to bring to the notice of your Excellency is one that is not only closely allied with the future management of this institution, but is now agitating the people of this and other States, and occupying the attention of the best minds of the country. I refer to the question of convict labor. While it is not my intention to go into a lengthy discussion of the questions involved, nor yet make any recommendations on the subject, I deem it my duty to express to your Excellency my views as to the result consequent upon the act of the Legislature abolishing contract labor in the New Jersey State Prison. In so doing I fully appreciate the weight of the responsibility I am incurring, and the adverse criticisms I will doubtless subject myself to in certain quarters. But my duty to the people of this State, to the convicts in my keeping, and the promptings of humanity in their behalf, as well as a regard for public policy, impel me to set aside all personal and political considerations in the attempt to unravel a problem so vital to the future conduct of this institution and of so much importance to the people. Having spent the major portion of my life among those who toil for their daily bread, I fully recognize the justice of their demand, "that convict labor should not be allowed to come in competition with theirs"; and I sincerely hope that in the near future such laws will be enacted as to accomplish that purpose without, on the other hand, making invalid the law which ordains that every convict shall be held to hard labor, working positive injury to the people of this State; or, that which concerns me most, making this institution a cage for nine hundred or a thousand unemployed people, a large percentage of whom will be driven to a mad-house or an early grave, by the idleness cruelly forced upon them.

I need not call the attention of your Excellency to the fact that the law makes it incumbent upon the judges to add the "hard labor clause" to every State Prison sentence imposed. That law is still in force, not having been repealed by any of the recent acts relating to convict labor. In order to carry out that law, I must have employment for these convicts, and it is highly improbable that any law will ever be on the statute books making any and all convict labor unlawful. Such action would not only burden the taxpayers with an annual outlay of about $150,000 for the support of these convicts in idleness, but it would be cruel and inhuman in the extreme to enforce such penalty upon them. Only those acquainted with prison management, and who have time and again heard the piteous appeals of convicts deprived of work to be restored to the same, can form some idea of the terror of the punishment inflicted by the State upon its convicts in keeping them confined to their cells in idleness, and how the maintenance of discipline and the enforcement of the rules for health and cleanliness are made almost impossible under such a state of affairs.

But your Excellency will doubtless observe that convict labor has not been abolished by the Legislature, and that only the contracting out of such labor has been prohibited. True. Yet I am of the opinion that it would be a very hazardous experiment to work the convict after the expiration of the contract on the 1st of July next, under the now existing laws, and unless the Legislature very materially adds to the same, and in a much more explicit and comprehensive manner ordains what shall be done, by whom, and fixes the limit of the money allowed to be expended, I very much fear that idleness in this institution will be the result.

At the expiration of the present contracts we will only be allowed to pursue one of two courses, that is, adopt either the "public account" or "piece-price" system. Yet both appear to me impracticable unless improved or perfected by additional legislation. The public account system would entail an immediate and an immense outlay on the part of the State, and would be extremely demoralizing in its tendencies. The system has been tried, with disastrous results, in other States. Under this plan, the State becomes a manufacturer, and instead of selling only the labor of the convicts, as under the contract system, the State also puts in the capital required, and thus enters into double competition with free labor. It is a well established fact that a State cannot work as advantageously as a private firm or corporation, and would therefore have to dispose of its goods at a great sacrifice. The adoption of that system would make it necessary to purchase large quantities of machinery (for it should be remembered that we are not allowed to work more than one hundred men at any one industry), the building of additional shops, the employment of purchasing agents, salesmen, book-keepers, foremen and instructors; in short, the State would have to conduct six or seven factories, in each of which one hundred men are employed, and for the business conduct of which many additional offices will have to be created. To conduct these various factories, a large amount of money would have to be drawn out of the public treasury, each month, with no likelihood of a full return being made by the sale of the goods. In conclusion, it should also be remembered that, in the event of the adoption of the public account system, it would take many months after the completion of our present contracts, to put the same into force and the consequent idleness of all our convicts.

As to the second, the piece-price plan, the objections are not so numerous, yet they are of sufficient force to make its adoption by the State a very doubtful and expensive experiment. First of all, the hardships entailed by convict upon free labor are not at all alleviated by the adoption of this latter system. To be candid, it is a distinction without a difference. Were it to be put in force the contractors would still control the work of the convicts, the only difference being that, instead of paying the State a given price per day for the labor of each convict employed, so much a piece, a dozen, or a gross would be paid for the article manufactured in the institution. It stands to reason that the price would have to be fixed far below that paid to free labor for the same kind of work, as otherwise manufacturers would not submit to the annoyance of doing their work under the guidance and rules of the State Prison authorities. And assuredly these contractors would arrange their prices in keeping with the figures paid for the labor heretofore, so that they will be enabled to dispose of their wares as advantageously as in the past. Thus it will be seen that a change from the contract to the piece-price system will have not the slightest tendency to relieve free labor from the evils complained of, while on the other hand it will greatly add to the duties of the Prison authorities and incur much extra expense to the State.

These, in brief, are my views on the subject of the adoption of either the public account or the piece-price system, under the laws thus far enacted. If, however, in the wisdom of the Legislature, it is determined upon that either of the above systems is to be put in operation in this institution after the expiration (July 1st, 1885) of our present contracts, then that body should promptly pass laws at the ensuing session making it possible to carry out the same, by providing for the employment of the extra help such a change would entail, and voting the large sums of money that will be required.[1]

3. COMPARATIVE MERITS OF THE OPERATION OF THE "PIECE-PRICE" AND "LEASE" SYSTEMS OF CONTRACT LABOR AS APPLIED IN THE NEW JERSEY STATE PRISON.

The following reports of the Supervisor of the State Prison in 1890 and 1892, which were compiled by William A. Hall, Clerk of the Supervisor, concisely summarize the relative productivity of the lease and the "piece-price" systems of contracting for the labor of the inmates of the State Prison after 1884.

[1] *Annual Report of Keeper P. H. Laverty,* 1884; pp. 32–34; *New Jersey Legislative Documents,* 1885.

STATEMENT B.

Showing number of Convicts, annual cost of subsistence and maintenance separately. Also total cost, including all expenses per man, with amount of earnings and net loss to State for fiscal years 1880 to 1890, inclusive.[1]

Years	1880	1881	1882	1883	1884	1885
Number of Convicts	830	794	831	817	815	863
Total Cost of Maintenance	$50,135 14	$51,362 90	$62,502 80	$62,462 83	$59,248 71	$58,927 00
Salaries of Deputy Keepers	45,504 62	46,345 19	51,073 81	56,209 64	56,973 83	57,530 21
Salaries of Officers and Inspectors	9,500 00	9,207 34	9,000 00	9,000 00	9,000 00	9,000 00
Total Expenses	115,932 77	119,590 68	129,762 94	133,473 19	132,417 58	133,156 91
Credit by Amount of Earnings	68,572 50	50,702 74	68,599 67	72,706 88	61,846 21	45,319 55
Total Loss to State	$47,360 28	$68,887 94	$61,163 27	$60,766 31	$70,571 37	$87,837 36

Years	1886	1887	1888	1889	1890
Number of Convicts	892	893	874	965	973
Total Cost of Maintenance	$62,552 82	$69,340 46	$67,000 76	$72,798 48	$74,721 88
Salaries of Deputy Keepers	62,578 06	63,955 86	64,323 56	65,480 31	67,384 80
Salaries of Officers and Inspectors	9,000 00	9,000 00	9,000 00	9,000 00	9,000 00
Total Expenses	151,053 28	162,858 64	151,048 81	154,565 55	158,661 39
Credit by Amount of Earnings	66,411 03	65,617 16	57,287 13	54,985 94	61,082 64
Total Loss to State	$84,642 25	$97,241 48	$93,761 68	$99,579 61	$97,878 75

[1] Annual Report of the State Prison, 1890; p. 45.

ADDENDA—PIECE-PRICE SYSTEM.

Showing the number of days' work performed, earnings per capita, total earnings, and amount that the contract system of working the prisoners would have yielded at the usual price paid (50 cents a day) for the same period.

Years.	Number of Men at work.	Per diem per man average earnings.	Total earnings.	Earnings under contract system at 50 cents per diem.	Difference.
1886	163,797	.3998c	$65,485 96	$81,898 50	$16,412 54
1887	157,128	.4049c	63,634 64	78,564 00	14,929 36
1888	142,623	.3981c	56,786 69	71,311 50	14,524 81
1889	127,806	.4256c	54,387 89	63,903 00	9,515 11
1890	143,132	.4212c	60,284 85	71,566 00	11,281 15
1891	161,769	.4577c	74,047 21	80,884 50	6,837 29
1892	156,729½	.4944c	77,483 83	78,364 75	880 92
Total ...	1,052,984½	.4294c	$452,111 07	$526,492 25	$74,381 18

In total number of men at work for years 1891 and 1892 are included 17,582¾ and 8,391, respectively, these men being returned as idle, contractors not availing themselves of their services.[1]

4. THE INDUSTRIAL DISTRIBUTION OF THE STATE PRISON POPULATION IN 1893.

The following excerpt from the report of the keeper of the State Prison in 1893, concisely summarizes the industrial distribution of the State Prison population at that time.[2]

HOW EMPLOYED.

The 940 male convicts at this date are accounted for as follows:
On hosiery contract 95
On shoe contract 86
On mats and matting contract 74

[1] *Annual Report of the State Prison,* 1892. Statistics of the Supervisor, p. 31.
[2] *Annual Report of State Prison,* 1893; pp. 15–16; in *Legislative Documents,* 1894.

On brush contract	82
On shirt contract	83
On pants contract	95
On block contract	19
Shop runners and cleaners	24
Hall runners and whitewashers	46
Bakers	11
Cook-House	12
Wash-House	14
Barbers	5
Tailors	4
Shoemakers	5
Engineer	1
Firemen	5
Firemen's helpers	5
Blacksmiths	2
Blacksmith's helpers	2
Machinists	2
Masons	2
Masons' helpers	2
Tinsmiths	3
Locksmiths	1
Bookbinders	1
Librarians	2
Painters	3
Carpenters	3
Plumbers	2
Steamfitters	2
Electricians	2
Bucketmen	3
Gatemen	2
Gardeners and yardmen	10
Shop-hall runners	2
Shop-hall scrubbers	3
Shop-hall truckmen	3
Shop-hall whitewashers and cleaners	2
Slug heater	1
Woodchopper	1
Gatemen, shop-yard	2
Towermen	2
Lampman	1
Store-room	5
Old, infirm and unemployed	166
Sick in cells	21
Sick in hospital	18
Hospial attendants	3
	———
Total males	940

II. Prison Administration and Prison Reform Since 1885.

I. The Views of Keeper John H. Patterson, Regarding the Fundamental Problems of Prison Administration, 1890–1892.

John H. Patterson, keeper of the State Prison from 1886 to 1896, was the most efficient administrator of the prison during the second half of the 19th century. The following excerpts from his annual reports of 1890 to 1892 indicate his views upon the most vital phases of prison administration. While it is strongly maintained by a number of the prison authorities that these reports were written by William A. Hall, financial clerk of the prison, the very fact that a majority of the same deputies were in office before and after Patterson's administration, would seem to indicate that much of the credit for the acknowledged superiority of Mr. Patterson's administration was due to his own energy.

RECOMMENDATIONS (1890).

I would recommend that the convicts be paid for overwork, and their earnings be placed to their credit in the office, so that they would be enabled to help their dependent families during the term of their imprisonment and assist them to live honestly until they could procure employment.

Many convicts leave the prison with a determination to live honestly, but the few dollars given them to pay their expenses home, and the prejudices they have to overcome, cause them to be discouraged and they are forced back to their old habits.

I recommend the indeterminate sentence, for the reason that if a prisoner is returned the second and third times, he is not fit to be intrusted with his liberty, and society is rid of a dangerous person.

I recommend the Bertillion system of measurement for habitual criminals, as adopted by the Prison Wardens' Association of the United States.

There is much sentimentalism about this system, and while I believe that that there are a great many in Prison who are not of the general class of criminals, yet the burglar, the man who has committed arson, and the man who commits rape, for the first time, I feel no scruple in branding him, if I can, by identification, nor would I withhold his description if in my power to do so.

Society should know that he has been convicted of a crime of that sort, because it is not the result of impulse.

He is not in the same category with a man who has been on a spree, and struck his fellow-man down in hot blood. We all know that such crimes are crimes of deliberation, then why screen the offender because this is his first offense?

The French measurement is so accurate by meters, centimeters and millimeters, that his identification cannot be disputed.

I would recommend that as soon as practicable, the $100,000 appropriated for the construction of a new wing—chapel and hospital—as provided for in the bill passed by the Legislature of 1890, be raised to complete the work which is so much needed. In our crowded condition of the Prison, it is impossible to comply with the law requiring separate confinement.

CONCLUSION.

I tender my sincere thanks to Governor Abbett, Board of Inspectors, Supervisor and other officers of the Prison, both in their personal and official capacity, for the valuable suggestions and aid they have given me in the management of the Prison. It is also due to the Deputy Keepers to say that they have been uniformly courteous and vigilant.[1]

Respectfully submitted,

JOHN H. PATTERSON.

PAROLE (1891).

I believe the parole law, as being executed in New Jersey, the best parole system anywhere in the United States, and if its faithful operation can be continued it will prove a valuable factor in the reduction of crime; but should its execution fall under illegitimate influences it would then prove a law dangerous to the good order of society.

Of the whole number paroled under this law none have been returned to this institution.

Regular employment being absolutely essential to the granting of a parole, I would suggest as wise that some organized agency be adopted as a means of securing that employment previous to the egress of the criminal.

A parole should be possible only after the prisoner has had a positive experience of the rigor of the law, and been compelled to appreciate the certainty of punishment as consequent on the infraction of that law; it should be dependent also on good standing acquired by the prisoner whilst in prison; it should be admissible only on the certain assurance of the steady occupation of the prisoner after his exit from the Prison; it should be granted only on a satisfactory assurance of its being acceptable to the general sentiment of the reputable citizens of that community from which the prisoner was received; it should not be applicable in any case of second conviction for crime.

[1] *Annual Report of John H. Patterson, Keeper of the State Prison,* 1890; *Legislative Documents,* 1891; Vol. V, pp. 24–25.

GENERAL REMARKS.

The increase of crime in the United States is certainly a cause for alarm. Owing to the Federal System of government it is almost impossible to estimate accurately how much is spent in the prevention and punishment of crime in this country, but Mr. Worms calculates, on fair premises, that this cost amounts to fifteen millions of dollars annually.

In Great Britain the cost of criminal justice and its administration is constantly on the increase, and it never was as high as at the present time; the ulterior cost of criminal proceedings added to these makes a total expenditure in the United Kingdom of seven and one-half millions pounds sterling. Apart from the accompanying danger to the community these figures afford ample food for most serious reflection. Already in the United States, to say nothing about the maintenance of prisons, penitentiaries and reformatories, the support of the police force alone involves an amount equal to one-tenth of the national expenditure.

England, with her industrial schools, has no doubt done much towards limiting crime, but notwithstanding the beneficent effects of these, the criminal classes still keep pace with the annual growth of her population.

In our own land, when we take into consideration the vast immigration from all climes and countries under the sun, and most of this from the lowest strata of society, as an addition to our own criminal classes, it is not surprising that leading penologists have sounded an alarm they make the lamentable admission that crime is not only increasing in our midst, but increasing faster in proportion than the growth of population; nearly all statisticians tell the same story; such increase is more to be dreaded than war—war has become a transitory incident, but crime is far from being a passing incident; there appears to be not the faintest prospect of its coming to an end. While not affecting so seriously those who have passed the meridian of life, it must inevitably constitute conditions baneful to the prosperity of generations to come after us. When in a hundred years from now, excepting the casualties of war, our population will have become as dense as that of India, and farms reduced to one or two acres, these conditions will have become so exaggerated as to constitute a state of society absolutely appalling. What could possibly be done with such a vast army of criminals, produced through hereditary viciousness, parental neglect, diseased organism, with the host of accompanying deleterious environments?

It is impossible to discuss here the subject of the causation of crime. We can but glance at some of the reasons for its increase. Such increase is no doubt in some degree attributable to the unhealthy concentration of population in our large cities, where the inducements to crime, the opportunities for crime, the facilities for instruction in crime and for concealing the same are greater than elsewhere.

A prominent divine but lately observed, in a public oration, that the problem of the age was the reaching of the people through religious and moral influences; that this in the large cities—festering sores on the body politic of the nation—was not being accomplished by the pulpit; that the means and appliances for effecting this purpose were not co-ordinate with the relative increase of population and crime.

Let us consider the influences of legislation on crime. Its present tendency seems bound to produce more crime. All law by its nature is coercive, but so long as the coercion is confined to a limited space and operates only at rare intervals, it has very little effect on the volume of crime; but when a law affects every member of a community every day of his life, such a law is certain to increase the population of gaols. The present legislative tendency seems to be towards the increasing passage of such laws, and so long as this is the case, the annual amount of crime will increase and a corresponding taint be cast on a larger body of the population so made candidates or recruits for the large army of criminals.

A crime, as it concerns us, is defined as that act which the law declares to be a crime and for which the State recognizes punishment. In the annals of history crime has been declared to exist in telling the truth, in exercising the body, and even in eating, except under certain restrictions; there is, in fact, no conduct which may not be criminal if the dominant power in any country enacts a law to punish it. On the other hand, the transgressor of the law, who, by his transgression, becomes a criminal, may be, according to his own ideas, entirely innocent, both in intention and action; the law may be even most extreme. At one time in England a man would hang for sweating a penny or snaring a hare.

Legal efforts to correct and punish crime may, accordingly, be unwittingly injurious by the excessive multiplication of penal statutes, seeming necessary because of the over-magnifying of the infraction of moral rules and by sweeping into one capacious and over-finely meshed net too great a variety of minor offenses elevated into crimes and too extended and remote grades of criminals.

A man goes to prison, for instance, for disobeying some municipal law; he comes out of prison the friend and associate of habitual criminals; he is transformed from a comparatively harmless member of society into a dangerous thief or a house-breaker. One person of this character is a greater menace to the community than a hundred offenders against municipal regulations. The present system of law-making undoubtedly tends to multiply this class of men.

The subject of criminal classification is much discussed. In my experience, the most dangerous class of criminals are under thirty-five years, and the greatest amount of crime is committed by those between twenty and forty years. The older criminals, who have passed the meridian of life almost constantly in one prison or another, have become comparatively physically disqualified for bold enterprises, and by being shut up have lost their knowledge of persons and places; though feeling as strangers to the community, they are nevertheless, so well remembered by the police that for the slightest offense they are again incarcerated. On the other hand, the young offender is familiar with all the tricks of the trade, and is competent to teach even the older offender.

PUNISHMENT AS A CORRECTION OF CRIME.

A criminal is one who has committed a crime, as defined by the law, and by the same, pronounced as deserving of punishment, but being at the same time morally diseased. The prison is the remedy intended to effect a cure, and chiefly through the means of judicious punishment. Punishment, then, has a true object; punishment which ceases to be, or is imperfectly punitive, is little less than a farce; no false philanthropy or maudlin sentimentalism should be allowed to thwart its real purpose; that purpose is not solely founded on the "Lex Talionis" (an eye for an eye, and a tooth for a tooth), nor, in justice to the criminal, could it be inflicted only for the protection of society, nor simply to deter others from similar crimes.

In every sense is it as true and vital today as it was nearly two hundred years ago, that motto inscribed over the first separate-cell penitentiary (that of San Michele), built by Fontana, the architect of Clement XII., at Rome, in the year 1703—"Parvum est coercere improbos nisi probos efficias disciplina," *i. e.* it is of little use to restrain the wicked by punishment unless you make them virtuous by discipline.

Punishment is an expiatory discipline necessary to the preservation of the organic and fundamental order of society; at the same time the most effectual way to protect society is to reform the criminal; any means used effectually outside may be legitimate inside, but not necessarily politic or admissible. Under no circumstances in accord with the satisfaction of justice should a punitive receptacle for criminals be converted into a play-house.

Punishment should be inflicted with such a just positiveness that the criminal shall be impressed with the fact that it is a certain and necessary consequence of crime, and yet he should be made to understand that he is the object of a kindly sympathy which would legitimately assist in making him a better man.

The determinal sentence as recommended in the report of last year, for reasons therein stated, is again approved, and for an additional reason, which would seem conclusive in its favor. Heredity must be accepted as one of the powerful agents in the reproduction and continuance of crime; the personality of individuals as comprised in their physical, mental and moral characteristics, fixed in their constitution by strong and continued habit, is certainly to be found impressed on their progeny. This source of the propagation of crime through lineal descent is undeniably preventable by the continued seclusion of the habitual criminal from society; as through prison confinement, as also by the absolute separation of the sexes in all prisons, almshouses, and asylums used as receptacles for criminals, or those physically or mentally prostrated or depraved.

In the conduct of a prison at which punishment and reformation are equally the object, there is a continuous need of sagacious and conscientious officials.

The head of the Danish Prison Department at the Stockholm Prison Congress is represented as saying, "Give me the best possible regulations and bad directors, and there will be no success, but give me good directors, even with mediocre regulations, and I will answer for it that everything will go marvelously well."

Capable and reliable officials, while insisting with inflexible firmness on the enforcement of discipline, are able at the same time by tact and kindliness to diffuse around them a moralizing and helpful atmosphere.

If so fortunate as to have a corps of such officials trained to regard their duties from an honorable and elevated standpoint, a Warden, through the personal confidence established between the prisoner and such officials, can accomplish a power of good by discerning the private character, habits and capabilities of the prisoner, and in the direction of such personal discipline or indulgence as would best promote the true objects of punishment and the reform of the prisoner.

RECOMMENDATIONS.

I reiterate the recommendation made last year, that the convicts be paid for over-work, and their earnings placed to their credit, so that they could help their dependent families during the term of imprisonment, and to assist them to live honestly when they return to society, until they can procure employment. Many leave the prison with good intentions, but because of the great prejudice to overcome and lack of funds they become discouraged and drift back to their old associates and old habits. The State will gain by this arrangement, for the reason every prisoner will have an incentive in doing his task in order to earn something for himself, and thereby avoiding the constant reprimanding, and forcing the prisoner to do a fair day's work will be avoided and better discipline secured in the shops.

In view of the impossibility, in the present inadequate condition of the Prison space, of carrying out the requirements of the law as to solitary confinement, I would urge an increase of accommodations, as provided for in the appropriation of one hundred thousand dollars, made three years ago, for the erection of an additional wing, a hospital and a chapel. This increased accommodation is, in addition to a necessity for the execution of the law, further appealed for on the following grounds, viz.:

As a necessity to the preservation of the individuality of the criminal, without which reformatory efforts might readily be misdirected; also, because isolated cell life is more positively expressive of the individual loss of liberty, in itself a powerful factor in the infliction of punishment; also, as a preventive of mutual contamination, or, at least, of the opportunity of education from a lower to a higher grade of vice; lastly, as a preservative of good order and discipline in the prevention of the tyranny of brute force, as in the stronger occupant of the cell compelling the servility of the weaker.

As to the recognized necessity for increased accommodations for a hospital and chapel, the respective reports of Physician and Moral Instructors are referred to.

CONCLUSION.

I herein express my appreciation of the services rendered me by Your Excellency, for the uniform courtesies and advice you have given me in the performance of my duties, also to the Board of Inspectors, the Supervisor and all public officials and subordinates, who have advised and assisted me in discerning and executing the duties of my position.[1]

Respectfully submitted,

JOHN H. PATTERSON,

Keeper.

PAROLE (1892).

So far, and especially as recidivation is concerned, the Parole law of this State, as now upon her statute-books, has met our fullest expectations, 78 convicts having been paroled, only two of whom have been returned to this Prison. From experience with this law, the salutary inference has been reached that the paroled are under restraining influences which prevent them from indulgence in those excesses leading to crime. They appreciate the fact of being under a ban, and their license to be at large is a constant reminder that if they violate the conditions of their parole they will be returned to prison, and summarily and without process of law; and will also be compelled to forfeit the remission of time previously gained by good behavior. Hence it is safer, both to the law and to society, to parole a convict than to pardon him, a pardon being unconditional but the parole conditional. Under the former he is free and unrestrained, under the latter his freedom depends on his good conduct and acts as a restraining influence in keeping him from his old companions in crime, guards him against indulgence in vice, affords him an opportunity to maintain his dependent family and helps on the road to ultimate reformation.

Again, it is believed that the paroled prisoner will be received back by the community he has offended under conditions more propitious to his success than would one who has been pardoned. This for the reason that being still under the surveillance of the punishing power he can be more promptly returned to confinement and without appeal (as in the case of a pardon) to the perhaps uncertain decision of the arm of the law.

For the perfection of a just exercise of the prerogatives of the parole it is but fair to the Warden of a prison, who, under the rules and regulations governing it, is required to state that "in the judgment of the Keeper or other official" he, the convict, has been a good prisoner and is "a proper person to be paroled;" that there should be placed in the Keeper's power adequate means and facilities for the classification of prisoners, whereby he can protect himself against all accusations of prejudice or unfairness in the indorsement of parties to be paroled.

He should be able to ground his decision upon an open reference to the list of merit or demerit in which the prisoner's name appears. One absolutely essential condition to such classification or grading of the convict as to worthy demeanor or faithfully-performed work, is an increase of separate cell-room in this Prison, for which increase, were there no other potent

---

[1] *Annual Report of John H. Patterson, Keeper of the State Prison*, 1891; pp. 16–21; *Legislative Documents* 1892.

reason, the simple requirement of the existing law as to the separate confinement of prisoners, should be amply sufficient.

REMARKS.

As the sentence of the law enjoins confinement at "hard labor," and because labor is one of the most valuable of reformatory agents, it is plainly advisable that, save in exceptional cases, all criminals should be steadily employed. Accordingly the scope of employment should be so varied, and the field so large, as to give occupation to every culprit capable of work.

As, however, with a large class of prisoners labor is looked upon simply as a punitive measure, to make it reformatory it should be accompanied by a system of reward as well as punishment. If a penalty follows failure to complete an allotted task, so a reward for faithful performance of duty should be as constantly and fairly held in view. On this principle some amount of pecuniary return, small though it be, will popularize labor. Wage-sharing by the culprit doubtless acts as an incentive to industry, as it is also in some degree preventive of the attempt of the malingerer to avoid work by many cunning devices. It would afford more willing workers for the shops, as well as assist in providing a moderate fund for the temporary support of the convict on his exit from the Prison, and until he could secure a supporting employment. It should be allowable for the convict to contribute some portion of his earnings to the support of a needy family outside of the Prison, and surely, when so doing, his fellow-workman in the outer world could hardly brand his labor with being any other than "honest labor."

As the present law seems inoperative, a new law should be enacted, making provision for a return to the faithfully-working convict of a definite proportion of what is gained by his labor.

Healthy popular sentiment has been aroused, and is in fruitful operation in several of the States, as to the conjoined duty of the community and the State in providing for the discharged convict who desires to become an honest citizen, prompt employment or temporary shelter and sustenance until employment can be obtained. Such efforts are highly commendable, both for the protection of society as also to prevent the return of the discharged man to the Prison, a most frequent occurrence, and sometimes for the third and fourth time, and for the alleged reason of his being unable to procure employment by his unaided efforts, and of existing prejudices of the community, which combat him at every point.

The worthy pride of the prosperous State of New Jersey should stimulate her to put herself in this direction on a progressive parity with her sister States, if not to excell them, in all efforts to elevate the tone of her citizenship, by assisting in the reform of her criminal classes. She should cheerfully lend some pecuniary aid to those charitable organizations formed for the purpose of encouraging and assisting the reformed convict, and should have, or contribute to the support of, some paid agent or officer to have already secured, or to secure, employment for him when released from confinement. Such action is taken, and successfully, in other States of the

Union, and there is no reason why a similar course of action would not be to the advantage of our own State. The employment of such an agent or officer, and a fair appropriation for the object above set forth, are earnestly recommended.

So far as finances would permit, desirable changes have been made in the sanitary arrangements and appliances of the Prison. The low mortality rate among the convicts, many of whom enter the Prison enfeebled and broken in health, shows that a fair sanitation as regards heat, light, ablution, apparel, cleanliness, diet, &c., is faithfully preserved; and the good physical condition of the men on their egrees from prison is confirmatory of the fact that the best of care is taken to return them to the community in a condition favorable to self-support. As previously urged, and for reason set forth in the reports of the medical officers of the Prison, an increase of hospital accommodations is strongly recommended.

In addition to the moral advantages to be derived from the construction of a chapel, for which the disbursement of the appropriation already made should be no longer delayed, such building would afford room-space for a school sufficient to accommodate the night classes, the present rooms being entirely inadequate and unsuitable for the purposes for which they are used. While in consideration of the classes of men admitted to prison more stress is laid on the necessity of manual training in the acquirement of some trade which will fit them for self-support, the advisability of teaching every candidate for citizenship to read and write is neither deprecated nor ignored. In the acquisition of such accomplishments the prisoner feels more inspired and better qualified to battle with the difficulties of life, and more hopeful of ultimate success.

The conduct of the female wing of the prison, while reflecting credit on its officers, would, in the silent but effectual methods of its daily routine, hardly suggest the presence of a female prisoner in the institution. Under the judicious organization and management of the Matron and her assistants, this wing is remarkable both for the little trouble it gives to the rest of the Prison and for the large amount of work accomplished by its industrious inmates. It is a model of neatness, cleanliness and good order.

I exceedingly regret the loss of the Rev. Father Fidelis, Moral Instructor, who has been called to another field of labor. His services in this institution were valuable indeed; indefatigable in his work—the night was never too dark and stormy to keep him from his duties—he was a genial companion, a good friend, and a wise counselor.

CONCLUSION.

I have diligently tried to conduct the office of the Prison so as to have a healthy, salutary influence upon the prisoners, with a view to encourage reformation and, at the same time, to give them to understand that they are deprived of liberty because they are violators of the law, and society demands their punishment. While I treat them humanely, and impress them that I am their friend and not an enemy, I demand they shall be governed by the strictest rules and discipline.

Permit me to express my appreciation to Your Excellency of the interest that you have always manifested in the work of the Prison, and your uniform courtesy and advice and the attention that I have always received from you with reference to Prison matters; and also to the Board of Inspectors, the Supervisor, and all public officials with whom I have been connected in the management of my office.[1]

Very respectfully,
JOHN H. PATTERSON,
Keeper.

2. REPORT OF THE DEPENDENCY AND CRIMES COMMISSION OF 1908.

In 1908 the Governor of New Jersey upon the authority of the Legislature appointed a commission, which was directed to make an investigation as to the causes of dependency and criminality in their broadest and most fundamental aspects. The report of the commission is important merely as an analysis of the situation as to dependency and crime in 1908, but it is immensely more significant as marking a recognition on the part of the community in general and the Commission in particular that the problem of criminality is not an isolated metaphysical, theological, and juridical phenomenon, but is an inevitable product of defects in the social environment produced by abnormal biological and psychological forces and influences. While the specific information contained in the report as to the conditions described was neither new nor revolutionary, the appointment and work of this commission was really epoch-making in the history of social economy in New Jersey in that it constituted the first public recognition of the broad sociological foundations of social pathology, and the necessity of attacking the problem as a unity which could not be met by sporadic and isolated efforts to combat some of its particular manifestations. The following reprint of this important report reproduces only those portions which are germane to the subject under discussion in this work, namely, the condition of the penal, reformatory, and correctional institutions of the state and the problems of their administration.

[1] *Annual Report of John H. Patterson, Keeper of the State Prison, 1892; Legislative Documents,* 1893; Vol. III, pp. 91–94.

REPORT OF THE DEPENDENCY AND CRIMES COMMISSION.

Appointed by Virtue of Chapter 140, Laws of 1908.

REPORT.

To His Excellency, John Franklin Fort, Governor of the State of New Jersey:

The Commission appointed by your Excellency, under and by virtue of Chapter 140 of the Laws of 1908, to investigate into the causes of dependency in all forms, and the causes of criminality, begs leave to submit the following preliminary report:

The Commission was charged with an investigation into questions of great and vital importance, covering a large field of work. In the short time alloted to the Commission since its appointment, it has been unable to practically complete all of its labors, as required of it under the provisions of the law above referred to, hence there are many other important problems and principles affecting the causes of dependency and crime which are not referred to in this report.

The following are the subjects which the Commission deem to be matters for attention in this report:

1. *This Commission recommends the abolishing of all the State Boards of Managers.*

2. This Commission also recommends the appointment by the Governor, with the consent of the Senate, of a Commissioner of Charities, who shall be a specialist in all phases of the work in the institution of this State, who shall know thoroughly the principles that should govern the penal institutions (prisons, reformatories, county jails and penitentiaries), also who shall be in touch with the best known methods for governing and regulating hospitals for the insane, State and county, and the care of the feeble-minded, epileptic and all other wards of the State, dependents, defectives and delinquents.

The said Commissioner to be the President of the Board of Managers hereinafter referred to, and to have equal powers with the other members of the Board.

3. This Commission also recommends that the said Commissioner of Charities shall have a secretary, who shall be known as "First Assistant," and that there shall be appointed a clerk. Sufficient appropriation should also be made for the employment of a stenographer and other necessary expenses.

4. This Commission also recommends that the Governor appoint a Board of Charities and Corrections of nine members, two of whom shall be women and two physicians, to have direction and control of the Department of Charities and Corrections, said Board to serve without compensation, but their expenses to be paid; said Board to have the right to conduct investigations, and, with the consent of the Governor, to issue subpœnas to compel attendance of witnesses in such investigations.

The said Board to have control of all the affairs of the State Prison, Rahway Reformatory, State Home for Boys, State Home for Girls, the two

State Hospitals for the Insane, the Skillman Colony for Epileptics, the Training School for Feeble-Minded, the State Home for Feeble-Minded, the State Sanitarium for Tuberculosis, and the State Home for Feeble-Minded Women and Girls; and shall have a general supervision of all other State institutions for the care of defectives, delinquents, and dependents.

, The Commissioner of Charities, subject to the rules of the Board of Charities and Corrections, shall have the power to place patients in the State and county institutions, and also to transfer patients from one institution to another.

5. That the said Board of Charities and Corrections shall meet in the State House, in the Department of Charities and Corrections, bi-monthly; the Board shall be divided into committees, whose work shall be specific, and whose duty it shall be to visit each institution bi-monthly and to report to the whole Board at each bi-monthly meeting.

6. That there shall be a fiscal agent who shall, with the approval of the Board, purchase all supplies for all the State institutions, and who shall, with a committee of the Board, audit all accounts, and who shall also collect all amounts due from parents or guardians.

7. That there shall be a State Training School for Nurses and Attendants, which shall be managed by the Commissioner of Charities and Corrections under the direction of the Board and under the supervision of the Civil Service Commission.

8. That the committees appointed by the said Board shall be, in part, as follows:

(a) An Educational Committee, having in charge the manual training work.

(b) An Industrial Committee, under whose charge should be the work done, not as to the amount of money directly earned, but as to the training of the inmates to become self-supporting; the work of this committee to include agriculture where they can regulate the products of the different institutions, according to the soil and conditions.

(c) A Committee on Maintenance and Management of Institutions.

This Commission believes that the centralization of authority, control and management of the State institutions would be far reaching in its effect. All the needs of the institutions would be of equal interest to the Board, and a definite policy would be established in regard to the needs of all the institutions, which would result in the abolition of the present unsatisfactory and extravagant methods now used in securing appropriations for new buildings and other necessities. One institution after another could be completed, taking them in the order of their needs, and the industries of each institution could be so planned that a perfect chain could be made, whereby each institution would supply some one or more wants of the other institutions; that is, the mattresses and furniture for all could be made at one institution, shoes and clothing at another, nurseries for providing plants and trees could be established at another, and so on.

This would allow for many more occupations, indoors and out, and thus provide adequate employment for all who are in a condition to work.

The State is now spending large sums of money each year, and has in the past invested millions in the different institutions for dependents, defectives and delinquents. The maintenance of these institutions, with the necessary buildings, presents a business proposition ever becoming greater and more complicated. The keynote of twentieth century activity along the line of philanthropy is research into causes. Therefore, it should be the duty of the Commissioner of Charities to have complete histories of all cases of the State's dependents, defectives and delinquents, including all the criminal classes, on file in his office. As at present constituted, each State institution is governed by its own board of managers, and is a unit having little or no reference to other institutions, the managers of which, living frequently at a distance from the institution, are unable to do more than irregularly attend meetings, and at those meetings have to depend upon the reports of the superintendent for the knowledge of the work for which they are responsible. The best results are not achieved either for the institution or the State.

This plan might be considered expensive in the beginning, but the Commission believes that it would lead to efficiency and economy in the future, and would be of greater force in reforming delinquents.

The Commission further recommends that a systematic compilation of all crimes committed in this State should be made annually and published by the State.

The Commission also recommends that there shall be appointed by the Governor, with the consent of the Senate, a medical inspector, who shall be a physician, and who shall be charged with visiting and inspecting all institutions from the hygienic and medical standpoint.

COUNTY JAILS NEED OVERHAULING.

Our present system of county jails demand a thorough overhauling. As they are at present conducted, it can be said that almost all of them are hotbeds of vice and schools for crime. The amount of harm done to the first offender, especially if he be young, by placing him in close contact with the hardened offenders, as is so commonly done, is very hard to undo, if at all possible.

To place in the county jail, in close contact with such offenders, persons who are detained as witnesses or who are accused of crime, and who may be innocent, is inexcusable and in itself criminal.

We favor the enactment of a law which would compel every county to maintain a separate building for the care of juveniles and witnesses; while the county jails are *only* to be used for the *detention* of persons awaiting trial and pending removal and the disposition of their cases. . . .

STATE PRISON.

After a careful and thorough investigation of the State Prison at Trenton, we find that it is a very unhealthy place. The shops in the prison are in a shocking condition; they are foul, with no proper sanitary arrangements, and

36 P

no proper air space for the prisoners at work. The prison, as it stands to-day, is a hotbed of disease and a menace to the health of the State, and it should be condemned by the State Board of Health at once.

We recommend the abandonment of the present prison, and urge that a modern prison be built in some available place where a large farm could be attached and plenty of sunlight and fresh air admitted within the walls of the prison, with proper yards for exercise, also with plenty of sunlight and air, and where all the prison buildings shall have proper sunlight and air. One of the things that man is entitled to under God's law is plenty of sunlight and air. There should be a drill ground in connection with the prison.

All the young officers should be brought before the Civil Service Commission, and those who have passed beyond the proper age limit should be removed. Many of these officers have spent their lives in the service, and have become aged and unfit to properly and fully discharge their duties. We believe that younger and sturdier men should take their places to successfully cope with desperate situations which may arise at any moment. We believe that it would be the essence of ingratitude to discharge them for inability, but, in the interest of the institution, they ought to go. The Commission believes that some recompense should be made, and advises retirement on one-half pay upon the arrival at a given age after a fixed period of service.

We desire to commend the present warden for the kind way in which he handles his prisoners under the serious difficulties herein set forth.

We recommend the abolishment of the trusty system now in use in the shops. We believe that it leads to abuse on the part of the inmates, and enables them to injure from personal motives men who otherwise would not be reported.

We also condemn the whole contract system in the State Prison, and believe that the work of the prisoners should be done for other institutions. These prisoners should be engaged in such work as would inure to the benefit of the State. For example, in the establishment of a large farm, which is hereinbefore recommended, from the labor of these prisoners enough products could be raised which could be furnished to some or all of our other State institutions.

We also find the woman's wing in the State Prison is greatly overcrowded.

WOMAN'S REFORMATORY.

We recommend that a Woman's Reformatory should be built at once, to relieve the conditions at the State Prison as well as at the State Home for Girls.

STATE HOME FOR GIRLS.

We recommend the enactment of a law providing that no girls over seventeen years of age be committed to this institution. We believe that girls of that age and older should be sent to a woman's reformatory. We find that at the State Home for Girls there are a large number of inmates who are over seventeen years of age, who mingle with the younger children in the institution. They should not be sent to this Home, they should be committed to a woman's reformatory.

We recommend that the Commissioner of Charities should be required immediately to secure from the superintendent of this institution the history of the girls under eleven years of age and over seventeen years of age, with a view to the removal of the younger ones to relatives who can be found to provide proper homes for them, as under no circumstances should girls of such tender age be sent to such an institution, unless their crime has been of a heinous nature.

The punishment room in this institution should be padded and should be light, with proper sanitary arrangements, and should be located in a place where it is directly under the eye of the superintendent. Bread and water, which makes the body weak and the brain inactive, is not an effective adjunct of punishment, nor is a lack of proper employment. Solitary confinement, without employment, is not a good reformatory measure. Dark cells are a thing of the past. At the State Prison they have been abolished.

Corporal punishment should be abolished, as its use leads to over-action, and its application to women cannot help reformation, as it breaks down self-respect, which is a quality to be encouraged, and not discouraged, in a reformatory.

The present superintendent is a woman of good principles, with a desire to accomplish the best results.

The tone of the institution is good, and the girls, generally, are healthy and well, and a spirit of good-fellowship exists between the superintendent and the girls. She is humane and kind, and, with the elimination of the present punishment rooms, the doing away with the leather whip, and the getting away from the institution of the man or any man who has in the past helped in the infliction of the punishment, there is no better managed institution in the land. . . .

STATE HOME FOR BOYS.

We recommend the system of this institution of "families" of "groups." But the overcrowding at this institution is serious. We believe that five hundred boys should not be together in any one institution. Individual training here is impossible.

We recommend that the Commissioner of Charities should be at once required to secure from the superintendent the histories of boys who, in his judgment, should not have been sent to the institution. We believe that boys should not be sent to this institution for truancy, that counties and cities should be required to build and maintain parental schools.

We also believe that the parole system is not as effective as it might be, owing, we believe, to the insufficient number of parole officers at the home.

We believe that the visiting of boys in their homes is one of the most, if not the most, important power for good.

We recommend that the contract system should be abolished, and the employment of boys when out of school should be of a simple and useful character, such as horticulture, the making of their own clothes and shoes, and working, if necessary, to produce commodities to be used by the dependents and inmates in our other State institutions.

MATRONS IN COUNTY JAILS.

An examination of the county jails of this State shows that in many of them there is no matron to care for the women prisoners, and, in at least one institution, this has been a direct cause of dependency.

We recommend that a law be enacted compelling the placing of a matron in every county jail of this State.

INACTIVITY OF PRISONERS IN COUNTY INSTITUTIONS.

We find in the county jails throughout the State that prisoners who are incarcerated there for minor offences, for short and for long terms, are afforded no opportunity for work or proper opportunity for exercise, and we, therefore, recommend that it be compulsory upon the counties to either provide within their own limits, or by combination with other counties, a county penitentiary or workhouse, to which all short-term prisoners be committed, and in which they be compelled to labor. And we also recommend that the county jails be reserved for the incarceration of persons awaiting trial, and witnesses, and for no other purpose.

MEDICAL EXAMINATION OF PRISONERS ON ADMISSION.

Our investigation shows an alarming condition, due to the intermingling in our State and county institutions of tuberculous inmates with healthy inmates. This condition was taken cognizance of by the United States Government.

We recommend that no person committed to any institution in this State, whether under State auspices or county auspices, be allowed to mingle with other inmates until he has undergone a physical examination by a physician, and that for the purpose of carrying out this recommendation there be established in all institutions detention rooms, or quarantine rooms, where newly admitted inmates may be kept pending such examination; and, we further recommend that all tuberculous inmates be kept at all times separate and apart from other inmates.

JUVENILE PRISONERS SEPARATE FROM ADULT PRISONERS.

As a measure to lessen juvenile crime, much of which is caused by the mingling of juvenile with older offenders, we would recommend that all children under sixteen years of age who are arrested be either paroled or kept in a separate place of confinement from the older offenders, pending trial or arraignment.

All of which is respectfully submitted, with the testimony, at Trenton, this fifteenth day of December, 1908.

MICHAEL T. BARRETT, *President,*
EMILY E. WILLIAMSON,
CAROLINE BAYARD ALEXANDER,
BENJAMIN BOISSEAU BOBBITT,
CHAS. A. RESENWASSER,
BENJAMIN MURPHY,
E. A. RANSOM, JR., *Secretary.*

CHAPTERS VII AND VIII

DOCUMENTS RELATING TO THE STATE HOME
FOR BOYS AT JAMESBURG, AND STATE
HOME FOR GIRLS AT TRENTON.

CHAPTERS VII AND VIII

DOCUMENTS RELATING TO THE STATE HOME FOR BOYS AT
JAMESBURG AND THE STATE HOME FOR GIRLS AT TRENTON.

I. THE ORIGIN OF THE STATE HOME FOR BOYS.

1. THE ATTEMPT TO FOUND A "HOUSE OF REFUGE" AT KINGSTON, 1850–1852.

The imperative need for a reformatory for juvenile offenders had been recognized in New Jersey as early as 1833 when the New Jersey Howard Society made an earnest plea for the provision of such an institution. No practical move was made in this direction, however, until the agitation was renewed by the New Jersey Prison Reform Association in 1849. In 1850 a law was secured which authorized the erection of a "House of Refuge" for juvenile delinquents in New Jersey. Though a site was selected at Kingston and the building partially erected, the funds appropriated for the institution were coveted by the political forces at the capital and the project was abandoned, greatly to the disgust of the exponents of penal reform in New Jersey. The following reports of the majority and minority of the committee of the Legislature appointed to investigate the desirability of continuing the erection of the "House of Refuge" admirably sum up the different arguments in the controversy.

REPORTS OF THE COMMITTEE OF THE MAJORITY AND MINORITY, ON THE HOUSE OF REFUGE, TRENTON, 1851.

REPORT.

To the General Assembly of the State of New Jersey:

The undersigned, a majority of the committee of one member from each county of the state appointed in virtue of the following resolution:

Resolved, That so much of the governor's message as refers to the House of Refuge, be referred to a committee of one member from each county, who shall examine and inquire as to the progress of the same, and make all other necessary inquiries and make report to the House, take leave to REPORT:

That your committee have diligently and carefully examined all the facts connected with the duties of their appointment; and in view of the importance of the subject, and the great solicitude in regard to it manifested by the great body of their constituents, as well as by the citizens at large, they have deemed it proper to present a full report of their proceedings and opinions.

At the last session of the legislature, the *"act to authorize the establishment of a House of Refuge"* was passed, by which commissioners were appointed to select *"a suitable site on which to erect buildings, to be called the New Jersey House of Refuge, in which may be kept, employed and instructed, such minors as may have been convicted of crimes by the courts, or who have been arrested as vagrants, or whose parents and guardians may desire their being committed to the institution hereby authorized to be erected."*

The purchase money of the said site was limited to $6,000.

The governor was directed to appoint three commissioners *"to contract for the erection of the said House of Refuge, on such terms and plans as they may deem just and proper, subject to the approbation of the governor;* and the Treasurer was directed to pay to the Commissioners, out of any unappropriated money in his hands, on the warrant of the governor, *"such sum or sums of money as they may require for the said House of Refuge, not exceeding fifteen thousand dollars."*

In virtue of this act the work was undertaken; a site was selected and purchased for $5,600.

Your committee have visited it, and are of opinion that it is well selected and not dearly purchased.

The cellars of the building have been excavated, and the foundation walls partly erected.

The apparatus for raising water by Hydraulic Rams from an adjoining brook are nearly completed; and will be a matter of great utility and comfort, if the brook, which apparently has not a very abundant supply, does not become dry in the summer months.

This is all the work as yet executed on the spot, although there has been a considerable quantity of sand, stone and brick, placed there.

Your committee having been furnished with merely informal statements of the probable cost of the building intended to be erected, were desirous to obtain for your guidance, as well as for their own, some information necessary to a correct decision on this important subject, of an authentic character, and therefore a communication was addressed to the Commissioners, a copy of which communication is hereto annexed, (marked A,) to which your committee received a reply, (marked B.)

This reply being from only a single Commissioner, and not being definite in its character, your committee are still obliged to have recourse, in addition thereto, to the statements which had been already in their possession, which are:

1st. A communication from Mr. McClurg, one of the Commissioners, which states that the contracts entered into amount (based on an estimate of gross, not having a copy of the original contracts in his possession,) to $53,825.

2d. Another rough estimate obtained from the Commissioners, without signature, and which makes the amount $72,711; and

3d. The message of Governor Haines, which states that "the central building and one wing can be finished in a plain, substantial and appropriate manner, of the best materials, for about $42,000. The additional wing may be enclosed without its range of dormitories, for the further sum of $12,000; and the whole edifice, with accommodations for 190, for $64,000; which sums may be increased indefinitely by additional or ornamental work, or diminished by inferior or inappropriate work."

From these statements, and the result of their own judgment, your committee believe that the House of Refuge, including cost of land, fences, out-buildings and improvements thereon, with heating and cooking apparatus, furniture, &c., &c., cannot be completed to answer any useful purpose for less than $100,000.

As to the other points contained in their inquiries to the Commissioners, being without data upon which to found an opinion, they will not venture any.

The members of the House may determine for themselves, as well as their committee can, what the probable annual expenditure to the state will be for the maintenance of such an institution.

From a review of what has been set forth, your committee desire firstly to remark that in their opinion, the legislature in passing the act authorizing the construction of a House of Refuge, could not have contemplated, by any means, the authorization of so large an expenditure. They have adopted this conclusion from facts within the recollection of those who were members of the last legislature, as well as from the fact that the sum to be drawn from the Treasury, under the warrant of the governor, was limited to only $15,000.—(Fifteen thousand dollars.)

If it had been considered that this work would have cost $100,000, surely an appropriation greater than the sum named would have been made for the first outlay. And your committee are impressed with the conviction, that had there existed the least suspicion that so large an expenditure would have been necessary for the completion of this work, the act in question would not have passed.

Your committee are fully convinced of the benevolent motives of those who originated this matter, and they are not the less convinced of the utility of providing some mode of punishment, correction and improvement for delinquents, who have not arrived at years of maturity and discretion; they believe all that has been said in behalf of a system which will separate the youthful, perhaps thoughtless or ignorant offenders from the more ad-vanced and practiced criminal; and which will remove from our judicial authorities the difficulty arising from the necessity of either sentencing youths to incarceration in our common prisons, or to let them go "unwhipped of justice." And if the advantages to be derived from such an institution could not be obtained, except by so large an appropriation, bearing so unequally and unjustly as this will do upon the different sections of the state, they would perhaps feel themselves warranted in looking upon it with favor; but they think that without erecting another state institution, involving a very large outlay, and a considerable annual expenditure, chargeable upon the *people* of *the state at large,* all the evils of the present system may be more effectually avoided by enactments which will give to the counties respectively, the power to construct Houses of Refuge, if they be needed, or to arrange their prison discipline so as to meet the object designed; this may be either done by single counties, or by the union of two or more adjoining counties.

In this manner, the expense would be equitably arranged. Counties which have few or no juvenile offenders to receive the benefits of the institution, would not have to contribute for those which have.

The expense of transporting delinquents would be more fairly apportioned.

The mode of treatment adapted to the disposition, habits and faults of offenders, would be better understood by officials in the immediate neighbor-hood of such offenders.

The influence of relatives and friends could be brought in aid of a cor-rective discipline practiced upon offenders in their near vicinity; and the expenditure drawn from the pockets of the people of the counties, would, in a measure, be restored by its outlay among themselves.

Again: Your committee would beg leave to observe, that although the revenue of the state may be fully capable of meeting more than its ordinary expenditure, it is questionable with many whether a sound policy would warrant the appropriation of the whole of the probable excess for many years in advance of its receipt; contingencies may arise, which might make it desirable that the financial condition of the state should be in a perfectly independent position, having a surplus on hand rather than a deficit, as now in fact exists. In truth, the wholesome practice of possessing means before we expend them, is as salutary for states as for individuals.

But still another consideration is deemed worthy of observation at this time. It is well known to every one, that a universal and loud cry is sent up from every part of the state in favor of a system of Free Schools, and the argument is used with much force, that the education of the children of the state being a matter of universal interest, and of universal advantage to the people of the entire state, it should be a matter for state appropria-tion.

Shall this cry be sent up to this legislature in vain? Shall it be said that the income of the state is not sufficient to satisfy this just demand made upon it, whilst it authorizes the expenditure of that income in a manner not asked for by the people, and as this committee believes, contrary to general sentiment?

Besides, your committee believe that one of the best preventives of vice and crime is education; and your committee believe that by the establishment of Free Schools, amply provided for throughout the length and breadth of the land, the necessity of a House of Refuge would be much diminished, if it be not rendered entirely unnecessary.

The children of indigent persons, who are unable to pay for their schooling, are, for the most part, allowed to pass their youth in idleness, the fruitful mother of vice; their associations are bad; and they fall into error, perhaps crime, and become fit occupants of a House of Refuge. But if gratuitous education had been afforded them, if their early days had been passed in the pursuit of learning, subject to the discipline of a school, their minds would have taken a turn leading to virtue; ambition for worldly advancement, tempered by the lessons of morality and of religion, would have given another current to their destiny.

Therefore, your committee respectfully submit, whether it would be wise to continue to make appropriations for this House of Refuge in the face of this and the other reasons which your committee have deemed it their duty to present.

And in conclusion, your committee would take leave to recommend:

That an act be passed suspending the operation of the act which authorizes the construction of the House of Refuge, and authorizing the governor of the state to appoint three Commissioners, or to retain the Commissioners now in charge of the erection of said building, (as in his judgment he may deem best,) to negotiate and arrange for the termination or suspension of the contracts, upon such terms as may be deemed by the Commissioners, under sanction of the governor, just and equitable, and for the care of the materials already delivered, and of the lands purchased for the said purpose.

Your committee are induced to make this recommendation, under the belief that the great expenditure for the work is not only uncalled for, but is disapproved by the people of the state; and its adoption will afford time for the representatives of the people to be instructed as to their will.

All of which is respectfully submitted.

BENJAMIN FRITTS, Chairman.

MINORITY REPORT.

To the Honorable, the House of Assembly of the State of New Jersey:

The undersigned, members of the Committee who were appointed to examine and report upon the progress of the House of Refuge, beg leave respectfully to present to your honorable body, this brief expression of their dissent from the conclusions to which the majority of that Committee have arrived.

We have made diligent inquiries of those persons who are supposed to be most capable of communicating accurate information in regard to all matters bearing directly upon the subject presented for our examination, and we take this occasion to say that the Commissioners, the Architect and the Contractors have each evinced a readiness in giving us every facility, which has rendered this part of our duty a pleasant rather than an irksome task. The objects to which our inquiries were more particularly directed may be stated as follows, viz:

Whether any or what contracts had been entered into.

Whether said contracts were absolute and without reservation, or conditional.

Whether, if absolute, the State or the Commissioners personally, were to be held liable for their faithful execution.

What expense has already been incurred.

What amount of money will be required to complete the work in accordance with the contracts already made.

What will be the probable cost of annulling said contracts, and suspending or entirely abandoning the further prosecution of the projected enterprise.

The answers to these inquiries may be briefly stated as follows:

Contracts have been made for the completion of the work, which has already been commenced, and the progress of which is partially detailed in the report of the majority of this Committee.

These contracts are positive and absolute in every respect, except that the condition is reserved to the commissioners, that the work may be stopped after the completion of the centre building and one wing, leaving the additional wing to be erected at the discretion of the Commissioners.

The opinion seems to have been entertained by some members of this House that the Commissioners personally, and not the State, whose agents they are, are responsible to the contractors for the faithful performance of the obligation which they have incurred. This opinion, if correct, could have no weight in the decision to which we have arrived, for we cannot allow ourselves to suppose that the State of New Jersey would permit her citizens and agents to suffer loss for what, at most, could only be characterized as a venial error of judgment, while in the conscientious performance of their duty. But the opinion is not correct. We learn that the Attorney General of the State has said, that the Commissioners have not transcended their powers and that the State is "held and firmly bound" for the fulfillment of the engagements made by them as her lawful agents. Several gentlemen of eminence in the profession coincide in this opinion.

The amount of money appropriated by the Legislature, last year, for the purpose of commencing this work, was $15,000. Of this sum, $8,000 have been drawn from the treasury, leaving $7,000 still available.

The additional amount required for the completion of the building, as at present proposed, is estimated at not exceeding $30,000. This will finish the centre building and one wing, giving ample accommodation to ninety-six inmates, of the class for whose reception this institution is designed, together with the necessary attendants.

The estimated loss to the State, in case the project should be abandoned, is stated by the Commissioners, or some of them, at about $30,000. The Architect informs us that "the loss to the State by stopping the work in its present condition, would be fully equal to one half the estimated cost of the building."

These appear to be very liberal estimates, and possibly are somewhat too large, but we feel it to be our duty to present them to the House as we received them. It must be borne in mind that a large quantity of materials have been collected and prepared for use, many, perhaps most of which will be entirely useless for any other purpose than that for which they were originally designed, a large proportion of the cost of which is caused by the labor which has been bestowed upon them rather than the value of the original material. These considerations are so obvious that we would leave the subject without further notice, but for our desire that the House should receive more minute and special information in regard to this matter than is contained in the report of the majority of the Committee. That report—so far as we recollect, not having a copy before us,—ascribes the present situation of the work as it appears upon inspection at the site selected for the building. In addition to the excavations, grading, foundation walls, &c., &c., which have already been brought before the notice of the House, we desire to add the following particulars, viz:

Messrs. Bottom, Tiffany & Co., the contractors for the iron work, have expended large sums of money in the purchase of machinery and materials, and in the preparation of patterns; and they have already executed several tons of castings and wrought iron work. This contract has prevented them from taking orders for other work, as the capacity of their shop is taxed to the utmost, and they have engaged, and are now employing many workmen in addition to their regular force.

John Grant, the contractor for the stone work, has rented a stone quarry for the express purpose of filling this contract. He states that he "has already quarried large quantities of stone and dressed the same according to the specifications" in regard to dimensions, &c., "all of which," he adds, "would be useless for any other purpose." He has employed many additional workmen, including stone-cutters and others, and has rented houses for their accommodation. He has made contracts with other persons for transporting the stone to Kingston and has contracted for the building of a boat for the same purpose, at a cost of $1,100. He has also purchased all the scaffolding, poles, &c., and has already received the sand necessary for making the mortar. He has "made various other contracts and has perfected arrangements for the vigorous prosecution of the work."

Messrs. Biles & Hunt, contractors for the carpenters' work, have purchased all the timber required for the building, and have already worked out a large portion of the same, which, it is said, will be entirely useless for other purposes, this is especially the case with the large window and door frames, window sashes, &c. They have had heavy timber cut to order, some of which is said to be of unusual dimensions. They have also contracted for the painting and glazing. They have rented a large shop with power attached, employed a large increase of workmen, and made every arrangement necessary for the faithful performance of their engagements.

Messrs. Lafaucherie & Kahnwailler, contractors for furnishing brick, have purchased a lot of ground containing the clay necessary for their purpose, employed additional workmen and rented houses for their accommodation, and have contracted heavy expenses necessary for the due performance of their obligations.

Each and all of these parties have entered into bonds and given heavy securities for the punctual and faithful fulfillment of the contracts which they have taken. There are several matters of minor importance which might be mentioned in this connection, but to which we have not thought it necessary specially to ask the attention of the House.

It will be perceived from these statements that the arrangements for the erection of the building are all completed, and that a large portion of the expense has already been incurred.

Although giving this prominent place to the pecuniary aspect of the question, the undersigned do not desire that the House should therefore entertain the idea that the expense is the one controlling consideration which has alone induced them to ask the indulgence of the House of Assembly for presenting this report. While we acknowledge that a due regard for the financial condition of the State requires a provident and economical administration of its affairs, we also take occasion to express our conviction that a wise and liberal expenditure of money is sometimes an evidence of sound judgment and a dictate of true statesmanship.

Taking this view of the case, we are happy to express our hearty concurrence with the sentiments expressed by the majority of the committee in regard to the importance of an improvement in our school system, and we must be permitted to declare ourselves favorable to an increased expenditure for the purposes of education. No member of this House can set a higher value upon the proper cultivation of the faculties of the intellect and the affections of the heart, and none can more earnestly desire the coming of that day when the diffusion of intelligence shall be free and universal among the masses of the people, than does each and every one of the undersigned. We are therefore happy in being enabled to state, as we do by the authority of the late executive, (Ex-Gov. Haines) that the proposed House of Refuge can be built as was originally contemplated and that ten thousand dollars can also be added to the amount of the last appropriation for the purposes of education, thus making the sum of $50,000 available for distribution among the school districts of the State during the present fiscal year. We are informed that this desirable result can be attained without any inconvenience, merely by continuing the special loan of 1847, the payment which is not desired nor asked for. We do therefore respectfully submit, that the additional appropriation for schools will not necessarily interfere with the erection of the House of Refuge.

The recent message of Ex-Gov. Haines represents the finances of the State to be in a flourishing condition, and her resources to be fully adequate to the demands which may be made upon the treasury. The Joint Committee upon the Treasurer's accounts fully sustain the statements made in the message. We must therefore respectfully insist that there is no evidence before us to justify an abandonment of this important work in consequence of anticipated difficulty in making the payments stipulated in the contracts.

Nor can we concur with the majority of the Committee in the opinion that the several counties should attempt the attainment of the ends proposed, and which the majority admit to be praiseworthy and desirable. Leaving out of view the fact, which we assume to be incontrovertible, that the aggregate expense of erecting and properly furnishing the necessary buildings, together with the salaries of the persons who would be required to superintend these establishments which, though containing but few inmates, will for that very reason, if properly managed, be vastly more expensive in proportion than can possibly be the case in an extensive central institution; we venture to express the opinion that the youth who are the proper subjects for the discipline of a House of Refuge, ought to be removed from the vicinity and influence of their companions in vice and crime. Hence we consider the argument of the majority to be based upon an untenable position, and one which is in direct opposition to the principle which lies at the very foundation of the whole system of prison discipline as it is now generally administered, and from which the ideas establishing Houses of Refuge and their kindred institutions are naturally derived. The influence of parents and relatives so pathetically invoked in the report of the majority of the Committee, is in a vast majority of cases, especially to be deprecated. The precocious development of evil passions and vicious habits may not unfrequently be traced directly to parental example and to the contaminating influence of constant association with depraved relatives and companions. A very large proportion of those who are proper subjects for the restraints of this institution are orphans, either literally, or by the operation of our criminal laws, which have consigned their natural protectors to the cells of a prison. We are impelled by a conscientious conviction of the responsibilities resting upon us as philanthropists, as Christians, as good citizens and lovers of our country, to say to your honorable body, that the State should assume the parental relation, and that considerations of State policy no less than those of humanity, should induce us, the almoners of her bounty, to provide from her treasury the means of instructing and saving her otherwise friendless children.

The majority of the Committee refer us to a system of free schools as a panacea for this disease which now so deeply affects the well being, and the increasing virulence of which threatens still more extensive injury—we might even say danger—to the body politic. As we have already said, we are ready to stand in the foremost rank of those who look upon such a system as "a consummation most devoutly to be wished for," and we will venture to promise that no member of the majority of this Committee will make greater sacrifices for the attainment of that desirable object than ourselves. But the youth in whose behalf we present this report, are not those who will be sent or even permitted, to attend the public schools unless—as

37 P

is the case in Prussia—their parents or guardians are compelled by law to place them there. Those whose inclination might lead them towards the door of a school room are generally dependent upon their own exertions for the means of sustaining a miserable existence, while the vast majority occupy a place in society which presents no inducements for mental or moral improvement.

It has been objected to the erection of the House of Refuge, that the counties would be unequally taxed for its support. The undersigned can see no difficulty in making such arrangements as will entirely obviate any injustice which may be anticipated. The means of doing so in a satisfactory manner are so simple and obvious that we forbear further allusions to the objection.

To set forth in detail the manifold advantages of such an institution as is contemplated in the act establishing the House of Refuge, and to attempt a defence of the liberal and humane policy which prompted its originators in their efforts to accomplish this laudable enterprise, would argue an indifference to the condition of an important and increasing class of our population and a disregard of the true interests of the State, for which the undersigned are not willing to be held responsible. The uniform testimony of those who are familiar with the practical operation of this and similar measures of an enlarged benevolence, together with the beneficial results attending the establishment of Houses of Refuge for juvenile offenders and vagrants in other states is such, as to leave no doubt upon our minds that it is at least *desirable* that the design of the last Legislature should be carried out. We are decidedly of the opinion that, if desirable, it is also practicable, and that as an appropriation will be required to extinguish liabilities to contractors and others, the small additional amount which will be necessary to complete the centre building and one wing—which is all that is now proposed—will not occasion any inconvenience or embarrassment to the treasury. We beg leave also to suggest an opinion founded upon conversations with large numbers of the people of the state, that but a short time can elapse before the need of such an institution will be still more sensibly felt than it now is, and that a true economy would be observed by continuing the erection of the building already commenced.

While, therefore, we must in candor admit, that if the question of *commencing* this work, were now presented for our consideration, we should hesitate long and deliberate carefully before recommending the project to the favorable notice of this House—we are not now placed in such an embarrassing position. If the work is discontinued a heavy loss of money, is inevitable, and for that loss there is no reciprocal benefit. With a comparatively small increase of appropriations, we obtain a benefit vastly disproportioned to the increased expenditure.

In view of the above brief and imperfect statement of facts and estimates, and with a profound sense of our responsibility to the state and to society, we do respectfully submit, that New Jersey can well afford to erect and keep in active operation this asylum for her unfortunate and erring children, who being thus removed from the influence of the tempter, may—and as experience in similar establishments has, in numerous instances proved, will—grow up to manhood and become, that surest, best defence of a free state, "a virtuous intelligent yeomanry." [1]

All of which is respectfully submitted.

> W. M. WHITEHEAD, Essex.
> JOHN B. JOHNSON, Middlesex.
> BENJAMIN C. TATEM, Gloucester.
> J. VAN VORST, Hudson.
> BENJAMIN AYRES, Cumberland.
> MACKEY WILLIAMS, Cape May.

Trenton, Feb. 11, 1851.

2. THE COMMISSION ON THE REFORM OF JUVENILE OFFENDERS RECOMMENDS THE ERECTION OF A REFORM SCHOOL FOR JUVENILE OFFENDERS, 1865.

In his annual message for 1864, Governor Parker vigorously recommended the provision of an institution for the confinement of juvenile offenders. The report of the commissioners who were appointed to report on this section of the Governor's message, which is here reprinted in part, was the determining factor in securing the provision of the State Reform School for Juvenile Delinquents at Jamesburg.

REPORT OF COMMISSIONERS ON REFORM OF JUVENILE OFFENDERS.

REPORT.

At the last session of the legislature, Governor Parker, in his annual message, Jan., 1864, made the following remarks:

"Some place other than the State Prison should be provided for the incarceration of youth. In many instances the disgrace of confinement in the penitentiary, and the evil communications which unavoidably attend the least contact with hardened offenders, prevent reformation. The object of imprisonment is to reform as well as punish, and the state owes it to the youthful criminal to place him in circumstances that will tend to soften his pliant nature rather than render him more obdurate."

This brief but decided paragraph was referred to a joint committee of both houses of the legislature, who reported as follows:

[1] *Reports of the Committee of the Majority and Minority on the House of Refuge;* Trenton, 1851. A copy of this report is preserved in the New York Public Library.

To the Senate and General Assembly of the State of New Jersey:

The joint committee to which was referred that portion of the Governor's message which relates to juvenile offenders, beg leave respectfully to report—

That they have not been able, with so many other duties pressing upon them, to give the subject that full attention which its gravity demands; but the more they have considered it the more earnest has become their conviction of the truth of the language of the Governor—"The object of imprisonment is to reform as well as punish, and the state owes it to the youthful criminal to place him in circumstances that will tend to soften his pliant nature rather than render him more obdurate."

We have failed, in our legislation, to recognize this debt, and still doom to a prison and to a downward course of ruin, children whom the kindly ministry of wise instruction would in many cases lead upward to lives of honorable usefulness. Your committee think that *now, as of old,* a child should be *trained* "in the way that he should go." New Jersey, as a long-living parent, has a deep interest in every child she rears. And if from penury, or orphanage, or neglect, or the direct evil training of parents, any of her youth are in danger of becoming criminals, it is her *right*—it is her *duty*—to take care of *her own* and of *their* future, to remove them from evil influences and to provide them with virtuous instructors. Thus, by a wise and economic foresight, will she bless herself and them.

We have not, however, thought it would be prudent, in the midst of the engrossments of a busy session, to urge upon the legislature any measure hastily prepared. We have thought it better to inquire and wait. Within the past few years the attention of many Christian philanthropists has been turned to this subject, and the result has been an advance in the proper appreciation of reformatory influences. Other states, also, have labored to elevate their unfortunate criminal youth, and their experience may throw light upon our path. With this view we have prepared the following joint resolutions, for which we ask your favorable consideration:

JOINT RESOLUTIONS.

Be it Resolved by the Senate and General Assembly of the State of New Jersey, That the Governor be authorized to appoint three commissioners whose duty it shall be, carefully to inquire into the character and influences of institutions in other states designed for the reformation of criminal or vagrant youth, and from their experience to collate a system of reform which they shall deem best adapted to supply the wants of New Jersey; to ascertain the probable number of children whose course of life demands the care of the state, and the manner in which criminal youth are at present dealt with; to propose such laws as may be necessary for the establishment of a suitable school or schools, and to report to the Governor the result of their labors, in order that he may present it to the legislature at its next annual session.

And be it resolved, That the treasurer of the state be directed to pay to the commissioners a sum not exceeding three dollars per diem for the time they may be engaged in actual service, with such reasonable expenses as the Governor may approve.

> Edward W. Scudder,
> Richard M. Acton,
>> Committee of Senate.
> James H. West,
> Daniel Corey,
> David H. Wikoff,
>> Committee of House of Assembly.

These resolutions were unanimously adopted in both houses, and approved by the Governor March 29th, 1864.

———

State of New Jersey, Executive Department, Trenton, April 1, 1864. }

By virtue of joint resolutions authorizing the appointment of commissioners to report laws for the reformation of juvenile offenders, approved March 29th, 1864;

I, Joel Parker, Governor of the State of New Jersey, hereby appoint as such commissioners, the following gentlemen, who will proceed to the discharge of their duties under provisions of said joint resolutions, viz: George T. Cobb, Phineas B. Kennedy, Samuel Allinson.

> Joel Parker.

———

COMMISSIONERS' REPORT.

To Joel Parker, Esq., *Governor of the State of New Jersey:*

The commissioners appointed by the Governor in pursuance of the foregoing resolutions, respectfully present to him the following report:

In entering upon the important work assigned to us, we conluded that our first step should be to take measures for ascertaining the statistics of juvenile crime in the state. With this view we prepared and printed a circular, a copy of which is appended, and forwarded it to several officers of each county, and to other individuals who would probably aid us in the work. A few answers have been received, but a large part of those to whom it was addressed, and on whose assistance we counted, have failed to reply. These imperfect returns, with information received from other sources, have satisfied us that in our towns and cities, and even in the villages of our agricultural districts, a large number of children are growing up without proper parental control, and in habits of idleness, vagrancy and crime. They become accustomed to the use of tobacco and intoxicating drinks at an early age; hazard their little possessions in various games of chance; hang about low theatres and taverns, and learn to scoff at the restraints of religion and morality. They absent themselves from the daily and sabbath school, congregate at the corners of streets, insult the passers by with ribald jests or profane language, get up alarms of fire and run with the engines, and become prepared for a continual progression in evil. In many instances the example and direct teaching of parents have trained them to thefts and other misdemeanors. Several cases have occurred of bands of youthful burglars successfully plying their trade. A distinguished lawyer, who was prosecutor of the pleas in one of our counties, was called on to examine a young culprit preliminary to his commitment for robbing stores. He gave the names of several boys as his accomplices, and among them that of the attorney's much trusted office-keeper. This threw discredit upon the whole statement, but the accused lad being inquired of, acknowledged his guilt, and that the office of the prosecutor, of which he had the key, was the midnight rendezvous of the gang for the division of their spoils. Instances have come to our knowledge of boys prowling about on the sabbath and robbing farm-houses when the families had gone to their places of worship. One of the supreme judges told us of a boy who invited another to go with him and *see some fun.* He went, and a barn was burned for their amusement. Great damage is some times done to steam engines and machinery, by cutting off expensive portions for the paltry purpose of selling the fragments as old brass. The engineer of some works, thus injured, said $1,000 would not repair the damage, though the boys received less than ten dollars as the proceeds of this wanton and wicked spoilation. Little beggars too, with piteous tales of sorrow, are found to be adroit pilferers when opportunity offers. But we need not swell this report with the thronging evidences of youthful depravity. Alas, they are patent to all, and no observant man can be ignorant of numerous cases. On every hand we see youthful insubordination growing out of the want of firm parental treatment. The father is engaged in his daily business; the mother with her household claims; absorbed in their own present they forget the great duty of training their infant charge for a bright future. The child is left to seek its own associates and amusement. He finds them with the idle and the vicious, and soon astonishes his parents with his obstinacy in wrong doing. The tendency of unrestrained human nature is downward. Besides this, many parents are themselves profane and godless, and unfit to have the charge of children. They squander their time and money in bar-rooms and beer-houses, and children half-clad, half-fed, dishonest, false and ignorant, tell of the criminal neglect. Society has too much at stake to permit this course and this result. Such parents forfeit all claim to their own offspring, and the state should see that the child, which is hereafter to be invested with the priceless rights and duties of American citizenship, shall become fitted for them. The right of election is too pure and holy a boon to be thrust upon young men so debased by crimes that they must shrink from and oppose wholesome laws and honest

officers. General virtue and intelligence should be the inseparable con-
comitants of universal suffrage.

We have rejoiced to find, in different parts of the State, institutions
established by private benevolence, as temporary homes for the little ones
whom orphanage or other causes have made destitute. They are fed and
clothed and taught with maternal care and when opportunity offers, placed
out in families to earn their own bread, and be fitted for life's duties. We
wish our citizens more generally felt the importance of these "Homes,"
(the fruits generally of the outgushing sympathies of a few Christian
women,) as among the surest *preventives of crime*. They are well managed, are productive of great good, and there can be no comparison between
them and the only legal alternative—the poor-house.

A young child cannot, in the view of the law, commit a crime; but, with
increasing years and knowledge, it becomes responsible. Society is forced
to protect itself from the acts of the wrongdoer, and does so by the infliction of penalties. At what age legal responsibility should commence is
a mooted question, but youth and ignorance and inexperience may claim
some mitigation of the penalty justly due to adult criminals.

Persons often decline to complain of young criminals. They think of
the probable ruin consequent upon exposure and conviction, and satisfy
themselves with threats or counsel. Grand juries pity, and ignore bills.
Petit juries pity, and find "not guilty". Courts pity, and impose light punishment or suspend sentence. The whole moral nature of our judges and
juries rises up against the strict execution of laws which consign to the
ignominy of a prison, children who have acted "without discernment," and
whose great need is to be snatched from the perilous guardianship of their
own parents, and to be led into the paths of virtue. This lenity, in some
instances, is followed by amendment—in others, it hardens. But confinement in a prison also hardens. A warden said to us: "Boys are taught
much evil here, and go out thinking it is not such a bad thing, after all,
to be in jail." They associate familiarly with older and more accomplished
criminals. In a cell of one county jail, a little fellow, afterward proved
to be innocent, was locked up with a practiced burglar. In another we saw
a boy of eleven years of age, charged with theft, the companion of a man
committed for murder. An orphan boy, eleven years old, was found by a
city missionary in a county jail, herded with criminal men and boys. On
the death of his parents he lived with his grandfather, but he, too, died,
and the child was homeless, and was committed to prison solely for his
destitution. There must be criminal apathy in a civilized community where
such horrible injustice is permitted. We stand aghast at the murder of
supernumerary infants in China and on the Ganges, yet such deeds as these
in our midst awaken little feeling.

We have had reported to us but two jails where there is systematic employment (another report says, none but *"card playing"*), and none where
there is systematic instruction in literature or morals. In some there is
Sabbath preaching; but there is no reform. It seems a necessity that the
mind of the child should be tendered by the kindly influence of human

charity (and what do these poor imprisoned outcasts know of that?) ere they can receive the glad tidings of redemption. The heart is saddened to see in how many instances reconviction follows close upon release. A boy of fifteen we saw in jail after his thirteenth conviction! May we not say, in the language of an eminent citizen of our State, "New Jersey is *cruel* to her poor wicked children."

The question before us now seemed to be, What is the duty of the State? How, out of these lost, degraded children, shall it make God-fearing men and women—law-abiding, law-sustaining citizens? Correspondence had been opened with persons conversant with the subject, in different parts of the country, and much valuable information and important suggestions were thus received. The annual reports of numerous institutions, for the reformation of criminal children, in other States were also procured and examined. We found a wide difference existing in the modes of treatment, and became convinced that we could not satisfactorily decide on the merits of the various systems without personal observation and conversation with the officers. We accordingly visited the reform schools of Connecticut, Massachusetts and Ohio, and the houses of refuge at Providence and Cincinnati, and a part of our number those of Philadelphia, New York and Pittsburg. We desire here to express our grateful sense of the kindness and courtesies of the officers of these institutions, who furnished us with documents, and in other ways facilitated our object. We subjoin a brief description of a number of the reformatories (See Appendix) showing somewhat of their mode of operation. Whilst in every one of them there were points to admire and imitate,[1] we were united in preferring as model institutions—

1st. The State Reform Farm School, at Lancaster, Ohio, for boys under fourteen years of age.

2d. The Massachusetts Nautical School Ship, for boys above that age; and

3d. The Industrial School for Girls, at Lancaster, Massachusetts, for young females who, through corrupt influence, have fallen into evil ways, or are imminently exposed to danger.

1. Of the necessity for a school of reform of the first class—boys under fourteen—we think no doubt can exist. *We* feel none, that the State should assume the duty. Experience has demonstrated that, if left to counties, it is left to be utterly neglected. The erring children of a few years ago, who might have been rescued by the exercise of parental public effort, are now our hardened criminals. By separation into families and classes, two hundred boys can be admitted into one institution, and we think the State should provide for that number. We need scarcely say that the officers should be carefully selected. The principal, especially, should feel an inward call to the work, and that he is laboring for a reward above all that the State can give.

Our reasons for preferring the farm school to the house of refuge are, briefly, that the former develops the bodily and mental powers naturally and healthfully; the varied influences of agricultural life being far more

---

[1] Especially was this the case in the Westborough school, in some respects without its compeer.

exhilarating and ennobling than those of the workshop. But above all do we prefer it because of its freedom from that ignominious restrain of grate and lock which sickens the heart of many a refuge boy, and impels him to risk his life in efforts at escape though surrounded by comforts, advantages and opportunities unknown to him before. The power of truth and love and right, on which the family system farm school *must* rely, is a wonderful lever in lifting degraded children up to a level where the light of science and morals and religion can reach them. The sins of their past lives become visible to them when seen from their new stand-point, and a bright prospect for their future dawns upon them of which they had hope or desire before. It seems to us, too, that, for the sake of confining two or three desperate boys in one hundred who could not be controlled on the farm, it would be manifestly unwise and unjust to *imprison* the ninety-seven or ninety-eight Let the few who will not yield to kindness, be more severely dealt with.

2. The experience of reformatory institutions is against having older boys associated with younger. Crime has become more habitual to those approaching manhood, and they are not so readily reached by moral appliances. They have become accustomed to take care of themselves, and would be more likely to escape during a novitiate, from an open farm school. Their age and size give to their example, if it be evil, a dangerous power. "Do not take boys above fourteen into your school," was the advice to us of a gentleman who had been for more than thirty years laboring efficiently as a manager in the Philadelphia House of Refuge. Other provision must, therefore, be made for them. New Jersey cannot afford to give up to a life of crime her wayward boys of fourteen and upwards, turning them over, without effort for their reclamation, to the degradation of a prison. The thought of adopting such an alternative was saddening to us. In our dark doubtfulness, therefore, with regard to this class, the example and experience of a sister state, in her school ship, "The Massachusetts" were indeed cheering. (For account of this school see pp. 20, 37.) The benefits which would result from placing these restless, reckless boys under such a course of training appear to us to be great. Their old corrupting associations would be broken off, and they would be fitted for usefulness in life. When honorably discharged there would be no insurmountable stain upon their characters. The foreign and coasting trade of citizens of our own State would afford opportunities for procuring excellent situations for these educated young mariners, who would be desirable acquisitions in any crew. The extended sea and river coast of the State would afford ample circuit for the summer cruising of the ship in visiting various ports, from Fort Lee to Burlington, and a safe, commodious winter harbor.

3. The necessity for an institution where destitute or criminal young females may be shielded or reclaimed, must be manifest to every thoughtful observer. In some aspects it appears even more needful than one for boys. It is of incalculable importance to a state to raise high the standard of female purity and virtue. Woman, as the presiding genius of the home circle, moulds it according to her own ideas of excellence. And if those ideas are cor-

rupted by unholy living, the sweetest and purest charities of human existence spring not along her pathway. Her influence is for evil. The annals of our criminal courts show an increasing number of girls who, for larceny, disorderly conduct, or other violations of law, claim their attention. That our jails are suitable homes for them, no one will affirm. There is no place to which a magistrate can commit them with the belief that such action will benefit them or the State. There is no place where a parent or friend can send an obstinate or morally endangered daughter or ward with any hope of reformation. This ought not to be in such a commonwealth as ours. We would, therefore, earnestly recommend the establishment of an industrial school for girls on the plan of that at Lancaster, Mass., for an account of which see p. 21.

Beside the direct benefit of the reform schools to the pupils themselves, we think there will be a reflex influence of great value. If a boy or girl is taken from its parents because they allow it to grow up in vagrancy and lapse into crime, the parents of its young associates will feel that they can no longer permit their children to run the streets in neglected ignorance; that they must restrain or lose them.

We believe that three such institutions as we have suggested, under proper management, would arrest in their downward course to ruin many children, whom destitution, and ignorance, and evil influence have led astray, enabling them to walk honorably through life, in the light of Christian principle. We anticipate the prompt response, that three such establishments would be costly appendages to the State. So is our State Prison; so are our county jails; so is all the machinery of our criminal jurisprudence; so are our blind, our mute and our idiotic children. New Jersey appropriates for the education of each of these afflicted ones $200 per annum, for four years. And she does wisely, generously, well. She provides, in her system of common schools, for the instruction of all her children, rich and poor alike, at a public cost of more than $400,000 per annum. For the benefit of those laboring under one of the severest of earthly afflictions, she provides her Lunatic Asylum, an honor to the State. This has cost her $300,000; but what high-minded Jerseyman grudges the expense? And shall her destitute youth, falling into evil ways from ignorance and want, be left in their sad condition, to sink yet deeper into crime, or be cast into prison, and thus be doomed to ignominy and confirmed in guilt, when, by timely care, a large proportion might be rescued. The awakened conscience of the State will surely demand the effort.

The proper question is, will the necessary expenditure be compensated by future benefits? To answer this correctly, we must consider that the children of whom we are treating are *already of us*. Their destiny for weal or for woe is connected with *our* community. The evil seed has even now been sown in their hearts, and if we look on in apathy, we shall in due time be compelled to reap the fearful harvest which will follow. May a merciful Providence avert it, by turning the hearts of our people to a wise consideration of our own enduring interest, leading us to cherish with affectionate parental interest these moral orphans, the least favored members of our commonwealth, and train them up in the paths of learning and virtue, to appreciate the rich blessings of our equal inheritance of religion, of liberty, and of law.

To meet the needful expenditure in purchasing land, erecting buildings, &c., for the proposed schools, $100,000 would probably be required. This, considering the heavy burdens already existing, is a large sum. But the State, by an arrangement of last session, is to receive more for but a fraction of its lands lying under water, near Jersey City. We would therefore very respectfully suggest that a further portion of this now unproductive inheritance might be sold, and the proceeds be devoted to the reformation and instruction of her sadly neglected children. The reclamation of the lands which would follow would add to the common wealth, but the reclamation of the children, telling on their eternal destiny, would be a nobler, more enduring triumph.

To carry into effect the conclusions to which the Commissioners have come in the foregoing report, they would further propose:

The establishment by law of a Board of Control of Reform Schools, to consist of the Governor, the Chancellor, and the Chief Justice of the State, whose duty it shall be to appoint a sufficient number of discreet and suitable persons as trustees of said schools.

That the trustees of the State Reform Farm School, for criminal or vagrant boys under fourteen years of age, shall have authority to receive or purchase a tract of land, of sufficient area for the establishment of said school, to erect suitable buildings thereon, and to enact by-laws for their own government; these several particulars to be subject to the approval of the Board of Control.

That under the said by-laws, they shall appoint the superintendent and other officers, and have the management and control of said school and farm, making an annual report of their proceedings, the condition of the school and its finances, to the Governor, that he may present it to the Legislature.

That boys under fourteen years of age, who, from parental neglect or otherwise, are vagrants, have fallen into crime, or are imminently in danger of doing so, shall, on complaint, be examined by two magistrates, or by a judge of any court of record who shall be authorized to commit them to the reform school, with such provision for appeal as may be thought advisable.

That the board of trustees be empowered to detain, employ, and instruct such boys, indenture them when reformed, and be clothed with all needful authority.

That the trustees of the nautical school for boys, and of the industrial school for girls, should such institutions be established by the Legislature, have similar powers, varied to suit their different circumstances.

The Attorney-General has kindly offered to prepare laws adapted to such reformatory schools.

In the absence of sufficient statistics, we cannot report the number of criminal children of the different classes. A synopsis of the information received will be found in the Appendix.

In concluding our deeply interesting labors, which we feel have been very inadequately performed, we may remark that the more we have investigated the subject assigned to us by the Governor, the stronger has become our conviction of its importance. We trust that the deliberations of the Legislature will result in a recognition of the claims of the neglected *children of the State,* and provision for throwing pure and elevating influences around them.[1]

GEORGE T. COBB,
P. B. KENNEDY,
SAMUEL ALLINSON.

3. CRITICISM OF THE MANAGEMENT OF THE REFORM SCHOOL
FOR JUVENILE OFFENDERS AT JAMESBURG, 1886.

While the State Reform School for Juvenile Delinquents at Jamesburg had been founded upon the cottage system, and was designed to provide for a flexible system of management, which would offer something approximating an adequate substitute for the family life of which the boys had either been temporarily deprived, or had never enjoyed, the institution soon drifted into a mechanical routine. The following report of the Legislative Committee appointed to examine the operation of the Reform School, presents a clear analysis of the relative failure of the institution, after twenty years of its existence, to provide a proper social environment or adequate reformatory influences for the boys committed to the institution. The report of this Committee is not only important as presenting a picture of the situation at Jamesburg in 1886, but is also significant in that it touched upon what has always been the weakest aspect of the system of management which has been practiced in the institution.

REPORT TO THE LEGISLATURE OF THE JOINT COMMITTEE ON REFORM SCHOOL.

REPORT.

To the Senate and House of Assembly of the State of New Jersey:
Your Committee of the Reform School for Boys would respectfully report that they have attended at the school on several days and have, as far as

[1] *Legislative Documents,* 1865; Document No. 13; pp. 1–13.

possible, investigated its working and management. They could not do more or act in the way of change for want of the appropriation which was made in the law passed by the legislature at the last session, but was not approved by the Governor.

It may be well to give a general description of the school, so that the members may get a proper idea of its working. It consists of an average of over 300 boys, who are distributed in families of fifty, in separate buildings. Over each "family" there is a head or "officer," who has the charge of that family, night and day. The first story of such a family building is arranged as a school-room; in the basement are the dining and play-rooms, and the bath, and the whole upper floor forms a sleeping-room, furnished with fifty cots and straw beds. There are likewise apartments used by the "officer" and his family. Besides these family buildings there is a central office, a hospital, a kitchen and a shirt factory furnished with steam-power, and sewing machines.

The whole are on a farm of several hundred acres, suitably provided with barns and out-buildings, and distant two or three miles from Jamesburg.

The school-day is always much the same. The morning begins with a breakfast of coffee, milk and bread; then follow over four hours of work till dinner-time, when the boys get as much soup as they will and the meat and vegetables that were boiled in it; then comes work again for two hours, then three hours of schooling, supper and bed.

Thus the family of fifty sleep together in the same room, work together under the officer, or study and recite together in the family school-room to the teacher, who is often the "officer's" wife. Their work is on the farm or in the shirt factory, except that a few help in tailoring, or rough shoe-making, or in the kitchen.

The cooking is better than at the committee's visit in the spring. The fare is honest and wholesome, though served like prison messes, in silence. The treatment is kind.

The farm is well tilled in the plain way that it is managed; the work in the shirt-room is not too hard and is well done, though the hours are too long. But what we have to lament in the school is the lack of employment or instruction that will fit the scholars for the business of life or encourage healthy emulation. The schooling is naturally limited to the English branches. But it is not right, as we think, that there should be no graded classes or chance for the ambitious student, no grades or rewards for study or work, nothing to be earned and nothing to own. The work even is task work. Each boy is given his task and is expected to perform it, and the only good that he gets from good work is that he gets to his play sooner.

A boy in the factory could formerly earn a little pocket-money by extra work, but that was stopped as unfair to the farm boys.

That years of a growing boy's life should be given up altogether to task work, locked up at night by fifties in one room, cut off from books, newspapers, and all the machinery of civilization, does not seem to your committee the province of a school. For a reform school is not a prison. It is founded on the just and merciful theory that lying and pilfering and the crimes for which these boys are sent here, are not always the results of depravity, but the faults of almost all children, developed in these boys by bad breeding, or poverty, or even by the romance of our dime novels.

We have built this school not so much to punish—for the disgrace of going there is all to much of that—but to reform, to educate, to bring out and draw forth all the powers of mind and body; to give occupation and training of the active powers; to excite interest, curiosity, love of learning and work, emulation, ambition, love of their teachers, their fellows and their kind; and to send them forth to make their place in society.

In proportion only as it does this work is it a school. It is not enough for a school to prevent, repress and forbid what is evil. It must draw out latent powers, direct growing activities, encourage honest desires and build up character. If it does not do this it does not do its work of reform.

In these qualities the system of this school is defective. There is little training and little chance for emulation or education in study or work. Shirt-making is not a profitable trade. Nor does plain farming pay in this State— the work is task work; the hours are too long.

The committee learn from the superintendent that the following is the established order of the day for the boys: They are called at 5:30 and have breakfast at 6:15. They go to work at 7 and continue until 11:45, with a recess from 10 to 10:30. They have dinner at 12, returning to work at 12:45. They quit work at 2:15 to go to school at 3, where they are kept until 6. After this they have their supper and at 8 they retire.

This schedule of a day's work is all that could be required of a man who had reached a full and vigorous physical maturity. When it is remembered that it is adopted for boys from eight to sixteen years of age, half of whom are under fourteen and a large proportion of whom are under twelve, it may be regarded as severe. The committee understand fully the class of boys usually found at a reform school, as well as the source from whence they come, but they feel that the chances for reform will be very much increased if the boys can be trained to take pride in their work, that they may feel that it is honorable and desirable. Nor do they believe that study can be made attractive if the physical strength of the boys is exhausted by a hard day's labor before school hours begin. The committee suppose that the present schedule was adopted that the school might be as nearly self-supporting as possible, but they submit that the primary purpose of the school is not so much to make money as it is to make good citizens.

The committee, therefore, have suggested to the Trustees that much shorter hours of work and longer hours of play be given the boys. They are clearly of the opinion that the school hours should be in the morning, and they recommend that the hours from nine to twelve, with a recess, be set apart for that purpose. They also recommend that four hours in the afternoon, say from one to five, be given to work, and that the balance of the day be allowed for recreation.

These rules, of course, will be subject to proper exceptions as to farm work as suggested by the season.

The committee desire also to offer some practical suggestions as to the school that they think will be, in a part at least, feasible and beneficial. There should be more variety in the farming. It would not cost much to add to the farm a garden, a cheap glass house for early vegetables, and the humanizing culture of fruits and flowers. This farm is in a fruit and vegetable district where that work is profitable. There might be a poultry yard; it would cheapen the kitchen, and the care of and love of animals is always interesting and humanizing to boys. For these boys, cut off from all home ties, there is nothing more necessary. Those who wish and deserve it might perhaps have their own little garden plot, and by extra work earn something for themselves.

But whether all this is practical or not in this exact shape, there must be some form of reward for work to teach the pride of honest earning. Work should be paid for—in grade and privilege, if not in pocket-money.

So, too, in the shops. There should be some form of useful employment learned. They now make their own brick and sell some. There has been an improvement since last session, in that more boys are employed in the shoe shop. There are now five making plain, rough shoes. There used to be only two cobbling. The school cannot perhaps go into trade, but they can make almost everything that they themselves require. More carpenter work could, we think, be found for them to do, and they should, at least, be taught the use of the tools and of the turning lathe.

In some degree we should aim at a manual training school, at least in the carpenter, shoe and blacksmith shop of the school. In the Ohio Reform School report of 1884 we find the following, to show the lines in which such effort may be made:

"Since the last annual report several useful departments have been added. The first was a telegraph office, where twelve boys are being taught telegraphy. Next, a small printing office was established, where ten boys are taught printing. Sufficient material has been purchased to print a seven-column folio paper. A paper is now published weekly, named 'The Ohio Industrial School Journal.' A competent foreman has been employed, and the boys under his charge are learning to set type quite rapidly. This seems to be the favorite trade for our most intelligent boys. We hope our facilities for printing will soon be such as will necessitate a much larger number of boys in the office than are now engaged in it. Some of the boys contribute articles to the paper each week, which are very creditable to persons of their age. The publishing of our paper is having a refining influence on our boys, and they look forward each week quite anxiously for a copy of their journal. We think, after the first year, the office will be self-sustaining.

"The polytechnic department, just being organized for the purpose of teaching a number of our boys to be good mechanics, will no doubt prove to be a valuable acquisition. A great many of the boys have a natural taste for working with machinery, drawing, framing and carving in wood. This department has been organized to accommodate those who prefer mechanics to other pursuits, and to qualify them for good situations when they leave the farm."

But if the boys learned no trade at the school there would be much more hope for them if the schooling were better. There cannot be good work with the present system. There should be at least one upper school, with a skilled teacher for the better scholars, who should be admitted after competition in the family schools. There should be graded classes, marks and grades. We would recommend that the State Superintendent be consulted by the Trustees from time to time on the school and its educational needs, and that he visit it officially and include it in his annual report.

There should be time to read, a good supply of books, newspapers and magazines, a reading and sitting room, or the right to use the school rooms as such; plenty of letter paper and encouragement to write to their friends.

These are not visionary projects. They are already in almost every large reform school in the Union. Some schools add military drill; always a good thing for boys. The Michigan school took the prize on company drill in the militia review of the State. Habits of obedience and command, self-respect and the honest pride that comes from the possession of a shoulder-strap are no small means to awaken the dormant ambition and love of the applause of his fellows that exist in every mind and are the great motives to success in life. The very strictness of military discipline gives opportunity for more real freedom, for a march to church in town on Sundays, and occasional excursions from the bare walls and fields of what is now a quasi-prison.

More than all, when boys have shown that they can be trusted, they should be. In no other way can we train self-respect. And there is no first-rate reform school that does not allow its best pupils to go out on parole and even on vacations. When that is done the disgrace that attends a boy who has been in such a school is practically taken away. He has become a man among his fellows.

In conclusion, the committee would recommend that for this year the appropriation for the school should be much enlarged. Some part of these moneys will be required for the supply of water, which has proved insufficient for the growth of the school. But the committee do not desire needlessly to fetter the Trustees in the expenditure of the appropriation, but to give them liberal means for the improvement of the school in such direction as may be best.[1]

> GEORGE O. VANDERBILT,
> L. A. THOMPSON,
> T. G. CHATTLE,
>   Senate Committee.
> FRANKLIN MURPHY,
> RICHARD WAYNE PARKER,
> A. JUDSON RUE,
> THOS. FLYNN,
> J. SEWARD WILLS,
>   House Committee.

[1] Document No. 42, in *Legislative Documents* for 1886, Vol. III.

II. Defects in the Management of the State Home for Girls at Trenton.

1. REPORT OF THE INVESTIGATING COMMITTEE OF THE LEGIS- LATURE IN 1900 WITH RESPECT TO THE ADMINISTRATIVE DEFECTS AT THE STATE HOME FOR GIRLS.

The following report of the Committee of the Legislature appointed to investigate the charges against the State Home for Girls is extremely significant as revealing the "slip-shod" methods of administration which apparently had been in vogue from the origin of the institution. While the defects were as much, if not more, due to the faults in the legal basis of the ad- ministration of the institution as to the mistakes of the man- aging authorities, it is significant that the authorities should have allowed these glaring weaknesses to have persisted. The dis- coveries of the investigating committee of 1900 and the recom- mendations submitted by them, resulted in the sweeping re-organ- ization of the administrative organization of the institution, as well as in the change of its name to that of the State Home for Girls. This administrative re-organization served to put the in- stitution on a fairly high plane of efficiency, and it was not until 1914 that another important investigation took place. This in- vestigation of 1914, which is amply dealt with in the text, re- sulted in the act of April 17, 1914, which furnishes the legal basis for the present administration of the institution.

W. Mungle, chairman of the Committee on the Industrial School for Girls, made the following report:

To the House of Assembly:

Your special committee appointed under the resolution of February 21st, last, to investigate the charges made with relation to the management of the State Industrial School for Girls, and to report with all convenient speed, respectively report as follows:

Pursuant to the direction and authority contained in said resolution, your committee at once began an investigation of the matter referred to it and is still engaged in that work. A large amount of testimony had been taken, both in support of said charges and on behalf of the management. Although

38 P

your committee has diligently prosecuted the work assigned to it, we have not been able as yet to conclude our work. A large number of witnesses remain to be examined and we have had no opportunity at all to go over and digest the testimony already taken. Your committee has therefore unanimously concluded that it will be impossible to present a final report to this session of the Legislature. They therefore recommend the adoption of the resolution hereto annexed authorizing the committee to continue the investigation during the recess of the Legislature so far as in their judgment the same may be necessary, with power to report to the Governor as soon as their labors are concluded and a final report can be prepared.

Your committee is at this time prepared to report as follows:

We had not proceeded far in our investigation of the affairs of the school before we became satisfied that the existing statutes regulating the school were in some important respects defective, and in others wholly wrong. The school was established under the act of April 4, 1871. This act was modeled largely upon the act of 1865 establishing the Boys' School and contained all the defects which have been found necessary to remove from that act.

The more important of these defects may, in the judgment of your committee, be stated as follows:

First. The powers and duties of the lady managers are no where defined. The act provides that "the trustees shall appoint six lady managers, who shall be associated with them in the management, care and oversight of the inmates of the school." This act, however, confers all governing powers on the trustees alone; and the lady managers cannot be said to exist as an independent board, and they are not trustees. Through no fault either of the trustees or the lady managers confusion and uncertainty as to their respective duties and responsibilities must follow from this state of the law. Your committee believes that the services of women in the management of an institution of this kind are indispensable, and that they should have authoritative voice in its management.

Second. The act of 1871 is defective in that it contains no provisions as to the proper subjects for the school, or as to commitments thereto, or as to methods and forms of procedure, or as to discharge of inmates, except in so far as the provisions of the Boys' School act are made applicable to this school.

Third. The authorities of the school have been constantly and greatly hampered and embarrassed in their work of caring for and reforming girls committed to their charge for lack of essential information as to the previous conduct and character of the girls and the specific causes of their commitment. Experience in this and similar institutions shows that there are three things concerning each girl committed to this school which it is essential that the committing papers should show on their face, viz.: The age, as near as may be, of the girl; her place of residence at the time of her commitment and the specific cause of her committal. Under the law as it now exists the committing papers do not in most cases disclose the cause or reason for committing the girl to the school. The commitment describes her simply as a "fit subject", and the authorities of the school do not know whether she has committed a crime, or is immoral, or is simply incorrigible. This defect in the law we regard as serious.

Fourth. The state of the law is such that there is at least some doubt whether the trustees now have the power to discharge a girl as reformed before she attains the age of twenty-one, unless she has been indentured, no matter how thorough her reformation may be. Certainly all doubt on this point should be removed, and the trustees should have the unquestioned right to discharge, as reformed, a girl who in their judgment is thoroughly reformed.

Fifth. Whatever conclusion may be finally reached as to the power of the trustees to discharge a girl as reformed, they certainly have not the power to parole a girl with the right to take her back if the conditions of her parole are violated. The power to parole exists even as to the inmates of our penal institutions and should certainly be given to the trustees of this school. The existence of such a power and the likelihood of its being exercised as a reward for good conduct would be an inspiration to the girls to so conduct themselves as to be thought worthy of a trial on parole. Parole would thus become a preliminary step to a full discharge as reformed.

Sixth. The law now provides that a girl over seven years of age may be committed to this institution. All agree that this age limit is too young, and it is the opinion of your committee that no girl under ten years of age should be committed to this school.

In view of these and other palpable defects in the law regulating this school, your committee caused to be prepared a bill remedying these defects and containing such new features as to your committee seemed wise. This bill we present herewith and recommend its passage. The defects above pointed out have been remedied and some new features in accord with modern methods and ideas have been inserted. In its general scope and plan the bill is simply a re-enactment of the existing laws with their defects cured and their omissions supplied.

Your committee believes that the enactment of this bill will greatly facilitate the work of the management of the school and prove a substantial benefit to its inmates.[1]

Respectfully submitted,

WILLIAM MUNGLE,
ELLIS R. MEEKER,
ELLIS H. MARSHALL,
LEON ABBETT,
EDMUND W. WAKELEE.

[1] *Minutes of the Assembly,* 1900; pp. 452–454.

DOCUMENTS RELATING TO THE STATE REFORMATORY FOR MEN AT RAHWAY.

CHAPTER IX

DOCUMENTS RELATING TO THE STATE REFORMATORY FOR MEN AT RAHWAY.

I. The Origin of the State Reformatory for Men at Rahway.
    1. The Commission on an Intermediate Prison Recommends the Provision of a Reformatory for Adult Delinquents in the State of New Jersey, 1878.
    2. Report of the Commission of 1890 Recommending the Provision of a Reformatory for Men.

I. The Origin of the State Reformatory for Men at Rahway.

1. The Commissioners on an Intermediate Prison Recommend the Provision of a Reformatory for Adult Delinquents in the State of New Jersey.

In the period of the "Seventies" there was a noticeable movement throughout the United States toward the provision of reformatories for first offenders and those convicted of the less serious crimes. The influence of this movement upon New Jersey is evident in the following report of the commissioners, appointed in 1877, to report upon the desirability of a reformatory or an "intermediate prison" in New Jersey. The report of the commissioners, submitted in 1878, is significant not only for its vigorous recommendation of a reformatory, but also for its comments upon the existing prison system and its recommendation of a state board to provide a centralized supervision of the penal, reformatory and correctional institutions of the State.

REPORT OF THE COMMISSIONERS ON PRISON SYSTEM OF NEW JERSEY, AND ON AN INTERMEDIATE PRISON. UNDER JOINT RESOLUTION, APPROVED APRIL 9, 1877.

To the Senate and General Assembly of the State of New Jersey:

The Commissioners appointed by the Governor, in accordance with the joint resolution approved March 9th, 1877, "to examine and report to the next Legislature on the present prison system of the State, to suggest any plans for its improvement, and if such plans shall include the establishment of any penitentiary or intermediate prison, to report an act for its establishment and government, and to recommend a plan and site for the same," respectfully report, that in October last, soon after their appointment, they met and considered the duties devolving upon them in the execution of this trust, and proceeded to collect information by a personal inspection of the county prisons of the State. Into a particular detail of these visits it is perhaps needless here to enter. Suffice it to say, that in several of the counties the old jails, whose appointments were so justly complained of by the Prison Commissioners of 1868, have given place to new and greatly improved buildings, and to better arrangements. Of some of our prisons it must be confessed that, from careless indifference on the part of keeper and of inmates, their condition was far from nice, and practices abhorrent to correct feeling were allowed. Of a larger number, it may with great satisfaction be stated that the apartments, bedding, table furniture, &c., are kept with scrupulous neatness, and that personal cleanliness is rigorously insisted upon. We heard no where complaint of insufficient quantities or improper quality of food, and in some cases the fare was the subject of unsolicited commendation.

But whilst the physical condition of most of our prisons is a source of gratulation, there is another aspect which fills us with sadness. We refer to the indiscriminate mingling together of the prisoners in enforced idleness, with little effort to give them instruction, religious, or moral or literary.

With the exception of the penitentiaries of Essex, and Hudson, there is no steady labor demanded, even from convicts, in any county jail of the State, beyond the family wants of the establishment. Spasmodic efforts have been made in several of the counties to remedy the evil but the industries have been dropped as impracticable. Work may not be demanded of persons merely held for trial. The convicts, being few in number, will not repay the cost of instruction, attendance, &c., nor will the more numerous police prisoners, idle, awkward and enfeebled by debauch. In a few of these places of confinement, the prisoners are, to some extent, classified, but in a great majority of cases the male prisoners associate in the common hall throughout the whole day, with little supervision; and in two jails the *women* were added to the crowd. Hardened convicts, witnesses, untried (perhaps only *suspected*) offenders, comparatively innocent youth and adult criminals, mixing together in such companionship as they desire, what that is not incorruptible can escape corruption? If an inmate be ignorant of the advance secrets of the brotherhood, there will not lack a *professor* to give him the password, and aid him to graduate in these county schools of crime. Prisons so conducted are pest houses which need abatement. What must be the moral and mental status of a community which, from decade to decade, allows such plague spots in their midst to go uncorrected? Our well-to-do citizens, like the priest and the Levite of old, ignore the claims of humanity, and "pass by on the other side". We sneer at the whipping post of an adjoining State, and yet subject our own petty offenders to less deterrent and far more corrupting influences. Lazy vagrants and criminals *seek,* in our jails, a winter refuge from cold and hunger and *labor.* They gladly submit to the confinement, for the sake of the attendant substantial and prolonged benefits. The brief, inexpensive discipline of Delaware *is not sought;* and its recipients alter their habits or shun the jurisdiction.

We are not advocates for brutalizing punishments, for the restoration of the whipping post, the bastinado, or the pillory; but alas, for the progress of mental enlightenment and christian civilization, if there be no better plan for the treatment of incipient offenders than that upon which we have fallen.

New Jersey, however, is not singular in possessing prisons which are far below the demands of humanity. The evils are inherent in the present system, and prevail wherever local jails are under the care of frequently changing and uninstructed officers, without supervision of competent board. For an admirable presentation of this subject see article on "County Jail System", by F. H. Wines, LL.D., Secretary of Illinois State Board of Charities, in proceedings of National Prison Congress, held in New York, 1876.

The remedy we apprehend, will be found in a great change of the system upon which our jails are conducted. Persons convicted and sentenced to the State Prison or reformatory, should, with all convenient despatch, be transferred to the place assigned them. To an individual held as a witness for the public benefit in an impending trial, the obvious duty of society is to protect him from association with criminal prisoners. Such also is the law. But a knowledge of the rights of a confined witness seems not to have reached some prison-keepers and Boards of Freeholders. Persons committed as charged with crime, and from whom labor cannot be exacted, should also be kept in strict seclusion for their own sake and for that of society. If innocent, criminal association is a wrong to *them.* If guilty, they should not be allowed to contaminate *others.* "This doctrine", says Dr. E. C. Wines, "is as old as the Roman jurisprudence, which distinguishes sharply between the *suspected* and the *convicted,* calling the former the *hostage of justice,* the latter the *slave of punishment.*" A speedy trial, a conviction or an acquittal, is the proper solution of their case.

In the much more numerous instances of commitments for short terms by the police magistrates, for disorderly conduct, petty thefts, drunkenness, etc., a more appropriate remedy than association with old comrades and others with like instincts, in a common hall, would be *strict cellular confinement, and very meager diet.* These points should be rigorously insisted upon. Several repetitions of such misdemeanors, showing habits injurious to society, should subject the offender to a sentence so prolonged, and to such discipline, as would give opportunity for a changed purpose in life. We were told of one person thus arrested and imprisoned thirty-seven times for terms of a few days and of another "nearly one hundred times". To tamper thus with such offenders, is beneath the dignity of the law, and of its administrators. A sentence of a year's duration in these cases would have saved the expense of continual arrests and trials, and would have relieved the community of a nuisance. It would greatly increase the hope of restoration to honorable citizenship.

TRAMPS OR VAGRANTS.

The "Act to define and suppress tramps," approved April 9th, 1876, has not yet produced its designed effect. Indeed, its provisions appear not to be generally known. If public attention were called to its provisions by its publication in handbill form or otherwise, and if citizens annoyed by this most undesirable population would insist upon the enforcement of the law, the evil would be lessened. We have been astonished at the number of tramps reported in towns and cities throughout the state.

Rigid surveillance and compulsory labor are indispensable conditions in the adequate treatment of these wandering idlers, who seem to regard themselves as exempted from the ordinary condition of humanity, "In the sweat of thy brow shalt thou eat bread". There is often great difficulty in procuring employment of a character which can be enforced upon such vagrants in the points where they congregate. In those parts of the State where suitable stone is found, it might be brought to a convenient place and broken for township roads. In others fire wood might be sent to be sawed and split for private citizens. In an agricultural region some heavy farm work, as clearing land of stones or stumps, grubbing, digging of drains, etc., ought to be insisted upon as a compensation for food and lodging. In cities or towns the grading and paving of streets and cutting down of embankments, might sometimes be kept in reserve for these unwelcome guests, sure to arrive. A benevolent lady whose kitchen door had frequent visitors, lessened their attendance by connecting her unfailing charity with the sweeping of her pavement and other employments. "NOTHING FOR NOTHING" should be the unfailing condition of aid, public or private, for able-bodied beggars.

A bill aiming at the permanent suppression of this evil is now before the Legislature of New York. It provides for the appointment of a Superintendent of work-houses, who with the approval of the Board of State Charities is to establish such institutions in rented premises at proper points; and it is made the duty of magistrates to send to them convicted vagrants, for from three to six months. On a second conviction the sentence is to be from six months to a year, and for a third to be of indefinite duration. Tramping, with its attendant arsons, thefts, and outrages would not flourish under the enforcement of such a law.

PUNISHMENTS IN PRISON.

The subject of legal punishment is one which has occupied attention in all ages. In the not distant past the laws of some nations may be said to have been "written in blood". But gradually the leavening influence of Christianity has effected a great change in public and in private life, subjecting both the prison and the family more and more to the operation of moral forces. One of the great poets of our time exultingly proclaims this onward movement. "Thank God!" says Whittier,

> "That I have lived to see the time
> When the great truth begins at last to find
> An utterance from the deep heart of mankind,
>   Earnest and clear, that ALL REVENGE IS CRIME!
> That man is holier than a creed,—that all
>   Restraint upon him must consult his good,
> Hope's sunshine linger on his prison wall,
>   And love look in upon his solitude."

A fatal objection to the reliance on physical suffering as a last resort in prison discipline, is that if the infliction be light it is the subject of contempt and ridicule; if severe and protracted by the determination of the convict not to yield, the cry is readily raised, and some times not without reason, of cruelty and brutality. The venomous whisper of a subordinate, some act of injustice unknown to the warden, perchance a taint of insanity, may have stung the culprit to almost superhuman endurance of pain, rather than submit to utter the simple words "I will obey." An estimable officer who, without anger or unworthy motive, enforces such punishment, under a belief that it is essential to the preservation of good order, may thus become unintentionally a vehicle of wrong, and the subject of scurrilous abuse and widespread calumny.

In many prisons of the United States a solitary cell, spare diet and deprivation of employment, is the extreme penalty for the violation of prison rules. In others the cell is darkened, and in flagrant cases, the hands are fastened to the wall, *not higher than the shoulders.* But whatever disciplinary regulations may be adopted there should never be wanting a loving pity for the erring and fallen brother, (the victim perhaps of "evil parentage and vile surroundings,") and a warm desire to lift him up into a Christian manhood. An unexpected and wholly undeserved kindness to a moody prisoner in such restraint, a walk in the fresh air, a delicacy from the officers' table, a few genial words, the reading of some simple story (good *will* finds a good *way*) may revolutionize the man, and win him to the right. We live in a professedly Christian land—a land of bibles and of churches. Surely it is not too much to expect that the management of our prisons shall be permeated with a Christian spirit.

Ex-Governor G. F. Fort wrote ten years since "Observations made in the prisons of other states, satisfied us that the kind and degree of punishment defined by the N. J. statute, without discretionary powers of further infliction by either keeper or inspectors, is amply sufficient to control and subdue all refractory cases, unless there is defective management in the prison. Gen. Amos Pilsbury, the able and efficient chief of the Albany

Penitentiary, who has for forty years presided most successfully over penal institutions in New Hampshire, Connecticut and New York, assured the commissioners that corporal or painful punishment was never necessary in a well regulated prison, and that seventy-five per cent of his men passed through their time *without a harsh word.* Mr. Haynes, Warden of Massachusetts State Prison, Capt. Robbins, of the South Boston House of Correction, and others, were equally explicit on that point, and agreed fully with Gen. Pilsbury. Mr. Brockway says 'coercive measures are only resorted to by unqualified officers.' "

The New Jersey law allows punishment in her State Prison "not exceeding close confinement in a dark cell, on bread and water, with chain on the leg, or handcuffs, or both, for six days," and "further punishment as the acting Inspectors shall think proper; *provided,* that corporal punishment shall in no case be inflicted."

The obvious meaning of this passage is that corporal *pain* shall never be inflicted as a punishment in the prison; not merely that the *lash* is abolished, and the thumb-screw, the rack or other devices of vindictive ingenuity, allowed as a substitute. All experience shows that abuses, sooner or later, follow where the infliction of bodily pain becomes the established mode for the correction of misconduct. Our statute is right, and ought to be maintained. But must discipline be abandoned, misrule be inaugurated, and all profitable industry be abandoned in our prisons? By no means. It is an absolute necessity, in such a family, that good order be maintained, that obedience be prompt, and that labor, both for discipline and sustenance, be exacted and performed.

THE COMMUTATION LAW.

It was with the intent to secure these ends, that the Legislature, in 1869, enacted what is known as the Commutation Law. This offers to the prisoner a powerful incentive to do right, by providing that for every month of satisfactory performance of assigned labor, *two days* of his sentence shall be remitted; for every month of orderly deportment, *two days;* and for every month of manifest effort at self-improvement, *one day;* for twelve months of continuous good record, an additional day per month may be given; thus deducting seventy-two days from a sentence of fifteen months or over. For the second year of good record, another day per month is granted; and so an added day per month for each year progressively.

Could any more beneficent provision be asked by the prisoner than this? Could any more efficient disciplinary power be asked by the officers?

It must be acknowledged, however, that the law has never produced, in our prison, the effects contemplated by its friends. But the cause of this is patent. To avoid trouble in the keeping of accounts, the plan was adopted of giving to every prisoner credit *in advance* for all his "good time," and entering as the day of his exit the shortest possible date which he could earn by faultless conduct. Punishments for misconduct were directed to be charged, with intent to prolong the time of imprisonment for each offense. But the account seems to have been carelessly kept, and sometimes wiped out; so that complaints have been made of uncertainty and injustice. The present administration receiving the record books and the established practices continued through several of its predecessors, naturally adopted their arrangement, as no objection was urged; but we understand it has carefully complied with the section of law forbidding commutation in any month when punishment has been inflicted.

The great aim should be to prevent all need of punishment, by securing to this end the hearty purpose of the convict. Every inmate on entering the prison should be made to understand the benevolent intent of the law in its several particulars; and be assured of the desire of the officers, justly and impartially to give him its full benefit, on condition that he shall deserve it. He should be furnished with a book containing a printed explanation of the plan and the permanent rules of the institution, and blank pages for the entry month by month of the credits or debits of his account for labor, conduct and self-improvement, as they appear on the books of the Prison. If the record be deemed by him unjust, he should, while the facts are all fresh in the memory be allowed the opportunity to ask its correction of the Keeper, the Moral Instructor, or an Inspector. If the entry be right, it could be kindly explained to him, whilst if an error has unwittingly occurred, an honorable officer will sedulously rectify it. Who would rob a helpless convict of his legal earnings?

The difference in effect in carrying out the commutation law upon the plan we, have indicated and that which was unfortunately adopted nine years ago—the moral forces made continuously operative in elevating the prisoner on the one hand, and the great want of them on the other, must be evident to any thoughtful mind.

THE REPRESSION OF CRIME.

Within a few years past the question of the best methods for repressing crime, has occupied the attention of philanthropists in this and other lands; and congresses, national and international, have discussed the whole subject in a calm, philosophical and Christian spirit, and with an interest unknown to any previous part of the world's history. Principles eliminated with much thought and toil, the result of struggles and experiments and theories formed in prison life, by Maconochie at the penal colony on Norfolk Island, by Montesinos at Valencia in Spain, and by other patient workers and advance thinkers—the separate system in Pennsylvania, and the silent or congregate system of Auburn—the working of approved plans adopted in Great Britain and Ireland, and the various countries of continental Europe, have been in these congresses brought to public notice, considered and discussed. The labors of our Dwight and Lieber, of Wines and Harris, have aided in the good work. The result has been a marked advance in penological science; and improvements, almost world-wide, have been made in systems and in practices.

THE IRISH PRISON SYSTEM.

The most prominent instance of improved practical results has been in the system of prisons and of discipline adopted in Ireland under Sir Walter Crofton in 1853. Under it the convicts are treated as erring and reasonable beings. They are instructed in the obligations of law, human and divine, and plied with motives to do right. As they manifest improvement in mental culture, in morals and in labor, they are advanced to higher grades, with increased privileges, till the last months of prison life, if it can be called *prison* life, are passed on an open farm.

To the wonderful results of this mode of treatment in the elevation and reformation of the convicts, statesmen and philanthropists have borne abundant testimony. And their testimony finds ready credence, for it is in accordance with our intuitive convictions of right. The system acts with nature. The path of the reforming convict is purposely made rugged, but industry and integrity smooth his passage, and hope beckons him onward till the goal is won. It is said that of 1,000 men who passed through the penal farm at Lusk *but two* attempted to escape.

THE NEW YORK STATE REFORMATORY.

A most hopeful experiment, because better adapted to our state of society in America, is that which has been recently inaugurated at Elmira, New York, the result of careful thought and labor by members of the N. Y. Prison Association. This institution is startlingly unique in its character, and meets wants long felt and acknowledged in our prison arrangements. It is designed for young men between 16 and 30 years of age, sentenced to it for criminal offence, who are not known to have been previously confined in *any* State Prison or penitentiary on conviction for a felony.

The buildings are arranged for three grades of prisoners. On admission all are received in the second grade. They are here comfortably fed and clad, eat in messes at tables in hall, and are allowed to see and correspond with friends. Six months of good record in conduct, labor, and study entitle an inmate to promotion to first grade, where improved diet, clothing and privileges await him. By gross misconduct in either of these grades a prisoner may fall to the number three grade, where a coarse gray dress is worn, the diet is meager and eaten in the cell, and intercourse with friends, even by letter, is denied. Three months of good conduct is required to reinstate him in number two.

The different grades meet together at labor, in school and in chapel under supervision. At other times they are separate. Two evenings of the week are devoted to the active recitation of lessons prepared on other evenings in the cells, where gas light is furnished. The progress is marked even in the most backward students. Prisoners, who do not know their letters, on admission, a few months after were reading in Third Reader and ciphering in Fractions. A number of advanced scholars were employed as teachers— a Normal School for their special instruction being held one evening in the week. Idleness in the cell on study evenings, manifesting itself in the recitation class, will give the careless pupils undesirable marks. The active prosecution of study or the perusal of instructive books is considered absolutely essential to their moral and mental renovation. Their lessons and questions growing out of them, being objects of common interest, form themes for conversation when they meet, instead of debasing or unimproving talk.

A mark system, strictly enforced, gives to the men deserving it at the end of every month a number three mark for good conduct, for effective labor and for diligent study—making an aggregate of nine marks. Each man has his little *bank* book in which these monthly credits are entered. Ungentlemanly behavior at table or elsewhere, or other misconduct, non-accomplishment of satisfactory results in labor or in studies, causing bad numbers, operate as checks, and reduce his balance, thus arresting his advance to a higher grade.

To an inquiry by the Commissioners in reference to the sources from whence this conduct record is derived, the General Superintendent, Z. R. Brockway, writes us: "The manner of making up the record in each case is briefly as follows—each keeper is required to keep an accurate account of the manner and amount of labor performed by the prisoners under his charge—so of the demeanor. The teacher keeps a similar account of school performance. A synopsis of this record made on blanks prepared, is sent to my office weekly, containing full notes of explanation when any defect is reported. At the end of each month these reports are examined and audited by the General Superintendent, and the clerk from this audit enters the marks earned for the month in the ledger. From the ledger the prisoner's pass books are written up as is a bank book in a bank, and returned to the prisoner."

But the most marked feature of the Reformatory is the indeterminate sentence. Inmates are sent with no limit to their imprisonment but the maximum term provided by law for the crime of which they were convicted. The act says, "when it shall appear to the managers that there is a strong or reasonable probability that he will live and remain at liberty without violating the law, and that his release is not incompatible with the welfare of society, then they shall issue to such prisoner an absolute release from imprisonment, and shall certify the fact of such release and the grounds thereof to the governor, who may thereupon, in his discretion, restore such person to citizenship. But no petition or other form of application shall be entertained by the managers." The Board of Managers also have power "to establish rules and regulations under which prisoners within the Reformatory may be allowed to go upon parole outside of the building and enclosure, but to remain while on parole in the legal custody and under the control of the board of managers, and subject at any time to be taken back within the enclosure of said Reformatory."

The principle underlying "the indefinite sentence" of the New York law is one which is continually acted upon under analogous circumstances. An insane person is taken to an asylum, not for any specified time, but *to be restored* to soundness of mind. A diseased patient, or one with fractured limbs, goes to a hospital, not to be treated for twenty or ninety days, but to be cured. When, in the judgment of the superintendent of the asylum or hospital, the inmate may with safety to himself and the community be restored to society, arrangements to that end are made. And all men say "it is right". So, when the legal discipline to which an offender has been sentenced has wrought in him a just sense of his relations to society and a respect for the rights of others, it is eminently fitting that he should be released from confinement. The state has no vengence for a truly repentant son. But when the moral sense of a convict is dormant, and a reform purpose of life is manifestly not attained, the community should be protected from his assaults for the full term to which he could have been sentenced.

In determining the fitness of a prisoner for parole or discharge, the managers have before them a certified copy of the whole legal proceedings in his case, the charge and the evidence pro and con; 2d, his previous history as recorded by the superintendent, after careful investigation; 3d, his whole prison record; and 4th, the testimony of the officers, and, if desirable, a conference with the man himself. From these various sources they will be able to arrive at conclusions so generally correct as to justify the adoption of the flexible sentence.

From a copy of the report of the Reformatory for 1877, not yet printed, but kindly furnished us in manuscript by the General Superintendent, we extract a few passages:

"The act of 1877, chapter 173, together with the early completion of the Reformatory, will afford a rare opportunity for an investigation by actual experiment, as to whether imprisonment for crime can be made beneficial to society by the reclamation of offenders. Under it stronger motives and better means for self-improvement may be supplied, and *the relations* of *the prisoner to the prison administration is radically changed.* This is not so much from any special feature of the law as from the whole act taken together, and the various provisions are so related to each other that to have altered them in any essential particular would have destroyed its usefulness, and it is therefore cause for gratulation that the law stands upon the statutes so free from faults."

"The principle of parole or provisional release is new in the prison discipline of this country, and imposes upon the managers a very delicate duty; but it is believed to be of the greatest importance. It has not yet been put to the test of practical experience here, only because from the brief period of time since the enactment of the law, and the absence of any case specially requiring it, there has been no demand for it. Experience has shown that there are certain weak characters among prisoners, not positively vicious, who, having a recognized abiding place in society, with reputable friends and relations to aid them, may be released with advantage to all concerned, if the moral force alone of their legal relations to their custodians may remain. And often such prisoners not only make much more rapid improvement when in usual social circumstances than if detained in durance, but if imprisoned too long they do actually deteriorate.

Great care will be exercised that only suitable prisoners shall be paroled *and that a place is prepared for them before they go out.* The managers, in fixing upon a uniform plan to determine the conditions upon which the prisoners may obtain increased privileges and ultimately their release from custody, have sought to carefully guard society against the return to any community, of confirmed criminals, or others likely to fall again into crime; to put before the prisoner the greatest inducements to the exercise of self-control and efforts for self-culture and to stimulate the self-regarding virtues; also, at the same time, they have sought to guard the prisoner against unjust imprisonment, either in kind or duration. To these ends they have adopted the present system of marks of merit and demerit and of social grades."

"The standard of conduct entitling prisoners to promotion from one grade to another is designed to be not only satisfactory, as relates to good order and the discipline of the reformatory generally, but also to induce habits opposed to those of the criminal cast of character. Therefore, it is made to embrace

First.—The general demeanor, the moral, social and economic features of it.

Second.—The industrious habit, whether forced, assisted or voluntarily diligent, and what degree of effective results; and

Third.—The interest in books and study, together with the progress in education actually made.

Of course, in finally determining the date of parole or absolute release, the impressions of those brought constantly in contact with a prisoner, will be sought, in addition to any systematic records and the personal examination by the managers."

There are in our State Prison nearly five hundred prisoners under thirty years of age, many of whom are in on their first conviction. Others are under sentence for offences hastily committed, whose lives have not been criminal. We would earnestly press upon the Legislature, for the treatment of such offenders, the establishment of a Reformatory upon the New York model.

If we have seemed to be diffuse in treating upon the subject of this novel and interesting experiment in American prisons, our apology must be the importance of a sufficiently full presentation of its claims. A visit at the institution and a careful consideration of its rules satisfied us that its establishment is the beginning of a new era of penitentiary discipline, to be carried on with a new aim, by new methods and destined, we confidently trust, to produce greatly improved results. The general Superintendent, Z. R. Brockway, is no novice at the work. He has had long years of successful experience as an educator of imprisoned men, and has entered upon this new field of advanced opportunities with noble purposes and high hopes.

39 P

A BOARD OF STATE CHARITIES.

Several of our sister commonwealths have derived much benefit from the appointment of a Board of State Charities for the purpose of examining into the condition and practices of the various penal and charitable institutions of their respective States. They report to the Governor or Legislature annually, making such suggestions as they may deem proper, with reference to the more economical or efficient working of these institutions, and the harmonious accomplishment of the beneficent purposes of the State. The appointment of such a board consisting of five or six judicious, philanthropic citizens, to serve without compensation, (their necessary expenses of course being paid,) would, we think, result in much good. Various evils have come to the knowledge of this commission which such a Board might have corrected or prevented.

A CHAPEL IN STATE PRISON.

The Keeper and Moral Instructor have both called the attention of the Legislature to the great need of a suitable room in the State Prison for the purpose of public worship. We think the State has eminently failed in its duty by so long neglecting provision for supplying this want. The proclamation of the Gospel of the Redeemer, the fullness of His love and mercy, is the most effective of all means of restoration for fallen man. The repetition of religious services to six different congregations of prisoners, mostly out of sight in their cells, is dispiriting both to minister and to hearers. Indeed, of those supposed to be hearers, many, from position, cannot be so, and others from apathy or indifference, will not. The magnetic sympathy of an audience with a speaker in solemn earnest laboring for their good, manifested in kindling eyes and serious, upturned faces, stimulates and compensates his efforts; but it is impossible if he talks *to the corridors*. A gentleman who walked down the aisle during a sermon, to look within the cells, found many convicts giving serious attention, but some at paltry occupations, or lying in bed, a few amusing themselves with games.

Surely such a state of things should be promptly remedied. We know of no large prison where the religious wants of those committed to it are not better provided for. Ministers of different denominations would often gladly address the inmates but for the physical barriers. As a lecture room where instructive addresses on various topics could be delivered, and also as a school room, such an apartment would be a signal benefit, and inmates guilty of improper conduct in any of these collections could be debarred from the privilege of attendance. The experience of other prisons forbids the expectation of serious difficulty.

The conclusions at which the commissioners have arrived are:

1st. That the county jails are not suitable places for the prolonged detention and employment of persons convicted for crimes and misdemeanors.

2d. That our State Prison is of sufficient capacity for the confinement of all persons convicted for crimes of the higher grade, and that mainly to such it should be hereafter restricted.

3d. That a House of Correction or State Reformatory should be established for criminals of lesser turpitude, and for young offenders on first conviction. In the strict disciplinary arrangements of the Reformatory, continuous encouragement should be given to the inmates in the formation of corrective habits of thought and action, fitting them as far as possible, for their restoration to society.

4th. That a Board of State Charities should be appointed, with advisory power over all penal and charitable institutions of the State, which are supported in whole or in part by State or municipal funds, in order that the beneficient purposes of the State may be efficiently, economically and harmoniously accomplished.

5th. That the provisions of the Commutation Law, passed April 19th, 1869, designed to act as a continuous encouragement of the convicts in good order, efficient labor and mental self-improvement, should be so carried out that month by month each man may know by a record furnished him, his allowance of "good time".

6th. That a commodious apartment ought to be provided in the State Prison for the purposes of religious worship, which could also be advantageously used for lectures on various improving and interesting topics, and for a school room.

7th. That to some officer connected with the State Prison should be assigned the duty of aiding discharged prisoners in securing suitable employment and homes.

We have been able to give but little attention to the selection of a site for the proposed State Reformatory. For the facility of receiving materials and of forwarding the products of the labor of the inmates it ought to be of easy access to both railroad and water communication. There are also reasons why it should be near some center of trade and varied industries. A plan for the requisite buildings has been promised us, and when received will be presented to the legislative committee.

In accordance with the terms of the joint resolution under which we have acted, we present herewith for the consideration of the Legislature, "An Act to provide for a New Jersey State Reformatory".[1]

All of which is respectfully submitted.

SAMUEL ALLINSON
JOHN CLEMENT
F. H. TEESE

Trenton, February 23d, 1878.

2. REPORT OF THE COMMISSION OF 1890 RECOMMENDING THE PROVISION OF A REFORMATORY FOR MEN.

While the report of the commissioners of 1878 was noteworthy for its enlightened opinions on the subject of penology, and for its commendable recommendations, no practical accomplishments

[1] Report cited, pp. 3–16. Copies of this report are preserved in the Library of the New Jersey Historical Society at Newark, and in the State Library at Trenton.

resulted from its activities.   Not until the prison at Trenton had again become seriously overcrowded and the need of lessening the pressure of the prison population on the facilities for confinement had come to the aid of the humanitarian argument in favor of a reformatory, was the agitation renewed with any degree of vigor. In 1889 a commission was appointed to examine the various reformatory systems then in existence in the United States and to submit plans and recommendations for the provision of a reformatory for men in the State of New Jersey.   While no immediate results ensued from the report of this commission submitted in 1890, the report was nevertheless the turning point in the agitation for a reformatory.   In 1895 a law was passed which authorized the State to proceed in putting into operation the recommendations of the commission of 1890 relative to the erection of a reformatory.

REPORT.

To His Excellency, Leon Abbett, Governor of New Jersey:

The undersigned commissioners, appointed by the Governor in pursuance of chapter 216 of the Laws of 1889, respectfully report as follows:

On May 6th, 1889, the following act having been duly passed by both houses of the General Assembly, was approved by the Governor:

"An Act relating to the state reformatory.

"Whereas, it is deemed advisable that there shall be a state reformatory in this state for the custody and imprisonment of criminals between the ages of sixteen and thirty, who have not been previously sentenced to a state prison in this or any other state or country, and of persons convicted for the first time of crime not involving moral turpitude; therefore,

"1. *Be it enacted by the General Assembly of the State of New Jersey,* That the governor shall appoint five persons as a board of commissioners, who shall be authorized to visit and examine any of the intermediate reformatories erected and in operation in other states, and shall make report to the governor of their inspection and judgment as to the best institution and system.

"2. *And be it enacted,* That they shall thereafter select from any available property owned by the sinking fund a suitable site for a state reformatory, and in case there is no suitable site among such properties they shall select one elsewhere; they shall make a report of the site selected and the value thereof to the governor and comptroller, and if approved of by them, in case the same does not belong to the sinking fund, they shall procure an option of its purchase in behalf of the state, and for a price not greater than the sum so approved of.

"3. *And be it enacted,* That the said commissioners shall be authorized to employ an architect or architects, and to procure plans or designs for the construction of suitable buildings for the state reformatory, which shall have a capacity of not less than five hundred prisoners, and to be so constructed as to admit of the classification of prisoners; they shall report to the governor the plan which they shall be of the opinion is the best adapted to the purpose, with an estimate of its probable cost; the governor shall report to the next legislature the said plan and estimate.

"4. *And be it enacted,* That the said commissioners shall be entitled to receive their traveling and other official expenses, which, with the cost of such plans and estimates, shall be paid, under the approval of the governor, by the treasurer, on the warrant of the comptroller.

"5. *And be it enacted,* That this act shall take effect immediately."

On or about January 3d, 1890, your predecessor in office, Governor Robert S. Green, appointed the undersigned as commissioners under this act, and a commission was duly issued to each of us, under the seal of the State. At the request of the Governor, the commission met at the Executive department on Tuesday, January 7th, and organized by choosing Charlton T. Lewis as Chairman and Robert W. Elliott as Secretary. We now report as our general conclusions:

First. That, on the whole, the best institution and system now in operation in any other State of the Union as an intermediate reformatory is the institution known as the New York State Reformatory, at Elmira, and the system of government and discipline there practiced.

Second. That among the available property owned by the Sinking Fund, there is one, and only one, suitable site for a State Reformatory, namely, the property known as the Edgar farm, in the city of Rahway, Union County; that this site is, in our judgment, better adapted to the purpose than any available property which has been offered to the commission for sale by private owners, and that we cordially recommend the appropriation of it for the erection of such an institution.

Thirdly. That the plans which, in our opinion, are the best adapted to the purpose of such an institution are substantially those which are appended to this report. They have been prepared and submitted by J. R. Thomas, architect, and embody the ideas and arrangements which have been found most useful in similar structures, freed from certain errors and defects which experience has revealed in prisons and reformatories hitherto constructed. We believe that they combine economy of construction and conduct, with convenience and security, in a degree not hitherto attained; and that by utilizing the labor of State prisoners and of the inmates of the reformatory, the entire structure can be completed in two years, at a cost to the State of three hundred thousand dollars.

In support and in explanation of these conclusions, we respectfully submit the following facts and considerations:

The only intermediate reformatories of the class contemplated in the act above recited, and which are now in successful operation in other States, are the New York State Reformatory at Elmira, the Pennsylvania Industrial Reformatory at Huntingdon, and the Massachusetts State Reformatory at Concord. Each of these has been visited and carefully inspected by the commissioners in a body, with the guidance and aid of the officers in charge. We have, upon the ground in each case, investigated the plans and the construction of the buildings, the laws regulating the commitment, maintenance, employment, instruction and discipline of prisoners, the methods of keeping records and accounts, the condition and products of the industries carried on, the practical workings of the system in all these respects, and the results thus far attained in the reformation of convicts. The first institution of the class in which reformation was distinctly set in view as the principal object of confinement, was erected in New York, under a law passed in 1870. Upon the completion of the buildings, the general principles of its administration were defined by an act passed in 1877, and since several times amended in details, and the reformatory has now been in successful operation for twelve years. The Massachusetts Reformatory was opened in 1885, and the Pennsylvania Industrial Reformatory early in 1889. In each of these the Elmira system has been adopted, with some modifications, and except in a few details, of education, discipline and labor, all that is most valuable in them is modeled after the New York institution. The buildings at Elmira are, on the whole, admirably adapted to their purpose, but were built without careful regard to economy, and have since been enlarged in disregard of the original plan, so that their cost has been far greater than would now suffice to construct an edifice of the same capacity and utility. The buildings at Concord are those of the State Prison converted into a reformatory, and are not in all respects so well constructed for the purpose. Those at Huntingdon have been built on imperfectly digested plans and apparently at a needless cost.

The principal differences in the laws which govern these several institutions relate to the selection of inmates. The law of Massachusetts, in this respect, was at first conspicuously imperfect, permitting the commitment to the institution of all classes of prisoners, including those guilty of the most aggravated felonies, as well as tramps, vagrants, stubborn children and common drunkards, and without any limitation to exclude persons advanced in life, or habitual or professional criminals. The law has been amended in this respect, but still permits the commitment to the institution of large numbers of criminals who are very doubtful subjects of its discipline; and it seems clear that the law of New York, which contemplates the commitment to the reformatory only of those who have been guilty of a serious offense, and yet of none except first offenders, and those who are comparatively youthful, is in all respects preferable. But even in New York we find that the spirit of the law has not been carefully observed by the courts, and partly because of a lack of careful discrimination in the infliction of sentence, and partly, perhaps, because of the crowded state of other penal institutions, a considerable number of habitual or professional criminals have been sent to the reformatory, and have been kept there to the injury of its proper work. It seems essential to the best results in such an institution that the subjects of its discipline should be selected with care. It is impossible by statute to lay down any fixed rule, founded either upon the nature of the offense, the age of the offender, or the number of previous convictions, which shall secure a proper selection. It is much better that a careful consideration of each particular case shall be made by the court passing the sentence, and that those offenders shall be committed to the reformatory, and those only, who, on such an investigation, are found to be probably susceptible of moral influence and capable of receiving such discipline and education as may fit them to become self-supporting citizens.

Apart from the law regulating the selection of inmates, the most important differences between the systems of discipline prevailing in the New York and the Massachusetts institutions respectively, are to be referred to the difference in character and policy between the heads of the respective institutions. No doubt a large discretion must necessarily be left to the competent superintendent of such an institution, but your commission have been profoundly impressed by the fact that an experiment has been tried on a large scale in the Massachusetts Reformatory, which has no parallel, so far as we are aware, in any other penal institution. The prisoners are allowed a freedom of social intercourse which is without precedent, and which has been regarded by many experienced students of the subject as questionable, if not fraught with peril. The highest class of convicts, who have won this position in the institution by a considerable period of good behavior, industry, and diligence in study, and who constitute a large percentage of the whole, are permitted to form clubs and societies, which assemble without the supervision of officers, and conduct their literary exercises and their amusements on fixed evenings of the week, in halls furnished for the purpose. After several years of experience, the officers of the institution declare that the liberty thus granted has never been abused, and that the results of it have been eminently beneficial; that these societies are a support to the moral order and good discipline of the institution, as well as a powerful stimulus to its intellectual activity. And this is said to be true in spite of the fact that the institution was originally peopled by a large detachment of prisoners from the State Prison. If it had begun with a small number of carefully selected subjects, and had gradually grown by the commitment of suitable persons selected for it by the courts, the same public spirit might have been still more easily built up, and the excellent result would have been less surprising.

While the law of Massachusetts for the selection of subjects for the reformatory seems to us inferior to that of New York, there are some respects in which the Commonwealth of Massachusetts has embodied improvements in the statute law relating to prisoners which experience has proved to be valuable, and which have, as yet, no complete parallel in the legislation of any other State. We refer particularly to the provision made for the supervision by a State agent of all juvenile offenders, and for the appointment in any city or town of the Commonwealth of a probation officer. It is the business of these officers carefully to inquire into the character and offense of every person arrested for crime, in order to ascertain whether the accused may be expected to reform without punishment; and in case he is satisfied, on investigation, that the best interests of the public and of the accused would be subserved by placing him upon probation instead of consigning him to prison, the court, upon his recommendation, may permit the accused to be thus released upon probation, upon such terms as it may deem best, always having regard to the reformation of the prisoner. A person thus released upon probation is subject to the supervision of the probation officer, who becomes, in a certain sense, responsible for his good conduct, and who may at any time re-arrest him, with the approval of the police authorities, without any further warrant, and bring him again before the court for sentence. The State Agent for Juvenile Offenders and his assistants have similar powers over all persons of tender age who are accused of crime, wrong-doing, or vagrancy, and may take charge of them and find places for them in which the influences upon their characters are likely to be much more beneficial than those in which they would be subject in a county jail. The combined work of these officers for a series of years has had the effect of diminishing vagrancy and crime in the Commonwealth of Massachusetts to an extraordinary degree, and it forms part of a system of penal jurisprudence which is so vast an improvement upon the methods commonly practiced that it deserves the careful consideration of all other civilized Commonwealths.

The act providing for the release on parole of prisoners whose conduct character indicate that they are fitted for it, which is now pending in the Legislature and has been received with so much favor, seems to indicate that the State of New Jersey is ready for a general revision of its criminal jurisprudence on the lines of the best modern practice. While such an act cannot, of course, be justified merely by the desire to relieve the penal institutions of the State from their over-crowded condition, it is, we believe, a wise measure, in the interest of a more intelligent and statesmanlike method of dealing with crime than has been hitherto practiced. It seems to us that while the establishment of a State Reformatory is a pressing necessity and will be of great value to the community, yet it can only be made useful in the highest degree if it is a part of a comprehensive system of dealing with the criminal classes which contemplates the utmost efforts in the reach of society for their entire elimination; and such a system must keep in view certain principles which have come to be admitted by all special students of the subject of crime, but which as yet have had little influence on the legislation of most civilized communities. The first and highest of those principles is that criminal jurisprudence, to accomplish its best ends, must have regard less to the particular offense which has been committed than to the person who has committed it. Hitherto it has been customary in penal laws to attempt to graduate punishments in accordance with the supposed enormity of offense, these offenses being crudely defined by certain vague and general names. This custom has grown out of the traditional and antiquated notion that imprisonment, when inflicted by law, is a sort of retaliation for the offense which has been committed against the law—that the law, in short, in punishing an offense, avenges itself by inflicting an equivalent for the offense upon the offender, yet in reality this notion is admitted to have no foundation. The object of the infliction of punishment is the welfare of society, which must be protected by the restraint of persons who would be dangerous to its peace and prosperity, and must be further protected, if possible, by the reformation of the offender. These two ends—the restraint of a criminal from the practice of criminality, and his reformation in order that he may be restored to honest and self-supporting industry—are the only ends which a wise statesmanship can hold in view in its penal laws; and this being admitted, it is the evident duty of the Legislature and of the administrator of the law to study not the offense, but the offender, and to inflict precisely that punishment, and no other, which is best adapted to restrain the offender, where there is danger of further acts of crime, and to reform him. All students of criminal jurisprudence are now agreed that the old notion of deterring prisoners from crime by the terror of punishment has broken down entirely, and must be abandoned. Prisons, then, should be retained only for those whose restraint is required by the interests of society, or those of whom there is hope that imprisonment will reform them. It is doubtful whether, in a large proportion of cases, the effect of imprisonment has not been to make criminals rather than to reduce their number; and, in any case, it is the part of wisdom to keep men out of prison, when imprisonment would injure them.

The great work which can be accomplished in a nation by a well digested and firmly administered prison system is illustrated by the recent history of crime in Great Britain. It is now about forty years since reformatory schools for the reception of boys and girls who had fallen into crime began to be established in Great Britain, and from that time to the present the entire system of prisons and jails throughout the country has been made the subject of careful study on the part of the Government, and has been improved by successive acts of Parliament until a complete reformatory system has been introduced in all the prisons, and every local jail has been brought under the same central administration. The result of these combined efforts is seen in the fact, shown by official statistics, that for forty years the number of criminals and the number of crimes of every grade in England and Wales have steadily and continuously declined, and during the last five years the average number of persons sentenced for both felonies and misdemeanors has been less than one-half of what it was from 1841 to 1845, although the population of the kingdom has increased about seventy per cent. It is clear that the prison system of England, on the whole, steadily diminishes the number of criminals, while in most of the States of the Union there is no comprehensive system of dealing with prisoners, or none which is equally effective. Yet, even in the English prisons, we believe that no such results have been obtained in the reformation of criminals as can be shown in the experience of the reformatories at Elmira, in New York, and at Concord, in Massachusetts.

It is impossible in this report to recount at length the principles of discipline which shall control the administration of such an institution as it is proposed to establish. Experience has shown that a large proportion of those who are first arrested for crime are susceptible to moral influences, and can be rescued from criminality if they are brought under the power of an institution thoroughly organized for the purpose. The means which it possesses for this purpose consist, first, of physical training and improvement, including exercise, cleanliness and diet; next, of industrial education intended to build up the habit of industry, and also to confer such special skill as will render the pupil capable of self-support, and, finally, of the education of the whole man, including the development to the utmost extent of his intellectual capacities. It is an ascertained fact that less than one-fifth of one per cent. of the crime in the United States is committed by persons who can be called educated. In addition to these influences, every moral and religious power which can be brought to bear on the prisoners should be utilized for their benefit. As the result of twelve years' experience in the Elmira Reformatory, it is now claimed that not less than eighty per cent. of those who have been subjects of education in that institution, and who are now free, are doing well, are supporting themselves and are free from criminal habits and associations. All precise statistics upon such a subject are open to criticism, but it seems to be a well ascertained fact that the proportion of criminals who have been restored to independence and to respectable citizenship through the agency of this institution is very large, including, perhaps, a decided majority, at least, of all those who have been subjects of its work. Such an institution must be regarded, not merely as a vast charity, which is an honor to the community instituting it, but further, as one of the best investments of money which can be made by any government for the benefit of the people.

In order to define as clearly as possible the nature, extent and organization of the proposed institution, the commission have embodied in the annexed draft of a bill the legislation on the subject which they deem necessary and appropriate at the present time; and they respectfully present it as a part of this report, for the consideration of the Governor and Legislature.[1]

> CHARLTON T. LEWIS, Chairman.
> PATRICK FARRELL,
> DAVID M. CHAMBERS,
> IRA OTTERSON,
> ROBT. W. ELLIOTT, Secretary.

At Trenton, N. J., April 2d, 1890.

[1] *Minutes of the Votes and Proceedings of the One Hundred and Fourteenth General Assembly of the State of New Jersey*, 1890; pp. 783–791.

Chapter X

DOCUMENTS RELATING TO THE STATE
REFORMATORY FOR WOMEN AT
CLINTON FARMS.

CHAPTER X

DOCUMENTS RELATING TO THE STATE REFORMATORY FOR WOMEN AT CLINTON FARMS.

I. The Origin of the State Reformatory for Women at Clinton Farms.
  1. The Joint Committee of 1886 Recommends the Provision of a Reformatory for Women.
  2. The Commission of 1903 Repeats the Demand of the Committee of 1886 for a State Reformatory for Women.

I. THE ORIGIN OF THE STATE REFORMATORY FOR WOMEN AT CLINTON FARMS.

1. THE JOINT COMMITTEE OF 1886 RECOMMENDS THE PROVISION OF A REFORMATORY FOR WOMEN.

The agitation for reformatories in the last quarter of the 19th century in New Jersey was not limited to a demand for a reformatory for men. In 1886 a joint committee appointed by the Legislature reported strongly in favor of the provision of a State Reformatory for Women. While the Legislature passed a resolution approving this report no practical action was taken toward providing for the erection of such an institution.

REPORT OF THE JOINT COMMITTEE ON FEMALE PRISON AND REFORMATORY

REPORT.

To the Senate and General Assembly of the State of New Jersey:

We, the Committee appointed by the Legislature of 1886, in accordance with Joint Resolution No. 7, to consider the advisability of establishing a prison for female convicts and reformatory for women in our State, respectfully submit the following report:

We have visited the prisons and reformatories for women at Indianapolis, Ind., Sherborn, Mass., and at Hudson, N. Y., and by correspondence and otherwise, have inquired into the management of female convicts in the prisons of different States, and the county jails and penitentiaries of our own State.

The institution at Indianapolis has both a penal and reformatory department. At the time of our visit there were one hundred and twenty-nine in the reformatory, and fifty-four in the penal department. The inmates of both departments of sufficient age and strength, are required to perform useful labor. Schools are maintained in the institution in which the girls receive a good common education, and the prisoners are taught the rudimentary branches. Many of them take much interest in the lessons and the improvement is generally satisfactory. In the studies that are prescribed, and in the labor required, the future welfare of the inmates is primarily regarded.

The girls are instructed in such useful labors as will enable them to provide for their own wants and render them independent of public charity, and prepare them for useful and honorable lives.

The aim of the discipline of the prison is to arouse ambition and inspire to better endeavors; to bring the prisoner under the control of her will instead of her inclinations. Obedience to the rules is strictly required, which helps to develop the will power and enables the prisoner to form the habit of using it.

As soon as the girls in the reformatory are fitted for work, good homes are provided for them in private families and they are sent out on ticket of leave, but they remain under the supervision of the institution until they become of age. All money thus earned by her is placed to her credit and paid to her at the expiration of her term.

The Reformatory Prison for Women, at Sherborn, Mass., was opened in November, 1877, and had under its care at the beginning of last year, two hundred and sixty-one women and girls, of which seventy-four were out to service on ticket of leave.

The system of grading and classification was adopted in 1881, and is so fully described in the report of that year, that we quote the description here:

"Each prisoner upon her admission to the prison is placed in a 'probation-room', so-called—a comfortable room, not a cell—in which she remains, secluded from other prisoners, for one month. If she has previously been an inmate of the prison, she is kept in this seclusion an additional month. While in the probation-room, she has opportunity for reflection, and obtains her first impressions of the purpose of her imprisonment. She is required to work steadily during her stay in this room.

Classification.

"In classifying the prisoners they are separated into four divisions, the lowest being division one and the highest division four. A prisoner who has not been an inmate of the prison before, enters division two (the next to the lowest grade), if she has a sentence not exceeding two years. If she has been an inmate previously, or has a sentence of more than two years, she enters the lowest grade, division one. The time passed in a probation-room is reckoned as a part of the time she is required to spend in her entrance grade."

They also have a system of promotion as follows: The prisoners are divided into four divisions, and are promoted from the lower to the higher grade, in accordance with credit marks received and retained during a given time.

The discipline of the prison is strict and rigidly though kindly enforced. The aim, as in the institution at Indianapolis, is to thoroughly reform the inmates and lead them to honorable and useful lives. The women and girls here are trained in such a manner as to fit them for household duties, etc. Having a farm connected with the prison, a dairy is successfully conducted.

The school is doing a good work—and the chapel services, conducted by the chaplain, aided by the clergy of South Farmingham, are heartily partici- pated in by all the inmates.

At Indianapolis, the board of managers is composed exclusively of females as are all the officers. Three men are employed on the premises as follows, viz: one engineer, one day and one night watchman.

At Sherborn the board of managers consists of two ladies and three gentlemen. The officers of the prison are all females. They have two male employes within the building, viz., the engineer and fireman—and twelve men employed outside as farm hands and day and night watchmen.

Both of these institutions (the one having a history of fourteen years and the other of eight years) have been successful beyond the highest anticipa- tions of their projectors, and have thoroughly shown that women are entirely competent for the control and management of women.

The State of New York has just completed a set of buildings—on the cottage system—at Hudson, N. Y. They have erected four cottages, one prison building, one hospital and a main building, with furniture and equip- ments, at a cost of one hundred and twenty thousand dollars.

The board of managers, as at Sherborn, will be composed of ladies and gentlemen, but will be officered exclusively by ladies.

We find that in our State more than thirty-five hundred women have been committed to county jails and penitentiaries during the past year, for terms of from two days to six months; average length of terms, nineteen and a half days. Many of the above arrests and commitments were of persons who had repeatedly been committed, and are illustrations of the evils of our present jail system with its short sentences and its failure to reform.

As a sample of some letters received by your Committee we hand the following from the Warden of the Hudson County Penitentiary:

HUDSON COUNTY PENITENTIARY ⎰
January 1st, 1887.　　　　　　⎱

GENTLEMEN—You ask in your letter for any further information which may be useful to the Committee. I should say, from my experience, that where a separate prison cannot be erected for females, that separate pro- vision in separate institutions for these two classes of prisoners, or separate and distinct departments where the regulations will prohibit intercourse and communication between the inmates, as though they were inmates of entirely separate institutions, should be made by law. All who have had any experience in keeping of male and female prisoners, condemn the keeping of them under the same roof, and I think it very injurious to both male and females, as they certainly do not require the same discipline or the same treatment. In regard to the officers in charge of female prisons, my opinion is they should be women, and should be selected with great care. They should be women of education, experience, keenness and courage, thoroughly practical, with strong motherly gifts. Discipline should be strict, punishment should be on the cumulative plan, beginning with a light punishment and increasing its severity with each succeeding offense. I am greatly in favor of grading prisoners, classifying them according to crime; each prisoner entering the lowest class and having the power to pass to the highest upon good behavior. The plan at Elmira meets my views; there no term is specified, but each prisoner has his term dependent upon his own conduct and reformation. I think one year should be the shortest term they should be committed for, and when a prisoner is discharged some suitable place should be provided where she could work and earn her living. No one should be allowed to leave the prison until suitable employment is secured. This is a good undertaking, and I hope to see your honorable committee successful in establishing such an institution, and if not for the whole State, my opinion is, would be a grand thing for the counties of Essex and Hudson to have such a prison jointly.

Your obedient servant,

JOHN GRIMES, Warden.

During its investigations your Committee also visited the State Prison at Joliet, Illinois, having understood that a female reformatory department was connected with that institution. It was found, however, that it was conducted on the same plan as that in operation in the like department in our own State Prison, having reference more to the punishment for crime than to any reformation of the criminal, by the proper surroundings and fitting education.

As penal institutions, both the New Jersey Prison and that at Joliet are as successful and as well conducted as any in the States, but both fail to reach the ultimate effect desired and sought to be accomplished by a female reformatory.

In view of the fact that so many women and girls are annually committed to our county jails and penitentiaries at an enormous expense to the taxpayers—an expense which is largely increasing each year, without any possibility of their reformation—and because of the success of the institutions named in reforming this class of females (eighty per cent. of those committed to their care, according to statistics, being thoroughly reformed), we, your Committee, recommend that a similar institution be erected in this State, and that an appropriation of seventy-five thousand dollars be made and a commission appointed to supervise the erection of such an institution.

We further recommend that said institution be located in Middlesex or Union counties, on lands now held by the State.[1]

Respectfully,
WM. H. CARTER,
T. G. CHATTLE,
THOMAS J. ALCOTT,
JOHN MARTIN,
R. B. SEYMOUR,
Committee.

2. THE COMMISSION OF 1903–4 REPEATS THE DEMAND OF THE COMMITTEE OF 1886 FOR A STATE REFORMATORY FOR WOMEN.

The Report of the committee of 1886 in favor of a reformatory brought no practical results. From 1886 to 1896 the women's ward at the State Prison was under the efficient management of Mrs. John H. Patterson. Her competent administration together with an appropriation of fourteen thousand dollars in 1899 for the improvement of the women's wing of the prison, tended to lessen to some degree the pressure of public opinion for the provision of a reformatory for women. However, the agitation was begun with even greater vigor in the early years of the present century, and the commissions appointed by the Legislature in 1903–4 vigorously recommended the establishment of a State Reformatory for Women. It was some little time, however, before any practical results were achieved as a result of the recommendations of the committee. In 1907 a law passed the House providing for the erection of a reformatory for women, but failed in the Senate. However, the law of April 1st, 1910, brought to a successful conclusion the agitation for the provision of a reformatory for women which had extended over more than a quarter of a century.

[1] *Legislative Documents,* 1887. Document No. 39, Vol. III, pp. 1–7.

40 P

REPORT OF THE WOMEN'S REFORMATORY COMMISSION APPOINTED BY VIRTUE OF
JOINT RESOLUTION NO. 2 OF THE LEGISLATURE OF 1903.

NEWARK, N. J., Jan. 30th, 1904.

MY DEAR SIR—I beg leave to hand you herewith report of the Commission appointed by you under the authority of Joint Resolution No. 2 of the Legislature of 1903, to investigate into and report upon the advisability of establishing a State Reformatory for Women.

A bill embodying the ideas of the Commission is in course of preparation, and will be handed to some member of the Legislature for introduction at an early day.

Yours very respectfully,

EDWIN G. ADAMS,

Secretary of Commission.

HON. FRANKLIN MURPHY,

Governor of New Jersey,

Trenton, N. J.

REPORT.

To the Senate and General Assembly of the State of New Jersey:

The members of the Commission appointed by His Excellency the Governor, in pursuance of Joint Resolution No. 2 of the Legislature of 1903, respectfully report:

Since their appointment, the members of the Commission have visited and inspected the State's Prison, the penitentiaries of Essex and Hudson counties and the principal county jails. All of the county institutions not visited have reported to us in writing, in reply to written interrogatories submitted to them. The Commission has also visited the Women's Reformatory, at Bedford, New York, the Women's Reformatory at Sherburn, Massachusetts, and the State Home for Girls at Lancaster, Massachusetts. The discharge of the duty devolved upon us necessarily included not only the visitation and inspection aforesaid, but also an examination into the principles and system of penology in general, especially in its relation to women offenders.

The objects of imprisonment for crime and lesser offenses against the law are (1) the punishment of the offender, (2) the prevention of further offenses by the offender, (3) the deterrent effect upon others, and (4) the reformation of the offender. Our examination of the various institutions and our study of this subject convinces us that the present method of punishment of women offenders employed in our State, accomplishes in some cases, but not in all, the *first* of these objects, and probably also accomplishes the *third;* but that it utterly fails to attain either of the other two important objects; while a reformatory prison for women, exclusively officered and managed by women, and under a systematic and thoroughly organized method of classification, education, training, example and life, would effectively accomplish all of these purposes.

During the year ending December 1, 1903, eighteen hundred women have been confined in the State's Prison, penitentiaries and jails of New Jersey. Many of them we have seen, and having come upon them unexpectedly, we have observed them in their ordinary daily life in the institutions. Most of them, coming from the humblest walks of life and with perhaps inherited tendencies to vice, owe their imprisonment directly or indirectly to alcoholism and prostitution. There is no classification or gradation of offenders; and, except in two or three jails, women and girls detained as witnesses, or accused of an offense of which they may be proved innocent, are confined in the same corridor with women convicts, as well as with women awaiting trial who may be guilty of serious offenses. Thus a young girl, held as witness, is brought into daily association with drunkards, prostitutes and perhaps murderesses. No systematic industries are maintained in the county jails, and therefore these unfortunate women spend most of their time in indolence, except the few hours devoted to sewing or the manual labor of scrubbing, cleaning and perhaps cooking, with full opportunity for debasing and demoralizing conversation.

In the county jails the women are under the direct charge of men keepers. The attitude of these keepers toward the women is, in some instances at least, distinctly demoralizing. It is undoubtedly true that these jails, designed to prevent crime, actually engender it; that women witnesses, women held for trial, and first offenders serving short sentences for minor offenses are influenced by the debasing conversation, the demoralizing atmosphere and the attitude of the jail authorities, to a life of moral depravity. Of the eighteen hundred women confined in the penal institutions of our State during the year ending December 1, 1903, fully fifty per cent. were "habitual offenders". This, of itself, would seem to demonstrate that the method of punishment of women offenders which we now employ fails utterly to accomplish the prevention of further offenses, or the reformation of the offender. In the two penitentiaries and the State's Prison, occupation is provided and women attendants are in charge; but the work done cannot be of an educational nature, and there is no opportunity for gradation, according to conduct. These institutions are prisons and not reformatories, and the respective jailors have expressed themselves, from their practical experience, as heartily in favor of a separate reformatory for women.

A reformatory for women, established upon proper lines, suitably equipped, managed by a body of specially trained, intelligent women, would accomplish not only the punishment of the offender and the repression of offenses by others, but also, in a large majority of instances, the prevention of further offenses by the individual, and her reformation. This statement is abundantly proved by the results attained by the Massachusetts Reformatory for Women, after an experience of twenty-five years. At this institution the inmates are assigned to such industrial pursuits as the authorities deem most advisable in each individual case. Care is taken to thoroughly train each woman in the line of work to which she is assigned, so that when released she will be qualified to earn an honest living. Every effort is made to surround the inmates with good influences, and to prevent any communication between them except in the presence of a matron. The inmates are graded into three classes. A "credit system" prevails, whereby a certain number of credits are given daily to each woman, for perfect conduct and industry; for misconduct, marks already earned are forfeited. Upon the numbers of marks obtained within a certain period depends the advancement of the woman into the higher grade, or her reduction to the lower grade. In the highest grade, absolutely perfect conduct and industry for a period are requisite before she can be released. So anxious are the women to excel that at the time this Commission visited this reformatory in November last, out of the two hundred and twenty women inmates there was not one in the third or lowest grade.

In our opinion, this system can be still further improved under the cottage plan, which is used at Bedford, New York. There the newly arrived inmate is placed in the reception house and thence promoted as her conduct warrants from one cottage to the next until she reaches the highest cottage, where she receives many small but valued privileges and comparative liberty.

In all the reformatories visited, work is found for the inmates upon their release. The majority of them go out to service, and the demand is greater than the supply. The authorities report that the return of a woman who has once served a sentence is rare—a situation in marked contrast to that of the "habitual offenders" who constitute fifty per cent. of the women inmates of our institutions. If these habitual offenders cannot now be reclaimed, at least New Jersey has the opportunity of preventing more women from becoming confirmed criminals. Is it not real economy to turn three-quarters of our women offenders into self-respecting members of society, rather than to allow at least one-half to spread the contamination for which the State itself is responsible, and thus feed the supply of criminals and defectives, which must in their turn become an ever increasing expense to the State?

We earnestly recommend the establishment of a reformatory for women on the cottage plan, to be under the exclusive management of women as officers and attendants, and to be organized along the general lines adopted in Massachusetts and New York, and we suggest to the Legislature the urgent need of enacting the necessary legislation at its coming session. We believe that the only possible objection that can be raised to the establishment of such an institution would be on the ground of its initial cost. While we feel that the obvious duty of our State in this matter is such as not to admit of the consideration of any such objection, yet we suggest that the ultimate cost of caring for unfortunate women would be lessened through the reduction by reformation of the number to be cared for.

We recommend the purchase of about one hundred and fifty acres of farming land in a location as easily accessible as possible to the large cities of the State, and the ultimate erection thereon of five brick cottages, with other necessary and suitable buildings. The estimated cost of the land, buildings and equipment necessary for one hundred and fifty women is as follows:

Five cottages at $20,000 each, ... $100,000 00
Superintendent's house,.............................   6,000 00

Farmer's house,	1,500 00
Stable, barns, etc.,	3,000 00
Sewerage, water, etc.,	5,000 00
Land—150 acres at $50,	7,500 00
Furnishing and equipment,	15,000 00
Contingencies and expenses,	10,000 00

$148,000 00

Each cottage should accommodate from twenty-five to thirty inmates, a matron, housekeeper and teacher. The annual cost of maintaining the establishment herein indicated, with the cottages filled, is estimated at about $240 per capita.

We recommend, however, an appropriation by the Legislature of $75,-000, which sum will be sufficient to purchase the land and establish the entire plant indicated above, except three cottages. The two cottages thus to be erected would be sufficient to care for all the younger women who may be sentenced by the various courts and magistrates for a first or second offense. The plant could later be increased by the building of additional cottages, so that all women convicts in the State, except as herein indicated, could be confined in such reformatory.

Such an institution should be in charge of a board of managers of five persons, carefully chosen, at least two of whom should be women, and should be under the direct care of a woman superintendent, experienced in reformatory work.

In order to fully accomplish the essential objects of such a reformatory, we recommend that after the establishment thereof, the present laws of this State be amended so as to mandatorily require the commitment to the women's reformatory of all women between the ages of sixteen and thirty, except those committed for life, unless the sentence shall be for a term of more than five years. We believe, however, that the present probationary law should not be modified or transgressed upon.

The Commission has no bill of expenses to present to the State.

Respectfully submitted,

CAROLINE BAYARD ALEXANDER,
EMMA L. BLACKWELL,
LEROY H. ANDERSON,
EDWIN G. ADAMS.

SUPPLEMENTAL REPORT OF THE WOMEN'S REFORMATORY COMMISSION RENDERED BY VIRTUE OF JOINT RESOLUTION NO. 2 OF THE LEGISLATURE OF 1904.

SUPPLEMENTAL REPORT.

To the Senate and General Assembly of the State of New Jersey:

Pursuant to the requirements of Joint Resolution No. 2 of the Legislature of 1904, the Commission appointed to report upon the advisability of establishing a women's reformatory, makes the following report as follows:

The Commission has further examined into the present facilities and accommodations of the State, for the imprisonment and care of women offenders; and (2) has made inquiries as to the number of women confined in houses of correction, refuges, missions, or homes of like character, for the care of delinquent women of the State, who have been placed in such institutions at the request of any judge of any court of this State, or of any probation officer; and (3) has also inquired into the number of women under the care of the probation officers of the several counties and the nature of their offenses; and (4) has also inquired as to the character of the work required of women in the jails and penal institutions in the State, and the average number of hours each day in which they are employed.

We find no improvement in the facilities and accommodations of the State for the imprisonment and care of women offenders over those shown in our former report. We believe that no improvement is possible until the Legislature provides for the establishment of a women's reformatory.

Our inquiry as to the number of women confined in houses of correction, refuge, missions or homes of like character, for the care of delinquent women, has been made of the county judge in each county and of the several probation officers. We have found that in three counties, namely, Hudson, Essex and Union, a number of women convicted of crime, or of being disorderly persons, have been placed in private institutions. The reason assigned for this was that such women needed the restraining influences of some institution, and in the opinion of the judges and probation officers, they should not be subjected to the degradation of a jail or penitentiary sentence. In each of such cases, sentence was suspended upon the woman, and she was placed under probation, upon condition that she go to such house of correction, refuge, mission or home, as the court should determine. In Hudson county sixteen women were placed in private institutions; in Essex county twenty-one women were placed in private institutions; and in Union county eight women were placed in such institutions.

Further inquiry has been made of the probation officers of several counties as to the number of women under their care. We have ascertained that eight counties have no probation officers, namely, Cape May, Gloucester, Hunterdon, Monmouth, Ocean, Salem, Somerset and Warren. . . .

We find no change in the character of the work required of women in the various penal institutions in the State, since the submission of our former report. In the county jails there is no systematic work required; and in the penitentiaries of Essex and Hudson counties and in the State's Prison the nature of the work is necessarily restricted, and has little educational value.

The need of a women's reformatory grows more urgent each year. The Commission therefore earnestly recommends the establishment of such a reformatory as outlined in its former report. A bill looking to this end has been prepared, under the supervision of the Commission, and will be introduced at the present session of the Legislature.[1]

Dated January 28, 1905.

> Respectfully submitted,
> LEROY H. ANDERSON,
> EMMA L. BLACKWELL,
> CAROLINE BAYARD ALEXANDER,
> MARY PHILBROOK,
> EDWIN G. ADAMS.

[1] *Legislative Documents*, 1904; Vol. V, Document No. 57.

CHAPTER XI

DOCUMENTS RELATING TO THE JAILS OF NEW JERSEY.

CHAPTER XI

DOCUMENTS RELATING TO THE JAILS OF NEW JERSEY.

I. DISTRESSING ABUSES IN THE NEW JERSEY JAILS.

I. IMPRISONMENT FOR DEBT IN THE JAILS OF NEW JERSEY, 1831.

Until 1846, New Jersey, in common with many of the other States retained the barbarous and irrational practice of confining debtors in the jails and prisons of the State. The following comments on the situation in New Jersey in 1831, taken from the annual report of the Prison Discipline Society of Boston, illustrate the deplorable situation of debtors in county jails at that time.

NEW JERSEY.

Imprisonment for Debt.—On this subject we know of nothing worse, in the whole length and breadth of the land, than in New Jersey. The number committed to Prison for debt, according to the population; their filthy and neglected condition while incarcerated; the small sums for which it is done; the expense to some of the counties of this most fruitless mode of collecting debts; the leaving of debtors in Prison without any provision by law for their support;—these things cannot so remain. The laws of New Jersey, says a humane sheriff of one of the counties, provide food, bedding and fuel for criminals; but for debtors, nothing is provided but walls, bars, and bolts. A member of the legislature in New Jersey described the condition of a jail in that State, where he had attempted to go among the criminals and debtors, in one common mass of corruption, but the air was in such a state that he could not do it. Like a member of Congress from Pennsylvania, who attempted to enter an apartment of the old jail in Washington city, a few years ago, he was obliged to retreat. We wish the retreat to the halls of legislation, in the former case, as in the latter, may be attended with the same result—the passing of a law for the renovation of the whole system. We are not, however, apprized of any modification of the laws of New Jersey in regard to imprisonment for debt, during the last year. But from all we have heard in conversation, learned by letter, or observed personally, in regard to imprisonment for debt in New Jersey, we think the necessity for it is imperious.[1]

2. CONDITION OF THE JAILS IN NEW JERSEY IN THE MIDDLE OF THE 19TH CENTURY.

In their famous memorial to the Legislature in 1850, the New Jersey Prison Reform Association admirably summed up the condition of the county jails at that time. The most obvious evils of the system, namely, unhygienic living quarters for the inmates, promiscuous association, and uniform idleness, have from the colonial period been the chief defects of the New Jersey jails, as they have indeed of the general jail system in the United States.

MEMORIAL OF THE NEW JERSEY PRISON REFORM ASSOCIATION, IN RELATION TO THE IMPROVEMENT OF COUNTY JAILS.

Communicated to the Legislature, January 25, 1850, and ordered to be printed.

MEMORIAL.

To the Honorable the Senate
and General Assembly of New Jersey:

The undersigned, a committee appointed by the New Jersey Prison Reform Association, at its annual meeting in Trenton, on the 16th instant, to lay before your honorable body the facts reported by the several county executive committees of the Association, relating to the condition, management and discipline of the county jails of the state, and to ask such legislative action as may remedy the evils shown to exist, beg leave respectfully to represent:

That by the Constitution of the society, it is made the duty of each executive committee to examine the jail of the county where they reside, and to report at each annual meeting of the society, all their proceedings, and all the information they may have obtained.

In accordance with this requirement, reports were made from thirteen counties, stating at length the condition of the jails, and the mode of treating those confined in them. From these reports it may be said, without hesitation, that it appears there is, throughout the state, with hardly an exception, a defective system of management in our county jails, resulting in increased moral degradation to the criminal, serious expense to the counties, and injury to the community at large.

[1] *Sixth Annual Report of Boston Prison Discipline Society of Boston,* 1831.

There seem to be four evils conspicuous in our present system, which can by judicious regulations be remedied, and for which the enactment of a general law, applicable throughout the state, would be necessary.

These are, the want of employment among the prisoners, the absence of any classification of criminals, (in some instances the sexes not even being separated), inattention to the cleanliness and comfort of those confined, and the neglect of all moral discipline.

As to the first of these evils, want of employment, it is believed to exist throughout the state; although your memorialists are happy to say that in a new jail recently erected in one of our counties, there are arrangements made for workshops, and it is contemplated to provide some employment for the criminals there confined. With this exception, no county of the thirteen from which reports were received, has ever established either a workhouse within its limits, or a workshop in connection with the county jail; and it is fair to presume that this is the case throughout the state. By a statute passed February 20th, 1799, and to be found on page 619 Revised Statutes, the chosen freeholders are authorized to establish workhouses in their respective counties; and by the supplemental act of March 4th, 1847, they are empowered to connect workshops with the jails; but as far as the examination of the county committees have extended, it does not appear that the boards of chosen freeholders have acted under these powers. As it is optional with the boards to act or not by the terms of these provisions, they have, either from doubts as to the wisdom of the measure, or from apprehension of increased expense, neglected to introduce this much desired reform, from which your memorialists are convinced, both by the facts now revealed in the reports already made, and by the experience of other states, the greatest good might be reasonably expected in the economy of our jail, and in the improvement of the criminals.

The want of a proper classification of prisoners as to age, sex and degree of criminality, is made a matter of severe comment from every county committee. As a natural consequence of the indiscriminate intercourse among the prisoners, most of our county jails are but schools of vice, where moral pollution and knowledge of evil spread and grow till all alike become degraded, adepts equally in crime, and prepared, after a short confinement, to issue forth, prey upon the community, hardened in vice, and skilled in every species of villainy.

As if, too, to increase the sad results, the absence of all regulations for the moral improvement of the criminal, and the negligence evinced as to his comfort and cleanliness, are shown to exist in nearly every jail within the scope of our reports. Your memorialists would not, in urging attention to these last mentioned evils, be understood as advocating such changes as would make our jails desirable places of refuge for the offender; while, however, they at the same time *do* contend, that such improvements should be made as shall conduce to the reformation of the offender, while also his punishment is secured. It cannot but be evident to the most casual observer, that our jails, with their promiscuous intercourse, their idleness, their scenes of drunkenness, and, your memorialists regret to add, their loathsome filthiness, cannot be otherwise than sources of great moral evil to the community.

This character may not, perhaps, apply to all our county jails, but it is not to be denied that it is but too faithful a picture of their condition in those counties containing a large and mixed population. In the punishment of the criminal, both for the prevention of crime and the security of the public, it certainly is no necessary teacher that the offender should be so treated as to sink him deeper in degradation, to destroy every moral principle, and divest him of the last remnant of self-respect. But no other result can be looked for, if he be shut up in common with a crowd of degraded beings like himself, in a cold and filthy cell, with scarcely clothes enough for decency, not even straw to lie upon, no occupation but that of imparting or learning lessons of vice—without books—without a word of good advice, and almost without hope. That these things are so, the reports of the county committees prove, and the experience of our judges confirms. Let then wise, well considered, and judicious enactments be passed, that shall provide for the strict enforcement of *hard labor,* for the proper separation of the hardened criminal from those younger in vice, and from those merely committed for trial, as also of the sexes; for a reformation in the treatment of prisoners as regards cleanliness, the ventilation and warming of the jails, and the providing of decent clothing, and for the introduction of some degree of moral discipline.

Your memorialists trust that they can confidently appeal to the moral sense, justice and intelligence of your honorable body, to give this truly important matter a calm and favorable consideration, not doubting that you will be prompt in applying such remedies as in your judgment may seem best adapted to correct the evil.

OLIVER S. STRONG,
D. NAAR,
WM. J. ALLINSON.
Committee of New Jersey Prison Reform Association.
Trenton, January, 1850.

BIBLIOGRAPHIC NOTE.

BIBLIOGRAPHIC NOTE

An investigator of the history of the penal, reformatory and correctional institutions is particularly fortunate in having at his disposal two magnificent guides to the documents. These are John Hood's *Index of the Colonial and State Laws of New Jersey, 1663–1903,* and Adelaide R. Hasse's *Index of Economic Material in the Documents of New Jersey,* 1789–1904. These two exhaustive guides indicate, classify and describe the location of practically every important public document bearing on the history of the penal and correctional institutions of the state, and are not only indispensible to any attempt at a thorough study of the subject, but also alone make possible a rapid survey of the subject.

Hood's *Index* gives the laws relating to these institutions according to the proper alphabetical entry. Miss Hasse's analysis of the public documents relating to the penal, reformatory, and correctional institutions of the state is contained in the section under the general heading "Maintenance." The following is the arrangement:

> State Prison, pp. 490–501.
> Rahway Reformatory, 483–84.
> State Home for Boys, Jamesburg, pp. 486–88.
> State Home for Girls, Trenton, pp. 488–490.
> Conferences of Charities and Corrections,
> Prison Reform Associations, etc., pp. 457–8.
> Defectives, pp. 458–64.
> Delinquents, pp. 464–66.

New Jersey has been one of the states which have published in a very complete form the serial and non-serial reports dealing with all phases of the history of their penal, reformatory and correctional institutions. The annual and special reports dealing with the state prison down to 1862 are to be found in the *Votes of the Assembly,* the *Journal of the Legislative Council,* and the *Appendices to the House and Senate Journals.* From 1862 onward they are found in the volumes of the *Legislative Documents.*

The documents concerning the State Home for Boys at James-burg, the State Home for Girls at Trenton, and the two reformatories are found in the *Legislative Documents,* as their histories all fall within the period since 1862. By consulting Miss Hasse's admirably classified list of documents one can learn in a few minutes the nature and location of the documents dealing with any of the public institutions of New Jersey from 1789 to 1904.

In addition to the session laws, which are indexed by Hood, there are a number of valuable collections of New Jersey laws compiled from time to time since 1732. The laws of New Jersey from 1665–1702 are gathered together in the famous compilation of Leaming and Spicer, *The Grants, Concessions, and Original Constitutions of the Province of New Jersey* (1758). The important laws passed from 1703 to 1730 are compiled in William and Andrew Bradford's *The Acts of the General Assembly of New Jersey,* 1703–1730 (1732). A more voluminous compilation giving the significant laws passed during the whole period of the royal province is Samuel Allinson's, *The Acts of the General Assembly of New Jersey,* 1702–1776 (1776). The earliest compilation of state laws is to be found in Peter Wilson's *Compilation of the Laws of New Jersey,* 1776–1784 (1784). This is followed by William Paterson's *The Laws of the State of New Jersey* (1800). The earliest compilation in the last century was that of Joseph Bloomfield, *The Laws of New Jersey* (1811). A voluminous compilation of all the laws in force in 1820 was published by Joseph Justice in 1821 as *The Laws of the State of New Jersey,* 1703–1821 (Trenton, 1821). The next important compilation was that of Josiah Harrison, *A Compilation of the Laws of New Jersey* (1833). The laws passed in the mid-century period were gathered and classified in the successive editions of Lucius Quintius Cincinnatus Elmer's *Digest of the Laws of New Jersey,* the last editions of which was edited by Nixon as the Elmer-Nixon *Digest of the Laws of New Jersey* (1855, 1868). The most pretentious compilation that had yet appeared was the one known as *The Revised Statutes of 1877,* prepared by G. D. W. Vroom and J. H. Stewart (1878). The laws of the next decade were compiled by Vroom and Wm. Lanning and issued as *The Supplement to the Revision of 1877* (1886). Ten years later, Vroom and Lanning produced the greatest of all compilations of New Jersey laws, *The General Statutes of New Jersey,* 1895, in 3 volumes (1896). This work was truly a marvel of legal accuracy, convenient arrangement, and skillful editing. An equally voluminous but not as well edited work brought the compilation down to 1911—*The Compiled Statutes of New Jersey,* 1911, in 5 volumes (1911). A new compilation is now in press—*The Supplement to the Compiled Statutes of 1911,* which will bring the classified list of New Jersey laws down to date.

With the original sources so readily available and so well indexed, one has little need for any secondary works, though there are two scholarly monographs dealing with the colonial period— E. P. Tanner, *The Province of New Jersey, 1664–1738,* and E. J. Fisher, *New Jersey as a Royal Province, 1738–1776.* New Jersey is greatly in need of an equally good account of its history since 1776, and nothing approaching an adequate social history of New Jersey has ever appeared. A readable general history of New Jersey is the composite work edited by Francis Bazely Lee, *New Jersey as a Colony and a State.* The voluminous county and municipal histories are of some value in throwing light upon penological ideas and practices in the early period.

INDEX.

This Index should be supplemented by the analytical Table of Contents at the opening of this volume

VITA.

Harry Elmer Barnes was born at Port Byron, New York, on June 15, 1889. He received his secondary school education at Port Byron High School, graduating in 1906. Between 1906 and 1909 he was engaged in engineering work and as a teacher in the public schools. In 1909 he entered Syracuse University. From this institution he received the degree of Bachelor of Arts, *summa cum laude*, in 1913, and of Master of Arts in 1914. During the years 1913–1915 he held the position of Instructor in Historical Sociology in Syracuse University. In 1915 he entered Columbia University as a graduate student, electing major work in the History of Thought and Culture. During the year 1915–1916 he attended the lectures of Professors James T. Shotwell, James Harvey Robinson, William A. Dunning, and Franklin H. Giddings. During this year he attended the seminars of Professors Shotwell and Giddings. In the year 1915–1916 he held a University Fellowship in Historical Sociology. In the following year he was appointed Cutting Traveling Fellow in the History of Thought and Culture. This year (1916–1917) was spent in research at Harvard University, where material was gathered for a work soon to be published on *The Contributions of Sociology to the History of Political Theories*. He was appointed Lecturer in History in Columbia University in 1917.

Criminal Justice in America

AN ARNO PRESS COLLECTION

Administration of Justice in the United States. 1910

Barnes, Harry Elmer. **A History of the Penal, Reformatory and Correctional Institutions of the State of New Jersey.** 1918

Capital Punishment: Nineteenth-Century Arguments. 1974

Chicago Community Trust. **Reports Comprising the Survey of the Cook County Jail.** [1923]

Connecticut General Assembly. **Minutes of the Testimony Taken Before John Q. Wilson, Joseph Eaton, and Morris Woodruff, Committee from the General Assembly, to Inquire Into the Condition of Connecticut State Prison.** 1834

Criminal Courts in New York State, 1909/1910

Finley, James B[radley]. **Memorials of Prison Life.** 1855

Georgia General Assembly. **Proceedings of the Joint Committee Appointed to Investigate the Condition of the Georgia Penitentiary.** 1870

Glueck, Sheldon, editor. **Probation and Criminal Justice.** 1933

Goldman, Mayer C[larence]. **The Public Defender.** 1917

Howe, S[amuel] G[ridley]. **An Essay on Separate and Congregate Systems of Prison Discipline.** 1846

Kohn, Aaron, editor. **The Kohn Report: Crime and Politics in Chicago.** 1953

Lawes, Lewis E. **Twenty Thousand Years in Sing Sing.** 1932

Los Angeles Police Department (Chief August Vollmer). **Law Enforcement in Los Angeles:** Los Angeles Police Department Annual Report, 1924. New Introduction by Joseph G. Woods. 1924

Maine Joint Special Committee. **Report of the Joint Special Committee on Investigation of the Affairs of the Maine State Prison.** 1874

Massachusetts, Commonwealth of. **Report of the Special Commission on Investigation of the Judicial System.** 1936

Moley, Raymond. **Our Criminal Courts.** 1930

Morse, Wayne L. and Ronald H. Beattie. **Survey of the Administration of Criminal Justice in Oregon.** 1932

National Conference on Bail and Criminal Justice. **Proceedings of May 27-29, 1964 and Interim Report, May 1964-April 1965.** 1965

New York. Kings County, Grand Jury. **A Presentment Concerning the Enforcement by the Police Department of the City of New York of the Laws Against Gambling by the Grand Jury for the Additional Extraordinary Special and Trial Term.** 1942

New York State. **Proceedings of the Governor's Conference on Crime, the Criminal and Society.** 1935

New York State. **Report of the Crime Commission, 1928.** 1928

New York State Committee on State Prisons. **Investigation of the New York State Prisons.** 1883

New York State Crime Commission. **Crime and the Community.** 1930

New York State Supreme Court, Apellate Division. **The Investigation of the Magistrates' Courts in the First Judicial Department.** 1932

O'Sullivan, John L. **Report in Favor of the Abolition of the Punishment of Death by Law, Made to the Legislature of the State of New York.** 1841

Pennsylvania Parole Commission. **The Report of the Pennsylvania State Parole Commission to the Legislature.** 1927. Two volumes in one.

Pennsylvania Special Grand Jury. **Investigation of Vice, Crime and Law Enforcement.** 1939

Reform of the Criminal Law and Procedure. 1911

Reporter of the Post. **Selections from the Court Reports Originally Published in the Boston Morning Post, From 1834-1837.** 1837

Shalloo, J. P., editor. **Crime in the United States.** 1941

Smith, Bruce. **Rural Crime Control.** 1933

Smith, Ralph Lee. **The Tarnished Badge.** 1965

Society for the Prevention of Pauperism. **Report on the Penitentiary System in the United States.** 1822

South Carolina General Assembly. **Report of Joint Committee Created Under Joint Resolution 662 of 1937 to Investigate Law Enforcement.** 1937

Sutherland, Edwin H. and Thorsten Sellin, editors. **Prisons of Tomorrow.** 1931

Texas Penitentiary Investigating Committee. **A Record of Evidence and Statements Before the Penitentiary Investigating Committee.** [1913]

Train, Arthur. **Courts and Criminals.** 1926

Train, Arthur. **The Prisoner at the Bar.** 1906

United States Department of Justice. **Attorney General's Survey of Release Procedures.** Volume II : Probation. 1939

United States Department of Justice. **Attorney General's Survey of Release Procedures.** Volume IV : Parole. 1939

United States. House of Representatives. Committee on the District of Columbia. **Investigation of the Metropolitan Police Department.** 1941

Waite, John Barker. **Criminal Law in Action.** 1934

Warner, Sam Bass. **Crime and Criminal Statistics in Boston.** 1934

Warner, Sam Bass and Henry B. Cabot. **Judges and Law Reform.** 1936

Wiretapping in New York City. 1916